Evaluation Studies

EVALUATION STUDIES REVIEW ANNUAL
Volume 12

Review Annual

Evaluation Studies

Review Annual

Volume 12   1987

Edited by
William R. Shadish, Jr.
and
Charles S. Reichardt

SAGE PUBLICATIONS
The Publishers of Professional Social Science
Newbury Park   Beverly Hills   London   New Delhi

For information address:

SAGE Publications, Inc.
2111 West Hillcrest Drive
Newbury Park, California 91320

SAGE Publications Inc.   SAGE Publications Ltd.
275 South Beverly Drive   28 Banner Street
Beverly Hills   London EC1Y 8QE
California 90212   England

SAGE PUBLICATIONS India Pvt. Ltd.
M-32 Market
Greater Kailash I
New Delhi 110 048 India

Printed in the United States of America

International Standard Book Number 0-8039-2941-2

International Standard Series Number 0364-7390

Library of Congress Catalog Card No. 76-15865

FIRST PRINTING

CONTENTS

DEDICATED: With love and affection,
to my wife, Betty Duke Shadish;
to my sister, Linda Reichardt.

ABOUT THE EDITORS

WILLIAM R. SHADISH, Jr., is an Associate Professor with the Center for Applied Psychological Research in the Department of Psychology at Memphis State University. His Ph.D. in clinical psychology was taken at Purdue University in 1978, with dual minor areas in statistics and measurement theory. He then spent three years as a Postdoctoral Fellow in Methodology and Evaluation Research in the Psychology Department at Northwestern University. His research interests include evaluation theory, mental health policy, and social studies of science. His articles and chapters on these topics have appeared in such outlets as the *American Psychologist,* the *Handbook of Social Psychology,* and the *Annual Review of Psychology.* His forthcoming books include one on evaluation theory (coauthored with Thomas D. Cook and Laura C. Leviton) and a second on the psychology of science (coedited with Barry Gholson, Robert A. Neimeyer, and Arthur C. Houts).

CHARLES S. REICHARDT is an Associate Professor of Psychology at the University of Denver. He is the coeditor of *Qualitative and Quantitative Methods in Evaluation Research* (with Thomas D. Cook) and has been a statistical consultant on local and national evaluations. He received the President's Prize from the Evaluation Research Society and has served on the Board of Directors of the Evaluation Network.

PART I

Overview

The Intellectual Foundations of Social Program Evaluation
The Development of Evaluation Theory

William R. Shadish, Jr., and Charles S. Reichardt

The maturity of a discipline is reflected partly by the clarity with which problems facing the discipline are understood, and partly by the sophistication with which solutions to problems are devised and practiced. Such developments take time, but are eventually codified in the theoretical literature of a field. After 20 years of development, the discipline of program evaluation is beginning to show its age along these dimensions. Our intent in the present volume is to document this progress: to present the most recent thinking both about the nature of the problems that face evaluation and about potential solutions to those problems. In the process, especially with the remarks in this opening chapter, we hope to shed some light on the development of the theoretical literature that forms the intellectual foundations of our specialty.

The readings in this volume begin with a chapter by Cook and Shadish (1986) that identifies five fundamental problems in program evaluation, and that summarizes past and present trends in addressing these problems. Following their organization, this volume is divided into five sections, one for each problem: (1) *Social Programming:* the role of social programs in social problem solving and social change, and especially the issue of program improvement; (2) *Knowledge Use:* the use of evaluative information in social programming; (3) *Valuing:* the role of values in evaluative inquiry; (4) *Knowledge Construction:* how evaluative knowledge should be created; and in view of the answers to these first four problems; (5) *Evaluation Practice:* how evaluation ought to be practiced, especially given the practical constraints that evaluation practitioners face. Of course, as with any descriptive classification, this particular conceptualization of the problems of social program evaluation is partly arbitrary. But by the end of this volume, we hope the reader will agree that the conceptualization captures most of the important debates and problems in the field.

SOURCES OF EVALUATION THEORY:
PROBLEMS, PRACTICES, SCHOLARLY TRADITIONS

In the early days of social program evaluation, the field had little detailed sense of what problems it should be addressing, or of what strategies and tactics it ought to use to address the task. Consequently, it adapted the problems, methods, and paradigms existing in the disciplines from which the first evaluators came. Understandably, some parochialism and naïveté resulted, for example, as noted in the Stanford Evaluation Consortium's (1976) criticisms of the early *Handbook of Evaluation Research* (Guttentag & Struening, 1975). Evaluators from a testing tradition were often accustomed to defining the problem as measuring achievement and to defining the solution as achievement testing. Evaluators from the tradition of experimentation in psychology and public health tended to see the problem as assessing program effectiveness, and the solution as experimental or quasi-experimental methods. Similarly, evaluators from economics focused more on causal modelling techniques, quantitative sociologists focused on survey research, and qualitative sociologists and anthropologists emphasized case studies so as to understand social programs from the participants' point of view.

In typical evolutionary fashion, however, the realities of evaluation practice exerted a winnowing influence on this diversity. First, the problems faced by evaluators—roughly, to construct knowledge about the value of the operations and consequences of programs, knowledge that could be used to improve social programs and social problem solving in the short-term—proved far broader than did any of the narrow disciplinary approaches. Methodological problems were also encountered that prevented any one discipline from dominating the field. For example, experiments proved more difficult to implement successfully than was first anticipated; selection biases routinely compromised causal modelling techniques; achievement testing failed to reflect significant processes and effects of education; surveys provided limited information about causal effects; and case studies proved difficult to market to federal and state level policymakers. Over 20 years, then, these realities have forced program evaluation to focus more on its own set of problems, and to develop or adapt methods suited more specifically to those problems.

In short, the theoretical literature in program evaluation resulted from a complex interplay among the problems identified and faced by evaluators, the practices those evaluators brought to bear, and the scholarly traditions and theories within the disciplinary heritage of each evaluator—all winnowed by the vagaries and regularities of over 20 years experience in the field. The chapters in this volume reflect this reciprocal, interactive interplay among problems, practices, and scholarly traditions. Of course, none of the individual works we reprint is by itself a complete evaluation theory. But each is theoretical in the functional sense that any theory aspires to: helping us to organize, categorize, describe, predict, explain, and otherwise aid our understanding and control of evaluation. They are the fragments of a more complete evaluation theory that is still (and perhaps always will be) emerging.

Sources of Evaluation Theory
in the Problems of Program Evaluation

The works reprinted in this volume—indeed, most theoretical work in evaluation—can be viewed as a response to one or more of the five problems around which this volume is organized. These problems are foundational because each must be confronted, either implicitly or explicitly, whenever an evaluation is put into the field. They are also foundational in that they allow no easy or automatic solutions. No matter how far the specialty of social program evaluation advances, thoughtful evaluators will continue to puzzle over these problems. Since Cook and Shadish (1986) describe these five foundational problems in more detail in their paper, we describe them only briefly here.

The Problem of Social Programming. In the early days, evaluations often were based on naive assumptions about the way social programs operated and were improved, about the nature of the social problems that these programs were meant to ameliorate, and about the ease with which important social change could be encouraged (Campbell, 1969; Suchman, 1967). Evaluators often assumed that social problems were easy to alleviate, and that large effects could be produced by social interventions. As a result, weak designs and blunt observational methods were not seen to be serious handicaps. Similarly, evaluators often assumed incorrectly that programs were likely to be implemented as planned. As a result, evaluators misattributed small effects to the ineffectiveness of the treatment-as-proposed rather than to the ineffectiveness of the treatment-as-implemented. Because they often assumed that programs varied relatively little from site to site, evaluators failed to learn about the differential effectiveness of program variations. Evaluators often failed to realize that programs take time to get up and running, and so assessed the effectiveness of programs before they were operating efficiently. Evaluators often assumed that managers could and would accurately represent the goals of programs. By failing to recognize that their studies could be threatening, evaluators were unprepared when managers and staff sabotaged the research. By failing to recognize which aspects of programs and policies were most amenable to improvement, evaluators often wasted resources studying program modifications and demonstrations that had little payoff.

In short, evaluators found that social programs were heterogeneous entities across sites and times, with diffuse aims among which social problem solving was not always the highest priority, and were resistant to a more than incremental change in the short term (Weiss, 1972). Evaluations that were conducted under faulty assumptions about how such changes occurred resulted in minimal change (Shadish, 1984), and so evaluators faced the problem of how to contribute to important social problem solving in a context that was inherently conservative in nature. Beginning with such theorists as Wholey (Wholey, Nay, Scanlon, & Schmidt, 1975) and Weiss (1972, 1973), evaluators began to struggle toward a more realistic understanding of social programming, and of how, when, and where programs can be improved. The chapters in the first section of this volume address many of these issues, including ways to cope with the vagaries of program implementation, ways to increase the success of incremental change, and suggestions for moving beyond incrementalism. Today, evaluation theory reflects the fruits of this struggle. Implementation theory is widely viewed as central to understanding social program improvement, since it most directly addresses methods for bringing about incremental change in programs. In this volume, for example, Weick's (1984) plea to redefine the scale of social problems by aiming for "small wins" is a prototypical incrementalist position. But the limits of an incremental approach to social change are better understood, as well; even though it is usually the most feasible change, incremental change solves social problems very slowly, and sometimes never, as Lindblom (1986) reminds us.

Parenthetically, we should note Scriven's constant reminder that evaluation is broader than social program evaluation; it also should incorporate product and personnel evaluation, for example. Our inclusion of a section on social programming is not intended to ignore Scriven's point, but rather to reflect the emphasis in the present volume on social program evaluation. In a broader sense, though, the problem of social programming is just a special case of the problem of how anything being evaluated can be improved. Product evaluation needs its theory of product change and improvement, and personnel evaluation must have its theory of personnel change and improvement.

The Problem of Knowledge Use. Early thinking was that the results of evaluations would be used instrumentally to make direct changes in social programs, replacing ineffective programs and projects with more effective ones, cutting or adding to budgets where evaluations indicated most good would be done, and adding improvements to programs that would be widely disseminated (Campbell, 1969). But in the 1970s evaluators found that such instrumental use was less common than was anticipated, and that evaluations could be misused as well. In response, some evaluators focused on finding ways to facilitate incremental use by studying the characteristics of evaluative information that managers and policymakers found most useful (Patton, 1978; Wholey et al., 1975). Other evaluators searched for alternative kinds of use for evaluative information (Weiss, 1978), proposing "enlightenment" (Weiss, 1977), "naturalistic generalization" (Stake, 1978), and "demystification" (Berk & Rossi, 1977) as central kinds of use to strive for. During that time, instrumental use was relegated to a less central position in justifying evaluative inquiry—although as we will see in the present volume, it is currently making a minor comeback as more instrumental uses of evaluation are being located. Today evaluative theory has a more finely differentiated understanding of the kinds of uses that are possible, and of the kinds of evaluative inquiry that facilitate each kind of use. The readings in the present volume contribute to these efforts by debunking some myths about use as well as by providing examples both of highly successful uses and of unexpected negative consequences.

The Problem of Valuing in Evaluation. The traditional view was that science can and should be value free. According to this view, program evaluation should produce knowledge without imposing anyone's values, and values should be brought to bear only by decision makers in the political process of taking action. But the work of such authors as Scriven (1966, 1967) forced evaluators to recognize that they were somehow involved in making value judgments about programs. Today, many evaluators realize that their own evaluative methods and findings are inherently value laden, and they strive to make those values both explicit and appropriate to the context of evaluation. For example, it is becoming clear to most evaluators that values are involved whenever evaluators (a) agree to provide evaluation services for one client and not another, (b) choose to study one kind of question about, say, program outcome rather than program process, (c) choose the measures upon which to assess programs, (d) suggest that changes be made to improve a program, or (e) decide that a program is or is not sufficiently effective to justify the cost.

Because values cannot be avoided in conducting evaluations, evaluators need to consider the role that values should play, and how to go about applying values appropriately. The evaluation literature has taken up these questions in earnest. Stakeholder approaches to evaluation, for example, have been developed in part to ensure that a pluralistic array of values are represented in an evaluation (Bryk, 1983). House (1980), with his proposal that evaluators adopt Rawls's theory of justice, has successfully put prescriptive ethical considerations onto the evaluation agenda even though his proposal elicited strong reactions (Borich, 1981; Kenny, 1982; Wortman, 1982). Throughout it all, Scriven (1980, 1983) continued to develop the logical structure of the valuing process in evaluation. Today, although values are still approached gingerly by many evaluators, there is a better sense of the terms of inquiry into values, and of the role of evaluation in passing value judgments on programs. The readings we offer in this volume continue the discussion about values. Among other topics, the readings present prescriptive options for assigning value, reveal the values that are often hidden in our work, and provide mechanisms for adjudicating value disputes.

The Problem of Knowledge Creation. One of the principle tasks of evaluation is to gather and interpret data so as to create knowledge about social programs and problems. Though there is universal agreement about this goal, there is great uncertainty about how it is best accomplished, and many of the most interesting and salient debates in evaluation have concerned this issue (Cook & Reichardt, 1979). The debates have been partly methodological as evaluators from different disciplinary backgrounds brought their own favorite methods to bear on evaluation problems. Evaluators have adapted methods from social experimentation, survey research, econometric modelling, multiattribute-utility theory, and case-study methodology; and they have invented new methods to fit their own unique circumstances, including the *modus operandi* method, evaluability assessment, and service delivery assessments. But debates about knowledge construction have also been debates about epistemology and ontology. Some theorists have claimed that different worldviews undergird different evaluation methods, and that some of these views are better suited for evaluation than are others. Such theories as naturalistic inquiry (Lincoln & Guba, 1985) and evolutionary epistemology (Campbell, 1974a) have evolved at least partly in the context of these debates in program evaluation. Nearly every issue of the major evaluation journals now has at least one article that discusses such epistemological matters. Modern evaluators are no longer naive about the complexities of knowledge construction. In the readings we have reprinted, these debates are continued, and strategies for improving knowledge creation are offered.

The Problem of Evaluation Practice. If one problem is central to the foundations of evaluation, it has to be the problem of evaluation practice. Program evaluation is a field that is dominated by practitioners (AEA, 1986). While all evaluation practice depends ultimately, implicitly or not, on abstract debates about epistemology, ethics, use, and social change, such debates are most relevant to practitioners of evaluation when they obviously inform decisions about practice. Such decisions include the agreement to evaluate, the role the evaluator is to play, the sources of possible questions to be asked, the final selection of questions, the selection of methods, the implementation and management of the study, analysis and interpretation of data, reporting of results during and after the study, and activities that might facilitate use of results. Complicating matters further, all these decisions often have to be made under significant constraints of time, money, and staffing (Hendricks, 1986). Given these constraints, it is probably no accident that the methods uniquely invented for program evaluation—for example, modus operandi, service delivery assessment, evaluability assessment—are all ways to gather relevant information as quickly, cheaply, and pragmatically as possible. Compared to the practical decisions faced every day by most evaluators, abstract discussions of whether or not there is a reality, or whether evaluators should wear Rawls's (1971) "veil of ignorance" when judging the merits of social programs, must seem of secondary importance or less. The problem of practice is central to the intellectual foundations of social program evaluation.

Sources of Evaluation Theory in Evaluation Practice

For those of us in academic settings, it is temptingly egocentric to think that evaluation theory drives evaluation practice—that practicing evaluators both read and consider our academic opinions before deciding how to do their craft. But in many important respects, the situation is probably just the opposite, with evaluation theory being shaped by developments in evaluation practice. Some historians of science have argued that action and technology tend to precede theory development in any discipline.

> Kuhn (1971) illustrates how up to the nineteenth century, a pattern of technology preceding science has been the rule. Practical inventions were not the product of applied theoretical science. They resulted from alert handy men who hit upon new combinations of actions and procedures to yield effects that already had some value or that turned out to be valuable. Afterwards, scientists, partly intrigued by some of these results, developed conceptual systems to account for such effects. (DeMey, 1982, p. 237)

Program evaluation seems prototypical of this assertion. For example, Wholey did not first develop evaluability assessment in an academic setting, then go out to find a practical setting in which it might apply; rather, the theoretical presentation of evaluability assessment followed his experience trying to do evaluations in practical settings (Wholey et al., 1975). Examples of works of this genre in the present volume include McLaughlin (1986), Ozawa & Susskind (1986), and Bangert-Drowns (1986).

Of course, it is only the proposed solutions that are codified in written form that ever find their way into the literature by way of publication. The wisdom of evaluation practitioners is rarely codified directly in this manner, but provides a large repertoire of workable solutions that have been tried in the field. In this latter regard, the recently initiated series of interviews with practicing evaluators in *Evaluation Practice* is a laudable attempt to provide such evaluators with a forum for participation in the professional literature (Eichelberger, 1986; Hendricks, 1986).

Practice also finds its way into theory through studies of evaluation practice, with the results being used to discover and revise ideas about how evaluation should be done. Examples are numerous. Bernstein and Freeman (1975) used six criteria for evaluating the technical quality of some evaluations commissioned by the Department of Health, Education, and Welfare. McTavish and his colleagues (Minnesota Systems Research, 1976) used about 100 items for the same purpose. House (1980) developed criteria of "objectivity, fairness, and justice" by which he then examined the evaluations of the Follow Through educational program. Boruch and Cordray (1980) used a broad array of criteria for assessing federal evaluations in education. Studies of evaluation practice—surveys of practice, metaevaluation, meta-analysis, critical commentaries—provide both a fertile source of ideas and an empirical data base with which to generate and against which to test and revise theories about how to do evaluation. Examples in the present volume include the critical commentary by Stake, and the studies of use by Leviton and Boruch, Rossi and Wright, Saxe, and Wholey.

The relationship between theory and practice is not always complimentary, of course. One commentator on the differences between academic work and professional practice observed, "Academic disciplines are engaged in the constant questioning of accepted knowledge; practice professionals are committed to respect accepted knowledge until new knowledge is tested and accepted"(Austin, 1981, p. 350). There can sometimes be an implicit antagonism between academic evaluation and evaluation practice. Such antagonism can lead to both beneficial and detrimental effects, and we should constantly try to minimize the latter. On the positive side, it can engender a creative tension as both sides struggle to answer each other's criticisms, leading to new ways of thinking about and doing evaluation. Examples such as Wholey's evaluability assessment, Scriven's modus operandi, and Hendricks's service delivery assessment speak eloquently to the beneficial effects of such tensions. But on the negative side, such tensions can split an organization if the aims and needs of practitioners and academics diverge too much. We see a current example of this in the American Psychological Association, where the divergence between practicing clinicians and academic psychologists has led to a loss of academic membership in APA, a rethinking of the scientist-practitioner model that has dominated clinical psychology for 40 years, and a proposed reorganization of APA into scientific versus practitioner assemblies with separate goals, dues structures, and convention agendas. Of course, the differences between AEA and APA are probably greater than are these similarities, so that these observations are not meant to sound a premature alarm. But academics and practitioners have so much to learn from each other that it would be a shame to see a similar divergence develop in our profession.

Sources of Theory in Scholarly Traditions

Disciplinary Diversity and Program Evaluation Theory. Professional program evaluators come from diverse disciplinary backgrounds, including psychology, education, economics, sociology, and political science. Even that bastion of product evaluation, Consumers Union, recently announced its interest in evaluating poverty programs (Karpatkin, 1987). In response to this diversity, evaluation theory has become extraordinarily catholic in the topics, methods, and substantive theories it addresses.

This diversity makes it difficult for evaluators to keep abreast of the interdisciplinary developments relevant to their work. Much of the value of *Evaluation Studies Review Annual* is in the service it provides evaluators by reprinting relevant work that evaluators might otherwise miss. To illustrate the point, we reviewed all 10 ESRA volumes that had appeared in print by 1986, identifying the number of papers reprinted from different sources. A total of 396 items were reprinted in these 10 volumes, of which 288 came from periodicals, 72 from unpublished manuscripts, and 36 from books. The periodicals included 110 different journals from 12 substantive areas (economics, 39 articles; education, 31; evaluation, 52; law, 12; management, 10; medicine, 25; psychology, 43; public health, 23; public policy and political science, 20; sociology, 23; statistics, 1; miscellaneous, 9). Of these 110 journals, only five contributed more than 10 articles reprinted in past ESRA volumes: *Journal of Human Resources* (N = 15), *Harvard Educational Review* (11), *Evaluation Quarterly/ Review* (26), *Ameri-*

can Psychologist (11), and *American Journal of Public Health* (13). The modal number of contributions from any one journal was one.

Similarly, in choosing works to reprint in this volume, the present authors located and reviewed 156 journals that were potentially relevant to our theme, limiting our search for practical reasons to journals in our own personal or university libraries. Reflecting this professional diversity, the present volume reprints works by philosophers (Glymour & Scheines, 1986; Phillips, 1985), political scientists (Quirk, 1986), sociologists (Rossi & Wright, 1985), physicians (Goodwin & Goodwin, 1984), educators (Wood, Peterson, DeGracie, & Zaharis, 1986), policy analysts (Ascher, 1986), economists (Haveman, 1986; LaLonde, 1986), and psychologists (Finney & Moos, 1986). It is a tribute to our field that we value the contributions of these diverse disciplines.

We have always considered this professional diversity to be one of the strengths of evaluation. Therefore, we worry that in at least some of the professional forums in which evaluators interact, too few specialties are represented for us to take full advantage of the opportunity to learn from other fields. For example, the recent directory of the American Evaluation Association (1986) shows that the majority of members come from only three groups: education (28%), psychology (21%), and research/statistical methods (13%). By contrast, AEA has not so successfully attracted the membership of evaluators from sociology (6%), political science (3%), economics (1%) or a host of other disciplines. The reason for the disparity is that political scientists and economists who are interested in evaluation issues have tended to join associations focused on public policy analysis such as the Policy Studies Organization or the Association for Public Policy Analysis and Management (Nagel, 1985). Such a situation is, we think, severely detrimental to all parties concerned. Nagel (1985), for example, described many of the similarities and differences between policy studies and evaluation research, and discussed the mutual benefits that might ensue from more interaction between the two fields. Conversely, Wargo (Hendricks, 1986) warned that evaluation is often not known as an independent specialty in many important federal circles, and that it ultimately may have to be incorporated into policy analysis. Should we be so concerned with maintaining our professional identity that we sacrifice extensive interactions with colleagues in other specialties? We do not think so. Evaluators cannot afford, either intellectually or organizationally, to become parochial and isolated from these interdisciplinary sources of ideas, contacts, and substantive problems.

Diversity of Research Traditions. Much of evaluation theory, including the work reprinted in the present volume, arises within the context of existing research traditions that are often orthogonal to any particular discipline. The concept of research traditions (Lakatos, 1978; Laudan, 1977) expresses the idea of an ongoing set of loosely articulated methodological and theoretical guides to approaching a problem. Such traditions are composed of multiple theories that are related in their overall agreement as to which theoretical and empirical paths to pursue and which to avoid. The individual theories within each tradition can and often do change in important ways, and often turn over completely as better theories come along that share similar assumptions about which paths to pursue or avoid. We will discuss such theories in the next section. But unlike theories, traditions tends to be stable over a longer period of time.

For example, one problem evaluators face is how to measure program effects. Research traditions that have developed in response to this problem include the experimental tradition, the causal modelling tradition, the program monitoring tradition, and the case study tradition. Within, say, the case study tradition, we can identify such distinct theoretical approaches as Lincoln and Guba's (1985) naturalistic inquiry, Campbell's (1974b; 1979b) qualitative knowing and "degrees of freedom" approach, and Scriven's (1976) *modus operandi* method. These traditions and theories have become foundational to future attempts to solve the program effectiveness problem, because it will be difficult to address the problem without returning to these past accomplishments for terminology, concepts, and data about their successes and failures. In many respects, these past accomplishments define the structural and intellectual context in which future developments will take place.

Similarly, at least three traditions have emerged to deal with the problem of valuing in evaluation. The most common approach might be called the descriptive tradition. Members of this tradition share the common assumption that the values imposed and studied by evaluators ought to be those held by the important stakeholders to a program. Within the descriptive tradition, however, there are many individual theories. One theory, for example, is the local stakeholder approach championed by Stake (1978; 1986), which assigns priority to the values held by the diverse local interest groups associated with a project, and which gives less attention to the values held by federal and state managers and policymakers. A contrasting theory in the descriptive tradition is that of Wholey (1979; 1983), who assigns the opposite set of priorities compared to Stake. In the present volume, Wood et al. (1986) illustrate this descriptive tradition.

Two less common research traditions exist in approaching the problem of values. One is the prescriptive tradition, which champions the application of specific theories and concepts from moral and ethical philosophy. Prescriptive theories share the assumptions that not all stakeholders' opinions are equally valid, that thousands of years of thinking about ethics and morality have resulted in a better understanding of the merits of different criteria of merit, and that these criteria should be applied to evaluating social programs. One salient example is House's (1980) application of Rawls's (1971) theory of justice, which entails ascribing priority to social programs that meet the material needs of the disadvantaged. House's proposal engendered a good deal of controversy (Borich, 1981; Kenny, 1982; Wortman, 1982), which, if read carefully, could be interpreted as a clash between the descriptive tradition's emphasis on the priority of stakeholders' values and the prescriptive tradition's emphasis on the priority of ethical theory. In the present volume, Bunda (1985) represents this prescriptive tradition in valuing.

Finally, there is the metatheoretical tradition, concerned mostly with the logic and justification for the role of values in evaluation. Scriven's (1980) logic of evaluation is clearly the most identifiable theory within this tradition, with its concern about such matters as what differentiates value statements from other kinds of knowledge, and what procedures must be followed in order to construct value statements. Other examples include Smith (1985), who describes the nature of moral problems in evaluation; Hendricks (1985), who demonstrates the role that evaluators should play in forming value judgments; and, in the present volume, Lynn, discusses the inevitability of values in any applied science. Members of this tradition assume that value claims are generated and adjudicated according to procedures that are independent of the descriptive or prescriptive values that are given priority in a particular evaluation. Often such theorists try to avoid taking a stance about which prescriptive or descriptive position evaluators ought to adopt.

Such traditions can be identified for each of the problems around which this volume is organized, although their identification is at least partly a construction of the observer, so that several legitimate ways of construing these traditions are possible. For example, social programming traditions include incrementalism, policy innovation, and system change; knowledge use has instrumentalist and enlightenment traditions; knowledge creation has realist and idealist traditions; and practice has "manipulable solution," "generalizable explanation," and "stakeholder service" traditions (Cook & Shadish, 1986). Some articles representing each of these traditions are now chapters in this volume. We hope that future volumes of ESRA will follow suit, since these traditions will remain relatively stable over time in their basic assumptions. For example, at least for the foreseeable future, some evaluation theorists will focus mainly on incremental program improvement, while others will continue to believe that such change is too slow and conservative to be important. Conversely, we should be wary of evaluators who say that one and only one tradition in any of these areas is "what evaluators should be doing." Especially when a tradition has survived and been used successfully in some sphere of evaluation, it must be assumed that it has a role in evaluation theory.

Sources of Evaluation Theory in Theory Group Development. Traditions are comprehensive entities that encompass multiple scientists, theories, and schools, but individual theories are more discrete, often espoused initially by a single scientist who may or may not attract significant attention to the work. Sociologists of science have studied the process of theory and theory group development, and their findings have plausible exemplars in the development of evaluation theory. Mullins (1973), for example, postulated a four-stage process of theory group development. In the *normal stage* of theory development, the scientific communication structure about a problem is unorganized and ill-defined. The literature about that problem is scattered among many scientists and institutions, most of whom would not consider themselves part of any organized or identifiable effort to solve a problem. For example, before the early 1960s, people scattered throughout the public, private, and academic sectors were concerned with assessing the effectiveness of policies and programs. Cronbach and colleagues (1980) summarize some of those early efforts, which included Roethlisberger and Dickson's (1939) controlled experiments in the Western Electric Plant at Hawthorne, IL, Kurt Lewin's (1948) action research, and studies of the effectiveness of psychotherapy (Herzog, 1959). None of these people thought of themselves as part of an organized social experimentation network, nor probably of any focused network, for that matter.

The start of the second phase of theory group development according to Mullins's theory, the *network stage,* is often marked by the appearance of an exciting intellectual product that attracts the attention and work of several researchers. Communication among these researchers increases, they recruit like-minded students and colleagues, and early research or theoretical successes support a developing consensus that the direction is worth pursuing. In the case we are discussing, the appearance of Campbell & Stanley's (1963) *Experimental and Quasi-Experimental Designs for Research,* based partly on Campbell's (1957) earlier work on that same topic, catalyzed interests in a social experimentation approach to studying program effectiveness. This work attracted colleagues at Northwestern University, such as Robert Boruch and Lee Sechrest, students at Northwestern, such as David Kenny, and scientists at other universities, such as Edward Suchman at the University of Pittsburgh. Early successes included Campbell's (1969) "Reforms as Experiments," as well as successful applications of the social experimentation theory in, for example, the "Manhattan Bail Bond Experiment" (Ares, Rankin, & Sturz, 1963). This second stage often culminates in a program statement that codifies the style and content of the work to be done by the theory group members, the best example of which is Campbell's (1971) "Methods for the Experimenting Society" (see also Riecken et al., 1974).

In the *cluster stage*, training and research centers for the theory are institutionalized at one or two universities. The number of colleagues and students working in the theory group increases, and their relationships become more formalized through teaching and collaborative writing. As the products of the group increase in number, the theory attracts the attention of its parent field, which accepts it as a constructive contribution or rejects it as too revolutionary. During this period, secondary materials and critical work begin to appear. This stage is clearly illustrated at Northwestern, where the 1970s saw the institutionalization of a training program in methodology and evaluation research, with a number of associated faculty (Campbell, Boruch, Sechrest, Wortman, Cook), a slew of pre- and postdoctoral students, and training grants from federal agencies. The frequent productivity and coauthorships of this theory group are illustrated by a host of secondary works (Boruch, Wortman, & Cordray, 1981; Brewer & Collins, 1981; Cook & Campbell, 1979; Kenny, 1979; Morell, 1979; Riecken et al., 1974; Wortman, 1981). At the same time, works critical of the theory also appeared both from within (Campbell, 1974b, 1979b) and outside the theory (Cronbach et al., 1980; Cronbach, 1982; Guba & Lincoln, 1981).

However, the reaction of the parent fields to this theory group (both evaluation and psychology) were on the whole positive, and both the theory and the theory group members achieved such indicators of institutional success as routine mention of the theory in relevant textbooks, and for members came editorial board membership, professional awards, and lucrative job offers.

This very success begins to usher in the *specialty stage* of theory group development. Prominent students and faculty are hired away from the original group or retire, replacements are hired who may not share the original interests of the group, old collaborations among theory group members are replaced by new interests that are not always within the program statement of the original work, and a more diverse network of scientists begins to do scholarly work in the theory. At Northwestern, for example, Lee Sechrest left early on, followed by Wortman and Campbell. While some of the replacements such as Dave Cordray shared an interest in the theory group, some other replacements had little or no interest in either evaluation research or social experimentation. Collaborations among the original theory group members have decreased in frequency (Cook & Campbell, 1986), while at the same time the theory has become institutionalized within both psychology and evaluation so that a wider group of scientists are now working on aspects of it as an established specialty area (McCleary & Hay, 1980; Rossi & Freeman, 1985; Saxe & Fine, 1981; Trochim, 1984), but without the same social organization and coherence that was characteristic of the previous stage. The methodology and evaluation research program at Northwestern, of course, is active and productive, with a rich legacy from the social experimentation theory group; but that group is no longer the sole influence in the program.

The social experimentation theory group is just one of many such groups that have developed as part of the response of evaluators to the problems they face. Other groups include, for example, the Stanford Evaluation Consortium, most prominently associated with Cronbach and his colleagues (Cronbach et al., 1980; Stanford Evaluation Consortium, 1976), the UC Berkeley/USF group formed around Michael Scriven, and the University of Illinois group associated with such evaluators as Robert Stake, Ernest House, and Nick Smith. Each of these groups produced their own exciting intellectual products and program statements, had their own empirical and theoretical successes, and attracted many students and faculty colleagues into mentor and collaborative relationships. A thorough history of evaluation theory would discuss each of them in more detail; and many of the dynamics described above for Northwestern would pertain to these groups as well.

Of course, most efforts to respond to the foundational problems of evaluation never progress through the four stages just described. After all, the production of a work that is so intellectually exciting that it attracts other faculty and students away from their own interests is a rare event in itself, precluding most work from ever entering the second stage. Consequently many excellent pieces of scholarship exist that do not lead to the development of a theory group eventually institutionalized into the parent discipline. These articles nonetheless have a measurable impact on the development of evaluation, as assessed by citation analysis, for example (DeMey, 1982; Smith, 1981). Even when an exciting intellectual work is produced, however, many factors can prevent the development of the social organization needed to pass through the second and third stages. Sometimes the failure of an intellectual leader to be sufficiently charismatic, or to "sell" the theory's merits to a cadre of students, will prevent it from thriving at least temporarily—as Campbell (1979a) describes when comparing the relative fates of Tolman and Spence in learning theory. Other times a hostile or indifferent organizational environment can have the same effect if it is unwilling to provide the resources needed to hire additional faculty, fund student stipends, or even retain the original theorist.

PROGRESS IN EVALUATION THEORY: TOWARD A CONTINGENT THEORY OF PROGRAM EVALUATION

The important question, of course, is whether or not evaluation theory has made progress as it responds to the influences outlined in this chapter. We think it has. In general, evaluation theory displays a better sense now than it did 20 years ago of what evaluation practices work under what conditions to solve various problems evaluators face. So for example, evaluators now know that program goals should rarely be taken as complete or even accurate statements of what programs are doing, that randomized experiments are more likely to be successfully concluded and useful when there are relatively greater resources and fewer time constraints than is true for many other methods, and that expecting evaluation to produce major social change in the short term is not a very realistic goal. Cook and Shadish (1986) list many other examples of such progress in our understanding of evaluation.

At the same time, evaluation's theoretical literature appears to be more fragmented than one would hope. As Glass and Ellett (1980) put it, "Evaluation—more than any science—is what people say it is; and people currently are saying it is many different things" (p. 211). Their point is well taken. If one were to read, say, Stake (1978) on the case study method or Wholey (1979) on the sequential purchase of evaluation, one would think evaluation was a very different thing than if one read, say, Campbell's (1971) "Methods for the Experimenting Society" or Chen and Rossi's (1981) theory-driven evaluation. It is not immediately apparent what all these approaches have in common that warrant the label evaluation. Yet each is part of our heritage, and one can find examples of each working well.

The existence of these diverse alternatives poses a problem—most evaluators can think of some situations in which the advice of each of these authors is worth following, but no single approach offers advice that adequately addresses all situations. Knowing when to choose which approach is the key, but most authors are not sufficiently specific and detailed in providing guides to exactly when, where, and why their advice should be followed. When authors begin to spell out these contingencies more clearly, telling evaluators how to adopt the best from multiple approaches rather than trying to fit all evaluation situations into the same strategic mold, we may be surprised to find that more agreement underlies our diversity than we first thought. Rossi and Freeman's (1985) concept of "tailoring evaluations" perhaps comes closest to the kind of contingent theory of evaluation we have in mind.

Of course, we do not think we will ever see the day when a single, grand evaluation theory will be widely accepted. The field is too young, with too much yet to learn; and it may never prove possible to resolve some differences of opinion. But the first generation of evaluators generated an enormous amount of theoretical and practical wisdom, priming the discipline for a second generation of progress in theory and practice. We hope that the present volume helps lay the groundwork for this second generation.

REFERENCES

American Evaluation Association. (1986). *Membership directory.* Charlottesville, VA: Evaluation Research Center, Curry School of Education, University of Virginia.

Ares, C. E., Rankin, A., & Sturz, H. (1963). The Manhattan bail bond project: An interim report on the use of pre-trial parole. *New York University Law Review, 38,* 67-95.

Austin, D. (1981). Comments on the preceding article: The development of clinical sociology. *Journal of Applied Behavioral Science, 17,* 347-350.

Berk, R. A., & Rossi, P. H. (1977). Doing good or worse: Evaluation research politically reexamined. In G. V. Glass (Ed.), *Evaluation studies review annual* (Vol. 2, pp. 77-89). Newbury Park, CA: Sage.

Bernstein, I., & Freeman, H. E. (1975). *Academic and entrepreneurial research.* New York: Russell Sage.

Borich, G. D. (1981). All the "least privileged" please stand up! *Contemporary Psychology, 26,* 834-835.

Boruch, R. F., & Cordray, D. S. (1980). *An appraisal of educational program evaluations: Federal, state, and local agencies.* Report to the Office of Education.

Boruch, R. F., Wortman, P. M., & Cordray, D. S. (1981). *Reanalyzing program evaluations.* San Francisco: Jossey-Bass.

Brewer, M. B., & Collins, B. E. (Eds.). (1981). *Scientific inquiry and the social sciences: A volume in honor of Donald T. Campbell.* San Francisco: Jossey-Bass.

Bryk, A. S. (Ed.). (1983). *Stakeholder-based evaluation.* San Francisco: Jossey-Bass.

Bunda, M. A. (1985). Alternative systems of ethics and their application to education and evaluation. *Evaluation and Program Planning, 8,* 25-36.

Campbell, D. T. (1957). Factors relevant to the validity of experiments in social settings. *Psychological Bulletin, 54,* 297-312.

Campbell, D. T. (1969) Reforms as experiments. *American Psychologist, 24,* 409-429.

Campbell, D. T. (1971). *Methods for the experimenting society.* Paper presented to the Eastern Psychological Association, New York, and to the American Psychological Association, Washington, DC.

Campbell, D. T. (1974a). Evolutionary epistemology. In P. A. Schlipp (Ed.), *The philosophy of Karl Popper.* La Salle, IL: Open Court Publishing.

Campbell, D. T. (1974b, September). *Qualitative knowing in action research.* Kurt Lewin Award

Address, Society for the Psychological Study of Social Issues meeting with the American Psychological Association, New Orleans.

Campbell, D. T. (1979a). A tribal model of the social system vehicle carrying scientific knowledge. *Knowledge: Creation, Diffusion, Utilization, 1,* 181-201.

Campbell, D. T. (1979b). "Degrees of freedom" and the case study. In T. D. Cook & C. S. Reichardt (Eds.). *Qualitative and quantitative methods in evaluation research* (pp. 49-67). Newbury Park, CA: Sage.

Campbell, D. T., & Stanley, J. C. (1963). *Experimental and quasi-experimental designs for research.* Chicago: Rand-McNally.

Chen, H., & Rossi, P. H. (1981). The multi-goal, theory-driven approach to evaluation: A model linking basic and applied social science. In H. E. Freeman & M. A. Solomon (Eds.), *Evaluation studies review annual* (Vol. 6, pp. 38-54). Newbury Park, CA: Sage.

Cook, T. D., & Campbell, D. T. (1979). *Quasi-experimentation: design and analysis issues for field settings.* Chicago: Rand-McNally.

Cook, T. D., & Campbell, D. T. (1986). The causal assumptions of quasi-experimental practice. *Synthese, 68,* 141-180.

Cook, T. D., & Reichardt, C. S. (Eds.). (1979). *Qualitative and quantitative methods in evaluation research.* Newbury Park, CA: Sage.

Cook, T. D., & Shadish, W. R. (1986). Program evaluation: The worldly science. *Annual Review of Psychology, 37,* 193-232.

Cronbach, L. J. (1982). *Designing evaluations of educational and social programs.* San Francisco: Jossey-Bass.

Cronbach, L. J., Ambron, S. R., Dornbusch, S. M., Hess, R. D., Hornick, R. C., Phillips, D. C., Walker, D. F., & Weiner, S. S. (1980). *Toward reform of program evaluation.* San Francisco: Jossey-Bass.

DeMey, M. (1982). *The cognitive paradigm.* Dordrecht, Holland: D. Reidel.

Eichelberger, R. T. (1986). Interview with Jeff Schiller: A "Dinosaur" in federal government evaluation. *Evaluation Practice, 7,* 25-34.

Glass, G. V, & Ellett, F. S. (1980). Evaluation Research. In M. R. Rosenzweig & L. W. Porter (Eds.), *Annual Review of Psychology* (Vol. 31). Palo Alto, CA: Annual Reviews.

Guba, E. G., & Lincoln, Y. S. (1981). *Effective evaluation: Improving the usefulness of evaluation results through responsive and naturalistic approaches.* San Francisco: Jossey-Bass.

Guttentag, M., & Struening, E. (1975). *Handbook of evaluation research* (Vols. 1 & 2). Newbury Park, CA: Sage.

Hendricks, M. (1985). Should evaluators judge whether services are appropriate? *Evaluation and Program Planning, 8,* 37-44.

Hendricks, M. (1986). A conversation with Michael Wargo. *Evaluation Practice, 7,* 24-34.

Herzog, E. (1959). *Some guidelines for evaluating research* (Children's Bureau Publication, No. 375). Washington, DC: Department of Health, Education, and Welfare.

House, E. R. (1980). *Evaluating with validity.* Newbury Park, CA: Sage.

Karpatkin, R. H. (1987, February). Memo to members. *Consumer Reports,* p. 71.

Kenny, D. A. (1979). *Correlation and causality.* New York: John Wiley.

Kenny, D. A. (1982). Review of evaluating with validity. *Educational Evaluation and Policy Analysis, 4,* 121-122.

Lakatos, I. (1978). *The methodology of scientific research programmes.* Cambridge: Cambridge University Press.

Laudan, L. (1977). *Progress and its problems: Towards a theory of scientific growth.* Berkeley: University of California Press.

Lewin, K. (1948). *Resolving social conflicts: Selected papers on group dynamics.* New York: Harper & Row.

Lincoln, Y. S., & Guba, E. G. (1985). *Naturalistic inquiry.* Newbury Park, CA: Sage.

McCleary, R., & Hay, R. (1980). *Applied time series analysis for the social sciences.* Newbury Park, CA: Sage.

Minnesota Systems Research, Inc. (1976). *Final report: Evaluation and prediction of methodological adequacy of research and evaluation studies.* Minneapolis: Author.

Morell, J. A. (1979). *Program evaluation in social research.* New York: Pergamon.

Mullins, N. C. (1973). *Theories and theory groups in contemporary American sociology.* New York: Harper & Row.

Nagel, S. S. (1985). Evaluation research and policy studies. *Evaluation News, 6,* 59-65.

Patton, M. Q. (1978). *Utilization-focused evaluation.* Newbury Park, CA: Sage.

Rawls, J. (1971). *A theory of justice.* Cambridge, MA: Harvard University Press.

Riecken, H. W., Boruch, R. F., Campbell, D. T., Caplan, N., Glennan, T. K., Pratt, J. W., Rees, A., & Williams, W. (1974). *Social experimentation: A method for planning and evaluating social intervention.* New York: Academic Press.

Roethlisberger, F., & Dickson, W. J. (1939). *Management and the worker.* Cambridge, MA: Harvard University Press.

Rossi, P. H., & Freeman, H. E. (1985). *Evaluation: A systematic approach* (3rd Ed.). Newbury Park, CA: Sage.

Saxe, L., & Fine, M. (1981). *Social experiments: Methods for design and evaluation.* Newbury Park, CA: Sage.

Scriven, M. (1966). *Value claims in the social sciences* (Publication #123 of the Social Science Education Consortium). Lafayette, IN: Purdue University Press.

Scriven, M. (1967). The methodology of evaluation. In R. W. Tyler, R. M. Gagne, & M. Scriven (Eds.), *Perspectives on curriculum evaluation.* Chicago: Rand-McNally.

Scriven, M. (1976). Maximizing the power of causal investigation: The modus operandi method. In G. V Glass (Ed.), *Evaluation studies review annual* (Vol. 1). Newbury Park, CA: Sage.

Scriven, M. (1980). *The logic of evaluation.* Inverness, CA: Edgepress.

Scriven, M. (1983). Evaluation ideologies. In G. F. Madaus, M. Scriven, & D. L. Stufflebeam (Eds.), *Evaluation models: Viewpoints on educational and human services evaluation* (pp. 229-260). Boston: Kluwer-Nijhoff.

Shadish, W. R. (1984). Policy research: Lessons from the implementation of deinstitutionalization. *American Psychologist, 39,* 725-738.

Smith, N. L. (1981). Classic 1960s articles in educational evaluation. *Evaluation and Program Planning, 4,* 177-183.

Smith, N. L. (1985). Some characteristics of moral problems in evaluation practice. *Evaluation and Program Planning, 8,* 5-11.

Stake, R. E. (1978). The case study method in social inquiry. *Educational Researcher, 7,* 5-8.

Stake, R. E. (1986). *Quieting reform.* Urbana: University of Illinois Press.

Stanford Evaluation Consortium. (1976). Review essay: Evaluating the handbook of evaluation research. In G. V Glass (Ed.), *Evaluation studies review annual* (Vol. 1). Newbury Park, CA: Sage.

Suchman, E. A. (1967). *Evaluative research: Principles and practice in public service and social action programs.* New York: Russell Sage.

Trochim, W.M.K. (1984). *Research design for program evaluation: The regression-discontinuity approach.* Newbury Park, CA: Sage.

Weiss, C. H. (1972). The politicization of evaluation research. In C. H. Weiss (Ed.), *Evaluating action programs: Readings in social action and education* (pp. 327-338). Boston: Allyn and Bacon.

Weiss, C. H. (1973). Where politics and evaluation research meet. *Evaluation, 1,* 37-45.

Weiss, C. H. (1977). Research for policy's sake: The enlightenment function of social research. *Policy Analysis, 3,* 531-545.

Weiss, C. H. (1978). Improving the linkage between social research and public policy. In L. E. Lynn (Ed.), *Knowledge and policy: The uncertain connection* (pp. 23-81). Washington, DC: National Academy of Sciences.

Wholey, J. S. (1979). *Evaluation: Promise and performance.* Washington, DC: The Urban Institute.

Wholey, J. S. (1983). *Evaluation and effective public management.* Boston: Little, Brown.

Wholey, J. S., Nay, J. N., Scanlon, J. W., & Schmidt, R. E. (1975). If you don't care where you get to, then it doesn't matter which way you go. In G. M. Lyons (Ed.), *Social research and public policies: The Dartmouth/OECD conference* (pp. 175-197). Hanover, NH: Dartmouth College.

Wortman, P. M. (Ed.). (1981). *Methods for evaluating health services.* Newbury Park, CA: Sage.

Wortman, P. M. (1982). Review of evaluating with validity. *Educational Evaluation and Policy Analysis, 4,* 22-25.

1

Program Evaluation
The Worldly Science

Thomas D. Cook and William R. Shadish, Jr.

INTRODUCTION

Social program evaluation produces knowledge about the value of social programs and their constituent parts, knowledge that can be used in the short term to make the programs more responsive to the social problems they are meant to ameliorate. In the title of this chapter we call program evaluation the worldly science. We have several reasons for this. Unlike many other sciences, evaluation makes no distinction between applied and basic research. The real world of social programs is its only home; there is no laboratory into which to return; and even theoretical work is concerned with constructing better guides to evaluation practice. Because evaluators are paid to improve social programs, they must interact with programs on the latter's terms. They have to embrace the whole messy world of social programming, knowing that its boundaries do not respect those of the disciplines in which they were trained, while also realizing that they will have to learn practical lessons they could not have been taught, or would not have appreciated, during their training.

The ways in which the real world has returned the evaluator's embrace have resulted in some embarassment and a considerable loss of naivete when com-

From Thomas D. Cook and Williams R. Shadish, Jr., "Program Evaluation: The Worldly Science," *Annual Review of Psychology,* Vol. 37, pp. 193-232. Reproduced, with permission, from the *Annual Review of Psychology,* Vol. 37 © 1986 by Annual ᴚeviews Inc.

pared to the state of affairs 20 years ago when systematic program evaluation began. Evaluators have emerged from the 20-year embrace more sophisticated about the complexity of their task and more realistic about the political realities that exist in social programs and about how social science information is used in social problem solving. Evaluators now find themselves addressing an expanded list of theoretical and practical issues, most of which were identified as lessons learned from the earlier years of evaluation practice. Debates in the field have now acquired a remarkably catholic, interdisciplinary, and grounded character, some of which we hope to capture as we summarize the theoretical literature on evaluation.

Briefly, we will suggest that accumulated experiences have indicated that at least four knowledge bases are needed for a comprehensive theory of evaluation. First, evaluators should understand social programs so as to identify where they are most and least amenable to productive change; second, they need to know how social science knowledge is and is not used to influence social programming; third, they need an explicit theory of *value* so as to distinguish good from bad programs; and finally, they need ways of constructing valid knowledge about programs.

But these four bases are not enough. They have to feed into a theory of evaluation practice that guide' question and method choice within the limits set by budget, time, and staff constraints and in light of the trade-offs that inevitably follow once particular issue or method choices have been made. While only a theory of practice is essential to evaluation, our assumption is that such a theory will not be useful if it is naive or wrong in its underlying assumptions about any of the four knowledge bases. Consequently, the present chapter seeks to describe the lessons learned over the last 20 years in each of the areas. We begin with the lessons learned about social programs because, more than anything else, it was these that robbed evaluators of their early innocence.

KNOWLEDGE BASE ABOUT SOCIAL PROGRAMS

Concepts

The 1960s were characterized by optimism about ameliorating significant social problems through large social programs such as Job Corps, the Community Mental Health Center Program, Aid to Families with Dependent Children, and Model Cities, to name just a few. In these early years, program evaluators made many optimistic assumptions about solving social problems through social programs, believing 1. that social science theory would point to clear causes of target problems and would suggest interventions for overcoming them; 2. that these interventions would be implemented and then evaluated in ways that provided unambiguous answers; 3. that the evaluated "successes" would be welcomed by policy makers, service deliverers, and program managers who would willingly adopt them; so that 4. a significant amelioration of the original social problem would occur (Suchman 1967). But the world of social programming proved greatly inconsistent with these early assumptions, and within the policy-making community in general, optimism about social reform gave way to disillusionment about the efficacy of most federal efforts at social change other than the provision of income support and health services to the elderly and poor.

The reasons for this disappointment are complex. Some relate to intrinsic difficulties in creating major changes in "advanced" societies where many of the problems less fortunate societies now face have already been solved to a generally satisfactory degree. The problems that remain are the stubborn ones for which inexpensive solutions do not yet exist. Also, multiple groups have a stake in how most "advanced" societies are organized and changed. In the United States, such groups include Congress, officials from federal, state, and local agencies, and organizations representing professional service providers and social groups in need. Most of these groups are politically active but differ both in the priority they assign to various problems and in the preferences they hold for proposed solutions. Hence, most plans for action have to be watered down as a political precondition for being implemented as policy. To be implemented also requires that a proposed change be consistent with majority beliefs about the kind of society that is desirable and the kinds of changes that are feasible. Consequently, few policies are approved if they call for more than marginal changes in the status quo (Shadish 1984), further predisposing social change attempts toward those that are less conceptually bold.

To be acted upon, every policy has to be embodied as a program. However strong aspirations to standardize programs might be, the reality in the United States is that most federal programs are implemented in heterogeneous fashion across the 50 states and 78,000 local governments that make up the nation's administrative structure (Lindblom 1977). With the exception of income support programs such as Social Security, social "programs" are little more than administrative umbrellas for distributing funds and issuing regulations aimed at managing the many local "projects" that are physically located in city or county agencies where service provision actually takes place. Even when they receive funds from the same program, local projects differ from each other in the mix of services provided, in local traditions about service provision, in client characteristics, in the training staff members have had, and in the mix of other state and federal programs from which operating funds have been received. Social programs are diffuse, heterogeneous, and ever-changing entities, usually composed of a central program staff and many local projects that receive funds and directives from program personnel but that administer the services themselves.

Each project is itself not much more than a set of service "elements" presumed to be useful for ameliorating a social problem. Thus, the Women Infant Children program of the U.S. Department of Agriculture has many local project offices where the elements of service include medical checkups, nutrition counseling, and well-baby care, and where the elements of management include outreach, intake, record keeping, and service coordination. Since elements make up projects and projects make up programs, a complex chain of relationships connects the central program officials who are accountable for project performance to the many managers and service providers at the local level whose practice has to change if clients are to be better helped and programs improved. But the vast majority of project personnel have established ways of doing things, enjoy considerable discretion in what they do, and are only loosely coupled to program headquarters.

All social programs need political constituencies to be funded initially; and once implemented, they tend to develop even larger constituencies of those who benefit from the program through employment, power, or services. This leads to a political impactedness that makes nearly all social programs permanent features of the policy world. Local projects are subject to similar entrenchment dynamics; even so, they are not as impacted as programs. Some projects do close down for want of human energy or because of budget changes, while new projects may be added to a program as budgets expand. Such project turnover creates the opportunity to modify the mix of program-funded projects in ways that might improve the program as a whole. But since any one local project reaches only a small fraction of a program's total pool of clients, its potential for program improvement is necessarily limited. Elements are not as impacted as programs or projects, so more latitude exists to add or remove elements from projects so as to improve their functioning and that of the social programs of which they are a part. Though some elements have the advantage of being manipulable and capable of transfer across projects, most suffer from the disadvantage that they have only a puny potential to influence individual lives and are often only a small part of the total set of services a client receives.

Here we see one of the great paradoxes of evaluation. Programs reach more people than projects and promise larger individual effects than elements, but they are so politically entrenched that they cannot be modified easily by evaluation results. Projects turn over more than programs, and by influencing the number and mix of projects in a program one can influence the program itself. Yet project turnover is presumably a slow process that can only be speeded within limits. Elements have potentially the most leverage if they can be added to the repertoires of those who deliver or manage services without much disruption of routine. Unfortunately, most elements that meet these specifications will usually promise little change in the lives of individual clients. There is a mismatch here between (a) the ability to introduce new practices—lowest with programs and highest with elements; (b) the number of people who receive new or improved services—lowest with individual projects and highest with programs; and (c) the degree of anticipated influence on individual lives—lowest with individual elements and highest with programs and projects.

Being concerned with ameliorating social problems, evaluation would seem to have a well-ordered place in any rational problem-solving model which requires that: 1. problems are first clearly defined; 2. then a wide array of potential solutions is generated; 3. some of these potential solutions are then implemented and 4. *eventually evaluated.* 5. Knowledge of the successful solutions is then widely disseminated with the expectation that 6. policy makers will use the knowledge in making decisions. Unfortunately, the real world of social programming is not as rational as this decision-making model requires. In the real world, problems are ill defined and stakeholders disagree about the priority each definition deserves (Bryk 1983); program objects can be vague or contradictory (Wholey 1983); the change attempts actually implemented are marginal (Shadish 1984); program structures involve long chains of communication that hinder the accurate dissemination of information between program and project staff (McLaughlin 1985); and sources of authority for local decision making are typically diffuse, with directives from a program central office often playing only a minor role in determining the decisions made (Weiss 1978). Such realities make problematic each step in the formal problem-solving model above, forcing evaluators out of the cool world of pure analysis into a maelstrom of political and administrative complexity. With the exception of Weiss (1972), early evaluators were not very aware of the intransigence of social programs, of the descriptive inaccuracy of normative theories of decision making, and of the limited role evaluation plays as only one of the many steps in formal models of social problem solving.

As this contextual complexity became more salient, it influenced most of the social scientists who had hoped that their substantive input would improve program functioning. They gained a new appreciation of the rationality and tenacity with which policy makers, program officials, and project employees pursue their primary goals of keeping or improving their jobs and of promoting their beliefs, assigning these a higher priority than the evaluator's goal of identifying technically superior options for problem definition, program design, or problem amelioration. These same lessons also influenced many evaluators. They came to realize that because of the way programs are embedded in the world of politics, they would rarely be called upon to evaluate bold new programs or fundamental changes that had been made in existing programs. Hence, "large" effects could not be expected. Moreover, since projects are so different from each other and respond so variably to requests for change from central program authorities, most evaluators also came to realize that they could not expect the effects obtained in some projects to be consistent across all the projects in a program. Of all effects, probably the most difficult to uncover are those that are both small on the average and variable in where they are manifest.

Social Programming Methods

We might posit three action strategies for creating social changes to ameliorate social problems, each of which has different implications for program evaluation. The most frequent strategy involves creating incremental modifications in existing social programs so as to improve their functioning, usually through adding projects to a program or changing some elements in the package of services provided. The need for such change is usually felt when budgets shift, clients complain, service providers seek better ways to do things, or managers and auditors detect specific troubles.

One crucial assumption of this incrementalist approach is that by modifying projects or programs at the margin, they will become more effective and will eventually contribute to ameliorating some target social problem. Yet if the basic assumptions of a program or project are flawed, evaluation may help make a project function more efficiently without improving clients' lives. A major challenge to those who advocate incrementalism is to identify the types of programmatic change that are most likely to result in nontrivial improvements in programs that have a significant potential for ameliorating a particular problem. Such changes might require combining many novel elements or identifying the attributes of those single elements that are most likely to create significant change. While presumably rare, some elements with these attributes do exist. In mental health, for example, we can point to phenothiazine medications for treating psychotic disorders and to systematic desensitization procedures for treating phobias. We might surmise that their importance depends on a number of factors that various theorists of evaluation have emphasized in their search for approaches to evaluation that might "make a difference"— namely, each is a manipulable practice (Campbell 1969), difficult to implement incorrectly (Sechrest et al 1979), consonant with the values of the professionals who use it (Fullan 1982), keyed to an easily identified problem (Williams

1980), and robust in its effects across different types of clients and service providers (Cronbach 1982). Moreover, each is inexpensive, can be used to influence many lives, and through significantly reducing symptoms will demonstrably lead to enhanced individual functioning by criteria which everyone would agree are important (F. L. Cook 1982).

A second strategy of social change involves the use of demonstration projects to test the efficacy of planned innovations before deciding whether to introduce them as approved policy. Many things can be demonstrated, although in the later 1960s and early 1970s the emphasis seems to have been on new philosophies of service with different assumptions from the then dominant practice. Thus, experimental demonstrations of a negative income tax were launched, predicated on the notion that in times of need every citizen ought to be able to rely on a guaranteed income rather than be provided with social services (Rossi & Lyall 1976). Also, Fairweather (1980) experimented with a demonstration predicated on the assumption that chronic mental patients can look after themselves in small group living arrangements without the help of hospitals and mental health professionals. Largely because options are explored in highly circumscribed settings and are not advocated as current policy, demonstrations can be more bold than incremental changes. They are most likely to be funded when existing programs are widely acknowledged to be ineffective and difficult to improve at the margin, and our impression is that demonstrations of novel projects reached their zenith in the early 1970s. They have declined in frequency since then, as a more laissez-faire approach to social welfare came to predominate that ascribed less importance to bold innovation and preferred to use demonstrations as clinical trials of new elements that might be added to existing philosophies of service.

Demonstrations have their drawbacks. They have never been initiated as often as program or project elements have been changed. They can never convincingly indicate what would happen if an intervention were to become policy because the time frame of a demonstration is limited and the staff's commitment usually exceeds that of the persons who would implement the demonstrated activities if they became bureaucratically routinized. The utility of demonstrations is also reduced because, with the rapid turnover of federal officials and "hot" policy issues, demonstration results are sometimes provided when windows of opportunity have closed or the persons receiving the results are not those who fought to set up the demonstration. Also, although demonstrations are labeled as "tentative" or "experimental," they occur in the real world and are affected by it. In the first negative income tax experiment, for example, implementation of a minimum guaranteed income was hampered by local welfare authorities who wanted to ensure that the households receiving benefits from the demonstration were reporting them in full when filing for their regular welfare entitlements. Finally, the transition from a successful demon-stration to a fully funded social program is strewn with obstacles, as the fate of Fairweather's Lodge illustrates. Despite positive evaluation results and many recommendations to implement the concept widely, we still do not have many Lodges, probably because its assumptions are too radically different for most mental health professionals (Shadish 1984). Though successful evaluation results may raise the likelihood that a demonstration's activities will be used as a basis for policy, this felicitous outcome is not at all guaranteed.

The third strategy of social change involves changes in basic social structures and beliefs that touch on such fundamental matters as the nature and locus of political authority, the form of the economy, and the distribution of income and wealth. Such system change is rare, although during the Depression major changes did occur in many American beliefs and in the structure and responsibilities of the federal government. However, such changes are not part of the routine government functioning that evaluators aspire to improve and so are more properly the purview of historians, sociologists, and political scien-tists.

KNOWLEDGE BASE ABOUT EVALUATION USAGE

Concepts

With the wisdom of hindsight, we can now see the naivete of early conceptions of how evaluation results would improve social programs. The dominant notion in the 1960s was that evaluative feedback about which programs did and did not work would be used to maintain or expand effective programs and to discontin-ue or radically change ineffective ones (Suchman 1967). But discontinuing social programs is rare, and discontinuing them because of evaluation results is unheard of. This is partly because evaluations are never so compelling, and their findings usually lead to dispute rather than consensus (Lindblom & Cohen 1979). It is also because evaluation is in many ways just another political act that occurs in a context where power, ideology, and interests are more powerful determinants of decision making than feedback about programs.

It is not clear how often evaluation results influence program budgets, increasing them when effectiveness is indicated and decreasing them when it is not. This is a less stringent criterion than discontinuance, although it retains the same connotation of evaluation results being used to shape the decisions made by formal decision makers. Claims have been made that some past evaluations did influence funding levels, as with the decision to phase out the small summer component of Head Start (Weiss & Rein 1970). However, it is difficult to attribute any single decision to evaluation findings alone, given the complexity of the world of politics. Nonetheless, the consensus among evaluators is that in the short term, evaluations rarely influence program budget levels.

Somewhat stronger, but still indirect, evidence suggests that evaluation findings can influence the internal priorities of programs, affecting the mix of services made available, the manner of their provision, the target beneficiaries of preference, how regulations are enforced, etc. While obviously political, such changes are less so when compared to changes in budget levels, for the latter transmit powerful symbolic messages about the social problems being addressed on a priority basis and about the client groups and professional guilds that are to benefit from a program's provisions. Still, we know little that is systematic about the frequency with which evaluation results lead to short-term changes in internal program priorities.

The foregoing discussion has emphasized the instrumental use of evaluations designed to summarize the achievements of national programs and demonstrations that might later become national programs. This is not the only model of short-term instrumental usage. A small number of federal programs mandated self-evaluation by local projects under the assumption that evaluators employed by a project are more trusted than external evaluators and know the project and its operations better. The expectation was such that in-house evaluators would be better at identifying where evaluative results might have leverage, at collecting high-quality data, and at getting evaluation results used. Self-evaluation was mandated for all the projects receiving program funds so that the feedback provided would improve each project and in so doing would enhance the overall program to which each project belonged.

Unfortunately, there is little empirical support for this project-level theory of instrumental usage, except with some types of educational television (Cook & Curtin 1986). In community mental health (Cook & Shadish 1982), community crime prevention (Feeley & Sarat 1980), and local Title I projects in education (David 1982), the theory seems to have run afoul of several realities. First, project managers rarely want systematic information based on social science methods and instead prefer ammunition to help with their project's public relations. Second, in-house evaluators tend to have little power and multiple responsibilities, and are named as the "evaluator" only because someone has to have this title and they know something about social science methodology. Finally, in-house evaluators are sometimes seen as allies of project management. Hence, if factions are competing for power within a project, the evaluator may be seen as taking sides and may lose the very advantages she or he is supposed to have over external evaluators. While some exceptions undoubtedly exist, the administrative conditions required by the local project model of instrumental usage may not occur often.

The emphasis on immediate instrumental usage by elected officials or the managers of programs and projects is now less salient than it used to be in evaluation. This is probably because disappointingly few large effects have been discovered, and because few clear incidences of instrumental usage have been documented. It is not easy to document such usage, for when results and decisions coincide, the evaluation results could have been used to justify decisions already made on other (and more political) grounds. As currently practiced, few evaluations seem to be of a clearly demonstrated, short-term instrumental utility, though exceptions exist (see Leviton & Boruch 1984).

Empirical attacks on the instrumental conception of evaluation use were accompanied by some evaluators beginning to ask: What should the role of evaluative information be in an open, democratic society (Cook 1983)? Should decisions not be influenced by enduring cultural values and the give and take of political compromise every bit as much as by the type of feedback that evaluation provides? Normative reflections like these were probably partly responsible for decoupling the definition of evaluation usage from an exclusive emphasis on results constituting decisions and for enlarging the definition to include evaluations being cited in policy deliberations where they might function as just one of many inputs and not have any clear link to a particular decision. The dissociation of usage from decision making was also furthered by the realization that prior decisions often leave decision makers with little freedom for present action (Weiss 1980). To label the choices they eventually make as "decisions" suggests a greater freedom to select among options than is actually warranted, and to believe that evaluation results influence such preempted "decisions" is naive. If many political decisions are preempted, and if theories of democracy do not imply that evaluation feedback should determine political decisions, no rationale exists for defining the use of evaluation results solely in terms of results causing decisions.

A second shift in the conceptualization of usage followed from learning that individuals in decision-making groups are exposed to many different sources of information, some of which use evaluation findings in ways that suit their own purposes but are not closely linked to the evaluator's major stated conclusions. Thus, lobbyists or journalists might sometimes refer to findings about one program in deliberations about other programs, or they might cite results to help make points about the needs of a particular social group or about the length of time it might take for a new program to impact on national-level statistics. They might do this, even though none of these points was explicitly made in the evaluation report they cite and though none of these uses speaks directly to short-term instrumental usage. Rather, they concern a more diffuse and indirect type of use called "enlightenment" (Weiss 1977), that deals with the influences knowledge has on cognitive frameworks. For instance, enlightenment occurs when knowledge clarifies the theoretical assumptions undergirding a program, when it highlights relationships among the values of various stakeholder groups, or when it illuminates the priorities that different problems deserve. In altering cognitive frameworks rather than uncovering and teaching specific "facts," enlightenment decouples usage both from a dependence on reports about a single program and from the notion that usage should occur soon after an evaluation is completed. For Cronbach and his associates (1980, 1982) and Guba & Lincoln (1981), enlightenment came to replace short-term decision making as the ultimate justification for evaluation.

Another shift decoupled the definition of evaluation usage from usage by particular decision makers. Pluralist conceptions of evaluation stress that multiple groups have a stake in programs. Of these, program managers and funders originally received most attention, and some theories of evaluation were specifically tailored to meeting their information needs (e.g. Patton 1978, Wholey 1983). But with time other stakeholders came to be seen as equally important, especially service deliverers (Cronbach et al 1980) and consumers of services (Scriven 1980). Their importance increased even more after it was realized that while evaluations might be used to modify the regulations coming from a program central office, these regulations did not always influence local practices that are shaped by many other forces, some more immediately pressing than program regulations. Growing awareness of the partial independence of local practitioners also led to an interest in how they learn about evaluation findings—through in-service training, books and journals that cite evaluations, or observing colleagues whose own practice has been influenced by evaluations (Leviton & Boruch 1983). Congruent with this was a growing interest in how evaluations are used to train future professionals who will later deliver services in local projects as teachers, social workers, nurses, and the like (Leviton & Cook 1984). These themes all reject the notion that the use of evaluations should be expected only from senior program and project managers.

A further shift decoupled usage from dependence on the formal conclusions presented in an evaluation report. Research suggested that potential users sometimes raise issues with evaluators that transcend the information gained from a single study (Leviton & Hughes 1981, Mielke & Chen 1981). Instead, the issues require knowledge synthesized from the total body of prior studies, from the incidental observations made by evaluators during their work, or even from their own reflections on the program, project, or element they have studied. Being able to respond on the basis of such incidental knowledge can prove helpful in ways that transcend the major conclusions explicitly drawn in a particular evaluative study.

By 1985 the concept of usage was much broader than in 1965. It encompassed evaluations constituting decisions, playing a codeterminative role in constituting decisions, being cited in formal and informal debates, being used in the in-service training of working professionals, being used in the education of future practitioners, and being used to enhance the enlightenment of all stakeholders so that they might conceptualize past and future social programs and problems in a different manner. The agent of influence was no longer a single evaluation report presented to formal decision makers. Literature reviews were also involved, as was knowledge gained from incidental reading and interactions with substantive experts and practitioners. Even the sources for disseminating knowledge were now more broadly understood. Instead of being restricted to evaluation reports and briefings targeted at funders, they now included reports aimed at audiences of scholars and practitioners, ad hoc media presentations of findings, and even unanticipated conversations with important persons at informal events.

Methods to Stimulate Usage

Empirical and conceptual work suggests that the usage of evaluations is promoted in three major and related ways: through the choice of issues addressed; through the roles the evaluator adopts regarding potential users; and through the communication channels chosen for disseminating evaluation results.

To help create a descriptive language for discussing how evaluation issues are framed, Cook et al (1985) distinguished between issues framed at the program, project, or element level and issues framed around issues of (a) targeting (who receives or distributes services?); (b) implementation (what are the program inputs, processes, and cost, and how can the treatment be specified?); (c) effectiveness (what changes have occurred in the units receiving services?); and (d) impacts (how do the services influence the social and other systems with which persons in need interact—e.g. their families, neighborhoods, other service projects?). Cook et al (1985) also distinguished between issues framed in a more descriptive or explanatory mode. The former would be involved when one asks: "Which types of clients received services more often?," or "What are the program's effects?" The more explanatory mode would be involved when one asks: "Why did this group receive more services than another?", or "Why did the intervention have the effects attributed to it?" We now use these distinctions to discuss how methods for stimulating usage depend on the framing of an evaluative issue.

Since programs rarely die, the powerful consensus in more recent evaluation theory is that orienting evaluation exclusively toward the description of program effects and impacts provides little leverage for short-term usage. More utility is assigned to describing and explaining the targeting and implementation of program services on the dual grounds that describing program operations (a) will help identify problems of implementation that occur widely across the projects in a program, and (b) will generate practical suggestions for improving projects, with the suggestions coming from common sense, current professional practice, and knowledge of what has been implemented at the superior sites among those studied. The ultimate hope is that once a source of improvement has been identified, knowledge of it will be disseminated throughout a program and will be adopted (or adapted) by a significant number of projects (Wholey 1983).

A second source of leverage at the program level is presumed to come from explanatory studies that model the theoretical and operational logic behind a program. The hope is to trace all the time-bound relationships through which program inputs are supposed to influence project processes that in their turn are supposed to bring about effects on clients' lives and ultimately impact on indicators of a social problem. Once such models have been made explicit, they can be critically examined prior to data collection to estimate whether the financial, human, and material resources they postulate as necessary are available and whether the hypothesized relationships between inputs, processes, and outcomes are congruent with relevant, substantive theory. It is surprising how often such preevaluative model building reveals failures of program planning, even though no primary data have been collected. Nonetheless, collecting such data is crucial for assessing the correspondence between program operations and planners' assumptions. Although armchair analysis and ad hoc reports from practitioners provide useful preevaluative knowledge, they cannot be relied upon for a comprehensive or veridical description of what actually happens within a program (Rossi & Freeman 1982).

A third source of leverage at the program level involves the description of effects attributable to elements that central program administrators can control. (These will be quite different from the elements that local project officials can control.) While many program elements are puny in the effects anticipated on individuals, their potential to reach so many clients can make their aggregate impact considerable. Thus, a minor change in the application forms for free and reduced-price school lunches that was sponsored by central program authorities reduced fraudulent applications by a small percentage; but since about a billion lunches of these types are served each year, the savings in the first year were estimated to be about seven million dollars (Applied Management Services 1984). The need is to identify the types of program element that can be changed and are most likely to result in improving program operations in socially significant ways.

If we move from the program to the project level, we note that considerable leverage was once anticipated from evaluations describing the targeting, implementation, and effects achieved in each of the individual projects making up a program. Indeed, the payoff anticipated from this source was once enough to justify mandating local project evaluations for many programs. However, for reasons mentioned earlier, this path to program improvement now appears less promising. More emphasis is now placed on identifying projects that are particularly successful by the most important effect criteria in the hope that such knowledge will eventually influence program managers to modify the mix of projects funded and will persuade local project personnel to change the mix of service elements they provide. However, research on this leverage point has not had an auspicious history, since (*a*) most past procedures for identifying successful projects concentrated on *single* exemplary instances even though many were unique in ways that precluded effective transfer elsewhere—often because of the charisma of project developers; (*b*) active disagreement emerged about the criteria of success and standards of methodological adequacy that should be used to identify exemplary projects; and (*c*) the identification procedures rarely emphasized those elements within projects that were responsible for success, even though such explanatory knowledge might facilitate transfer to other projects.

Because of these limitations, it has been suggested that evaluation should be directed at identifying the *types* of projects that are so effective by major outcome criteria that they deserve to be more widely distributed throughout a program (Cook et al 1985). The logic behind this is that the number of projects in a program does wax and wane since projects terminate voluntarily, program budgets change, and projects occasionally seek to change their operating philosophy. However, it would be naive to pretend either that project-level turnover is high or that evaluators can easily identify the more successful types of projects in a program. The latter task requires constructing a typology of project types and then sampling some individual projects from within each type. Inevitably there will be considerable variability within each type, and the more there is the less useful is the concept of type.

If we turn to the level of project elements, there are undoubtedly some novel elements of practice that, if introduced into projects, would improve many of them and thus enhance the overall program of which they are a part. In these current times of fiscal stringency, much leverage is attributed to identifying manipulable practices that practitioners can adopt (or adapt) into their repertoire without changing the essence of their practice (McLaughlin 1985). Some theorists emphasize locating such practices through identifying the elements to which the success of exemplary projects can be attributed. However, there is no need to focus only on exemplary projects, and our guess is that much of the research aimed at identifying successful elements occurs in evaluations of more ordinary projects where data on the implementation of services is used to try to explain the pattern of obtained results.

Causal explanation is not the only source of knowledge about transferrable project manipulanda. Many developers gear their work to improving the tools practitioners use; some practitioners actively experiment in their own work in the hope of identifying better procedures; and in each policy sector new substantive theories develop from which implications for practice are abstracted. Each of these instances can lead to a clinical trial (or demonstration) in which a particular element serves as the independent variable in a focused study designed to identify successful elements that deserve to be made available for general practice or even reimbursement (Pacht et al 1980, Bunker 1985).

Clinical trials of possible future practices do not link reimbursement to current professional practice and so are less threatening than clinical trials of elements of present practice. Indeed, many professional associations will resist the latter type of study, but such instances do occur. However, when clinical trials are used to identify successful elements of local practice, it is difficult for program authorities to monitor practitioner compliance with any specific behaviors that might be recommended because of clinical trials. If such monitoring is conducted independently and on site, it tends to be expensive and obtrusive; but if it is done through fellow professionals employed at the same agency or through self-reports from practitioners, the monitoring is likely to be biased toward obtaining exaggerated levels of compliance with the recommendations or prescriptions of program personnel.

The degree of leverage for getting evaluation results used does not depend solely on how evaluation issues are framed. It is also associated with the nature of the persons setting evaluative questions and with the role relationships evaluators adopt regarding these persons. For instance, Wholey (1983) assigns a major role to program managers, reasoning that their job puts them in a special position to suggest and enforce changes in program guidelines. Hence, Wholey believes that evaluators should look to program managers to provide the guiding evaluation questions. However, he believes that evaluators should not be passive in doing this. They need to help managers formulate questions that are clear, important, and answerable within the constraints of time and budget, and they also need to keep regular contact with managers. Indeed, almost all theorists of evaluation agree that usage is stimulated by frequent, close contact between evaluators and prospective users.

The type of contact they recommend varies somewhat. Campbell (1969) favors the evaluator as servant to the honest administrator, but as a "whistle blower" to the dishonest administrator; Wholey (1983) sees him or her as a faithful retainer who also seeks to educate managers about how to evaluate more usefully; Cronbach (Cronbach et al 1980) also favors an educator role, but one that takes theory and past research findings into greater account than is the case with Wholey and that tilts more toward representing the needs of those who directly deliver or manage services at the local level; Berman & McLaughlin (1977) see the evaluator as an information broker; while Scriven (1983) sees him as a consumer consultant who tells prospective purchasers about the best buys from among the competing alternatives. A few case studies suggest that short-term usage is associated with the evaluator playing more of a proactive than reactive role, responding flexibly if the information needs of potential users change during a study and, when required, invoking background knowledge of the social problem and social program under analysis instead of sticking only to preformulated evaluative issues (Leviton & Hughes 1981, Leviton &

Boruch 1983). Thus, the pendulum has now swung closer to the conception of Cronbach and of Berman and McLaughlin, or perhaps even of Wholey, than to the conception of Campbell or Scriven.

Roles have to do with communication, and we assume that some ways of communicating are more likely than others to lead to the dissemination and eventual utilization of evaluative results. All theorists are agreed that communication should be informal and cast in simple language devoid of jargon. Many theorists also contend that evaluation reports might be in several different forms tailored to the unique information needs and communication patterns of different stakeholder groups. All except Campbell argue that the action implications of the evaluation findings should be spelled out and defended but without obscuring the basic findings or inadvertently promoting the evaluators' values. The theorists also believe that evaluators should do all they can to get publicity for their findings in the mass media and professional outlets. The assumption is that such exposure will increase the number of stakeholder groups that learn of the evaluation findings and hence might use them for their own enlightenment even if they do not use them as guides to immediate changes in what they do.

KNOWLEDGE BASE ABOUT VALUING

Concepts

In its early years, evaluation gave little explicit attention to the role of values. Scriven (1983) suggests that this was because evaluators naively believed that their activities could and should be value-free. But many evaluators learned from experience that it was impossible in the political world of social programming to make most of the choices they had to make without values becoming salient, perhaps most clearly when evaluative criteria were being selected and justified. While evaluators have increasingly come to acknowledge that values deserve more attention, they have not known how to proceed in this delicate task, for most evaluators were trained to believe that values are not part of "science."

To address issues of value, a few evaluators have used metatheoretical approaches to construct frameworks from which statements about the value, merit, or "goodness" of any entity can be deduced. Scriven's (1980) approach is the best known, and his general logic involves four steps. First, justifiable criteria of merit have to be developed that specify what an evaluand has to influence as a condition for being labeled good. Second, justifiable standards of performance have to be selected for each criterion that specify how well the evaluand ought to perform in order to attain a specified level of merit. Third, performance has to be measured on each criterion so as to estimate whether specified standards of quality performance have been reached. And finally, where multiple criteria are involved, the measured results have to be integrated into a single statement about the overall goodness or value of the evaluand.

A form of logic like Scriven's is heavily used in several areas. Consider product evaluations. In evaluating automobiles, the criteria of merit would include purchase price, gas mileage, passenger capacity, and comfort. Standards of performance might specify minimal standards of safe handling under emergency conditions which, if not met, would lead to a car not being recommended. Yet standards can also be relative, as when several automobile models in the same size and price range are compared because they are the alternatives from which potential consumers will actually have to choose. After performance standards have been set comes the measurement of performance, which can involve test drives, owner surveys, interviews with automobile engineers, or laboratory tests. Finally, the results are somehow synthesized across the various measures to recommend the "best buy" from among the standards considered. Traditional quantitative research practice follows the same metatheoretic logic. Criteria are called dependent variables; standards of performance are called comparison or control groups; data collection retains the same name; while global synthesis is achieved through decision-making statistical procedures. However, in social science the object being evaluated is usually a theoretical hypothesis rather than an automobile or a social program.

Metatheoretic approaches do not specify which criteria or standards to use or how to measure and synthesize. Prescriptive ethical theories could be a source of such criteria, on the rationale that evaluators participate in a moral act by providing data to improve social programs aimed at poverty, racism, crime, and the like (Warnock 1971). One such prescriptive theory is Rawls's (1971) egalitarian theory of justice, which states that social goods and services ought to be distributed to alleviate those material needs of the disadvantaged that, if not met, will result in unacceptable harm. In suggesting how to operationalize his otherwise apparently neutral metatheoretic logic of valuing, Scriven (1980) adopts a similar position, suggesting that a program or element is good to the extent it meets needs, with the latter being inferred when an unacceptably high cost is incurred in the absence of the service being evaluated. House (1980) is even more explicit than Scriven, arguing that Rawls's theory should be used to guide the selection and weighting of evaluative criteria and performance standards.

However, few evaluators are willing to rely on prescriptive ethics for criteria selection. This is largely because no compelling reason currently exists for preferring one prescriptive theory over another. In the case of theories of justice, a number of credible alternatives to Rawls have been constructed, most notably Nozick's (1974) libertarian theory. Moreover, while justice is a central moral concern in evaluation, it is not the only relevant concern. Criteria can also be justified in terms of their relationship to human rights, equality, liberty, utility, and many other such abstract concepts. Evaluators may also be unwilling to endorse particular prescriptive ethics because few data have been advanced thus far to support particular philosophers' claims that a better society will result if one ethic is followed rather than another and because the American political system has traditionally preferred to foster a pluralism of values. Promoting a single prescriptive ethic is therefore inconsistent with the political context in which evaluation occurs. While evaluators will benefit from being generally informed about the prescriptive implications of criteria selections so that they can help others reason about the values and kind of society that particular choices seem to imply, it is difficult to justify a more extensive role than this.

A descriptive approach to valuing is better suited to the political context in which evaluators actually function, since decision making depends more on the values held by relevant legislators, managers, voters, lobbyists, etc, than on any single prescriptive calculus of value. Hence, knowledge of stakeholder values can be used to help select criteria so that no criteria are overlooked that are of crucial importance to particular groups. More is at issue here than conformity with a pluralist ethic. Without an understanding of stakeholder values the process of conducting an evaluation may be more difficult. Stakeholders may not be cooperative with data collection and may even challenge the eventual evaluation findings on grounds of evaluator partisanship.

Descriptive approaches are now popular in evaluation, but are limited by the wisdom of the values held by the various participants in the political process. Many participants do not have the time, interest, or experience to express their values with the degree of articulation found among theorists of ethics or among organized stakeholders who seek to clothe their self-interest with ethical-sounding rationales for or against particular government programs. Descriptive approaches are also limited because, although values are interrelated in complex ways, many Americans have been socialized to believe in the special priority of certain values—e.g. life, liberty, and the pursuit of happiness—and may have a limited understanding of how promoting these values could hinder the attainment of others. Moreover, while knowing the values of different groups may be enlightening, it cannot easily generate specific principles for justifying the selection of some criteria and standards over others. The description of values generates a list and not a justified procedure for setting priorities.

Methods for Valuing

As Scriven's first step in his metatheoretic logic of valuing suggests, to know how good a program is requires criteria of merit. In the early years of evaluation, it was standard practice to use program goals to set criteria. This was not unreasonable. Programs have goals, and since they are usually formulated through give-and-take in the political arena, they presumably reflect some conjunction of the many interests participating in the democratic process. Nonetheless, exclusive reliance on program goals proved to be an error because 1. goals are often vague, contradictory, or latent (Weiss 1977, Scriven 1983); 2. program implementation is so heterogeneous and locally controlled that the goals of program officials do not overlap heavily with the goals of local officials and service deliverers; and 3. programs have unintended effects that sometimes turn out to be just as important as planned goals. Also, 4. if they have enough control over goal specification, program managers are often tempted to specify excessively modest goals on the grounds that it is better to succeed at something less important than to fail at something more important. And 5. when they have less control over goal specification, managers are likely to find themselves stuck with unrealistically high goals that mirror the overpromises that program advocates gave to secure initial funding. Finally, 6. to know that a program or project reached its goals says nothing about whether it represents the most efficient available way of meeting these goals.

Although goals have been rejected as the sole source of criteria of merit, no replacement has yet been agreed upon. Candidates for criteria now include: 1. examining the claims that clients, service deliverers, and program managers make about what a program is achieving and about the factors that led to success or failure (Guba & Lincoln 1981); 2. studying factors that will feed into decisions that policy makers or managers have to make in the near future (Weiss 1972); 3. assessing any substantive system models that have been developed to explain how program inputs should be related to subsequent processes and outcomes (Chen & Rossi 1983); 4. estimating the degree to which the material needs of clients have been met (Scriven 1980); and 5. catering to the information needs of multiple stakeholder groups (Bryk 1983) or of just managers and policy makers (Wholey 1983). By itself, none of these options results in a neat set of criteria or priority judgments. Procedures for prioritizing do exist, of which the most noteworthy are decision-theoretic in their origins (see Edwards et al 1975). But these procedures are more easily implemented with fewer stakeholder groups, and have been used most often in the management-centered evaluations that Wholey prefers. When multiple stakeholder interests are taken into account and no a priori reason exists for weighting some interests more than others, no perfect method currently exists for generating a prioritized list of criteria of merit.

Once a goal-based approach to valuing is rejected, the value of an evaluand must depend on the total set of effects it achieves, whether intended or not, harmful or beneficial. A serious practical problem is to know how to identify the unintended effects that might occur. Chen & Rossi (1983) suggest that substantive social science theories will often provide clues to such effects if the theories are used to help articulate the links relating program inputs to subsequent processes, effects, and impacts. Scriven (1980) suggests that potential side effects may be discovered if evaluators come to know the evaluand in detail before collecting more formal evaluation data. Interviews with clients, service providers, and program managers might be used for this purpose, with particular attention being paid to passionate advocates and opponents of the program, since no one is more likely than they to have thought about potential beneficial or harmful side effects. However, no perfect method exists for informing evaluators about unplanned effects.

The second step in Scriven's metatheoretic logic of valuing concerns the construction of standards for ranking performance. Two possibilities are suggested. Absolute standards link evaluative rankings to prespecified levels of performance, as when criterion-referenced tests are used in education to assign letter grades or to certify competency for graduation from high school. Since the results of such tests do not depend on how classmates perform, they differ from the results that follow from using comparative performance standards, as when school grades are assigned on a curve or alternative automobile models are directly compared. These last examples are instructive, for with grading on a curve students can perform very well and still receive a D; and an automobile can be totally satisfactory but not be recommended for purchase because it performs less well than an alternative.

Although social programs can be held to either absolute or comparative standards, the latter are more easily justified and in fact predominate in evaluation practice. Of the five comparative standards used to date, Campbell (1969) is most closely identified with the selection of *no-treatment control group* standards that represent what would have happened to respondents in the absence of the evaluand. Evaluators hope to learn from this standard whether exposure to a program, project, or element is better than no such exposure, even though receiving no exposure does not prevent control group members from exercising their initiative and receiving comparable services from nonprogram sources.

A *no-services baseline* restricts the counterfactual conditions to those where it can be presumed that the controls receive no ameliorative services whatsoever. A precondition for this is a measure of service implementation that includes measures of help from sources other than those being evaluated, so that a group can be constructed of persons with no sources of help at all. The preference for no-service controls is often associated with a preference for purified treatment groups that are restricted to those persons who demonstrably received more or better services. This permits a "high or maximal dosage" group to be constructed that can be contrasted with the "no-service" or "no-dosage" control group.

Scriven (1980) suggests that comparisons should be with the *available alternatives* among which the "consumers" of programs, projects, or elements have to choose in determining how to act. He argues that no consumer needs to choose between a particular automobile model and having no car at all, and that decision makers in the social policy world rarely have to choose between a program or no program, or even between a current program and a single alternative. Campbell's work on evolutionary epistemology (1974) also implies the same preference for identifying the better performers among multiple viable alternatives, and it buttresses his advocacy that evaluations are particularly useful if they are linked to demonstration studies that examine multiple "planned variations" and are not restricted to a single program or a single plan for a program.

Cronbach (1963) opposes the use of comparative standards from outside a program or project, arguing that social problem solving is best facilitated by improving the evaluand relative to itself in the past. He argues that studies of variants cannot identify how to improve current practices, and he further maintains that the variants examined rarely pursue the same set of goals, rarely prioritize their shared goals the same way, and rarely postulate the same time frames in which effects and impacts should be expected. Hence, he believes it is misleading to treat social variants as though they were functionally equivalent, and he cautions anyone who commissions an evaluation with this premise that they are likely to engender in project developers and personnel an apprehension about being evaluated that may be counterproductive. This is because project personnel tend to see the services they provide as unique, and they fear that their work will be insensitively tested if evaluation activities are limited to those consequences that the evaluators believe all the projects under analysis should achieve.

Light (1983) has added another relative standard of performance to the list. He notes that in many areas of social welfare the planned interventions involve attention being paid to clients, and he suggests that the marginal contribution of an evaluand be assessed over and above any results attributable to such attention. His rationale is presumably that while attention is an intrinsic component of many interventions, it is a less expensive form of treatment than the total package of services provided, it may not have the same long-term effects, and it does not define what is unique about a program or project. At issue here is a *placebo control group*.

In selecting relative standards: 1. a concern for maximizing the likelihood of obtaining some treatment effects impels evaluators toward the strategy of contrasting maximally implemented services with the total absence of such services; 2. a concern for comparing future alternatives with current ones impels evaluators toward the comparison of treatments-as-implemented with no-treatment controls who are free to seek out alternative services; 3. a concern for comparing the major alternatives available for service provision impels evaluators toward studies of planned variations; 4. a concern to attribute effects to the specific services that define a treatment's uniqueness impels the evaluator toward the use of placebo controls; and 5. a concern to improve an evaluand on its own terms impels an evaluator toward before-after measurement on the evaluand, especially if there is no reason to believe that maturation or testing will increase performance over time. Since so much depends on the choice of comparative standards, since so many standards exist, and since they have not been well discussed to date in the evaluation literature, our guess is that much more debate on standards of comparison will occur in the future. Two issues might then be worth developing.

First, no algorithm yet exists for helping evaluators select among the various relative standards. Yet the choice of a standard can have profound implications, for it is not unreasonable to assume that the likelihood of effects will generally be lowest when an evaluand is compared to an alternative, next lowest when compared to a placebo control group, and next lowest when compared to a no-treatment group. Effectiveness is more likely when no-services baselines are used or when before-after changes are contrasted, particularly when treatment groups are defined in terms of the subgroup of persons manifestly receiving high-quality services. Fortunately, the choice of comparison standards does not require selecting a single option, and evaluations can be designed with multiple controls. When resources permit, this is clearly the preferred strategy (Light 1983), but no choice algorithm yet exists.

Second, the comparison standards that are most likely to result in "effects" seem to be more heavily advocated by evaluation theorists today. This probably reflects their belief that past evaluations chronically underestimated the potential of treatments because of inadequate evaluation designs (Cronbach 1982, Light & Pillemer 1984), suboptimally implemented program activities (Sechrest et al 1979), and operational plans that were not well linked to the social science theory undergirding program design (Chen & Rossi 1983). From such concerns arises the recent attention to implementation and its emphasis on no-service baselines and before-after changes. However, it is important to distinguish between impediments to implementation that are the result of inherent structural constraints and those that result from temporary problems that might be corrected with better knowledge, more resources, or keener commitment. To select standards of performance assessing what services might achieve if they were implemented well makes sense if past impediments to high-quality implementation are likely to be corrigible. Evaluators can then orient future work to probing ways to improve the implementation of those factors that improve performance, while ceasing work on those elements of practice that are ineffective even when evaluated by standards designed to maximize effectiveness. However, if evidence strongly suggests that the impediments to high-quality implementation are structural, it makes little sense to evaluate a program under conditions that maximize the contrast between no services and services implemented at their best, for it will not be possible to implement on a routine basis those conditions associated with highest quality implementation.

As for measuring performance—the third step in his metatheoretical logic—Scriven cautions evaluators that this is a limited task. It does not include for him the preevaluative tasks of describing the evaluand or assessing opinions about its value. Nor does it include postevaluative analyses of why an evaluand was effective or of how the evaluation results might be used. While all of these tasks result in knowledge useful for the program improvement that Cronbach prefers, Scriven contends that such measurements are not necessary for the evaluative purpose he most prizes—summarizing the value of an entity. For this purpose, Scriven contends that only measurement of each alternative on each pre-specified criterion is required, provided that the measurement is sensitive enough to permit strong inferences about whether absolute standards were reached or true comparative differences detected. Although measurement is a restricted concept for Scriven, it does entail more than performance assessment alone. To make statements about an evaluand's value, it must be clear that it was the evaluand, and not some force correlated with it, that caused the changes observed in the criteria of merit (see Campbell 1969). Hence, inferences about causal connections are necessarily implied by Scriven's concept of measurement.

For Scriven (1980), valuing is not complete until a fourth step has been made and a final synthesis about merit has been achieved. Since all synthesis requires weighting criteria and then summing them, measurements have to be converted into a common metric. Benefit-cost analysis attempts to do this by converting all program inputs and outputs into money terms so that the ratio of costs to benefits can be computed. However, it is difficult to assign a monetary value to outcomes such as increased marital happiness, decreased fear of crime, or higher self-concept, and so the weighting schemes used in benefit-cost analysis are especially assumption-riddled at their core. Consequently, some economists in evaluation prefer cost-effectiveness analysis (Levin 1983). This also requires converting program inputs into monetary terms; but unlike with benefit-cost analysis, effects and impacts are left in the original metric so that statements can be made about how much financial input is required to cause a particular unit of change in any outcome. Syntheses of individual studies can also be achieved through descriptive weighting techniques that measure the values of the persons who might eventually use the evaluation results and then using these values to assign different weights to different patterns of results. The most common methods for doing this are Bayesian but are rarely used today (Edwards et al 1975).

It would be wrong to think of synthesis as being restricted to a single evaluation. Because it puts all effect size estimates onto the same standardized scale, metaanalysis (Glass et al 1981) has been widely used in recent years to synthesize results across multiple evaluations of a program, project, or element. Metaanalysis permits evaluators to escape from the limitations of statistical power and contextual uniqueness that attend single studies, but it also requires assumptions about weights, especially as concerns weighting effect sizes by the sample sizes used to achieve them and weighting studies by the quality of their methodology. Considerable interest has been shown recently in techniques for qualitatively integrating single evaluative studies into the findings from earlier research and into the knowledge base of professional wisdom (see Cronbach et al 1980). Like metaanalysis, qualitative integration techniques can help in drawing conclusions about the robustness of findings, in identifying situational or personological factors on which effect sizes might depend, and in providing a more comprehensive picture of an evaluand's total influence by adding information about important variables that were left out of a particular evaluation.

Evaluators do not seem to be very concerned with methods for synthesizing results, particularly across different outcome constructs. Cronbach (1982) argues that separate conclusions should be presented for each criterion, because different conclusions warrant different degrees of confidence, and individual conclusions are less likely to be challenged if they stand alone than if they are part of a criterion synthesis that depends on a weighting system with which some stakeholders will disagree. Moreover, letting each conclusion stand by itself gives readers the chance to assign their own weights to findings, perhaps eventually coming to an overall conclusion that differs from the evaluator's. After all, very tall readers of automobile evaluations in *Consumer Reports* are likely to weight front leg room more highly than the magazine's staff, and so are likely to buy different cars! Evaluators can reduce the problem of parochial weighting by constructing multiple value positions—often representing different stakeholder groups—from which different sets of weights can be generated. For example, Cook et al's (1975) review of data on *Sesame Street* resulted in the conclusion that if one values learning about two or three letters of the alphabet in six months, and if one does not object to the fact that economically advantaged children learn more from *Sesame Street* in the aggregate than disadvantaged children, then *Sesame Street* is good; but if one objects to either of these premises, then the program is not good.

Yet despite these reasons for not constructing a single system of weights and summing across criteria, it is worth noting that both benefit-cost and metaanalysis have proven spectacularly appealing in the world of public policy, probably because they lead to simple, quantified results that are general in application, can be readily remembered, and are not hindered by multiple caveats. Perhaps the lesson to be learned is that while a good overall synthesis may be compatible with the political system's struggle for simple answers to complex issues, individual findings need nonetheless to be respected so that those who can justify a unique weighting system can construct their own syntheses.

KNOWLEDGE BASE ABOUT CONSTRUCTING VALID KNOWLEDGE

Concepts

Like most social science, evaluation originally looked to versions of logical positivism to justify method choices. Congruent with this was a preference for using program goals to formulate causal hypotheses which could then be tested using experiments (Suchman 1967, Campbell 1969). This strategy assumes that programs are relatively homogeneous, have goals that are totally explicit, postulate effects that can be validly measured, and can be assessed using feasible experimental designs that rule out all spurious interpretations of a treatment effect. All these assumptions have come under attack, not only in evaluation, but also in science at large. Of special importance are three themes that Kuhn (1962, 1970) has popularized: 1. since all observations are theory-laden, no "objective" measurement is possible; 2. since all theories are in-commensurable and "squishy," disconfirming evidence can always be rejected; and 3. being conducted by humans, science relies heavily on intuition and background knowledge, sometimes preferring theories on aesthetic or social grounds rather than strictly logical ones.

These attacks were especially relevant to evaluation. Realization of the vague, contradictory, and latent nature of program goals made it questionable to assume that goals could function like theoretical hypotheses. Of the alternative sources of evaluative issues that were forwarded, some did not necessarily imply the primacy of causal analysis that is built into the hypothetico-deductive model. For instance, from a pluralist perspective on question formulation, multiple stakeholders should be consulted to learn of their information needs. Program managers constitute one relevant stakeholder group, and because they are held accountable for the smooth operation of programs, they are more likely to be interested in the more descriptive issues of targeting and implementation than in the more inferential and causal issues associated with assessing effects and impacts. A further justification for deemphasizing the description of causal connections came from the ambiguity of results from evaluations of the early Great Society programs. Did these programs achieve so little because of 1. deficiencies in the substantive theories that buttressed program design, 2. the operational activities constituted poor representation of core theoretical constructs, or 3. the evaluations were too insensitive to detect the smaller-than-expected effects that actually occurred? Such uncertainty led to more emphasis on describing program and project activities, justifying the wider use of implementation measures and of theoretical excursions into the "black box."

While experiments probe causal connections between manipulanda and outcomes, they cannot by themselves explain why a treatment is or is not effective. Causal explanation requires a description of program process and the identification of those factors that are necessary and sufficient for the causally efficacious components of a program to influence the causally affected components of effect and impact measures. Full explanation of why a program achieves its effects is extremely useful because it specifies the factors that have to be present if a program or project is to be effective when transferred elsewhere (Cronbach 1982). As program descriptions revealed more variability than had been expected both within and between projects, the need for explanatory knowledge as a guide to transfer became all the more obvious. By 1985, explaining effects (or non-effects) had a higher profile than describing them, especially for Cronbach (1982), Guba & Lincoln (1981), and Rossi & Freeman (1982).

More sensitivity also developed to the utility of letting evaluation issues emerge from intensive on-site knowledge as opposed to formulating them prior to data collection. While such openness is obviously beneficial for detecting unanticipated side effects, the advocacy of grounded discovery went beyond this (Patton 1978, Guba & Lincoln 1981). Since programs are evolving entities characterized by considerable local discretion in the form and scheduling of services, it is presumptuous of evaluators either to maintain they know in advance the most useful research questions to ask or to believe that the issues of greatest importance at the beginning of a study will remain so by its end. Since they assume a nonstationary target for evaluation, some evaluation theorists have rejected quantitative research altogether and have turned to qualitative methods. Their expectation is that intensive on-site observation and interviews will lead to the formulation of explanatory hypotheses about process and effects that can be iteratively tested and reformulated in the field until a satisfactory fit is achieved between the data and the explanation. This rationale is based on the use of both ethnographic and hermeneutic techniques (Habermas 1972, Dunn 1982), with the latter being particularly used to provide closure on the interpretations of events. Ethnographers and hermeneuticists make quite different epistemological assumptions from those of quantitative social scientists who prefer a hypothetico-deductive research strategy based on prespecified program goals and formal experimental designs.

By 1985, the world evaluators assumed what they were studying was no longer universally considered to be real and consisting of simple causal connections from programs to outcomes, as the work of Suchman (1967) and Campbell (1969) had implied. Some evaluators abjured realism in favor of an idealism which emphasized how humans cognitively create their own worlds and, in communicating their creations to others, help generate a shared social reality whose links to the outside world are unclear. Indeed, if one assumes humans respond to social constructions of the world rather than to the world itself (Patton 1978, Guba & Lincoln 1981), then the whole issue of how these cognitive links relate to reality is of no practical interest. Even among those scholars who retained realist assumptions, their ontological world view changed. It came to encompass a multivariate world of complex, interdependent causal forces rather than a simpler world of bivariate pushes and pulls. As with epistemological options, the ontological options from which evaluators had to select in 1985 were far more numerous and diverse than 20 years earlier.

New options for knowledge construction also followed from attacks on the positivist assumption that theory-neutral measurement is possible. The attacks came mainly from those historians and sociologists of science who illustrated how scientific observation is theory-impregnated 1. in the choice of constructs, 2. in the way constructs are conceptually "defined," 3. in the theoretical irrelevancies operational representations contain, 4. in the theory components particular operational instances fail to include, and 5. in the weights implicitly assigned to factors in the multidimensional measures that social scientists invariably use. These attacks led nearly all evaluators into some form of fallibilism, often taking the form of a critical multiplism that justified the selection of multiple operations, multiple methods, and the integration of any one study into the (usually) multiple relevant studies that had preceded it (Cook 1985). In cases where observational practice did not change because of the attacks on theory-neutral measurement, many evaluators must have felt less certain about their results, especially after receiving commentary on them, for the commentary often occurred in a context of cacophonous dispute about the constructs selected (and not selected) for measurement and about the ways particular measures were constructed (Lindblom & Cohen 1979). The attacks on "objective" measurement also caused some evaluators to firm their belief that anthropology and journalism, rather than experimental psychology (Guba & Lincoln 1981), should provide the appropriate models for constructing knowledge in evaluation.

Claims also began to surface that evaluation should abjure not only positivist forms of constructing knowledge but also traditional scientific standards of inference. Cronbach (1980, 1982) asserted that the potential users of evaluation are less concerned than academics with reducing the final few grains of uncertainty about knowledge claims; that prospective users are also more willing to trust their own experience and tacit knowledge for ruling out validity threats; and that they also expect to act upon whatever knowledge base is available, however serious its deficiencies. Like Rossi & Freeman (1982), Cronbach maintained that each evaluation should seek to generate many findings, even at the cost of achieving less certainty about any one of them. In his own terminology, "bandwidth" should be preferred over "fidelity."

Cronbach particularly objected to the traditional scientific preference for resolving method trade-offs in favor of enhancing internal validity or external validity defined as generalizing from the samples of persons, settings, times, and constructs studied to the target universes they are meant to represent. Cronbach favors making method trade-offs so as to enhance his own conception of external validity which is based on generalizing from the samples achieved in a study to populations with different characteristics from those of the samples studied. Cronbach justifies this preference on two grounds. First, social programs are so heterogeneous that sampling plans cannot by themselves provide knowledge that is demonstrably applicable to the unique characteristics of single projects, particularly those not yet studied. Second, evaluation results tend to be used in mostly unexpected ways that speak less to "instrumental usage" than to the "enlightenment" associated with generalized explanatory knowledge about practical procedures and substantive theories that are more or less successful and that might therefore guide transfer to other projects and programs.

Knowledge Methods

In the 1960s the methods for acquiring knowledge from evaluation could have been laid out according to something like the following schema: 1. The most important questions in evaluation concern the causal consequences of programs or projects. To examine such consequences, randomized experiments should be used or, failing this, strong quasi-experiments based on interrupted time-series or regression-discontinuity designs. 2. Since it is sometimes important to make general causal statements, evaluators should try to sample people and settings at random. If this is not possible—as will often be the case—the samples should at least be heterogeneous in composition so that final inferences are not restricted to a small range of settings and persons. 3. For those who insist on causal explanation—as opposed to descriptive causal connections—substantive theory should be used to identify the constructs worth measuring and then some form of causal modeling should be carried out. If such modeling is not possible, one should at least "correlate" each potential explanatory construct with the degree of change obtained on major effect and impact measures.

By 1985, the experiment had lost its hegemony. In part this was because of the increased importance of noncausal issues and of questions about causal explanation for which the experiment was not designed. The loss in hegemony was also the result of a growing awareness of the limitations of experimentation. Randomized experiments came under attack because (a) they are only relevant to causal forces that can be manipulated; (b) ethical and political concerns sometimes preclude assignment by lottery in favor of assignment by need, merit, or "first come, first served"; (c) because most social programs are ameliorative in intent and provide valued treatments, attrition is often treatment-related and so violates the most critical assumption of all experimentation that the various treatment groups are probabilistically equivalent on all characteristics other than treatment assignment; and (d) respondents in one group may sometimes compare the treatment they receive with what others receive, leading to compensatory rivalry, resentful demoralization, treatment diffusion, or compensatory equalization (Cook & Campbell 1979). Quasi-experiments also came under attack, mostly from advocates of randomized experimentation who focused on the quasi-experimental design most used in evaluation that requires pretest and posttest data from treatment groups that are initially nonequivalent. Critics maintained that equivocal causal inferences usually result from this design because the processes leading to treatment-related selection are rarely, if ever, completely understood and so cannot be statistically modeled with confidence. The disturbing possibility was also noted that in some substantive areas a single source of selection bias may plague all the evaluations conducted, creating an impressive convergence of results on the same wrong answer (Campbell & Boruch 1975)!

Probably as important as awareness of the limitations of experimental methods were claims that alternative methods existed that could fulfill the experiment's function of probing causal connections while simultaneously probing other evaluation-relevant issues. Within quantitative traditions, the challenge to experiments came principally from causal modeling, especially in the latent trait models exemplified by LISREL and in the econometric methods developed by Heckman (1980) that have recently come under attack (Lalonde 1985, Murnane et al 1985). Within the more qualitative tradition, the challenge came from case studies (Yin 1985), especially after Campbell (1975) pointed out that a case study with multiple dependent variables could under certain (rare) conditions achieve a pattern of results fit by only one causal explanation. The desirability of alternatives to the experiment increased because they seemed more generally applicable, more flexible in the types of knowledge achieved, and hardly worse for facilitating inferences about causal connections.

The preference for functionally plastic methods also influenced how causal explanations came to be studied. Primitive forms of causal modeling were espoused in the late 1960s, principally multiple regression. More sophisticated, maximum-likelihood models came to be preferred later, partly because they are sensitive to issues of unreliability and partial invalidity of measurement and partly because they are capable of simultaneously interrelating client characteristics, program inputs, program processes, third variable spurious causes, and intended outcomes measured at different points along a distal time chain (Flay & Cook 1982). However, quantitative causal modeling does not provide the only means for explaining program results. Advocates of qualitative research emphasize the explanatory knowledge that can emerge from juxtaposing prior knowledge, expert opinion, practitioner belief, logical analysis, and qualitative knowledge acquired on site, and to these Cronbach adds knowledge gained from quantitative studies relating input, process, and outcome variables. It is also possible to extend the sampling and measurement frameworks of most experiments so as to probe issues of process in addition to issues of causal connections. Ironically, the form of analysis that results from such an extension involves the very same explanatory modeling techniques that are advocated for nonexperimental data! Since multiple method options are now available for studying causal explanation, the formerly preferred option based on the quantitative causal modeling of process and other forms of contingency has lost its hegemony, though not to the same extent that experiments have lost theirs in the area of probing causal connections.

We turn now to the task of constructing generalized knowledge. The initially preferred techniques required sampling with known probability from some clearly designated universe, but it is difficult to define some types of universe, particularly when historical times or physical situations are at issue. Also, the variability between projects, and between clients and practitioners within projects, requires that samples have to be "large" (and hence more expensive) if formal representativeness is to be achieved within "reasonable" limits.

For both reasons, the respectability of various forms of purposive sampling increased, particularly those that emphasize selecting instances from within a population that is either presumptively modal or manifestly heterogeneous. The rationale for selecting modal instances is to ascertain whether causal relationships can be generalized to the most frequently occurring types of persons or settings. One rationale for selecting heterogeneous instances is to probe whether a causal relationship can be inferred despite the heterogeneity in respondents and settings; the other is to analyze whether similar findings are obtained when different subgroups of persons and settings are separately examined (Cook & Campbell 1979). It is only a small step from haphazard heterogeneous sampling within individual studies to metaanalysis and its unsystematic sampling of studies that are heterogeneous on many important attributes. Formally, metaanalysis assumes that the achieved effect sizes under review constitute a random sample of all the effect sizes that could have been achieved with a particular class of treatment. Since this assumption cannot be sensitively tested, metaanalysts actually operate on the less restrictive assumption that the effect sizes under review come from a less formally representative set of studies with considerable heterogeneity in the populations and settings sampled. This makes the generalization metaanalysis achieves more like a product of purposive sampling than of formal random sampling.

Generalization is not only a product of sampling strategies. As Cronbach (1982) emphasizes, it is also a product of causal explanation. The more we know about the plethora of contingencies on which program or project effectiveness depends, the more likely it is that we will be able to transfer successful practices to other sites that have not yet been studied. As the realization grew that generalization can follow from a number of different sampling procedures and from theoretical explanation, so it became clearer that multiple methods exist for generalizing. As a result, the initially favorite method based on random selection lost its hegemony.

When we turn to a fourth research function—discovering novel issues and questions—the degree of functional blurring between methods is not as noticeable as it is with causal issues and generalization. Intensive on-site observation and interviews have always been preferred for gaining knowledge that could not have been preformulated as hypotheses. These methods remained the distinct favorites. What changed with time were attitudes about the priority that discovery deserved, probably because of the demise of the goal-centered approaches to evaluation that had implicitly devalued discovery in favor of hypothesis testing. What also changed was appreciation of the functional plasticity of the methods advocated for discovery, given the way Yin (1985) and Campbell (1975) linked intensive on-site knowledge to causal connections and the way Cronbach (1982) linked it to the causal explanation he favors for evaluation.

It would be wrong to leave the impression that over the 20 years since Suchman's (1967) advocacy of causal questions and experimental designs, the only changes in thinking about methods has been to blur former certainties about question and method preferences and to raise the priority accorded to discovery and causal explanation. Two other changes are worth comment. First, growing consciousness of the inevitable fallibility of observation is reflected, not only in the growth of multiplist methods of data collection, but also in the advocacy of multiple investigators analyzing the same data set and in the advocacy of data analysis in more of an exploratory than confirmatory mode. In this last regard, a philosophy of data analysis akin to Tukey's (1977) seems to be taking hold in the more quantitative tradition within evaluation, with individual substantive issues being approached several different ways predicated upon different methodological and substantive assumptions. While the popularity of confirmatory factor analytic models like LISREL seems to be an exception, even here the advocated strategy is to pit multiple models against each other and to measure each construct in several different ways, creating a more exploratory flavor than when the data are used to generate a single best-fit model and there is only one measure for most of the constructs in the model. An analogous development in the more qualitative tradition is that multiple observers are now advocated for each site instead of single observers, and in some research where this has been done the observers have honestly struggled to reconcile the different interpretations that resulted (e.g. Stake & Easley 1978). There are even some cases where both qualitative and quantitative methods were used in the same study and at first seemed to generate results that had different implications for the overall evaluation conclusion, leading to a creative tension that was only resolved after many iterations (Trend 1978). Whatever the data collection mode, multiple tentative probes seem now to be the watchword, replacing older and more positivist conceptions based on theory-free observation, single definitive tests, and crucial single studies.

The recognition that evaluation has both social and logical components and is built upon necessarily fallible methods has been associated with increased interest in methods for making evaluations more critical in the questions and methods selected for study. Among the methods advocated to increase the critical component are commentaries on research plans by heterogeneous groups of experts and other stakeholders; more extensive monitoring of the implementation of evaluations by federal program officers and scientific advisory groups; calls for the simultaneous funding of several independent evaluations of the same program, project, or element; recommendations to conduct secondary analyses of collected data; and the advocacy of including in final evaluation reports comments by personnel from the program evaluated (Hennigan et al 1980). Also heard have been calls to force out the latent assumptions behind evaluation designs and the interpretations offered for results, usually through some form of adversarial legal process or through a committee of substantive experts (Cronbach 1982). All evaluations can be evaluated according to publicly justifiable criteria of merit and standards of performance, and data can be collected to determine how good an evaluation is. The need for metaevaluation (Cook 1974) implies a frank recognition of the limitations of all social science methods, including evaluation.

THEORIES OF EVALUATION PRACTICE

At a minimum, a theory of evaluation practice should use logic and the last 20 years of experience with evaluation to specify and justify the types of knowledge that are supposed to have leverage because it is presumed they will help improve social programs and ameliorate social problems. A theory of practice should also use the 20 years of experience to specify critically assessed and practical methods that are relevant to the types of knowledge presumed to have most leverage. Such a theory should also detail the most productive roles evaluators can play in furthering the conduct of evaluations that are likely to be used in one of the many ways usage is now understood. But that is not enough. A theory of practice should also use past experience to highlight the constraints under which evaluators will most likely have to work—constraints of budget, time, staff capabilities, and sponsor sophistication about evaluation—for these constraints independently influence the issues, methods, and roles that can be selected for a particular evaluation assignment. Finally, a theory of evaluation practice has to be detailed about the steps to follow in physically conducting an evaluation once issues with leverage have been determined, general stances about methods and roles have been adopted, and constraints have been fully understood. All evaluations require that plans for sampling, measurement, and data collection have to be implemented, and a theory of practice should describe the options available for each of these tasks. In particular, it should outline the strengths and weaknesses of each option, the trade-offs between them, the signs that indicate when a preferred option is being inadequately implemented, and the fallback positions that are available should a breakdown occur in implementing some option. Since we cannot discuss all these issues in the space available, we will concentrate only on the most general level of discussion of evaluation practice in the literature. Fortunately, many of the lower-order issues can be inferred from the more general.

All the theorists discussed here agree that evaluation should help ameliorate social problems; but they disagree about what evaluators ought to do to achieve that purpose. All seem to take one of three general approaches to prescribing evaluation practice, which we might call approaches based on 1. "identifying manipulable solutions," 2. "identifying generalizable explanations," and 3. "providing stakeholder service." Most of the differences among the approaches are related to specific disagreements about one or more of the knowledge bases covered in this chapter, although the differences are sometimes more implicit than explicit in the writings of particular theorists. Nonetheless, we will attempt to make the most important differences explicit so that they can be publicly scrutinized on logical and empirical grounds, for this should eventually help assess their relative strengths and weaknesses as guides to evaluation practice.

Campbell's (1969, 1971) experimenting society and Scriven's (1983) consumer model of evaluation epitomize the "manipulable solution" approach. This mounts a frontal assault on social problems by orienting evaluation toward the discovery of manipulable solutions, postulating that it is far less important to know how and why purported solutions work than to know to what extent they work. Campbell and Scriven view evaluation as a service in the "public interest" more than in the interests of specific stakeholders; they place a premium on studying multiple potential solutions to a problem so as to increase the chances of discovering one that works or of discovering the most efficient; they emphasize truth about effects over reducing uncertainty about elements that might improve a program; and their concern with effectiveness leads them to be most explicit about methods for causal inference and about the selection of criteria that speak to obvious social needs. Finally, they believe that the political and economic system should determine how an effective solution is used, with the evaluator playing only a small role in this process.

The "manipulable solution" approach was dominant in the early years of social program evaluation, but its popularity is currently on the wane. This is largely because of the purported disconfirmation of its most crucial single assumption: that novel solutions to problems can be readily identified through the use of evaluative techniques. Randomized experiments and planned variation studies were advocated for this purpose, but early experience suggested that they were fundamentally flawed as models for evaluation practice. A second crucial assumption of the manipulable solution approach is that, once identified, novel solutions will be widely disseminated through society. Once again, experience indicated that dissemination and adoption are not so easy in the real world of social programming. The approach also tends to relegate analyses of program implementation and causal mediation to a subordinate position; but some interpretations of experience during the past 20 years suggest that analyses of implementation and causal mediation are crucial in evaluation for they promote explanation, and explanation may be crucial for the transfer of evaluation findings to new settings and populations. Moreover, empirical studies of use suggest that the restricted role evaluators are urged to adopt by Campbell and Scriven may not facilitate evaluation results being used, especially in the short term. By the middle 1970s, the assumptions buttressing the "manipulable solution" approach were under heavy attack, and alternative models for social program evaluation were beginning to be formulated.

Cronbach (1982) and the later writings of both Rossi (Chen & Rossi 1980, 1983) and Weiss (1977, 1978) represent the generalized explanation alternative. Where manipulability theorists believe that many solutions will be robust enough in their effects that it will be rare to discover negative relationships within any of the subpopulations of relevance, explanatory theorists believe that the world is so ontologically complex that it is best described, not in terms of simple main effects, but in terms of higher-order statistical interactions which indicate that a particular effect may be present under some conditions but absent or reversed under others. Hence, knowledge of the complex interrelationships among multiple causal determinants is believed necessary for generalizability and for transferring findings from the samples studied to other projects in a program. Where manipulability theorists believe that the implementation of identified solutions can proceed smoothly, explanatory theorists contend that such instrumental usage is far less likely than enlightenment and that if it is to be useful, instrumental use must occur at the site of local service delivery rather than in the offices of central program officials.

Where manipulability theorists believe that summative questions about effects and impacts are sufficient to justify evaluation, generalizability theorists seek to achieve some uncertainty reduction about many questions of many different forms. Descriptions of causal connections constitute only one such form. Thus, they also tend to deal with issues of implementation, targeting, or costs in both an explanatory and descriptive mode, preferring methods that are functionally plastic over methods developed for highly specific purposes. Above all, theorists of generalizable explanation seek to test the substantive theory that underlies the program so as to achieve a complete understanding of all its operations and consequences. This emphasis on "enlightenment" and "demystification" favors external validity in Cronbach's sense over internal validity, and it stresses multivariate causal models over simple causal connections from a program variable to effects.

The generalizable explanation approach requires great fath in our ability to construct social theories that relate program inputs, processes, and effects. It also assumes that generalizable knowledge facilitates the transfer of knowledge to such an extent that social problems are eventually ameliorated. Moreover, in placing a higher premium on explanation than description, evaluators may expend considerable effort explaining complex causal relationships in which the basic causal connection between the evaluand and a major outcome is not itself well justified. And Cronbach's exhortation—which Rossi does not seem to share—that evaluators should adopt lower inferential standards than academics flies in the face of some case study findings which suggest that decision makers at the federal level ask social scientists for findings that are beyond reproach, believing these to be the only findings they can effectively use in the political process (Boeckman 1974).

As represented by Wholey's (1983) management-centered evaluation, Stake's (Stake & Easley 1978) responsive evaluation, and Patton's (1978) utilization-focused evaluation, proponents of the "stakeholder service" approach postulate that evaluations will ameliorate social problems only if they are explicitly tailored to the information needs of stakeholders who have close relationships with the specific projects or programs being evaluated. Theorists who take this approach subordinate all other aspects of evaluation to producing usable information for stakeholders, although they differ as to who those stakeholders should be. Wholey and Patton focus mostly on program managers, probably reasoning that they have more responsibility for changes in social programming than any other actors. But Stake, and Guba & Lincoln (1981), try to serve a broader array of stakeholders that includes managers, program clients, service providers, and local boards. However, all the theorists who adopt a stakeholders service approach agree that evaluations should not be concerned with generalizing evaluation findings to other programs or projects. The priority is on the particular program or project under highly particularistic study. Theorists who favor this approach want stakeholders to play the major role in deciding on problems, questions, and interventions, with the evaluator serving as a consciousness-raising educator. They also prefer methods that provide quick answers to a wide array of questions rather than methods that might provide higher quality answers to a narrower set of questions. They also seek to maintain close contact with the evaluation clients at all times so as to be responsive to their changing needs and to maximize the eventual use of the results.

Adherents of the stakeholder service approach criticize other theorists on several grounds. One is for being too concerned with traditional social science theory and methodology at the expense of serving individuals and groups with a direct stake in a program or project. Another is for concocting an ephemeral "public interest" that serves to justify particular evaluator stances but is divorced from real people with real information needs. A third is for being insufficiently concerned with providing rapid results that can be profitably used in the short term. And a final criticism is for presuming that they can construct better understandings of social problems and social programs than service-providers who have much more frequent and direct contact with clients and with the social world from which these clients come.

Several criticisms of the "stakeholder service" approach can be made. First, its connection to social problem solving is dependent on locating a stakeholder who wants information about important social problems and their solution. But stakeholders may ask uninformed, trivial, or self-centered questions, and the resulting information, while usable, may have minimal relevance to important social problems. Second, the idea that the evaluator will often educate stakeholders to ask better questions and want better methodology will sometimes be inconsistent with political and economic realities. Practicing evaluators make their living by securing contracts, and those who contract with evaluators are free to give future work to other evaluators if they do not like the education current contractors are providing. Finally, the trade-offs between the accuracy, timeliness, and comprehensiveness of results are not yet well known, but adherents of the stakeholders service approach run the risk of providing timely information that is wrong in its claims or is misleading because of its incompleteness.

It is not yet possible to judge the merit of these three approaches to evaluation practice. For one thing, proponents often speak as if they were inevitably distinct. However, the manipulable solution approach comes close to the generalized explanation approach once evaluation uses formal sampling, metaanalysis, simultaneous replications, or other methods yet being developed (Cook et al 1985) in order to identify main effects that are demonstrably robust. Similarly, the stakeholder service approach can regain a focus on social problem solving through an informed choice of stakeholders, for some stakeholders are more actively concerned with social problem solving than others. For instance, when members of Congressional committees request evaluations from the General Accounting Office, the resulting work will often have a clearer link to acts that might help ameliorate important social problems on a broad scale than would be the case if a local project manager asked an evaluator to upgrade his record-keeping system for billing purposes.

It is also difficult to choose between these three approaches to evaluation practice because data-based argumentation is still sadly lacking. Advocates of the generalizable explanation approach depend heavily on the assumption that short-term instrumental usage is rare, but there is some empirical evidence to the contrary (Leviton and Boruch 1983). The techniques that Wholey has promoted for so long rely heavily on stimulating short-term use by program managers. Would they have continued funding such work for so long if it were not useful in some immediate way? Advocates of both the generalized solution and the stakeholder service approaches write as though failures of randomized experiments and planned variation studies are well documented. While their arguments are well taken, it may nonetheless be premature to conclude that the experimental option in evaluation is dead, especially if the early failures of social experiments were due as much to inexperience in implementing the research designs as to any intrinsic limitations randomized experiments are supposed to have. Indeed, recent successful experiments with multiple planned variations warrant more study than they have had in order to determine the conditions under which such efforts can be undertaken fruitfully (Cook 1986). A similar need for data applies to most other arguments in the field. Do case studies really foster use in readers, and if so, of what kind? What loss in accuracy is incurred from the use of "quick and dirty" methods for providing fast feedback? How educable are evaluation clients in the question formation process? Where does nontrivial social change take place in social systems, and how can it be catalyzed by evaluation? How accurate are the inferences about causal connections produced by different methods? Evaluation theorists should be no different from other social science theorists in subjecting their claims and counterclaims to logical and empirical scrutiny.

Our brief discussion of the relative merits of these three approaches should not mislead the reader into thinking that evaluators ought to be choosing from among them. Proponents of each approach provide intelligent and often persuasive arguments in favor of their different positions on the same issue. Indeed, it is sometimes easy to believe that all of them may be correct and that the positions appear inconsistent only because our theories of evaluation are not yet complex enough to specify the contingencies that will eventually lead to integrating the apparent disagreements. It may be that our classification scheme overlooked some more integrative approaches to evaluation that go beyond the theories we analyzed, although the partial similarity of our scheme to others (e.g. Stufflebeam & Shinkfield 1985) leads us to be optimistic that our sins of omission are few and minor. Rather than encouraging evaluators to choose any one approach, we hope that the present discussion will encourage them to get to know each approach on its own terms; to explore how well each is grounded in the knowledge bases we outlined; to seek ways to resolve apparent differences between the approaches; and to base their practice choices on considerations from each approach instead of relying exclusively on a single one.

CONCLUSION

Our review of the field of evaluation leaves us impressed with the intellectual vigor and yield of the many debates in which evaluation theorists are currently engaged. To be sure, the simplicity of the early years of evaluation has been replaced by a complexity that must seem bewildering to some, by a keen sense of the limitations of evaluation and social programming, and by an active search for novel evaluation approaches. All this is consonant with the major lesson of the last 20 years: that program evaluation should be predicated on knowledge about how social programs really operate and use social science information.

In taking this important lesson to heart, our hope is that evaluators will not forget the tasks of knowledge construction and value analysis that loom less salient today because of the emphasis on fitting evaluation into the world of social programs. Evaluation does indeed need to be worldly in the sense of seeing the world of social programs as it really is. However, it also needs to be worldly in the second sense of the term that connotes responding to the world by working hard to achieve such grace and style that, in evaluation's case, it would be rare to generate inaccurate knowledge or place a wrong set of values on research findings. Evaluators must be careful lest knowledge construction and value analysis are drowned in the sea of accommodation to the complexity and intransigence of social programs and to the ways in which program officials do and do not use evaluation findings.

ACKNOWLEDGMENTS

The authors would like to thank the Center for Applied Psychological Research at Memphis State University for providing a congenial and supportive setting in which to write this paper.

Literature Cited

Applied Management Services Inc. 1984. Income verification pilot project Phase II: Results of the quality-assurance evaluation, 1982–1983 school year. 962 Wayne Ave., Silver Spring, MD

Berman, P., McLaughlin, M. W. 1977. *Federal programs supporting educational change.* Vol. 8: *Factors affecting implementation and continuation.* Santa Monica, CA: Rand Corp.

Boeckmann, M. E. 1974. Policy impacts of the New Jersey income maintenance experiment. *Policy Sci.* 7:53–76

Bryk, A. S., ed. 1983. *Stakeholder-Based Evaluation.* San Francisco: Jossey-Bass

Bunker, J. P. 1985. When doctors disagree. *NY Rev. Books* 32:7–12

Campbell, D. T. 1969. Reforms as experiments. *Am. Psychol.* 24:409–28

Campbell, D. T. 1974. Evolutionary epistemology. *The Philosophy of Karl Popper,* ed. P. A. Schilpp, 14:413–63. LaSalle, IL: Open Court Pub.

Campbell, D. T. 1975. "Degrees of freedom" and the case study. *Comp. Polit. Stud.* 8: 178–93

Campbell, D. T., Boruch, R. F. 1975. Making the case for randomized assignment to treatments by considering the alternatives: Six ways in which quasi-experimental evaluations in compensatory education tend to underestimate effects. In *Evaluation and Experiments: Some Critical Issues in Assessing Social Programs*, ed. C. A. Bennett, A. A. Lumsdaine, pp. 195–296. New York: Academic

Chen, H., Rossi, P. H. 1980. The multi-goal, theory-driven approach to evaluation: A model linking basic and applied social science. *Soc. Forces* 59:106–22

Chen, H., Rossi, P. H. 1983. Evaluating with sense: The theory-driven approach. *Eval. Rev.* 7:283–302

Cook, F. L. 1982. Assessing age as an eligibility criterion. In *Age or Need? Public Policies for Older People*, ed. B. L. Neugarten. Beverly Hills, CA: Sage

Cook, T. D. 1974. The potential and limitations of secondary evaluations. In *Educational Evaluation: Analysis and Responsibility*, ed. M. W. Apple, M. J. Subkoviak, H. S. Lufler Jr. Berkeley, CA: McCutchan

Cook, T. D. 1983. Evaluation: Whose questions should be answered? In *Making and Managing Policy: Formulation, Analysis, Evaluation*, ed. G. R. Gilbert. New York: Dekker

Cook, T. D. 1986. Evaluating health education curricula: An exemplary planned variations study that should have failed. *Int. J. Educ.* In press

Cook, T. D. 1985. Post-positivist critical multiplism. In *Social Science and Social Policy*, ed. R. L. Shotland, M. M. Mark. Beverly Hills, CA: Sage

Cook, T. D., Appleton, H., Conner, R. F., Shaffer, A., Tamkin, G., Weber, S. J. 1975. *"Sesame Street" Revisited*. New York: Sage Found.

Cook, T. D., Campbell, D. T. 1979. *Quasi-experimentation: Design and Analysis Issues for Field Settings*. Boston: Houghton Mifflin

Cook, T. D., Curtin, T. R. 1986. An evaluation of the models used to evaluate educational television series. In *Public Communication and Behavior*, ed. G. A. Comstock, New York: Academic. In press

Cook, T. D., Leviton, L. C., Shadish, W. R. 1985. Program evaluation. In *Handbook of Social Psychology*, ed. G. Lindzey, E. Aronson. New York: Random House. 3rd ed.

Cook, T. D., Shadish, W. R. 1982. Metaevaluation: An evaluation of the congressionally-mandated evaluation system for community mental health centers. In *Innovative Approaches to Mental Health Evaluation*, ed. G. Stahler, W. R. Tash. New York: Academic

Cronbach, L. J. 1963. Evaluation for course improvement. *Teachers Coll. Bull.* 64:672–83

Cronbach, L. J. 1982. *Designing Evaluations of Educational and Social Programs*. San Francisco: Jossey-Bass

Cronbach, L. J., Ambron, S. R., Dornbusch, S. M., Hess, R. D., Hornik, R. C., et al. 1980. *Toward Reform of Program Evaluation*. San Francisco: Jossey-Bass

David, J. L. 1982. Local uses of Title I evaluations. In *Evaluation Studies Review Annual*, Vol. 7, ed. E. House. Beverly Hills, CA: Sage

Dunn, W. 1982. Reforms as arguments. *Knowledge: Creation, Diffusion, Utilization* 3:293–326

Edwards, W., Guttentag, M., Snapper, K. 1975. A decision theoretic approach to evaluation research. In *Handbook of Evaluation Research*, Vol. 1. Beverly Hills, CA: Sage

Fairweather, G. W. 1980. *The Fairweather Lodge: A Twenty-five-year Retrospective*. San Francisco: Jossey-Bass

Feeley, M. M., Sarat, A. D. 1980. *The Policy Dilemma: Federal Crime Policy and the Law Enforcement Assistance Administration*. Minneapolis: Univ. Minn. Press

Flay, B. R., Cook, T. D. 1982. The evaluation of mass media prevention campaigns. In *Public Communication Campaigns*, ed. R. E. Rice, W. J. Paisley. Beverly Hills, CA: Sage

Fullan, M. 1982. *The Meaning of Educational Change*. New York: Teachers College Press

Glass, G. V., McGaw, B., Smith, M. L. 1981. *Meta-analysis in Social Research*. Beverly Hills, CA: Sage

Guba, E. G., Lincoln, Y. S. 1981. *Effective Evaluation: Improving the Usefulness of Evaluation Results Through Responsive and Naturalistic Approaches*. San Francisco: Jossey-Bass

Habermas, J. 1972. *Knowledge and Human Interests*. London: Heinemann

Heckman, J. J. 1980. Sample selection bias as a specification error. In *Evaluation Studies Review Annual*, Vol. 5, ed. E. W. Stromsdorfer, G. Farkas. Beverly Hills, CA: Sage

Hennigan, K. M., Flay, B. R., Cook, T. D. 1980. "Give me the facts": The use of social science evidence in formulating national policy. In *Advances in Applied Social Psychology*, Vol. 1, ed. R. F. Kidd, M. J. Saks. Hillsdale, NJ: Erlbaum

House, E. R. 1980. *Evaluating with Validity*. Beverly Hills, CA: Sage

Kuhn, T. S. 1962. *The Structure of Scientific Revolutions*. Chicago: Univ. Chicago Press. 1st ed.

Kuhn, T. S. 1970. *The Structure of Scientific Revolutions*. Chicago: Univ. Chicago Press. 2nd ed.

Lalonde, R. J. 1985. Evaluating the econometric evaluations of training programs with experimental data, Working Pap. 183, Industrial Relations Section. Princeton, NJ: Princeton Univ.

Levin, H. M. 1983. *Cost-effectiveness: A Primer*. Beverly Hills, CA: Sage

Leviton, L. C., Boruch, R. F. 1983. Contributions of evaluation to education programs and policy. *Eval. Rev.* 7:563–98

Leviton, L. C., Boruch, R. F. 1984. Why compensatory education evaluation was useful. *J. Policy Anal. Manage.* 3:299–305

Leviton, L. C., Cook, T. D. 1984. Use of evaluations in textbooks in education and social work. *Eval. Rev.* 7:497–518

Leviton, L. C., Hughes, E. F. X. 1981. Research on the utilization of evaluations: Review and synthesis. *Eval. Rev.* 5:528–48

Light, R. J. 1983. *Evaluation Studies Review Annual*, Vol. 8. Beverly Hills, CA: Sage

Light, R. J., Pillemer, D. B. 1984. *Summing Up: The Science of Reviewing Research*. Cambridge, MA: Harvard Univ. Press

Lindblom, C. E. 1977. *Politics and Markets: The World's Political and Economic Systems*. New York: Basic Books

Lindblom, C. E., Cohen, D. K. 1979. *Usable Knowledge: Social Science and Social Problem Solving*. New Haven, CT: Yale Univ. Press

McLaughlin, M. W. 1985. Implementation realities and evaluation design. In *Social Science and Social Policy*, ed. R. L. Shotland, M. M. Mark. Beverly Hills, CA: Sage

Mielke, K. W., Chen, M. 1981. *Children, Television and Science: An overview of the formative research for 3-2-1 contact*. New York: Children's Television Workshop

Murnane, R. J., Newstead, S., Olsen, R. J. 1985. Comparing public and private schools: The puzzling role of selectivity bias. *J. Bus. Econ. Stat.* 3:23–35

Nozick, R. 1974. *Anarchy, State, and Utopia*. New York: Basic Books

Pacht, A. R., Bent, R., Cook, T. D., Klebanoff, L. B., Rodgers, D. A., et al. 1980. Continuing evaluation and accountability controls for a national health insurance program. *Am. Psychol.* 33:305–13

Patton, M. Q. 1978. *Utilization-Focused Evaluation*. Beverly Hills, CA: Sage

Rawls, J. 1971. *A Theory of Justice*. Cambridge, MA: Harvard Univ. Press

Rossi, P. H., Freeman, H. E. 1982. *Evaluation: A Systematic Approach*. Beverly Hills, CA: Sage. 2nd ed.

Rossi, P. H., Lyall, K. C. 1976. *Reforming Public Welfare: A Critique of the Negative Income Tax Experiment*. New York: Sage Found.

Scriven, M. S. 1980. *The Logic of Evaluation*. Inverness, CA: Edgepress

Scriven, M. S. 1983. Evaluation ideologies. In *Evaluation Models: Viewpoints on Educational and Human Services Evaluation*, ed. G. F. Madaus, M. Scriven, D. L. Stufflebeam. Boston, MA: Kluwer-Nijhoff

Sechrest, L., West, S. G., Phillips, M. A., Redner, R., Yeaton, W. 1979. Some neglected problems in evaluation research: Strength and integrity of treatments. In *Evaluation Studies Review Annual*, Vol. 4, ed. L. Sechrest, S. G. West, M. A. Phillips, R. Redner, W. Yeaton. Beverly Hills, CA: Sage

Shadish, W. R. 1984. Policy research: Lessons from the implementation of deinstitutionalization. *Am. Psychol.* 39:725–38

Stake, R. E. 1982. A peer response: A review of "Program Evaluation in Education": When? How? To what ends? In *Evaluation Studies Review Annual*, Vol. 7, ed. E. R. House. Beverly Hills, CA: Sage

Stake, R. E., Easley, J. A. 1978. *Case Studies in Science Education*. Champaign: Univ. Ill. Cent. Instruct. Res. Curriculum Eval., and Comm. on Cult. Cognit.

Stufflebeam, D. L., Shinkfield, A. J. 1985. *Systematic Evaluation*. Boston, MA: Kluwer-Nijhoff

Suchman, E. 1967. *Evaluative Research*. New York: Sage Found.

Trend, M. G. 1978. On the reconciliation of qualitative and quantitative analyses: A case study. *Hum. Organ.* 37:345–54

Tukey, J. W. 1977. *Exploratory Data Analysis*. Reading, MA: Addison-Wesley

Warnock, G. J. 1971. *The Object of Morality*. London: Methuen

Weiss, C. H. 1972. *Evaluation Research: Methods for Assessing Program Effectiveness*. Englewood Cliffs, NJ: Prentice-Hall

Weiss, C. H. 1977. Research for policy's sake: The enlightenment function of social research. *Policy Anal.* 3:531–45

Weiss, C. H. 1978. Improving the linkage between social research and public policy. In *Knowledge and Policy: The Uncertain Connection*, ed. L. E. Lynn. Washington, DC: Natl. Acad. Sci.

Weiss, C. H. 1980. Knowledge creep and decision accretion. *Knowledge: Creation, Diffusion, Utilization* 1:381–404

Weiss, R. S., Rein, M. 1970. The evaluation of broad-aim programs: Experimental design, its difficulties, and an alternative. *Admin. Sci. Organ.* 15:97–113

Wholey, J. S. 1983. *Evaluation and Effective Public Management*. Boston, MA: Little Brown

Williams, W. 1980. *The Implementation Perspective*. Berkeley: Univ. Calif. Press

Yin, R. K. 1985. *Case Study Research: Design and Methods*. Beverly Hills, CA: Sage

PART II

Social Programming

Cook and Shadish (1986) describe three successively less frequent and feasible action strategies for ameliorating social problems: incremental modification of existing projects and programs, the introduction of new projects and programs, and alterations of the basic social structures and beliefs in which programs and projects are embedded. The articles reprinted in the present section illustrate each of these three strategies.

The majority of these articles concern incremental modifications. The first article (McLaughlin, 1985) contends that traditional approaches to evaluation are at odds with the realities of program implementation and that as a result, traditional evaluations provide results of limited value. McLaughlin suggests five lessons about program implementation realities and their implications for program evaluation. In the next article, Levin and Ferman (1986) describe conditions that contribute to the effective implementation of social programs. They argue that implementation is greatly aided by program managers who can anticipate obstacles to implementation, create interest convergence, and encourage simple program designs with modest goals. In these ways, an adaptable and realistic manager provides a "political hand" for the public sector that is analogous to the "invisible hand" in a free market. In the following article, Higgins (1986) suggests that certain pitfalls in implementing a program sometimes cannot be avoided and that as a result it is possible to become overcommitted to an infeasible program "whose time has not come." Higgins illustrates his point with short case studies of two demonstration programs that he attempted to implement in vain. Finally, Weick (1984) completes the set of incremental-change articles by arguing that defining social problems on too large a scale can reduce the likelihood that they will be solved. Instead, he suggests breaking down social problems into "small wins," which are bounded problems with achievable solutions in the short-term, and he argues that this strategy will be more effective in the long run than will be striving for big wins.

The creation of new programs and policy initiatives can be an effective approach to problem solving. But the introduction of such innovations occurs less frequently than do incremental changes in existing programs; consequently, articles to reprint proved difficult to locate. Two recent books on the topics of policy innovation and agenda setting by Kingdon (1984) and by Polsby (1984) were obviously too long to reprint. Instead, we have included an extended review of and commentary on those books by Quirk (1986). Quirk makes a number of points potentially relevant to evaluators' roles in policy innovation, especially in his discussion of the "garbage-can model" of public policymaking.

The last article represents the comparatively rare and radical "system change" approach to social problem solving, where the aim is not just to introduce new programs or improve old programs, but to alter political or economic structures in some fundamental way. This approach is illustrated with a chapter by Rahman (1985) on the "participatory action research" paradigm. Rahman's examples reveal how radical evaluation might appear if evaluators followed House's (1980) suggestion to judge the merits of social programs according to how well they meet the material needs of the disadvantaged. By contrast, we can see more clearly the inherently conservative nature of program evaluation. What Rahman suggests is partly research but also partly social action, reminiscent of the work of community organizers such as Saul Alinsky (Heller et al., 1984), whose work is also praised in Weick's (1984) article on small wins.

REFERENCES

Heller, K., Price, R. H., Reinharz, S., Riger, S., & Wandersman, A. (1984). *Psychology and community change: Challenges of the future.* Homewood, IL: Dorsey.

House, E. R. (1980). *Evaluating with validity.* Newbury Park, CA: Sage.

Kingdon, J. W. (1984). *Agendas, alternatives, and public policies.* Boston: Little, Brown.

Polsby, N. W. (1984). *Political innovation in America: The politics of policy initiation.* New Haven, CT: Yale University Press.

2

Implementation Realities and Evaluation Design

Milbrey Wallin McLaughlin

In most planning, policy, and evaluation agencies, the received view
of evaluation is the rational, hypotheticodeductive or "impact" model
(Rossi & Freeman, 1982; Boruch & Cordray, 1980.) This approach
to evaluation has several defining characteristics. It assumes clear, operationally specified goals, stable program parameters, and specific criteria
for success. It rests on a correlational model in which "inputs" generally
are considered in the static terms of the experimental paradigm and
"outputs" typically are presented as estimates of treatment effect. Both
inputs and outputs are framed in unidimensional, constant terms that
reference program features but seldom incorporate contextual or process factors. This evaluation paradigm assumes a simple environment
with single component goal structures, a hierarchical authority structure, few complex interactions, and a rational reward structure. Concomitant assumptions describe a 1:1 relationship between what can
be learned about social settings and what can be affected in them.
Natural science provides the intellectual reference for this dominant
evaluation paradigm; its rules of evidence, accordingly, are rooted in
canons of the classic scientific method.

The hypotheticodeductive model for evaluating programs and policies
has strong conceptual appeal. It has refined methods, clear rules of
evidence, and agreed-upon strategies of proof. Criteria of an evalua-

*AUTHOR'S NOTE: Thanks go to Melvin M. Mark and R. Lance Shotland of
Pennsylvania State University for organizing this volume and playing an unusually active
editorial role in bringing it to completion. Their comments and those of my Stanford
colleague, Henry M. Levin, substantially improved this chapter; I am grateful for their review.*

tion's acceptability are grounded in methodological codes that are well-developed and known to the field. Armed with this expertise, an evaluator can be confident of doing a "good job."

However, experience with social programs gained over the past decade or so suggests that reality is much more complex than this dominant evaluation model acknowledges and that our trust in the efficacy of these methods is exaggerated. Efforts to understand and evaluate the spate of special programs generated by the Great Society's social policies and their legislative descendants have shown that traditional correlational or experimental models too often misrepresent the nature of treatment, the notion of program effects, and the relationship between inputs and outputs. Experience gained largely in the 1970s underscores the importance of program implementation and the context in which project efforts are carried out. Yet these issues are seldom treated beyond *ceteris paribus* assumptions or randomization strategies in traditional evaluation models. But the implementation realities that characterize social programs mean that these process and contextual issues are more than academic curiosities or "externalities." They are central to the conduct and effects of special project efforts. To ignore them results in evaluations of limited use to practitioners and assessments that risk misspecification of both treatment and effect.

This chapter draws on experience with program implementation to consider questions of program evaluation. The first section reviews major lessons for evaluation from the past decade's experience with program implementation. The second section discusses implications for evaluation and guidelines for rethinking approaches to social program evaluation. Section three presents a summary and conclusions.

IMPLEMENTATION REALITIES

Implementation is the process whereby programs or policies are carried out; it denotes the translation of plans into practice. Less than a decade ago, there was little research or theory about implementation. Indeed, implementation was not even considered an issue requiring an evaluator's attention. Instead, analysts embraced the "black box" metaphor. The black box represented a reality that accepted program inputs and produced program outputs but whose supposedly idiosyncratic content defied systematic attention from analysts. Further it was also assumed that the black box process whereby inputs were transformed into outputs was not of great significance because of the strong and direct relationship posited between treatment and effects.

However, the avalanche of federal social policy activities associated with Great Society programs and their concomitant evaluation mandates forced analysts to look inside the black box. They sought to explain the frequent and disappointing findings of "no significant difference" associated with these special program efforts. This look at the actuality of how programs were defined and carried out raised fundamental questions about learning from social programs and assessing their effects. Five lessons from experience with social program implementation appear especially central to thinking about evaluation research:

(1) treatment effects are indirect;
(2) implementation choices dominate program outcomes;
(3) implementation is a multistage, developmental process;
(4) implementors pursue multiple and often competing goals; and
(5) decisions made closest to the delivery level are most influential.

Treatment Effects Are Indirect

Correlational or impact designs assume a direct relationship between treatment or program inputs and program effects. However, this relationship seldom exists in reality. "Treatment effects," be they improved student achievement scores, enhanced teacher capacity, or lowered dropout rates, are the result of complex and multiple interactions between program inputs, e.g., technology, training, materials, money, technical assistance, and factors in the program's institutional setting. Social programs are carried out *within* and *through* their institutional setting.

At the local level, factors such as staff background and training, administrator commitment, competing or conflicting system demands, or constituent support are primary determinants of how and how well a program is carried out (Berman & McLaughlin, 1978; Fullan, 1982). Given the central influence of these local institutional factors, the common finding that similar programs have different effects in different settings—or even in the same setting over time—is not at all surprising. Education technologies are, in this sense, "soft"; specific outcomes are people-dependent and context-bound. Direct (or main) effects are institutional or contextual. Programs or policies influence local practices only indirectly and at the margins. Thus as Gilbert, Light, and Mosteller (1975) remark, education treatments (or other social program interventions) cannot provide the "slam-bang" effect many planners, policymakers, and evaluators hoped for.

This implementation reality also means that what is delivered—the "treatment"—varies by setting. This fact generates what can be called the "label fallacy." Programs ostensibly operating under the same level, e.g., the Bank Street model of early education; the Southwest Regional Laboratory reading program, cannot be assumed to be the same program in practice. The factors associated with each institutional setting can result in treatments that are substantively and significantly different even though they may operate under the same manner. Treatment as provided may depart in crucial ways from treatment as planned or designed. Indeed, treatment as experienced by the recipient may have little or nothing to do with project plans.

Implementation Choices Dominate Outcomes

What a program is, research tells us consistently, matters less to program outcomes than how it is carried out (Bardach, 1977; Berman & McLaughlin, 1978; Fullan, 1982; Nakamura & Smallwood, 1980; Sabatier & Mazmanian, 1979). Local choices about how to put a project into practice determine the extent to which a new program, technology, or curriculum fulfills its promise, whether the benefits reach the intended target group, or in fact whether a new policy is implemented at all. Project success is as much an issue of procedure as of substance.

Features of the local institutional environment clearly influence implementation choices; available technical expertise, for example, will affect training choices; staff experience and sophistication can influence project choices; labor disputes can attenuate planning time for a new project. But there are also implementation decisions to be taken that represent discretionary choices for local staff. Examples of such choices are the type and amount of staff participation in planning, the role of building principals in teacher training activities, the distribution of project resources across schools, the frequency of staff meetings to discuss project activities (rather than school or district administrative matters), strategies for evaluating project activities, and strategies for mobilizing support.

Differences in these local implementation decisions can mean that similar (or indeed identical) project designs will be carried out very differently and with substantially different results in various settings. Although a good idea or a promising technology is important to the quality of a planned change effort, local choices about how to put the idea or technology into practice ultimately play a major role in determining how an effort fares in a particular institutional setting. In practice, the relationship between "treatment" and strategy is elastic because any given treatment can be supported by a number of different strategic arrangements.

Implementation Is a Multistage Developmental Process

In general, implementation is a multistage developmental process. Except when policies or program objectives contain all of the information necessary to carry them out, e.g., distributional formulas, or when adoption of a new technology or procedure constitutes implementation, e.g., installation of a more sophisticated electronic communication system within a building, implementation is a complex, multistage process of institutional and individual learning. Policies that direct the allocation of funds among targeted interests are essentially different from policies that direct state or local officials to provide more effective services for particular categories of students. The former tells officials all that they need to know to "succeed"; the latter suggests broad objectives but do not specify the necessary knowledge or processes.

In one sense the process of implementation is heuristic; it is a process of learning and adjusting rather than a process of installation. Further, two and sometimes three substantively disparate kinds of learning are necessary to carry out many program and policy objectives. Policies often require not only new practices or means for service provision but also new organizational processes of targeting, allocating, evaluating, and accounting. One kind of learning necessary to program implementation, then, is learning to comply; that is, learning to administer the program efficiently and within its regulatory framework.

A second kind of learning assumed by those programs or policies that seek change in institutional routines is learning to provide the practices consistent with program goals; for example, classroom activities that are effective for educationally disadvantaged youngsters. This kind of learning involves the development of new activities, the acquisition of new skills, and integration of new practices and expertise into ongoing routines.

When programs or policies represent a normative position, for example, bilingual education or school desegregation, effective implementation can require yet a third kind of learning: The acquisition of new norms and beliefs about appropriate activities and system priorities. For example, federal policies addressing bilingual education, education of handicapped children, and racial balance in the public schools all intend a reordering of state and local priorities for allocating resources and educational service provisions. This kind of learning involves more than marginal adjustment in system routines; it comprises a fundamental change in the normative assumptions that structure system action.

These quite different kinds of learning usually do not and cannot occur simultaneously. In most cases, institutions need to learn the rules of the game before substantial and confident attention can be devoted to learning how to make practice more effective. For example, disappointing program outcomes were common during the early years of programs sponsored by Title I of the 1965 Elementary and Secondary Education Act, the federal government's massive compensatory education program (McLaughlin, 1975). However, evaluations were mistaken to conclude on the basis of these outcomes that Title I "did not work." Practitioners were engaged in determining accounting, delivery, and oversight strategies that were consistent with the program's regulatory framework. It was not until broad compliance issues generally were resolved that effective program activities began to be developed (Kirst & Jung, 1980). Developmental activities of this nature generally require implementor confidence that administrative or regulatory issues have been resolved. Doing it right usually takes precedence over doing it better. The third kind of learning—change in the value structure directing organizational choices—is necessary to the sustained presence of an initiative based on a normative position different from that of the implementing system. Yet for programs of this type, it is a process that takes a long time in most settings and indeed may never transpire.[2]

Substantively different activities accompany these different types of learning. For example, compliance is associated with allocation of funds to activities and stewardship in accounting for expenditures to constituents and others. Learning how to provide effective practice requires program development that translates regulatory requirements into program activities. All three kinds of institutional learning are enhanced by the mobilization of effective political and professional incentives and by the establishment of norms of good practice to guide program activities.

The further one moves through these stages and activities, the more complex is the learning required and the less susceptible is performance to command and control types of decisions and assessment practices. The problems and issues that dominate the process also change as the process evolves. The question central to a newly adopted program or policy are quite different from those associated with a mature, well-established practice. In the early stages of implementation, for example, problems are likely to be technical, procedural, and political. What are the technical requirements of the project and how can they be met? How can support for the project be generated? How can resistance be overcome? How can new practices be integrated with ongoing routines? Subsequent problems tend to be defined primarily as developmental issues: How can practices be refined? Modified?

The process of implementation, in short, is complex and multistaged. At each stage, it involves somewhat different activities and problems of learning, and different actors dominate. Further, at each stage, the "treatment" may be modified as emphases shift, corrections are made, goals and strategies are clarified, or unanticipated demands change the priorities that guide practice.

Implementors Pursue Multiple and Often Competing Goals

Although most evaluations describe a one-dimensional focus on delivery goals—increased student achievement scores, integration of handicapped youngsters into mainstream classrooms, decreased drop-out rates and vandalism, for example—implementors throughout the system in fact pursue multiple goals. In addition to the delivery (or the formal) program goals, implementors also must attend to political and bureaucratic interests. Implementation certainly will be shaped by the extent to which program (or delivery) goals are compatible with or eclipsed by bureaucratic and political objectives.

For example, I visited one midwestern elementary school in which a principal was about to terminate an apparently successful follow-through program. In his view, the high level of parent involvement achieved by the program made it extraordinarily difficult for him to run his school. His bureaucratic interests, in other words, conflicted with and superseded the delivery objectives of the follow-through effort. Similarly, studies of local allocation decisions under the deregulated Model Cities program show that municipal administrators were unable to continue targeting funds to disadvantaged neighborhoods under the new federal policies. Political pressures from more powerful (and advantaged) constituencies meant that funds were expended instead for more general municipal purposes such as parks and recreation facilities or on maintenance in middle-income areas (U.S. Advisory Commission on Intergovernmental Relations, 1981).

The question of relevant goals is complicated by additional factors: Policies have multiple dimensions and categories. A single policy, for example, can have a number of simultaneous purposes. For example, a single policy can seek to redistribute resources, to remedy a specific concern, and provide support for general maintenance. Title I of the 1965 Elementary and Secondary Education Act (now Chapter 1 of the 1981 Education Consolidation and Improvement Act), which provides federal support to state and local agencies for programs targeted at educationally disadvantaged youngsters, is an example. The act supports state level activities such as technical assistance and evaluation, distributes funds according to a formula based on a measure of economic disadvantage, and assumes the development of special programs for educationally disadvantaged youngsters. State and local response to this legislation has been shaped by the priorities assigned particular goals by state and local staff (McDonnell & McLaughlin, 1982).

To complicate matters further, policies also use multiple strategies, or policy implements. Bardach (1980), for example, outlines three categories of public policy implements: Enforcement, inducement, and benefaction. Enforcement involves standard-setting, oversight, and the invocation of sanctions. Inducement uses various means to motivate people to behave in ways consistent with policy objectives such as rewards for performance, competitive awards, tax incentives, and matching grants. Benefaction employs technologies such as transfer payments, technical assistance, and entitlement grants. Most policies typically employ a strategic mix of the three that can shift dramatically depending on particular implementors and actual program focus (Elmore & McLaughlin, 1982).

This multiplicity of goals and policy dimensions molds implementation. Participants in the policy system select and emphasize certain dimensions of a program or policy (Steinberger, 1981). This selection, which occurs as programs are defined, implemented, evaluated, and institutionalized, reflects the constellation of system goals shaping activities at a given point in time (i.e., bureaucratic, political, and delivery concerns) as well as perceptions about the central goals, importance, relevance, utility, and feasibility of the policy to be implemented.

Seen in this way, the illusion of a holistic notion of program or policy goals is apparent. The goals and concerns that drive policy and program decisions will reflect an individual actor's perceptions of the policy and priorities operating in the institutional context. And because multiple actors are involved at different levels of the policy system, a program or policy can be transformed in multiple or inconsistent ways as it moves through the policy system and even at the same level of the system over time. The interaction between implementing system priorities and perceptions about policy objectives means that in reality there are as many "goals" driving implementation as there are implementation points in the policy process.[3]

Decisions Made Closest to the Delivery Level Are Most Influential

In a complex policy system, a policy must pass through many organizational levels and multiple decision points. At each, someone makes a decision (by commission or omission) about policy goals and how they are to be addressed. In this way policy is further developed by the implementation process. Predetermined policy is not simply put into practice. Instead, policy is clarified, specified, and modified as it moves through the policy system. The final decision point, and the one that typically has the most impact on the way programs or policies are carried out, is at the "bottom" of the delivery system; it rests with the "street-level bureaucrat" who interprets policies and programs adopted by the larger system and translates them into services.[4]

For example, in education it is axiomatic that in schools it is the classroom teachers who have the most effect on how students are treated and the services they receive. But the evidence on policy implementation takes this truism one step further. Weatherley, for example, demonstrates in his analysis of Massachusetts special education reform that one effect of imposing a new policy on an already crowded system is to force teachers, principals, and diagnostic personnel to simplify, adapt, adjust, and, in some cases, distort policy just to get their jobs done. Weatherley's (1979) conclusions are consistent with studies of PL 94-142, the Education of All Handicapped Children Act (Hargrove et al., 1981), and with research that portrays the strategic autonomy of teachers in the privacy of their classrooms (Lortie, 1975; Jackson, 1968; Goodlad, Klein, & Associates, 1974). There is, in short, no necessary or 1:1 relationship between what administrators say, or regulations mandate, and what teachers do. The success or failure of a policy or program ultimately depends on what teachers or street-level bureaucrats think and do. Planners and policymakers at higher levels of the system must rely on individuals at the bottom to understand their intent, to endorse it, and to be willing and able to carry it out.

Summary

Implementation realities, in summary, comprise a complex, multistage process in which the phenomenon typically of interest to an evaluator—the relationship between program inputs and system outputs—is indirect and achieved against a noisy and constantly changing institutional setting. Further, the target for an evaluation—a program or policy—is in flux as well. It is created and recreated at various levels of the policy system in ways that are consistent with the interests, goals, skills, and perceptions of various actors. The unitary and apparently fixed "policy" or "program" as defined by an evaluation instrument or report has questionable basis in reality.

IMPLICATIONS FOR EVALUATION

These features of the implementation process raise fundamental questions about the conduct and use of evaluation. Implementation realities have important implications for evaluation both as a mode of inquiry and as a strategy to promote organizational learning, program improvement, or even accountability. Experience with the process of change and social program implementation suggests fundamental rethinking of evaluation design and conduct in five major areas:

(1) evaluation objectives,
(2) unit of analysis,
(3) outcome measures,
(4) differentiation of evaluation strategies, and
(5) concepts of use.

Evaluation Objectives

Contrary to the canons of traditional evaluation design, the effects of social programs cannot be "proven" with certainty or truth in the way that a principle of physics or a geometric theorem can be proven. Proof in this sense requires satisfying a number of conditions, among them that all sources of variance be controlled and that specific program or policy effects can be estimated against the clamor and complexity of the institutional setting.

But satisfying these and other conditions necessary for "proof" is no easy task. For example, the effect of a new reading program on student achievement will represent the combined effect of factors such as student characteristics, teacher expertise, teacher commitment to the curriculum, other responsibilities demanding teacher attention, the emphasis placed on successful implementation by district administrators, and previous reading programs in the students' experience. The list of factors that influence so-called treatment effects is extensive indeed:

> Once we attend to interactions, we enter a hall of mirrors that extends to infinity. However far we carry out analysis—to third order or fifth order or any order—untested interactions of a still higher order can be envisioned. (Cronbach, 1975, p. 119)

In theory, random assignment can control for such situational interactions, thereby isolating treatment effects. However, given the potential significance of third- and fourth-order interactions for program outcomes, vast amounts of data are required to identify and specify higher-order interactions. Consequently, control through randomized assignment would be practically (if not absolutely) impossible. The sample size required by such a strategy would far exceed the budgets or the sites available to evaluators (Cronbach, 1975, p. 124). Nonetheless, higher order interactions cannot be simply dismissed as "noise" or as "externalities." Nature, Cronbach reminds us, does not distinguish between main effects and interactions or between orders of interactions (Cronbach, 1982, pp. 152-153) in terms of the consequences for program effectiveness. However, main effects and higher-order interactions may have considerably different implications for policy, and the possibility of higher-order interactions should therefore not be overlooked.

The importance of site-specific interactions also means that evaluators labor under the burden of "cultural relativism." The factors affecting program outcomes will behave differently and will combine differently in various settings. Thus beyond broad categories of influences (such as the importance of concrete in-service education for new program implementation), the causal and conditional statements associated with an evaluation in one setting are likely to have questionable relevance to program operations in another setting.

The *ceteris paribus* conditions assumed by traditional evaluation design, in short, do not exist. In the fluid, complex, and often random complex reality of the social program setting, scientific proof is not possible. And even if it were possible to "prove" program effects and confidently assign causality, the relevance of this accomplishment would be short-lived from both a scientific and a practical perspective. Social systems are not "self-sealing."[5] They are dynamic—open to their environment, random internal fluctuation, unanticipated pressures, and exogeneous pressures beyond their control. The "effects" demonstrated by last year's evaluation, as well as their "causes," then, may well be ephemeral.

The now classic tale of the *It Works* series illustrates dramatically the erosion of conclusions and generalizations (Hawkridge, Compeau & Roberts, 1969). In the late 1960s, Congress was anxious to hear good news about local programs supported by the massive federal compensatory education effort, Title I of the 1965 Elementary and Secondary Education Act. The American Institutes for Research was awarded a contract to identify and describe a series of exemplary federally funded compensatory education programs. The results were published under the upbeat title, *It Works*. But when evalautors returned to these sites a year or two later they found that these successful projects were no longer "working" (McLaughlin, 1975). Evaluators discovered that the essential contextual components of success, and so the outcomes themselves, had shifted with time. Because main effects are associated with the contextual and institutional factors that determine how a program is carried out, generalizations and findings based in this fluid reality break down over time. As Cronbach put it: "We tend to speak of a scientific conclusion as if it were eternal, but in every field emprical relations change. . .[and] generalizations decay" (Cronbach, 1975, p. 122).

The reality of social program implementation means that evaluations limited to goals traditionally associated with the hypotheticodeductive model, that is, estimates of effect and specification of causality, face substantial obstacles. Social program evaluation cannot control all of the things that "matter" to outcomes; evaluation cannot lead to final statements about causal relationships between program inputs and outputs; evaluation cannot result in detailed prescriptions relevant to other social settings; and social program evaluation rarely can furnish scientific proof.

But this does not mean that evaluation cannot serve its assigned function in the policy system: Support for learning and control. Rather than search for proof about program effects and fine-tuned outcome estimates, a more realistic and useful goal for evaluation would incorporate assessments about the value of a practice relative to other practices in the system and to practices that it replaced. For example, on dimensions such as efficiency, ease of implementation, support for program objectives, to what extent and how is the practice under examination better than former or present practices? Moving away from standards of proof and toward notions of "better than," evaluation can reduce the uncertainty about such relationships and inform practitioners about the conditional nature of social program choices.

Such an approach would reflect more accurately the problems of *learning* about social programs as well as the problems of *effecting* social settings. The changeable nature of social settings means that it is not possible to solve problems—they can be moved, transformed, and hopefully improved, but not forevermore "fixed" (Majone, 1981). Evaluations designed to examine a program's stature vis-á-vis its environment, rather than to generate scientific estimates of effect, can provide valuable procedural advice. (Of course, these two functions may not be mutually exclusive.) Because they stress the relative outcomes of various program choices and outcomes, evaluations of this type support understanding of the conditions under which alternative program or policy choices seem more or less desirable.

These suggestions for reassessing evaluation objectives leave unaddressed the question of "acceptability." If criteria associated with methods of scientific proof largely are inappropriate to evaluation research, what other criteria of acceptability can be applied? Several philosophers of science and social analysts have suggested that the criteria of "goodness" associated with research in the natural sciences be replaced with something no more exotic than common sense. In this view (which is expressed by a number of analysts and philosophers, in particular, Lindblom & Cohen, 1979; Majone, 1981; Kaplan, 1964; Ziman, 1978), criteria of acceptability in evaluation would be derived from craft knowledge and experience. Do the results of evaluation square with common knowledge about policy and practice? Do they incorporate the complexity of relevant decision-making settings? Do evaluations frame recommendations in terms of the actions and choices actually available to practitioners? In considering this view, it is important to recognize that although "acceptability" is grounded in craft knowledge and experience, it is capable of modifying such common sense by force of persuasion.

Majone extends this homely notion of acceptability to methods and data as colleagues make judgments about the quality of one another's work. Generally accepted criteria of adequacy in the domain of policy studies and social program evaluations should reflect the actuality in which programs as well as evaluations must be carried out.

> Such criteria are derived not from abstract logical canons but from craft experience, depending as they do on the special features of the problem, on the quality of data and limitations of available tools, on the time constraints imposed on the analyst, and on the requirements of the client. (Majone, 1981, p. 17)

Unit of Analysis

Almost all evaluations adopt what can be called a "project model" of research in which the project is taken as the unit of analysis without reference to its institutional setting. Most of the history of evaluation is written in such project-specific terms. Yet as we have seen, "treatment" and outcome are the result of complex interactions between project factors and the implementing system. This implementation reality raises questions about the appropriate unit of analysis for an evaluation. Clearly an evaluation that looks at a project in isolation from its institutional setting misspecifies the nature of the process: So-called treatment effects consequently will be misestimated to an unknown degree. This "project model" approach also risks wrong conclusions or advice because of the false dichotomy implicit in its partitioning of reality into problem/nonproblem and treatment/nontreatment. The complex interactions that define treatment make a treatment/nontreatment distinction spurious at best. Similarly, the multiple goals that shape actions and choices within an implementation make project-specific notions of "the problem" meaningless. Advice resulting from a evaluation that draws effectively arbitrary boundaries in terms of the "project" or treatment, then, is bound to be limited and misleading.

Instead of the isolated project, the appropriate unit of analysis for evaluation is what has been variously termed the "implementing system" (McLaughlin 1980), the "policy environment" (Nakamura & Smallwood, 1980) or the "policy space" (Majone, 1981). The reality of program implementation not only requires evaluators to cast a wide net around the project in order to capture important main- and lower-order influences; it also "requires evaluators to attend to the related sequence of decisions and actions together with their behavioral, cognitive, and ideological supports" rather than discrete decisions and actions" (Majone, 1981, p. 20).

This broader view also captures unanticipated consequences or spin-off effects associated with program implementation. These associated effects are often of more than academic interest. They can have major import for an evaluation's conclusions. For example, imagine an instance in which evaluators judged the development and implementation of an arts magnet school highly successful on multiple measures—the quality of the curriculum in place, student achievement in the area of art history and art criticism, as well as the making of art, parent support for the program, and teacher satisfaction. Yet a look at the project within the broader system context may show that the resources, energy, and attention devoted to the art magnet drained and demoralized art education in the regular district program. From this perspective, then, the arts magnet would represent a net loss in the quality of the district's art program.

Outcome Measures

The so-called "goal model" dominates evaluation theory and practice. Majone (1981) calls this strategy "evaluation by results"; Deutscher (1977) warns of the "goal trap." Implementation realities define a number of problems with this time-honored evaluation approach. First, implementors and implementing systems pursue multiple goals, and program or policy goals may be interpreted differently by different actors in various parts of the system. Most evaluations, however, address only a single goal: The ostensible delivery goal of the program being assessed. There are risks in failing to attend to other goals that influence program-related decisions and other system goals or interests (e.g., political and bureaucratic concerns): The relationship between program activities and program effects can be misunderstood, and the evaluation can provide information of only limited utility to policymakers and practitioners. A policy could be effective in terms of a single goal (e.g., delivery), but fail in terms of other system objectives. In a social policy setting, effectiveness is a complex, heterogeneous concept that must incorporate the variegated character of the implementing system as well as differences in perceptions about policy relevance and objectives. Acknowledging the existence and import of multiple goals, important questions arise:

- How does an evaluator determine and decide which "impact" to assess?
- How can multiple and competing policy definitions and emphases be identified and reconciled?
- Given the multiplicity of perceptions about the intent of a program or policy and the dominant system priorities, whose perception "carries the day?" Whose is most important to program or policy outcomes?
- How can shifts and modifications over time and across the implementing system be recognized and estimated? (Maynard-Moody, 1983)

Second, a goal-focused evaluation often pays only minimal attention to the procedures and the implementation choices that shape program outcomes. Goal-focused evaluations typically ask questions of "how much" without examining organizational questions of how and why. Consequently, it shifts attention away from the factors that matter to an important user group: Individuals charged with improving practice. Not only do implementation decisions fix program outcomes, they often are among the most powerful policy variables an evaluator might consider. Ironically, "treatment" may be among the least manipulable of factors now that fiscal retrenchment severely constrains administrator ability to initiate new programs or introduce new materials. For the foreseeable future, administrators are unlikely to be debating whether or not to adopt a new curriculum (that choice may be prohibited by budgetary stringency), but will be instead deliberating about how to get better performance out of existing investments in people, materials, and technologies. This, at its root, is an implementation question.

Third, a goal-focused evaluation typically assumes a well-developed theory of relationship between ends and means—project inputs and program outcomes—as well as agreement on goals among planners, policymakers, evaluators, and implementors. However, such well-developed theories about means and ends generally do not exist. But more importantly, experience with social program implementation shows that policies and programs are transformed in the process of implementation and that agreement on goals cannot be assumed to exist at all or to endure over time. Thus the specificity of most goal-focused evaluations effectively *constructs* a reality that does not necessarily exist in practice. It risks imposing casual models on projects or programs that have only scant resemblance to the "models" upon which staff base program activities.

Differentiated Evaluation Strategies

The realities of program implementation make it clear that a unidimensional evaluation design can neither accurately portray all evaluation situations nor adequately respond to the needs of different evaluation consumers. For example, the methodologies and questions appropriate to the later or mature stages of a program effort are likely to misrepresent activities and accomplishments during the early stages. The presence of disagreement about preferred program practices when a program has been in operation for some time can signal distress. However, this same observation in early stages of implementation can mean something quite different: The beginning of the "unfreezing" of ongoing practices necessary to the learning of new routines. (A California observer of planned change efforts in education dubbed this necessary stage the "thermal period.")

Similarly, the "outcomes" of each stage differ. Assessment of project effects on student achievement is inappropriate to a project still struggling to get off the ground. However, assessment of factors such as the political support available for the project, teacher commitment to carrying out project plans, and administrator support for the project is relevant to this stage of program operation. Actors and organizational locations most important to project activities and outcomes also change through the process of development and implementation; central staff typically are most central in the early stages whereas individuals with direct implementation responsibility have the most influence during later stages.

An examination of art education practices sponsored by the Getty Trust used an analytical scheme that differentiates actors and outcomes by stage of the change process (McLaughlin & Thomas, 1984). At the initiation or adoption stage, relevant outcomes were defined as successful marshaling of the multiple resources necessary to carry out the program and the generation of support for the program throughout the district. For the implementation stage of the change process, outcomes were conceptualized as teacher confidence in carrying out the new practices and demonstrated ability to do so, a high quality of practice across participating schools and classrooms, and activities that are consistent with program goals. Institutionalization is the final stage of the planned change process. At this point, special project status must be replaced by routinized support and activity. Outcomes of interest here include teacher commitment, central office support for the project, provision for the program's continuing developmental needs, and the incorporation of program activities into ongoing district routines. The multiple goals and interests relevant to programs or policies also call for a differentiated evaluation strategy. It is difficult to envision an evaluation that could address all salient goals with the same rigor and scope. Although any evaluation must attend to the several objectives relevant to decision makers, a number of different outcomes could shape the major focus of an evaluation effort including program delivery goals, political support, efficiency, user satisfaction, and the like (Maynard-Moody, 1983).

Mode of analysis and instrumentation is another area in which differentiation would enhance the validity and utility of program evaluation. The dominant evaluation model is quantitative, representing "hard" data and notions of statistical proof. For example, Bernstein and Freeman's 1975 assessment of the "quality" of evaluation research developed a quality index with which to assess more than 200 evaluation research projects (Bernstein & Freeman, 1975). Their major ratings (with the higher numbers indicating higher quality evaluation) underscore the dominance of this quantitative model. Three indicators were assigned for data analysis:

Quantitative (2)

Qualitative and quantitative (1)

Qualitative (0)

Ratings for statistical procedures reflected the same paradign (Patton, 1978, p. 206):

Multivariate (4)

Descriptive (3)

Ratings from qualitative data (2).

Narrative data only (1)

No systematic material (0)

By this rating scheme, qualitative evaluations are judged to have no value and mixed method studies to be seriously flawed. Yet experience with social program implementation shows that quantitative methods pursued alone cannot capture the complex processes, indeterminate factors, and often subtle influences that shape program outcomes. The institutional reality of social program implementation defeats attempts to apply unilaterally the abstract formalism represented by mathematics and the logic of numbers.

First, statistical differences and substantive significance do not always coincide. Statistical significance simply refers to whether an observed difference is likely to be due to chance. Substantive significance refers to the *consequence* of differences in a social setting. How meaningful, for example, is it to know that the level of parent participation has increased significantly unless one also knows who the new participants are (i.e., is the configuration of parent participation changed) and how they participate (i.e., pro forma attendance at meetings or involvement in decisions about school activities)? What practical meaning do significant statistical differences among students have if they represent only a single item difference on a standarized achievement test?

Second, determinant tools often are incompatible with central features of the process of program implementation. Policies and practices change over time as a practice is carried out. Determinant tools, such as a fixed coefficient model, risk misrepresenting transformation in key variables. Relationships and effects that held at time 1 often do not obtain at time 2. Early teacher resistance, for example, may have been overcome by an effective in-service education program. An early and unamended estimate of the level of teacher resistance to a new program and its effect on program outcomes would, in this case, lead to wrong conclusions. Or, particular factors—principal support—may be more or less important at different points in the process of carrying out a new practice. A one-shot, fixed determinant model would miss the shifting "weight" of this important factor. (More complex, time-dependent models could be constructed but are rare in practice and difficult to institute.) The search for simplification implicit in such models may in fact be counterproductive because it ignores differences, interactions, and complexities that are crucially important to effective performance.

Three, the things that matter to program outcomes may be difficult to quantify. For example, the quality of teacher involvement in school decision making or the values and beliefs associated with particular program choices often elude quantification. For any evaluation, there will be information that can be best gotten through quantitative methods, distributions and frequencies, for example. But the state of the art and the realities of social setting defies comprehensive learning with a single method. Evaluation involves more than the logic of numbers and the enumeration and scaling central to quantitative models; it involves the logic of classes that characterizes qualitative research. For example, understanding the institutional norms, statuses, and goals as well as the individual beliefs and values that shape program activities and results requires largely qualitative methods of interviewing and observation.

A unitary evaluation model, in short, is ill-equipped to capture the emergence and resolution (or lack of resolution) of the factors, issues, and quandaries associated with implementation. An evaluation that differentiates methodological choice by the type of information required and the nature of the problem to be addressed is more likely to represent reality accurately and to serve the needs of evaluation users.

Concepts of Use

Evaluations have many purposes ranging from the political to the practical (Goldenberg, 1983). Leaving aside patently political interests, the multiple specific purposes of evaluation can be described by two broad goals: Learning and control (Elmore, 1980). Evaluations are undertaken (1) to learn about program activities and outcomes so practices can be improved and (2) to control the behavior of those responsible for implementation. However, evaluators agree that neither purpose generally has been well served (Pincus, 1980; Wholey, 1979; David, 1982; Patton, 1978).

Implementation realities suggest reasons for this assessment and thus pose fundamental questions about the concepts of use that underlie most evaluations. For example, the typical impact model is designed by higher-ups in the policy system (or even outside the system) with little involvement on the part of those responsible for program implementation. Further, evaluation findings are delivered only to system managers; little effort is made to communicate or explain results to those whose performance was examined. This approach to evaluation ignores the role of the street-level bureaucrat and misunderstands the conditions under which the learning and control assumed by evaluation take place. The concept of use implicit in this model disregards how learning relevant to improved outcomes takes place as well as the nature of effective control in most social policy settings (Elmore, 1980).

To learn, individuals need to reflect on action; to learn how to do better, individuals need regular feedback about their performance (Schon, 1983; Good, 1983). Most evaluations provide little information to support reflection on action; instead evaluations report on the extent to which formal goals have been met. Most evaluations provide summative, one-shot assessments rather than intermittent information about performance.

But even if evaluations addressed these concerns, they would still fall short of their goals because, in the main, they do not direct information to those individuals whose "learning" and performance is of most import to program outcomes: The individuals responsible for service delivery. Most evaluations are built on a command-and-control view of the social system that assumes an effective hierarchy of authority and closely linked operating units. As experience shows, the facts of institutional life in most social policy settings diverge substantially from this platonic notion of concentrated power and responsibility. Yet evaluations seldom leave the management and supervisory units; little effort is made to convey evaluation findings to those charged directly with implementation (David, 1982). Nor, interestingly, does it appear that the people who receive evaluation have the authority to act on their findings (Kennedy, 1980, p. 47). Primary decision makers at the "top" of the system, who are important to changing conditions of support or sanction for implementers, usually are bypassed as well.

In most cases, however, if evaluations were shared with street-level bureaucrats, they would find them questionably relevant. Typically, goals are defined and expressed in the evaluator's terms, not the deliverer's terms. Few evaluators ask individuals responsible for delivery what they intend and what they would like to learn about program operations. In many cases, the evaluator's questions hold limited import for the street-level bureaucrat. Relevance is confounded by format. The language evaluators use to talk to each other usually is practically meaningless to deliverers. For the street-level bureaucrats, meaningful evaluation must be based in the craft knowledge, language, and experience of their professional world (Kennedy, 1980; Lindblom & Cohen, 1980).

Most evaluations, in short, do not collect or target the information that could promote the learning most directly related to program outcomes. In the final analysis, learning acquired at the top of the system requires concomitant learning at the bottom in order for evaluation findings to translate into meaningful program improvement. Evaluation seldom can fulfill its intended purpose if a single decision maker or a solitary center of influence describes its focus. And exclusion of the street-level bureaucrat excludes those most influential in determining program outcomes.

The command-and-control view of authority also misunderstands what effective control means in many social policy systems. As the preceding section argued, there is no necessary and direct correspondence between what administrators (or legislators) mandate and what actors responsible for implementation actually do. Evaluations rooted exclusively in a formal oversight model miss opportunities to exercise the most effective kind of control—control based in professional incentives and motivation. Most people want to do better. Evaluations that provide information to deliverers about the quality of their performance in a way that is relevant and comprehensible are among the most effective mechanisms for control available to an organization.[6] Evaluations that support rational calculation to the exclusion of learning from experience miss significant opportunities to support institutional growth and development.

SUMMARY AND CONCLUSIONS

Since its inception, evaluation research has aimed to describe "lawful relations" between program inputs and outcomes (Cronbach, 1975, p. 121). This standard has been used to identify "good" evaluation questions as well as "good" evaluation methods. Experience with social program implementation, however, points to serious if not insurmountable obstacles to such aspirations. Assumptions essential to the dominant evaluation model, the hypotheticodeductive paradigm, find little support in reality. Whereas traditional evaluation designs generally assume that project treatment or inputs have main effects on program outcomes, these project factors in fact have only indirect and marginal effects because they must operate through the implementing system.

The essentially static notions of treatment found in most evaluation designs seriously misrepresent the variable and changing nature of social programs as they are transformed by implementation choices at different levels of the policy system. Further, these implementation choices are affected by more than just features of the implementing system such as resources, expertise, and relative need. They also are molded by the multiple goals that shape implementer priorities, rather than only by the single delivery goal most evaluations address. For all of these reasons, the classic models for estimating effects and specifying causality as well as scientific standards of proof are largely inappropriate to learning about social programs and assessing their effects.

The concepts of use and usefulness implicit in most evaluations also misrepresent reality. Rather than the hierarchical authority structure assumed by most evaluation and reporting schemes, social settings have multiple sources of power and influence. And the ultimate influence lies with the street-level bureaucrats, individuals who are responsible for carrying out policy, programs, and mandates but who seldom are consulted in the design of evaluations and specification of items to be assessed or involved in the presentation of findings. Implementation realities suggest that notions of learning and control found in most evaluations misunderstand both how learning occurs in social systems and the nature of effective authority.

Finally, in contrast to the search for universals and axioms associated with the dominant evaluation model, evaluation findings are not ageless. The institutional context in which social programs are implemented is fluid, unstable, complex, and often unpredictable. As a result, findings, conclusions, and generalizations break down over time. Social scientists are bound to be disappointed if they hope to emulate the timeless relations of natural science.

What are reasonable expectations, then, for evaluation? What kind of evaluation makes sense? What will be most useful to policymakers and practitioners? The fundamental lack of fit between traditional evaluation paradigms and implementation realities means that it is not a question of "fixing" our old way of doing evaluation business. Experience with social program implementation suggests that different questions and methods are in order. A focus on process questions, for example, clearly is an important evaluation task and one that is largely ignored by most goal-driven evaluation designs. But, because implementation choices dominate project outcomes, advice to policymakers and practitioners needs to specify the nature of these choices, the trade-offs surrounding them, and the process whereby they are carried out. This argues for evaluation that attends as much to *how* something is done and *why* it is done as it does to *what* is done.

Because generalizations decay, and because few social programs are undertaken in the go/no-go spirit of experimentation, evaluation profitably could move from a focus on conclusionary statements of effect toward goals of short-term control and correction. Evaluations could address issues of targeting and implementation, for example, as ways to assist practitioners and policymakers in achieving various program goals. Regular feedback about performance, evidence of success, and suggestions for improvement are crucial to implementer improvement and effectiveness. This provides short-run control of the highest order. It also suggests an approach to evaluation that adopts a regularized strategy for information collection and analysis and abandons the evaluation-as-event, as a once a year way of learning about program activities.

Experience with social program implementation also suggests that evaluations should move from notions of "proof" and static conclusions toward judgments of "better than" and an emphasis on the conditional knowledge to be gained from a special program effort. Among the questions to be asked are: What institutional factors (e.g., existing knowledge base, resource constraints) shaped program choices? What factors impeded or supported implementation? What was the interaction between existing staff capacity and program expectations?

What ancillary effects are associated with program operations? Are some program participants affected differently than others by program activities? This kind of information about program processes and the institutional effects of various program and implementation choices provides practitioners with information they need to make sense of the alternatives before them. It also can furnish the information policymakers need to consider issues central to the crafting of policy, for example, the policy mechanisms most appropriate to particular policy objectives; strategies for differentiation of resources; incentives or sanctions; reasonable expectations; and standards for program operations.

At the very least, experience with social program implementation underscores the fact that traditional evaluation models are only one, and an inherently limited, way of conceiving of the evaluation task and the role of evaluation in social settings. This experience makes it evident that new ways of thinking about evaluation are necessary for generating and integrating new insights and, indeed, for learning from experience.

NOTES

1. This section draws heavily on an earlier essay by Richard F. Elmore and Milbrey W. McLaughlin, "The Federal Role in Education: Learning From Experience," *Education and Urban Society, 15,3,* 1983, 309-330.

2. This fact provides a major rationale for a continued and vigorous federal role in areas that are seen as national priorities but which have uneven support at state and local levels.

3. This is the thesis of J. Pressman and A. Wildavky's landmark study, *Implementation* (1973).

4. "Street-level bureaucrat" is the very apt term used by R. Weatherley and M. Lipsky, "Street-Level Bureaucrats and Institutional Innovation: Implementing Special Education Reform," *Harvard Educational Review, 47,2,* 171-197, 1977.

5. C. Argyris and D. Shon (1978) use this very descriptive phase in *Organizational Learning: A Theory of Action Perspective* (1978) to underline the permeability of organizational boundaries.

6. This conclusion is prominently displayed in T. Peters and R. Waterman, *In Search of Excellence,* New York: Harper & Row, 1982.

REFERENCES

Argyris, C., & Shon, D. A. (1978). *Organizational learning: A theory of action perspective.* Reading, MA: Addison-Wesley.
Bardach, E. (1977). *The implementation game.* Cambridge, MA: MIT Press.

Bardach, E. (1980). *Implementation studies and the study of implements.* Paper presented at the Annual Meeting of the American Political Science Association, Washington, DC.

Berman, P., & McLaughlin, M. W. (1978). *Federal programs supporting educational change: Vol. 8, implementing and sustaining innovations.* Santa Monica, CA: The Rand Corporation.

Bernstein, I., & Freeman, H. (1975). *Academic and entrepreneurial research: The consequences of diversity in federal evaluation studies.* New York: Russell Sage.

Boruch, R. F., & Cordray, D. S. (1980). An appraisal of educational program evaluations: Federal, state and local agencies. Evanston, IL: Northwestern University.

Cronbach, L. J. (1975). Beyond the two disciplines of scientific psychology. *American Psychologist,* 116-127.

Cronbach, L. J. (1982). *Designing evaluations of educational and social programs.* San Francisco: Jossey-Bass.

David, J. L. (1982). Local uses of Title I evaluations. In E. R. House et al. (Eds.), *Evaluation Studies Review Annual* (Vol. 7). Beverly Hills, CA: Sage.

Deutscher, I. (1977). Toward avoiding the goal-trap in evaluation. In F. Carol (Ed.), *The evaluation of social action programs.* New York: Russell Sage.

Elmore, R. F. (1980). *Evaluation, control and learning in organizations.* Paper presented at the Western Political Science Association Meetings, San Francisco, CA.

Elmore, R. F., & McLaughlin, M. W. (1982). Strategic choice in federal education policy: The compliance-assistance trade-off. In A. Lieberman & M. W. McLaughlin (Eds.), *Policy making in education: The 81st Yearbook of the National Society for the Study of Education.* Chicago, IL: University of Chicago Press.

Elmore, R. F. & McLaughlin, M. W. (1983). The federal role in education: Learning from experience. *Education and Urban Society, 15,* 309-333.

Fullan, M. (1982). *The meaning of educational change.* New York: Teachers College Press.

Gilbert, J. P., Light, R. J., Mosteller, F. (1975). Assessing social innovations: An empirical base for policy. In C. A. Bennett & A. A. Lumsdaine (Eds.) *Evaluation and experiment.* New York: Academic Press.

Goldenberg, E. N. The three faces of evaluation. *Journal of Policy Analysis and Management, 2* (4), 515-525.

Good, T. (1983). Research on classroom teaching. In L. Shulman & G. Sykes (Eds.), *Handbook of teaching and policy.* New York: Longman.

Goodlad, J., Klein, M. F., & Associates (1974). *Looking behind the classroom door.* Worthington, OH: Charles A. Jones.

Hargrove, E., et al. (1981). *Regulations and schools: The implementation of equal education for handicapped children.* Nashville, TN: Institute for Public Policy Studies, Vanderbilt University.

Hawkridge, D. G., Campeau, P., & Roberts, A. O. H. (1969). *A study of exemplary programs for education of disadvantaged children.* Palo Alto, CA: American Institutes for Research.

Jackson, P. W. (1968). *Life in classrooms.* New York: Holt, Rinehart & Winston.

Kaplan, A. (1964). *The conduct of inquiry.* San Francisco: Chandler.

Kennedy, M. (1980). *The role of evaluation and test information in the public schools.* Cambridge, MA: Huron Institute.

Kirst, M., & Jung, R. (1980). The utility of the longitudinal approach in assessing implementation: A thirteen-year view of Title I, ESEA. *Educational Evaluation and Policy Analysis, 2,* 17-33.

Lindblom, C. E., & Cohen, D. K. (1980). *Usable knowledge.* New Haven, CT: Yale University Press.

Lortie, D. C. (1975). *Schoolteacher.* Chicago, IL: University of Chicago Press.

Majone, G. (1981). Policies as theories. In I. L. Horowitz (Ed.), *Policy studies review annual* (Vol. 5). Beverly Hills, CA: Sage.

Maynard-Moody, S. (1983). Program evaluation and administrative control. *Policy Studies Review, 2,* 371-390.

McDonnell, L. M., & McLaughlin, M. W. (1982). *Education policy and the rule of the states.* Santa Monica, CA: The Rand Corporation.

McLaughlin, M. W. (1975). *Evaluation and reform: The case of ESEA Title I.* Cambridge, MA: Ballinger.

McLaughlin, M. W. (1980). Evaluation and alchemy. In J. Pincus (Ed.), *Educational evaluation and the public policy setting.* Santa Monica, CA: The Rand Corporation.

McLaughlin, M. W., & Thomas, M. (1984). *History, criticism and production: An examination of the process of art education in selected school districts, Vol. 1: Comparing the process of change across school districts.* Santa Monica, CA: The Rand Corporation.

Nakamura, R. T., & Smallwood, F. (1980). *The politics of policy implementation.* New York: Saint Martin's Press.

Patton, M. Q. (1978). *Utilization focused evaluation.* Beverly Hills, CA: Sage.

Peters, T. J., & Waterman, R. H., Jr. (1982). *In search of excellence.* Cambridge, MA: Harper & Row.

Pincus, J. (Ed.). (1980). *Educational evaluation in the public policy setting.* Santa Monica, CA: The Rand Corporation.

Pressman, J., & Wildavsky, A. (1973). *Implementation.* Berkeley: University of California Press.

Raizen, S. A. & Rossi, P. H. (1982). Summary of program evaluation in education: When? How? To what ends? In E. R. House et al. (Eds.), *Evaluation studies review annual* (Vol. 7). Beverly Hills, CA: Sage.

Rossi, P. H. (1982). Some dissenting comments on Stake's review. In E. R. House et al. (Eds.), *Evaluation studies review annual* (Vol. 7). Beverly Hills, CA: Sage.

Rossi, P. H., & Freeman, H. E. (1982). *Evaluation.* Beverly Hills, CA: Sage.

Sabatier, P., & Mazmanian, D. (1979). The conditions of effective implementation: A guide to accomplishing policy objectives. *Policy Analysis, 5,* 481-504.

Schon, D. A. (1983). *The reflective practitioner: How professionals think in action.* New York: Basic Books.

Stake, R. E. (1982). A peer response. In E. R. House et al. (Eds.), *Evaluation studies review annual* (Vol. 7). Beverly Hills, CA: Sage.

Steinberger, P. J. (1981). Typologies of public policy: Meaning construction and the policy process. In I. L. Horowitz (Ed.), *Policy studies review annual* (Vol. 5). Beverly Hills, CA: Sage.

U.S. Advisory Commission on Intergovernmental Relations (1981). *The future of federalism in the 1980s: Reports and papers from the conference on the future of federalism.* Washington, DC: ACIR.

Weatherley, R. (1979). *Reforming special education: Policy implementation from state to street level.* Cambridge, MA: MIT Press.

Wholey, J. S. (1979). *Evaluation: Promise and performance.* Washington, DC: The Urban Institute.

Ziman, J. (1978). *Reliable knowledge.* London: Cambridge University Press.

3

The Political Hand
Policy Implementation and Youth Employment Programs

Martin Levin and Barbara Ferman

Outstanding studies in the past decade have illuminated the sources of ineffective implementation and thus have suggested what not to do. To learn more about what to do, we analyzed a broad range of cases of effective implementation of youth employment programs in eight cities. The goal was to build an impressionistic model of the conditions contributing to effective implementation. We found that executives in the successful

Abstract *programs often acted as "fixers," repairing the implementation process and protecting and correcting their programs, especially through coalition building and constant intervention in administrative detail. Some executives created patterns of interest convergence among the relevant actors, using incentives to turn mild interests into active support. They thus provided the public sector's missing "political hand," analogous to the market's "invisible hand."*

In the early 1970s, the implementation problems of the Economic Development Administration (EDA) and the Office of Economic Opportunity (OEO), as well as other programs such as Model Cities, New Towns-in-Town, and federal aid to education, were considered to be largely the result of overly ambitious social engineering by liberal Democrats. It was often said that these liberal plans were immodest and that the liberals themselves were both too optimistic and uninterested in the actual details of implementing their "bright ideas."

By the end of the 1970s decade, experience suggested that such diagnoses of the problems of implementation probably missed the mark. Domestic policies of conservative Republican administra-

* We wish to thank Frank Levy, Tom Glynn, Gene Bardach, Aaron Wildavsky, and Martin Shapiro for their invaluable comments on an earlier draft. Support for the preparation of this article came from the James Gordon Foundation of Chicago and the Office of Youth of the Department of Labor.

tions—often with rather modest goals—also foundered at the implementation stage. This was true for both the swine flu vaccination program and the Community Development Block Grant program.

It seems that more is needed than good intentions or even good program designs to achieve effective policies. In the past two decades, implementation has been identified as the knottiest aspect of policymaking. One critical source of these difficulties, it is now clear, is the fact that in the heterogeneous society and fragmented political system that characterize the United States, there are numerous possibilities for disagreement, delay, and resistance. Thus, the legislative successes of yesterday often become the implementation problems of today.

YOUTH EMPLOYMENT In the past few decades, youth unemployment has become a serious national problem. The existence and persistence of high teenage unemployment rates, especially the disparities between teenage and adult rates, and between the rates of white and black teenagers, are now well known. Also well known is the fact that a relatively small proportion of youths—approximately 10%—accounts for almost half the unemployment of the youth group as a whole; this is a subset that is unemployed for long spells, six months or more.[1] Some suggest that the size of this relatively small subpopulation in the totals means that the problem is less serious than is usually supposed; others take the opposite view.[2] Whatever side one espouses, it is clear that any programs to reduce youth unemployment ought to be shaped by considerations of how to improve the lot of this specific subset.

Programs such as those authorized by the 1977 Youth Employment Demonstration Project Act (YEDPA) are especially suited to targeting specific groups. The implementation of nine of these programs in eight cities provides a rich basis for observing the role of the political hand in the implementation process. At its inception, YEDPA represented a new federal initiative to alleviate youth unemployment. In the first 18 months of its operation beginning in 1978, YEDPA expanded to a program that served some 450,000 youths at an expenditure of $1.7 billion. Projects under YEDPA focused on both developing new jobs and providing youths with the training, experience, and placement assistance to fill jobs. The training involved remedial reading, practical arithmetic, and on-the-job experience. All of the nine projects we analyzed included efforts to develop sound work habits and discipline. The youths in the nine YEDPA programs were aged 16 to 21, with family incomes not over about $9400 (the benchmark figure actually varied somewhat by region). Over 80% of the youths in the YEDPA came from low-income families, and 51% were black or Hispanic. In some programs, most were still in school, and in others most were not. Whether in school or not, most youths in these programs were difficult to work with—they showed poor academic development, lack of discipline, and poor work habits.

LEARNING WHAT
WORKS

Like many social programs, YEDPA had implementation problems. But the nine YEDPA programs analyzed here differ from most of these other programs in a number of ways. First, the implementation obstacles YEDPA faced were somewhat different from those of other programs. In general, there are three major types of implementation obstacles: resistance—some actors resist implementation because they feel it is not in their interests; imperfect convergence of interests—some actors create delay or threaten to delay in order to expand their benefits; disorganized interests—others create obstacles simply because they are unclear where their interests lie or are unable to organize themselves to respond to their convergent interests. The first two types of obstacles are common to most programs. The obstacles of disorganized interests, on the other hand, are often overlooked in implementation analyses even though they are more formidable than is typically recognized. The problems of this sort encountered by the YEDPA programs provided a fine opportunity to examine the dynamics of disorganized interests.

Another way in which these YEDPA programs differ from most others is that they provide more insights than the analyst usually encounters regarding what works. Several outstanding studies in the past decade have illuminated the sources of ineffective implementation.[3] Because these studies concentrated on programs whose performance appeared inadequate, their chief virtue is in telling one what not to do. The YEDPA study, on the other hand, was motivated in large part by the desire to learn more about what to do; the goal was to build an impressionistic model of the conditions contributing to effective implementation.

In seven of the nine programs studied, we concluded that implementation had been effective; the two remaining programs seemed on the borderline. These seven satisfied three broad criteria for effective implementation. First, was the program able to hold delay to a reasonable level? Second, was it able to hold financial costs to a reasonable level? Third, was it able to meet its original objectives without significant alteration or underachievement of these objectives?

Among the factors that played an important role in overcoming the obstacles to effective implementation were the actions of the executives in these nine programs, especially their actions as "fixers." As "fixers," they were constantly repairing and adjusting the machinery used for executing their programs, constantly putting together coalitions to support, protect, and sometimes expand those programs.[4] Some of these executives also created patterns of interest convergence among the relevant actors, using incentives to turn mild interests into active support. They thus provided the public sector's missing "political hand," analogous to the market's "invisible hand," and facilitated a public use of private interest. There also was the growth of a local policy infrastructure in these cities that resulted in local actors contributing positively rather than negatively to the implementation of federal programs. This seems to be a significant change from the 1960s.

But there are significant limits to how effective the implementation can become. Thus, program executives should develop an anticipatory and "dirty-minded" perspective: the ability to anticipate and predict implementation difficulties and to be attuned to conflicting interests and their likelihood of delaying, even outright resisting, implementation. A "dirty-minded" implementor, for example, might have better predicted the major implementation difficulties that the swine flu vaccination program would face and would have suggested precisely the actions and thoughts that those in charge of that program did not take.

To the extent that these nine YEDPA programs were effectively implemented, their performance seemed to be explained by the existence of some specific structural conditions in the environment in which they operated and some specific behavioral patterns on the part of their managers. The behavioral patterns have already been mentioned: an ability of managers to build piece by piece and to play the role of fixer. The environmental conditions are described and explored below. The distinction between structural and behavioral elements is useful. But like any such concept, it tends to simplify reality—all of these conditions interact significantly and tend to constitute a package of interrelated and interdependent elements. An executive pursuing the fixer strategies, for instance, would have little success in some environments. But, as will be argued below, talent is more scarce than either money or good ideas, especially at the executive level. Thus, favorable structural conditions are a secondary factor, supplementing or conditioning the effects of the behavioral patterns. At times, they can help produce favorable results even when highly talented executives are not available.

THE STUDY'S METHODOLOGY The aim here, as suggested, is to build an impressionistic model of the conditions that contribute to effective implementation. Therefore, these nine programs were selected from a larger pool of about 100 programs for which there was preliminary evidence of effective implementation.[5] They were selected because they were among the most effectively implemented and because they represented a diversity in size, region, and ethnicity of the youths in the program. The nine included programs in Pittsburgh, New Haven, Portland (Oregon), Syracuse, Albuquerque (two programs), San Antonio, Newark, and Baltimore.

For each of these nine programs, in addition to collecting statistical and documentary data, we conducted over a dozen interviews with a variety of actors. The interviews were systematic, although open-ended, and each lasted 45 min to 2 h. Drafts of all nine case studies were submitted to several actors in each program, including each program executive, in an attempt to check our findings and incorporate feedback. We have benefited from their suggestions. In the case of only one individual—apparently motivated by the fear of political fallout in Washington—did they differ from our conclusions. And this difference eventually was resolved to that actor's satisfaction.

Within these limits of our data, which are quite common to policy analysis in general and implementation studies in particular, we are confident of our generalizations. Nevertheless, while our data are strongly suggestive of the conclusions reached, in most instances they cannot demonstrate them conclusively. We have not followed the usual social science practice of using pseudonyms for the cities analyzed. We hope this will ameliorate any evidentiary issues by encouraging other researchers to check our findings by analyzing these programs themselves.

STRUCTURAL CONDITIONS FOR EFFECTIVE IMPLEMENTATION

Programs often are stillborn because nobody views them as being in their direct interest. Lacking such interests, the characteristic inertia of the governmental process tends to block effective implementation.

YEDPA was a good idea with a good program design. But the support of those who were concerned about youth employment, such as civil rights groups and local political leaders, was insufficient to implement these nine programs. They needed the support of those with more immediate interests in the programs, such as city governments and their agencies and private companies that received free labor, as well as the schools that were directly involved in executing the programs.[6]

The Political Hand

In some cases, groups that would benefit from the programs were not aware of those prospective benefits. The challenge for the executives was to create a convergence of interest. They used incentives and inducements to develop interests; they turned mild interests into active support. This seems to have contributed greatly to effective implementation.

For instance, New Haven, Portland, and San Antonio public housing authorities were in a position to receive free labor to support their programs for conserving and rehabilitating old structures, provided they took certain preliminary measures. One was to designate worksites for the program. The programs also needed general support from construction unions, as well as more direct contributions that included providing crew supervisors and apprenticeship positions for the youths who graduated from the programs. In turn, the programs offered unions an opportunity for preapprenticeship training at reduced costs, a referral service that helped unions satisfy affirmative action requirements, and the possibility of some additional jobs for union journeymen at a time when some in that category were unemployed.

Interest convergence is a pattern in which private (or individual) and public interests come to coincide. This resembles the (ideal) pattern of individuals in a private market. But in public sector activities like the implementation of a complex public program, there is no "invisible hand" to lead interests to coincide. Indeed, the inherent tension between private and public interests is a constant obstacle to socially desirable actions in the public sector. These YEDPA executives' actions in creating interest convergence in effect provided the public sectors' missing *"political hand"*[7] and created a *public use of private interest.*

One is reminded of Barnard's classic statement on the function of the executive, "to facilitate the synthesis in concrete action of contradictory forces, to reconcile conflicting forces, instincts, interests, conditions, positions, and ideals."[8] Others have suggested that the executive's principal tool in that process is communication aimed at mediating between groups and educating groups to their interests.[9] Through this ability for role taking, the executive becomes a medium for communication. These YEDPA executives communicated (as well as created) the incentives to those actors who merely had latent or potential positive interests to gain from YEDPA.

Using the Local Policy Infrastructure   In pursuing their role, YEDPA executives seem to have been helped by the existence of a recently developed policy infrastructure at the local level in these cities. The individuals and organizations comprising this infrastructure were oriented toward innovation and social progress. Many were alumni of Great Society programs and their foundation spinoffs; others came from post-Great Society innovative programs of the Federal Departments of Labor and Housing and Urban Development. The accumulated experiences of many federal social programs taught a great deal to both individuals and institutions. The individuals represented a new generation of activist bureaucrats. They functioned in a real sense as "organizers," and likening them to community or labor organizers captures a good deal of their political background and personal predilection. But they played a larger role because they were also skilled bureaucrats.

The term "infrastructure" is used to emphasize the rich organizational—rather than merely personal—legacy found in these cities. Numerous community-based organizations, new public agencies, and special programs within public agencies have developed and have become experienced, effective, and relatively prosperous. They know how to develop monetary and political support. For example, the Mexican–American Unity Council (MAUC) is a community development corporation that operates San Antonio's YCCIP. It was formed in 1967 and became involved in a broad range of community development projects, including major roles in the financing of large downtown construction projects. It is a politically influential organization, locally through alliance with activist priests, and nationally through its director's contacts with federal bureaucrats.

The growth in local infrastructure produced complex organizational and personal networks linking persons and organizations and gave them overlapping interests. The networks are built on past relationships and trust. This greatly facilitates securing the joint action and program assembly necessary for effective implementation. For instance, the assistant director of the prime sponsor in Pittsburgh and the program's director worked together as Neighborhood Youth Corps counselors in the late 1960s and early 1970s. Personal trust and cooperation developed over the years enabled them to avoid the suspicion that has existed between prime sponsor and schools in other cities, and which has led to implementation delays.

These policy infrastructures are an important social development of the last two decades, and using them could aid the implementation of a wide variety of other programs. A good deal of organization and many outstanding administrators remain from adult CETA and earlier manpower programs. YEDPA benefited greatly from the positive and negative lessons of the adult CETA programs. For example, the negative publicity that surrounded CETA nationally encouraged YEDPA prime sponsors and RDOL's to adopt stringent cost-monitoring devices. Without CETA (or any of its predecessors such as the Neighborhood Youth Corps and the Manpower Demonstration Training Act), YEDPA's implementation would almost certainly have been slower and less effective. There would have been more learning on-the-job and fewer program managers with the experience needed to anticipate implementation pitfalls and thus be better able to develop ways of avoiding, coping, or overcoming them.

Modest and Straightforward Design Although effective implementation depends on good local administration, that is not sufficient in itself. Even when a local program has a talented executive, implementation may founder simply because of the complexity of the program design. Thus, the modest, straightforward, and even simple designs of these YEDPA programs seem to have contributed markedly to effective implementation.

These designs maintained YEDPA's focus on the goals of job development, experience, training, and placement. YEDPA programs were not intended to redistribute political power or create political autonomy in low-income neighborhoods, as the Office of Economic Opportunity and Model Cities sought to do. By keeping to modest, specific goals, YEDPA's implementation was able to avoid the implementation pitfalls that have beset other social programs since the mid-1960s. For instance, the bulk of YEDPA expenditures have gone for youth wages and benefits. In fact, there was a formal and rigorously enforced regulation in the two largest categories of programs that 65% of each program's budget must go directly for youth wages and benefits. By contrast, the complex design and implementation processes of many earlier social programs often were major contributors to ineffective implementation and poor outcomes. The indirect design of EDA described in Jeffrey Pressman and Aaron Wildavsky's classic study of Oakland is a good example. They subsidized the capital of business—rather than their wage bill—on the promise that they would later hire low-skilled minority persons.[10]

Anticipating Pitfalls Even with modest designs, all of these nine programs experienced many implementation difficulties. But the implementors took several steps to anticipate these pitfalls. Thus, they were better able to develop ways of avoiding or coping with them.

First, often they did not attempt to start from scratch. Many YEDPA programs were built (Portland, Pittsburgh, and Newark) or modeled (San Antonio and New Haven) on previously successful ones. For instance, Pittsburgh's was built upon previously successful programs that had been designed for less disadvantaged youths. This enabled Pittsburgh to avoid most of the ordinary implementation difficulties: key actors—at both the worksites and the schools—had already worked together successfully for seven years.

Second, in several of these programs, internal evaluation and reassessment led to the detection and correction of serious implementation problems. In effect, they created a second phase for these programs that could be effectively implemented after initial problems were detected. The test of a good policy or a good program is not the absence of error but the ability to detect errors and then correct them.[9] In Baltimore, for example, after the first few months of operation there appeared published reports, citizen complaints, and mayoral inquiries that made it clear to the heads of the prime sponsor and the program that there were serious implementation problems (i.e., significant administrative difficulties—such as breakdown of the payroll systems for youths—resulting from the overcentralization of a large program). They assembled a task force of their top staff to review operations and develop recommendations. The subsequent changes (greater decentralization; in particular, the responsibility for supervision, counseling, and payroll was shifted to smaller units) greatly improved implementation. A similarly successful reassessment and reorganization was undertaken in San Antonio.

BEHAVIORAL CONDITIONS

Fixers Fixer strategies are crucial to effective implementation. The program assembly process will not run by itself. It has to be put together piece by piece. It should be guided by a strong executive. Actors and interests have to be cajoled, convinced, and persuaded into joint action. Adjustments and adaptations have to be made. Coalitions have to be built. Numerous compensating actions were taken by these program executives in response to intentional omissions at the design and formulation stages (designers felt that it was not politically or financially feasible to include them earlier). One occurred in Albuquerque's WORP where planners knew it would be difficult for program youths to use the city's small public transportation system to get to the distant worksite, but needed to avoid an expensive transportation item in their proposal lest they lose out to less costly competitors. After the program was funded and many youths began to get fired because they could not get to their jobs on time using public transportation, the program executive renegotiated the grant to obtain transportation funds. Other compensating actions were in response to inadvertent omissions, which are endemic: at the earlier stages nobody can fully anticipate the difficulties and resistance that may surface in implementation.

Coalition building is a central element of the fixer strategy. The most significant element of coalition building pursued by these YEDPA executives was the creation of the patterns of interest convergence described above. There were also other instances of coalition building by these fixers. In San Antonio, the prime sponsor director created a coalition behind the YCCIP program by developing support for it from local construction unions and from the Six Parish Coalition (a group previously formed by activist priests to organize barrio residents).

Other recent studies also point to the major contributions to effective implementation made by program executives. For instance, studies of the "Effective Schools" movement, successful black schools, and a broad range of London schools all indicate that the role of the schools' staffs as shaped by the "program executive"—the Principal—is much more important in achieving improved academic performance and improved behavior than educational innovations such as new teaching techniques, special programs, and new facilities.[12]

Bridging Agents Several program executives made major contributions to effective implementation by acting as "bridging agents." This role consisted of securing joint action among various interests through the executive's standing and membership in more than one of the relevant implementation camps. One bridging agent assembled Albuquerque's "THE" program by bringing together the hotel industry (providing worksites, jobs, and training) and the public schools. She was head of vocational training in the public schools, and her husband was a hotel executive and leader in the local hotel industry. The idea for "THE" came from her husband's constant complaint that he could not find enough trained people to work in his hotel. She also had a number of important contacts in the hotel industry that facilitated "THE's" initial implementation.

Similarly, the person who conceived, designed, and was *de facto* director of the Syracuse program had extremely helpful positions in several camps: he was a black officer at the Air Force base worksite (and head of its social action training program) who had been active in a broad range of black community affairs in the city and once worked in its Human Rights Department with a current executive in the prime sponsor's office. Like other bridging agents, the officer also had knowledge of labor shortages in the worksites to which he was close. And he thought that the base's labor shortage could be ameliorated by the YEDPA youths.

LIMITS TO ACTION Talented program executives, especially those able to act as "fixers," were a key to the success of implementation in these nine cases. But there seem to be significant limits to their availability.

Effective executive action in implementation requires the ability to carry it out, the resources, and the incentives. Ability is scarce. Even in a period of tight budget constraints, talent usually is more scarce than money, especially at the executive level. As James Q. Wilson has argued,

The supply of able, experienced executives is not increasing nearly as fast as the number of problems being addressed by public policy . . . Anyone who opposed a bold new program on the grounds that there was nobody around able to run it would be accused of being a pettifogger at best and a reactionary do-nothing at worst. Everywhere, except in government, it seems, the scarcity of talent is accepted as a fact of life . . . The government—at least publicly—seems to act as if the supply of able political executives were infinitely elastic, though people setting up new agencies will often admit privately that they are so frustrated and appalled by the shortage of talent that the only wonder is why disaster is so long in coming.[13]

Even when there is a potentially strong executive for implementation with the ability, he or she must have sufficient resources for the task. But often the able person does not. Nevertheless, a significant number of persons have the ability and resources, yet many of them do not have sufficient incentives. Indeed, the scarcity of these incentives seems to be the most significant limit. Most incentives for executives to become active in implementation run in the wrong direction, and the few positive incentives are weak. The electoral imperative is the biggest disincentive. American public officials feel their first job is to get themselves or their bosses reelected (or elected in the first place). This creates a short-run orientation and pressure for fast action. The constraint is the next election, which typically is in less than four years (less than two years for Congressman and many state legislators). All this goes against the grain of working on implementation or even developing an interest in it. Instead, potential implementation leaders opt for the dramatic; it need not be a dramatic achievement. A dramatic disclosure or proposal may be sufficient for one's electorate or superior. By contrast, implementation of an older proposal (even if effective) is not dramatic or fast; often it is downright dull.

These pressures also create incentives for symbolic politics rather than substantive activity. To convey a symbol—or effort, position, or commitment—it often may be sufficient for the official to take a stand, make a proposal, or sometimes initiate a program. Often this satisfies the electoral imperative without actually having to lead the implementation effort. In the extreme, officials "proclaim and abandon": they are more interested in a podium for policymaking rather than actual policy adoption and implementation.

THE POLITICAL HAND AND INTEREST CONVERGENCE Another replicability problem is that positive incentives for innovative social programs often are not present. Sometimes the innovation is supported by organizations and actors who favor it on

general material or ideological grounds, but are not direct beneficiaries. This leads to less than total commitment. Even more commonly, the major beneficiary of the program is that most amor-
phous group—citizens and taxpayers as a whole. The public
interest is notoriously difficult to organize, especially to press for
something as unglamorous as policy implementation that follows
high-visibility legislative struggles. The difficulty is compounded
when benefits are widely dispersed.

Thus, a pattern of interest convergence must usually be developed. For too long we have either acted as if a "political hand"
would appear spontaneously or simply bemoaned its absence in
the public sector. But interest convergence is at best difficult to
develop, probably even more difficult in policy areas other than
youth employment. Indeed, the positive contributions of local
unions that we found probably are not typical of other cities and
other unions. Moreover, the development of interest convergence
seems to be very dependent on the actions of a "fixer," and these
people are scarce.

There are, however, other conditions that are likely to be replicated in other policy areas.

LOCAL POLICY INFRASTRUCTURE Current local conditions surrounding the implementation of
YEDPA seem to be significantly more favorable than they were 15
or even 10 years earlier. Implementation difficulties then often
seemed to be caused by local actors; at worst there was active
resistance, and at best an inability to make programs work. By
contrast, today local conditions and actors tend to provide an extra boost to the implementation of federal programs. Employment
and other social programs of the 1960s and 1970s provided many
lessons—positive as well as negative—and helped develop local
infrastructures which have contributed toward effective implementation. It seems likely that this learning and infrastructure
development also occurred in other policy areas and in other cities. For instance, Paul Hill's analysis of federal education programs found that the development of informal networks of state
and local officials facilitated the implementation of Title I.[14]

MODEST DESIGNS AND MODEST GOALS Modest, straightforward program designs also seem to be replicable, as are modest program goals. Since some conditions depend
on able program executives to activate them and since talented
executives are scarce, such modest designs and goals are especially
important because average executives can carry them out.

To practical persons, our emphasis on the importance of talented executives and simple, modest program designs may seem
obvious matters of common sense. But experience shows that program designers in particular, and staff people in general, tend to
overlook both of these issues. Intellectuals of all political stripes
overemphasize bright ideas as the most important element in
achieving effective policies. Whether they are staff people in Wash-

ington or designers at City Hall, they tend to look at elegant designs as sufficient in themselves and to forget about what is going to happen at the front line. However, these YEDPA cases and a host of other studies show that programs do not start up automatically.

Overlooking the importance of a simple design is part of this same tendency. Program designers often confuse complexity with superiority and forget that average administrators will be carrying out their complex designs.

THE IMPLEMENTORS' CREDO: "DIRTY MINDEDNESS" Given that modest and simple program design facilitates effective implementation, the operational questions of what an executive actually should do still remain. These YEDPA cases suggest the importance of executives approaching their task with the view that implementation will be difficult. Several of these YEDPA executives tried to anticipate pitfalls in three ways. First, they gave high priority to the task of internal evaluation and reassessments to detect and correct errors, and in doing this, they performed the very important function of implementation of error correction.

Second, several of these program executives acted as if they had what has been called a "dirty mind": the ability to anticipate and predict implementation difficulties and to be attuned to conflicting interests and their likelihood of delaying, even outright resisting, implementation.[15] Most importantly, the "dirty-minded" implementor is aware that most implementation difficulties cannot be anticipated fully (What else can we expect but the unexpected?) and that a program's implementation cannot even come close to being free of error.

This awareness leads to the third way in which these several programs executives tried to anticipate implementation pitfalls—scenario writing. While accepting the fact that implementation difficulties can never be anticipated fully, a shrewd and dirty-minded implementor will try to improve and formalize his anticipation as much as possible. Scenario writing can help do this. Scenario writing involves the imaginative construction of future sequences of actions, the resulting conditions and reactions, and in turn, the further conditions and reactions that are developed by all actors and organizations involved in the implementation process. At its best, it should sensitize the program executive to the obstacles that lie ahead. It brings the likely flaws and problems to the forefront.[16] Thus, it forces designers and program executives to try to take account of them.

ADAPTABLE AND REALISTIC IMPLEMENTORS YEDPA's modest and straightforward design was important. But a major element of its success was the flexibility and improvisation that it allowed program executives. Previous experience seems to have been more important than preconceived plans for program details. These YEDPA cases suggest the importance of a strategy of flexibility and improvisation for policy implementation, as opposed to fixed battle plans. Elegant designs, especially when developed from the top (the federal level in this case) may be less important for success than the conditions and personnel at program sites. The advantages of a strategy of improvisation over fixed battle plans suggest some ways to train better implementors. First, the training should be directed toward changing implementors' expectations: make them more realistic about the high probability of error and ineffective implementation. Second, in the face of these more realistic expectations, we ought to train implementors to be more adaptable so that they might be better able to cope with these constant difficulties. They should be trained to view implementation as a process of avoiding pitfalls. In part, this can be done by reacting to circumstances. As Edmund Burke put it so well, "Circumstances give in reality to every political principle its distinguishing colour and discriminating effect. The circumstances are what render every civil and political scheme beneficial or noxious . . ."[17]

CURRENT CIRCUMSTANCES AND REALISTIC EXPECTATIONS This emphasis on adaptable implementors is a necessary balance to the earlier stress on the importance of anticipatory approaches in general and scenario writing in particular. But of course both strategies are needed. The specification of the conditions under which one should be preferred seems to depend largely on the context.

Fifteen years ago the lessons that needed to be emphasized were different than our focus on caution, modesty, and anticipatory strategy. In 1967, in his "strategy for economic development," Albert Hirschman in effect argued against modesty and foresight. He suggested that imbalance, ignorance of all the conditions at hand, and hence all the limitations, and even a touch of foolhardiness were needed to give initial impetus to the development. He urged executives to ignore the overly cautious conclusion that usually is developed by focusing on the obstacles to implementation. He also urged them to overextend their reach and not to be constrained by knowledge of implementation difficulties in economic development. By contrast with the lessons of the present study, Hirschman felt that foresight and knowledge of these conditions and obstacles too often tended to discourage people and immobilize the process.[18]

However, circumstances are a paramount policy consideration. Hirschman in part seems to have been reacting against the circumstances of the 1950s and 1960s—the call for "balanced development" with much emphasis on planning for contingency and little on the need for risk taking. By contrast, we are responding to the circumstances in domestic social policy of the past two decades: insufficient modesty, overly complicated program designs, and little appreciation of the virtue or necessity of simple design. For two decades, the predominant view has been that a good program design, or in some cases merely good intentions and substantial funding, would be sufficient to bring about effective implementation. It has been a period with insufficient focus on the importance of the task of implementation qua implementation. In particular, there has been insufficient focus on the importance of talented executives (and all the component characteristics and strategies) in achieving effective implementation or on the problem of the scarcity of executive talent.

Perhaps the message of more realistic expectations about implementation difficulties is needed less during the Reagan administration—a time of social policy retrenchment. But even assuming continued retrenchment for the next several years, this does not alter the need for realism about implementation. Indeed, we would speculate that significant budget cuts in domestic programs probably will mitigate the development of realistic expectations about implementation. And they will retard the process of "governmental learning" in which organizational memories about the nature of policy implementation can be developed.[19] As suggested, funding is an important and necessary element for effective implementation, but as countless studies indicate, it is not a sufficient element. In this period of budget cuts, it seems likely that there will be a tendency to blame program deficiencies largely on these cuts. There probably will be the commensurate tendency to overlook more general implementation difficulties, inadequacies, and the whole issue of institutional capacity. We speculate that the view will develop, as has developed during other recent periods of budget cuts (the Ford and Nixon administrations, the New York City fiscal crises, Propositions 13 and 2½), that "if only the money would be restored, we could accomplish almost everything that we intended." And thus there will be a tendency to forget about the other continuing generic problems of policy implementation that exist even with adequate funds.

MARTIN LEVIN is with the Department of Politics, Brandeis University. BARBARA FERMAN is with Barnard College of Columbia University.

NOTES 1. Clark, Kim and Summers, Lawrence, "The Dynamics of Youth Unemployment," in *The Youth Labor Market Problem: Its Nature, Causes and Consequences*, Freeman and D. Wise, Eds. (Chicago: University of Chicago Press, 1982), pp. 194–234.
2. For example, see the opposing views of, on the one hand, Martin Feldstein and David Ellwood ("Teenage Unemployment: What is the Problem?" in Freeman and Wise) and, on the other, Clark and Summers, and the various supporting views that each cite.
3. Pressman, Jeffrey and Wildavsky, Aaron, *Implementation*, 2nd ed. (Berkeley: University of California Press, 1979); Bardach, Eugene, *The Implementation Game* (Cambridge: MIT PRess, 1977); Derthick, Martha, *New Towns In-Town: Why a Federal Program Failed* (Washington: The Brookings Institution, 1973); Hargrove, Erwin, *The Missing Link* (Washington: The Urban Institute, 1975); Murphy, Jerome, "Title I of ESSEA: The Politics of Implementing Federal Education Reform," *Harvard Educational Review*, *41*(1) (1971): 35–63; Berman, Paul, "The Study of Macro- and Micro-Implementation," *Public Policy*, *26*(2) (1978): 157–184; Binstock, Robert, and Levin, Martin, "The Political Dilemmas of Intervention Policies," in Binstock, Robert, and Shavas,

Ethel, *Handbook of Aging and the Social Sciences* (New York: Van Nostrand Reinhold, 1976); Ingram, Helen, "Policy Implementation Through Bargaining: The Case of Federal Grants-in-Aid," *Public Policy, 25*(4) (1977); 499–526; Mazmanian, Daniel, and Sabatier, Paul, *Effective Policy Implementation* (Lexington, MA: Lexington Books, 1981); Nakamura, Robert, and Smallwood, Frank, *The Politics of Implementation* (New York: St. Martin's, 1980); Radin, Beryl, *Implementation, Change, and the Federal Bureaucracy* (New York: Columbia University Press, 1975); Williams, Walter, *The Implementation Perspective* (Berkeley: University of California Press, 1980).

4. Bardach, Eugene, *The Implementation Game*, chap. 11.

5. These 9 were selected from a larger pool of about 100 programs for which there was preliminary evidence of effective implementation. These 100 programs were selected on the basis of the following published studies and interviews with Department of Labor officials in Washington and program officials and prime sponsors from all areas of the country. Wurzburg, G., et al., "Initial Youth Employment Demonstration Projects Act Experience at the Local Level," National Council on Employment Policy, Washington, DC, 1978; Wurzburg, G., et al., "The Unfolding Youth Initiative Employment Policy"; Ball, J., et al., "The Youth Entitlement Demonstration Program: A Summary Report on the Start-Up Period of the Youth Incentive Entitlement Pilot Projects," Manpower Demonstration Research Corporation, New York; Ball, J., et al., "An Interim Report on Program Implementation," Manpower Demonstration Research Corporation, New York, 1979.

6. See our forthcoming book, *The Political Hand* (New York: Pergamon, 1985), for a more detailed discussion.

7. We are indebted to Eugene Bardach for suggesting this analogy.

8. Barnard, Chester, *The Functions of the Executive* (Cambridge: Harvard University Press, 1938), p. 243).

9. Mead, George, *Mind, Self, and Society* (Chicago: University of Chicago Press, 1934).

10. Pressman and Wildavsky, *Implementation*.

11. Wildavsky, Aaron, "The Past and Future Presidency," *The Public Interest, 41* (Fall 1975): 56–76.

12. Sowell, Thomas, "Patterns of Black Excellence," *The Public Interest, 43* (Spring 1976): 26–58; Rutter, M., et al., *Fifteen Thousand Hours: Secondary Schools and Their Effects on Children* (Cambridge: Harvard University Press, 1979).

13. Wilson, James, "The Bureaucracy Problem," *The Public Interest, 6* (Winter 1967): 3–9.

14. Hill, Paul, "Enforcement and Informal Pressure in the Management of Federal Categorical Programs in Education," Rand Corporation, Santa Monica, CA, 1979.

15. Bardach, Eugene, "On Designing Implementable Programs," in *Pitfalls of Analyses and Analyses of Pitfalls*, E. Quade and G. Majone, Eds. (New York: Wiley, 1978).

16. Bardach, Eugene, *The Implementable Game.*

17. Edmund Burke, quoted in Kristol, Irving, "Decentralization for What," *The Public Interest, 11* (Spring 1968): 10–21.

18. Hirschman, Albert, "The Principle of the Hiding Hand," *The Public Interest, 6* (1968): 10–23.

19. Etheridge, Lynn, *Government Learning* (New York: Pergamon, 1985).

4

Implementation Revisited
The Case of Federal Demonstrations

Thomas J. Higgins

Policy analysts rightfully worry about whether their recommendations can be implemented in practice. Their first dose of caution often comes from reading *Implementation* by Jeffrey Pressman and Aaron Wildavsky.[1] Many pitfalls, surprises, and reformulations lurk on the road from policy concept to program provisions, to actual consequences. Implementation problems loom especially large for federally funded programs aimed at local problems. Whether in health, housing, welfare, or transportation, "great expectations in Washington" often are "dashed in Oakland"; truly, "it is amazing federal programs work at all," as Pressman and Wildavsky observe. How can analysts and federal program managers improve their chances? Or, when can they and when can't they? Current thinking seems to go little farther than *Implementation's* suggestion:[2]

> The great problem, as we understand it, is to make the difficulties of implementation a part of the initial formulation of policy. Implementation must not be conceived as a process that takes place after, and independent of, the design of policy.

The following brief saga suggests some further answers based on demonstration projects of the federal Urban Mass Transportation Administration (UMTA) in the late 1970s. My experience with these federal efforts to help localities reduce traffic through tolls and higher parking prices shows that training in implementation and political feasibility may indeed help the analyst in the planning stages of a project. But it can also cause him or her to work too long and hard to gain implementation of improbable and ultimately infeasible demonstration ideas. Consequently, analysts should not only be carefully selected for their skills but also deployed so as not to confuse roles of analyst, advocate, and assessor. I also conclude that certain risks and pitfalls simply cannot be avoided. The final

---

* The views expressed here do not necessarily reflect those of the Urban Institute or UMTA.

From Thomas J. Higgins, "Implementation Revisited: The Case of Federal Demonstrations," *Journal of Policy Analysis and Management*, Vol. 4, pp. 436-440. Copyright © 1985 by the Association for Public Policy Analysis and Management. Reprinted by permission of John Wiley & Sons, Inc.

important step for implementation is to inform other localities about successful demonstrations, once good work and some luck bring success.

Road Tolls: The Bewitching of Analysts Some ideas can bewitch public policy analysts. Consider this scenario: A common local problem cries out for solution. The Congress asks a federal agency to help. Federal administrators then turn to a think tank. Analysts at the think tank propose a theoretically promising but little used solution—at least for a test. The agency agrees to fund demonstrations. The analysts seek out likely sites. At first, a few cities seem strongly interested, but prospects soon deteriorate. Newspapers scoff. Citizens rise up in protest. Decision-makers squirm. But the analysts only dig in. Especially if trained in implementation analysis, they go on trying to find elusive fixes. In short, they have been bewitched by trying to put across an idea whose time has not come. After much wasted effort, and no small embarrassment to all, no demonstration ever takes place. The analysts and federal program managers finally realize a second or third best solution would be more practical.

Such is the story of UMTA's late-1970s effort to promote tolls for major streets in or leading to cities. The goal was to cut traffic congestion and encourage mass transit and carpools. Tolls would be imposed at congested times and places, or on solo drivers or both. Tolls wouldn't be collected through booths. The plan was to use the same simple permits which had dramatically reduced congestion in Singapore.[3] For about three years, I and others at the Urban Institute in Washington, DC, helped UMTA try to get U.S. cities to plan and test such tolls.

Despite early interest in the concept, toll plans eventually were dashed in Berkeley, Madison, Honolulu, and Ann Arbor. Precisely what went wrong and why, and what unsuccessful compromises, federal protections, and communication nuances were tried along the way is related elsewhere.[4] The important point here is how thoroughly I and other policy analysts at the Urban Institute were "swept away" in a vain effort. Early on, I expressed my concerns that there was no lobby for efficiency,[5] but then quickly set out to give road tolls their best chances. Soon, I became a mix of issue advocate, fixer, and neurotic. As a student of implementation literature, I dutifully followed the standard advice:[6] nurture local constituencies and mesh with local priorities. I stayed on the scene, "in touch," trying harder where congestion was worst, where advocates were strongest, where mass transit had extra peak capacity, and where carpooling and vanpooling were feasible. In brief, I was bewitched into trying to fly the very contraption I had already claimed wouldn't take off.

Prices for Parking: Second Best Muddles Along With the road-tolling proposal in tatters, UMTA administrators and Urban Institute analysts met to consider repairs. What could be done to resuscitate the anticongestion demonstration? Implementation, or rather an attempt at it, was about to alter program policy.[7] A close substitute for road tolls is higher prices for parking, a near second best for efficiently reducing traffic.[8] Some cities control many downtown parking spaces and might discourage congestion by raising rates at public garages, at parking meters, or for new permits. Through-traffic escapes such efforts, and it can be substantial. Yet, cities are familiar with parking pricing, so no great leaps of faith are required to envision effective implementation.

With the analysts' blessing, UMTA decided to promote several experiments in the use of prices for parking. Now very concerned with local acceptance, Institute analysts soon realized that recreational communities might be good demonstration sites. Cramped coastal and mountain jurisdictions that suffered from outsider traffic ought to be willing to test parking prices for nonresident tourists. Although results might not apply to all urban areas, they would teach important practical lessons about administration, enforcement, costs, revenues, and political acceptance.

By late 1984, UMTA has funded four demonstrations with some success. However, the outcome at each site has depended on local variables hard to predict at the outset and continually subject to change. For example, in Madison, Wisconsin, a morning surcharge was put on some downtown parking lots. The city also provided park-and-ride lots around downtown and offered shuttle buses to and from the lots. However, surprisingly strong business resistance stopped the city from placing the surcharges that had been planned for most of its lots. The main reaction of commuters was to shift to private and public lots not subject to the surcharge, rather than to the shuttle bus.

In Santa Cruz, an equally unexpected but much more satisfactory result occurred. For summer weekends, the county set a daily charge for parking along three miles of coastal neighborhoods. Neighborhood residents got free annual permits for up to two vehicles. As intended, beach-goer parking fell by at least one-third and revenues from permits and citations rose to exceed operating costs. However, irate county residents not living in the zone resented being charged like tourists and almost killed the demonstration. Then, smart administrators solved the problem by offering nominally priced summer-long permits for frequent beach users. This measure eased the burden on county residents but maintained the daily price for most tourists. Fortunately, sharp administrators had been hired because the chairperson of the Board of Supervisors, spurred on by support from residents *in* the zone, strongly favored the program. Without the attentive eye of the board chairperson, all might have gone differently. With it, the program became effective, self-sustaining, and accepted.

In another California coastal community, Hermosa Beach, management weakness crippled the successful Santa Cruz model. At first, all seemed well. Then, newly elected council members objected on principle to federal money and federal ideas. Supporters backed off, and the project became neglected. Inexperienced, low-paid people, sometimes turning over twice per summer, "coordinated" the project from the Planning Department. They had little authority, no operational staff, and failed to cope with inevitable problems. Finally, the Council stepped in. Acting against advice from Institute analysts, they decided to give resident permits to anyone living in the city. The Supreme Court had found resident permit programs to be constitutional *only* for areas like the beach neighborhoods, which suffer from significant nonresident parking and traffic. Eventually, a lawsuit halted the entire program.

Early prospects in Eugene, Oregon, were good. Capable project managers were located in the right departments. A committee of residents, institutions, and businesses worked hard for months to arrive at an acceptable program. All participants agreed on a $15 per month permit for parking in certain neighborhoods, residents exempted, and congestion dropped. Nonetheless, a surprising turnabout may yet halt the young project. One affected group of commuter parkers marched on city hall in protest, contending that they were ignored in the planning, that parking prices are excessive, and that carpooling and transit could not suit their needs. Even an elaborate planning process can neglect an important affected party, to everyone's surprise.

Conclusions: Toward a Better Way

One obvious caution emerges from the UMTA experience—yes, indeed, it is hard to design federal programs for local implementation. Moreover, analysts should be particularly wary of innovations that do no more than promise efficiency, because such programs often have no local constituency. Even with local support, pitfalls are waiting. Local commitment may waver and ruin the idea with compromises, as in Madison. Unforeseeable opposition may threaten a successful start, as in Eugene. Weak management may sink even a proven concept, as in Hermosa Beach. However, some failures do not invalidate the concept of a demonstration program. The repeatedly rejected road tolls deserved an earlier grave, but not parking pricing. Good planning for implementation helps, as does capable technical assistance during local implementation. But, it is very difficult to make realistic "implementation estimates"[9] before trying an untried idea, and there are no guarantees.

Second, reformers had better choose analysts carefully, perhaps selecting different analysts for different jobs. Even analysts sensitive to implementation issues may well fail to recognize infeasibility when they stumble over it, and instead devote all their talents to prolonging the inevitable demise. The Urban Institute team recognized many problems early on, but was too slow to give up the battle to try out tolls. It seems implementation training in the hands of advocate analysts may lead to stubborn and prolonged attempts at creating constituencies, packaging information, and finding compromises all for naught.

Perhaps the main lesson, though, is to deploy analysts appropriately. Different perspectives are useful as an idea moves from theory, to program planning for implementation, to actual implementation, to final results and assessment. UMTA was right to seek out analysts knowledgeable about the economics and technical feasibility of road tolls before deciding on demonstrations. The fact that some of these analysts were also advocates was not in itself a problem. However, UMTA should have asked impartial implementation analysts to assess prospects of demonstration. Instead, as the analyst deemed most sensitive to implementation issues, I was assigned as an integral part of a team to make the demonstration happen. Only after tolls failed did UMTA get the best from me as an implementation analyst. Then, I could usefully suggest sites for the promotion of parking pricing, and could play the role of fixer with some prospects of success.

In the long view, successful implementation must go beyond viable demonstrations to win broad acceptance of new ideas. What ultimate effects will the parking demonstrations have? Will they lead to successful replications elsewhere? How should the agency disseminate demonstration results? So far, no other coastal or mountain communities even know about the successful program in Santa Cruz. If Eugene succeeds, few cities may find out. UMTA does commission reports, publish project briefs, and make presentations at conferences. But all this information reaches only transportation analysts, not program managers or decision-makers. UMTA should target results to local parking administrators and planners through their professional associations and trade magazines. If the federal government is to promote local innovation, it certainly ought to tout its successes. Such successes are hard-won indeed.

THOMAS J. HIGGINS is a private consultant based in Oakland, California.

NOTES 1. Pressman, Jeffrey L., and Wildavsky, Aaron, *Implementation, 2nd ed.* (Berkeley, CA: University of California Press, 1973).

2. *Ibid.*, p. 147.

3. Higgins, Thomas J., "Road Pricing, Should and Might It Happen?" *Transportation, 8* (1979): 99.

4. Higgins, Thomas J., "A Clash of Analysis and Politics: The Case of Road Pricing," *Policy Analysis, 6* (7) (Winter 1981): 71.

5. See Behn, Robert D., "Policy Analysis and Policy Politics," *Policy Analysis, 7* (2) (Spring 1981): 216.

6. See, for example, Sebatier, Paul, and Mazmahian, Daniel, "The Conditions of Effective Implementation: A Guide to Accomplishing Policy Objectives," *Policy Analysis, 5* (4) (Fall 1979): 496; and Meltsner, Arnold J., "Don't Slight Communication: Some Problems of Analytical Practice," *Policy Analysis, 5* (3) (Summer 1979): 367.

7. Pressman, *op. cit.*, p. 192.

8. Higgins, *Transportation, op. cit.*

9. Hargrove, Erwin, C., and Dean, Gillian, "Federal Authority and Grassroots Accountability: The Case of CETA," *Policy Analysis, 6* (2) (Spring 1980): 144.

5

Small Wins
Redefining the Scale of Social Problems

Karl E. Weick

ABSTRACT: The massive scale on which social problems are conceived precludes innovative action because bounded rationality is exceeded and dysfunctional levels of arousal are induced. Reformulation of social issues as mere problems allows for a strategy of small wins wherein a series of concrete, complete outcomes of moderate importance build a pattern that attracts allies and deters opponents. The strategy of small wins incorporates sound psychology and is sensitive to the pragmatics of policymaking.

There is widespread agreement that social science research has done relatively little to solve social problems (Berger, 1976; Cook, 1979; Kohn, 1976). Common to these assessments is the assumption that social science is best suited to generate solutions, when in fact it may be better equipped to address how problems get defined in the first place.

A shift of attention away from outcomes toward inputs is not trivial, because the content of appropriate solutions is often implied by the definition of what needs to be solved. To focus on the process of problem definition is to incorporate a more substantial portion of psychology, specifically, its understanding of processes of appraisal, social construction of reality, problem finding, and definition of the situation.

Whether social problems are perceived as phenomena that have a serious negative impact on sizable segments of society (Kohn, 1976, p. 94), as substantial discrepancies between widely shared social standards and actual conditions of life (Merton, 1971), or as assertions of grievances or claims with respect to alleged conditions (Spector & Kitsuse, 1977, p. 75), there is agreement that they are big problems. And that's the problem.

The massive scale on which social problems are conceived often precludes innovative action because the limits of bounded rationality are exceeded and arousal is raised to dysfunctionally high levels. People often define social problems in ways that overwhelm their ability to do anything about them.

To understand this phenomenon, consider the following descriptions of the problems of hunger, crime, heart disease, traffic congestion, and pollution.

To reduce domestic hunger we grow more food, which requires greater use of energy for farm equip-ment, fertilizers, and transportation, adding to the price of energy, which raises the cost of food, putting it out of the price range of the needy.

To solve the problem of soaring crime rates, cities expand the enforcement establishment, which draws funds away from other services such as schools, welfare, and job training, which leads to more poverty, addiction, prostitution, and more crime.

To ward off coronary heart disease, people who live in cities spend more time jogging and cycling, which exposes their lungs to more air pollution than normal, increasing the risk of coronary illness.

To ease traffic congestion, multilane highways are built, which draws people away from mass transit so that the new road soon becomes as overcrowded as the old road.

To reduce energy use and pollution, cities invest in mass transit, which raises municipal debt, leading to a reduction in frequency and quality of service and an increase in fares, which reduces ridership, which further raises the municipal debt (Sale, 1980).

When social problems are described this way, efforts to convey their gravity disable the very resources of thought and action necessary to change them. When the magnitude of problems is scaled upward in the interest of mobilizing action, the quality of thought and action declines, because processes such as frustration, arousal, and helplessness are activated.

Ironically, people often can't solve problems unless they think they aren't problems. If heightened arousal interferes with diagnosis and action, then attacking a less arousing "mere problem" should allow attention to be broader and action to be more complex. Responses that are more complex, more recently learned, and more responsive to more stimuli in changing situations usually have a better chance of producing a lasting change in dynamic problems.

To recast larger problems into smaller, less arousing problems, people can identify a series of controllable opportunities of modest size that produce visible results and that can be gathered into synoptic solutions. This strategy of small wins addresses social problems by working directly on their construction and indirectly on their resolution. Problems are constructed to stabilize arousal at moderate intensities where its contribution to performance of complex tasks is most beneficial.

From Karl E. Weick, "Small Wins: Redefining the Scale of Social Problems," *American Psychologist*, Vol. 39, pp. 40-49. Copyright © 1984 by the American Psychological Association. Reprinted by permission of the publisher and author.

Arousal and Social Problems

The following analysis of small wins assumes that arousal varies among people concerned with social problems, but tends to be relatively high, which affects the quality of performance directed at these problems. Arousal is treated as a generic concept under which is assembled a variety of findings that cohere because of their mutual relevance to the Yerkes-Dodson Law (Broadhurst, 1959). Although arousal mechanisms are neither simple nor unidimensional, they do seem to be localized in at least two physiological sites (reticular formation, limbic system), are visible under conditions of sensory deprivation, produce differences in the quality of learning and performance, and have observable physiological effects.

The specific effects of arousal on performance associated with the Yerkes-Dodson Law are that (a) there is an inverted-U relationship between arousal and the efficiency of performance with increasing levels of arousal, first improving and then impairing performance and (b) the optimal level of arousal for performance varies inversely with task difficulty. Even though these coarse propositions have been amended, tuned more finely, and differentiated, they remain basic principles in which an analysis of social problem solving can be anchored.

Key assertions for the present analysis culled from previous investigations of arousal and performance include the following:

1. Arousal coincides with variation in degrees of activation and varies along at least two dimensions, energy–sleep and tension–placidity (Eysenck, 1982; Thayer, 1978a, 1978b).

2. As arousal increases, attention to cues becomes more selective and this editing is especially detrimental to performance of difficult tasks (Easterbrook, 1959, although this generalization has received mixed support. See Baddeley, 1972; Pearson & Lane, 1983; Weltman, Smith, & Egstrom, 1971, for representative work).

3. At relatively high levels of arousal, coping responses become more primitive in at least three ways (Staw, Sandelands, & Dutton, 1981): (a) people who try to cope with problems often revert to more dominant, first learned actions; (b) patterns of responding that have been learned recently are the first

ones to disappear, which means that those responses that are most finely tuned to the current environment are the first ones to go; and (c) people treat novel stimuli as if they are more similar to older stimuli than in fact they are, so that clues indicating change are missed.

To invert this list, highly aroused people find it difficult to learn a novel response, to brainstorm, to concentrate, to resist old categories, to perform complex responses, to delegate, and to resist information that supports positions they have taken (Holsti, 1978).

When these findings are focused on problem solving, they suggest that to call a problem serious is to raise arousal, which is appropriate if people know what to do and have a well-developed response to deal with the problem. This is analogous to the situation of a simple task, the performance of which improves over a considerable range of activation because selective attention does not delete the few cues that are essential for performance. High arousal can improve performance if it occurs after a person has decided what to do and after she or he has overlearned how to do it.

To call a problem minor rather than serious is to lower arousal, which is also appropriate if people don't know what to do or are unable to do it. If we assume that most people overlook the fine-grain detail of problems, think only in terms of force as a response (Nettler, 1980), and overlook minor leverage points from which the problem might be attacked, then it is clear they have neither the diagnoses nor the responses to cope. This means that people need lower arousal to keep diagnostic interference at a minimum and to allow for the practice of relatively complex skills. To keep problem-related arousal at modest intensities, people need to work for small wins.

Sometimes problem solving suffers from too little arousal. When people think too much or feel too powerless, issues become depersonalized. This lowers arousal, leading to inactivity or apathetic performance. The prospect of a small win has an immediacy, tangibility, and controllability that could reverse these effects. Alinsky (1972, pp. 114–115) persuaded a demoralized neighborhood group to picket for reinstatement of Infant Medical Care, which he knew would be granted if they merely asked. Organizing for the protest, making the demand, and then receiving what they asked for energized people who had basically given up.

Examples of Small Wins

Small wins have been designed and implemented in a variety of settings. For example, the Pittsburgh Steelers in the National Football League have won 88 games and lost 27 under their coach Chuck Noll (as of February 4, 1980). Those statistics become more interesting if they are partitioned on the basis of

Tom Peters's (1977) original description of small wins was a crucial point of departure for this formulation. Subsequent discussions with Peters, as well as with Linda Pike, Richard Thaler, Joseph McGrath, Sharon McCarthy, David Anderson, Marianne LaFrance, and students and faculty of the Psychology Department at Rice University contributed to my understanding of this phenomenon and I am grateful to all of them for their help.

Requests for reprints should be sent to Karl E. Weick, Cornell University, Graduate School of Administration, Malott Hall, Ithaca, New York 14853.

whether the Steelers were playing against teams with winning records or teams with losing records ("Superbowls," 1980). Against opponents who won more than half of their games, the Steelers won 29 and lost 26, or slightly more than half of these games (53%). However, against opponents with winning percentages below .500, the Steelers' record was 59-1, meaning they won 98% of these games.

Thus a professional team renowned for its power got that way by consistently and frequently doing the easy stuff. The Steelers did not become great by winning the big one. Against tough opponents, they did no better than anyone else. These data suggest that winning teams distinguish themselves by more consistent behavior in games in which their skill advantage should make a difference, a condition that is part of the prototype for a small win. Thus, the best indication of good coaching may be the ability to induce consistent high performance against weak opponents rather than against strong opponents (Peters, 1977, p. 286).

The successful effort by the Task Force on Gay Liberation to change the way in which the Library of Congress classified books on the gay liberation movement is another example of a small win. Prior to 1972, books on this topic were assigned numbers reserved for books on abnormal sexual relations, sexual crimes, and sexual perversions (HQ 71-471). After 1972, the classifications were changed so that homosexuality was no longer a subcategory of abnormal relations, and all entries formerly described as "abnormal sex relations" were now described as varieties of sexual life (Spector & Kitsuse, 1977, pp. 13–14). Labels and technical classifications, the mundane work of catalogers, have become the turf on which claims are staked, wins are frequent, and seemingly small changes attract attention, recruit allies, and give opponents second thoughts.

The feminist campaign against sexism has been more successful with the smaller win of desexing English than with the larger win of desexing legislation (ERA). The success of attempts to make people more self-conscious about words implying sex bias is somewhat surprising, because it represents an imposition of taboos at a time when taboos in general are being removed. "For even as books, periodicals and dictionaries (not all, to be sure) are liberally opening their pages to obscenities and vulgarisms, they are unliberally leaning over backward to ostracize all usage deemed offensive to the sexes" (Steinmetz, 1982, p. 8). This hypocrisy notwithstanding, the reforms have been adopted with little objection, due in part to their size, specificity, visibility, and completeness. As one commentator on Steinmetz's essay put it, "winning equality in the language was necessary; and while the winning shouldn't be overestimated, it will work—the drops of water on the rock—to change

consciousness, and in time, unconsciousness" (Williams, 1982, p. 46).

When William Ruckelshaus became the first administrator of the U.S. Environmental Protection Agency in the early 1970s, he laid aside his mandate to clean up all aspects of the environment and went instead for a small win.

He discovered some obscure 80-year-old legislation that permitted him to go after some cities on water pollution. He took advantage of the legislation, effectively narrowing his practical agenda for the first year or two to "getting started on water pollution." On day one of the agency's formal existence, Ruckelshaus announced five major lawsuits against major American cities. The impact was electrifying. The homework had been meticulously done. Noticeable progress was made quickly. It formed the beachhead for a long series of successes and distinguished EPA from most of its sister agencies. (Peters, 1979, p. 5)

Ruckelshaus did not tackle everything nor did he even tackle the most visible source of pollution, which is air pollution. Ruckelshaus identified quick, opportunistic, tangible first steps only modestly related to a final outcome. The first steps were driven less by logical decision trees, grand strategy, or noble rhetoric than by action that could be built upon, action that signaled intent as well as competence.

Alcoholics Anonymous has been successful in helping alcoholics, partly because it does not insist that they become totally abstinent for the rest of their lives. Although this is the goal of the program, alcoholics are told to stay sober one day at a time, or one hour at a time if temptation is severe. The impossibility of lifetime abstinence is scaled down to the more workable task of not taking a drink for the next 24 hours, drastically reducing the size of a win necessary to maintain sobriety. Actually gaining that small win is then aided by several other small measures such as phone calls, one-hour meetings, slogans, pamphlets, and meditations, which themselves are easy to acquire and implement.

Several studies of micro-innovation are also compatible with the idea of small wins. For example, Hollander's (1965) closely documented microeconomic study of decreases in production costs of viscose rayon yarn manufacturing at five DuPont plants between 1929 and 1960 demonstrates that minor technical changes—rather than major changes—accounted for over two thirds of the reductions. A technical change is a change "in the technique of production of given commodities by specific plants, designed to reduce unit production costs" (p. 23). Major technical changes (e.g., introduction of compensation spinning) differ from minor changes (e.g., introduction of forklift trucks) in time, skill, effort, and expense required to produce them.

Analyses showed that the cost reductions were substantial (e.g., from 53.51 to 17.55 cents per pound of rayon from 1929 to 1951 at the Old Hickory plant). Technical changes, as opposed to changes in quality of pulp input, management practices, quality of labor, and plant size, accounted for approximately 75% of the reductions, and most of these technical changes were minor (specific percentage of reduction attributable to minor changes in the five plants was 83%, 80%, 79%, 100%, and 46%, the last being a new plant making a new product, tire cord yarn).

The minor technical changes were small improvement inventions, rather than major inventions, made by people familiar with current operations (p. 205). Experience with the process was crucial, since the very acts of production that created the problems in the first place were also the sources of the minor improvements that could solve the problem. People learned by doing.

Left for further research is the interesting possibility in this study that minor innovations were dependent on preceding major innovations. Ten to fifteen years after a major change, the number of minor changes that were improvements was close to zero (pp. 205–206). Small alterations in technique can improve productivity for some time after a major change, but these improvements may not go on indefinitely.

Implied in Hollander's analysis is the possibility that older plants can produce almost as efficiently as newly built plants if technical changes are identified and funds are invested in them. Thus, contemporary fascination with quality circles may be appropriate if it aids in identifying needed minor technical changes.

The point to be drawn from Hollander's analysis is summarized by Machlup (1962):

A technological invention is a big step forward in the useful arts. Small steps forward are not given this designation; they are just "minor improvements" in technology. But a succession of many minor improvements add up to a big advance in technology. It is natural that we hail the big, single step forward, while leaving the many small steps all but unnoticed. It is understandable, therefore, that we eulogize the great inventor, while overlooking the small improvers. Looking backward, however, it is by no means certain that the increase in productivity over a longer period of time is chiefly due to the great inventors and their inventions. It may well be true that the sum total of all minor improvements, each too small to be called an invention, has contributed to the increase in productivity more than the great inventions have. (p. 164)

Characteristics of Small Wins

A small win is a concrete, complete, implemented outcome of moderate importance. By itself, one small win may seem unimportant. A series of wins at small but significant tasks, however, reveals a pattern that may attract allies, deter opponents, and lower resistance to subsequent proposals. Small wins are controllable opportunities that produce visible results.

The size of wins can be arranged along a continuum from small to large. Lindblom's (1979) example of monetary control makes this point. Raising or lowering the discount rate is a smaller win than is the decision to use the discount rate as a method of monetary control. Both of those actions are smaller than introducing the Federal Reserve system, which is smaller than a change that eliminates the use of money entirely. Lindblom summarizes the example by drawing the generalization that a small change is either a change in a relatively unimportant variable (people tend to agree on what is an important change) or a relatively unimportant change in an important variable (Braybrooke & Lindblom, 1963, p. 64).

Small wins often originate as solutions that single out and define as problems those specific, limited conditions for which they can serve as the complete remedy. I emphasize the importance of *limits* for both the solution and the problem to distinguish the solutions of small wins from the larger, more open-ended solutions that define problems more diffusely (e.g., "burn the system down").

Once a small win has been accomplished, forces are set in motion that favor another small win. When a solution is put in place, the next solvable problem often becomes more visible. This occurs because new allies bring new solutions with them and old opponents change their habits. Additional resources also flow toward winners, which means that slightly larger wins can be attempted.

It is important to realize that the next solvable problem seldom coincides with the next "logical" step as judged by a detached observer. Small wins do not combine in a neat, linear, serial form, with each step being a demonstrable step closer to some predetermined goal. More common is the circumstance where small wins are scattered and cohere only in the sense that they move in the same general direction or all move away from some deplorable condition. Ideals, broad abstract ends, and lasting ambitions are less influential in defining a means–ends structure for a series of small wins than they are in articulating the specific trade-offs that occur when each win improves something at the expense of something else (Lindblom, 1979, p. 519).

A series of small wins can be gathered into a retrospective summary that imputes a consistent line of development, but this post hoc construction should not be mistaken for orderly implementation. Small wins have a fragmentary character driven by opportunism and dynamically changing situations. Small wins stir up settings, which means that each subsequent attempt at another win occurs in a different context. Careful plotting of a series of wins to achieve a major change is impossible because conditions do not remain constant. Much of the artfulness in working with small wins lies in identifying, gathering, and labeling several small changes that are present but unnoticed (e.g., the Aquarian conspiracy, megatrends, back to basics), changes that in actuality could be gathered under a variety of labels.

Small wins provide information that facilitates learning and adaptation. Small wins are like miniature experiments that test implicit theories about resistance and opportunity and uncover both resources and barriers that were invisible before the situation was stirred up. Attempts to induce self-consciousness about sex references in speech revealed that language was more susceptible to change than had been thought earlier (e.g., Basic English never took hold); that opponents to language change were more dispersed, more stuffy, and less formidable than anticipated; that sex-biased language was more pervasive and therefore a stronger leverage point than people realized; and that language reform could be incorporated into a wide variety of agendas (e.g., APA *Publication Manual* revision). Language experiments uncovered entrenched sexism that had been invisible and created a more differentiated picture of allies, opponents, bystanders, and issues.

A series of small wins is also more structurally sound than a large win because small wins are stable building blocks. This characteristic is implicit in Simon's (1962) analysis of nearly decomposable systems and is illustrated by a fable (Kuhn & Beam, 1982):

Your task is to count out a thousand sheets of paper, while you are subject to periodic interruptions. Each interruption causes you to lose track of the count and forces you to start over. If you count the thousand as a single sequence, then an interruption could cause you, at worst, to lose a count of as many as 999. If the sheets are put into stacks of 100, however, and each stack remains undisturbed by interruptions, then the worst possible count loss from interruption is 108. That number represents the recounting of the nine stacks of 100 each plus the 99 single sheets. Further, if sheets are first put into stacks of ten, which are then joined into stacks of 100, the worst possible loss from interruption would be 27. That number represents nine stacks of 100 plus nine stacks of ten plus nine single sheets. Not only is far less recounting time lost by putting the paper into "subsystems" of tens and hundreds, but the chances of completing the count are vastly higher. (pp. 249–250)

Small wins are like short stacks. They preserve gains, they cannot unravel, each one requires less coordination to execute, interruptions such as might occur when there is a change in political administration have limited effects, and subparts can be assembled into different configurations. To execute a large win such as ratification of the Equal Rights Amendment requires much greater coordination because interdependencies are more dense, timing is more crucial, and defections are a greater threat. If one crucial piece is missing, the attempted solution fails and has to be restarted.

Parts of Saul Alinsky's (1972) model for building community organization parallel the notion of small wins. Alinsky's three criteria for working goals are that the goals be highly specific, realizable, and immediate (Peabody, 1971, p. 525). If people work for something concrete, if people have an opportunity for visible success from which they draw confidence, and if people can translate their excitement and optimism into immediate action, then a small win is probable, as is their heightened interest in attempting a second win.

As an example of how these goals might be directed toward solving the problem of pollution, Alinsky suggests that people try to influence polluters by influencing the polluters' bankers. To do this, the normal time-consuming process of opening and closing a savings account is turned to advantage by having 1000 people enter the bank, each with $5, to open a savings account. Although this volume of business may paralyze the bank, it is not illegal and no bank is eager to be known as an institution that forcibly ejects depositors. Once the deposits have been made, the people come back a day later, close their accounts—again a time-consuming activity—and the process continues until this secondary target, being punished for someone else's sins, brings pressure to bear on the offender. Making mass changes in savings accounts is a specific, realizable, immediate, small, and controllable opportunity. It is just like defeating a second-rate team, changing the card catalog, finding a chairperson, suing five cities, staying sober for an hour, or introducing a forklift into a work procedure.

The Psychology of Small Wins

From a psychological perspective, small wins make good sense. This is evident if we review what is known about cognitive limitations, affective limitations, stress, and the enactment of environments.

Cognitive Limitations

Given the reality of bounded rationality (March, 1978; Perrow, 1981), small wins may be effective as much because they are "small" as because they are "wins." The growing documentation of ways in which people take cognitive shortcuts on larger problems (e.g., Kahneman, Slovic, & Tversky, 1982; Kiesler & Sproull, 1982; Miller & Cantor, 1982) suggests that smaller wins may suffer less distortion from these heuristics. People with limited rationality have sufficient variety to visualize, manage, and monitor the smaller amount of variety present in scaled-down problem environments. When people initiate small-scale projects there is less play between cause and effect; local regularities can be created, observed, and trusted; and feedback is immediate and can be used to revise theories. Events cohere and can be observed in their entirety when their scale is reduced.

An example of scaling down problems to more manageable size is an incident that occurred during the Apollo 13 mission when the astronauts staged what some regard as the first strike in space on December 27, 1973. Mission control had been sending more and more directions, corrections, and orders to the astronauts until finally Commander Gerald Carr said, "You have given us too much to do. We're not going to do a thing until you get your act in better order." He then shut off communications for 12 hours and the astronauts spent their day catching up and looking out the windows. They regained control over their circumstance. They did so partly by complicating themselves—an astronaut who both disobeys and obeys mission control is a more complicated individual than one who merely obeys, and partly by simplifying their system—they cut off one whole set of demands and reduced their problems simply to dealing with their own preferences. Their system became simpler because they had fewer demands to accommodate and simpler schedules to follow.

To gain some control over interdependent problems, people can disconnect the parts so they don't affect each other. Problems escalate only because they are tied together in a circular fashion and become vicious circles. A system with fewer interdependent events is a simpler system. It is easier to comprehend, easier to control, easier to improve.

Small wins disconnect incomprehensible systems such as the Library of Congress, a DuPont factory, EPA, or NASA. Once the system is disconnected, people then focus their attention on specific events that have been stripped out of their context, specific events such as the HQ portion of the Library classification system or a sequence of space experiments. What is common in instances such as these is that the "mere problem" that people finally end up with becomes manageable, understandable, and controllable by fallible individuals and stays that way until the larger system is reconnected. Arousal is reduced because control and predictability increase. The mere problem is also seen more clearly, which improves the chances that a small, specific solution that fits it will be invented. The resulting small win becomes a visible change in a highly inertial world. The change was made possible because the bounds of rationality were not exceeded. The change also becomes more visible to other people because its size is compatible with their own bounded rationality.

Affective Limitations

Repeatedly, psychologists have demonstrated that small changes are preferred to large changes. The small scale of small wins is important affectively as well as cognitively. Examples are plentiful.

Successive small requests are more likely to produce compliance (Freedman & Fraser, 1966). Changes

in level of aspiration are most satisfying when they occur in small increments. Positions advocated within the latitude of acceptance modify opinions more often than does advocacy that exceeds these limits. Orders within the zone of indifference are followed more quickly and reliably. The central measure of perception is the *just noticeable* difference. Theories are judged interesting when they disconfirm assumptions held with moderate intensity (Davis, 1971). People whose positions are close to one's own are the targets of intensive persuasion, while those whose positions are farther away are dismissed, isolated, or derogated. Social comparison is more stable the more similar the comparison other is. Small discrepancies from an adaptation level are experienced as more pleasurable than are larger discrepancies. Brief therapy is most successful when the client is persuaded to do just one thing differently that interdicts the pattern of attempted solutions up to that point. Extremely easy or extremely difficult goals are less compelling than are goals set closer to perceived capabilities. Learning tends to occur in small increments rather than in an all-or-none fashion (this generalization is highly sensitive to the size of the building blocks that are postulated in all-or-none positions such as stimulus sampling theory). Programmed learning works best when there is a gradual progression to complex repertoires and a gradual fading out of stimulus prompts for answers. Retention is better when people are in the same emotional state in which they learned the original material (Bower, Monteiro, & Gilligan, 1978). Numerous other examples could be given. The point is that incremental phenomena such as small wins have a basic compatibility with human preferences for learning, perception, and motivation.

Small wins are not only easier to comprehend but more pleasurable to experience. While no one would deny that winning big is a thrill, big wins can also be disorienting and can lead to unexpected negative consequences. The disruptiveness of big wins is evident in the high stress scores associated with positive changes in Life Events Scales (e.g., Dohrenwend, Krasnoff, Askenasy, & Dohrenwend, 1978). Big wins evoke big countermeasures and altered expectations, both of which make it more difficult to gain the next win (e.g., attention paid to Nobel prize winners often makes it impossible for them to do any further significant work).

Stress

Since arousal is a central construct in stress research, the soundness of small wins should be evident when stress formulations are examined. Recent work by McGrath (1976) and Kobasa (1979) reveals just such a fit. McGrath argued that there is a potential for stress when people perceive that demands exceed capabilities under conditions where it would be extremely costly to ignore the issue (p. 1352). The severity of perceived stress becomes stronger as uncertainty about the outcome increases. Uncertainty intensifies the closer the perceived demand is to the perceived ability. Large demand–capability discrepancies in either direction virtually assure successful or unsuccessful outcomes compared with situations of smaller discrepancy in which the outcome could go either way.

When people scale up the gravity of social problems, they raise at least the importance of the issue and the magnitude of the demand. The crucial question then becomes: What happens to the third variable of perceived capability to cope with demands?

Although numerous assumptions about perceived ability are possible, it would seem that the generic statement, "This problem affects you, and you can make a difference," reduces the perceived discrepancy between demands and abilities. If people respond to "you can make a difference" with the retort, "that's nonsense," then larger discrepancies will be created and stress will be minimal. If, however, people respond with a different reaction such as "that might just be true," then the demand–capability discrepancy is narrowed, which makes the outcome more uncertain and the stress more intense. As stress increases, the disruptive effects of arousal on problem solving increase. Just when people feel most encouraged to do something about a problem, they become least capable of translating that growing optimism into detailed diagnoses and complex responses. They become disabled by their own optimism, because it intensifies the perceived uncertainty of outcomes.

Once the gap between ability and demand begins to narrow, it becomes crucial that people see how their abilities can unequivocally *exceed* demands in order to remove some uncertainty. This assurance of success is precisely what people begin to feel when they define their situation as one of working for a small win. When a large problem is broken down into a series of small wins, three things happen. First, the importance of any single win is reduced in the sense that the costs of failure are small and the rewards of success considerable. Second, the size of the demand itself is reduced (e.g., all we need to do is get one city to discipline local polluters). And third, existing skills are perceived as sufficient to deal with the modest demands that will be confronted.

A small win reduces importance ("this is no big deal"), reduces demands ("that's all that needs to be done"), and raises perceived skill levels ("I can do at least that"). When reappraisals of problems take this form, arousal becomes less of a deterrent to solving them.

The potential attractiveness of a small win is that it operates simultaneously on importance, demands, and resources and defines situations away from

the "close calls" where higher uncertainty and higher stress reduce problem-solving performance. Small wins induce a degree of certainty that allows greater access to the very resources that can insure more positive outcomes.

Additional recent research on resistance to stress, especially Kobasa's work with hardiness (Kobasa, 1979, 1982; Kobasa, Maddi, & Kahn, 1982), suggests the psychological soundness of the strategy of small wins. While Kobasa has interpreted hardiness as a personality disposition, pursuit of a small wins strategy could induce more generally the perceptions associated with this disposition.

Hardiness is composed of commitment, control, and challenge. Commitment refers to involvement and a generalized sense of purpose that allows people to impose meaning on things, events, and persons. Control is the tendency to act and feel as if one can have a definite influence (not *the* influence) on situations through the exercise of imagination, knowledge, skill, and choice. People with a sense of control tend to experience events as natural outgrowths of their actions rather than as foreign, overwhelming events. Challenge is the belief that change is an incentive to grow rather than a threat to security. Thus, incongruent events are opportunities rather than disasters.

Deliberate cultivation of a strategy of small wins infuses situations with comprehensible and specific meaning (commitment), reinforces the perception that people can exert some influence over what happens to them (control), and produces changes of manageable size that serve as incentives to expand the repertory of skills (challenge). Continued pursuit of small wins could build increasing resistance to stress in people not originally predisposed toward hardiness.

Enactment of Environments

Small wins build order into unpredictable environments, which should reduce agitation and improve performance. Most "reality" surrounding social problems is disorganized, fragmented, piecemeal. When people confront situations that contain gaps and uncertainties, they first think their way across these gaps. Having tied the elements together cognitively, they then actually tie partial events together when they act toward them and impose contingencies. This sequence is similar to sequences associated with self-fulfilling prophecies (Snyder, Tanke, & Berscheid, 1977).

A crucial element in thoughtful action consists of "presumptions of logic" (Weick, 1979, p. 138) about situations that will be confronted. These presumptions draw people into situations in anticipation that the situations will make sense. This anticipation sets the stage for the second half of the process where, finding themselves in a presumably sensible situation, people take action. In doing so, they create patterns and consolidate scattered elements, both of which create the sensible situation that was anticipated.

This sequence of events is especially probable in the case of small wins. A small win is a bounded, comprehensible, plausible scenario that coheres sufficiently that people presume in advance that a forthcoming situation will be orderly. Having imposed the logic of small wins on a situation cognitively, the person then wades into the situation and acts with persistence, confidence, and forcefulness (Moscovici, 1980). Such decisive action is appropriate for an ostensibly orderly situation which, of course, has actually become more orderly precisely because forceful action consolidated it. Forceful action monopolizes the attention of other actors and becomes a causal variable in their construction of the situation. As a result, their actions become more interdependent and more orderly than they were before the intervention occurred.

Even though the actions associated with small wins are brief, specific, and localized, they can have a deterministic effect on many problem situations, because those situations are often even less coherent than the actions directed at them. The situations are loosely coupled, subject to multiple interpretations, and monitored regularly by only a handful of people. The confidence that flows from a pursuit of small wins frequently enacts environments in which the original problem becomes less severe and the next improvement more clear.

The Politics of Small Wins

Small wins can penetrate the main occupational hazard in Washington—information overload. The pace of work in Washington is fast, incessant, and unavoidable. The Obey Commission in 1977 found that in an average 11-hour day, a House member has only 11 minutes for discretionary reading (O'Donnell, 1981). That is where small wins have power. Small wins are compact, tangible, upbeat, noncontroversial, and relatively rare. They catch the attention of people with short time perspectives who have only 11 minutes to read.

Small wins also attract the attention of the opposition, though this is not inevitable. Opponents often assume that big effects require big causes, which means that they discount the importance of small wins. Opponents also often assume that attempted solutions cluster. Since small wins are dispersed, they are harder to find and attack than is one big win that is noticed by everyone who wants to win big somewhere else and who defines the world as a zero-sum game.

Because someone's small win is someone else's small loss, the stakes are reduced, which encourages the losers to bear their loss without disrupting the social system. A vague consensus is preserved by small wins because basic values are not challenged. People can accept a specific outcome even if they disagree on the values that drive it or the goals toward which it is instrumental.

The fact that small wins attract attention is not their only political virtue. In the world of policy, there are seldom clear decisions or clear problems (Weiss, 1980). Outcomes are built from bits and pieces of action, policy, and advice that are lying about. Since small wins are of a size that lets them supplement rather than dominate policy, they are more likely to be incorporated than are other more conspicuous solutions (McNaugher, 1980; Redman, 1973).

Despite their apparent political advantages, however, small wins may sound hopelessly naive, since they rely heavily on resources such as hope, faith, prophecies, presumptions, optimism, and positive reappraisals. Authors of many of the policy articles that have appeared in the *American Psychologist* have criticized psychologists for being naive and knowing relatively little about playing "hardball" with constituencies that have serious resources and know the game (e.g., Bazelon, 1982; Dörken, 1981; Hager, 1982; Sarason, 1978). Psychologists have responded by deprecating the game (e.g., March, 1979), making efforts to learn hardball (e.g., DeLeon et al., 1982), or by defining new games (e.g., Fishman & Neigher, 1982). The thrust of the present analysis, however, is that we need to be less apologetic for our apparent naivete than we have been.

First, being naive simply means that we reject received wisdom that something *is* a problem. Being naive means nothing more than that. We are always naive relative to some definition of the situation, and if we try to become less so, we may accept a definition that confines the definition of small wins to narrower issues than is necessary.

Second, being naive probably does have a grain of denial embedded in it. But denial can lower arousal to more optimal levels, so that more complex actions can be developed and more detailed analyses can be made.

Third, to be naive is to start with fewer preconceptions. Since it's usually true that believing is seeing, strong a priori beliefs narrow what is noticed (e.g., concern with sexism leads people to ignore threats that could annihilate both sexes). People with naive preconceptions will see a different set of features and are less likely to become fixated on specific features.

Fourth, naive beliefs favor optimism. Many of the central action mechanisms for small wins, such as self-fulfilling prophecies, affirmation, self-confirming faith that life is worth living (as first described by William James), the presumption of logic, trust, the belief in personal control, and positive self-statements, all gain their energy from the initial belief that people can make a difference. That belief is not naive when the world is tied together loosely. Firm actions couple events. And firm actions are more likely to occur when belief is strongly positive than when it is hesitant, doubtful, or cynical.

Optimism is also not naive if we can deny the relevance of hopelessness for the spirit of optimism. We justify what we do, not by belief in its efficacy but by an acceptance of its necessity. That is the basis on which Don Quixote survives.

Don Quixote embraces the foolishness of obligatory action. Justification for knight-errantry lies not in anticipation of effectiveness but in an enthusiasm for the pointless heroics of a good life. The celebration of life lies in the pleasures of pursuing the demands of duty. (March, 1975, p. 14)

One can argue that it is our duty as psychologists to be optimistic. To view optimism as a duty rather than as something tied to unsteady expectations of success is to position oneself in a sufficient variety of places with sufficient confidence that events may be set in motion that provide substance for that hope. Small wins may amount to little, but they are after all wins, and wins encourage us to put the most favorable construction on actions and events.

Naivete can be a problem when optimistic expectations are disconfirmed (small flops), for although it increases the likelihood that good things will happen, it does not guarantee they will. Disconfirmation often leads people to abandon their expectations and adopt skepticism and inaction as inoculation against future setbacks. The important tactic for dealing with the flops implicit in trying for small wins is to localize the disconfirmation of expectations. Cognitive theories of depression (e.g., Beck et al., 1979) suggest that people often generalize disconfirmed expectations far beyond the incident in which they originated. The faith that makes life worth living can suffer setbacks, but these setbacks are specific and, in the case of small flops, limited. Highly aroused people who have flopped attempting a large win can't see those specifics, so they abandon all faith and all possible scenarios for how life might unfold. That is the generalizing that needs to be contained and often is contained by trying for smaller wins, with smaller stakes.

Conclusion

The preceding analysis leaves several questions unanswered. For example, is the concept of arousal really necessary to understand why attempts to cope with large problems are self-defeating? Cognitive explanations (e.g., "I simply can't cure cancer so I'll work to make terminally ill patients more comfortable") may make it unnecessary to resort to motivational explanations. I favor motivational explanations under the assumption that social problems are emotional issues argued under emotionally charged conditions.

What is the natural distribution of arousal around social problems? The preceding analyses assume that most people feel intensely about social problems most of the time, or at least at those crucial times when they try to diagnose what is wrong and rehearse what to do about it. That assumption is a simplification, because it is clear that participation is uneven, unpredictable, and easily distracted (Weiner, 1976). Furthermore, interest in a given issue soon diminishes and bored people wander off to other problems (Koestler, 1970). Nevertheless, there are problem elites, opinion leaders, and hubs in networks. These people are central because they feel strongly about issues. Those strong feelings can affect their thought and action directly, and others who model this thought and action indirectly.

What role do individual differences in arousability or sensation seeking (Zuckerman, 1979) play in strategies to cope with social problems? Implicit in the preceding argument is a rule of thumb: If you can tolerate high levels of arousal, go for big wins; if you can't, go for small wins.

Questions such as this notwithstanding, it seems useful to consider the possibility that social problems seldom get solved, because people define these problems in ways that overwhelm their ability to do anything about them. Changing the scale of a problem can change the quality of resources that are directed at it. Calling a situation a mere problem that necessitates a small win moderates arousal, improves diagnosis, preserves gains, and encourages innovation. Calling a situation a serious problem that necessitates a larger win may be when the problem starts.

REFERENCES

Alinsky, S. D. (1972). *Rules for radicals.* New York: Vintage.
Baddeley, A. D. (1972). Selective attention and performance in dangerous environments. *British Journal of Psychology, 63,* 537–546.
Bazelon, D. L. (1982). Veils, values, and social responsibility. *American Psychologist, 37,* 115–121.
Beck, A. T., Rush, A. J., Shaw, B. F., & Emery, G. (1979). *Cognitive theory of depression.* New York: Guilford.
Berger, B. M. (1976). Comments on Mel Kohn's paper. *Social Problems, 24,* 115–120.
Bower, G. H., Monteiro, K. P., & Gilligan, S. G. (1978). Emotional mood as a context for learning and recall. *Journal of Verbal Learning and Verbal Behavior, 17,* 573–585.
Braybrooke, D., & Lindblom, C. E. (1963). *A strategy of decision.* Glencoe, IL: Free Press.
Broadhurst, P. L. (1959). The interaction of task difficulty and motivation: The Yerkes-Dodson Law revived. *Acta Psychologica, 16,* 321–338.
Cook, S. W. (1979). Social science and school desegregation: Did we mislead the Supreme Court? *Personality and Social Psychology Bulletin, 5,* 420–437.
Davis, M. S. (1971). That's interesting: Towards a phenomenology of sociology and a sociology of phenomenology. *Philosophy of Social Science, 1,* 309–344.
DeLeon, P. H., O'Keefe, A. M., VandenBos, G. R., & Kraut, A. G. (1982). How to influence public policy: A blueprint for activism. *American Psychologist, 37,* 476–485.

Dohrenwend, B. S., Krasnoff, L., Askenasy, A. R., & Dohrenwend, B. P. (1978). Exemplification of a method for scaling life events: The PERI life events scale. *Journal of Health and Social Behavior, 19,* 205–229.

Dörken, H. (1981). Coming of age legislatively: In 21 steps. *American Psychologist, 36,* 165–173.

Easterbrook, J. A. (1959). The effect of emotion on cue utilization and the organization of behavior. *Psychological Review, 66,* 183–201.

Eysenck, M. W. (1982). *Attention and arousal: Cognition and performance.* New York: Springer.

Fishman, D. B., & Neigher, W. (1982). American psychology in the eighties: Who will buy? *American Psychologist, 37,* 533–546.

Freedman, J. L., & Fraser, S. C. (1966). Compliance without pressure: The foot-in-the-door technique. *Journal of Personality and Social Psychology, 4,* 195–202.

Hager, M. G. (1982). The myth of objectivity. *American Psychologist, 37,* 576–579.

Hollander, S. (1965). *The sources of increased efficiency: A study of DuPont rayon plants.* Cambridge, MA: MIT Press.

Holsti, O. R. (1978). Limitations of cognitive abilities in the face of crisis. In C. F. Smart & W. T. Stanbury (Eds.), *Studies on crisis management* (pp. 35–55). Toronto: Butterworth.

Kahneman, D., Slovic, P., & Tversky, A. (Eds.). (1982). *Judgement under uncertainty: Heuristics and biases.* Cambridge, England: Cambridge University Press.

Kiesler, S., & Sproull, L. (1982). Managerial response to changing environments: Perspectives on problem sensing from social cognition. *Administrative Science Quarterly, 27,* 548–570.

Kobasa, S. C. (1979). Stressful life events, personality, and health: An inquiry into hardiness. *Journal of Personality and Social Psychology, 37,* 1–11.

Kobasa, S. C. (1982). Commitment and coping in stress resistance among lawyers. *Journal of Personality and Social Psychology, 42,* 707–717.

Kobasa, S. C., Maddi, S. R., & Kahn, S. (1982). Hardiness and health: A prospective study. *Journal of Personality and Social Psychology, 42,* 168–177.

Koestler, A. (1970). Literature and the law of diminishing returns. *Encounter, 34,* 39–45.

Kohn, M. L. (1976). Looking back—A 25-year review and appraisal of social problems research. *Social Problems, 24,* 94–112.

Kuhn, A., & Beam, R. D. (1982). *The logic of organizations.* San Francisco: Jossey-Bass.

Lindblom, C. E. (1979). Still muddling, not yet through. *Public Administration Review, 39,* 517–526.

Machlup, F. (1962). *The production and distribution of knowledge in the United States.* Princeton, NJ: Princeton University Press.

March, J. G. (1975). Education and the pursuit of optimism. *Texas Tech Journal of Education, 2,* 5–17.

March, J. G. (1978). Bounded rationality, ambiguity, and the engineering of choice. *The Bell Journal of Economics, 9,* 587–608.

March, J. G. (1979). Science, politics, and Mrs. Gruenberg. In *The National Research Council in 1979* (pp. 27–36). Washington, DC: National Academy of Sciences.

McGrath, J. E. (1976). Stress and behavior in organizations. In M. D. Dunnette (Ed.), *Handbook of industrial and organizational psychology* (pp. 1351–1395). Chicago: Rand McNally.

McNaugher, T. L. (1980). Marksmanship, McNamara, and the M16 rifle: Innovation in military organizations. *Public Policy, 28,* 1–37.

Merton, R. K. (1971). Epilogue: Social problems and sociological theory. In R. Merton & R. Nisbet (Eds.), *Contemporary social problems* (pp. 793–846). New York: Harcourt Brace Jovanovich.

Miller, G. A., & Cantor, N. (1982). Book review of Nisbett and Ross, "Human Inference." *Social Cognition, 1,* 83–93.

Moscovici, S. (1980). Toward a theory of conversion behavior. In L. Berkowitz (Ed.), *Advances in experimental social psychology* (Vol. 13, pp. 209–239). New York: Academic Press.

Nettler, G. (1980). Notes on society; sociologist as advocate. *Canadian Journal of Sociology, 5,* 31–53.

O'Donnell, T. J. (1981). Controlling legislative time. In J. Cooper & G. C. Mackenzie (Eds.), *The house at work* (pp. 127–150). Austin: University of Texas Press.

Peabody, G. L. (1971). Power, Alinsky, and other thoughts. In H. A. Hornstein, B. B. Bunker, W. W. Burke, M. Gindes, & R. J. Lewicki (Eds.), *Social intervention: A behavioral science approach* (pp. 521–532). New York: Free Press.

Pearson, D. A., & Lane, D. M. (1983). *The effect of arousal on attention.* Unpublished manuscript, Rice University.

Perrow, C. (1981). Disintegrating social sciences. *New York University Educational Quarterly, 12,* 2–9.

Peters, T. J. (1977). *Patterns of winning and losing: Effects on approach and avoidance by friends and enemies.* Unpublished doctoral dissertation, Stanford University.

Peters, T. J. (1979). *Designing and executing "real" tasks.* Unpublished manuscript, Stanford University.

Redman, E. (1973). *The dance of legislation.* New York: Simon & Schuster.

Sale, K. (1980). *Human scale.* New York: Putnam.

Sarason, S. B. (1978). The nature of problem solving in social action. *American Psychologist, 33,* 370–380.

Simon, H. A. (1962). The architecture of complexity. *Proceedings of the American Philosophical Society, 106,* 467–482.

Snyder, M., Tanke, E. D., & Berscheid, E. (1977). Social perception and interpersonal behavior: On the self-fulfilling nature of social stereotypes. *Journal of Personality and Social Psychology, 35,* 656–666.

Spector, M., & Kitsuse, J. I. (1977). *Constructing social problems.* Menlo Park, CA: Cummings.

Staw, B. M., Sandelands, L. E., & Dutton, J. E. (1981). Threat-rigidity effects in organizational behavior: A multi-level analysis. *Administrative Science Quarterly, 26,* 501–524.

Steinmetz, S. (1982, August 1). The desexing of English. *The New York Times Magazine,* pp. 6, 8.

Superbowls super coach. (1980, February 4). *Time Magazine,* p. 58.

Thayer, R. E. (1978a). Factor analytic and reliability studies on the activation–deactivation adjective check list. *Psychological Reports, 42,* 747–756.

Thayer, R. E. (1978b). Toward a psychological theory of multidimensional activation (arousal). *Motivation and Emotion, 2,* 1–34.

Weick, K. W. (1979). *The social psychology of organizing* (2nd ed.). Reading, MA: Addison-Wesley.

Weiner, S. S. (1976). Participation, deadlines, and choice. In J. G. March & J. P. Olsen (Eds.), *Ambiguity and choice in organizations* (pp. 225–250). Bergen, Norway: Universitetsforlaget.

Weiss, C. H. (1980). Knowledge creep and decision accretion. *Knowledge: Creation, Diffusion, Utilization, 1,* 381–404.

Weltman, G., Smith, J. E., & Egstrom, G. H. (1971). Perceptual narrowing during simulated pressure-chamber exposure. *Human Factors, 13,* 99–107.

Williams, C. T. (1982, September 5). Letter to the editor about "Desexing the English language." *The New York Times Magazine,* p. 46.

Zuckerman, M. (1979). *Sensation seeking: Beyond the optimal level of arousal.* Hillsdale, NJ: Erlbaum.

6

Agenda-Setting
A Review Essay

Paul J. Quirk

The question of how policy proposals are initiated and obtain a place on the governmental agenda has long been a neglected item, so to speak, on the agenda for political research. E. E. Schattschneider stressed the significance of the agenda in his classic 1960 book, *The Semi-Sovereign People*, putting forth the bold proposition that "the definition of the alternatives is the supreme instrument of power." Discounted in some degree for the rhetorical flourish, his claim gained general assent among political scientists, for whom it became a familiar nostrum. Until recently, nevertheless, few political scientists had tried to improve our understanding of the agenda or its role in policymaking by conducting empirical research.

In the books under review, two distinguished students of American politics turn their attention to the agenda. Polsby's study (begun in 1969 but set aside for more than a decade) is based on a series of eight brief case studies of policy development in the federal government. Ranging from the immediate post-World War II era to the mid-1960s, the cases were selected to represent "political innovations"—defined by Polsby as governmental actions that meet the three criteria of "large scale and visibility, break with preceding habit, and lasting consequences." The cases chosen include three such innovations in postwar science policy, namely, civilian control of atomic energy, the National Science Foundation, and the Nuclear Test Ban Treaty; two in foreign policy, the Truman Doctrine (specifically aid to Greece and Turkey) and the Peace Corps; and three in domestic policy, the Council of Economic Advisers, Medicare, and local participation in Community Action Programs.

Polsby wrote each of the case studies from narratives originally drafted by research assistants, who worked exclusively from secondary sources. He is interested partly in testing the common belief that policy initiation in American politics is mostly a function of the presidency. But more generally, he aims in each case to treat several "descriptive dimensions" of policy initiation: the length of time between proposal and enactment; the relative roles of specialists and generalists in shaping alternatives; the degree of elite consensus about the need for action; the degree of reliance on systematic research in formulating policy; and the temporal separation or fusion of the processes of invention and search.

Polsby is not altogether direct and consistent in saying whether the study is about innovation, meaning the whole process of adopt-

From Paul J. Quirk, "Public Policy," *Journal of Policy Analysis and Management*, Vol. 5, pp. 607-613. Copyright © 1986 by the Association for Public Policy Analysis and Management. Reprinted by permission of John Wiley & Sons, Inc.

ing policies that are in some way especially novel, or rather initiation, meaning the act of proposing or providing early impetus behind any policy change, novel or not. As I have mentioned, the cases selected for analysis are intended to qualify as innovations. But the questions about the cases have to do—for the most part, although not exclusively—with how problems are first identified and proposals to deal with them are devised. The resulting ambiguity is not resolved by the book's title, which mentions both innovation and initiation, or by Polsby's announcement in an uncharacteristically opaque passage that he uses the two terms "more or less interchangeably." In view of the research questions actually posed, the book should be read primarily as a study of policy initiation, that is, agenda setting—based on a sample of important policies. The innovative character of the cases does not figure prominently in the analysis.

In both obtaining and presenting information, the study is a model of economy. Besides being derived from secondary sources, the case studies are quite brief, presented two and three to a chapter. Yet they provide intelligible narrative accounts of the several policy changes while reciting the evidence needed for a substantial and often ingenious comparative discussion at the end of the book.

The analytic findings, barely hinted at before the concluding chapter, may be disappointing to some in that they do not suggest a great deal of structure or regularity in the initiation process. They are useful nevertheless. "Subject matter alone," Polsby observes, referring to the division of the cases into science policy, foreign policy, and domestic policy, "does not conclusively determine the process by which policy is initiated." Citing the two foreign policy cases as illustration, he notes that the Truman Doctrine was "the product of the activity of a governmental elite," whereas the Peace Corps emerged "almost by accident, bubbling up from a number of sources."

Instead of substantive categories, Polsby proposes that some of the variation across the cases can be accounted for by distinguishing between two types of innovation. In "acute" innovation—exemplified by civilian control of atomic energy, Community Action Programs, and the Truman Doctrine—"the lapse of time between the first surfacing of an idea within the subculture of decision makers and its enactment is short." The cases in this category also resembled each other in that they exhibited improvised solutions, a unified process of invention and search, and low levels of partisan conflict. In contrast, "incubated" innovation—found in the cases of Medicare, the Peace Corps, and the Council of Economic Advisers—"takes place slowly, frequently over many years." In these cases proposals were based on elaborate research; they were invented well before the system began actively searching for solutions; and partisan and ideological conflict was considerable.

The distinction between acute and incubated innovation is persuasive. But, as Polsby himself emphasizes, it leaves a large amount of variation unexplained. Two of the eight cases, the nuclear test ban treaty and the National Science Foundation, fall in neither category, and three of the seven descriptive dimensions—specialization, subculture agreement, and public salience—have no strong associations with the typology. As he remarks, the limitations of the typology "should occasion no surprise, except to those who believe the world is a very simple place." The variety of patterns also belies the notion of presidential dominance of policy initiation. Indeed, Polsby argues, much of the capacity for policy change in our political system results from the presence of a variety of actors—presidents certainly, but also senators, bureaucrats, and interest group leaders—who have reasons to initiate policy change on a routine basis.

The product of a much more ambitious project—with a massive data-gathering effort, and a novel, carefully constructed theoretical argument—Kingdon's study is one of the most innovative and intellectually challenging works on American politics in recent years. The purpose of Kingdon's investigation is to find out something about two processes that occur prior to actual decisionmaking and which, he points out, previous research has largely overlooked: "We seek to understand why some subjects become prominent on the policy agenda and others do not, and why some alternatives for choice are seriously considered while others are neglected."

To help answer these questions Kingdon developed two complementary sets of data. The one principally relied on is a series of nearly 250 interviews that Kingdon conducted personally, in four annual waves from 1976 to 1979, with participants in policymaking in two areas of federal activity, health and transportation. The respondents included officials in the White House and other agencies of the executive branch; congressional staff; interest group representatives; and miscellaneous others such as journalists, consultants, and academics. The main questions put to them were simple: "What major problems are you and others in the health (transportation) area most concerned with these days? Why? What proposals are on the front burner? Why?" In addition, Kingdon and some research assistants developed a set of 23 case studies, representing instances of "policy initiation and noninitiation" over three decades in the same two policy areas. Altogether it is a rich body of data, and Kingdon puts it to good use.

The first part of the analysis aims to sort out the relative roles in setting the agenda of a number of presumptive sources of influence, from presidents to bureaucrats, and policy experts to public opinion. Kingdon finds that no single actor, category of participant, or other source of influence dominates the agenda; and none is consistently ahead of the others in giving attention to new subjects. The most important category of actors consists of elected officials—among whom the President is clearly, but not overwhelmingly, preeminent. In explaining why a subject was receiving attention, few of the respondents attributed it to the actions or preferences of civil servants.

Kingdon argues that although the "hidden cluster" of lower-level participants, such as civil servants and policy analysts, have slight influence in determining what problems are on the agenda, they have much greater influence in shaping the alternatives. It would be surprising, however, if civil servants and policy analysts had any more discretion over the value-laden, politically significant choices in the design of proposals than they have in the selection of problems. They may appear more prominent in policy design merely because that phase involves a larger number of subordinate decisions.

The major contribution of Kingdon's book, however, is in the second part of the analysis, where he treats agenda-setting processes and develops a version of Cohen, March, and Olsen's so-called "garbage-can model" of organizational choice. Others have noticed the possible pertinence of this model, originally designed to describe "organized anarchies" such as universities, to public policymaking. Kingdon's achievement is to perform the task—thoroughly, systematically, and insightfully—of working out the application. As modified by Kingdon for the political context, the garbage-can model views the policy agenda as being formed by the coming together of three "process streams"—concerned respectively with problems, policies, and politics. Its central idea, in contrast with more structured, conventional views of decisonmaking, is that the three streams are largely independent: Each follows its own course and responds to its own set of influences.

In the first stream, problems "come to occupy the attention of people in and around government." This happens partly through their monitoring of systematic indicators—highway deaths, consumer prices, and the like—but also, in a less orderly or predictable way, because of "focusing events" like crises or disasters or through "a powerful symbol that catches on." About half of the respondents prominently mentioned some kind of systematic indicator and one third cited a crucial event. Kingdon points out a number of subtleties of this process, observing, for example, that a focusing event will have a powerful effect mainly when it reinforces a preexisting perception of a problem.

The second stream consists of "the formation and refining of policy proposals." In this process, the domain mostly of experts working in loosely organized policy communities, ideas are invented, laboriously researched, and endlessly amended. They may be put forth repeatedly during a long "softening up" period before they are ever taken seriously. Most of the ideas die out. The ones that succeed are those that meet demanding criteria for survival. Kingdon argues that some of the criteria—such as equity, efficiency, and technical feasibility—are defined and enforced by the policy community itself. Finally there is a political stream, "composed of such things as public mood, pressure group campaigns, election results, partisan or ideological distributions in Congress, and changes of administration"—all of which, for well known reasons, exert large effects on the agenda.

Policy change can occur, then, when the process streams happen to converge so as to create what Kingdon calls a "policy window," a brief period in which circumstances are propitious for action on a given proposal. To put a subject on the agenda for immediate decision, developments two or more of the streams must fit together: "An alternative floating in the policy stream, for instance, becomes coupled either to a prominent problem or to events in the political stream in order to be considered seriously in a context broader than the community of specialists." The key requirement for a successful policy entrepreneur, accordingly, is persistence and skill in finding these couplings. Kingdon does not exaggerate the calculation this involves: "You keep your gun loaded and you look for opportunities to come along," explained a respondent. *"Have idea, will shoot."*

Taken literally, the garbage-can model (in either Kingdon's or the original version) is hyperbolic. The frequent convergence of the three process streams is more than merely accidental. As a more straightforward, perhaps stodgier analysis would have it, the streams are linked in manifold ways: Political trends largely determine which problems are regarded as serious, and that largely determines which proposals get developed. Policy alternatives do not really float about seeking problems without first having been put forth as solutions to other problems. Even so, the essential insight of the garbage-can model—the often marked looseness and variability of these linkages—is both valid and important. A key task for future work on policy formation, therefore, is to clarify the relations among problem recognition, alternative design, and political change. How and how far do changes in public mood and party power govern the attention given to problems? How much support and momentum develops behind proposals, independent of the problems they are created to solve? Because such questions will not be easily answered, Kingdon's book should be discussed for years to come.

Considered together, the studies by Polsby and Kingdon bear in unexpected ways on some basic issues of political analysis. Ironically, they end up casting doubt on what is in one sense the central premise of both studies—namely, that the setting of the agenda is a behaviorally distinct and enduringly consequential phase of the policy process. The assumption, in other words, is that the agenda is shaped by influences that differ at least in their weights from those that shape final decisions—and that it then constrains those decisions. These two stipulations are what makes the agenda both a subject requiring separate investigation and one that is worthy of it.

On the evidence of these two books, however, neither stipulation is clearly correct. The agenda is not evidentally behaviorally distinct. Rather, the selection criteria and tests of support that determine which proposals get on the agenda seem to be similar (except for being applied earlier with lower threshholds) to those that determine which proposals on the agenda get adopted. Kingdon's measures of the influence of various participants on the agenda, for example, would be entirely plausible as measures of their influence on actual decisions. It seems that proposals get on the agenda above all because they appear with some modest level of probability to have the necessary attributes for adoption. To put this point a different way, instead of the agenda constraining decisions, expectations about decisions define the agenda.

Nor does the agenda as it stands at any given moment exert an enduring, independent influence over decisions. If the balance of political forces changes (and sometimes even if it doesn't), so will the agenda. Proposals are subject to radical revision throughout the process of decision. "An administration proposes a bill," Kingdon remarks, "then is unable to control subsequent happenings and predict the result." The proposed Council of Economic Advisers, observes Polsby, "changed over the years from a control instrument of the corporate state via comprehensive interest-group representation to a statistical service bureau, and then to a central agency of presidential fiscal planning." The effect of these books should not be, of course, to throw cold water on the whole subject of the agenda. Rather, they should help establish a more seamless conception of the policy process—one in which distinct phases are replaced by a continuous progression of issues and proposals, under relatively constant criteria of selection, from obscurity to adoption.

Neither Polsby nor Kingdon discusses the implications of his work for economic theories of public choice. But the entire conception of the agenda and policymaking that emerges in both books, supported by a variety of empirical evidence, contradicts basic assumptions of efforts to apply public choice theory to the policy process. Public-choice theorists take for granted that there is at all times a large set of potential policy changes that, if put up for votes in Congress, would be adopted—a reflection of the numerous possible ways to assemble majorities. The actual outcomes are therefore almost entirely a function of which proposals happen to be voted on, and in what order. Recently, in a conclusion highly unflattering to democratic processes, both the content and the observed stability of public policy have been ascribed merely to institutions, such as congressional committees, that are said to dictate outcomes by controlling the agenda.

These notions, however, have little or no resemblance to what Polsby describes in his cases or what Kingdon's respondents are concerned with. Opportunities for substantial policy change with readily available majority support are not superabundant. To policy entrepreneurs' constant regret, such opportunities are quite scarce. The adoption of a new policy does not usually represent merely a new way of assembling a majority. It generally reflects an observable change in the demands that prevailing values, problems facing the public, and the distribution of political resources make effective. And no actor or institutional unit has reliable control of the agenda. The agenda is shaped by a pluralistic process responsive to the same complex set of forces as actual decisions.

The erroneous suppositions result, I would argue, from the use of an analytic model—decisionmaking under majority rule—that although superficially appropriate is nevertheless deeply flawed as a representation of the dynamics of policy formation. The majority-

rule model ignores very evident aspects of the behavior of participants in the policy process. First, individual politicians not only
respond to the numbers of supporters and opponents of a given
policy change (and to their other political resources), as the majority-rule model holds; they take into account the views of losers
as well as winners and weight preferences by their intensity. This
amounts to an implicit and highly imperfect system of "utilitarian" voting—that is, one using cardinal measures of preference
and, thus, not subject to the indeterminacy of majority rule. Second, there is a bias against action and in favor of the status quo,
partly because a group's resistance to a threatened loss tends to be
more intense than its pursuit of an equivalent prospective gain.
This bias, which is notorious, rules out the kind of serial redistribution in all directions implicit in the public-choice notion of cycli-
cal majorities. And third, the selection of proposals for consideration is not random or arbitrary with respect to welfare. Presented
a choice among feasible proposals, politicians in positions of leadership prefer to act on those whose potential support exceeds what
is necessary for passage by the largest margin.

Democratic processes thus emerge in a more favorable light:
governmental agendas and public policy are shaped far more by
values and preferences, and far less by accident and manipulation,
than the majority-rule model would suggest.

*PAUL J. QUIRK is Assistant Professor of Political Science at the
University of Pennsylvania.*

7

The Theory and Practice of
Participatory Action Research

Muhammad Anisur Rahman

Consciousness of the Oppressed

Q. Do you know who is Lakshmi and who is Swaraswati?
Adivasi. Yes.
Q. Who is Lakshmi?
Adivasi. Rice, clothes, hut.
Q. And Swaraswati?
Adivasi. Sawkar's knowledge.
Q. If you could have only one of them, what is your preference?
Adivasi. Swaraswati.
Q. Why?
Adivasi. If everyone has knowledge, then no one can cheat others. Then only
we can have true equality.

(A dialogue with a tribal (Adivasi) poor peasant in Junglepatti, Thane district,
Maharastra, India. 'Lakshmi' and 'Swaraswati' are the Hindu goddesses of
prosperity and knowledge respectively. 'Sawkar' is the money-lending
landlord/trader/rich farmer.)

I. INTRODUCTION

The tradition of intellectuals stimulating and assisting popular
struggles is an age-old one. This tradition seems to be gaining some
momentum in recent times, and developing links not only within but
also across national boundaries. Two major factors may be
contributing to this: (1) convergence of national systems into elite
domination over the masses, of both 'right' and 'left' varieties,
which is generating its own counter-consciousness; and (2)
increasing facilities for communicating between the resulting
counter-culture.

This counter-culture has taken on a wide variety of characters,
with some carrying a conscious-research (knowledge-generation)
interest. The latter variety has sometimes been referred to as 'action
research', sometimes as 'participatory research'. The terminology
has not yet converged.

From Muhammad Anisur Rahman, "The Theory and Practice of Participatory Action Research,"
Orlando Fals Borda, ed., *The Challenge of Social Change,* pp. 108-132. Copyright © 1983 by the
International Labour Organisation, Geneva. Reprinted by permisssion.

Orlando Fals Borda favours the term 'participatory action research' — henceforth abbreviated to PAR — and I feel that this is a useful term because it emphasizes the point that we are talking about action research that is participatory and participatory research that unites with action (for transforming reality).

It cannot be claimed that PAR has as yet a convergent theoretical position. But certain concerns are being increasingly shared in common, ideological positions are being taken (not necessarily in writing) that are broadly similar, and methodological similarities in action are being observed. From this an ideological position may be inferred, and theoretical questions can be raised and discussed, all in a tentative way, as a contribution to the progressive articulation of the standpoint of PAR. This chapter is a modest attempt in this direction.

There is no space to do justice to the vast practice of PAR in this short chapter, and I have a language barrier myself in undertaking such a job. In observing some highlights from this practice, I have confined myself to a few initiatives which are:

(a) relatively recent, as these directly challenge us as contemporary intellectuals to respond;
(b) relatively well documented; and
(c) those of whose ideological concerns I have a better sense than others, through a combination of reading and personal dialogues with people involved in these initiatives.

These highlights from the practice of PAR are presented in section II. Section III discusses the emerging ideology of PAR and questions relating to its contribution to social transformation. The final section discusses PAR as a means of generating scientific knowledge for guidance of social practice.

II. THE PRACTICE OF PAR

Bhoomi Sena — India

A number of acutely oppressed tribal peasants in the Junglepatti belt in the Thane district of India joined the 'land-grab' movement initiated by the left-wing parties of 1970. The movement ended in the area merely with the temporary jailing of the participants, with no resolution of the land question. Disillusioned by this 'symbolic' character of the movement, the tribal leaders who participated in this initiated after coming out of jail an independent militant movement called 'Bhoomi Sena' (Land Army), against illegal usurpation by the money-lending 'sawkars' of lands belonging to the tribal people. A few thousand acres of land were recovered by force (De Silva et al., 1979: 2; Rahman, 1981).

There was, however, no clear thinking beyond this action to carry the movement forward, and its leadership submitted to paternalistic assistance of some social workers from outside who brought sophisticated technology and massive bank loans to help them. Economic programmes were now undertaken which were managed by the outsiders without any involvement of the people. It so happened that this non-participatory experiment ended in financial disaster due to mismanagement, and the tribal people were shocked into a consciousness against external paternalism.

At the same time late in 1975, a new phase of the Bhoomi Sena movement started in which the tribal people were committed to decide their course of action themselves. A few outsiders who had come with the earlier team of social workers but had been looking for a role in the promotion of people's self-reliance, remained with the movement and assisted it to develop a participatory, self-directed course. In particular an educationist contributed significantly to 'conscientization' of the tribal people in this new phase, by a pedagogic technique in which the tribal people got together in 'camps' where they recounted their oppressive life's experiences individually and listened to others doing so, and then discussed the commonality of these experiences in order to move towards appreciation of the 'structure' of their environment, and from there to collective decision-making and action.

The leadership of the movement encouraged the tribal people to take local action in their own villages according to their own priorities and collective deliberations. The role of the 'centre' — a small vanguard — that now developed consisted of catalytic, supportive, co-ordinating and synthesizing tasks, for instance, learning from village-level struggles and disseminating their experiences and methods to other villages; coming to the assistance of local struggles when needed; organizing and co-ordinating mass demonstrations on specific issues; initiating investigations on the nature and causes of injustice and exploitation; and organizing periodic camps for collective analysis by the tribal people of the experiences of their struggle. The ongoing collective deliberations of the tribal people and their leadership progressively conceptualized the meaning of their struggle.

The resurgence of spontaneous action by the people resulted in confrontation again with the sawkars for liberation from 'bonded-labour' conditions and to reclaim land illegally held by the latter, and struggles for implementation of the legal minimum wage for work done for the sawkars. Gradually people's organizations emerged at the village level, taking charge of village-level struggles, management of collective savings funds and various economic and social functions. Late in 1978 Bhoomi Sena initiated the formation of an agricultural workers' union in the Thane district while continuing itself as an independent movement.

In the initial stages of this new phase of the movement, the assistance of the outsiders led by the educationist was critical, in particular in the development of collective critical thinking of the tribal people. They have achieved considerable self-reliance in this regard by now, and the educationist has for all practical purposes withdrawn from the area, maintaining a loose, friendly contact with the movement.

The Change Agents Programme — Sri Lanka

The Change Agents Programme was initiated in 1978 as an Action Research Project supported by the United Nations Development Programme (UNDP) under the Ministry of Rural Development of the Sri Lankan government (Tilakratna, 1982). It aimed at evolving a methodology for catalytic intervention in the rural sector, to stimulate self-reliant mobilization of the rural poor to overcome their poverty through the generation of internal leaders (change agents) and participatory processes. Conceptual leadership in developing the methodology was provided by a Sri Lankan social scientist assisted by an Indian action researcher, both of whom had interacted intimately with the Bhoomi Sena movement in India.

A four-member team of development workers visited a village about thirty-five miles from Colombo, in which practically all the poor families were betel producers. The team established rapport with the villagers and settled down in the village, setting out to stimulate the poor betel producers to get together, to investigate their socio-economic situation and discuss the causes of their poverty. A process of investigation and analysis by the people themselves followed, supplemented by research by the development workers. This revealed to the betel producers that the bulk of the surplus of their labour was being appropriated by the trading middlemen who carried their products to exporting organizations. Action followed, initiated by a group of producers in January 1979 who set up an informal Betel Producers' Association. After several attempts the association succeeded in getting an export organization to buy from them directly. The resulting benefit to the producers was considerable. Producers from a number of neighbouring villages started joining the association, and its membership increased to over 200 by mid-1981 from 35 in March 1979. Resistance from private traders in collusion with other export organizations was faced and gradually overcome by various strategies and tactics.

As the association grew in size, the issue of membership participation in its decision-making, vis-à-vis its office bearers, came in the forefront. Eventually the association split into five small organizations, each undertaking its own marketing work and operating as autonomous units with active participation of its members. Together, they are developing into a force to be reckoned with in the area.

Similar methods of intervention in a village in the southern coastal belt of Sri Lanka resulted in a group of coir yarn producers getting together, first to build a small capital fund by saving in kind — that is, by setting apart a few pieces of yarn as saving — out of each day's production. After building some saving the group sold the saved stock at a higher price to an outside trader, bypassing the village trader, and used the proceeds to buy raw materials, also from a new source. Eventually the group found direct market outlets for their product at a very favourable price in Colombo. Other small coir producers joined, and a collective marketing organization was formed whose membership rose from 31 in March 1980 to 214 by December. By now the process has spread into neighbouring villages, and similar marketing organizations have emerged in six more of them. The producers have evolved their own organizational forms — for example, in the first village the primary organizational unit is a small group of between fifteen and twenty families with ten such groups in all, linked together by a central committee consisting of representatives from each group. All members in each primary unit undertake the marketing and handling work on a rotating basis with no hierarchy of officials. All primary groups hold meetings every week, and the ten groups meet in a general session once a month.

The village organizations have federated into an inter-village organization of coir producers to promote their common cause, through activities such as joint negotiation with export organizations, negotiation with the government for various facilities, and expansion of the movement into new villages.

Neither the betel producers' nor the coir producers' organizations are now dependent on the initial teams of development workers who stimulated their self-reliant development. These development workers left the respective villages by June 1981 and have since been initiating similar processes in other areas, occasionally visiting the earlier villages where they started their work.

As a whole the Change Agents Programme is developing into a small-scale movement. It is now working also with other small rural producers such as tea and rubber smallholders, milk producers, rural artisans and fishermen. Besides the Ministry of Rural Development in the government, the programme is now being carried forward also by a newly formed non-government organization (NGO) — Participatory Institute for Development Alternatives (PIDA) — set up by a group of persons who were involved with the original UNDP-sponsored project. PIDA is being co-ordinated by a senior university professor after the untimely death of the programme's first intellectual leader.

Proshika — Bangladesh

'Proshika' was established in 1976 by a team of educated young activists, as a non-government development agency (Hossain, 1982). The word 'Proshika' is an acronym signifying development education, training and action, three essential elements integral to Proshika's approach to rural development. It is funded by the Canadian International Development Agency (CIDA) through the Canadian University Service Overseas (CUSO). The primary aim of Proshika is to help the rural underprivileged achieve self-awareness, see their own problems and find their own ways of solving them. There are seven main steps in Proshika's approach: (1) individuals and groups are identified from among the villagers who have expressed interest or shown initiative in sustained development activities; (2) these people are then invited to visit an existing Proshika development centre; (3) Proshika then encourages them to receive training in leadership and organizational skills, with emphasis on analysis by the underprivileged themselves of the society, by drawing examples from their own life's situations; (4) after such initial training, Proshika encourages them to organize a group composed of members with homogeneous characteristics — for example, landless or marginal farmers, fishermen, etc. A Proshika 'animator' works as a guide in the group-formation process; (5) the group is urged from the outset to build a joint saving fund irrespective of what the initial contributions may be. It is asked also to meet regularly to discuss the problems of its members and to identify common action to solve them according to their own priorities. Emphasis is laid on the undertaking of co-operative income-generating projects; (6) after a group has identified a project, Proshika provides the specific skills-training required by the group; (7) when the group is ready and able to take on an income-generating project with its own funds, Proshika makes available a small loan, if required, on a matching grant basis.

Proshika has established two regional centres and sixteen development centres in eight districts. Each of these centres offers training facilities to Proshika's field workers and members of Proshika groups, besides serving as places for review of experiences and exchanges between the trainers and group members. These development centres by now cover more than 4,000 Proshika groups with an average size of between fifteen and twenty families in each group.

While emphasizing group action for income generation, Proshika gives considerable importance to organization building, group solidarity and collective action for realization of the basic economic and social rights of the underprivileged. In different places several Proshika groups are meeting together to discuss acts of social injustice and oppression by the rural elites, and are taking co-ordinated action to resist them, often with signficant success. In some places Proshika groups have federated into intergroup organizations. Through Proshika's intervention the underprivileged in the Proshika areas are emerging as a strong countervailing force at the local level.

Cross-fertilization

The schemes mentioned above are some of the more widely known attempts by educated activists to generate participatory grass-roots processes for improvement of the economic and social status of the underprivileged in South Asia. But there are many more, and the number is growing (Tandon, 1980). A process of cross-fertilization between them is ongoing, both at the national and international levels. Workshops bringing together several NGOs and voluntary groups engaged in such work is commonplace in India and Bangladesh. One NGO in India — the People's Institute for Development and Training (PIDT, New Delhi), itself engaged in PAR with the rural underprivileged in several parts of India — has initiated with the sponsorship of the International Labour Organization (ILO) a process of People's Research on Forestry, Ecology and the Oppressed, in which ten forest-based poor people's movements (including Bhoomi Sena) in different parts of India are getting together over a series of grass-roots workshops and are conducting joint fact-finding investigations, with the assistance of sympathetic professionals to develop and articulate their joint position on the question of forestry management.

At an inter-country level, Proshika, PIDT and the Change Agents Programme have been interacting closely: the development workers in the Change Agents Programme visited the other two initiatives before starting their own work in Sri Lanka, and more recently these three have interacted systematically at the leadership level for cross-fertilization in an ILO-sponsored exchange project. The latter also involved an initiative of the Rural Workers' Office of the Ministry of Labour in the Government of the Philippines — Group Action Among Landless and Near-landless Workers in the Sugar Crop Dominated Regions — which was initially rather paternalistic in its approach, oriented primarily towards the mobilization of external resources to generate employment and incomes for the under-privileged; as a result of interaction with Proshika, PIDT and the Change Agents Programme, it is now working under the name of 'Sarilakas' (own strength), to stimulate grass-roots self-reliance, seeking to generate processes of people's own deliberation and action according to their own priorities. A number of village-level rural workers' organizations have emerged as a result, with their self-deliberated efforts directed primarily at resisting injustice and exploitation by local and external vested interests. Needless to say, in the Philippines itself there are several other such initiatives.

Methodology

Naturally while such works have many differences in their approaches, broad similarities can be observed in many of them. For those that are in close touch with one another, a methodological and, indeed, ideological convergence seems to be approaching. Methodologically converging trends in the following directions may be observed:

1. Catalytic initiatives are taken by persons coming from the well-educated class (university graduates and above), independent of macrosocial organizations such as political parties, to promote self-mobilization of the rural underprivileged for group or organized action to emerge from out of their own deliberations.

2. The starting point in generating such grass-roots processes is the stimulation of the underprivileged to get together to inquire why they are poor and oppressed through social investigation and analysis of their own, which promotes their critical self-awareness of their environment.

3. The underprivileged are encouraged to discuss what they could do by uniting to overcome poverty and oppression. They are encouraged to form groups or organizations absolutely of their own, whose structure and functioning are to be decided by them, and through these to take economic and social action according to their self-deliberated priorities.

4. An attempt is made to generate a self-reliance consciousness among the underprivileged, and an attitude of assertion of their knowledge, views and decisions vis-à-vis outsiders. Materially, external resources and expertise are not considered to be primary in solving their problems — these are offered only as supplements when needed and available to the mobilization of the people's own resources and skills. In the use of external resources emphasis is placed on the further development of people's own resources and skills for them to achieve progressively greater self-reliance.

5. The people are encouraged to meet periodically in camps or 'people's workshops' in order to review of their experiences, to undertake periodic fact-finding investigations of their environment, and to take decisions for subsequent action based on their own research thus conducted. They seek thereby to generate a process of 'people's praxis', that is, a progressive rhythm of action and reflection.

6. The people, once they have developed experience in mobilizing and in organized action, are encouraged to stimulate and assist other underprivileged people to start similar action, and to gradually form higher level organizations by federating smaller ones and to develop links with other organizations of this type.

7. Dependence of the people on the initial catalysts is supposed to cease, through the generation and development of internal leadership, cadres and skills. This does not necessarily mean actual physical withdrawal of the catalysts from people's processes; but the people should within a reasonable time be able to carry on with their collective activities on their own, while a catalyst may continue his or her association with such processes and seek new roles in their progressive development.

8. The initiators of such action have not only a practical, but also a research interest, in generating and assisting such self-reliant people's processes. This includes a search for a methodology sensitive to self-reliant catalytic action, for a role for intellectuals in the development of people's praxis and 'people's power', and inquiry into the implications of such interaction for social transformation. This research, however, is subordinate to the people's collective interests as perceived by them, and to a commitment to protect information whose dissemination might be contrary to this interest.

The Freirian Work

There are such activities in other parts of the world as well (Callaway, 1980; Mustafa, 1981) which can, however, be competently discussed only by colleagues more familiar with them. Mention may be made of the work of Paulo Freire, a legend in PAR, which has stimulated a world-wide movement in the pedagogy of literacy, besides influencing action research not directly focused on literacy as such. Indeed most of the Asian initiatives referred to above have used the concept of 'conscientization' in the same sense as Freire — that is, stimulation of the self-reflective critical awareness of the oppressed people of their social reality and of their ability to transform it by conscious action. The rejection of 'aid' and 'extension' as solutions to the problem of people's development ('liberation'), which is implicit in the Asian initiatives, has also found its sharpest expression in Freirian work and thinking.

However, the pedagogy of literacy as a method of conscientization has not featured very much in the particular Asian cases observed; instead the thrust has been the stimulation of immediate social investigation and analysis by the oppressed people — social research — collectively.

Work in Colombia

Among other PAR activities outside Asia, one of the most illuminating reviews has been done by Fals Borda (1979) of the work that he and his colleagues did with grass-roots groups in Colombia. A major focus of this work has been the legitimization of popular knowledge and its development into 'scientific knowledge', with the aim of assisting in the development of a 'science of the proletariat' with which the masses could conduct their own struggle for social transformation. Fals Borda's self-critique of this work brings home the paramount care that is needed in the methodology of such effort. With his characteristic sensitivity and frankness, Fals Borda reports that the search for a way to achieve the intended objective has so far been inconclusive. While the intellectuals conducting this search were able to develop considerable rapport with the masses, the latter were not stimulated to take over the initiative in the intellectual inquiry. In the end

> with characteristic impatience, it was the action researchers and their intellectual allies who were forced to define 'popular science' ..., and inject their own definition of it into the context of reality. The result was a special application of the notion of insertion into the social process in order to 'place knowledge at the service of popular interests', but such knowledge did not derive from the objective conditions of the proletariat as would have been theoretically more correct. . . . As historical materialism was almost an exclusive heritage of action researchers and committed intellectuals, they consequently had to diffuse it among the grass roots as an ideology. This led to the adoption as 'special mediating categories' of what in a classic manner, are expounded upon as general Marxist postulates. In this manner, what was termed 'popular science' had to be an ideological replica of certain general theses of historical materialism as developed in other contexts and social formations. This is to say that the groups fell victim to the worst historical form of dogmatism, that of 'mimesis'. (Fals Borda, 1979: 49)

Here Fals Borda touches on the source of elite domination over the masses in many radical attempts at social transformation, and PAR continues in its search for ways of avoiding this tragic pitfall.

III. PAR AND SOCIAL TRANSFORMATION

The Ideology

Whatever the successes, or failures, underlying all such work is the idea that a self-conscious people, those who are currently poor and oppressed, will progressively transform their environment by their own praxis. In this process others may play a catalytic and supportive role, but will not dominate.

Many participatory action researchers claim to have been inspired by the ideals of historical materialism. Indeed the notion of 'class struggle' as opposed to class harmony is implicit in PAR's approach which selects the poor and oppressed for self-conscious mobilization to assert themselves; the resulting actions of the oppressed are inevitably constituting class struggles of different forms, testifying to the inherent class consciousness of the oppressed.

Historical materialism, however, has passed through many hands, in theory as well as in application, and there seems no longer to be any broad consensus as to its operational meaning. The recent growth of PAR as an activity independent from left-wing political parties suggests that it is opposed at least to a certain interpretation of this ideology that views social transformation as primarily the task of a 'vanguard' party which will assume (itself) to have a consciousness that is 'advanced' relative to the consciousness of the oppressed masses, and who will mobilize the masses for social revolution and social reconstruction. One feels from interaction with PAR activists that, in fact, the growth of PAR owes itself to the crisis of the left as well as to the crisis of the right: application of the 'vanguard' party theory has produced structural change in a number of situations, but there is evidence that in several of them newer forms of domination over the masses have emerged, and to this the vanguards have not shown much sensitivity. People's liberation in many 'revolutionary' societies has as a result remained elusive. The ultimate caricature of the revolutionary ideal of liberation is visible today (January 1981) in Poland where the self-generated countervailing power of the working class vis-à-vis the vanguard is being militarily suppressed in the name of protecting 'socialism', which seemed to be a strategy of development based on paternalistic deliveries to the people through expertise and with massive borrowed finance. This strategy, which was managed without involving the people, has failed even in its own terms and has led the country into economic and financial bankruptcy — a case of Bhoomi Sena, in its first phase, on a national scale.

Dual Transformation

Historical experience of this nature calls for rethinking of the meaning of 'liberation'. Surely liberation must be opposed to all forms of elite domination over the masses. The dominant view of social transformation has been preoccupied with the need for changing existing, oppressive structures of relations in material production. This is certainly a necessary task. But — and this is the distinctive viewpoint of PAR — domination of masses by elites is rooted not only in the polarization of control over the means of material production but also over the means of knowledge production including, as in the former case, the social power to determine what is valid or useful knowledge. Irrespective of which of these two polarizations sets off a process of domination, it can be argued that one reinforces the other in augmenting and perpetuating this process. By now in most polarized societies the gap between those who have social power over the process of knowledge generation — an important form of 'capital' inasmuch as knowledge is a form of social power — and those who have not, has reached dimensions no less formidable than the gap in access to the means of physical production. History is showing that a convergence of the latter gap in no way ensures convergence of the former; on the contrary, existence of the latter has been seen to offset the advantages of revolutionary closures of the former and has set off processes of domination once again.

In order to improve the possibility of liberation, therefore, these two gaps should be attacked, wherever feasible, simultaneously. This is not accomplished by the masses merely being mobilized by a vanguard body with the latter's 'advanced' consciousness. People cannot be liberated by a consciousness and knowledge other than their own, and a strategy such as the above inevitably contains seeds of new forms of domination. It is absolutely essential, therefore, that the people develop their own endogenous process of consciousness raising and knowledge generation, and that this process acquires the social power to assert itself vis-à-vis all elite consciousness and knowledge. The theoretical basis for this assertion is discussed in the final section of this chapter.

The change in the relations of knowledge that is being conceived goes beyond the concept of 'from the masses, to the masses' (Mao Zedong, 1968). The Chinese revolution did seek to legitimize people's knowledge and thought, and asked elites to go to the masses and learn from them. But the task of systematizing people's thought was given, it seems, to the elites (intellectuals) and not to the masses, with the presumption that the people are incapable of systematizing their own thought — that is, of building their own science. In this view revolutionary theory rests ultimately with the elites. Whether Mao Zedong's thought correctly reflected the people's thought or not, the process of its systematization was apparently external to the process of the people's own collective reflection, and the knowledge that was built was in the end handed down to the people. The wisdom of all great religions can be traced to the wisdom or ordinary people revealed at a certain point in some particular context; but systematized religion descending from above and preached as a faith, rather than (scientifically) rationalized through processes of people's own (collective) self-reflection (see section II), is alienating rather than liberating. It can also be replaced by another religion if the faith does not work or if the 'prophet' dies.

PAR and Macrosocial Structure

PAR is a search for ways of promoting the dual transformation process conceived above by generating and assisting processes of people's own praxis. It starts at the grass roots as a microlevel activity, and seeks to stimulate and assist grass-roots processes to develop into a wider movement. How far this can go from any given situation cannot be usefully speculated about in the abstract. PAR, and the development of people's praxis which it seeks to promote, are creative acts that must move with skill and tact in order to create and expand space for their own continued growth. In this sense there is no theory of how PAR may, if at all, bring about macrostructural change by itself or through the processes that it generates. In fact the notion of praxis is opposed to theorizing that asks and presumes to answer questions on the course of progressive creative encounters between social forces.

In places where sustained PAR is possible, there is evidence of the generation of social transformation processes at the local level, in terms of both of the two relations mentioned above. This shows that objective conditions are favourable for the development of such processes in these places, at least up to a point. For the Asian experiences in particular it appears that a sporting chance exists for the oppressed to be able to unite and for their collective power to wrest significant gains at least from their immediate exploiters.

Specific explanation for the existence of such space in any given country should be derived from the specific socio-political context, and this will not be attempted in this short chapter. Broadly speaking, one would surmise that the strength of the link between the status quo of macropower and the local elites will be a factor in explaining this phenomenon. The stronger this link is, the likelier it is for macroforces to come to the protection of local vested interests in the event of any threat to the latter from organized action by the oppressed, thereby making it difficult for local action by itself to achieve much. On the face of it, this link is a question of the dynamics of political alliance between national and local elites, a relation that by itself may vary both over time and space, permitting independent grass-roots mobilization, more in certain times and areas than in others. There may be some role in a more basic sense of the economic worth of local elites to the national elites, by way of the dependence of the privileges of the latter on the appropriation of economic surplus by the former at the local level.

For Bhoomi Sena this conjecture is corroborated by a participatory study of the movement that observes the money-lending sawkars to be an unproductive class that has been contributing little to developing the productive forces of Junglepatti in order to be able to make any significant surplus available for use at 'higher' levels (De Silva et al., 1979). Indeed one of the reasons Bhoomi Sena has come as far as it has may be ascribed to the contradiction between the feudal money-lending class against which the tribal people's struggle is chiefly aimed, and the emerging class of capitalist farmers in the areas, with power at the state level no longer committed to bail out the former parasitic class. In Sri Lanka attempts (now being withdrawn) to create a welfare state rather than develop the productive forces resulted in the creation of a soft society as a whole, where the 'traditional' sector has been subsidized with resources raised through taxation of the 'modern' sector supplemented by foreign aid (Haque, 1977). And in Bangladesh the rulers in recent times have given the impression of being quite content with the image of an 'international basket case', with success of government policy often equated with the amount of foreign aid it is able to obtain, domestic resource mobilization remaining at an acutely low level (Alamgir, 1976). In such situations the economic worth of local-level elites to the national elites is low and in places negative, so that popular movements confronting the former alone may not be viewed by the latter as an immediate threat to its material interests. Within limits the national elites may actually be induced to patronize such movements as examples of democratic tolerance and concern for the wellbeing and rights of the poor, a gesture that may be stimulated also by the support to such movements of foreign donor agencies, for obvious reasons. It is, however, also not improbable that sections within the national elites may cherish some nationalistic sentiments and may be attracted by initiatives in search of an alternative development strategy in the direction of greater national self-reliance, and the support of such quarters may actually have played a role in the development of grass-roots people's movements in the Asian region.

Notwithstanding objective conditions such as the above favouring the growth of PAR in some countries, there may be limits to this growth in any one of them, given ultimately by the macrostructure of the society that progressive development of grass-roots processes and their interlinking may eventually confront. In other societies with different objective conditions very little activity of this nature may be possible. If such a limit is reached, it would be necessary to seek to change the macrostructure by appropriate means in order to enable the further development of the people's praxis. Unless people's self-conscious mobilization itself has developed already to a point at which they are able to take on this task, PAR has the responsibility to ally with other progressive social forces for confronting the macrostructure at appropriate times.

PAR in the 'Womb of the Old Order'

It is important, however, to note that the development of genuine people's praxis after macrostructural change is likely to be limited by the kind of social processes that have preceded it. The classic work of Bettelheim (1976) on the Soviet revolution reveals, sector by sector, the almost total unpreparedness of the Soviet working class to self-manage the task of post-revolutionary reconstruction, so that 'experts' were able to take over and consolidate their power and eventually establish a dictatorship over the people. All revolutions witness this struggle for power after the old order is overthrown between forces committed to the release of people's initiatives and those seeking to dominate the people in new ways. It may be suggested that a crucial factor by which this struggle may be won or lost is the relations of knowledge — more specifically whether the people can assert their right to apply their own knowledge in reconstructing society, and their autonomy of choice of outside knowledge rather than submitting to external expertise in a state of helplessness.

The earlier people's praxis starts, the greater should be the consciousness and confidence of the people at any stage to resist an invasion of expertise. Accordingly the liberational potential of the destruction of an old order should be greater the more advanced is people's praxis at the time of this act of revolution. It is therefore never too early to start PAR, if space for this exists or can be created. Under such conditions vanguard praxis cannot be viewed as a substitute for people's praxis, if liberation indeed is the objective. The growth of PAR, and for that matter popular movements, in several countries in recent times demonstrates that people's praxis is possible, right now. This is a challenge to all vanguards to clarify their commitment. The possibility exists, unfortunately, that the further development of PAR, which even reactionary social structures may permit, may be pre-empted by the action of other macrosocial forces committed to some kind of structural change but indifferent to the development of self-assertive people's initiatives.

Notwithstanding many obstacles that are being and will be encountered, there is some assurance that the ongoing PAR in different countries may not be in vain. There is evidence already of the impact of the Freirian work on revolutionary thinking, and if it has not by itself yet made a 'revolution' in any single country, revolutionary leaderships after coming into power are seeking to adapt the Freirian method in educational programmes for reconstructing society (e.g. in Cuba, Nicaragua, Guinea Bissau). Thus even microlevel experiments within restricted space can develop liberation-promoting knowledge and methods that may find macrolevel application after space for this has been created by revolutionary action. The same may be said of the microlevel initiatives that are going on in Asia. Any national leadership in these countries which seeks ways of social reconstruction that will avoid an inglorious and often hopeless strategy of delivery of development from above and outside, will do well to consider the methodology of generating self-reliant people's processes that some of these initiatives are developing.

PAR's Own Tension

'At times this congress sounds like an intellectuals' meeting. If they want to hold a congress then let the intellectuals hold one without us.' — Jan Jedreze-jewski, a worker from Gdansk, at Solidarity's Congress on 29 September 1981 (*Financial Times*, 1981).

But PAR itself needs to be modest about its own role. It should be admitted that it constitutes a rather unusual interaction between two social classes: in terms of material production, intellectuals are primarily a consumer class vis-à-vis the class of direct producers, and in terms of knowledge production it is, traditionally, the opposite. It is significant to observe that PAR postulates eliminating the second class distinction but not the first, insofar as intellectuals are not supposed to engage in manual labour (Fals Borda, 1981a). Thus PAR postulates perpetuation of one of the 'great contradictions' in society. This must imply deep tensions in terms of the distribution of material privileges and social power from which PAR cannot be claimed to be immune.

PAR, after all, is threatening to become a respectable intellectual movement, and participatory researchers are gaining in social status, within and across national frontiers. PAR is getting institutionalized, and this will corrupt some in the movement at the same time as it will promote its growth. Finally PAR constitutes praxis of the participatory researcher as well as that of the people, and the two processes are different, rooted in the respective traditions and accumulated wisdoms of the two parties in this interaction. The consequent pairs of knowledge-building and self-transformative processes may not always be in harmony, aggravating the tension that is inherent in this interaction.

As one participatory action researcher — a 'community facilitator' in the Sarilakas project in the Philippines — told me recently: 'in this work you have to constantly fight your enemies, and the greatest enemy is yourself'.

IV. PAR AS RESEARCH

PAR is often viewed as a kind of research and a discussion of this aspect of its activity is in order here. As Paul Oquist (1977) has observed, the epistemological premises of action research conform to those of pragmatism and dialectical materialism as schools of scientific research. These schools hold that science should be purposive, aimed at the modification of reality, and should unite with efforts to do so. This also means that research should be value- or ideology-directed, a standpoint that is explicit in research of these two schools. The specific ideology of PAR that is elaborated in this chapter separates it from pragmatism which keeps the choice of ideology as an open question; the ideology of PAR may be considered, if one wishes, to be one of the several interpretations of dialectical (historical) materialism, but this is an immaterial question of labelling.

Value-Bias

The epistemological standpoint of PAR opposes that of other schools such as empiricism, logical positivism and structuralism, which reject social value-bias in what is considered to be 'scientific' research, and from the same principle adopt the detached observational method of social inquiry. It may be argued, however, that no research in the final analysis can be value-free, although some specific inquiries may not be consciously value-biased.

   In the first place, although research may be considered by some schools to be valid for its own sake irrespective of its social use, the 'social value added' by research — that is, the social effects of the application of the knowledge produced by those who are in a position to apply it — is an observable fact that cannot be dismissed. Given the structure of society, the products of specific research activities will be used more by some social classes than by others, naturally to the greater intended benefit of the former. It is in general possible by relatively elementary social analysis (which even the 'illiterate', oppressed poor are capable of doing) to discover which social class will be in a position to use a particular knowledge in efforts to promote its own interests. In this sense all research whose results may be applied in practice has class bias, and this ideological responsibility of research cannot be avoided.

   In the second place, there can be a more subtle value-bias implicit in the choice of the logical system of analysis in social research. Consider, for example, the system of formal logic vis-à-vis dialectical logic. The former postulates that something that is observed to be 'A' cannot be 'not-A' at the same time, thereby ruling out the possibility of a change from 'A' to 'not-A' in certain ways that are considered to be possible by the latter. Policy conclusions from research of the same phenomenon by the two logical systems may therefore differ, with possible ideological implications that may be important. Thus, for example, if the poor are observed to be incapable of doing social analysis, formal logic would tend to conclude that they should therefore receive education to do so; but dialectical logic, postulating that the observed incapability unites with its opposite into which it may transform itself in response to appropriate stimulation, might suggest a different kind of pedagogy (the kind discussed in section II) to provide this stimulation — an act of liberating the thought process — to the people rather than for outsiders to educate the poor. The profound ideological difference between the two conclusions should be obvious.

In the third place, ideological bias is direct in the detached observational method of social research that implies a 'subject-object' relationship between the researcher and the researched (the people) in contrast to the 'subject-subject' relationship of participatory action research. Research on oppressed people by external researchers with a subject-object relationship assumes and asserts the myth of the incapability of the people to participate in the research as equals. This humiliates the people, and alienates them from their own power of generating knowledge relevant for transforming their environment by their own initiative. This makes them wait for elite researchers to come and find out about them, to write about them and make policy recommendations for outsiders to solve their problems. This helps to perpetuate the domination of the people for which as we have observed not only their economic dependence, but also their intellectual dependence on privileged elites, are responsible.[1] In this way this research methodology has contributed to inaction of the people and has invited action by others, and has had therefore profound practical as well as ideological consequences. Needless to say, 'radical' research by the non-participatory method, including 'vanguard praxis' that has not involved the people, is also responsible in this matter.

Finally the methodological premise that knowledge must be produced by detached observation has also contributed to the creation and perpetuation of a class of intellectuals (experts, technocrats) distinct from the masses of direct producers, constituting a separation of mental from manual labour. This class has been seen to be politically active in controlling or influencing social power to promote its own privileges in both pre- and post-'revolutionary' situations. In this sense non-involvement is a myth — the social researcher is involved consciously or unconsciously in his or her own bid for social power, and the observational method of research serves as an instrument to promote this interest.

Objectivity

One may question also a claim to objectivity in research if this were to mean being free from subjective bias. The methodological biases discussed above are subjective biases. Such bias is inherent also in conceptualizing and categorizing most human phenomena, and full communicability of such concepts and categories requires a sharing of sensuous, subjective perceptions — that is, communication at a subjective level in addition to formal definitions if these are so defined.

There is, however, another sense in which research may be defined to be objective (or, for that matter, 'scientific'), that is, in the sense of the methodology and product having passed through a process of social verification. This produces social knowledge that is distinct from knowledge that is purely individual and subjective. Objectivity in this sense requires transition from the individual to a collective. This in turn requires that (a) a collective is defined; (b) codes of communication (language) exist or are developed within the collective; and (c) agreement be reached within the collective as to valid methods of investigation, reasoning and refutation of observations and arguments.

Research in all well-established schools has a verification system of this nature, explicitly or implicitly, and is objective if verified within its own paradigm. In the more advanced schools the method of verification has by now become more or less standardized, and verification is often possible by mechanical application of certain rules or arguments so that interpersonal communication may not be necessary for establishing its objectivity. It is important to recognize, however, that objectivity in this sense is relative and internal to the collective concerned (e.g. a research profession). For those not belonging to this collective, either because of a lack of communicability or because they do not accept its premises or rules, this knowledge either has no meaning or is not acceptable. There is in this sense no universality in any 'science' insofar as the entire human race does not constitute a collective for the purpose of scientific knowledge generation. If the Chinese have not followed the verification system of some Western schools in developing their knowledge, this does not make acupuncture, for example, a piece of 'unscientific' knowledge in the endogenous development of the Chinese medical science.[2]

PAR, an emerging school of research, also generates objective, scientific knowledge in this sense. Moser (1977, 1981) has discussed the verification process in people's collectives. This is in general the dialogical process of collective reflection when people 'withdraw' from action for review and decision-making during their rhythm of action and reflection (Fals Borda, 1981a). It is argumentative and dependent on consensus rather than on pre-established rules to be applied mechanically. This does not make this process any less objective or scientific than other types of research as long as the necessary criteria for objectivity are satisfied. The people are entitled to see their 'ghosts' as professional researchers see theirs (Cain, 1977), and regard them as part of their objective reality — as a scientific truth in their endogenous knowledge-building process — so long as their existence can be collectively verified, tentatively at a point of time, and is open to subsequent refutation.

An immediate objective of PAR is to return to the people the legitimacy of the knowledge they are capable of producing through their own collectives and verification systems, which they may decide to establish themselves as fully scientific, and their right to use this knowledge — not excluding any other knowledge but not dictated by it — as guide in their own action. The reappropriation of this right by the people and its assertion is considered by PAR to be fundamental in the promotion of its ideology of dual social transformation, for the elimination of a major source of dependence that is standing in the way of people's liberation in both pre- and post-'revolutionary' societies.

Two Research Streams

PAR also involves a knowledge-generation process for the participatory researchers, a scientific process in its own right. However, participatory reseachers being in general intellectuals coming from a tradition very different from the underprivileged masses with whom they work, communication between the two may not be good enough for the two research processes to converge into a single stream of knowledge building. PAR therefore may involve two different knowledge-generation streams, and this has implications for social relations between the people and participatory researchers to which reference has been made in the previous section.

V. SUMMARY

By participatory action research (PAR) we are talking about action research that is participatory, and participatory research that unites with action.

Short glimpses are given of PAR with the Bhoomi Sena movement in India, the Change Agents Programme in Sri Lanka and the work of Proshika in Bangladesh. Cross-fertilization between such activities within and across national boundaries is mentioned. A converging trend in the methodology of such work is observed in the direction of the catalytic work of educated activists who generate and promote the self-organization of the rural poor and processes of their own praxis. This organization becomes progressively independent of outside assistance.

Mention is made of the Freirian concept of 'conscientization' that is reflected in the Asian initiatives, which have, however, used literacy less as a method of conscientization and have stimulated immediate social investigation and analysis by the oppressed people. Finally the work in Colombia is cited, which sought to generate an endogenous 'science of the proletariat' but ended up with the reformulation by radical intellectuals of revolutionary dogmas developed in other contexts.

The ideological trend in PAR is elaborated in terms of the view that a self-conscious people will transform their environment by their own praxis, as opposed to a social revolution attempted by a vanguard party with 'advanced' consciousness gained primarily through vanguard praxis; the latter may produce structural change but has the seeds of newer forms of domination. It is suggested that liberation opposes domination of all forms, and requires the dual transformation of relations of production in both physical goods and knowledge, to be attempted simultaneously. PAR is a search for ways of promoting this.

It is observed that PAR starts as a microlevel activity and confronts vested interests at the local level. Its growth may be facilitated by a weak link between national elites and local elites, probably depending in part upon the economic worth of the latter in preserving the former's privileges. Eventually macroconstraints have to be encountered, to be overcome by macroaction. The dialectical relation between PAR and macrostructural change is discussed, observing in particular the role of PAR before structural change in advancing the possibility of liberational activity after such change.

It is noted that PAR has its own tensions, arising out of the differences in the two traditions involved in this interaction — the intellectual and the popular. It constitutes praxis of both the parties, and the two may not necessarily converge.

As a method of research, PAR and people's praxis are frankly social-value biased. It is argued that the ideological burden of the mainstream of research is heavy — the application of all research is class-biased and the bias may be anticipated so that responsibility for this cannot be avoided. It is also argued that the methodology of all social enquiry has ideological implications, which are discussed. This, it is observed, nevertheless permits research to be 'objective' in the sense of passing through a process of social verification. PAR and people's praxis are in this sense a valid, objective research method. An immediate objective of PAR is to return to the people as part of the dual transformation process the scientific legitimacy of the knowledge they are capable of producing by creating their own system of social verification.

NOTES

This chapter was first published as *The Theory and Practice of Participatory Research* (WEP 10/WP. 29), copyright © 1983, International Labour Office, Geneva.

1. This follows Heisenberg's principle that every act of observation changes the reality that is observed (Paranjape et al., 1981).

2. The relativity of scientific observation has long been established by Einstein's theory of relativity. Social life is a conglomeration of matter in motion, and it is a pity that notwithstanding the theory of relativity, the mainstream of social science has remained in the Newtonian age with its postulate of an absolute truth which scientists can discover from outside (Paranjape et al., 1981).

REFERENCES

Alamgir, Mohiuddin (1976) 'Economy of Bangladesh: Which Way are we Moving?' Background paper to the Presidential Address delivered at the Second Annual Conference of the Bangladesh Economic Association, Dhaka University, Dhaka, Bangladesh, 14–17 March (mimeographed).

Bettelheim, Charles (1976) *Class Struggles in the USSR, First Period: 1917–1923.* New York: Monthly Review Press.

Cain, Bonnie J. (1977) *Participatory Research: Research with Historic Consciousness.* Toronto: International Council for Adult Education.

Callaway, Helen (ed.) (1980) *Participation in Research, Case Studies of Participatory Research in Adult Education.* Amersfoort: Netherlands Centre for Research and Development in Adult Education.

De Silva, G.V.S., N. Mehta, A. Rahman and P. Wignaraja (1979) 'Bhoomi Sena: A Struggle for People's Power', *Development Dialogue*, 2: 3–70.

Fals Borda, Orlando (1979) 'Investigating Reality in Order to Transform it', *Dialectical Anthropology*, 4 (1): 33–56.

Fals Borda, Orlando (1981a) 'The Challenge of Action Research', *Development: Seeds of Change, Village through Global Order*, 1: 55–61.

Fals Borda, Orlando (1981b) 'Science and the Common People', *Journal of Social Studies*, 11.

Fals Borda, Orlando (1981c) 'Die Bedeutung der Sozialwissenschaft und die praktische Produktion von Wissen in der Dritten Welt: Die Herausforderung der Aktionsforschung', *Österreichische Zeitschrift für Politikwissenschaft*, 2.

Financial Times, London, 30 September 1981.

Haque, Wahidul, N. Mehta, A. Rahman and P. Wignaraja (1977) 'Towards a Theory of Rural Development', *Development Dialogue*, 2: 9–137.

Hossain, Mosharraf (1982) *Conscientising Rural Disadvantaged Peasants in Bangladesh: Intervention through Group Action, A Case Study of Proshika.* World Employment Programme Research Working Paper No. WEP 10/WP.27, International Labour Office, Geneva.

Mao Zedong (1968) 'Several Questions on the Method of Direction', *Selected Works 3*. Peking: Government Printing House.

Moser, Heinz (1977) 'Action Research as a New Research Paradigm in the Social Sciences,' Paper presented at the International Sociological Association Symposium on Action Research and Scientific Analysis, Cartagena, Colombia, April.

Moser, Heinz (1981) 'Participatory Action Research: The Aspect of Research.' Paper presented at the International Seminar on Participatory Research and Training in Local Development, Lepolampi, Finland 9–11 September.

Mustafa, Kemal (1981) 'Participatory Research Amongst Pastoralist Peasants in Tanzania: The Experience of the Jipemoyo Project in Bagamoyo District.' Mimeographed World Employment Programme Research Report, International Labour Office, Geneva.

Oquist, Paul (1977) 'The Epistemology of Action Research.' Paper presented at the

International Sociological Association Symposium on Action Research and Scientific Analysis, Cartagena, Colombia, April.

Paranjape, P.V., V. Kanhare, N. Sathe, S. Kulkarni and S. Gothoskar (1981) *Grassroots Self-Reliance in Shramik Sanghatana, Dhulia District, India.* World Employment Programme Research Working Paper No. WEP 10/WP.22, International Labour Office, Geneva.

Rahman, Md. Anisur (1981) *Some Dimensions of People's Participation in the Bhoomi Sena Movement.* Participation Occasional Paper, United Nations Research Institute for Social Development, Geneva.

Tandon, Rajesh (1980) *Participatory Research in Asia.* New Delhi: Centre for Continuing Education.

Tilakratna, S. (1981) *Grass-Roots Self-Reliance in Two Rural Locations in Sri Lanka: Organisations of Betel and Coir Yarn Producers.* World Employment Programme Research Working Paper No. WEP 10/WP.24, International Labour Office, Geneva.

PART III

In the early 1970s, evaluators were dismayed to find that the results of evaluations were not being used to improve social programs as often as they hoped. As a result, evaluators began to examine and redefine their notions about what constitutes use, and to study in earnest the characteristics of information that would foster instrumental use. Both the fruits and limitations of these efforts are evident in the articles that are reprinted in this section.

The first article, which is by Lindblom (1986), argues that four widely accepted principles of knowledge use are incorrect and that we would be better off acting contrary to these principles. For example, in place of the common advice to study only feasible solutions that can be implemented in practice, Lindblom suggests studying all options including those that appear infeasible, so as to free our thinking from the narrowness of current practice. In part, Lindblom is reminding us that social research can serve many purposes and that the traditional focus on facilitating its use among policymakers can impede the achievement of other worthwhile ends.

Next are a number of studies that document both instrumental and conceptual uses of evaluations and social science research by federal and state policymakers. These include Leviton and Boruch's (1984) description of the use of compensatory education evaluations, Rossi and Wright's (1985) discussion of social science research and the politics of gun control, Saxe's (1986) report of how the Office of Technology Assessment used social research in several different areas, and Wholey's (1986) presentation of how Congress used evaluative findings about the Job Corps. These studies highlight not only the role that individual evaluation studies can play in producing change, but also the role played by accumulated social science findings that are synthesized qualitatively or through such techniques as meta-analysis. Clearly, evaluation results are being used in many more ways than was first thought; and as these articles illustrate, evaluators now know more about how to make such use happen.

Goodwin and Goodwin (1984) coin the term *tomato effect* to denote the rejection of highly efficacious medical therapies because they do not appear sensible in light of accepted theories about disease mechanism and drug action, just as the tomato was once widely rejected because it was thought to be poisonous. The tomato effect is the counterpart in utilization theory to the implementability concept in social programming theory (see Shadish, 1984). In both cases, use is facilitated to the extent that the intervention is consistent with the system doing the using, whether that system is conceptual, political, or economic.

The final article is a critique by Stake (1986) of an evaluation of the federal Cities-in-Schools program, which attempted to reach out to disadvantaged youths. Stake argues that the evaluation diverted local attention away from the activities which the local stakeholders believed would be the most efficacious toward meeting the objectives set forth by the evaluators, thus making the program less effective and squelching local problem solving efforts. In this way, even though evaluators may be dedicated to social reform, their actions might lead to just the opposite effect: a quieting of reform.

REFERENCES

Shadish, W. R. (1984). Policy research: Lessons from the implementation of deinstitutionalization. *American Psychologist, 39,* 725-738.

8

Who Needs What Social Research for Policymaking?

Charles E. Lindblom

In reflecting on changes in policy analysis, the author notes the climate of suspicion for policy advising and some of the major errors or "sins" in the way policy analysts choose, define, and analyze problems. All too often policy analysts and their sponsors, the users of analysis, react to typical issues, have an investment in change, and ignore the imperatives of the policy process.

How best to use professional fact gathering, inquiry, and analysis to help us solve our society's problems? Today the question engages a wide audience, for social research has become a sizable—and expensive—industry, and institutions have sprung up to train policy analysts.

More important, we hear that power in contemporary society is passing from those who hold conventional sources of authority, like arms, public office, or wealth, to those who *know*. The more complex a society, the more specialized its division of labor; the more its reliance on technology, the more its affairs fall into the hands—or the powers—of those who have the skills, the time, and the funds for analyzing the society's problems. Only professional social researchers and social scientists have the time, skills, and funds for analyzing the larger social problems of society. As Bell (1972) says, the new great political struggle is between the professional and the populace.[1]

Editor's Note: This article is an abridged version of a talk prepared for the Nelson A. Rockefeller Institute of Government, State University of New York. The author and editors are grateful to the Institute for permission to publish the present abridged version of the original.

From Charles E. Lindblom, "Who Needs What Social Research for Policymaking?", *Knowledge: Creation, Diffusion, Utlization,* Vol. 7, pp. 345-366. Copyright © 1986 by Sage Publications, Inc.

The Conventional Rules
of Good Policy Research

Let us begin an examination of how best to use professional social inquiry by setting out in our minds some familiar bedrock principles of how in general orientation a social scientist or researcher should proceed.

The social scientist interested in science for its own sake, who ignores practical problems and simply follows his or her own curiosity, we shall ignore. What general guidelines are said to be appropriate for professionals who intend to make a contribution to public policy?

(I) The first principle, I suggest, is that in a democratic society the best professional researchers, social scientists, analysts—whatever the label—ought normally to be concerned in a nonpartisan way with the values or interests of the whole society rather than on some segment of society. An illustrative prescription is that good policy analysis "obligates the policy analyst to take the larger view. . . . It minimizes the opportunity for the instrusion of the analyst's own values" (Graham and Graham, 1976: 86).

(II) A second principle is that professional inquiry intended to aid public policy should usually avoid the irrelevance of investigating policy alternatives that are simply infeasible.

This second principle meets with some dissent—more so than does the first principle on the public interest. But its weight is evidenced by the character of instruction on the public policy schools. They train for the analysis of policies for the here and now, for practical policies that have some chance of winning political support, that respect the society's values, and that fit into other existing policies and institutions. In coping, say, with the problem of inflation or with problems of industrial relations, one would not expect a trained policy analyst to give a moment's thought to so unidiomatic a solution as in the Marxian slogan, "Abolish the wages system."

(III) A third principle might better be called an understanding, habit, or obvious rule of thumb rather than be dignified as a principle. It is that professional inquiry speaks to the people who have to make the policy decisions, as in Wildavsky's book title, *Speaking Truth to Power*. A National Research Council report tells us: "From the point of view of participants, policy-relevant research is research that helps them carry out their roles and achieve goals they consider important." Who are the participants? They are the policymakers, the public officials (see Lynn, 1978: 16).

(IV) A fourth principle applies only to those analysts who are very close to the decision maker—for example, a staff analyst in the Department of Agriculture. The principle is that policy analysis takes the form of examination of a question of policy, normally culminating in some *recommendations* as to what the decision maker ought to do.

Actual policy analysis does not follow this prescription. Its weight, however, is indicated by textbooks and curricula, as well as by the emergence in recent times of an academic theory of policy analysis, all of which cast policy analysis in this form: reach recommendations.[2]

The four guiding principles for making professional inquiry helpful to public policy are, then: nonpartisan pursuit of the public interest; a practical concern with feasible policies; meeting the needs of public officials; and, in particular, providing them with recommendations. I wonder if they do not seem so obvious as to have raised in your minds a question about why I bother to discuss them.

Public Interest and Partisanship

But there is more in these principles than meets the eye. Let's look further now at the first one: on the nonpartisan pursuit of the public interest.

What is good for General Motors is not on all points good for Chrysler. What is good for organized labor is often achieved at the expense of unorganized labor. If the so-called pro-life groups win, the so-called pro-choice groups lose.

Some of these conflicts can be settled by a formula; for example, by majority rule. But neither majority rule nor any other formula is applicable to most cases of conflict.

What, then, is the public or common interest? That the interests, say, of farmers, should yield to those of the urban work force? And if so, to what degree? That the interests of those who look for jobs in a proposed new shopping mall should yield to the interests of the local residents who want no further commercial development in their neighborhood?

To answer such questions, one first has to understand that the problem is not of knowing a right answer, but of deciding on, or willing, a defensible outcome. Given the conflict, there is not one correct solution. Any benefit sought will be at cost to someone. Some substantial groups will always be hurt. It is not possible, consequently, to *know* an answer; indeed there is no *answer*. There is only a choice to be made, a decision to be taken, an outcome to be achieved by commitments or acts of will. Only up to a point will knowledge help form the commitment; for example, by helping to rule out the worst of possible solutions.

A professional analyst can sometimes be useful in situations in which there are elements of common interest to be uncovered. Or a good analyst can sometimes discover solutions that ought to be avoided because they suit no one. In academic language, he can find a Pareto-efficient solution; specifically, a solution that is to the advantage of some persons and the disadvantage of no one (see Stokey and Zeckhauser, 1978: 270-272). If such a solution exists, *knowledge* that it exists can make a contribution to good policymaking.

But even in these cases, there remains conflict. Economists often blunder into the conclusion that policymakers should choose Pareto-efficient solutions because they help some persons and hurt no others. Not so. If, as is typically the case—and perhaps is always the case—there are still other solutions that bring substantial advantages to large numbers of persons, and these advantages are worth seeking even at loss to other persons—for example, protecting civil liberties of minorities even if doing so is greatly irritating and obstructive to others—then, there remains a conflict as to what is to be done. The Pareto-efficient solution is not necessarily the best choice.

When we ask a social scientist or researcher to formulate a version of the public interest and pursue his analysis in the light of it, we are asking him or her to go beyond knowlede to choice or commitment.[3]

Who, then, is to be considered competent on such weighings, evaluations, and choices? No one. Beyond some point, as I have just said, it is not a question of competence. Who, then, competent or not, ought to make such choices or give advice on them? The only defensible answer, I believe, is the political officials, elected or appointed (aside, of course, from some very few weighings and choices that citizens might make directly). My claim, that the job is theirs, rests less on their demonstration of competence than on the argument that, again, competence is not the issue. The question is, who is to make a choice that cannot be justified as correct or as competent but that nevertheless must be made?

In short, there is a place for knowledge, on one hand, and for commitment or choice, on the other, in the making of public policy. The two aspects should not be confused; and professional social inquiry should not confuse the two.

Not so fast, you may respond. This principle—the dispassionate pursuit of the public interest—does not propose that social researchers usurp a political function. They only *advise* the decision maker on how to weigh the interests of one group against another. It remains for the decision maker, who is an elected or appointed public official, to accept or reject the advice. True enough. My point, however, is that the professional researchers or social scientists have no special competence even to advise on the reconciliation of interests in conflict. Whether one group should prevail over, or be asked to give way to, another is not something on which he has knowledge—and knowledge is all he has to offer professionally. Again, one cannot *know* what is to be done in such a situation. What is required is an act of choice, commitment, or will.

Give the researcher or analyst, then, tasks more suited to his special training and abilities. What might they be? Before I suggest an answer, note an additional particular damage the professional researchers do in their attempts to hold to the principle of nonpartisan pursuit of the public interest.

According to Jefferson, Lincoln, Jesus, and Plato, among others, one major legitimate interest in every society, often limited, however, to no more than a small number of people, is an interest in either gradual or rapid transformation of the society—an interest in drastic, radical change. However, a dispassionate policy analyst or researcher cannot weigh that interest heavily. Nor can he weigh heavily any sharply dissenting small-group interest, one that seems bizarre, out of touch, or utopian to the great mass of people in society. His version of the public interest must always—if it is to be accepted as relevant—hold closer to conventional values and conventional weights among them.

Now this tendency for the public interest to be defined around conventional positions offers some advantages to the society. It means that social researchers, because their versions are all very similar, can talk easily with each other; and in turn they can talk easily to political leaders, who in turn can talk easily with each other. They all find that their thinking is very much alike. In addition, their easy agreements may make a contribution to political stability.

However, another result is that dissident interests are disproportionately deprived of the services of social scientists and researchers. When Eugene Debs and Norman Thomas dissented to advocate old-age pensions and other forms of social security in the late nineteenth and early twentieth centuries, social scientists disregarded them—they were socialists, and hence irrelevant to American public affairs. If someone had listened to them, we might not have been among the last industrial nations to design and inaugurate such programs, recognized today as essential in a humane society. Because dissidents, however irrelevant on the average, are an indispensable source of our future, they, above all, might be argued to need helpful professional social analysis.

At this point, I offer a replacement for the first principle. It is a principle that excuses the professional social researcher from tasks in reconciling conflict that go beyond his competence and that will also attend to the need to bring social research to the innovating points in society.

Scratch the principle of the impartial pursuit of the public interest. Put in its place the principle of thoughtful partisanship. (But let me explain the concept of partisanship before you let your possible hostility to partisanship distort the concept.) I mean by a partisan social scientist or researcher one who acknowledges that his work is guided by a selection of some among other possible interests and values; who, so far as feasible, reveals his selection; who makes no claims that his values or interests are good for everyone; who, in other words, acknowledges that they are to a degree injurious to some people; and who believes that it is impossible for him to do otherwise without deceiving himself and those who use his work. I do not mean someone who lies, conceals evidence, or violates conventional standards of scientific integrity except as just stated.

Among a number of reasons for recommending partisanship to all social scientists and researchers, the first is that everyone is in fact a partisan, whether he knows it or not. Obviously, a member of the National Rifle Association is. So also is a member of Common Cause of the League of Women Voters. I do not call them partisans because they are narrow minded, bigoted, ignorant, or opinionated, which they may or may not be. They are partisans because they wish to advance certain values over others, and thus the interests and preferences of some people over those of others. And my point is that everyone does so.

Like any president, President Eisenhower recognized an obligation to pursue the public interest and to respond to all legitimate interests, needs, and values in society. He went further than most presidents in a deliberate effort to "stay above the fray," to rise, or appear to rise, above party partisanship. But he could not avoid taking sides, no more than anyone else can. For example, he had at some point to stand for those monetary and fiscal policies that would respond to the interests of the unemployed, or those that would respond to the interest of employed and propertied groups that feared inflation. In doing so, he became, as we all do, a partisan: *for* some values, interests, and groups; *against* others.

Highly educated people who find their political antecedents in the Enlightenment and in the English liberal tradition, often deplore what they see as the narrowness of partisanship of benighted persons who appear to fasten on some single issue, like guns, abortion, or godlessness. But these allegedly single-issue partisans usually, in fact, take a broad view of values and interests. Passionate members of the National Rifle Association, for example, endorse a complex set of interlocked values, embracing guns, to be sure, but also personal independence, civil liberty, family autonomy, and patriotism. They are committed to a complex ideology or political philosophy. The same can be said for most or all of the other allegedly narrow partisan groups. They are not necessarily any more narrow in their partisanship than highly educated persons who fasten on the environmental issue or agitate for an equal rights amendment (for supporting evidence, see Tesh, 1983).

What I am proposing, then, is not that we neglect the public interest, but that we recognize that our versions of it are partisan, and that we give up any pretense of appearance of speaking from Olympus, or as neutrals, or as representing a nonpartisan integration of interests that is for the good of all and injurious to none.

Where are examples of social scientists who are thoroughly partisan, openly and honestly so? They are almost all Marxists who confess a commitment to the working class and acknowledge that their preferred policies would be injurious to propertied groups in society. Among mainstream social scientists and social researchers are many who are often called partisan—Milton Friedman, for example. But almost all of them, Friedman included, see themselves as nonpartisan, as speaking for everyone's best interests. If my argument is correct, they are deceiving themselves, and, if we believe them, they are also deceiving us. They are also distorting their research. If there are many partisan non-Marxist social scientists and social researchers who are trying to follow such a prescription as mine for thoughtfully acknowledged partisanship, not many of them have yet come out of the closet.[4]

One benefit of acknowledged partisanship is that it would free professionals to work for the full variety of groups who have legitimate interests in policy, including dissident groups. So long as professionals hide behind a myth of nonpartisanship, they can bring their analytic services to government agencies without losing their reputations for scholarly integrity and excellence, but they cannot do so either for the National Rifle Association or for the dissident or radical groups on which our future depends, just as they could not do so for Eugene Debs. They can return to the view that the purpose of new knowledge in all fields is subversion.

We sometimes characterize democracy, in Lord Bryce's phrase, as government by discussion. What is the character of that discussion? Theorists sometimes idealize it as a cooperative search for solutions in the light of agreed values (see, for example, Knight, 1947: 185, 190). But how does discussion actually proceed—face-to-face, through political negotiation, or through publications—when people are in conflict, as we have been arguing is always an element in public policymaking? The basic form, or paradigm, of discussion is this: You try to persuade me that the policies you want (because you think they suit your values) would in fact also suit my values. You, as a partisan, appeal to my partisan values. That is about as far as discussion can go.

Democratic political discussion is overwhelmingly partisan discussion. Its effectiveness lies in the frequency with which it turns out that your partisan values and mine, though different, can both be satisfied by one and the same policy. If social science and social research are to be made more fully helpful to public policy, they must enter into that partisan discussion, rather than obscure it with a pretence of neutrality. The potential quality of partisan analysis is illustrated by *The Federalist Papers*, designed to make the case for the new Constitution, and today still a magnificent piece of political analysis.

I can put this line of argument into even more familiar context. Many thoughtful people in liberal societies like ours have long celebrated the virtues of a competition of ideas for guiding social change. Accordingly, they have protected and even stimulated a diversity of groups, each encouraged to defend and advance values precious to it. They have claimed that the outcome of civilized contention among such groups, each bringing some special insight to public affairs, would be better for us than the solutions to our problems that would be proposed by a political, even if also intellectual, elite. All liberal democratic states have been greatly influenced by this line of thought, which bears the name of pluralism.

In the last two decades, pluralist thought has been heavily attacked, and with success. However, the main criticism has not been that pluralist diversity is not a good thing, but that the liberal democratic states have not sufficiently practiced it.[5] Central tendencies in politics, such as a dominant ideology, and interests in protecting the *status quo*, overwhelm the touted diversity. The competition of ideas is rigged.

In social research, the principle of nonpartisan pursuit of the public interest is one of the betrayals of pluralism. For reasons I have explained, it puts the influence of social science and research at the service of central, conventional, established interests and values. It sabotages a competition of ideas. It starves the growing or innovating points of desirable social change. By contrast, the principle of partisanship moves in the direction of allying social research with a still unrealized pluralist aspiration.

Perhaps one reason that professional analysts have betrayed pluralism with their principle of nonpartisan pursuit of the public interest is that they took their training not amidst the competition of ideas in politics, but through term papers and dissertations. Their trainers, having been mistrained by their trainers, oblige them to pretend to a role of neutrality to treat problems as though solutions could be *known*. To believe that a solution to a problem calls at some point not for further knowledge, but for a partisan commitment or act of will, would require that many term papers and dissertations be left unfinished.

A similar misconception of what social problem solving is all about persists in professional life in the myth or pedagogic assumption that there exists for each problem "the decision maker" to whom the professional brings advice. "Our perspective is that of a unitary decision maker," say the authors (Stokey and Zeckhauser, 1978: 23) of a leading text in policy analysis. The palpable fact about politics, however, is that there is no single "decision maker." There are many, and they are always to some degree in conflict—all partisans. The professional analyst feeds what he has to say into the process through one or more of these multiple conflicting participants in problem solving, either by serving on his staff, or by consultation with some participants, or by writing books, articles, and reports that directly or indirectly reach the mind of a participant.

If pluralism flourished, the results would be that every participant in policymaking could call on professional help in finding solutions consistent with his or her values, and on professional help in reconsidering them. In partisan contention with each other, the considerations and arguments advanced by one partisan, or by his partisan researcher, would be challenged by others. No one would labor under the misapprehension that any participant or any professional researcher had come close to grasping the whole truth or had spoken on behalf of everyone's values.

The competition of ideas I am describing, which many social researchers betray, is often described by the betrayers in such words as these from Wilson (1978: 92) when he described one common form of it.

> When [organizations] use social science at all, it will be on an ad hoc, improvised, quick-and-dirty basis. A key official, needing to take a position, respond to a crisis, or support a view that is under challenge, will ask an assistant to 'get me some facts.' . . . Social science is used as ammunition, not as a method, and the official's opponents will also use similar ammunition.

And, then, he comes to his punch line. He says, "There will be many shots fired, but few casualties except the truth" (Wilson, 1978: 92).

His generalization is false. I find it hard to understand what he would like in the place of the competition of ideas he has characterized with hostility. Of course, social research has to be tied to positions, and naturally it is ammunition. However, it is through the resulting challenge and counterchallenge that usable truth often emerges; and as imperfect as the process is, there is no feasible alternative for reaching an approximation to truth for social problem solving.

We have more to fear by an inadequate or rigged competition such as we now practice than by an excess of challenge and counterchallenge among informed advocates of competing values and interests.

Do I hear a voice anxiously asking, "If partisans abound, who will look after the common interest?" The answer is that, if there are genuinely *common* interests, they are the shared interests of *all* partisans, all of whom will consequently pursue them. If they are hidden, the possibility of discovering them lies in interchange among partisans, each of whom is motivated to find common ground in order to turn adversaries into allies. The more important answer to the anxious question is that, as already noted, partisans tend to develop alternative versions of the public interest, rather than ignore it. That is often the best a society can do: acknowledge conflicting versions and work out—politically, not analytically—a resolution.

Or, do you now ask: "If there are, as always, conflicting partisan versions of the public good, how do we resolve the conflict?" We all know the answer, even if theorists on policy analysis sometimes seem to forget it in their desire to find an excessively large role for analysis in the resolution. Usually, the outcome is not analyzed and decided upon, *for beyond some point it is not analyzable*, as we have seen. Instead, it is brought about by political acts, or some other form of action or interaction, not analysis. Some outcomes are decided by voting, some by negotiation, some by other forms of mutual influence of partisans on each other.

Remembering this helps us understand that research and analysis can at best be no more than a part of social problem solving, and that the shortcomings to be feared from partisan analysis are really inevitable limitations on any and every attempt to reach an outcome through research and analysis.

Research for Officials and Other Decision Makers

Let us now look into the third principle, skipping the second for the moment. The third is that research intended to help public policy usually should be designed to meet the needs of government officials and other key decision makers. Who else?

Who else? How about you and me?—millions of us, all of us, "we, the people." In a democracy, as in all other forms of government, officials are the immediate or proximate decision makers. But in a democracy, they make decisions within constraints, even if loose ones, laid down by public opinion. And to a degree at least, they respond to popular agitation. Ranges of possible policy choices are walled off by certain public rejection, and cannot be attempted by political leaders even if they were innovative enough to offer them.

So who most needs the type of enlightenment on social problems that research and social science can sometimes offer: leaders or ordinary citizens? It is not at all clear. By what argument has the research community come to fasten on leadership as its audience? By no argument at all. By thoughtless habit and the simple assumption that leaders are more worth talking to than the mass. One might suggest that the issue itself makes a good public policy question.

Because the question is large and endlessly complex, I shall have to be highly selective and inconclusive. I shall go only so far as to develop one line of argument: that the ordinary citizen's need for help from social science and social research is enormous and that great gains are to be had from a drastic redirection of social science and policy research to meet that need. That would be enough to destroy the third principle.

My argument will be roundabout. It will strike some of you as odd, and on that count alone you will be suspicious of it. It will irritate, perhaps enrage, some of you. But I believe it is of the greatest consequence; and I ask you to take it home with you, mull it over, and oblige youself not to reject it without good reason. I am audacious enough at this point to estimate that you will not find a good reason.

The argument that ordinary citizens need much more help from social science and research turns on the phenomenon of widespread social agreement on many big political and economic issues. For example, Americans widely agree, although not unanimously, on the merits of the American Constitution, on a presidential rather than parliamentary system, on private enterprise, on loyalty to country, on family solidarity, on improving one's condition through personal responsibility rather than changing the structure of society, on cooperation or going along rather than criticizing or agitation, and on playing the game instead of complaining "foul!"[6]

Most of us prize that agreement. It seems to make for social stability and social cooperation. Anthropologists tell us that without agreement on some fundamentals, a group of people cannot live peaceably together, and cannot constitute a society (Linton, 1936). In political science, it is frequently argued—in the words of Brzezinski and Huntington (1965: 5)—that "a political system is effective to the extent that the history behind it has brought about an underlying consensus." And it is often taken as not needing supporting argument that democracy can exist only when such agreement exists, for only then are disputes small enough that losers are willing to bear their losses rather than subvert the government in order to dominate their adversaries.

But set aside the question of whether agreement is desirable. I want to ask you to put a question to yourself: how does such agreement come about? Prize it or not, how do you *explain* it?

For agreement on many kinds of belief, explanation is easy—beliefs, for example, that the world is round, that battered children are often the children of parents battered in their childhood, or that some judges take bribes and some do not. We agree on many issues because we know. We have evidence. Competent people have inquired into the issue and found grounds for one belief rather than a diversity of them. Knowledge is a great source of agreement.

But we do not *know*, we only believe that the U.S. Constitution is superior to other written constitutions, that private enterprise is best for us, that a parliamentary system would not suit us, that loyalty to country is better than a more cosmopolitan loyalty to humankind, and so on. No one can know that these beliefs are correct; sufficient evidence is not available. Moreover—now consider this—those who inquire most deeply into these complex issues disagree more than do those who do not inquire. That is to say, knowledge on these issues creates diversity of belief rather than agreement.

"But," some of you may reply, "I know that ours is a superb constitution." My reply is that I can find at least a few persons as informed and thoughtful as you who believe that they know it is not. You believe that you know, but the fact that other equally qualified people believe that they know otherwise tells us that none of you know; you only fervently and confidently believe.

That leaves us in a quandary. Why do so many Americans venerate the Constitution, free enterprise, the family, patriotism, and the like? There is plenty of room for disagreement; and, to repeat, the more knowledgeable the person, the more likely he or she is to disagree. How, then, to repeat any question, can we explain widespread social agreement on these fundamental values? Would we not expect a great variety of minds, so complex are these questions, and so inconclusive our information, to come to a variety of conclusions?

Not at all, you reply? You will say that tradition passes down agreed beliefs from generation to generation. If you take that position, you must ask why tradition passes down agreement instead of a variety of beliefs. *Tradition* is a word referring to transfer from generation to generation; but family, school, and religious traditions can, and on some issues do, transfer a diversity, not a homogeneity.

Look at it another way. If you believe that one generation's homogeneity is sufficient to explain the next generation's, how do you explain the earlier generation's? Somehow, somewhere along the line, a possible diversity was converted into agreement. For example, somewhere the idea of the democratic nation state, once an entirely new idea to most people, and then an issue of controversy, came gradually to mark a point of at least rhetorical consensus in many Western societies. How did that agreement first come about, the agreement that tradition now passes on? We need an explanation.

I can find no possible explanation of why people agree on complex issues on which the absence of sufficient knowledge leaves room for thoughtful diversity of belief except for one. It is that we have thoughtlessly accepted an indoctrination. Our agreement is the result of not exercising our critical faculties. Had we exercised them, we would disagree much more than we do.

We are an insufficiently thoughtful, careless body of citizens. We fasten on formulas. We do not explore the variety of possibilities to which we might turn to solve our problems. We are mired in conventional thought, restricted to a narrow range of possibilities. The evidence that all this is true is, again, that we agree on matters on which critical thought could not possibly agree. And even if the Constitution is superb, and the private enterprise system is superior to all others, because we cannot—at least not yet—*know* either to be true, then agreeing that either is true is evidence of our thoughtlessness. For, again, in that we lack sufficient evidence to constitute knowledge, our critical faculties would produce diversity of belief among us on such issues.

In most of the world, and in all of Western Europe, small ruling groups long ago organized the rest of mankind so as to maintain social order, to organize production, and to develop various forms of exploitation. As far back as we can trace our social origins, we consequently find small dominant groups teaching obedience, loyalty, faith, respect for authority, and, thus, respect for wealth and property, political quiescence, inequality—and, over and over again, veneration for existing political and economic institutions.[7] In the Middle Ages, lord and priest taught these lessons. In more recent times, earlier agreements are modified, but nevertheless perpetuated—no longer through feudal authority, but through the influence of property and wealth.

Patterns of belief in obedience, authority, deference to wealth, veneration for existing institutions, inequality and the like having been established, they are now easily maintained through many channels of indoctrination: the public schools, for example. Parents themselves do much of the work of indoctrination, especially working-class parents who stress obedience and docility over critical independence of thought (Hess and Torney, 1967). And, of course, we are flooded with corporate communications that explicitly and implicitly teach the virtues of private enterprise, the Constitution, and our other fundamental institutions. So great is the disproportion of business-oriented communication—for no other group has even a fraction of the funds available to business for indoctrination—that the ordinary citizen is crippled in his ability to think clearly about public policy. Most ordinary citizens in the United States, for example, cannot even distinguish between political democracy and private enterprise, so often have the two been treated as identical in commercial, public school, and other indoctrinations. Even a recent president of Harvard appeared to suffer from the same difficulty when, in replying to critics of his economics department, he assured them that his economics faculty supported the American way of life, for—he said—they are all trying to make the private enterprise system continue to work (Pusey, 1963: 171).

My conclusion, then, is that the existence of social agreement on many complex issues on which free minds would be expected to disagree is itself sufficient evidence that the minds of ordinary citizens are greatly impaired and are in desperate need of help from social science and social research for solving their problems. The great body of citizens in the democracies—to say nothing of less liberated citizens elsewhere—have hardly begun to explore the possibilities for solving their problems, thus for improving their prospects.

The impairment, of course, afflicts our political leaders as well as the whole citizenry. But what is required to right it is not policy analysis directed largely to the special needs of political leadership, but analysis that constitutes an education and an enlightenment and liberation for leader and citizen alike.

What Does the Citizen Need?

Social science has given so little attention to the informational and analytic needs of the ordinary citizen that precisely what he needs has not yet been clarified. Sometimes the citizen is dismissed as a largely passive participant in politics—it is pointed out, for example, that only a few citizens ever go to political meetings or write their representatives (Verba and Nie, 1972: 31). Producing knowledge for the ordinary citizen, then, appears to be a waste of time and effort. That knowledge of the right kind, in the right channels at the right time, might turn him into an active citizen is not much speculated about, except for some political leaders and social scientists, like those on the Trilateral Commission Task Force on the Governability of Democracy, who seem to prefer to keep him passive.[8]

Perhaps one reason for neglecting the citizen's need for information is that many of us picture democratic politics as a process in which political leaders do all the work. And just what is the work to be done? It is to discover or invent policies that will respond to citizen preferences. All the citizen has to do is to reveal those preferences. The search for what the preferences are, of course, might itself be made a task for social research. If so, it could be turned over to political leadership to commission and use the research. But, fearful of letting anyone but the citizen himself say what his preferences are, most of us have apparently taken the position that the best authority on what A's preferences are is A himself. And he needs to research help: On reflection he knows what he wants, not perfectly, but well enough.

Where did the notion come from that a citizen can know what he wants in politics by simple reflection and without any helpful study? In social science circles, it comes, I suggest, from economic theory, in which the concept of preferences is a workhorse. It has been easy for political scientists to give political preferences the same formulation and role in political analysis as in economic analysis. Thus, the citizen's preference for private enterprise, or for the constitution, is treated like his preference for bananas: "I like what I like, and I know what I like. My preferences do not require study."

I find it impossible to describe this state of affairs in social science without finding it ludicrous. The attitude toward the Constitution is not at all like the taste for bananas. The preference for most goods and services is fairly simply constructed in the mind. You either like or do not like vanilla, either because you were built that way or because you have been reared in a vanilla-appreciating society. Whether you like vanilla or not is a fairly simple fact, it is not a moral choice. It is relatively independent of other preferences, and does not require prolonged investigation of consequences or implications.

For some more complicated market preferences, and for all political choices, the economist's concept of preferences is wildly inappropriate. Do you have a *preference* for a constitutional prohibition of abortion? It is a silly question. Making up your mind on abortion issues calls up a variety of tasks. You must grapple empirically with questions of fact, ranging from facts about the reproductive process to facts about the feasibility of administering any public policy. With moral or ethical questions, facts range from those on life itself to those pertaining to the rights of your fellow citizens. You also grapple with prudential questions: questions, for example, about practical rules for social cooperation and decision.

Your position on abortion, then, is no preference. Nor is it anything to be discovered. It is not a fact that you must ascertain. It is something you make, form, or create. Whatever thinking you do culminates not in a fact about you that is disclosed, but in a commitment upon which you decide by your choice, to some degree considered. It is a volition, far removed from what we call preference. Indeed you may—and often do—form a volition for an outcome, or policy, that at the simpler level of preferences you do not prefer. "I don't like what I have to do, but I think I ought," is familiar to us all.[9]

If, rather than uncovering preferences, citizens are engaged in the construction of volitions, then they need helpful empirical, prudential, and moral analysis, and must themselves engage in it through discussion. In instructing and constraining leadership, citizens need such studies as, among others, analyses of the range of possible social institutions and practices, the competences and incompetences of government and of alternative social machinery like the market system, of how to train and organize themselves for political participation, and of the history of constraints on their own habits of thought (a subject hardly touched in contemporary social science).

I do not suggest that all that citizens need is research and social science. The political and interactive part of policymaking is a necessary stimulus toward forming better volitions. To form our volitions, we need the specific experience of political life: discussion, agitation, voting, and the like.

Practical Research and Problem Solutions

In the light of rejection of our first and third principles, let us now look at the second and fourth.

The second prescribed that social research intended to be helpful to public policy be limited to the consideration of feasible policy alternatives, alternatives that fit into existing institutions and politics. If there is any validity to what I have just been saying, that principle has to be rejected as too constraining. It would deny the appropriateness of the very variety of studies I have just described.[10]

In particular, it would continue to turn citizens and leaders alike away from a pivotal question, the neglect of which has already done enough damage. The pivotal question is this: Are there some problem areas for which no satisfactory solutions can be found that are consistent with existing institutions? One of the blindnesses of much contemporary research is its assumption that all problems have solutions within the existing institutional order.

The fourth principle is that analysis close to the decision maker, analysis intended to have relatively immediate application to a decision, should be designed to culminate in a recommendation to a decision maker. That the foregoing analysis, if valid, destroys that principle, too, is perhaps less obvious. Clearly, if the foregoing is valid, citizens need a variety of studies, and only rarely need recommendations about specific solutions to specific problems. Such is also the case for officials and other leaders who, we point out, suffer from the same indoctrinations and impairment of critical faculties. Hence, all need a variety of kinds of analyses. It is striking that empirical studies of what officials say they need from social science often report that they, the officials, say they want no recommendations, but want challenges to their ways of thinking, new orientations of their thought, or enlightenment, rather than social engineering.[11]

If we go back to the beginning of the discussion on partisanship, we find still another reason for rejecting the fourth principle. If it is correct that social researchers go beyond their capacity in proposing resolutions of conflicts of interest and values, and if that resolution is a political rather than scholarly task, calling not finally for knowledge, but for a commitment or act of will, then social researchers should usually not be called on for recommendations. As for officials, they should ask researchers for critical facts and pieces of analysis that will enable political leadership to perform its task of conflict resolution. Faced with an urgent choice to be made, political leadership needs—depending on the situation—one or more of many specialized contributions available from social research. The political official may need a missing fact; or a sustained piece of analyis on interconnections he has not been able to work out in his mind; or a challenge to a conclusion tentatively reached on which he feels vulnerable; a hypothesis to stimulate his thinking; or a checklist of variables that he must take into account; or an array of possible solutions.

An example. Years ago in India, while working for the Agency for International Development, I encountered a situation that I still remember vividly. Indian officials had reached a tentative conclusion that to increase foodgrain production it would be necessary to guarantee farmers a minimum price to be announced before planting, so that farmers could be confident that it would be profitable to plant and to use fertilizer, insecticides, and improved seed. Before reaching a final decision, the officials had to answer many questions. For example, in an illiterate rural society, could they get the announcement of the program and the promised minimum price communicated to the farmers? Would the farmers believe the promise? If, in the coming harvest season, foodgrain prices threatened to fall below the announced minimum, could the civil service get grain purchasers out in the field to buy up the grain at the minimum?

The Indian officials asked for some research help from the American aid mission. They did not ask, however, for a recommendation from researchers in the mission, from their own researchers, or from any other researchers. Nor did they even ask for research help on whether they could make an announcement effective, whether farmers would believe, or whether the government could actually make millions of purchases in the field if necessary. On each of many such questions, they knew that good enough research could not be conducted in the time available. Moreover, they thought—correctly, I would guess—that their political and administrative judgment on answers to these questions was more competent than research was likely to be.

But one remaining question troubled them: whether farmers would plant the same regardless of their price expectations or would respond to price. On this they thought—correctly—that some research had been done; and they wanted its results. They got the results—findings that price mattered to farmers. Answering their other questions favorably, they went ahead with their program. Social research had been of great help because it had been focussed on a specific critical need, not because it had made any recommendation. In another situation, the critical need might have been entirely different; but critical need, rather than recommendation, was the key to useful social research. It was, and it is.

* * * *

I can recapitulate the analysis in a few words about the four principles with which I began.

(1) Instead of the pursuit of the public interest, partisanship.
(2) Instead of a preoccupation with feasible solutions, a variety of studies to free the mind from its impairments.
(3) Instead of serving the needs of officials alone, help for the ordinary citizen.
(4) Instead of recommendations, a tailoring of research to meet varying specific critical needs.

Notes

1. See Howe (1972: 164 ff.). As Galbraith (1978) argues it, power is shifting to people with knowledge, experience, and talent who are found together in organizations.

2. This is discussed in Gregg (1976). Nine of the authors comment on this principle—eight endorse it; only one questions it.

3. Leaving aside the very long run, most analysts and social researchers, of course, acknowledge that policies typically help some groups and hurt others. My point is that they are not competent to go on to find, invent, or propose a resolution of that conflict, as though there existed some intellectual ground for sacrificing one group's interests to another's and as though they as analysts possessed some *professional* competence to make such judgments. When agreed rules for resolution are absent, in the face of gains to some at the expense of other groups, social scientists, researchers, and analysts reach the limit of their competence (if not before).

4. One reasonable interpretation of Marxist thought is that it is partisan in the short and middle run but is directed by a concern for the good of all, with injury to none, in a distant classless and harmonious future. And many non-Marxists may regard their appearances of partisanship as illusory, for they, too, pursue a distant good for all. To this attempt to turn partisans into nonpartisans, I would offer two replies. First, no social scientist or researcher can tightly derive short-run and the middle-run interim steps from a model of a far distant, wholly harmonious society; instead he must take some partisan positions for the interim, positions that cannot be defended by reference to the distant future. Second, that there exists a model of society in the distant future in which gains impose no losses on anyone is not persuasively argued, even by Marxists.

5. For a summary of criticism, see Connolly (1969).

6. An insightful review and comment on the character of political agreement and disagreement is Mann (1970).

7. Among many other sources, see Rustow (1980).

8. See Crozier et al. (1975), especially, for example, their introduction.

9. A related argument: "Although preferences are important for the understanding of welfare, their proper place in the scheme of things must not be exaggerated, as a not inconsiderable sector of modern economics has been inclined to do. . . . the road from preference to welfare is too long and winding. A man's welfare may, indeed standardly does, bear *some* relationship to his preferences, but that does not result in their mutual assimilation. Preference is too gross an instrument to capture the subtle nuances of welfare. If Jones prefers apples to oranges—be it in general or in point of, say, appearance or flavor—this does not go far to indicate what his welfare consists in. Welfare is a thing of stability and solidity; preferences can be things of the fleeting moment, and indeed things that fly in the face of consciously reckoned benefits" (Rescher, 1976: 36-37).

10. There is a good deal of discontent with "practical" studies. For example, "The amount of really useful [research in support of] analysis relevant to major defense decisions has been limited . . . [w]hile hundreds or possibly thousands of studies are turned out each year, few of them are of any real use for decisions at the Secretary of Defense level. . . . This is not necessarily a criticism of the individuals participating in these studies, many of whom are highly capable. Nor do we believe that the problems addressed by these studies are so complex that they can never be understood. In part the problem stems in our judgment from the fact that nearly all such studies are oriented to near term program

decisions. Few, if any, ever attempt any 'basic research' on underlying areas where data and knowledge are lacking."

The quotation is from a highly experienced analyst, Alain Enthoven, in Williams (1971: 57).

11. See, for example, Weiss (1977). Other interesting evidence comes from a study of education policymaking in Sweden, where the frequent use of study commissions (assisted by researchers) to develop policy recommendations would seem to imply the use of researchers for just that specific purpose. Their actual usefulness to the commissions is of a different kind, closer to "enlightenment." See Prefors (1982: 15-96).

References

BELL, D. (1972) "Labor in the post-industrial society," in I. Howe (ed.) The World of the Blue-Collar Worker. New York: Quadrangle.

BRZEZINSKI, Z. and S. P. HUNTINGTON (1965) Political Power: USA/USSR. New York: Viking.

CONNOLLY, W. E. (1969) "The challenge to pluralist theory," in W. E. Connolly (ed.) The Bias of Pluralism. New York: Atherton.

CROZIER, M., S. P. HUNTINGTON, and J. WATANUKI (1975) The Crisis of Democracy New York. New York Univ. Press.

GALBRAITH, J. K. (1978) The New Industrial State. Boston: Houghton Mifflin.

GRAHAM, G. J., Jr. and S. G. GRAHAM (1976) "Evaluating Drift in Policy Systems," in P. M. Gregg (ed.) Problems of Theory in Policy Analysis. Lexington, MA: Lexington.

GREGG, P. M. [ed] (1976) Problems of Theory in Policy Analysis. Lexington, MA: D. C. Heath.

HESS, R. D. and J. V. TORNEY (1967) The Development of Political Attitudes in Children. Chicago: Aldine.

KNIGHT, F. (1947) Freedom and Reform. New York: Harper and Brothers.

LINTON, R. (1936) The Study of Man. New York: Appleton-Century-Crofts.

LYNN, L. E. [ed] (1978) Knowledge and Policy. Washington, DC: National Academy of Sciences.

MANN, M. (1970) "The social cohesion of liberal democracy." Amer. Soc. Rev. 35 (June).

PREFORS, R. (1982) "Research and policy-making in Swedish higher education." University of Stockholm Group for the Study of Higher Education and Research Policy, report 24.

PUSEY, N. M. (1963) The Age of the Scholar. Cambridge, MA: Harvard Univ. Press.

RESCHER, N. (1976) "The role of values in social science research," in C. Frankel (ed.) Controversies and Decisions. New York: Russell Sage Foundation.

RUSTOW, A. (1980) Freedom and Domination. Princeton, NJ: Princeton Univ. Press.

STOKEY, E. and ZECKHAUSER (1978) A Primer for Policy Analysis. New York: Norton.

TESH, S. (1983) "Upholding principles: a note in support of 'single' issue politics." Yale University Institution for Social and Policy Studies, working paper no. CHS-54.

VERBA, S. and N. H. NIE (1972) Participation in America. New York: Harper and Row.
WEISS, C. H. (1977) "Research for policy's sake: the enlightenment function of social research." Policy Analysis 3 (Fall).
WILLIAMS, W. (1971) Social Policy Research and Analysis. New York: American Elsevier Publishing Company.
WILSON, J. Q. (1978) "Social science and public policy," in L. E. Lynn (ed.) Knowledge and Policy. Washington, DC: National Academy of Sciences.

CHARLES E. LINDBLOM is Professor of Political Science and Economics at Yale University. Among his many well-known books are The Policy-Making Process *(1980) and* Usable Knowledge: Social Science and Social Problem Solving *(1979), cowritten with David K. Cohen.*

9

Why the Compensatory Education Evaluation was Useful

Laura C. Leviton and Robert F. Boruch

A common belief is that program evaluations are seldom incorporated into law or public management decisions.[1] Our recent work suggests this is not true for the federal education sector. A notable example is the Compensatory Education Study done by the National Institute of Education. In Volume 2, Number 2 of *JPAM*, Walter J. Jones analyzed why this study was used by Congress: He emphasizes that it is essential for evaluators to pay attention to variables that are politically relevant.[2]

We think there is even more to be learned. Jones' article briefly indicated that the evaluation was useful: In this note we list the specific ways in which the study was used. These specifics shed additional light on when and how evaluators can make an impact.[3]

We define "use" of evaluations as serious consideration of findings in debates about policy or programs.[4] Some readers may doubt that citations of the National Institute of Education study, numerous as they are throughout the House and Senate reports, were necessarily valued by the Congress for their informational, as opposed to rhetorical, content. Obviously, both are important, and using evaluations to support a political position is entirely legitimate. On the value of the information, we have only indirect evidence: the fact that hearings were organized around the reports, the statements of virtually all participants and observers, and the following excerpts from the House and Senate reports:

> The Committee has found the quality of research by NIE to be excellent and has consequently relied upon these reports in formulating Amendments to Title I.[5]
>
> The Committee wishes to commend the National Institute of Education for the uniformly high quality of its study, as well as its timeliness, as it proved invaluable to the committee in the formulation of the Education Amendments of 1978.[6]

History and Nature of the Study The National Institute of Education was mandated by Congress under Public Law 93-380, the Education Amendments of 1974, to examine the current operation of Title I of the Elementary and Secondary Education Act, and the probable effects of change in Title I legislation. Title I is the major source of compensatory education funding at the federal level. Dr. Paul Hill directed the study with the administrative support of the National Institute of Education.[7] The mandate of the Institute was unusual in that Congress took explicit priority over the administration as the

From Laura C. Leviton and Robert F. Boruch, "Why the Compensatory Education Evaluation was Useful," *Journal of Policy Analysis and Management*, Vol. 3, pp. 299-305. Copyright © 1984 by the Association for Public Policy Analysis and Management. Reprinted by permission of John Wiley & Sons, Inc.

major client of the evaluation. Moreover, Congress required reports in time for reauthorization hearings three years later. According to Hill, the Institute was "struggling for its life after a series of devastating reverses dealt by the Senate Appropriations Committee."[8] This facilitated the creation of a special unit within the Institute to report directly to Congress without prior clearance by the Department of Health, Education, and Welfare.

After extensive consultation with congressional staff and many interest groups, the study staff translated the broad mandate given by Congress into six major topics on which to focus their reports.[9] All those interviewed mentioned that even-handedness in the formulation of questions was essential to the success of the study. It was especially important since the chairman and the ranking minority member of the House subcommittee overseeing Title I had strongly differing views on the question of eligibility. The authors of the study elected not to make specific recommendations on every point. It was too easy to become embroiled in the eligibility problem. Instead, they presented options to Congress and described the likely consequences of acting on those options. In this way, they married evaluation and policy analysis.

The study staff continued to consult with congressional aides throughout the research. The reports were presented weeks before hearings began, giving aides and members a chance to digest the findings before they dealt with a deluge of other information. One result was that the hearings took their form directly from the topics of the different reports. The reports were relatively simple and clearly written, a synthesis of 35 original projects. After the hearings, the Congress requested the study group to analyze the Title I law in light of their reports, to identify ambiguities, and to develop model legislation to embody proposed changes. The National Institute of Education contracted with the Lawyer's Committee for Civil Rights Under Law to translate the findings into legislative language that Congress could use.

To summarize the climate of the study, Congress demanded credible information within three years from an agency which many members of Congress felt was of little value. Under a vague mandate the study staff had to tease out the issues and findings of interest. This appears to be true of many congressionally mandated studies in many policy sectors. Local evaluators and policy analysts also face this situation. Policy researchers should therefore be interested in the success of Dr. Hill's strategy, as analyzed in Jones' article and as further documented here.

Uses of the Study   *Reauthorization and funding of Title I.* The reports of both the House and Senate committees acknowledged the study's findings that Title I services were delivered to appropriate children and that the program, *when stable and well implemented,* enhanced student achievement.[10] According to the House report, "All these findings can be contrasted with earlier studies which showed that disadvantaged students fall more and more behind in their achievement levels."[11] Thus, the study appears to have challenged the belief, created by previous studies, that Title I did not increase achievement.[12] New information that Title I appeared to be effective gave the committee an argument for reauthorization and increased funding of Title I.

Some researchers have claimed that evaluations of outcome or impact are of little use or interest to policymakers.[13] This was not the case for the study, although its use certainly involved a measure of rhetoric. The doubts that past studies raised about effectiveness had to be dealt with in some way. Pressures on the budget were beginning to pinch, and the administration had suggested some severe changes in the program. Democrats knew they had to improve the program or they might eventually lose it. The study's positive findings helped beat back the more drastic proposals, while its caveat "when the programs are stable and well-implemented," opened the door to important administrative and legal changes.

Clarifying legal authority and enforcement. Both the House and Senate reports cited the study's conclusion that Title I was generally well administered at the federal level. However, the reports also frequently cited the study's findings of troublesome variations in state and local administration. According to the study these were due to vague regulations and inconsistent enforcement by the Office of Education.

The study noted that the Office of Education had no coherent guide to legal interpretation of Title I: So Congress required the Office to publish a policy manual for use by states and school districts.[14] Regulations, according to the study, were especially vague about requirements that schools not substitute Title I funds for local funds: So Congress directed the Office to publish tests of compliance and legal models of funds administration. The study concluded that an amendment was needed to require districts to give Title I children their fair share of locally funded services: As a result, a House amendment encouraged such sharing.[15] The study concluded too that regulations were vague concerning exemptions from requirements on excess costs and comparability of locally funded services, whereupon a new exemption was created for state programs being phased in, and a new provision required the Office of Education or the states to determine exemptions in advance.[16]

The study concluded that the Office had a poor record on audits. Citing the study, the committee reports proposed amendments requiring the HEW Inspector General to audit grantees regularly (these did not pass). The reports also outlined responsibilities of the Office of Education for auditing and required these to be described in regulations. The law was amended to require the Office to report to Congress on audits once a year.[17]

According to the study, states were uncertain about their authority to make rules, provide technical assistance, and monitor compliance. The House clarified this authority, as well as procedures for withholding funds and auditing projects.[18] The Senate cited the study in proposing similar amendments under a new Title V to consolidate state administration of Title I and Title IV.[19] Both houses required the Office of Education to revise regulations in this area and required states to develop monitoring and enforcement plans.[20]

Staffers to whom we spoke noted that Congress had been aware of these administrative problems prior to the study, but in the form of accusations and counteraccusations. The study provided a coherent and objective analysis.

Allocating resources. The study showed difficulties and abuses of the requirement that Title I funds be allocated to counties and then to school districts. Congress amended the law to permit allocation directly to school districts.[21] The study also revealed strong pressures upon school districts to expand Title I to more schools and to allocate funds on the basis of low achievement. Congress cited the study in amending the law to allow districts to allocate funds based on both poverty and low achievement.[22] The study concluded that urban areas had been at a disadvantage under the existing formula for determining Title I grants: Congress changed the formula.[23]

Improved targeting of services. The study reported that fewer than 4% of private school students received service in districts getting Title I funds. The study suggested that they may not have been aware of services or that services may not have been designed for them. Congress cited the study in requiring equal expenditures for eligible children in private schools. Also, the Office of Education was required to use its bypass authority to resolve promptly private schools' complaints.[24] This was another area in which accusations were replaced by quantitative evidence from the study.

The study found fewer than 1% of high school students were served, compared with 20% in elementary school. The reason was that administrators were uncertain about legally acceptable instruction methods in high school. To boost Title I service in high schools, Congress directed the Office of Education to publish legally acceptable models for high school instruction.

Title I funds per participating child were lowest in poor rural districts, according to the study. Congress cited the study in allocating supplemental grants to districts with high concentrations of poor children.[25] The study also found that in such districts, it was difficult to design programs that did not serve all children in a school. House and Senate reports cited the study in permitting programs for whole schools in very poor districts.[26]

Flexibility in local practices. The study expended much effort on exploring the "instructional dimensions" of Title I—the effectiveness of different methods to teach disadvantaged students. One finding was that taking students out of regular classrooms—the "pull out" model—was about as effective as instruction in the regular classroom. Other findings were equally inconclusive. Congress avoided legislating local practices and ordered the Office of Education explicitly to increase flexibility. The study discovered that many school officials believed the Office of Education preferred the "pull out" model. The Office was ordered to describe both "in class" and "pull out" models as acceptable in regulations.[27]

Why Was the Study Successful? Researchers point to several reasons for the study's success. The article by Jones in *JPAM* contrasted the study to the performance of the evaluation office of the Office of Education and concluded that an awareness of the political realities of Title I was essential to the study's success.[28] Hill's memoir makes clear the tremendous importance of timeliness, of consultation with stakeholders, and of constant communication with congressional staffers.[29] One analyst emphasizes Congress' need for factual information and the quality of the evidence the study had to provide.[30] Research is more likely to be used when clients feel "ownership"[31]: The study was designed so the Congress felt this ownership.

But why did members of Congress care about improving the program? And why were they interested in an evaluation? Our interviews and analysis suggest some clues to an answer:

- Most parties concerned with Title I had been around for several congressional cycles. They knew the issues, the accusations, and each other. Most importantly, they "owned" the problems and were interested in their resolution.
- The program was threatened by doubts about efficacy and proposals for drastic change. Democrats agreed with Republicans on the importance of improving operations as essential to the program's future.
- The program was, in the words of a staffer, "mature." Congressional feeling was, "OK, they've had enough time to shape up their act, let's treat them differently now."
- Congressional staff were qualified by training or experience to think about the problem. As one staff member put it, "We trusted each other's professionalism."

Although not usual, these arrangements and tensions are not uncommon in other policy sectors: Congress was playing what has been labeled the "fixer" role in policy implementation by "repairing" or "adjusting the elements . . . so as to lead to a more preferred outcome . . . in accord with the spirit of the original mandate."[32] It may be that evaluation can be useful only when the appropriate conditions open up an opportunity and that, in particular, an opportunity arises when Congress is in its "fixer" mode.

Conclusion The National Institute of Education study, "owned" by Congress and highly competent, was a remarkable success in doing what evaluations should do—inform, identify options, and assay their consequences. Many of its features are desirable in any evaluation—frequent consultation, timeliness, and supplying reliable, politically relevant information.[33] As suggested in a note by Lawrence and Cook in this journal, a far-ranging constituency analysis appears to be helpful, even when program managers are the clients, to refine the questions and head off later accusations of irrelevance and unfairness.[34] But since evaluators are likely to be of use when their input is wanted, an initial question may be the key question: Is there a client who is receptive to an evaluation?

This research was supported by contract #300-79-0467 from the Department of Education to Northwestern University. The authors thank Paul Hill, Launor Carter, Chris Cross, Jack Jennings, and Iris Rotberg.

LAURA C. LEVITON is an assistant professor at the University of Pittsburgh.
ROBERT F. BORUCH is a professor at Northwestern University.

NOTES   1. Patton, M. Q., et al., "In Search of Impact: An Analysis of the Utilization of Federal Health Evaluation Research," in *Using Social Research in Public Policy Making*, Weiss, C. H., Ed. (Lexington, MA: Lexington Books, 1977). Also see Cronbach, L. J., et al., *Toward Reform of Program Evaluation* (San Francisco: Jossey-Bass, 1980); and Guba, E. G., and Lincoln, Y. S., *Effective Evaluation* (San Francisco: Jossey-Bass, 1981).

2. Jones, W. J., "Can Evaluations Influence Programs? The Case of Compensatory Education," *Journal of Policy Analysis and Management, 2* (1983): 174–184.

3. Our methods and evidence are described fully in Leviton, L. C., and Boruch, R. F., "Illustrative Case Studies," in *An Appraisal of Educational Program Evaluations: Federal, State and Local Agencies*, Boruch, R. F., and Cordray, D. S., Eds. (Washington, DC: Department of Education, 1980) (ED 192 446).

4. Cook, T. D., and Pollard, W. E., "Guidelines: How to Recognize and Avoid Some Common Problems of Mis-utilization of Evaluation Research Findings," *Evaluation, 4* (1977): 161–164; and Weiss, C. H., "Improving the Linkage Between Social Research and Public Policy," in *Knowledge and Policy: The Uncertain Connection*, Lynn, L. E., Ed. (Washington, DC: National Research Council, 1978).

5. U.S. House of Representatives, Committee on Education and Labor, *Report: The Education Amendments of 1978, H.R. 15*, 95th Congr., 2nd Sess., Rep. No. 95-1137 (Washington, DC: U.S. GPO, May 11, 1978).

6. U.S. Senate, Committee on Human Resources, *Report: The Education Amendments of 1978, S. 1753*, 95th Congr., 2nd Sess., Rep. No. 95-856 (Washington, DC: U.S. GPO, May 15, 1978).

7. Description of the conduct of the study appears in Hill, P., "Evaluating Education Programs for Federal Policy Makers: Lessons from the NIE Compensatory Education Study," in *Educational Evaluation in the Public Policy Setting*, Pincus, J., Ed. (Santa Monica, CA: Rand Corporation, May, 1980) (R-2502-RC). Reprinted in Rist, R. C., Ed., *Policy Studies Review Annual, 6* (1982): 591–619.

8. *Ibid.*, p. 49.

9. National Institute of Education, *Administration of Compensatory Education* (Washington, DC: NIE, 1977); *Compensatory Education Services* (Washington, DC: NIE, 1977); *Demonstration Studies of Funds Allocation Within School Districts* (Washington, DC: NIE, 1977); *The Effects of Services on Student Development* (Washington, DC: NIE, 1977); *Title I Funds Allocation: The Current Formula* (Washington, DC: NIE, 1977); *Using Achievement Test Scores to Allocate Title I Funds* (Washington, DC: NIE, 1977). Other reports were released after the hearings ended; their use was not investigated.

10. Critiques and secondary analyses of this conclusion are only now in process. Our data deal with use, not with the quality of the findings.

11. House Report, p. 7.

12. For example, see Cohen, D. K., and Garet, M. S., "Reforming Educational Policy with Applied Social Research," *Harvard Educational Review, 45* (1975): 17–41. Also see Jones, *op. cit.*

13. E.g., Guba and Lincoln, *op. cit.*

14. This amendment appears in P.L. 95-561, Title I, Part D, Section 187.

15. Title I, Part A, Section 130.

16. Title I, Part A, Section 131.

17. Title I, Part D, Section 185.

18. Title I, Part C, Sections 165, 170, and 186.

19. Title V, Part A, Sections 504, 508, and 509.

20. Title I, Part C, Section 171.
21. Title I, Part A, Section 111.
22. Title I, Part A, Sections 122 and 123.
23. Title I, Part A, Section 112.
24. Title I, Part A, Section 130.
25. Title I, Part A, Section 117.
26. Title I, Part A, Section 133.
27. Congress did attempt to constrain one local practice, however. The study found that one-third of districts surveyed had no chairperson for a parent advisory council, while one-fourth had no council at all. Citing the study, the House revised requirements for such councils and directed the National Institute of Education to study parent involvement in Title I. Three amendments passed and a fourth was altered in final legislation (Title I, Part A, Section 125).
28. Jones, *op. cit.* However, we found many uses of Office of Education studies.
29. Hill, *op. cit.*
30. Singh, V. P., "Use of Social Science Knowledge and Data in Public Policy Making: The Deliberations on the Compensatory Educational Policy by the U.S. Congress," presented at the Conference on Knowledge Use, Vienna, Austria, 1980.
31. Patton, M. Q., *Utilization-Focused Evaluation* (Beverly Hills, CA: Sage, 1978).
32. Bardach, E., *The Implementation Game* (Cambridge, MA: MIT Press, 1977), p. 274.
33. Leviton, L. C., and Hughes, E. F. X., "Research on the Utilization of Evaluations: A Review and Synthesis," *Evaluation Review*, 5 (1981): 525–548.
34. Lawrence, J. S. E., and Cook, T. J., "Designing Program Evaluation with the Help of Stakeholders," *Journal of Policy Analysis and Management*, 2 (1982): 120–123. Also see Cronbach, et al., *op. cit.*; and Wholey, J. S., *Evaluation: Promise and Performance* (Washington, DC: Urban Institute, 1978).

10

Social Science Research and the
Politics of Gun Control

Peter H. Rossi and James D. Wright

This chapter is concerned generally with the relationship between social science research and public policy formation. Many interesting, and at times rather disconcerting, aspects of this relationship are illustrated in the uses made of social science research by partisans on both sides of "The Great American Gun War" (Bruce-Biggs, 1976)—the perennial debate in American political life over what to do about crime and the firearms with which crimes are committed.

It perhaps goes without saying that the gun control issue is an inordinately complex and hotly debated one, and, thus, one that has been argued in any number of manifestations. Some aspects of the larger political debate have progressed more or less independently of anything the social sciences have had to say. To illustrate, much of the disputation, at least in some quarters, revolves around one's interpretation of the intent of the Second Amendment, and here, social sciences clearly has had little to contribute.

There are, however, many aspects of the gun control debate in which social science has become at least peripherally involved, and at least

AUTHORS' NOTE: Preparation of this chapter was supported by Grant 78-NI-AX-0120 from the National Institute of Justice. We draw heavily here on research reported in J. D. Wright, P. H. Rossi, and K. Daly, Under the Gun: Weapons, Crime and Violence in America *(Hawthorne, NY: Aldine Publishing Co., 1983). The acknowledgement of support from the National Institute of Justice does not imply endorsement of the views expressed in this chapter, for which we bear sole responsibility.*

two areas in which the available social science research has played a distinctive, indeed, critical role. The first concerns the extent to which public opinion favors or opposes new and more stringent gun regulations. And the second concerns the question of whether gun control laws "work" in reducing the rates of violent crime. These two specific issues therefore constitute the substance of this chapter.

PUBLIC OPINION ON
GUN CONTROL ISSUES

Partisans in virtually every public policy debate find it convenient, whenever possible, to claim that public opinion is favorable to their point of view, and the gun control debate is certainly no exception. To illustrate, we can quote briefly from the Executive Summaries of two recent studies of this topic:

> Majorities of American voters believe that we do not need more laws governing the possession and use of firearms and that more firearms laws would *not* result in a decrease in the crime rate.

> It is clear that the vast majority of the public (both those who live with handguns and those who do not) want handgun licensing and registration. . . . [T]he American public wants some form of handgun control legislation.

Only the extremely naive would misidentify the sources of these two quotations. The first is from a report entitled, "Attitudes of the Electorate Toward Gun Control 1978," prepared by Decision-Making Information, Inc., of Santa Ana, California, for the National Rifle Association (NRA). The second quotation is from a report entitled, "An Analysis of Public Attitudes Toward Handgun Control," prepared by Cambridge Reports, Inc., for the Center for the Study and Prevention of Handgun Violence. Both studies are opinion surveys based on national probability samples, were done in the same few months (April through June of 1978), and deal ostensibly with the same subject matter. And yet the "policy conclusions" appear, at least initially, to be polar opposites.

These two surveys, of course, are not the first soundings of public opinion on gun control issues. Indeed, the first "gun control" poll was conducted by Gallup in the 1930s, and literally hundreds of polls on the topic have been conducted since (Erskine, 1972; Wright, Rossi, & Daly, 1983, Ch. 11). The two 1978 surveys differ from previous polls in devoting their entire questionnaires to gun control issues; indeed, taken as a set, these two polls are nearly encyclopedic in their coverage. But even here, each survey focuses on different aspects of the larger issue and poses those issues to respondents in very different ways. Indeed, a quick scanning of the two interview schedules brings to light two salient features of these surveys. First, the Caddell survey emphasizes in each item that the question refers to handguns and "handgun violence," whereas the DMI survey focuses on firearms generally and on "crime control." Second, although the two surveys are ostensibly on the same issue, there are very questions that deal with the same specific topic.

The differing emphases of the two surveys are themselves instructive. Many people who favor stricter controls over the ownership and use of handguns nonetheless oppose further controls over the ownership and use of shoulder weapons by the civilian population. Symbolically, handguns are nasty little things that evoke potent and emotional responses in many people; rifles and shotguns usually do not evoke the same kinds of responses. Interestingly, although perhaps not surprisingly, the Caddell poll emphasizes handguns in nearly every question, whereas in the DMI poll, specific references to handguns (as distinct from guns in general) tend to be avoided.

In the same vein, Caddell's questions emphasize "handgun violence, " whereas the DMI questions focused on crime and its control. "Handgun violence," symbolically, seems to be the sort of thing that sensible firearms policies might fruitfully address; "crime," again symbolically, is clearly a more obdurate problem, and one may appropriately wonder whether "gun control" per se would contribute anything to its solution. Thus, through phrasing and emphasis, both survey organizations provide contextual cues that, in comparison, clearly seem intended to elicit the "right" answers from their respondents.

The contrasts between the contents of the two surveys also indicate that public opinion on gun control is sufficiently complex and multifaceted that two entire surveys can be devoted to the topic and still touch upon relatively little common ground. This also means that considerable latitude is given to the researchers in defining the issue operationally, a condition that invites partisan selectivity.

The Caddell survey has a lengthy sequence of questions on specific handgun control measures, prefaced, as we have just indicated, by a lead-in statement that the measures in question are to be considered as devices to "control handgun violence." The DMI survey has relatively few questions on handgun control.

As in most prior polls on the topic, Caddell finds large majorities favoring most, but not all, of the handgun controls mentioned. Some of the larger majorities are registered for relatively innocuous items that are easy to agree with because they call only for an endorsement of the status quo. For example, we should not be surprised to learn that some 85 percent would favor a crackdown on illegal gun sales because "cracking down" on anything illegal is simply an endorsement of existing laws. Several of Caddell's larger majorities are obtained from items of this general sort.

Several items dealing with the registration of handguns and the issuing of permits for handgun ownership or possession all elicit sizable majorities in favor of them. One should again be wary, however, of reading more into these results than is warranted. Many states and local communities already have laws of these kinds on the books. For example, Cook and Blose (1981) report that about two-thirds of the American population reside in jurisdictions that require handgun purchasers to be screened by the police. Hence, many who favor this provision, or other similar provisions, may again simply be endorsing the status quo within their jurisidictions.

Measures more extreme than those currently in use in many jurisidictions do not enjoy much public support. Substantial majorities, for example, oppose a "buy back" law, such as was once tried in Baltimore and a few other places. The idea of an outright ban on the manufacture, sale, or ownership of handguns is also rejected by sizable majorities, with the exception of the fairly strong endorsement (70 percent in favor) of a ban on the manufacture of "cheap, low-quality handguns."

There is very little in the DMI survey to which the Caddell findings just summarized can be directly compared. One item shows that 13 percent believe that there are already too many laws governing the possession and use of firearms, a proportion roughly on the same magnitude as the proportions who oppose each of the Caddell items concerning registration and permits. Some 41 percent say that "the present laws are about right," and 44 percent—the plurality—believe that we need even more laws along these lines. We can only speculate about the additional laws that this 44 percent say they want, suspecting that many of them may already be on the statute and ordinance books in their home towns and states. Correspondingly, the fact that the majority does not want more laws is also ambiguous. Indeed, these findings are by no means inconsistent with the large majorities who favor many of the measures that were included in the Caddell survey; as we have already stressed, many of these measures are already on the books in many jurisdictions.

The finding that the "majority" of the population does not want more gun laws is, of course, heavily stressed in the DMI report and was, indeed, the finding that was summarized in the quotation from their report cited earlier. It will be quickly seen, given the actual empirical results, that the DMI summary is a masterfully rhetorical formulation. As we have just seen, the actual result is as follows: 13 percent believe there are too many gun laws already, 41 percent believe that the present laws are about right, and 44 percent believe we need more laws. Given these results, it is worth emphasizing that all three of the following are true (and equally misleading) statements: (1) The majority does *not* believe there are too many laws; (2) the majority does *not* believe present laws are about right; (3) the majority does *not* believe that we need more laws.

A final set of items that touch upon the same subject matter in both surveys—although in different ways—concerns endorsement of gun registration programs. The DMI item finds that 61 percent of the electorate opposes "the Federal government's spending four billion dollars to enact a gun registration program." On the surface, this finding appears to contradict the Caddell finding of large majorities favoring gun registration. But, there is obviously no inconsistency between wanting gun registration and also wanting it to cost less than four billion dollars.

Both surveys have comparable questions about proposals for an outright ban on handguns. The Caddell survey finds that 31 percent of the population would favor such a ban, 18 percent are neutral, and 51 percent are opposed. The comparable DMI item is somewhat different, especially in not allowing respondents to select a neutral position and in being phrased in an "agree-disagree" framework. DMI finds that more than 80 percent disagree with the statement that "no private individual should be allowed to own a handgun." It is thus plain in both studies that the majority of the U.S. population oppose outright bans on private ownership and use of handguns.

Both surveys also find very large majorities (80 to 90 percent) supporting the concept of severe mandatory prison sentences for persons who use a gun to commit a crime. Caddell finds that 55 percent would favor mandatory prison sentences for persons carrying unlicensed handguns, whereas DMI does not have a comparable item. Both surveys find large majorities (again, in the range of 80 to 90 percent) agreeing that criminals will always be able to arm themselves no matter what laws are passed.

On the expected effects of gun control, DMI asks whether respondents anticipate that crime rates would decrease or increase if more firearm laws were enacted. The plurality (43 percent) expect a decline in the crime rate, most by only a small amount; a large minority, 41 percent believe crime rates would be unaffected; and a smaller minority, 16 percent, believe that crime rates would actually increase. Caddell's version is an agree-disagree question with no middle or neutral category: He finds 49 percent who agree that licensing all handgun owners would reduce crime, 42 percent who disagree, and 10 percent holding no opinion. Despite the differences in the wording of the two items, the two surveys achieve close to identical results; roughly 40 percent to 50 percent of the population believe that crime would go down with stricter gun controls, with the remainder thinking that crime rates would either remain the same or increase. Our review of these two opinion polls, although brief, provides the basis for at least a few generalizations.

First, these two polls amply demonstrate (as if further demonstration were necessary!) the important point that "gun control" is an inherently ambiguous term, one that has been used to refer to a wide range of possible interventions spanning the entire policy space from simple registration and licensing requirements to mandatory sentences for using a gun in commiting a crime and, at the outer edge, outright bans on the manufacture, sale, and possession of certain types of guns. The polls also demonstrate that large majorities of the public do indeed favor *some kinds* of gun controls, and that equally large majorities oppose *other kinds* of gun controls. To say that the public somehow "favors" or "opposes" gun control *in general* is obviously to speak in meaningless ambiguities and thus to confuse rather than clarify the issue.

Second, when the two surveys are comparable in detail, results are similar at least in magnitude. Slightly different questions do not change the distributions (at least for this topic) by more than a few percentage points in either direction.

Third, the surveys differ primarily in the ways in which the many facets of the larger issue are covered or not covered in the respective questionnaires and ensuing reports—what specific topics are chosen for coverage, how questions are phrased, and, in particular, which findings are most heavily emphasized in the analysis. Thus, Caddell sticks to handguns and handgun violence throughout his survey and DMI phrases questions in terms of firearms and crime control. Caddell's survey contains many questions about specific handgun control measures whereas DMI asks rather vaguely about "more" or "less" firearms legislation.

The rough comparability of the actual empirical findings from these two surveys leads to an interesting thought experiment to wit: Could Caddell sit down with the DMI results in hand and write a report that would satisfy the Center for the Study and Prevention of Handgun

Violence? Could the DMI staff use Caddell's results to prepare a report that would satisfy the National Rifle Association? The answer to both questions is almost certainly yes. The studies differ primarily *not* in what they actually find, but in the emphasis and significance attached to the various findings. The *accuracy* of a finding is a matter about which all technically trained people would normally be able to agree; the *significance* of a finding derives mainly from one's prior values.

It does not take a very fertile or subtle imagination to see how these two questionnaires were constructed to fulfill the needs of the respective sponsoring organizations—in a word, to find "strong popular support" for the client's point of view. Given the five-decade history of public opinion polling on gun control issues, each of the client organizations (and both survey organizations) must have had considerable prior knowledge about the kinds of specific proposals and questions that would produce findings supporting or opposing "gun control." (DMI, in fact, had done an earlier 1975 poll on the topic, also in behalf of the NRA.) The end result, as we have seen, is a pair of surveys, each with remarkably convenient findings for its sponsor.

Social scientists, of course, are accustomed to the perils of specification errors, especially in the construction of explanatory models of social phenomena. The presence and consequence of specification errors in descriptive studies are not ordinarily pointed out in social science work, perhaps because we value descriptive studies so little. (To be sure, similar concerns are sometimes raised in terms of "construct validity.") In any event, the major faults in the two surveys reflect specification errors: Each survey incompletely, and therefore incorrectly, maps out the domain of gun control policy, gerrymandering more or less at will to exclude areas in which their clients could be expected to fare poorly and to include areas in which popular support would no doubt prove to be strong.

And yet, there are limits even here. Certain aspects of the gun control issue are so obviously central to the relevant policy domain that one omits them only at the risk of losing all credibility. Thus, Caddell had to include questions about an outright ban on handguns in his survey, knowing full well (or so one presumes) that those questions would elicit little popular support; and, likewise, the DMI survey had to include items on gun registration and licensing, again knowing in advance that majorities would be in favor of such measures. (In the latter case, of course, DMI managed to cope effectively with the problem with some highly "creative" versions of the relevant questions.)

Despite the limits we have just discussed, there remain obvious gaps in the topical coverage of each survey. Indeed, one will find entire sections in one of the questionnaires that have no counterpart in the other. Perhaps, the principle used is simply that if one does not ask the question, then one does not have to cope with the answer. This, clearly, is an extremely useful principle when the survey is meant to serve mainly polemical purposes. If the intent, however, is to inform the client (or legislators or the public) as fully and accurately as the state of public opinion measurement allows, then specification errors of the sort we have discussed are seriously misleading.

On the other hand, neither Caddell nor DMI is in the business of "informing" anyone "as fully and as accurately as possible." Both organizations sell services to clients, and like all other organizations, they have some obligation to be sensitive to the client's needs. If either of these surveys had been done as an academic poll of public opinion (for example, with funds from the National Science Foundation), one would immediately (and rightly) question the competence and integrity of the principal investigator. In the present case, it is clear that both clients pretty much got what they paid for: A technically competent poll that shows the client's viewpoint in the most favorable possible light.

Interestingly enough, however, in providing these services for their clients, the two organizations have also (inadvertently, no doubt) done the science of public opinion research a service as well. We know quite a bit more about the complexities of public thinking on the gun control issue than we knew before these two polls were conducted. In comparing the two polls, it becomes obvious not only what each of them managed to leave out, but what all the other, more academic polls on the topic have also left out. By raising some issues more pointedly than the more neutral polling firms would ever dare to, by considering in detail aspects of the issue that neutral pollsters would never touch, these two polls, unquestionably, have enlarged our understanding of public opinion and gun control, even though in isolation each poll is as much a political document as it is social science research.

ASSESSING THE EFFECTIVENESS
OF GUN CONTROL LEGISLATION

A second major area in which social science research has figured prominently in the gun control debate concerns the evaluation of firearms laws and their effects on the crime rates. Partisans on both sides of the issue have for many years argued vehemently over the question of whether gun control, in fact, reduces crime. Social science interest in the topic corresponds to the emergence over the past two decades of a strong interest in applied work in the various social science disciplines (Rossi & Wright, in press).

If we have learned anything from the spate of applied social research of the recent past, it is that the expected value of the effectiveness of any social program or policy intervention hovers close to zero. We have also learned something about why policies and programs tend to be ineffective or only marginally effective. First, policymakers and their staffs often do not have the basic social science knowledge that would enable them to design programs in consonance with existing knowledge. Second, the required basic knowledge is often missing altogether and/or incomplete or otherwise defective. Finally, our knowledge about how human organizations work in the implementation of policy is extremely fragmentary, and it is often a mystery why some policies seem to be implemented in ways that preserve the integrity of the social programs involved and why others are implemented so badly that serious distortions occur.

This litany of why programs fail generally is particularly appropriate to a discussion of the assessment of the impact of gun control policies. In a word, there have been failures all along the line: In basic social science knowledge, in the art of implementing policies, and in the expertise of policymakers and their advisers in designing policy interventions.

The debate over proper civilian firearms policy remains among the more hotly contested political issues in present-day America. Much of the heat (certainly not all!) is generated in disputes about whether "gun controls" are effective in reducing crime, and in such issues, social science becomes inevitably and inextricably involved. Crime, after all, is a *social* problem of the purest sort; it is hard to imagine a technological intervention that would somehow solve the crime problem. Policymakers who deal with crime therefore turn, inevitably, to the social sciences for guidance on intervention strategies.

It is possible to deal with the issue of effectiveness to some degree because our political jurisdictions have experimented with a wide variety of gun control measures. Indeed, it appears that there are at this moment some 20,000 federal, state, and local laws regulating firearms ownership or use in one way or another (Wright et al., 1983, Ch. 12). Thus, almost every proposal that has ever been put forward by the proponents of stricter firearms controls is likely already to be in effect in some jurisdiction somewhere in the United States.

Cross-Sectional Comparisons

The diversity of "gun control" measures presently in force in the United States suggests that there are opportunities to test the relative effectiveness of different approaches to gun control. In principle, all that appears to be necessary is to contrast crime rates in jurisdictions with certain kinds of regulatory strategies to the rates prevailing in otherwise "comparable" jurisdictions that employ different strategies. On the face of it, it seems that we should be able to learn quite a bit from these "natural experiments." As we have learned, however, the results of natural experiments are as difficult to interpret in this field as in any other area of social policy.

Ordinarily, the person who asks whether gun control "works" wants to know whether there is any evidence that gun control measures reduce crime levels. A candid and considered, if rather depressing, response to such a question is that *nothing* seems to work very well in reducing crime. As we all know, crime rates in the United States have shown a very distressing upward trend since World War II that only in the last few years appears to be levelling off, and then only slightly. Nothing that has been attempted in the way of policies and programs designed to reduce crime has influenced the post-World War II crime rate trends very much.

Despite the obvious problems in so doing, social scientists have tried in various ways to answer the question of whether gun control policies of one sort or another lower crime rates. One approach has attempted to estimate effects by contrasting political jurisdictions that have relatively strict gun control laws with jurisdictions that have less strict laws, thus capitalizing on the "natural experiment" opportunities discussed above.

In their crudest form, these attempts show up in the polemical literature as simple zero-order comparisons between nations. For example, as is well-known, Great Britain has much stricter gun control laws and much less crime than the United States. From this it has been concluded that strict gun laws reduce crime! The Swiss require every able-bodied male to be a member of the national militia and thus to keep a military weapon and ammunition ready in their homes. The result is that the proportional density of firearms possession is clearly higher in Switzerland than in the United States. And yet, the Swiss have much less crime. And from this it has been concluded that crime and gun ownership are not related!

No technically competent social scientist would mistake either of the above comparisons for real evidence on whether guns or gun laws are or are not related to crime. The methodological problem encountered here, however, is formally identical to the problem that arises in other apparently more sophisticated and persuasive studies; namely, deciding what to hold constant in the comparisons.

In general, any two political jurisdictions—be they nations, states, or local communities—will differ in many ways, any one or combination of which may constitute the explanation for the observed differences in crime rates. If we had a credible, empirically persuasive macrotheory of crime, we would know just what to hold constant in making jurisdictional comparisons of this sort. Because we possess no such theory, these studies have typically held constant whatever happened to be available in the data sets used in the hopes that these variables would serve as suitable proxies for a good theoretical model. The results of such shotgun approaches should come as no surprise: different studies, holding different jurisdictional characteristics constant, produce remarkably different results. Consider the following two quotations:

> The data indicate that gun control legislation is related to fewer deaths by homicide, suicide and accidents by firearms. (Geisel, Roll, & Wettick, 1969, p. 666)

> On the basis of these data, the conclusion is, inevitably, that gun control laws have no individual or collective effect in reducing rates of violent crime. (Murray, 1975, p. 88)

In both of the studies cited, the data consist of state-level crime rates (the dependent variable), coded variables indicating the stringency of each state's gun laws (as shown in a compendium of state gun control laws), and an ad hoc selection of state-level demographic and economic data to be used as statistical controls. However, each investigator used a slightly different ad hoc selection of control variables. Depending on what was held constant, the stringency of gun control laws was either related or not related to the state-level crime rates. Neither study, incidentally, provides a plausible theoretical rationale for the set of control variables employed; as such, it is impossible to decide which is the more correct specification and therefore equally impossible to decide which conclusion is more credible.

Implementation Studies

A second category of research on the impact of gun laws has generally been more informative, mainly because it is more descriptive and hence is less dependent on the existence of sensible theory. These are "process" or "implementation"studies, centered on describing the actual "delivery" of gun control policies using data gathered in field research.

The importance of implementation research has only recently been recognized in the applied social sciences, a recognition that resulted more or less directly from the persistent string of "no effects" findings in the major evaluation studies (Rossi & Wright, in press). In speculating on the reasons *why* most social policies appeared not to produce their intended effects, it became apparent that part of the explanation was that programs were often implemented in ways that subverted the original intent (or, in some cases, were simply not implemented at all). These days, as a result, implementation research is considered to be an integral part of a comprehensive evaluation and a necessary precursor of informative impact assessment studies: It is, after all, rather foolish to assess the impact of a policy until one is clear just what policy is actually being delivered in the field.

Leading examples of implementation research in the gun control area include Zimring's definitive (1975) study of the Gun Control Act of 1968 and Beha's (1977) analysis of the implementation of the Barley-Fox gun law in Massachusetts, a law that was intended to impose mandatory one-year sentence enhancements for the unlicensed carrying of firearms. Both studies demonstrate that legislative intent can be, and often is, modified in actual enforcement to conform to the organizational imperatives of the criminal justice system.

To illustrate, the Gun Control Act (GCA) of 1968 required Federal licenses for all over-the-counter retail firearms dealers. However, the legislation did not enact any sensible procedures by which these licensed dealers would be supervised; indeed, Congress appropriated no funds for the purpose. Congress also failed to anticipate that the nominal fee required for licensure would result in several hundreds of thousands of licenses being issued. The number of licensees vastly exceeded the supervisory capacity of the relevant Federal agency (the Bureau of Alcohol, Tobacco, and Firearms). What appeared on paper as a new method of regulating retail gun dealers proved, in fact, to amount to no regulation of them at all.

Other provisions of the GCA of 1968 forbid firearms sales to convicted felons, the mentally disturbed, and out-of-state residents, but again, no procedures were specified for ascertaining whether these disqualifications were obtained or not. The result was an overload of applicants, far too few resources to police the actions of licensees, and, thus, widespread and rather simple circumvention of the intent of the legislation.

The general point to be gleaned from these studies is that unenforced and unenforceable laws and regulations cannot possibly achieve their intended goals. Such laws tend to satisfy symbolic needs, to create the impression that something is being done about the problem, but usually little more.

Time-Series Analyses

Most recently, various analysts have used more or less sophisticated time-series research designs to investigate the crime reductive effects of gun control legislation. These studies take advantage of the fact that states or other political jurisdictions often enact new gun control laws. If the appropriate time series of data exist, one can compare the behavior of the time series before and after enactment of new legislation and learn at least something of value about the net impacts.

The studies in question range in sophistication from simple pre- and posttest studies without control groups to quite complex interrupted time-series designs. No matter how sophisticated, however, such studies are not exempt from criticism or rancorous dispute. The essence of an interrupted time-series analysis is deceptively simple. One first models the time series prior to enactment of new legislation. On this basis, one then projects what the likely postenactment trends would have been had no new legislation been introduced. Comparisons between these projections and the observed behavior of the time series postenactment therefore provide the measure of net impact.

Clearly, the critical step in the above process is the projection of what "might have been" absent the intervention, a projection that can only be as valid as the analyst's prior understanding of why the time series behaves as it does. Sensible projections therefore require, once again, a credible, empirically based theory of how crime rates are produced. Lacking such a theory, all time-series analysts must make more or less plausible assumptions about the processes that underlie the behavior of the time series, and on the basis of those assumptions, choose the seemingly most appropriate statistical models for the data analysis. Unsurprisingly, different analysts then get different results, depending on the analytical models chosen.

Thus, the time-series analysis by Deutsch and Alt (1977) of the effects of the Bartley-Fox law in Massachusetts was challenged by Hay and McCleary (1979) on the grounds that the original analysis employed inappropriate time-series models. A reanalysis of the data, using different models, produced different findings: The original analysis suggested a small reduction in armed robbery and gun assaults as a result of Bartley-Fox, whereas the reanalysis concluded that these effects were not statistically significant. Which of these is the correct conclusion depends entirely on what kinds of assumptions one is willing to make, absent an appropriate theory, about how crime in Massachusetts is generated.

The best available time-series analysis of Bartley-Fox was conducted in a multimethod fashion by Pierce and Bowers (1979). These investigators enlarged the time frame for the study, compared the observed trends in Massachusetts and in Boston with trends in other states and communities, and, unlike previous studies, considered trends outside of Boston as well as in Boston itself. All told, the Pierce-Bowers study is more detailed and comprehensive than any of the previous Bartley-Fox analyses and does report some modest effects that consist of statistically significant but substantively small reductions in some but not all categories of gun-related crimes.

Most recent time-series studies, however, have found no discernible effects at all, for example, Loftin and McDowell's (1981) study of Detriot's recently enacted add-on sentence enhancement law, or Jones's (1981) study of the seemingly drastic Washington, D.C., gun control law.

No study has shown (or even claimed to show) *dramatic* effects of gun control legislation on gun-related crimes or crime rates generally. None of the studies claiming modest effects has yet had a long enough run to determine whether the effects persist beyond the first 12 to 18 months. The principal generalization to be made from these studies is thus that gun laws have (at best) modest and (at worst) nonexistent crime reduction effects.

Is it legitimate, then, to conclude that social science has proved that "gun control doesn't work?" Not quite! First, we must remember that "gun control" refers to an exceedingly wide range of policy interventions; the studies reviewed above deal with a fairly narrow spectrum of the broader policy space—mainly, that part of the range that involves mandatory sentence enhancement strategies. Other strategies, once enacted and evaluated, may prove somewhat more efficacious toward their intended goals.

Even restricting ourselves to the kinds of strategies that have been evaluated, however, the most we can conclude is that if these kinds of gun control laws do reduce crime, they do not work strongly enough to overpower specification errors or any of the other infirmities in the current state of the social research art. Or, to state the same point somewhat differently, if there are crime reduction effects to be obtained from these kinds of gun control laws, they lie just at or somewhere beyond the threshold of detectability through present-day social research methods.

Why don't gun control laws of the sort that have been evaluated work better than we have been able so far to detect? Why does the criminal abuse of firearms seem to persist more or less unabated in the face of whatever gun control measures we have enacted? In speculating about the possible answers to this question, we can illustrate in some fairly concrete ways how social science research and data can contribute to the design of sensible civilian firearms policies.

Jurisdictionally Specific Laws

Many diverse answers have been given to the question of why gun laws do not seem to work very well. For example, persons who favor gun control as a crime reduction measure often argue that gun control laws in the United States have never worked very well because every jurisdiction has enacted different laws. The result is that jurisdictions with very strict gun control laws often border on jurisdictions that have very lax laws. Beyond all question, there is some merit in this position: No law can be very effective if it can be circumvented by driving to the next political jurisdiction. Studies of the flow of illegal firearms into Eastern cities with very restrictive firearms laws (e.g., Brill, 1977) amply document just how futile these jurisdictionally specific laws can be.

The American "Gun Culture"

Another serious obstacle is that gun ownership is so widespread among the civilian population. Regulating the ownership and use of firearms therefore presents a considerable problem of scale. For a variety of reasons discussed in Wright et al. (1983, Chs. 2 to 5), it is difficult to know with much precision just how many guns are "out there" in private hands; a reasonable guess, however, is that there are at the present time approximately 120–130 million firearms in the United States, with one or more firearms being held by half the households in the country. Furthermore, unlike other possessions that are licensed (e.g., automobiles), gun ownership as a household characteristic is not obvious in casual observation.

Although there are many firearms held by civilians, few of them are ever involved in the roughly 1,000,000 "unfortunate gun incidents" that occur annually (events ranging from minor accidents to homicides, which are calculated quite loosely; see Wright et al., 1983, Ch. 8, for details). Serious firearm abuses that define chargeable offenses in criminal law are much fewer—approximately 300,000 annually. Social research on private weapons ownership and on the incidences of firearms crimes has thus made it clear that persons who use their firearms legally and carefully outnumber the firearms abusers by about three orders of magnitude, even if we assume that each abuse involves a separate offender, a dubious assumption. This, of course, implies that if we want to control *criminal* firearms abuse by somehow keeping tabs on all civilian ownership and use of firearms, we will be wasting our effort about 99.9 percent of the time.

The Criminal Firearms Abuser

In line with this last point, advocates of gun control have tried to devise ways to distinguish between potential legitimate and illegitimate gun users in the hopes of hitting upon some way to regulate the one while leaving the other more or less untouched. For a period of time, attention was focused generally on handguns on the dual grounds that handguns had little or no legitimate sporting use and that handguns were the weapons of choice in the commission of crimes. Subsequent research (Wright et al., 1983, Ch. 3) has shown, however, that handguns are in fact used in all sorts of manifestly legitimate sporting ways by obviously legitimate gun owners who resent further restrictions on their prerogatives and activities. Furthermore, although the majority of gun crimes involves handguns, there is a fair-sized minority (15–30 percent) that involves shoulder weapons (see the studies reviewed in Wright et al., 1983, Ch. 9). In terms of types of weapons preferred, there appears to be a considerable overlap between legitimate and illegitimate users.

To keep guns out of the hands of illegitimate users means to regulate the sale and exchange of guns in order to interdict illegitimate users from obtaining weapons. In order to accomplish this properly, we have to have firm empirical knowledge about how the civilian weapons market works. Unfortunately, we know relatively little about this topic. We do know that a large fraction of all firearms transfers involves informal trading between private parties, does not involve retail brokers or merchants, and is therefore inherently very difficult to regulate (see, for example, Burr, 1977; Wright & Rossi, 1983). We also know that firearms are an important commodity on black markets in which stolen goods are bought and sold. The widespread theft of guns from private residences (about a quarter-million a year) and their subsequent sale in the black market tend to obliterate the distinctions between legitimate and illegitimate markets because any gun that can be acquired legitimately can be stolen from its legitimate owner and subsequently fall into criminal hands.

It is important to keep in mind that what we want to accomplish primarily with "gun control" is to lower the use of firearms in crimes. In order to do this, we obviously need to know why criminals carry guns in the first place, which, until recently, has been a virtually unresearched subject. In an attempt to uncover these motives, we have been interviewing convicted felons in state prisons throughout the nation, asking them about how they acquired their firearms and for what purposes such weapons are used (Wright & Rossi, 1983). Our preliminary tabulations strongly suggest that the primary motivation for carrying firearms is for self-protection and *not* specifically for use in committing crimes. The use of guns in ordinary crimes appears to be an almost incidental by-product of a strongly ingrained practice of carrying weapons as a means of surviving life on the streets.

Now the person who is habituated to being armed is a very different person than the criminal who arms himself for a specific criminal purpose. In the latter case, it may make some sense to think in terms of structuring sanctions so as to make the use of guns in such behavior too costly. But in the former (and, it appears, empirically more common) case, we would have to deal not only with the individual criminal but the entire environment of neighborhoods, and possibly with lifelong patterns of behavior whose roots may extend back into early childhood. Thus, the reasons why criminals carry guns—a topic now being researched for the first time—have immediate implications about how we might get them to stop it.

Mandatory Sentencing for Gun Abusers

Of course, it is sometimes argued that we should not try to prevent firearms abuse in advance, this being a largely hopeless enterprise, but rather should satisfy ourselves with punishing abuses after they occur. For this reason, several jurisdictions have recently enacted sentence enhancement measures that add one or two years on to a sentence if a firearm was used in the crime. Unfortunately, the appeal of this approach dissolves rather quickly: It is effective neither as a deterrent nor as a means of punishment.

First, as a before-the-fact deterrent, this approach faces the problem that most criminals do not expect to be caught in any case, a fairly common criminological finding. What might happen to them if they were caught therefore cannot be of much concern. Furthermore, most of the crimes that people commit with firearms already carry fairly stiff penalties. For example, a person charged with armed robbery faces a potential sentence of from 10 to 30 years. A one- or two-year add-on penalty may not significantly change the subjective magnitude of the sentence.

Second, research has also taught us that add-on penalties have a way of being assimilated into the sentencing practices of judges, who often reduce proportionately the sentence for the main charge, with the result that the total sentence for the main charge plus the add-on penalties remains the same. Judges, of course, are very much aware of the overcrowding of state prisons and appear to be reluctant to add to the ever-increasing burdens.

SUMMARY

Our main points can now be summarized: First, attempts to assess the impact of gun control legislation on crime have been fraught with specification errors. We do not yet know enough to model completely the use of guns in crime or to model the determinants of crime itself. Moreover, there is no reason to suspect that we *will* know enough to do so any time in the near future. Lacking this ability, our assessments of the impact of gun control legislation on crime cannot be completely credible. As in the case of public opinion on gun control issues, this lack of comprehensive knowledge about the uses of guns in crime makes it possible to obtain widely different results depending on the specification used. Also, as in the case of the polls, this again allows partisans to pick and choose a conveniently agreeable specification, a circumstance that turns research activity into partisan in-fighting.

Second, by piecing together fragments of knowledge about the elements that need to go into a correct specification of the problem, we have been able to show that the model-building issue is one of considerable complexity. Research assessing the impact of gun control legislation has shown inconclusive results mainly because of the problems involved in specifying a plausible and acceptable macromodel for crime rates or a micromodel for criminal behavior.

Third, we have shown that gun control legislation designed to affect the use of guns in crime has typically been developed without considering whether the legislation accords with any realistic understanding of how criminals acquire their guns and why guns are used in crime.

The fragmentary descriptions we have been able to put together imply that the roots of gun control legislation's ineffectiveness lie in the fact that criminals usually acquire their guns outside the legitimate, regulated gun market and carry guns mainly for reasons that have little to do with their criminal activities.

Social Science and Social Policy

As in most of the other political struggles of our times, advocates on both sides of the Great American Gun War have employed the findings of social science to add credibility to their political positions. Although some of the researchers in question may well resent the ensuing politicization of their work, there is little that can be done to prevent it. To publish one's results is to invite their political use—and misuse.

Not all social scientists try to keep their research findings out of the political arena; indeed, some enjoy and encourage it. Others insist on making their findings fully available to all partisans, acting on the principle that it is a researcher's responsibility to do so. Still others are themselves partisans and are particularly pleased when their findings bolster their own political positions. And then there are those whose talents are simply for hire, who are especially anxious to have their findings match the expectations of their clients.

There are few social scientists who are so above mundane concerns that they would actively prevent their findings from reaching lay audiences. Indeed, in these times, when the social science disciplines are scrambling to show their "relevance," the professions often reward those who find themselves in the limelight.

But, there are also very few—outside of the hired hands of social science—who have been completely happy with the political uses of their research. Subtleties tend to vanish when translated by journalists from even the best of the national media and suffer even more when lesser talents turn their hands to writing articles based on social science. Nor has social science research fared much better in the hands of the law. Many social scientists have had the experience of testifying in a court in which clever lawyers skillfully prevented them from doing complete justice to their research.

The coming together of social scientists and policymakers—hopefully for mutual benefit—is clearly problematic. It is easy to understand and discuss how political activists have misunderstood or misused the work of the social scientists, but there is another side to the story. What can we—the social scientists—possibly hope to contribute?

In the debate over gun control, as in most other political debates of equivalent duration and intensity, relatively little of what is at issue can, even in principle, be decided by more and better research. Partisans sometimes debate questions of fact, and, on such points, good research can sometimes be useful, especially in areas in which there is consensus over what are appropriate research procedures. But very often such "facts" are off on the periphery of a debate whose main terms center on value issues. The opponents and advocates of gun control are often debating world views, ideologies, and ways of life. On these usually far more important points, social science research at its best is mute. The best we can do is to make reasonable guesses at what might be the consequences of pursuing one or another policy innovation, but even here we are producing analyses that may be better than outright guesses, but perhaps only marginally so. And these days, the partisans are sufficiently sophisticated that the "iffy" nature of our conclusions will be quickly pointed out.

The major limitation of the social sciences in the policy arena stems from underdevelopment; simply put, we do not yet know enough to be able to predict with reasonable confidence what will be the consequences of pursuing one particular policy rather than another. Each of us has been asked to project the consequences of passing this or that piece of new legislation. For example, will a mandatory sentence enhancement reduce robbery rates? Usually, the best response we can give is, "Try it and we will see!" And even here, we will need long time series both before and after the legislation was passed, so by the time we have the answer, most policymakers will no longer care. In addition, we would need to carefully establish ceteris paribus conditions, an endeavor in which good theoretical understanding is needed on how crime rates are generated, a matter about which we have little knowledge.

If we want to be relevant and helpful, we might take our best shot, putting together the best measure we can find on the robbery rates and constructing reasonable models of crime rate generation that can make use of available data. We may then attempt several alternative specifications, picking the one that seems most reasonable to us, but still a judgment call. Being responsible social scientists, we may write up the results with pages and pages of caveats, disclaimers, and qualifications that are of little interest to anyone but fellow social scientists.

When the national media get their hands on the report, their accounts will likely contain few of the disclaimers and qualifications. The findings will also irritate one set of partisans and please another.

The irritated parties may hire a "methodological gun" to pick over the report and expose the flaws—flaws we felt were minor at the time, of course, but which, in the retelling, become major structural disorders.

Every piece of social science research is flawed to a lesser or greater degree and hence vulnerable to criticism. The spectacle of social scientists battling over whether particular defects are fatal or cosmetic cannot do anything but contribute to the image of social scientists as partisans whose skills are at the service of their values. Even in the best of circumstances, our ultimate input on policy formation will typically be modest.

Although it is undoubtably irritating to know that it is difficult for a social scientist to play a major role in the making of policy, this is, in fact, as it should be. A society in which social scientists play crucial policy roles through their research is a society in which human values have been subordinated to technocratic considerations, a world in which social scientists have become philosopher kings. In a truly democratic society, social science must be content with an advisory but not dominating role. Only the autocratic are confident enough in the righteousness of their own values to impose them on others. When policymakers ask of the social scientists, "Will it work?" we often have the skills, and therefore the obligation, to respond with the best research and analysis we can muster. But when they ask, "Is it just?" it is best if we leave the answer to others.

REFERENCES

Beha, J. A. (1977). "And nobody can get you out": The impact of a mandatory prison sentence for the illegal carrying of a firearm on the use of firearms and on the administration of criminal justice in Boston, Parts I and II. *Boston University Law Review, 57*(1), 96-146; and *57*(2), 289-333.

Brill, S. (1977). *Firearms abuse.* Washington, DC: The Police Foundation.

Bruce-Biggs, B. (1976). The Great American Gun War. *The Public Interest, 45,* 37-62.

Burr, D.E.S. (1977). *Handgun regulation.* Orlando, FL: Florida Bureau of Criminal Justice Planning and Assistance.

Cambridge Reports, Inc. (1978). *An analysis of public attitudes towards handgun control.* Cambridge, MA.

Cook, P. J., & Blose, J. (1981). State programs for screening handgun buyers. *Annals of the American Academy of Political and Social Sciences, 455,* 63-79.

Decision-Making Information, Inc. (1978). *Attitudes of the American electorate toward gun control.* Santa Ana, CA.

Deutsch, S. J., & Alt, F. B. (1977). The effect of Massachusetts gun control law on gun-related crimes in the city of Boston. *Evaluation Quarterly, 1,* 543-568.

Erskine, H. (1972). The polls: Gun control. *Public Opinion Quarterly, 36,* 455-469.

Geisel, M. S., Roll, R., & Wettick, R. S. (1969). The effectiveness of state and local regulation of handguns: a statistical analysis. *Duke University Law Journal, 4,* 647-676.

Hay, R., & McCleary, R. (1979). Box-Tiao time series models for impact assessment; A comment on the recent work of Deutsch and Alt. *Evaluation Quarterly, 3,* 277-314.

Jones, E., III (1981). The District of Columbia's "Firearms Control Regulations Act of 1975": The toughest handgun control law in the United States—or is it? *Annual of the American Academy of Political and Social Sciences, 455,* 138-149.

Loftin, C., & McDowell, D. (1981). "One with a gun gets you two": Mandatory sentencing and firearms violence in Detroit. *Annals of American Academy of Political and Social Sciences, 455,* 150-168.

Murray, D. R. (1975). Handguns, gun control laws, and firearms violence. *Social Problems, 23,* 81-93.

Pierce, G. H., & Bowers, W. J. (1979). *The impact of the Bartley-Fox Gun Law on crime in Massachusetts.* Unpublished paper, Northeastern University, Center for Applied Social Research, Boston, MA.

Rossi, P. H., & Wright, J. D. (in press). Evaluation research: An assessment. *Annual Review of Sociology.*

Wright, J. D., & Rossi, P. H. (1983, November). *The illicit firearms market: Preliminary results from a national survey.* Paper presented at the American Society of Criminology in Denver, CO.

Wright, J. D., Rossi, P. H., & Daly, K. (1983). *Under the gun: Weapons, crime, and violence in America.* New York: Aldine.

Zimring, F. E. (1975). Firearms and federal law: The Gun Control Act of 1968. *Journal of Legal Studies, 4,* 133-198.

11

Policymakers' Use
of Social Science Research
Technology Assessment in the U.S. Congress

Leonard Saxe

Technology assessment (TA) is one model for synthesizing social science research and theory for policymakers. TA requires an unbiased assessment of social research presented in understandable and policy-relevant form. This article describes the conduct of three studies for the Congressional Office of Technology Assessment (OTA) concerned with psychotherapy, treatment for alcoholism, and the conduct of polygraph tests. The studies indicate the potential for systematic integrations of social research and their function in a political and policy environment. Review of these studies suggests that theory is critical in policy research and that social research, rather than a decision-making tool, can serve an "educative" function aiding policymakers to understand complexity.

Unlike its European counterparts, the U.S. government is organized in three separate but equal branches. The president is chief executive, but his power is limited by both the Congress and the courts. The system is benignly referred to as one of "checks and balances," but homeostasis among the branches is often volatile. During the 1960s, it was believed that Congress was losing its influence and that the executive branch had become dominant. As a result, a number of structural reforms were implemented. One set of reforms was designed to provide Congress with independent information on which they could make policy decisions.

The establishment of the congressional Office of Technology Assessment (OTA) was one such development. OTA was established in 1972 to help legislators anticipate and plan for the consequences of technological change and to examine how technology affects people's lives

From Leonard Saxe, "Policymakers' Use of Social Science Research: Technology Assessment in the U.S. Congress," *Knowledge: Creation, Diffusion, Utilization,* Vol. 8, pp. 59-78. Copyright © 1986 by Sage Publications, Inc.

(Arnstein, 1977; Gibbons, 1984; Wood, 1982). The agency was designed to provide Congress with independent advice about scientific issues. OTA is overseen by a bipartisan board of 12 congresspeople and has a staff of about 150. It draws, however, upon thousands of consultants and advisors from academia and industry (see OTA, 1986). The agency has conducted over 200 major studies, has published 500+ reports, and testified hundreds of times before congressional committees. OTA has been an important experiment in the use of science to assist public policymaking.

The concept of techonology assessment (TA) was first articulated by a congressman, and arose from concerns about the effects of unbridled technology (see Arnstein, 1977). OTA's definition of technology is very broad: the exploration of physical, biological, economic, social, and political impacts that result from applications of scientific knowledge. This broad view of technology provides the opportunity for a variety of scientists, including social scientists, to contribute to its analysis. This article describes a number of efforts to utilize social science in the development of OTA's policy analyses. The present discussion is based on the unique circumstances of OTA, but it has a number of implications for how knowledge, based on social research, is utilized in public policy formation.

The work described here primarily concerns mental health and psychology-based technologies. The examples are drawn from my own experience at OTA, both as a staff person and as an external consultant. The issues described range from how to make reimbursement decisions for psychotherapy and alcoholism treatment to the use and validity of polygraph tests. Despite the specific content focus of this work, the issues are not particularistic. They represent both the problems and potential of using a social science as part of efforts to understand and ameliorate social problems. Congressional use of social research is, perhaps, a litmus test of our abilities as social scientists.

Process of Technology Assessment

Fears about the potential effects of "galloping technology," and that technology was creating new strains of "social diseases," although long-recognized (see Frank, 1966), have taken on added significance in recent years. OTA's work is designed, in part, to ameliorate these fears. It is interesting to note that OTA was conceptualized by legislators, rather than by the scientists. Although one might expect social scientists to express concerns about the effects of technology, congresspeople were articulating similar concerns. In the language of the legislation that created OTA, technological applications were seen to be large and growing in scale, "increasingly extensive, pervasive, and critical in the impact, beneficial and adverse, on the natural and social environment." It was deemed essential that the consequences of technological application be anticipated, understood, and considered in determining public policy.

Methods

TA methods are difficult to describe because the problems and available data differ across problems. Even at OTA, where many TAs have been conducted and efforts have been made to describe these procedures (e.g., Wood, 1982), it is clear that there are many options. At OTA, an assessment typically begins as a result of consultation with congressional committees. Most studies are conducted at the request of these committees, usually as a result of disscussions with OTA staff about feasibility.

Development of a study approach and methodology is done through staff preparation of a project proposal. Such proposals describe the rationale and logic of the assessment, its implications, and the staff and budget required. Proposals are reviewed internally and ultimately by the congressional board. Although it is infrequent that requests developed into proposals are rejected by the board, the consultation process often has a significant impact on the scope of the project.

An important structure at OTA, perhaps its most unique feature, is the use of advisory panels. At the top of the advisory hierarchy is a council that advises OTA on overall strategy. The council provides advice about areas to devote resources and strategy to conduct assessments. Council members are leading scientists, academicians, and members of the business community. Each project also has an advisory panel with 6 to 20 members. Formal advisory committees are supplemented by workshops.

Once a project is approved, there are a number of models for how the assessment is conducted. In almost all cases, the emphasis is on making sense of already collected data and, thus, literature reviews and methods for synthesizing research results are relied upon. In some cases, cost-benefit analyses are conducted, surveys developed, and computer models designed. The methods depend on the nature of the problem and the resources available for the study. When in-house resources are not available, elements of a project are contracted out to researchers in academia and industry.

Although the emphasis on evaluating currently available evidence makes OTA analyses somewhat unique, also unusual is the use of information. Throughout development of a report, staff are in contact with leading researchers and those affected by the technology. This occurs through contact with the advisory panel, contractors, and congressional staff. In addition, assistance is often provided by other congressional agencies: the Congressional Research Service (CRS), General Accounting Office (GAO), and the Congressional Budget Office (CBO). Each of these agencies has a mission similar to OTA's, although their methods and staff are organized differently (see Saxe and Koretz, 1980).

An additional feature of OTA assessments is how reports are written and reviewed. Although project staff receive substantial input from the panel and others, it is their responsibility to develop the report. With larger studies, an overall report will be written and supplemented by monograph-length case studies. The key word in guiding development of reports is evenhandedness. Analysts are expected to integrate various sources and to remain as unbiased as possible. When contro-versy exists, it is described so that policy readers can understand the nature of the conflict.

In all cases, reports go through an extensive review and revision process. Internal review by peers and managers occurs, supplemented by outside reviews from members of advisory panels, from stakeholders, and from others identified as having relevant information. Reports are edited by an in-house publication staff and presented both to the OTA director and to the board for review. Published reports are made available to each member of Congress and to the public. In some cases, OTA reports are republished commercially as books or, more typically, are the basis for journal articles.

Assessments of Social Technology

The best means to demonstrate how TAs are conducted is to describe several assessment projects. The projects to be described, on psychotherapy, treatment for alcoholism, and polygraph tests, reflect a relatively narrow substantive range. Nevertheless, they illustrate how social science knowledge can be utilized.

Psychotherapy

The provision of psychotherapy, and its public funding, has been a continuing policy problem. In recent years, as pressures have intensified within the United States for insurance coverage of psychotherapy treatment, controversy has raged. It is exacerbated by conflict among the multiple disciplines involved as providers of mental health services. Although an unusual technology problem, its policy significance is large.

Background. In 1979, the Senate Finance Committee held hearings and began a review of funding for mental health services. Their interest was stimulated by the President's Commission on Mental Health (1978), which had identified groups within the United States in need of mental health services who were unserved. Interest in mental health treatment was also prompted by increasingly effective lobbying activities of mental health professionals. A related issue was recognition that Medicare (government health insurance for the elderly and disabled) was financially out of control.

OTA was already conducting a study at the request of the Finance Committee on the use of cost-effectiveness/benefit analyses (CEA/CBA) for health policy decision making. Under the umbrella of the CEA/CBA study, the committee asked OTA to conduct a case study of psychotherapy. Accoring to the committee, there were "over 130 psychotherapies" and there was "an urgent need to detemine which of those were efective, which were ineffective, and which were reasonable, given their costs and particular outcomes." Although the request was based on a genuine interest in improved health policy, many involved in mental health services and research were displeased. For such experts, it was self-evident that no single entity could be called psychotherapy, and some were perturbed at characterizing psychotherapy as a technology, akin to medical procedures.

Given the disjuncture between how legislators described the problem and how psychotherapy was seen by some mental health professionals, a major focus of OTA's analysis was the nature of psychotherapy as well as how different types of research information could be used to evaluate its effects. As project director it was advantageous that my disciplinary base was in social psychology, not clinical. By dint of this background, I shared a common language with clinicians and researchers, but my stake in the outcome was minimal and I had no theoretical "ax to grind" (see Banta and Saxe, 1983; Saxe, 1982).

Findings. The study focused on four issues: (1) the definition and complexity of psychotherapeutic treatments; (2) the degree to which psychotherapy is amenable to scientific analysis; (3) the evidence of efficacy of psychotherapeutic treatments; and (4) the appropriateness and results of CEA/CBA studies of psychotherapy. The study found that psychotherapy is complex, yet evaluable by accepted scientific procedures. Its complexity included elements such as the theoretical orientation of the therapist, the nature of the problem, and the treatment setting. It was suggested that psychotherapy could not be described by simple labels. Nevertheless, various methods (e.g., randomized designs) that have been used to evaluate the effectiveness of treatment were described.

The report also summarized substantive findings of psychotherapy outcome research. This was the most difficult aspect of the study because of the enormous number of potentially relevant studies. Reviews of the psychotherapy literature and commentary generated by these reviews were a principal focus. Most reviews of psychotherapy were positive, and there seemed to be a clear trend: More recent reviews reported more positive findings. The report suggested that available evidence was more supportive of psychotherapy than of alternative explanations and that treatment seemed demonstrably better than no treatment. What was not possible was to indicate under which conditions psychotherapy would be effective.

The psychotherapy assessment involved explicating the nature of the interventions and marshalling evidence as to its effects. The effort differed from evaluations of psychotherapy typically conducted by mental health researchers in that it did not assume effectiveness and did not attempt to make the case for a particular treatment. As policy analysis, the TA attempted to be objective about the nature and outcomes of psychotherapeutic interventions. It also did not attempt to understand the process of therapy, but merely tried to develop a model that would explain its overall impact.

Policy Use. The psychotherapy report was released in 1980 (Office of Technology Assessment, 1980) and was completed in time to contribute to an evolving congressional debate about the Medicare program. The report was reviewed positively in the professional community, perhaps reflecting relief that a TA could identify positive benefits. The report's conclusion, however, left Congress with a dilemma. Considerable scientific evidence was presented that psychotherapy is effective, at least compared to the alternative of not providing treatment. The report also indicated that psychotherapy evaluation is relatively new and that only in recent years have data accumulated. Because rigorous evaluation was in a nascent state and changes were occurring rapidly in mental health treatment, many questions remained unanswered.

Stimulated by the report and by discussions with OTA, Finance Committee staff working with their senators devised an ingenious approach to the problem. Coverage for psychotherapy would be expanded based on evidence of efficacy and safety. As existing data were inadequate or inapplicable, a special commission would be established to advise the government as to the conditions under which reimbursement should be provided. The commission would synthesize existing research data, consider them in light of clinical experience, and make specific coverage recommendations. Referred to as the efficacy amendment, it was an interesting solution because it satisfied critics who thought psychotherapy would not pass research scrutiny. Proponents were more sanguine that such positive evidence could be provided.

The efficacy amendment did not become law, however, in part because the elections of 1980 led to change from Democratic to Republican control of the Senate and its committees. Since that time, the financial condition of the Medicare program has deteriorated and few proposals for expanded coverage have been considered.

Alcoholism

OTA's alcoholism project was an outgrowth of some of the same conditions that led to the demise of the efficacy amendment. By the time Congress organized in early 1981, it was clear that major changes to Medicare were required. Costs for Medicare (along with other health programs) were increasing faster than any other sector of the economy; in addition, deliberate efforts were being made by the new administration to shift spending priorities.

Background. As with the psychotherapy project, the requesting committee was the Senate Finance Committee. In the summer of 1982, the committee had agreed to reduce the Medicare budget over a 5-year period by $13 billion. Such a reduction could not be funded by administrative changes, and in order to reduce this amount, it was necessary to review specific benefits. Alcoholism treatment was a likely target. Treatment programs for alcoholics served a population believed responsible for their own problem. Unlike other patient groups, alcoholics were unlikely to have an organized lobby that could generate widespread public sympathy and support. In addition, as a result of initial investigation by committee staff, several examples of fraud and abuse were detected.

The most dramatic examples of alleged fraud concerned a proprietary hospital system. The hospitals were well known because of their use of aversive conditioning (pairing alcohol use with vomiting) as a centerpiece of inpatient alcohol treatment (Smith, 1982). The hospitals had been identified in the news as allegedly violating of Medicare rules, for example, by shifting patients across facilities to extend eligibility. Finance Committee staff were convinced that the high cost of inpatient treatment provided by such facilities was unjustified. They openly sought OTA's help to provide "scientific" documentation about the inefficacy of treatment for alcoholism.

Study. Similar to the psychotherapy project, this study was done as a "case study" within a larger assessment of the Medicare system. The charge was also similar to the psychotherapy project: to synthesize scientific evidence on efficacy and to assess the cost-effectiveness of alcoholism treatment. Because of budget and time constraints, the study would be reviewed by the advisory panel of the larger study, along with a large group of ad hoc reviewers. I worked with several colleagues as outside consultants supervised by the staff of the Medicare project.

The report that resulted from the study (Saxe et al., 1983) included an overview of the alcoholism problem and the multiple approaches to treatment. Even more explicitly than psychotherapy, alcoholism is dealt with by multiple disciplines, and much of the problem in understanding alcoholism deals with the extent to which it is a medical versus a social problem. The study attempted to describe the multiple etiological bases for alcoholism and their relationship to treatment programs. The report reviewed the range of research methods and findings about alcoholism. There appears to be substantial evidence to indicate that alcoholism can be treated. The problem, however, is that we do not know which of the available treatment methods work with whom. The conclusion that one is better off with treatment than without was sustained.

For policy purposes, probably the most important aspect of the report was its analysis of the costs of alcoholism and the effectiveness of treatments. It was estimated that alcoholism (in 1980 U.S. dollars) cost approximately $10,000 per alcoholic per year and, under such conditions almost any investment in treatment was likely to be beneficial. What surprised even those of us working on the report was the extent to which alcoholism had large and relatively easy-to-measure economic costs. Not only were data clear about the role of alcohol in traffic accidents and cirrhosis of the liver, but substantial evidence was available of the role of alcohol in virtually every form of criminal and antisocial activity, as well as its pervasive impact on health care and health costs.

As with the psychotherapy report, the conclusions of the alcoholism case study were disappointing to the requestors. They had sought ammunition to support funding cuts in alcohol treatment and the evidence suggested otherwise. Perhaps the most important outcome of the report was that hearings were not held to discuss the report. The report suggested that the amount spent on alcoholism treatment was minuscule in relation to the cost of the problem and implied that increases, rather than decreases in funding, were required.

Polygraph Testing

A very different substantive problem is represented by the assessment of polygraph testing (OTA, 1983; Saxe et al., 1985). Its genesis was a change in regulations proposed by the Department of Defense (DOD). The change would have resulted in the use of polygraph tests for preemployment and periodic security screening. This was followed by an even more far-reaching National Security Directive issued by President Reagan in February 1983, which instructed agencies to develop policies to permit personnel with access to classified information to be subjected to polygraph testing. The justification was the need to maintain security of critical national security information.

The proposed changes created an intense congressional reaction. The chairman of the House Committee on Government Operations was particularly concerned and asked both OTA and the GAO to study polygraph tests (see Brooks, 1985). OTA was specifically asked to assess the scientific validity of polygraph testing. In the Senate, the ranking minority member of the Committee on Armed Services engineered passage of an amendment to prevent DOD from implementing expanded polygraph testing until Congress had reviewed the matter.

Design. At OTA, although involvement in controversial issues was not new, the polygraph issue was novel. It was a relatively specific problem, but it was in an area that did not have a clear scientific disciplinary base. Because of the emphasis of the request on the underlying scientific issues assumed to be psychophysiological, the project was referred to the Health Program and, eventually, the work was contracted out to myself and colleagues (see Saxe et al., 1985). I was selected because of my methodological expertise, my neutrality about polygraph testing, and because of a track record with earlier OTA reports.

An important feature of how this study was structured was the use of an advisory panel. As with other OTA panels, its function was not to determine conclusions but to provide nonbinding advice to OTA on the scientific issues. A 12-member panel was selected, most of whom were scientists from psychology, medicine, and criminal justice. The panel included leading researchers on polygraph testing, as well as their critics, and several panel members had extensive experience as polygraph examiners. The number of proponents, opponents, and neutral scientists was carefully balanced.

Results. The relatively specific focus of this study enabled us to deal with the population of relevant research. Approximately 4,000 references were identified in the polygraph literature. Less than 10% of these sources, however, were empirical investigations, and of the almost 350 empirical studies, fewer than 40 were methodologically sound. Most empirical studies were uncontrolled case reports. Despite availability of a specific literature, definitional problems and the nature of the technology played an even more significant role in this study than in either of the studies on psychotherapy and alcoholism. What was learned is that there was little theory to explain polygraph test efficacy. Proponents and antagonists of testing often disagreed because they thought about testing differently and referred to different aspects of the technology.

As a result, much of the study consisted of developing an understanding of the mechanisms by which polygraph tests operated. It appeared that there were various uses, which could be roughly distinguished as being either screening (e.g., testing prospective employees for honesty) or specific incident testing (e.g., testing an individual about a specific crime). Although there are many nuances, screening uses different techniques than specific incident testing. Screening tests used a test in which physiological reactions to relevant questions are compared to reactions to irrelevant questions. A specific incident examination, in contrast, compares reactions to questions that are supposed to be arousing for all subjects compared to relevant questions about a specific incident.

Examination of the empirical data was revealing in a different way. First, despite extensive efforts, no evidence was available that directly investigated situations analogous to screening. Two studies came close, but there were enough differences to make them not generalizable. Almost all research evidence concerned the specific incident tests, either from actual cases (field studies) or from simulated situations (analogues). There were 10 field studies of the use of the CQT and another 25 analogue studies. Not only did these studies deal exclusively with specific incident situations, they dealt mostly with criminal cases in which crime against persons was involved. With perhaps one exception, no studies investigated national security situations. This suggested extreme restrictions to generalizability of the available data.

Even more important, when explanations of the deviations in response to polygraph tests were examined, a mechanism seemed clear. Using data from simulations using supposed polygraph tests (the "bogus pipeline"), results seemed to depend on the interaction between examiner and subject. If a subject is convinced of the efficacy of the test, then it may be effective. In addition, subjects' nervousness, sense of morality, intelligence, or psychopathy, as well as examiner training may affect test results, and test can be defeated. Perhaps the simplest countermeasure is to train people to believe that the polygraph cannot detect them. Other countermeasures include movement in response to control questions and the use of drugs to blunt arousal.

Utilization

The political history of the polygraph study is not yet complete. Following release of OTA's report, findings were presented at hearings of the Government Operations Committee. As a result, legislation was introduced that followed the line of argument of the report; that is, there was no evidence for screening uses of the polygraph. Parallel legislation was not introduced in the Senate, although as a result of the DOD amendment, there was a need to hold hearings. The results of hearings held both in the Senate and by the House, at which the OTA findings were presented,was that DOD did not go ahead with full implementation.

It is not clear what will happen at this point. Legislation is pending in both the House and Senate to prohibit use of polygraph tests in employment situations. Interestingly, the use of the OTA report seems to have been very literal. From my perspective, the most important conclusion had to do with the technique's lack of construct validity and the lack of research to validate most uses of testing. Yet the interpretation of the report was that there is limited validity for one type of use (specific incident testing) and no evidence for another (screening). In some respects, the underlying message about the lack of scientific theory has not been a focus. For proponents, it is an anathema and they cannot countenance the thought. Opponents of polygraph testing seem to regard concrete evidence (i.e., studies, however limited, or the lack of them) as the best offense. In the longer run, it is unclear what will be most important. It is hoped that it is the underlying ideas.

Implications

One summary of the examples of social TA described above is that complex problems were attacked with a variety of problem-solving techniques. The analytic techniques were drawn in a loose way from psychology. A number of implications of these assessments pertain to the use of social science knowledge. The theme underlying this analysis is that the utilization of social science is more substantial than is usually acknowledged, but that utilization occurs in much more complex ways than traditionally viewed. Social science, it will be argued, provides a perspective to understand complexity and is not a knowledge base that is merely "tapped." It permits a focus not on simplification, but on explanation of complexity.

Social scientists seem to have long clung to the view that "if only" policymakers would better use our theories and data, deleterious social problems could be solved (see Lindbloom and Cohen, 1979; Weiss, 1977). To be sure, this optimism has not been unbounded. Many who have advocated the greater use of social science have called for major reforms in the way social scientists approach application. Yet for some (e.g., Massad et al., 1983), improving knowledge utilization will happen when social researchers develop a better understanding of the policy process. Such understanding is important, but it is probably insufficient. Successful use of social science by policymakers is dependent on a host of factors. These include how problems are defined, the credibility of researchers, the nature of the arguments developed by researchers, the quality and availability of the research evidence, the ability of analysts to communicate their ideas and research findings, and the timeliness of the policymakers' interest in the issue.

Although the policymakers addressed by OTA's projects are unique, as are the problems, an analysis of how they functioned suggests a view of the policy application process that has wide relevance. It is a view of problem-driven research that both adheres to standards of conceptual rigor and is sensitive to utilization issues. This analysis suggests a number of alternative ways of viewing social scientists' contribution to and function in policy analysis.

Process

The starting point for any policy analysis conducted by OTA is a specific problem. Interestingly, in the TAs described above, the assessments drew on a variety of disciplines and substantive expertise was only of limited usefulness. This problem occurs in a variety of areas. Health problems, for example, are often expressed by policymakers as economic ones, much to the chagrin of medical practitioners. For policy purposes, the content of the problem may be different than the context within which it occurs. In many situations, a problem becomes a public policy issue because of the failure of substantive experts to solve it within their domain. Each of the cases described above reflects such failure.

Another feature of how policymakers present questions is that they describe them in global terms: Is psychotherapy cost-effective? Is treatment for alcoholism effective? Are polygraph tests valid? Such questions are not designed to be answered by single research studies. Although policymakers thrive on dramatic illustrations of problems, there is implicit recognition of the need to "weigh" the body of evidence. In the alcoholism project, for example, although charges of fraud and abuse were highlighted as part of Senate hearings, there was recognition that policy could not be altered without considering systematic evidence of effectiveness.

It is also true that policy problems are reframed for particular groups to answer. In the case of OTA, requesting committees need to shape their questions in a way that is amenable to syntheses of scientific findings. This necessitates that questions are stated neutrally and with an emphasis on objective analysis. A side benefit of OTA's bipartisan structure is that congressional staff are guided to frame questions scientifically. The requester of the polygraph study had strong initial beliefs, yet the request was made in a neutral way that did not necessitate a particular answer.

Credibility. Given that there are no universally accepted principles in social science, how does one gain credibility? In OTA's case, there are several important mechanisms: the organization's structure, its reputation, and the use of advisory panels. Each of these played an important role in determining the infuence generated by the social TAs described above. In contrast to research done by individual investigators, OTA's work is the result of a team effort. OTA is organized much like a university with departments ("programs") and schools ("divisions"), yet a strong collaborative norm exists. Individuals work on multiple projects and there is extensive review of projects, both internally and externally (Wood, 1982). Although intense disagreements sometimes arise about project conclusions, the process is designed to resolve these conflicts and produce a product that has broad acceptability.

The use of advisory panels is also key to how OTA gains credibility, and they are critical to how assessments are conducted. Panels do not determine project conclusions, but they provide important input about the focus of the projects and serve as key reviewers. Analysts attempt to incorporate the information provided by advisors and reviewers in the final report. Although this is not always possible because reviewers may contradict one another, be irrelevant or incorrect, knowing the preponderance of views (along with minority positions) is essential.

One effect of the team nature of projects and the use of advisory panels is that OTA reports have high credibility. Reports are not merely the opinions of their authors, but have the imprimatur of the U.S. Congress. Congressional staff have respect for the organization and seem to give OTA's views added weight. In part, this influence may be exaggerated. There is an assumption that science has clear-cut answers (hence, the nonpartisan structure of OTA), and when opinions are delivered by OTA they are regarded as the "best" of current knowledge.

Neutrality. OTA has been criticized (Dreyfus, 1977: 105) for not having "the time, or perhaps temerity, to offer policy judgments on politically charged issue[s]." This is intentional, and the key operating phrase at OTA is *evenhanded*. Analysts are expected to take a neutral stance and OTA reports never include explicit recommendations. Dreyfus suggests that OTA's early work was characterized by presentations of undigested facts. Although dull and perhaps unuseful analysis would be suggested by the phrase *evenhanded*, that does not characterize my own OTA work. How one chooses to organize a problem, from its definition to the nature of evidence used to assess effects, inherently involves an active processing of information and the inclusion of recommendations is irrelevant.

A key way in which evenhandedness is operationalized is in the choice of staff. Project staff may be chosen for their expertise in a particular problem area, but more often because of generic methodological or policy analysis skills. In my case, in none of the three projects was I initially expert. This relative ignorance was an advantage, as not having a particular theoretical view tied to the problem allowed greater objectivity. In the psychotherapy study, it make it possible to conceptualize mental health treatments as an entity and not emphasize either behavioral, humanistic, or dynamic approaches. In the alcoholism project, it made it possible to examine the overall impact of the problem and not become entangled, as was the literature, in disputes about matters such as controlled drinking and aversive conditioning. In the polygraph study, it was clear that if we had been advocates of a particular position it might not have been possible to form an advisory panel.

This is not to say that I am totally neutral. In fact, my perspective as a social psychologist played an important role in how the analyses were conducted (see Saxe, 1983). No doubt, I was influenced by this perspective to see problems as ones of interactions among individuals. In addition, I sought data that had high internal and construct validity (see Cook and Campbell, 1979; Saxe and Fine, 1981). Not to have any perspective would have made us incapable of conducting the studies. In the psychotherapy project, the principal conclusion was that efficacy is an interaction among a variety of factors: the treatment, setting, nature of the patient's problem, and characteristics of the therapist. Our solution to the policy dilemma was to propose establishment of a commission that could fund research and translate its results into reimbursement policy. In the alcoholism report, the conclusion was similar: that the problem is multiply caused and that a treatment system needs to be established that reflects the various factors. Again, the central idea was to use data to indicate policy. In an even clearer way, the polygraph study employed a social psychological model. The report suggests that, to the extent the technique has validity, it is due to what social psychologists have called the "bogus pipeline"; that is, convincing subjects that they can be detected.

It has long been recognized (e.g., Berg, 1975) that the TA process is not value-free. Analyses, although evenhanded, are guided by a set of values and a broad conceptual framework. In the assessments described here, the values concern improving social conditions and the framework is drawn from social psychology. There is an important distinction between such a framework and the usual way in which problems are examined. To some extent, the work of OTA is to monitor and control the application of science. What is needed is a framework that allows objective assessment of the implications of a technology from a perspective external to the technology. Thus, mental health technologies need to be evaluated by criteria other than those used by mental health professionals and the polygraph by nonpolygraphers. It is, in a sense, the operational definition of taking a societal policy perspective on a problem.

Problems and Potential

Below are two views of the process of TA in terms of social science knowledge. It is clear that the policy process is complex and that social science contributions are only one element.

Limited Role. My tone has been very positive with respect to the contributions that social science can make to national policymaking. A caveat needs to be provided, however, in terms of the peripheral role that social science has played at OTA. Despite its influence in the assessments described here, it is not the model for other analyses conducted at OTA. Each of the projects was not a full TA, and they were all done primarily by staff working outside of OTA (as a consultant/contractor). To date, there has not been a large-scale TA that is uniquely based on a social technology, such as a study of leadership or prejudice. The reason for this lack of direct social science involvement has to do as much with how social scientists view their contribution as with policymakers' views. Social scientists are, perhaps, defensive about their disciplinary identification and about the limits of their abilities to understand particular problems. Until social scientists become more secure about their contributions, it may be difficult for their perspective to be respected.

Dealing with Complexity. Although useful to consider what we might do given the opportunity, it is important to consider what we have accomplished. Particular national policy decisions have probably not been changed. What has happened, however, as a result of our work is that the debate about the issues we have studied is more informed. It is the "educative" function of social research. The level of debate in Congress has been affected, and we have provided policymakers with the tools to understand problems not previously available to them.

In some discussions, public policy is presented as a simple decision-making process. A series of yes/no decisions are made about specific problems. Experience, based on the projects described here, suggests that is not the case. First, decisions are inordinately complex, and the number of factors considered in any one decision is staggering. Even those who are cynical about the role of politics need to acknowedge that partisan concerns are complex. Policymakers need to include a large number of factors. In some ways, it is more complex that making a decision about the strength of evidence about a particular problem.

In the case of psychotherapy, although the initial question seemed simple (is or is not psychotherapy effective?), even policymakers did not expect that it could be answered in a simple fashion. More importantly, the political issues are not simple, Congressional staff opposed to increasing reimbursement for psychotherapy did not consider themselves "Neanderthals" and were interested in the welfare of the greatest number of people. Their concerns about psychotherapy were that it was a potentially uncontrollable technology (because demand is dependent on the client and practitioner) and that its value was dubious. Cost-benefit analysis was attractive because it was a formal way to make sense of a difficult set of trade-offs.

The issues were similar in the alcoholism study. In several respects, the complexity of the treatment system (its medical, psychological, and social welfare bases) misleads policymakers as to the nature of the problem. Debate within the mental health community about the best ways to deal with the problem only provided additional confusion. The analysis task was to develop a model of the problem, supported by data, that could explain this complexity and indicate how responsible social policy might be formulated.

Thus, problem conceptualization is critical. It is clear that the principal benefit of the polygraph study was its conceptualization of the technology as more than a gadget. A central theme of the analysis was that it was the way in which questions were structured and examiners related to subjects that determined the effectiveness of tests. Although policymakers did not utilize the conceptual information as much as we would have liked, our analysis changed the context of the discussion. Debate moved from one about values concerning privacy and civil liberties to one focusing on the nature of the technology and its function.

This view contradicts a prevailing view within social science disciplines of the differences between basis and applied research (e.g., Bickman, 1981). The characterization of basic research as a knowledge-driven search for causal relationships with applied research as focused on problem solving and prediction is an oversimplification. Applied research, in order to analyze adequately policy problems, must be driven by a conceptual search for relationships and causes. This view is supported by empirical data. In Weiss and Bucavalas's (1977) study of federal, state, and local mental health policymakers, survey data suggest that research is useful both when it helps to solve specific problems and when it questions perspectives and definitions of a problem. Research is useful, thus, when it challenges the conceptual status quo. These findings parallel those of Caplan (1975) and are supported by recent emphases on accumulative effects of knowledge (see Weiss, 1980).

Future

It should be clear that the OTA work described here is only one of several models for social scientists. Social scientists concerned about the utilization of knowledge need to proceed on a number of tracks: theory development, applied research, and policy analysis. One question is whether social scientists engaged in this myriad of activities can talk with one another and whether our work can crossfertilize one another's efforts. The answer is important, not only for parochial concerns about the health of social science but in terms of our ability to solve social problems. Social science is a voice that needs to be heard. We need to maintain our identity, but we also need to learn how to act in the world at large.

The view developed here is that social scientific analysis serves an educative function in the development of policy. It is a perspective on policy that, when developed in the context of specific problems, can offer policymakers useful understandings of their policy dilemmas. The examples provided here of analyses conducted for OTA indicate that such analysis is possible and that it can influence how national policy is formulated. Such work does not necessarily change policy; it does, however, influence policy. In a pluralistic society committed to democratic ideals, that is perhaps all that one should expect.

References

ARNSTEIN, S. (1977) "Technology assessment: opportunities and obstacles." IEEE Transactions on Systems, Man, and Cybernetics 7: 571-582.

BAMGORD, J. (1982) The Puzzle Palace. New York: Houghton Mifflin.

BANTA, H. D. and C. J. BEHNEY (1981) "Policy formulation and technology assessment." Milbank Memorial Fund Q. 51: 445-479.

BANTA, H. D. and L. SAXE (1983) "Reimbursement for psychotherapy: linking efficacy research and public policymaking." Amer. Psychologist 38: 918-923.

BARAM, M. (1973) "Technology assessment and social control." Science 180 (May 4): 465-472.

BERG, M. R. (1975) "The politics of technology assessment." J. of the Int. Society for Technology Assessment 1: 21-32.

BICKMAN, L. (1981) "Some distinctions between basic and applied approaches," in L. Bickman (ed.) Applied Social Psychology Annual. Beverly Hills, CA: Sage.

BROOKS, J. (1985) "Polygraph testing: thoughts of a skeptical legislator." Amer. Psychologist 40.

CAPLAN, N., A. MORRISON, and R. J. STRANBAUGH (1975) The Use of Social Science Knowledge in Policy Decisions at the National Level. Ann Arbor, MI: Institute for Social Research.

COOK, T. D. and D. T. CAMPBELL (1979) Quasi-Experimentation: Design and Analysis Issues For Field Settings. Chicago: Rand McNally.

DREYFUS, D. A. (1977) "The limitations of policy research in congressional decision making," in C. H. Weiss (ed.) Using Social Research in Public Policy Making, Lexington, MA: Lexington Books.

FRANK, J. D. (1966) "Galloping technology: a new social disease." J. of Social Issues 22, 4: 1-14.

GIBBONS, J. (1984) "Technology assessment for congress." Bridge, 2-8.

GLASS, G., B. McGAW, and M. L. SMITH (1981) Meta-Analysis in Social Research. Beverly Hills, CA: Sage.

KOPPEL, B. (1979) "Evaluating assessment: a comment and a perspective." Technological Forecasting and Social Change 14: 147-152.

LINDBLOM, C. E. and D. K. COHEN (1979) Usable Knowledge: Social Science and Social Problem Solving. New Haven, CT: Yale Univ. Press.

MASSAD, P. M., B. D. SALES, and E. ACOSTA (1983) "Utilizing social science information in the policy process: can psychologists help?" In R. F. Kidd and M. J. Saks (eds.) Advances in Applied Social Psychology. Hillsdale, NJ: Erlbaum.

Office of Technology Assessment (1980) The Efficacy and Cost-Effectiveness of Psychotherapy. Background Paper #3, Cost-Effectiveness of Medical Technology. Washington, DC: Government Printing Office.

ROSENTHAL, R. (1984) Meta-Analytic Procedures for Social Research. Beverly Hills, CA: Sage.

SAXE, L. (1982) "Public policy and psychotherapy: can evaluative research play a role?" in New Directions for Program Evaluation: Making Evaluation Useful to Congress. San Francisco: Jossey-Bass.

———(1983) "The perspective of social psychology: toward a viable model for application," pp. 231-255 in R. F. Kidd and M. J. Saks (eds.) Advances in Applied Social Psychology. Hillsdale, NJ: Erlbaum.

———and M. FINE (1981) Social Experiments: Methods for Design and Evaluation. Beverly Hills, CA: Sage.

SAXE, L. and D. KORETS [eds.] (1982) "Making evaluation research useful to Congress." New Directions for Program Evaluation 14 (June).

SAXE, L., D. DOUGHERTY, and T. CROSS (1985) "The validity of polygraph testing." Amer. Psychologist 40.

SAXE, L., D. DOUGHERTY, and K. ESTY (1985) "Alcoholism: a public policy perspective," in J. Mendelson and N. Mello (eds.) The Diagnosis and Treatment of Alcoholism. New York: Wiley.

———and M. FINE (1983) The Effectiveness of Treatment for Alcoholism. Washington, DC: Government Printing Office.

SMITH, J. W. (1982) "Treatment of alcoholism in aversion conditioning hospitals," in E. M. Pattison and E. Kaufman (eds.) Encyclopedic Handbook of Alcoholism. New York: Gardner Press.

WEISS, C. H. (1977) "Introduction," in C. H. Weiss (ed.) Using Social Research in Public Policy Making. Lexington, MA: Lexington Books.

———(1980) "Knowledge creep and decision accretion." Knowledge: Creation, Diffusion, Utilization 1: 381-404.

———and M. J. BUCUVALAS (1977) "The challenge of social research to decision making," pp. 213-230 in C. H. Weiss (ed.) Using Social Research in Public Policy Making. Lexington, MA: Lexington Press.

WOOD, F. B. (1982) "The status of technology assessment: a view from the congressional office of technology assessment." Technological Forecasting and Social Change 22: 211-222.

LEONARD SAXE is Director of the Center for Applied Social Science and Associate Professor of Psychology at Boston University. He has been a Congressional Fellow and consultant to the U.S. Congress, Office of Technology Assessment. He is a social psychologist interested in the conduct of social research and its application to public policy.

12

The Job Corps
Congressional Uses of Evaluation Findings

Joseph S. Wholey

I n the early 1980s, evaluation played a significant role in congressional decisions to maintain funding for the Job Corps in the face of Reagan administration attempts to eliminate or to curtail the program. The story goes on as this chapter is written. The Reagan administration again seeks to eliminate the Job Corps and a number of other domestic programs, and evaluation information is again being used in congressional decisions on the fate of the Job Corps.

Initiated twenty years ago under the Economic Opportunity Act, the Job Corps is a relatively high-cost training program designed to improve the employability of disadvantaged youth, all of whom are from poor families and most of whom are school dropouts. In addition to skills training, the Job Corps offers comprehensive services, including basic education and health care, in approximately 100 centers, most of which are operated by private contractors. By the early 1980s, the Job Corps was enrolling nearly 100,000 youth each year, at an annual cost of approximately $600 million. The Job Corps has frequently been questioned because of its high cost per training slot ("it would be cheaper to send them to Harvard"), because of issues related to administration or to particular centers, and as a symbol of the liberally oriented "War on Poverty."

The Reagan administration's efforts to reduce federal domestic expenditures have included proposals for large cuts in Job Corps funding. Though Congress agreed to a 60 percent reduction in federally funded employment and training programs between early 1981 and mid-1983, Congress maintained Job Corps funding at approximately $600 million per year. Congressional decisions not to accept the administration's Job Corps proposals appear to have been influenced by evaluation evidence that demonstrated that the program is effective and that its benefits to society outweigh its high cost.

This chapter examines a major evaluation of the Job Corps and the use of that evaluation by Congress.[1] The evaluation demonstrated that (1) Job Corps participants had better postprogram experiences than comparable

Reprinted by permission of the publisher, from *Performance and Credibility,* edited by Joseph S. Wholey, Mark A. Abramson, Christopher Bellavita (Lexington, Mass.: Lexington Books, D. C. Heath and Company, Copyright 1986, D. C. Heath and Company).

youth not enrolled in the program, (2) those enrolled in the Job Corps for longer periods had much better results, and (3) Job Corps' economic benefits to society exceed the high cost of the program. Though many factors influence budget decisions, the positive evaluation findings played a significant role as Congress decided to maintain Job Corps funding and enrollment levels in a different budget environment.

Job Corps Evaluations

Over the years there have been several evaluations of the Job Corps. For most of these evaluations, inadequate data or inadequate analytic methods made it difficult to estimate the extent to which the program was producing intended effects, and left study findings open to serious question.

In 1976, after a period in which the program was redirected and then stabilized, the Employment and Training Administration's (ETA's) Office of Policy, Evaluation and Research contracted for a major longitudinal evaluation of the benefits and costs of the Job Corps. This evaluation, which took six years and cost more than $2 million, compared the postprogram experience of a large sample of Corpsmembers participating in the program in the spring of 1977 with the experiences of a comparable group of disadvantaged youth who had not been in the Job Corps. The comparison group members were selected from school dropouts and employment service applicants in areas of the country that were similar to the areas from which Corpsmembers came, but in which the Job Corps did not recruit extensively. Baseline surveys were done in the spring of 1977; follow-up surveys were conducted at periods of 9, 24, and 54 months after the baseline survey to document postprogram experiences on a variety of relevant measures. The last survey included more than 3,900 youth, represented nearly 70 percent of the baseline observations, and included an average of forty-eight months of postprogram experiences of Corpsmembers.

In 1980, an interim report from this evaluation found that the Job Corps had a positive, sizable effect on participants in the first twenty-four months and estimated that the program's economic benefits to society were greater than its costs.[2] Estimates based on the interim evaluation indicated that the Job Corps returned $1.39 for every $1.00 expended on program services.[3]

In 1982, after the experiences of participants and comparison group members had been tracked for an additional thirty months, the final report from the evaluation stated that:

> During the first four postprogram years, we find that Job Corps is at least moderately successful in achieving its desired effects: (1) increasing employment and earnings, (2) improving labor-market opportunities through work

experience, military service, higher education and training, better health, and geographic mobility, (3) reducing dependency on welfare assistance and other public transfers, and (4) reducing criminality.[4]

The measured effects included the following (on a per-Corpsmember basis, including military jobs, and averaged over the four-year observation period):

1. An increase in employment (more than three weeks per year).

2. An increase in earnings of approximately $655 per year (more than 15 percent).

3. A very substantial increase in the probability of having a high school diploma or equivalent (a 27 percentage point increase).

4. Fewer serious health problems (a reduction of more than one week per year).

5. Less dependence on welfare (a reduction of two weeks per year).

6. Less dependence on unemployment insurance (a reduction of nearly one week per year).

7. No effect on arrests, but a significant shift from more to less serious crimes (fewer thefts and more traffic offenses).[5]

The evaluators concluded that:

8. A substantial positive correlation exists between the estimated Job Corps impacts and the proportion of the Job Corps completed. Impact estimates for those who completed the program were generally more than twice the overall program average, partial completers made only small gains, and early program dropouts made little or no gains over comparable nonparticipants.

9. The program's economic benefits to society were estimated to be approximately $7,400 per participant in 1977 dollars, in comparison with costs of approximately $5,100. Because more than 40,000 youths enrolled in Job Corps during 1977, net social benefits were estimated to be more than $90 million for that year.

10. A substantial part of the economic benefits of the Job Corps (approximately $2,900 per Corpsmember) were associated with reduction in criminal activity by Corpsmembers, particularly murder, robbery, and larceny (including substantial reductions of these and burglary during the program).

11. Additional unmeasured, intangible benefits would increase the estimates of net benefits to society if economic values were assigned to them; for

example, reductions in the psychological costs of crime for actual and potential victims and participants' satisfaction from working rather than receiving welfare.

12. Economic benefits exceed costs under a wide range of alternative assumptions, estimated effects, and values, without including any of the unmeasured benefits. As long as displacement in the labor markets that Corpsmembers enter was not severe and the observed crime reductions were at least minimally valued, Job Corps was estimated to be an economically efficient investment.[6]

Mathematica's Job Corps evaluation was impressive in its successful effort to maintain contact with participants and comparison group members over a four-year period. Equally impressive was its presentation of findings under a wide range of alternative assumptions; for example, alternative assumptions as to the persistance of the effects measured over the four-year period and alternative assumptions as to the discount rate that should be used for assigning present value to benefits to be received in future years. At the request of the Office of Management and Budget (OMB), the Department of Labor asked several reviewers to critique the Job Corps evaluation. Though the reviewers raised several technical questions and noted possible uncertainties (particularly about possibly inadequate control for selection bias in construction of the comparison group), the reviewers commended the evaluation as generally meeting such questions as well as the current state of the art permitted and concluded that the basic evaluation findings were strong and credible.[7]

Dissemination and Use of the Evaluation Findings

The findings of the 1980 interim evaluation of the Job Corps were widely disseminated by the ETA's Office of Policy, Evaluation and Research. The findings from the interim evaluation (which were confirmed in the longer time period covered in the final report) were made known, not only to the Job Corps staff and the contractors operating Job Corps centers, but also to the key officials in the Department of Labor and in the OMB, to congressional committee staffs, to key members of the House and Senate, and to the press. Any use of evaluation findings by private contractors has not been examined and is not covered here.

The OMB was not influenced by the evaluation, considering the Job Corps to be a high-cost program whatever its merits. OMB, which had long been a critic of Job Corps "wastefulness," regarded the program as an obvious target given the new administration's strong desire to reduce the federal role in, and federal expenditures for, social programs. OMB pressed for reduction of the Job Corps on grounds of the program's high unit cost. In addition, OMB stressed that most enrollees left the Job Corps quickly and that the program's benefits were concentrated on relatively new participants.

Early in 1981, as the Reagan administration was taking office and talk of budget cuts was everywhere, the *Washington Post* published an editorial on the Job Corps under the title, "A Social Program That Works." *The Post* characterized the Job Corps as effective: "Not an automatic ticket to the middle class but a long step in the right direction."[8]

On February 26, 1981, a key conservative republican, Orrin Hatch, took the Senate floor to encourage his colleagues to maintain the Job Corps. Hatch had been impressed by a Job Corps center in his state that was operated by a private contractor. He had been reassured that the center was representative. His staff had been made aware that a credible evaluation study showed that the Job Corps produced significant, lasting benefits. After quoting *The Post* editorial and referring to his recent visit to the Clearfield (Utah) Job Corps Center, Hatch continued:

> As the new chairman of the Senate Labor and Human Resources Committee, I am more committed than ever to insure the continuation of *The Post's* description of what "a social program can hope to achieve." Here at last, in that process of achievement, is a Government training program that provides jobs and saves more dollars than it expends. . . .

After describing both the national program and the Clearfield Center, he continued,

> These students who have enrolled in the Job Corps, according to both government statistics and an ongoing independent study by a private and independent research firm, have markedly increased their employment and earnings, reduced their dependence on welfare assistance and other public transfers, reduced criminality, reduced extramarital children, delayed family formation in females, and almost doubled the likelihood of entering the armed forces.
>
> Are these benefits worth the cost when measured against an average student staying six months with an average center operational cost of $3,800 per student? The comprehensive evaluation of the social benefits and costs back up observations that, indeed, the public investment in Job Corps is economically efficient. . . .

Senator Hatch concluded:

> To reduce inflation, I totally subscribe to federal budget cuts which will improve the economy. However, it would be foolhardy to reduce the Job Corps which is doing that already. . . .[9]

On March 1, 1981, the *Washington Post* reported that, "[T]he Job Corps, originally slated for a major reduction, has been largely spared after pleas from Congress."[10] Aside from attempts to achieve across-the-board cuts in Department of Labor programs later in 1981, the administration postponed its attempts to achieve major reductions in Job Corps funding. The Omnibus Budget Reconciliation Act of 1981 signaled major surgery for most programs funded under the Comprehensive Employment and Training Act (CETA), including elimination of the Public Service Employment program, but produced no change in the Job Corps.

In 1982 Congress again used information on Job Corps effectiveness in deciding to maintain the Job Corps. In its report on the Job Training Partnership Act of 1982 (P.L. 97–300), which made substantial program changes in replacing CETA, for example, the Senate Committee on Labor and Human Resources stated that:

> Title IV B of the Comprehensive Employment and Training Act authorizing the Job Corps is retained unamended.[11]

On the House side, the Committee on Education and Labor stated that:

> Because of the exemplary success which the Job Corps has demonstrated over a number of years in making the hardest-to-employ youth employable, the Committee believes that it is most important to continue this program without the disruption engendered by unnecessary changes in authorizing provisions. Therefore, most existing provisions of law are extended with little or no change.[12]

In 1982 Congress again rejected administration proposals for substantial reduction of Job Corps funding.

After President Reagan was re-elected in 1984, the administration again attempted to eliminate the Job Corps. Though congressional action on the administration's FY 1986 budget has not been completed as this is written, Senator Hatch, generally a supporter of federal budget restraint, has again opposed the administration's efforts to eliminate the Job Corps. Introducing a resolution to express the sense of the Congress that the Job Corps is effective and should not be eliminated, he stated that he had originally been opposed to the Job Corps but had become a supporter because the Job Corps is a benefit rather than a cost to society:

> The Job Corps, I once thought, was not much more than a handout for youth so we could start their welfare dependence much earlier in life.
>
> After I was elected a senator from Utah and was assigned to the Labor and Human Resources Committee, I began to learn much more about the Job Corps. I studied most of the reports on the effectiveness of the program and

the long-term success of its students. Perhaps more importantly, I was invited to visit the Clearfield Job Corps Center operated by the Management and Training Corporation. I was greatly impressed by what I saw and by the enthusiastic responses of the students. It was clear that the Job Corps was not a handout program at all, but a hand-up program designed to give youth a chance to learn lifetime skills.

After summarizing the findings of the Mathematica study and the findings of a study by the Upjohn Institute for Employment Research, Senator Hatch stated that:

In short, I support the Job Corps because it works. We can count the results, measured by those young people who become fully, contributing members of our society rather than welfare junkies.

Senator Hatch concluded:

I want to join Senator Cranston and other bipartisan supporters of the Job Corps in urging that budget reductions which may be necessary this year to control the federal deficit be made in the Job Corps Program as a last resort. If budget cuts are required for economic or equity reasons, they should not damage the essential elements of the Job Corps concept, namely its aim to provide life skills as well as job skills for those youth who are most in need.[13]

Budget Outcomes

Key Senate conservatives, who are ordinarily skeptical of federal social programs, have given considerable weight to evaluation findings that demonstrate the effectiveness of the Job Corps and its value to society. Their support of the Job Corps, based at least in part on its "demonstrated effectiveness," appears to have tilted the balance in favor of maintaining Job Corps funding.

The incoming Reagan administration moved quickly to change the direction of the federal government. Within four weeks of Inauguration Day, 1981, the new administration introduced a "Program for Economic Recovery" that included $35 billion in reductions from the expenditure levels in the FY 1982 budget that the outgoing Carter administration had just proposed. Three weeks later, the new administration produced a revised budget that included another $14 billion in proposed expenditure reductions.

Congress was strongly influenced by the administration's constant pressures to reduce spending in domestic programs: proposed rescissions for FY 1981, a revised budget for FY 1982, actual and threatened vetoes of appropriations that exceeded administration proposals for FY 1982, and proposals for further reduction for FY 1983 and FY 1984. In the Omnibus Budget Reconciliation Act of 1981 and the series of four continuing resolutions that financed the Department of Labor in FY 1982, Congress agreed to substantial reductions in employment and training programs (see table 19–1). Faced with actual and threatened vetoes, Congress made across-the-board cuts in FY 1982 appropriations for the Department of Labor but restored some of these cuts later in the fiscal year. Overall, the administration achieved a 60 percent reduction in funding for employment and training programs between January 1981 and July 1983.[14]

But both Orrin Hatch (chairman of the Senate Committee on Labor and Human Resources) and Dan Quayle (chairman of that committee's Employment and Productivity subcommittee), senators who supported many of the administration's proposed budget reductions, rejected the proposed cuts in Job Corps funding. Though Congress agreed to deep reductions in federally funded employment and training programs in response to Reagan administration proposals, Congress has maintained funding for the Job Corps at approximately $600 million per year. For FY 1982 Congress agreed to deep cuts in general employment and training programs and elimination of the Public Service Employment program, but slightly increased Job Corps funding. For FY 1983 the Administration proposed cutting Job Corps funding to $387 million,[15] but Congress again increased Job Corps funding. As the Congressional Budget Office has reported,

> This program—which has proven effective for those who complete it—has not undergone the more substantial reductions in real funding that have been made in most other employment programs for the disadvantaged.[16]

Conclusion

Information on program effectiveness was used in congressional decisions to maintain Job Corps funding and enrollment levels. Dealing with a very difficult client population, the Job Corps had been shown by a credible evaluation to be effective in terms of its objectives and to return more than its cost to society. An expensive longitudinal evaluation was needed to demonstrate the effectiveness and value of the Job Corps. The evaluation produced clear evidence that the Job Corps increases employment and earnings, increases the likelihood of subsequent education and training, reduces criminal activity, and reduces the need for public assistance and unemployment benefits.

The Job Corps' demonstrated effectiveness—and favorable benefit-cost ratio—appear to have been persuasive to key legislators otherwise disposed to reduction or elimination of social programs. Their support was pivotal in

Table 19–1
Trends in Federal Support for Selected Employment and Training Programs

| | | | *Total Obligations ($ Millions)* | | |
	1980	*1981*	*1982*	*1983*	*1984*
CETA/JTPA Block Grant	3,342	3,692	2,108	2,179	3,301
Job Corps	401	573	583	617	596
Public Service Employment	1,660	750	0	0	0

Source: Budget of the United States Government: Fiscal Years 1982–1986; Employment and Training Report of the President, Fiscal Years 1980 and 1981.

getting Congress to maintain the Job Corps despite the administration's desire to curtail the program during times of wide agreement on the need for budget stringency. The availability of information demonstrating program effectiveness—information that is lacking for most programs—apparently led to a more positive decision for the Job Corps than would have occurred if that information had not been available.

Again in 1985, as the Job Corps is threatened with termination, key conservatives are joining more liberal senators in a bipartisan effort to save a program of demonstrated effectiveness. While many factors influence budget decisions, evidence of a program's effectiveness can sometimes play an influential role.

Notes

1. This chapter expands on observations included in Joseph S. Wholey, "Executive Agency Retrenchment," in Gregory B. Mills and John L. Palmer (Eds.), *Federal Budget Policy in the 1980s* (Washington, D.C.: The Urban Institute, 1984), pp. 295–332. Information on the budget environment and on budget and program outcomes is reprinted with the permission of The Urban Institute Press. I am indebted to Seymour Brandwein for his critical comments and many constructive suggestions on the points made in this and earlier presentations.

2. Charles Mallar et al., "Evaluation of the Economic Impact of the Job Corps Program: Second Follow-up Report," Report prepared for the U.S. Department of Labor, Employment and Training Administration, Office of Policy, Evaluation and Research (Princeton, N.J.: Mathematica Policy Research, 1980).

3. Estimates by the National Council on Employment Policy based on the interim report just cited. See "CETA's Results and Their Implications, a Policy Statement by the National Council on Employment Policy, September, 1981," U.S. Congress, House, Committee on Education and Labor, Subcommittee on Employment Opportunities, "Oversight on CETA Reauthorization," Hearings, 97th Congress, 1st session, November 1981, pp. 154–162.

4. Charles Mallar et al., "Evaluation of the Economic Impact of the Job Corps Program: Third Follow-up Report," Report prepared for the U.S. Department of Labor, Employment and Training Administration, Office of Policy, Evaluation and Research (Princeton, N.J.: Mathematica Policy Research, 1982) and Office of Research and Evaluation, "Evaluation of the Economic Impact of the Job Corps Program: Management Summary" (Washington, D.C.: U.S. Department of Labor, Employment and Training Administration, November 1982).

5. *Ibid.*

6. *Ibid.*

7. Information provided by Employment and Training Administration staff, April 1985.

8. Orrin Hatch, "The Job Corps," *Congressional Record,* February 26, 1981, pp. S 1600–S 1601.

9. *Ibid.*

10. The *Washington Post,* March 1, 1981, p. A4.

11. U.S. Congress, Senate, Committee on Labor and Human Resources, 97th Congress, 2nd session, Senate Report No. 97–469, 1982, p. 8.

12. U.S. Congress, House, Committee on Education and Labor, 97th Congress, 2nd session, House Report No. 97–537, 1982, p. 29.

13. Orrin Hatch, "Favoring the Continuation of the Job Corps Program," *Congressional Record,* February 20, 1985, pp. S 1610–S 1611.

14. Congressional Budget Office, "Major Legislative Changes in Human Resources Programs Since January 1981: Staff Memorandum," Report prepared for Speaker Thomas P. O'Neill (Washington, D.C.: August 1983).

15. U.S. Congress, House, Committee on Education and Labor, "Oversight Hearings on 1983 Budget Request," Hearings, 97th Congress, 2nd session, March 1982, p. 194.

16. Congressional Budget Office, "Major Legislative Changes in Human Resources Programs since January 1981," Staff Memorandum, p. 67.

13

The Tomato Effect
Rejection of Highly Efficacious Therapies

James S. Goodwin and Jean M. Goodwin

THE TOMATO (*Lycopersicon esculentum*) is a New World plant, originally found in Peru and carried back to Spain from whence it quickly spread to Italy (pommidoro) and France, where it was known as the pomme d'amour and thought to have aphrodisiac properties (this is the first recorded confusion between the placebo effect and the tomato effect—described herein). By 1560, the tomato was becoming a staple of the continental European diet.

Of interest is that while this exotic fruit from South America (along with other novel products such as potatoes, corn, beans, cocoa, and tobacco) was revolutionizing European eating habits, at the same time it was ignored or actively shunned in North America.[1,2] During the 18th century, tomatoes were not even cultivated in North America. Not until the 1800s did North Americans accept the tomato as edible; commercial cultivation of tomatoes was rare until the 20th century, although in the past eight decades the tomato has grown to become our largest commercial crop.[1]

The reason tomatoes were not accepted until relatively recently in North America is simple: they were poisonous. Everyone knew they were poisonous, at least everyone in North America. It was obvious. Tomatoes belong to the nightshade (Solanaceae) family. The word "nightshade" is usually preceded by the word "deadly," and for good reason. The leaves and fruit of several plants in this family, for example, belladonna and mandrake, can cause death if ingested in sufficient quantity. The fact that the French and Italians were eating tomatoes in increasing quantities without seeming harm did not encourage colonial Americans to try them. It simply did not make sense to eat poisonous food. Not until 1820, when Robert Gibbon Johnson ate a tomato on the steps of the courthouse in Salem, NJ, and survived, did the people of America begin, grudgingly, we suspect, to consume tomatoes.

The previous paragraphs are meant to explain the derivation of the term "tomato effect." The tomato effect in medicine occurs when an efficacious treatment for a certain disease is ignored or rejected because it does not "make sense" in the light of accepted theories of disease mechanism and drug action. The tomato was ignored because it was clearly poisonous; it would have been foolish to eat one. In analogous fashion, there have been many therapies in the history of medicine that, while later proved highly efficacious, were at one time rejected because they did not make sense. The purpose of this article is to expand on this concept by describing three examples, all from the field of rheumatology. We contend that the tomato effect is in its own way every bit as influential in shaping modern therapeutics as the placebo effect. While the placebo effect has contributed to the enthusiastic and widespread acceptance of therapies later shown to be useless or harmful, the tomato effect has stimulated the rejection or nonrecognition of highly efficacious therapies. Recognition of the reality of the tomato effect, while not preventing future errors, may at least help us better understand our mistakes.

Colchicine

The use of colchicine for the specific treament of acute gout attacks dates back to the fifth century.[3] Colchicum is an extract from the corm of *Colchicum autumnale*, a crocuslike plant found along the eastern shores of the Mediterranean. In the fifth and sixth centuries, Christian and later Moslem physicians in Constantinople demonstrated a fair knowledge of the clinical pharmacology of such extracts—formulation, indications, dosages, and toxicity. Most medical writers of this period recommended the concomitant administration of aromatic spices to prevent the well-recognized gastrointestinal (GI) tract side effects of colchicum. During the next six centuries there were frequent references to the use of colchicum in both acute and chronic gout. Students of the medical school at Salerno, Italy, the first such school in western Europe, continued to learn how to use colchicum to treat gout during the so-called Dark Ages. After the 13th

From the Departments of Medicine (Dr James Goodwin) and Psychiatry (Dr Jean Goodwin), University of New Mexico School of Medicine, Albuquerque.

Reprint requests to Department of Medicine, University of New Mexico School of Medicine, Albuquerque, NM 87131 (Dr J. S. Goodwin).

century, however, all mention of col-chicum as a treatment for gout disap-peared from medical writings, al-though it was occasionally mentioned as a GI tract poison. Colchicum was not reintroduced in the West until 1780, when it reappeared as a major constituent of "l'eau medicinale d'Husson," an enormously successful patent medicine advertised for the treatment of gout and other ail-ments.[4] During the next four decades, colchicum once again became the pri-mary treatment for acute and chronic gout.

It is perhaps useful at this point to reflect on what a powerful and effica-cious medicine colchicum is, one of the few specific treatments ever dis-covered. Gout, a disease more preva-lent in the Middle Ages than at present,[3] is one of the most painful conditions afflicting mankind. Vol-umes of both medical and literary works were devoted to descriptions of the disease. It is clear from medical texts that colchicum extracts were as efficacious as modern-day colchicine in aborting acute gout attacks and preventing recurrences. In short, col-chicum was one of the most clearly efficacious medicines ever discovered. How could it be discarded for 400 years after centuries of successful use? As Copeman[3] has said, "this is a strange page in medical history." He also suggests an explanation. The abandonment of colchicum coincided with the Renaissance. "Then came the Renaissance and the dominance of scholars who, with all this written and practical evidence before them chose to see none of it—their learning seemed like a bandage round their eyes."[3](p46) The problem was that col-chicum and other specific treatments no longer made sense. The Renais-sance brought a return to the medical teachings and practices of Hippocra-tes and Galen, who saw all disease as resulting from a nonspecific imbal-ance of bodily constituents.[5] While specific cures for specific illnesses made sense to the medieval mind steeped in religion and magic, such concepts were repugnant to the enlightened classicists of the Renais-sance. Thus, the Renaissance brought a return to the "classical" therapies for gout—bleeding and purging—and these were still the major treatments when condemned by Sydenham[6] five

centuries later.

The success of l'eau medicinale d'Husson stimulated considerable ac-tivity within the medical community. For a time the sale of this patent medicine was banned in Paris. In 1814, James Watt discovered that the active ingredient was colchicum. At about this same time the kings of England and France were both suc-cessfully treated with colchicum, which conferred regal if not scientific patronage on this treatment. The last major medical holdout was Trous-seau, the French skeptic famed for his statement that we should use new remedies quickly before they lose their efficacy. Apparently he attrib-uted the success of colchicum to the placebo effect. This is the second recorded confusion between the place-bo effect and the tomato effect.

One final point about colchicum. While this treatment fell victim to the return of the holistic concepts of Hippocrates and Galen during the Renaissance, it should also be noted that the discovery of colchicum in all probability stemmed from these very same concepts. Extracts of plant bulbs and roots were frequently used by classical physicians to induce diar-rhea and/or vomiting, thereby purg-ing the body of excesses of particular humors. That one of these extracts, colchicum, had a specific therapeutic effect for a specific disease was recog-nized at about the time when Hippo-cratic and Galenic thought began to be challenged by other medical sys-tems, particularly those of the great Arabic civilization.

Gold

The discovery of the efficacy of gold therapy for rheumatoid arthritis was somewhat analogous to the discovery of colchicum treatments for gout. From 1900 until 1940, the preponder-ant theory of the pathogenesis of rheumatoid arthritis was that it either represented a direct infection of the joints or was a reaction to a chronic infection at another site in the body.[7] Indeed, "chronic infectious arthritis" was a synonym for rheu-matoid arthritis. The popular thera-pies for rheumatoid arthritis evolved directly from that theory. In 1931, Cecil[8] wrote that "the most important single factor in the treatment of rheumatoid arthritis is the removal

of foci of infection." This meant ton-sillectomy, adenoidectomy, and ex-traction of teeth, along with other procedures as indicated. "This de-mands very thorough investigation—there is no use in halfway measures" Osler's Modern Medicine is quoted as stating.[9] Other popular therapies in-cluded vaccination with killed strep-tococci and typhoid bacilli.[7]

The use of gold in the treatment of rheumatoid arthritis evolved directly from this infectious theory. At the end of the 19th century, Koch described the inhibition of the growth of tubercle bacillus in vitro by the salts of several heavy metals, includ-ing gold.[10] This finding led to trials of these compounds in patients with tuberculosis, syphilis, and other chronic infectious diseases, including rheumatoid arthritis. The first re-ported trial of gold salts for treat-ment of rheumatoid arthritis was in 1927, and this was followed by a series of reports both in Europe and the United States noting favorable results with this agent.[11] In 1945, the first double-blind, placebo-controlled trial of gold therapy produced dra-matic results favoring gold therapy. Unfortunately, this favorable report coincided with the discarding of the "infectious" theory of rheumatoid arthritis on which the rationale of gold therapy was based. All "activist" therapy based on the infectious theo-ry was disparaged.[12] Gold rapidly devolved from a scientific to a magical treatment. Without the support of the infectious theory, gold shots became uncomfortably reminiscent of alche-my. The next 20 years witnessed the decreasing popularity of gold therapy in the face of increasing evidence of its effectiveness. While some medical centers continued to inject gold, many ceased using it altogether during the 1950s and early 1960s. Therefore, one textbook of medicine published in 1956 does not mention gold as a therapy for rheumatoid arthritis,[13] while the 1960 edition of the same textbook notes that "it is still being used in many medical centers."[14] A 1966 textbook mentions the popu-larity of gold compounds in the past tense.[15] Gold started to regain its former popularity only when the medical community accepted both the evidence of gold's efficacy and medi-cine's ignorance of gold's mechanism of action. The fact that gold now has an unknown mechanism of action—is a truly idiopathic medicine—is no longer an impediment to its use, because rheumatoid arthritis has become an idiopathic disease.

Aspirin

Extracts of the bark of the willow tree (latin and salix) have been used off and on for almost three millennia for the relief of pain and fever.[7] After the commercial production of sodium salicylate and acetylsalicylic acid started in the late 1800s, high-dose salicylate therapy (12 to 24 aspirin per day) became the treatment of choice for acute rheumatic fever. High-dose salicylate therapy is also recognized today as the initial treatment of choice for rheumatoid arthritis, but this has been the case only since the mid-1950s. At the end of the 19th century there appeared several reports showing that high-dose salicylate therapy was highly efficacious in relieving the pain, swelling, stiffness, and malaise of rheumatoid arthritis. Coincident with the discovery of the efficacy of high doses of salicylates in the treatment of rheumatoid arthritis, however, came the acceptance of the infectious theory of the disease. It did not make sense that aspirin, a pain and fever medicine, could have any real effect on a chronic infectious process. Thus, from 1900 to 1950, every major textbook of medicine and every article on the treatment of rheumatoid arthritis that we reviewed[7] either did not mention aspirin treatment or made brief mention that low doses (eight aspirin or fewer daily) given intermittently could be a helpful adjunct in controlling pain. The only mention of high-dose aspirin therapy was in the context of a warning that one needed to watch patients carefully because of their tendency to become addicted to high doses of salicylates.[16] By the early 1950s the infectious theory was discarded, and rheumatoid arthritis was seen as a chronic inflammatory disease of unknown origin. In this same period, experiments in rats showed aspirin to possess substantial anti-inflammatory properties in addition to analgesia and antipyresis. Starting in the mid-1950s, most textbooks and review articles recommended aspirin in doses as high as

could be tolerated by patients with rheumatoid arthritis. Therefore, high doses of aspirin for rheumatoid arthritis became an accepted treatment some 70 years after the initial studies demonstrating its efficacy.

Other Tomatoes

The aforementioned discussion represents our attempt to show that colchicum, gold, and high-dose aspirin were tomatoes—efficacious medicines that were ignored or rejected for a time because their presumed mode of action did not fit the prevailing concepts of disease pathogenesis. These therapies simply did not make sense. In many cases, in rejecting these tomatoes, physicians of the time turned to various placebos that did make sense. Therefore, purgatives were the preponderant therapy for gout for six centuries and removal of foci of infections the major treatment for rheumatoid arthritis in the first half of the 20th century.

The status of tomatoes, like placebos, changes when they are recognized for what they are. For this reason it is difficult to identify present-day tomatoes. It would seem, however, that modern medicine is particularly vulnerable to the tomato effect. Pharmaceutical companies have increasingly turned to theoretical over practical arguments for using their drugs. Therefore, we are asked to use a new arthritis drug because it stops monocytes from crawling through a filter, a new antidepressant because it blocks re-uptake of serotonin but not norepinephrine into rat synaptosomes, a new antihypertensive because it blocks angiotensin generation, or an oral diabetes drug because it increases insulin receptors on monocytes. What gets lost in such discussions are the only three issues that matter in picking a therapy: Does it help? How toxic is it? How much does it cost? In this atmosphere we are at risk for rejecting a safe, inexpensive, effective therapy in favor of an alternative treatment perhaps less efficacious and more toxic, which is more interesting in terms of our latest views of disease pathogenesis. Such an attitude also increases the risk that we use a medication to "normalize" a laboratory value— blood glucose, uric acid, or cholesterol—regardless of whether it improves

our patient's state of health and even if it increases risks for morbidity and mortality.

We will conclude this discussion by providing two examples of modern therapies amenable to the tomato effect. One may very well be a tomato; the other is probably not, but in both we can trace the dynamics that allow us to make the mistake of rejecting an efficacious treatment.

Our first example is ergoloid mesylates (Hydergine), a combination of three ergot alkaloids marketed for the treatment of mild to moderate dementia. This drug was originally introduced as a peripheral and cerebral vasodilator, its presumed mechanism of action in improving memory and modifying behavior in elderly demented patients. During the 1960s several articles appeared reporting no effect of ergoloid mesylates on cerebral blood flow. Because of these reports the use of ergoloid mesylates fell into disrepute, especially in academic medicine. This occurred despite the publication of more than 20 double-blind, placebo-controlled trials showing that ergoloid mesylate administration was indeed associated with substantial improvements in objective measurements of memory and behavior.[17] The problem was that it seemingly did not work the way it was supposed to work; so it was rejected. We still do not know how it works.[18] Somehow, what became important was that the drug was proved in laboratory experiments not to increase blood flow to the brain.

The other contemporary example is the use of starch blockers for obesity. A recent article reported that these agents do not increase fecal caloric content.[19] The obvious conclusion was that starch blockers have no role in the treatment of obesity.[20] Here we have all the elements necessary for the tomato effect. A therapy (starch blockers) is claimed to cause weight loss. It is rejected because it does not increase fecal caloric excretion. What if it does indeed cause weight loss? We may never know.

There is no reason to think that starch blockers are effective. The point of the example is to demonstrate how a drug can be rejected for reasons other than a directly demonstrated lack of efficacy. The example brings up another risk factor for the tomato effect. If a treatment bypasses the medical establishment and is sold directly to the public, whether starch blockers, megavitamins, or l'eau d'Husson, the temptation in the medical community is to accept uncritically the first bad news that comes along.

We cannot progress in medicine without a theoretical structure. Structure by necessity limits our peripheral vision while allowing us to focus on a particular path. The benefit of such a structure far outweighs the detriment. However, we can reduce the detriment by asking, almost in ritual fashion, certain questions. Before we accept a treatment we should ask "Is this a placebo?" and before we reject a treatment we should ask "Is this a tomato?"

References

1. Rick CM: The tomato. *Sci Am* 1978;239:76-87.
2. Wittwer SH: Tomato, in Cayne BS (ed): *Encyclopedia Americana.* Danbury, Conn, Americana Corporation, 1978, vol 26, pp 832-833.
3. Copeman WSC: *A Short History of the Gout.* London, Cambridge University Press, 1964, pp 38-47.
4. Lawall CH: *Four Thousand Years of Pharmacy.* Philadelphia, JB Lippincott Co, 1927, p 418.
5. Sarton G: *Galen of Pergamon.* Lawrence, Kan, University of Kansas Press, 1954.
6. Sydenham T: *The Works of Thomas Sydenham, M.D.* London, Robinson, Otridge, Hayes, and Newbery, 1788.
7. Goodwin JS, Goodwin JM: Failure to recognize efficacious treatments: A history of salicylate therapy in rheumatoid arthritis. *Perspect Biol Med* 1981;31:78-92.
8. Cecil RL: Rheumatoid arthritis, in Cecil RL (ed): *A Textbook of Medicine.* Philadelphia, WB Saunders Co, 1931.
9. McCrae T: Arthritis deformans, in Osler W (ed): *Osler's Modern Medicine.* Philadelphia, Lea & Febiger, 1907, p 548.
10. Freyberg RH: Gold therapy for rheumatoid arthritis, in Hollander JL, McCarty DJ (eds): *Arthritis and Allied Conditions.* Philadelphia, Lea & Febiger, 1972, pp 455-482.
11. Hench PS, Bauer W, Boland E, et al: Rheumatism and arthritis: Review of American and English literature for 1940 (eighth rheumatism review). *Ann Intern Med* 1941;15:1001-1108.
12. Short CL, Bauer W: The treatment of rheumatoid arthritis. *N Engl J Med* 1942;227:442-450.
13. McCombs RP: *Internal Medicine.* Chicago, Year Book Medical Publishers Inc, 1956, pp 611-650.
14. McCombs RP: *Internal Medicine.* Chicago Year Book Medical Publishers Inc, 1960, p 660.
15. Shulman LE: Rheumatoid disease, in Harrison TR, Adams RD, Bennett IL, et al (eds): *Principles of Internal Medicine.* Wintrobe, NY, McGraw-Hill Book Co, 1966, pp 1352-1357.
16. Pemberton R: Arthritis: chronic, in Piersol GM (ed): *The Cyclopedia of Medicine.* Philadelphia, FA Davis Co, 1935, vol 2.
17. Yesavage JA, Tinklenberg JR, Hollister LE, et al: Vasodilators in senile dementia. *Arch Gen Psychiatry* 1979;36:220-223.
18. Yesavage JA, Westphal J, Rush L: Senile dementia: Combined pharmacologic and psychologic treatment. *J Am Geriatr Soc* 1981;29:164-171.
19. Bo-Linn GW, Santa Ana CA, Morawski SG, et al: Starch blockers—their effect on calorie absorption from a high starch meal. *N Engl J Med* 1982;307:1413-1416.
20. Rosenberg IH: Starch blockers—still no calorie-free lunch. *N Engl J Med* 1982;307:1444-1445.

14

The Evaluators' Accomplishment

Robert E. Stake

The troubling hypothesis represented by the title *Quieting Reform* is that this AIR research activity muted the services to youngsters—not only to the evaluated youth in Atlanta, Indianapolis, and New York City but to all urban youth. After an epistemological look at the knowledge AIR "produced" and after a practical look at the utility of the study to stakeholders, the effect of such research on efforts to reform social services will be discussed.

The Cities-in-Schools program brought together three propitious ideas: (1) personalization of human services, (2) integration of community agency service, and (3) ameliorative adult-youth interaction at school sites largely in the form of schoolwork. The *Final Report* indicated that CIS caseworkers were often able to establish rapport and to engage large numbers of youngsters in desirable activities. Relying heavily on political luminaries and corporate leaders for support, CIS nevertheless failed to gain substantial support from those more directly in charge of community agencies and schools. The program itself remained a possession of founders Harold Oostdyk, William Milliken, and associates. It did not draw the schools or agencies into vital partnerships. Nor did CIS achieve the officially designated intermediate goals for youth, i.e., aggregate improvements in attendance and scholastic achievement and reduction of juvenile delinquency.

A fact most obvious to the evaluators was that good data were extremely difficult to obtain. This was attributed in large part to poor project management in each of the three cities and at the na-

From Robert E. Stake, "The Evaluators' Accomplishment," in Robert E. Stake, eds., *Quieting Reform: Social Science and Social Action in an Urban Youth Program,* pp. 129-163. Copyright © 1986 by the Board of Trustees of the University of Illinois. Reprinted by permission.

tional level. There was a shortage of good case records, partly because the projects were not well organized. The evaluators at first blamed the poor organization on three factors: the inexperience of the founders, sudden expansions in program activity, and the "personalism" ethic (which encouraged caseworkers and projects to be individualistic). But in the end Charles Murray blamed even more the diverse requirements of separate funding sources, particularly the seven federal agencies. *One principal AIR conclusion was that efforts to redirect the most wayward urban youth should await major reconceptualization of the federal role in welfare—a timely theme with the new Reagan-appointed department heads.*

Encouraged collectively by NIE personnel, evaluation colleagues, and school officials—and loyal to the legacy of AIR's historic Project Talent—the evaluation team remained committed to a quantitative test of impact. Charles Murray had a rationale for studying "process"—for helping the project build better solutions—but the investigative energies of his research here were devoted to determining the outcomes of a treatment. Conceptually, the "treatment" was a generic form of Cities-in-Schools. This was to be a social science study featuring statistical analysis of aggregate scores to provide generalizations about social services delivery. Murray provided early formative assistance to projects so as to maximize the likelihood that such a test could occur. When it became apparent the data base would be too weak for such an analysis, individual student records were searched to determine the "best case" the program might make. Finding records for "the most helped youngsters" to be incomplete and problematic, Murray concluded that substantial gains had not occurred, certainly not an impact worthy of the federal investment of $10 million.

Cities-in-Schools did not deliver on many of its promises. No one disputes that. It did deliver something. Just what it did deliver remains in doubt. Even though AIR rhetoric emphasized the need for measuring incremental growth, these evaluators did not set their micrometers to just barely noticeable differences or to individualistic turnaround. Generally, AIR relied on measurements (i.e., observation and records) made by others: district test people, CIS evaluators, caseworkers, teachers. Those records indeed were not good enough. Clearly the data were incomplete. Apparently CIS caseworkers did not overstate progress, as might be expected if there were apprehension about the evaluation. They may have understated it. It has been suggested that some caseworkers distrusted the evaluators and did not cooperate with them. No one suggested there was widespread gain on the designated criterion variables that AIR failed to see, but program people cited instance after instance of good work, implying that AIR did not use its expertise to document the help CIS did provide.

Charles Murray wanted to carry out what AIR had promised. But he did not analyze CIS program outcomes as promised partly because CIS did not provide the program promised. Furthermore, school district officials did not provide data they had contracted to provide. Consequently, AIR reports described the projects in detail and arrived at a largely indisputable conclusion: "CIS impact was imperceptible." Could more have been expected of AIR? Yes.

The evaluation study was not as fair as it could have been to the CIS program and to protagonistic parents and youngsters. AIR people did not adequately inform CIS people that AIR's primary interest was in gathering information useful for guiding national development of CIS-like programs rather than on identification of local accomplishment. AIR evaluators did not organize their research to study cases or team processes. There was little formal observation of what was happening, and not happening, to these youngsters. The evidence Murray found was sufficient to justify the conclusion that what was promised to funders was not delivered. CIS students were not making what most readers would consider an "investment in society." But Murray responded only a little to program claims of widespread assistance, provision of good adult role-models, diminution of hostility, increased awareness of predicament, and more. Murray repeatedly asked CIS people to identify criteria by which CIS might better be assessed. They did not, possibly could not. But criterion identification is the expected forte of evaluators, not necessarily of paraprofessional social workers. CIS's inability to describe program quality did not justify so meager a search.

Even though CIS was a costly program, some would argue that the federal effort did not represent more than a fair share of the common wealth due those underprivileged youth. CIS advocates reminded us of a societal obligation to try to relieve conditions of impoverishment even when we do not know how much we will accomplish. They urged us to base evaluation more on whether their program is the most logical and compassionate of alternatives available, less on whether their program is the most efficient or effective.

Logic and compassion are not the usual criteria for formal assessment of government programs, but they too are defensible criteria. Furthermore, the usual criteria often lead us toward a "cease and desist" conclusion. Program opponents interpret *"No significant gains were observed"* to mean that *"No assistance is justified at this time."* Of course that is a misinterpretation of the finding, but if research is regularly misinterpreted in a way that deprives certain citizens of equity, then even well-reasoned criteria need to be reconsidered.

AIR began by looking for what CIS would surely do, and ended by finding what CIS had not done. A better description of what CIS was and what it actually did would have served some stakeholders better. It is unlikely but possible that if stakeholders knew what actually was accomplished, they would have judged it a successful program even if it did not fulfill grand intentions.[1]

Had AIR enthusiastically taken this more descriptive approach it would have been in trouble, opposed by most government officials, most program evaluation specialists, and most funding agency rep-

---

1. Reviewers of manuscript drafts have urged me to indicate more directly how *I* might have done this evaluation study. I fear that already I am drawing too much attention to my evaluation ideas at the expense of attention to those of Charles Murray, Norman Gold, and the ERS panelists. But it may be important here to say that in much evaluation research I personally find decision maker stakeholder values given too much emphasis, consumer stakeholder values too little. Even with my strong ideology I am displeased to see evaluation research driven by ideological purpose, including that great good aim: to reform governance. Evaluation studies usually should illuminate the activity at hand, engage ideological as well as practical issues, and indicate merit and shortcoming. I admire disciplined study and precision of measurement, yet oppose fixed designs insensitive to context, emerging issue, and program change. Evaluations are political, and equity is a consideration in design as well as in interpretation. Neither rigor nor empathy nor completeness nor clarity is virtuous beyond cost; each is part of trade-offs that the evaluator must resolve.

In this CIS case I would have sought a rich, balanced, frank description with less attention to uniform measurement of attendance, achievement, and trouble with police. I would have tried to study operator and consumer stakeholder issues more, some even though not hearing them voiced. I would not limit my attention to those issues, or try to present them in a way to advance their cause, or give "affirmative action" because they usually are undervalued. My conclusions as to program effect would probably have been the same as Murray's, but my description and implication of program worth would have ranged further.

resentatives. Many evaluators are sympathetic to the arguments for formative evaluation rather than summative, for the productivity of process-establishment rather than a productivity defined by intended-impact. Evaluators faced vexed critics, many not comprehending the limitations of impact analysis. If there was serious fault with AIR design, if it should have abandoned the hypothesis-testing approach sooner, the fault rests more with those who commissioned and sustained the faulty design. It is they who were the key *evaluation* stakeholders (as distinct from program stakeholders). They insisted on a rigorous test of the impact of CIS services integration. Many of them were personally identified and committed to "social science as quantification." In no small way they are responsible for the insufficiency of information about what Cities-in-Schools accomplished in three cities in 1978, 1979, and 1980.

Social science methods can be used to describe a complex array of actual accomplishments—but if used merely to find statistically significant differences or covariates, the result will be simplistic. An alternative design is needed. Evaluation specialists often debate the advantages of quantitative versus qualitative methods, but too seldom debate the utility of generalistic versus particularist evaluation designs—and implications for social reform.

The Production of Knowledge

The evaluation study was created by NIE to see if the *CIS idea* had merit. It was expected that project activities would be scrutinized at several sites in each of the three cities not so much to learn the good they would do for Atlanta, New York, and Indianapolis youngsters, but to learn whether CIS, as a general approach, could be counted on to do a better job of services integration and personal support to troubled and troublesome youth—at existing funding levels. As I said in the opening paragraph of this review, NIE and AIR were seeking policy-relevant generalizations for program administrators in cities, school districts, and funding agencies across the country.

Research methods can be sorted into two classes of inquiry. Designers of evaluation studies can design their inquiries (1) with relatively greater emphasis on producing statements of general relationship (among prominent elements or constructs) or (2) with relatively greater emphasis on producing descriptions of particular events (and their contingencies and contextuality). It is a choice between *generalization* and *particularization.*[2]

The first way, sometimes called the scientific,[3] the positivistic, the formalistic, or the rational approach, is preferred by most social scientists. They are seeking parsimonious, context-free, universal explanations, hopefully relevant in all situations though perhaps not revealing the determining influence in most. This approach usually makes its way to grand generalization by deliberate selection of a few key variables, careful identification of populations and samples, and analysis of measurements for large numbers of cases.

Disciplined researchers who follow the established procedures create new knowledge, new generalizations. They indicate tendencies to be expected in large numbers of subsequent observations. Just what will happen in the next single instance is of course not determined, but the chances are sometimes improved that the outcome will be predicted. Social science generalizations might indicate, for example, that charismatic leaders tend to create organizations which set unattainable goals for individual members. Whether or not that would pertain to the next Cities-in-Schools project of course is not thus determined, even if it were a sound generalization, for with social phenomena the descriptors are tenuous and exceptions to the rule are common. But with suitable cautions, the generalizations may improve program management.

The second way of designing evaluation studies, sometimes called the naturalistic, the phenomenological, the clinical, or the intuitive, is common in life's ordinary problem solving. Being more subjective, this way is considered suspect by many social scientists. Its advocates are often professional persons faced with problem situations, *each* of which has an essential importance. These practitioners seek historical, contextual, "personalistic" understandings,

---

2. In *The Reflective Practitioner* Donald Schön wrote of these options as a choice between rigor and relevance (p. 42, 1982). Fine reviews of these alternatives have been published by Georg Von Wright (1971) and David Hamilton (1977).The alternatives are prominent in the literature on philosophy of social science.

3. "Scientific" need not mean formalistic, analytic, quantitative, standardized, and grandly generalized. Science is any orderly, dispassionate quest for understanding. But those who have striven to make their research "more scientific" and their science more rigorous usually have emphasized these five characteristics.

hopefully relevant for the individual case whether or not a basis for understanding large numbers of cases. This approach makes its way toward conditional or limited generalization by: labored identification of critical moments or symptoms, attention to patterns of covariation within the context, recognition of classic examples, and careful exploration of the uniqueness of the situation. A case study may be prepared.

Highly experienced researchers who rely on this approach create new knowledge, new generalizations, but generalizations having narrower limits, situational constraints. These researchers recognize an immediate case's membership in a class or population of cases and may provide additional acquaintance with other members of the group. Just what will happen in the very next situation is of course not determined, but if the vicarious experience or typologizing is good, chances are sometimes improved that the next case will be better managed, or at least better understood.

The evaluation specialist may describe the activities and problems of an organization, noting the events, valuings, personalities— all in context. To again cite the example, program leadership might be charismatic and the member goals unattainable, but more additional information would be seen as pertinent. Whether or not this would aid preparations for a new Cities-in-Schools project is not assured, but knowledge of what seemed to work and not to work this one time might enrich the experience of the new managers to some extent and increase the chances of success. Many managers believe it does.

For the development of education and social institutions, which kind of knowledge will be more useful: grand generalizations or particularistic knowledge? Both are needed. But certain users or situations call for one kind more than the other. Evaluation specialists designing program evaluation studies expect to provide some of each. But because different specialists have different questions and different audiences and because the two approaches call for rather different allocation of resources, designers usually choose to emphasize one kind over the other.

In the case of Cities-in-Schools, support for just a small portion of the nation's urban youth was very expensive. It could be justified perhaps only if it could be said to be a "demonstration project"— developing knowledge or experience that would pay off in many other cities. Production of knowledge was a common responsibility of the CIS program and the AIR evaluation. The *general* idea of CIS needed to be tested.

Most scientists in AIR, NIE, and the Evaluation Research Society have a strong preference for the formalistic approach. The design had to be respectable in their eyes or it would not have been accepted.[4] Charles Murray preferred the formalistic approach. Not more than three members of his Technical Review Panel expressed doubt; one noted that AIR risked committing the entire budget to a few generalizations that might somehow turn out to be obscure or trivial. Murray was confident his previous field experience would draw him into adequate attention to contextual detail and that the national value of CIS would be better demonstrated in the formalistic ways suggested in the proposal.

"Knowledge production" (to use bureaucratic jargon) can be measured much more easily when it is formal, e.g., in written or symbolic form, than when it is formed by readers in their own minds from descriptive accounts. When social scientists talk about knowledge production, they are usually talking about generalizations written for widespread distribution and policy making. The attention in the remainder of this section will be on formal knowledge produced, with personal knowledge to be considered later in the section on utility of the study.

Problem Reduction vs. Solution Building

In his summary Chapter IV, "The Potential of CIS," Charles Murray made a substantial effort to provide generalizable knowledge. Much of it was negative. He opened the chapter with this brief summary of "lessons learned."

> We have learned that a program which is in a developmental phase, receives uncoordinated and irregular funding from multiple sources, is constrained to rely heavily on untrained Caseworkers, has limited access to the social service delivery system, and works with adolescents who have a history of severe problems—such a program is unable to make headway in solving those problems.
> We have also learned that, despite these constraints, the program can achieve a pattern of measureable benefits (Indianapolis, 1978–79). However, this success was not repeated when the staff was reduced and a strike cut two months from the school year. (P. 87.)

---

4. Peter Rossi once observed that program evaluation work is held in low esteem by academicians doing basic research (pp. 17–18, 1969).

He went on to discuss an alternative conceptualization or strategy: "solution building." He closed a lengthy review of student cases with the generalizations: "Who is most likely to benefit from CIS? Students who come with at least some sort of asset. The asset can be a strong parent, or the student's existing motivation. . . . The student without any visible assets—with problems at home, no signs of self-starting, behavioral problems, few basic academic skills—may be retrievable, but not by CIS alone" (p. 110).

In the report Murray went no further along this line than: "It is not at all clear that CIS is an answer for any appreciable number of the worst-of-the-worst among the nation's problem youth" (p. 117). But orally (for example, at the Atlanta stakeholder meeting, November 1980) Murray made explicit the *Report*'s implication that success was beyond the reach of the CIS approach unless the target group of youngsters was redefined as "less troubled" youngsters. This conclusion was unsettling.

Such a redefinitional conclusion dismayed social scientists on the Technical Review Panel. They believed the data were too few to justify such an important conclusion. It dismayed "liberals," who saw it as punitive, a declaration that the opportunities of education should be shared only among those whom society could recognize as redeemable. It upset school officials in Atlanta and Indianapolis, who saw their own programs as able to help delinquent students who wanted to change, but admitted needing help with students without visible assets. It dismayed CIS people, who saw themselves doing a good job with "worst cases." It threatened the appeal CIS had with funding agencies.

Murray recognized that his data base, including detailed case information on a small number of youngsters, was not sufficient for attribution of effect to the program and not a good basis for grand generalization, positive or negative. Yet the pressures from his colleagues in and outside AIR, his own sense of what a study should accomplish, and his contract made him want to say not only that CIS "did not" but "could not" achieve its aims under these conditions. But in his written reports he only declared that it "did not" and suggested reasons why.

Many readers were interested in what this particular CIS enterprise accomplished and failed to accomplish. For the conclusion that CIS fell short of its stated goals Murray had sufficient data. (It was summarized at the outset of this chapter.)

The major contribution to program development and evaluation to be found in the CIS experience, according to Murray, was the generalization that one should attend to successful provision of program elements or assistances. Following the advocacy of Paul Schwarz, AIR president and senior reviewer for the CIS evaluation study, Murray called this approach "solution building." For compensatory programs, e.g., Cities-in-Schools, where "return" to some norm is sought, heavy emphasis on the norm regularly has resulted in "no-difference" findings and "devaluation" of the program. Murray argued—not from data formally gathered but out of experience and on logical grounds—that any compensatory program should be recognized as partially enabling, possibly even necessary, but certainly not sufficient for elimination of "the problem." Or alone even for its reduction.

Thus Murray drew attention to the success of CIS in providing circumstances (pre-investment accomplishments) that were believed to facilitate "first-turnaround" investments by the students. He emphasized "personalism" and "the caseworker." He did not analyze personalism in a traditional social science or cite literature on diadic counseling relationships and caseworker roles, both heavily researched topics, but provided examples of relationships at CIS sites and interpretations.[5] He concluded that the "family" concept, small caseload structure, and avoidance of a particular problem orientation (an antispecialist view?) facilitated the relationships.

This argument for "solution building" or "incrementalism" follows a tradition in program evaluation sometimes identified with Lee Cronbach (1963) and often labeled "formative evaluation" or "instrumentalism." The emphasis is on leaving those in charge of education and social services in a better position for the next effort. Murray used the analogy: "CIS saw itself as baking pies (having major effects on a student's life). The evaluation was seen as counting how many pies were baked. The more accurate view of the situation is that CIS was the flour. An evaluation that counts pies is never going to be in a position to answer the more pertinent questions: How good is the flour? What else is needed to produce the pie?"

As indicated in the minutes of the retrospective Technical Re-

5. Technical Review Panelists Eugene Webb and David Wiley had encouraged Murray to do mini-experiments at single sites to increase the understanding of key factors.

view Panel meeting, this "solution building" rationale was taken by several of the social scientists as "letting CIS off the hook." They insisted on "impact" standards, following a tradition associated with Michael Scriven (1967) and sometimes called "summative evaluation" or "product evaluation." They applauded the fact that Murray had tried to produce knowledge about CIS impact and had in fact demonstrated low impact. Murray felt that to increase the general understanding of CIS he needed to discuss the degree to which CIS had been implemented, but these critics, strong advocates of general-knowledge production, objected because such discussion detracted from the findings of low impact.

The Extension of Theory

The *Final Report* of the evaluation of Cities-in-Schools has few bibliographic citations and no bibliography. In the large sense it is atheoretical and ahistorical. Other than citations of project documents the primary reference is to AIR President Schwarz's writing on program development and evaluation. Little before and outside the Atlanta, Indianapolis, and New York City projects is described. The conceptual effort was self-contained. The report is a document more of immediate record than of social science research.

Omitted, for example, was the fact that in 1971 Atlanta Superintendent John Letson created a new school, the John F. Kennedy School and Community Center. It was to be a model of social services integration. No mention of that effort appears in the AIR *Final Report*. Community education ("bring the neighborhood into the school!") was a growing specialization across the country during the 1960s and 1970s. It was written about and occasionally studied in a scholarly way.[6] A policy study entitled "the Potential Role of the School as a Site for Integrating Social Services" was prepared for the U.S. Office of Education in 1971 by the Educational Policy Research Center at Syracuse University. It pointed to several benefits of exploration of the idea and reminded that "little is known about the often highly personal and inter-personal ramifications of integrated services. The potential for institutional jealousies and rivalries, prompted by power and authority sensitivities, are almost limitless" (p. 62). The *Final Report* neither invited the reader to attend to that

6. Abt Associates, "Comparative Neighborhood Programs: A Synthesis of Research Findings," O.E.O. Contract #B99-4981 (November 1970).

literature nor contributed *directly* to general understanding of "institutional jealousies and rivalries" and other aspects of services integration.

The same can be said regarding AIR attention to the scholarly literature on "urban education," "social rehabilitation of delinquent youth," or "developmental programs under charismatic leadership," all themes important in the CIS experience. The philosopher of social science expects few studies to provide "breakthroughs" in understanding but hopes, rather, that they will make incremental contributions to what is known already. It is not the responsibility of every researcher to summarize what is already known but each should build upon theory and add to the storehouse of factual information, and to the collection of hunches. This study of CIS addressed itself little to that challenge and contributed little to scientific generalization.

Other than the social scientists involved, few evaluation study stakeholders cared about the report's contribution to social science. Of course they wanted the study to be respectable, along the lines that social science research is respectable: sufficiently quantitative, representative, explicitly operationalized, effectively managed. But most wanted the questions to be investigated to be the questions of practitioners, e.g., outreach assignment managers, caseworkers, and project officers in funding agencies. Just as key questions differ from one user group to another, the methods of questioning vary. The original AIR design and personnel assignments were organized to find relationships among quantitative indicators of program operation, but not to fit these relationships into a well-researched, theory-disciplined, knowledge base. And it could not have gone far in that direction. There can be a little social science in a program evaluation study, and a little program evaluation in a social science study, but the purposes are sufficiently different to deny accomplishing much of both in one study. Though atheoretic and ahistorical he was, Charles Murray designed a study which fulfilled his program evaluation contract.

Utility of the Study

Formal evaluation studies of educational programs are undertaken with the expectation that they will be useful. The investigators, the sponsors, the program staff, and various other stakeholders have different uses to which they may put the studies. The allocation of resources of research varies considerably as different potential uses are considered.

The term "utility" implies usage and the existence of users.[7] Much evaluation designing identifies the primary user as a "decision maker" and implies that the decision maker will be someone having substantial authority, possibly a sponsor—often persons having policy responsibilities for this and other programs. The orientation to decision makers was protested in the Stanford Consortium review of the Struening-Guttentag encyclopedia (in Glass, 1976), partly because it diminished the importance of information useful to stakeholders who had no immediate decisions to make but who wanted to understand the function and worth of the program. Decision making and policy setting are important consequences of evaluation study, but *understanding* alone is a consequence that indicates utility in evaluation studies.

The previous paragraph emphasized the "knowledge" utility of studies. It is important also to take account of the imprimatur of evaluation studies. The fact that evaluation is going on or has been completed can itself be a substantial utility. Program sponsors or directors often make use of the fact that "an evaluation is underway." Regardless of the findings of the study, the fact of having carried out an investigation carries certain sanctions. An evaluated program may be seen as more authentic. Those responsible for authorizing the evaluation may be seen as acting in "a responsible way." The utility of program evaluation includes such imprimaturs.

Evaluation studies also have utility for "signaling" the standards, expectations, and warnings of an authority. Evaluation requirements are messages about emphases and limits. Evaluation designs are indicators as to what will be under scrutiny—in this program and elsewhere. Not only are inputs and outcomes specified, but theories and philosophies are indicated as in or out of favor. One's design of evaluation research indicates much about one's belief in social change and improvement of services. Evaluation research can be said to have utility if its conduct informs people in these ways.

---

7. For more general discussion of metaevaluation utilities see Alkin, Daillak, and White (1979); Braskamp and Brown (1980); and King and Pechman (1982).

Such a broad definition of utility as a criterion for evaluating evaluation studies bothers some people. But Carol Weiss is one research analyst (among others) who has urged a broad construction. Weiss said: "We may like some uses and dislike others, but such judgments should not get in the way. We need to understand the consequences of research and evaluation for organizational practice. Only with a broad-gauge view will we make headway in the endeavor" (1981).

It was useful to federal supporters of Cities-in-Schools to be able to say that the program was being evaluated, that the funding was being handled in an accountable way. It was useful to NIE spokespersons to be able to say that they were contributing to the practical remedy of urban school problems by conducting this evaluation study. It was useful to CIS spokespersons to say, "We are being rigorously evaluated." The AIR evaluation of CIS had these imprimatur and signaling utilities.

Of course, the concept of utility should not be considered only in a positive sense. There can be negative utilities too. Investigation can postpone the delivery of services. Evaluation expenses often draw from operational funds (that was not the case here). The orientation of knowledge in the evaluation study may draw attention away from important realizations and impede needed decisions. The evaluation work may distract and discourage program personnel. As will be discussed in the final section, that disutility did occur here.

The following paragraphs summarize the use made of particular CIS information from the AIR evaluation team.

During the three-year study evaluators provided the program staff and stakeholders with descriptions of program arrangements, activities, and interim accomplishments. Faced with the growing reality of weak and unworkable data on program impact, Charles Murray increasingly portrayed weaknesses of management, staff competence, student selection, and caseworker record keeping. Program directors had been at least partially aware of these deficiencies, but the stimulus to strong remedial action was absent until AIR feedback arrived. Feedback on the ineffectiveness of pursuit of one original goal—to bring about a vital integration of social services—brought no more than the surprising response that this was not an objective of immediate priority.

Data on attendance, achievement, and delinquency—as well as information on the sparsity of such data—were widely distributed within the program. The response was acknowledgment, but improvement seldom followed.

The Indianapolis CIS people responded more directly to the feedback on shortfall than did those at the other two sites. There was feeling in New York and Atlanta, and a mention of it in Indianapolis too, that the evaluators were overly concerned with form, too little concerned with substance. CIS field site people recognized that a CIS organization more uniform from site to site, more fully committed to record keeping, would not necessarily play the *intended* role with youth any better. At the national level of Cities-in-Schools there was a high readiness to respond to the evaluation reports. Even while the AIR study was in progress (and partly because of it), a management information system was established to do similar monitoring within *their own* (CIS's) control.

By the time NIE had printed and circulated the *Final Report* in 1980, the findings were well known.[8] Some people found the conclusions too kind; some thought them too mechanical. I found the conclusions limited in scope, yet coherent, pertinent, interesting, and "contractually" correct. But little use was made of them. Charles Murray was disappointed with the program, with his *Report*, and with the reaction to it. Like CIS itself, the American Institutes for Research had promised more than it delivered. The utility of its evaluation reporting was limited largely to early feedback on operational difficulties.

The *Final Report* was not circulated widely within or outside the program. By the time it was printed and officially released, its findings were over a year old. (Lengthy delays of such reports are not uncommon.) No stakeholder group found it a source of critical planning information or evidence to back a key argument. The *Final Report* was occasionally cited, but its utility as a resource document was negligible.

The Stakeholders

The nature of the evaluation study was influenced by contemporary notions of research utility. To counter overemphasis on knowledge production, to assure attention to the immediate needs of people

---

8. The interactive nature of Murray's design for stakeholder evaluation had necessitated intermediate and final review of observations and interpretations.

faced with practical responsibility, the stakeholder orientation was set forth in the RFP and repeatedly insisted upon by Norman Gold.

CIS reformers had a large stake in the evaluation study. Not only might AIR's findings increase their understandings, but their political standing and opportunities for support could be enhanced or jeopardized by the study. In this effort to tease out whether or not the evaluation work blunted the reform of social services, it is important to re-examine AIR's commitment to stakeholders.

When Charles Murray spoke to the Evaluation Research Society in Minneapolis in 1977, he emphasized using the stakeholder concept to increase the *use* of evaluation findings: "The fundamental assertion about Stakeholders is that they can increase the likelihood that an evaluation will be used" (p. 2, partial draft of presentation, AIR files). Acknowledging that evaluation studies are often little used, Murray planned to make this CIS evaluation usable and useful.[9] The stakeholder, Murray said:

(1) can tell the evaluator what to measure,
(2) can tell the evaluator when and in what form the evaluation must be presented to be useful, and
(3) will be more likely to pay attention to the evaluation results when they are presented. (P. 2)

This utilitarian orientation did not rule out an evaluator's pursuit of grand generalizations, but gave higher priority to findings pertinent to CIS operations familiar to on-site stakeholders.

In a rationale for stakeholder evaluation prepared at NIE, Norman Gold emphasized concern for the utility of evaluation studies. He alluded to a 1977 report by Stephen Weiner of the Stanford Evaluation Consortium. Entitled "Pathology in Institutional Structures for Evaluation and a Possible Cure," Weiner's paper aimed at "increasing the influence of evaluators." Gold also alluded to contemporary interest in stakeholders as presented in writings by Stake

---

9. Stakeholders are often unrealistic in their presumptions of data utility and usage. To the amusement of the Technical Review Panel, Charles Murray once told of an instance of naive expectation for clear-cut finding and programmatic follow-up. Murray said: "I was stymied at the first White House meeting. I had said, 'We all know that many of the reasons why specific programs survive has nothing to do with technical criteria of success and failure.' The people at the table disagreed, saying, 'No. We will look at the data. If the program is shown to be effective we will make our decision accordingly.' My mouth dropped open. . . ."

on "responsive evaluation," House on concern for "fairness and justice," Stufflebeam on "effective decision-making," and Edwards and Guttentag on representing the "priorities of constituencies" (p. 2, Gold, 1981, draft).

The ERS Technical Review Panel heard Murray's words about increasing the evaluation study's utility. Malcolm Klein and other members seeking generalizable findings did not see the stakeholder approach as requiring a substantial departure from the pursuits of quantitative social science. Stakeholder evaluation was little discussed, and when discussed it was treated unenthusiastically—a constraint, perhaps a challenge, certainly not an opportunity. It was interpreted primarily as a basis for adding to the list of measurable variables. Without diminishing his advocacy of a stakeholder approach, Gold assured the panel at its first meeting that the AIR study was to be a "fundamentally sound piece of research." Everyone believed that everyone would profit by new and penetrating insights on grand multi-city efforts to provide services to urban youth.

Who were the *stakeholders* here? As indicated in Chapter One, Murray (with help from Redish) distinguished between local and national stakeholders. Locals included those deciding resource allocations, the program beneficiaries, and program staff. Nationals included funding agencies, federal policy makers, and evaluation researchers. In practice Murray found it useful to separate the locals into "decision makers" and "consumers," those who were more concerned about the project as a whole against those who directly or indirectly were recipients of program service. Project members such as Mary Jane McConahay and David Lewis were stakeholders not well represented by this arrangement. They had access to Murray's attention if they wanted it, but (unlike in the usual formative evaluation situation) their concerns were not considered high in priority. Officially, CIS staffers were stakeholders, but their conversation with evaluators was to serve the data needs of other stakeholders rather than their own.[10]

The questions AIR used to involve stakeholders were straightforward. Groups regularly were asked:

(1) What indicators would convince you that the project is successful?

---

10. Rodman and Kolodny once identified organizational arrangements which increase the distance between researchers and practitioners (1964). Such arrangements were apparent here.

(2) What are the most important of these indicators for you?
(3) When do you need feedback from the evaluation?
(4) In what form would you prefer that feedback to be? (Janice Redish, p. 4, Preliminary Report on User's Needs, January 1978)

As indicated here and at the outset of Chapter Two, Murray was setting the *evaluation study* as the focal point of the stakeholder approach rather than the stake stakeholders had in the program. He, for example, did not ask them:

(1) What is your stake in CIS?
(2) What do you have to gain or lose?
(3) What about CIS is important to protect?
(4) What about CIS concerns you?

These latter questions would probably have taken the study still further from a test of CIS's general approach, i.e., "personalistic" youth assistance and services integration. Murray's course was a compromise, attendant to the information needs of stakeholders who could identify them, but keeping the needs conceptualized as outcome indicators which would regress on treatment variables.

Community decision makers were comfortable with Murray's information delivery questions. The "consumers" (sometimes called "clients") found the questions hard to answer. Murray said:

The idea of using clients as stakeholders never really got off the ground. How do you get parents and kids together in Indianapolis? You have to use the program to get them together. So what do you get? You get the "Fan Club." You get parents who really like the program. They tell a lot. It's a wonderful data collection device for us because even though they're "fans" you really learn a lot listening to them. But this isn't having a stake in it. I don't see how you establish a stakeholder kind of relationship here. (ERS Panel, Chicago, 1980.)

All through the study Murray was holding meetings with the decision makers. He had more or less abandoned the consumers. They were unhelpful and seemingly uninvolved.[11] He could have served them better. He could have probed their apprehensions. Or he could have conceived issues about which they should have been concerned. He could have given study to questions that aggressively

---

11. In her commissioned evaluation of CIS for the Field Foundation, Judy Austermiller reported that Murray expressed reservations about the effectiveness of the stakeholder panels (unpublished document, 1978; see section on the federal period).

examined the well-being of students, teachers, and citizens, questions like:

(1) With Arsenal Tech's long-standing reputation for vocational education, is it right to deny these CIS students vocational courses, giving them instead an all-day immersion in basic (academic) skill training?

(2) Are ordinary classroom teachers using referral (banishment?) to CIS as a way of diminishing their problems of classroom control?

(3) Are CIS loyalties formed at the expense of family and neighborhood ties?

(4) Are "CIS family" interactions supportive of traditional ethical codes? Are they socially upgrading? Are they at least occasionally intellectually stimulating—as well being personally supportive and skill-developing?

(5) What gaps in social services *still* exist? Are there foolish redundancies?

Beset with many problems, Murray was not looking for ways to expand the study.[12] Working with decision-making stakeholders took time but was rewarding. Working with consumer stakeholders seemed fruitless.

It perhaps is important to note the stakeholder approach here was not carried to the point of probing social costs and fairness of the program. Risk is an essential implication of the word "stakeholder." A stake may be lost. It might be improved. Whether or not the stake is protected, even treated fairly, is part of the concept of stakeholder evaluation—as some see it.[13] The ultimate value of stakeholder approaches to program evaluation will probably involve the fairness and justice of educational and social provisions. These aspects were not studied here.

Stakeholding was perceived here within an information technology model. An advocate might say, "What evaluation studies do is produce information. People should use that information to guide

12. Part of the time problem resulted from Murray's interpretation of stakeholder evaluation as stakeholder-participative evaluation. He could have pursued more of their probable concerns and could have spent less time surveying their needs. But that would have diminished the hope of utility (and political safety) through shared ownership.

13. See Ernest House's "Justice in Evaluation."

decision making." According to NIE, what was to be demonstrated by AIR here was the proposition that if stakeholders are drawn into discussions of design and intermediate finding, the ultimate findings will be better used. When we discussed this rationale for his stakeholder approach. Murray and I both invoked several other criteria as well, particularly interim utility and sensitivity to the political role of evaluation research.[14]

In addition to the information generated, evaluation research is undertaken for its imprimatur and signaling uses (as defined in the previous section). Each use introduces additional stakeholders. The federal government in effect announced certain purposes and standards by commissioning this evaluation study. NIE leaders were looking for ways of demonstrating NIE usefulness and integrity. A good evaluation study was expected to help—a bad study could have hurt. Also, the American Institutes for Research could have been a big winner or loser, depending on how the study went. Evaluation Research Society officials took the unusual step (for a professional society of its kind) of contracting to provide an advisory panel. Panel members were not told to represent the organization, yet the organization (and more generally, the professional specialization) was at risk here. So NIE, AIR, and ERS all were stakeholders in the evaluation study. It should be noted again that they were *not* stakeholders in the CIS program but *were* stakeholders in the evaluation project.

The CIS reformers also were stakeholders in the evaluation study. Their interests in some ways coincided with other interests. But in certain ways reformer interests were in direct conflict with interests of the technical groups. NIE, AIR, and ERS had a common interest in producing a respectable piece of research—accurate, objective, tough. Cities-in-Schools people wanted a study that "understood" their true aims, was tolerant of their indifference to proper organization and management practice, commiserated with youngsters facing enormous social displacement, and gave credit for what CIS accomplished without concluding that its people "ought to be more like technocrats and engineers." To further their cause, they wanted not just sympathy, not just acknowledgment, but a "bottom

---

14. That there were also political purposes for this stakeholder approach was apparent in the minutes of the retrospective Technical Review Panel meeting, as reported in the final pages of Chapter Four.

line" so oriented. No respectable evaluator would give them all they wanted, but a stakeholder-based evaluation study should have presented their case more completely.

According to Charles Murray, almost all variables requested by the reformist stakeholders were already listed by the evaluators. Nor did the quality of research questions improve because of the meetings. The stakeholder meetings did apparently contribute to Murray's turn toward more practical matters. He said that the direct contact increased his admiration for their efforts and sympathy for their plight—even, in the eyes of at least one person (see Peter Rossi's comment in Chapter Four), to a certain degree of "co-option." The stakeholder approach appears to have made the evaluators more aware of sources of support and opposition to CIS. Sensitivities apparently were increased.

But in the world of Charles Murray (and most other evaluation researchers) the CIS stakes were small compared to those of AIR, NIE, and ERS. Professional affiliation and accepted standards of inquiry held sway. The *Final Report* acknowledged a certain integrity of the reform effort but declared Cities-in-Schools to be an unsound national investment.

In summary, the evaluation team did not take full advantage of the stakeholder concept, limiting formal consideration largely to "information enhancement." The effort did not improve the selection of issues studied, but did increase team interaction with community people. During the study CIS's use of evaluation feedback was enhanced by decision maker–stakeholder participation, but not after the *Final Report* was prepared. The primary effect of AIR involvement with these stakeholders probably was to draw temporary attention to local use of information and away from the production of generalizable knowledge—but in the end the program was considered not a success because hard evidence of student gain was not obtained.

Enervating Improvement

The closing sentence of Charles Murray's *Final Report* was: "The more reasonable assumption is that 'an inner-city school that works' will include as part of its resources something very like CIS, and that the most economical way to reach that goal is to build on the start that CIS has made" (p. 120). With these closing lines Mur-

ray intended not only to commend CIS for good intention and selected accomplishments but to diminish the report's negative pall.
A few pages earlier he had indicated that efforts to integrate social
services and bring youth offenders into the mainstream of society
needed more planning and better institutional commitments than
had occurred here. He said that Cities-in-Schools had failed. And
for any such program to succeed, many difficult (but not "exotic")
changes would first have to take place (p. 112).

The possibility that CIS could not have succeeded was raised.
Orally Murray put it bluntly; in writing he was less direct. His was
a devastating hypothesis: all here-and-now CIS-type efforts were
futile. Yet it could be true. In Murray's opinion present federal funding arrangements destined programs to fail.

His readers seemed not to take this notion seriously. CIS might
in fact have been destined to fail, but the local stakeholders, especially when displeased by evaluation findings, continued to believe
that federally funded "youthwork" services could be effective.

People believe that services can improve. Experience tells them
so. Research persuades them little one way or another—experience
and opinion dominate. And it would be their experience with variety
rather than with change and control, rather than with strict covariation, that tells them that services can improve. They do not have to
look far to see that some youth services are more humane, some
more effectively coordinated, some getting more favorable responses
from boys and girls. Even in any one program services get better
and worse over time. "What has been, can be!" Since variety and
change are ever with us, it is easy to believe that providing better
services in any one neighborhood or all across the nation is possible.

Within CIS the ebb and flow of enthusiasm to try was apparent.
And things had to be going right, fair winds blowing, for full enthusiasm to sustain: for a caseworker to keep working not knowing if
paychecks would continue, for a Chamber of Commerce director to
risk hassling with the gangs down there, for a pregnant girl to go
to school. Milliken and his following seemed to thrive on adversity,
but they had their down times. And negative feedback from the
evaluators brought both discouragement and a flurry of activity to
counter the findings.

Especially at first the words from AIR were tentative, couched
in apparent empathy and offers of assistance. But Murray pointed

out organizational disarray and CIS disregard for a host of promises made. What CIS got was not "news." What Murray had to say was already known to be needed but was now increasingly an imposed demand: better management; better student selection; better training of caseworkers; better records of activities, problems, and results.

Even in a novel enterprise such as CIS there are ordinary processes by which some things get done and others ignored. The compulsion within CIS was to get more staff members in closer contact with more youngsters. But no, the evaluators were saying: "hold off, plan ahead, spend more time training, read your own contracts, set up a "program," manage these things. Some CIS people seemed to agree, or at least acquiesced. The evaluators had a modest impact organizationally. Some things were rearranged. A little more time was spent on the records, a little less time was spent on the kids—probably not much changed. Still things were not going as well as they should have been. The evaluators were trying to help—but they were trying mostly to get a research study going. Getting that pregnant girl back in school was not the highest priority for them.

In no way could the AIR contract for evaluation research be construed as technical assistance to Cities-in-Schools. As is usual, however, researchers and clients alike presumed that the information being collected for program evaluation would be useful for program management. And as was stated earlier in the chapter, to an extent it was. Problems in spreading caseworker resources too thin *were* better realized after the first evaluation feedback came in. Murray pressed the feedback on CIS leaders, urging that operational priorities be changed. The program had been adapting to the circumstances at each school, fitting in, changing the original plan, giving the school's principal, for example, a voice in how the services should be arranged. The evaluators complained that the evaluation would not be effective, future expansion would not be soundly based, if "treatment across schools" were not uniform. The credibility of the evaluation was at stake. Future federal funding appeared to be at stake. The advice of the evaluators was not incompatible with CIS's national management *plans*. Ordinary operations *were* changed, at least a little, especially in Indianapolis. Whether or not they were changed for the better remains a debatable question.

Uniformity of treatment remained an important standard with AIR. Rather than accepting CIS as an emergent, locally adaptive process, the evaluators wanted to treat CIS as a generic process, potentially available for placement in all cities. They saw local circumstances already overly dissimilar. Effects were going to be very difficult to measure. The evaluators wanted to diminish the time needed to describe and understand the treatment. Uniformity across schools was not a standard with most program stakeholders—save school administrators and perhaps "the government." Yet uniformity, maintenance of the original written plan, and resistance to local adaptation became indicators of good programming, and were pressed upon CIS fieldworkers.

Good evaluation practice requires some uniformities within the program if representations are to be meaningful, especially if new installations of program concept are anticipated. Good evaluation practice also requires minimal interference in program operation. A balance needs to be found. Here it was clear to me that Murray pushed too hard for uniformity. Several ERS panelists judged Murray's pressure as not hard enough.

Evaluation is a natural, ubiquitous human activity, mostly carried on unconsciously, only occasionally made formal with *specification* of what needs to be known and what was found. From research and experience it is known that in the presence of a greater authority, e.g., a "better developed" evaluation system, individuals will lessen their own surveillance, be less attentive to their own warning signals. It is reasonable to suppose that in the presence of a major evaluative study, some diminution of evaluative surveillance occurred within CIS. (This supposition was neither confirmed nor denied in the interviews.) The power of controlling the repository of feedback data was apparent to CIS board members. Chairman Howard Samuels insisted that CIS institute its own management information system to provide more immediate feedback to the program and, if necessary, to counter hurtful information from federal evaluators. This also might have occurred had there been no federal evaluation study, but to some extent the constraint on informal evaluation and adaptation was apparent. *With* the evaluation, the CIS work was different from what it would have been without it.

The evaluators had a strong idea of what "a program" should be. AIR President Paul Schwarz had indicated that eventually he hoped AIR would have an opportunity to undertake such social action projects itself. They were well acquainted with the social science literature on innovation in education and the social services, the work of Ronald Havelock (1973) and Milbrey McLaughlin (1975), for example. The evaluators recognized the political nature of social work (Morris, 1979) and of evaluation research itself (Cohen, 1970; House, 1974). They were well acquainted with the problems of treating human affairs "rationally" and of expecting too much too soon. Yet the AIR notion was "rational" (and ultimately, I believe, expected too much). It is exemplified by Figure 3, a flow of energy and purpose through planning, operations, production, and feedback. Program activities needed to be stipulated, responsibilities realized, indicators monitored. AIR wanted to be creative about these things, but saw social science constructs as *essential* epistemological structure. If the CIS program was to be a success, if it was to be recommended to American cities, it *would* have such features. To be successful, it had to be describable. It had to be sufficiently uniform so that one description more or less would cover it all.

AIR did not devote a substantial portion of its budget to studying CIS operations so that they would be described most effectively, but Murray and his colleagues overviewed the processes. They did not see a sufficiency of the ingredients they were looking for. They did not see adequate manifestation of a workable central plan. Authority was obscure in CIS. Communication was informal, terms were inadequately defined. Training was haphazard. An ethic of basing future operations on present results was missing.

It is not clear whether traces of the ingredients were too subtle, too idiosyncratic—or whether the ingredients were missing. Murray soon presumed that it was clear that CIS was not going to be exportable to other cities, so he worried little about looking longer. There really is no dispute about one conclusion: management was one of CIS's weakest features.

In response to first-year charges of weak management, Elizabeth Baltz was asked to reorganize management of the Indianapolis project. Later she moved on to help run the national office. For reasons unclear, she was considered by some an interloper. She talked Murray's language; to some that alone seemed to make her a threat to "the real CIS." The more I heard the complaints the more I came to believe that what the corporate world sees as "good management" is not highly compatible with the central CIS ethic and offering: personalistic youthwork.

Howard Samuels had dedicated himself to running Cities-in-Schools as a business should be run. Burton Chamberlain was brought in as executive vice-president to set up a more competent program management. As far as I could see, neither of them (nor Charles Murray) dealt with the incompatibility in the two purviews. For the neighborhoods where CIS will be, good caseworkers are seldom going to be good record keepers. Ghetto fieldwork and corporate management have essential frictions. What is best for CIS is not always the corporate view.

Murray did not choose to study just how removed CIS management was from optimal management of the unique work being done. Early CIS management (and some later on) was considered disordered and negligent, particularly for failing to insist that the ideal CIS would be a unified, centrist program.

In a similar AIR evaluative study of federal support for Jesse Jackson's PUSH-to-Excellence project, Saundra Murray concluded that Jackson had never established "a program" (1982). Uniform activities, objectives, and accounting of results were not to be found in the several cities monitored. In a case study of the evaluation work (a companion piece to this one) Farrar and House (1982) stated that Jackson had never claimed to have a "program," that federal officials had defined it such so that they could fund his work under existing legislation, that it was more a movement than a program, and that it was held up to criteria that emerged from social science notions of "program" ill suited to a spiritualistic and inspirational movement. It is seldom that evaluators are challenged as to whether or not they used the right criteria, but it occurred with PUSH/Excel.

It happened again and again with Cities-in-Schools, but seldom in public. In the pain of first knowledge of AIR findings William Milliken moaned, "But did they ask the right questions?" Charles Murray reminded us that Milliken had countless opportunities to identify the right questions. Murray believed there were no better questions. Milliken knew that the worth of what he was doing was not indicated in Murray's data. Some people who know them both say that it must be possible for both to be right.

The Quieting That Occurred

Let me summarize the case I have tried to make in this book. It seems clear to me that CIS program people changed some practices, responding to suggestions (demands?) made by the evaluators. Certainly some discouragement followed evaluation feedback throughout the period. The evaluators believed that there was good reason to be discouraged and claimed that only with better organization could reform occur and could the reform be evaluated. To various degrees CIS program people both agreed and disagreed with the evaluator's claim.

It seems clear to me that the program people—these urban reformers—did turn away somewhat from previous experience, from their intuitive plan for providing support to the youth. Those who agreed to the evaluator-recommended changes felt that they might thus facilitate long-term expansion of CIS services. At least for the present, that expansion did not occur and the teams drifted apart. The concept of noneducator caseworkers working full-time in the schools, of all the city's social forces in "personalistic" collaboration, has largely disappeared. The reform quieted. It did not end, but it quieted.

Activities had at times been frenzied. Some quieting was welcome. Most CIS people agreed that better training and better record keeping were needed. It would take a while to get these in place. This was a quieting for the organization's good—but there was another. Some caseworkers and managers were disheartened. It was a while before some could throw themselves into it again; some dropped out.

Still another CIS reaction to the evaluation was contention. "How can we dismiss Murray's claims? How can we nullify this bad press?" Milliken attacked the criteria as simplistic. Joyce McWilliams wrote the rebuttal and prepared a "survival kit" for CIS spokespersons. Howard Samuels and Burton Chamberlain instituted CIS's own management information system. However needed or valid these responses, they were largely a response to the power of social science research to shape CIS destiny. Cities-in-Schools people diverted energies from something they were experts at (getting funds and developing personal relationships with the ghetto's problem youth) to address their organizational frailties. The reform work was quieted as CIS mobilized to defend itself. Some of the quieting was an indication of program debilitation.

What is not clear is how much the evaluative research operation contributed to the debilitating quiet. The evidence is good that the evaluation study had an effect, but I cannot separate the debilitating quiet from the restorative quiet.

CIS leaders were attentive to AIR feedback. Some staff members were defensive, some organized something of a counterattack.

They denied the accuracy of certain findings. Some were inclined to boycott the evaluation activity. The evaluation was a distraction, a continuing distraction. Some interesting charges were raised: that AIR fixed its gaze upon too few criteria, had set standards too high, had been overly fearful of recidivism, etc. The communal interest of evaluation research and innovative programming was called into question. The program was obligated to draw away from what it saw to be its work to attend to what it was not very good at doing.

There are alternative reasons why CIS activities peaked and began to wane. Funding was at risk because the government had other attentions. Opponents in each city opposed CIS continuation. Charles Murray was a convenient scapegoat. The evidence that the AIR evaluation caused the downfall of CIS activity is almost non-existent. It is not clear that AIR contributed to the debilitating quiet of reform but also not clear that it did not.

One argument, voiced by Charles Murray, is that the program was not effective the way it was, that it was not even ready to be evaluated, that it *should* have been quieted, or at least allowed time without evaluation to straighten itself out. He thought that the evaluation data contributed to a needed realization—and, yes, to a quieting.

An alternative argument, more or less William Milliken's, was that CIS was in fact operating effectively on a person-by-person basis, that it was the recording-keeping-for-evaluation that was not working, that the demands of the evaluators drew substantial energies from the personalized support system, and that if a true assessment were possible, it would show that CIS was doing as well as our society knows how, to move these youth toward productivity and respect in their communities.

As long as the evaluators and others maintained the view that AIR was providing at least an approximation of a true assessment, their lack of impact data and lack of support for CIS fieldwork probably contributed to diminution of the reform efforts. The evidence for this diminution is not strong. I looked for it and found nothing we would call causal evidence. Obviously at times efforts waned, and in the end the program in two cities greatly diminished, yet in the third, New York City, it took new life. I cannot conclude that the evaluative research effort quieted the reform, but I leave it to the reader as a possibility.

Another question remains as to whether AIR worked with standards set too high. It is not clear that every minimally successful CIS project *would* produce gains in reading scores and cutback in absenteeism and trouble with the law.[15] Suppose that some small change in "life perspective" did occur in each of the youngsters in CIS: a movement toward accepting common social values.[16] Somehow the changes might, but would not necessarily, show up on Murray's indicators.

What is minimal expectation for a $2,000 additional investment in an urban youth already in trouble? Or to put the issue more generally—as Jarvis Barnes did in Chapter Four—what is the cost effectiveness of Cities-in-Schools? For certain dollar costs, what minimum returns should we expect? How much should we as a society be willing to pay for small movements toward social acceptability?

We who are social scientists should be able to help people answer these questions. Perhaps we should be able to say what can be accomplished for what costs. But we cannot. Some specialists pretend to, but their estimates are presumptuous. With regard to innovative social and educational programs we cannot provide basic cost-effectiveness information.

The Cities-in-Schools situation at first appeared to provide one of the best opportunities ever to put a price tag on a few social service and educational arrangements. But not even the "pure form" was reduced to economic equation. Nor would it have been had Murray collected every datum identified in his full-blown proposal. And it is not reasonable to suggest that other researchers could have done the job proposed. It was not a failing of design or staffing.

It is reasonable to believe that for such services there is no way of determining cost figures that will generalize to different cities, across different administrations, remaining invariant as federal and local backup programs vary over time. It *is* important for us to conceptualize the problem as one of costs and benefits, but it is not reasonable for us to expect that for such programs, sound, useful cost-benefit data can be provided.

For district and federal decision making we will have to continue following the usual iterative process, asking—with careful

---

15. The AIR program evaluation rationale cautioned against setting too high a standard and advocated a more gradualistic turnabout.

16. Such changes would not necessarily be attributable to CIS, of course. Adolescents do mature. Some changes for the better would occur without social service intervention.

consideration of the distress—how much we can afford to spend, then asking how best can we use our funds to adjust our present services, back and forth.[17] It is irresponsible to say we should decide on the program needed, then find the money to pay for it. Responsible decisions are made by intuitive compromise among need, resources, and a program's potential for solution of the problems. To effect these compromises we need program indicators such as Murray gathered. And we also need to know more about day-to-day operations and more about individual caseworker-student interactions.

William Milliken told of the youngster who did not begin talking to his youthworker until after months of silence. Joyce Mc-Williams told of the 14-year-old girl with multiple physical problems, chronically absent, without parental backup—who came to CIS on her own, was tutored, shepherded, represented—who now had won a class math prize. There is no dispute as to whether or not these things happened. Charles Murray recognized such cases, but could not find evidence that collectively the youth were making substantial and enduring improvement. He looked for the evidence and found little. Still he concentrated on written records, not getting personally involved in individual cases.[18] Murray granted that commendable youth support occurred, but added that it did not aggregate to produce durable improvement in the youngsters, especially as evidenced in the three agreed-upon criteria.

At the outset, with concurrence from others, Murray had set what he considered to be standards easy to attain. CIS did not attain them. Neither Murray nor other evaluators continued to raise the issue as to whether or not those standards actually had been suitable. They *were* seen as suitable by many people in and out of Cities-in-Schools. Howard Samuels continued to endorse them—but he, too, could have been setting standards too high. The Milliken team asked, "Do such expectations adequately consider the uniqueness of a child's deviant behavior and the uniqueness of a restorative path? Or mostly reveal our wishes as to what the world should be?"

---

17. The notion of zero-base budgeting for social services comes not from practical experience but from desire that costs and services be drastically cut knowing that poorly defined services are vulnerable, even when valued.

18. In *Street Corner Society* W. F. Whyte indicated that a researcher had to be "hanging around" to discover what was happening in young people's lives.

Many CIS people said in effect that AIR standards were too high—the "walls too thick," the problems too complex, the road back too tortuous. They said the evaluators' thinking was just not compatible with their work. They had acquiesced earlier on the matter of standards because they, too, thought CIS would accomplish them and because they had no sense of the technical difficulty in using *common* criteria with students having greatly uncommon problems.

Is it possible that these fieldworkers were more right than the technical experts? Could their accomplishments, however poorly recorded, have been a source of national pride, even with disappointment that more was not accomplished? Should not the obligation to work with the youngsters continue, using the best people and ideas, with what resources we can afford, even if we are unable to measure the impact? Surely the evaluators should not decide the question of continuance, but they and the public should examine the logic connecting a shortfall on specified criteria with decisions to discontinue the effort.

The CIS fieldworkers seemed genuine in their belief that sometimes they made a difference—to be sure, in different ways with different kids. Some of them admitted that their organization had many deficiencies. But with many caseworkers and youngsters, they believed the additional "investment" paid off. One of the reasons the Carters are no longer in the White House is that they also believed these $2,000 purchases were reasonable. It seems indirectly that the majority of voters thought otherwise. Here in Reagan's first term, if United Way, the churches, and the schools cannot deal with the problems of urban youth, the country seems to have little confidence that federally funded social services can. The reform has quieted.

On one point the public, the scientists, and the federal establishment seem to agree. It will not be sufficient for Cities-in-Schools to draw deviant youth slightly toward socially approved behavior. To be deemed successful and to be continued, CIS needs to change children in ways that can be registered for skeptics to see. For things we personally are involved with, it is sufficient to have "experiential knowing" of their success. But for things we are distant from, geographically or culturally, we will require more than testimony. We will require (not just prefer, but require) formal evidence.

And that may mean we will go without sustained social reform efforts.

Knowing and Believing

It seems clear to me that the CIS program people and the AIR evaluation people did not agree on how reform works. They certainly did not agree about ways of recognizing whether or not reform is working. Formal criteria—relatively constant across people and places, not adapted to situations—are a central notion in most formal evaluation designs. CIS program people were inclined to carry out their work as obstacles permitted, then to decide whether or not they were making headway.

The program people agreed to demonstrate their effectiveness nationally, in fact asked for the opportunity to do so. But many of them did not understand that "effectiveness" is an econometric term. They did not comprehend what constitutes "a demonstration."

The on-site Cities-in-Schools staff perception of "effectiveness" was of services rendered, clients engaged, hurts mended. The science-government definition of "program effectiveness" was more in terms of information generated, information to be taken as evidence that funds were properly spent, results recorded, with a basis set for directing subsequent programs.

This latter way is a formal knowing, one that can be shared with a distant stranger—who indeed may work within a very different context. The earlier way was a personal knowing, Polanyi's tacit knowing (1962), an experience and private confidence. The knowing may be revealed in storytelling. But when there are many, many stories, the overall message is unlikely to be clear.

The project people did not understand the demonstration process the way the dissemination experts defined it. The CIS group wanted the benefits of demonstration funding and its opportunity for growth. They accepted the language and its implicit overpromising. They found the terms of program specification, institution building, and evaluative criteria somewhat amusing but not without meaning. But they did not realize how compelling would be the science-technology metaphors of effectiveness, productivity, and impact—pre-empting their own practitioner metaphors and valuings.

As have many philosophers of science, Abraham Kaplan distinguished between social science knowledge and common knowledge: "Scientific observation is deliberate search, carried out with care and forethought, as contrasted with the casual and largely passive perceptions of every day life. It is this deliberateness and control of the process of observation that is distinctive of science, not merely the use of special instruments (important as they are)" (p. 126, 1964).

Studying generalizations to be drawn from evaluation studies, Trumbull and I (1982) have noted the difference between social science knowledge and common knowledge as to their attachment to context. The social scientist searches for the parsimonious, the most context-free generalization, and treats as greatest in authority the information that has been gathered over a variety of contexts, indifferent to them all. The users of common knowledge (including scientists, of course) recognize the interaction of fact with context, the conditional nature of most important generalizations, and treat as most authoritative that knowledge which emanates from a context most relevant to the discussion at hand. The boundary line between general and social science knowledge is indistinct, but most evaluation specialists claim that the latter—more deliberately produced and less contextually bound—is preferable. Few clients are allowed to doubt that what is being offered by the social scientist is higher quality information. Science is said to provide a greater expression of authority.

Charles Lindblom and David Cohen have argued persuasively that social science knowledge cannot be authoritative without verification through common knowledge and that the pursuit of independently authoritative scientific knowledge is a misperception of the social scientists' responsibility (1979). Practitioners know that there are many more issues to consider than those the evaluator entertains, but the evaluator is indignant if his/her issues are not considered the prevailing ones. Especially when the practitioner is expected to identify central issues, he or she is reluctant to argue that the evaluators's plan is off target. In a world where everything is seen to be related to everything else, the evaluator makes a persuasive case that these few indicators can be counted on to represent a great variety of concerns. The practitioner is often quieted—and usually takes steps to assure that his/her performance *on those indicators* will be as robust as possible.

So, during program operation there is a considerable reactive effect—the evaluation work drawing operational pursuits toward a new "bottom line," i.e., what will be measured on the evaluator's instruments. Sometimes that will enhance the program's services. Not always. In the provision of social service there are always bottoms below bottom lines. Ultimate good is sometimes put off by the pursuit of immediate goals.

The key question here is what was the lasting effect of the evaluation presence. The question could be extended further: Did CIS emerge as a better force in its cities because of the evaluation? Were CIS reformers strengthened in their resolve and practice? Or still more grandly, have the many evaluation studies of Great Society programs improved the country's effort to reduce poverty and crime and enhance education and well being?

Formal evaluation probably did not make CIS a better program. In retrospect AIR appears to have contributed to a malaise, a distraction. Cause and effect are not clear. It is apparent that little direct attention was paid to the several AIR evaluation reports. (So it has been with most evaluation studies countrywide.) It is also apparent that the vitality of the effort to reform diminished, locally and beyond. There are surely many causes. It is reasonable to suppose that an unrealistic presumptuousness about what could be expected from federal remedial efforts contributed to present disillusionment. It is reasonable to conclude that the social scientist's literal operationalizations of goal aspirations and reliance on common gain as the indicator of success possibly has contributed as well.

Whether or not CIS deserved to survive is not a key factor in perceiving how social science may be part of the problem in social reform. This case study contributes little to perceptions of the essential worth and usefulness of Cities-in-Schools. Nor does it do much, of course, to resolve the worth and usefulness of social science. What it should have done is help clarify questions about evaluating social programs. The study helped us identify problems that accompany a strong orientation to "information" as a basis for decision making, problems that accompany research aimed at the production of generalizations, and problems that accompany rationality in a reform environment. Whether or not social science and its strongholds, such as AIR, ERS, and NIE, need themselves to reform does not depend on whether or not CIS deserves to survive.

Social science has been essential both to program development and evaluation. The danger that occurs to the observer of the evaluation of Cities-in-Schools is not reliance, but overreliance, on social science. Its thinking—disciplined and dispassionate at its best—provides much less than a complete guide to practice. When working with practitioners program evaluators have often been too much the advocates of social science knowledge, too little the facilitators of joint respect for scientific and experiential knowing. Evaluators should bring their best skeptical scrutinies to bear on their own role in social reform, on their attacks against "personalistic" reformers, and on their support for technocracy.

Administrators know that one way to blunt criticism is to appoint a study committee. Some years ago civil rights agitators came to realize that philanthropic foundations supporting their cause through "studies" succeeded in putting off action rather than fostering it. One intent of rational discourse is to quiet the shouting. Evaluation findings can provoke action, but much more often they postpone (and sometimes, in fact, terminate) action. Are we a better people shouting to right the wrongs or proceeding quietly with resolve? Evaluation philosophy presumes the latter.

But resolve is all too delicate, all too much a creation of its environment. Who pursues good intention without recollection, even without painful recollection? Today's painful recollection is that "it can't be done." We live in an age of constant communication. We know the excessive rainfall of the 48 contiguous states. We know the disorders of North Miami and the West Bank. Almost immediately we know of the world's calamities.

Silently it is announced that all the world's troubles are our troubles, that they are inevitable and unstoppable, that we are *spectators*. The impetus for reform diminishes.

In a minor way formal evaluation research contributes to the disillusionment. And so it strives. It seeks to help us shed our illusions. But without illusion we would find little worthy of attention. A world without curiosity and the aspiration to change, without the hope of "doing good," would rival any prospective calamity. Like the little blue engine, a nation needs to puff, "I think I can."

Program evaluation, as we social scientists have devised it, as Charles Murray and many others of us have practiced it, does little to keep those hopes alive. And sometimes, as here with Cities-in-Schools, it helps to muffle them.

PART IV

EDITORS' COMMENTS
Valuing

Cook and Shadish (1986) outline three classes of theories about valuing in evaluation: descriptive, prescriptive, and metatheories. Metatheories concern the logic of and justification for the role of values in evaluation. Two reprinted papers, by Lynn (1986) and Chalip (1985) fall into this category. Using an empirical survey, Lynn reveals how assessing and regulating environmental risks inextricably entails values. Chalip not only argues that scientists can't be value free—that "values provide the 'ground' on which facts are perceived as 'figure'"—but explains how "value-tinted controversy" assists that advance of knowledge.

Two more articles display characteristics of both the descriptive and the metatheoretical approaches. Wood, Peterson, DeGracie, and Zaharis (1986) describe how a judicial adversary procedure was used to resolve value conflicts successfully in an evaluation of politically sensitive programs for gifted and talented students. Similarly, Ozawa and Susskind (1985) propose using a mediation process to resolve value conflicts surrounding policy disputes. These two articles are metatheoretical in that they provide a method for resolving value disputes independent of a particular set of descriptive or prescriptive values. But they are descriptive in that the values they are mediating in both cases are the descriptive ones held by the stakeholders to the debate; prescriptive ethics are never raised.

Such prescriptive ethics are raised directly in the last two articles. Both of the articles extend the pioneering work by House (1980), who suggested that evaluators adhere to Rawls's theory of justice. Lane (1986) contrasts market justice and political justice, where the former emphasizes earning one's just deserts based on one's efforts, and the latter emphasizes concerns with equality and need. In explaining why political justice is less popular than market justice, Lane helps clarify the unfriendly reaction that House's suggestion received in the evaluation literature. Lane also makes recommendations for restoring political justice to favor. Bunda (1985) describes three schools of moral thought (utilitarianism, duty-based, rights-based) and explicates their implications for judging program worth. Bunda suggests that good practice in evaluation usually entails a blend of all three.

REFERENCES

Cook, T. D., & Shadish, W. R. (1986). Program evaluation: The worldly science. *Annual Review of Psychology, 33*, 193-233.
House, E. R. (1980). *Evaluating with validity.* Newbury Park, CA: Sage.

15

The Interplay of Science and Values in Assessing and Regulating Environmental Risks

Frances M. Lynn

In the late 1970s, the U.S. Occupational Safety and Health Administration (OSHA) proposed a standard for identifying, classifying, and regulating carcinogens.[1] The hearings for the standard attracted the largest number of participants in OSHA's rulemaking history and lasted for two months (May and June 1978). Although a standard was never implemented, OSHA's efforts stimulated a debate over the assumptions and decisionmaking process for assessing and regulating cancer risks which continues today. This debate about the methods for identifying and estimating occupational cancer risks appears at first to be predominantly scientific, but an analysis of the responses to OSHA's proposal led me to hypothesize that regulatory values and other social and political values influenced the selection among scientific assumptions and, furthermore, that these regulatory values seemed linked to place of employment.

To test these hypotheses, I designed an empirical study that explored the impact of regulatory values, institutional affiliation, and other social and political attributes on occupational health scientists' selection among assumptions used in the OSHA standard. I conducted 136 interviews with occupational physicians and industrial hygienists working for industry, academia, and government.

This article describes some of the results of that study and focuses on the role of science and scientists in the decisionmaking process for determin-

Frances Lynn is Research Assistant Professor, Institute for Environmental Studies, The University of North Carolina at Chapel Hill, Chapel Hill, NC 27514.

ing whether a product or technology is acceptably safe. It addresses the question of how to incorporate expertise into the formation of regulatory policy, while at the same time protecting democratic control of the final decision. The article is divided into three sections: A detailed look at the policy context surrounding discussions of risk, analysis of the interview findings, and a discussion of the study's conclusions and policy implications. In an appendix, I describe, in more detail, the choice, construction, and evaluation of the research instrument, the sampling process and data analysis techniques.

Policy Context

In the last ten years, a quiet but persistent effort has developed to incorporate different types of formal analytic methods such as cost-benefit analysis and risk analysis into environmental decisionmaking. Supporters of these techniques view them as a means to make environmental decisionmaking more rational and less highly charged. Critics challenge their use both on the grounds of methodological flaws and also because they believe that embedded within the techniques are value-laden assumptions often missed in the false precision suggested by the use of numbers and statistics.

Risk analysis, particularly as applied to the risk of contracting cancer from exposure to chemicals, is currently receiving widespread attention. Following OSHA's efforts to adopt its carcinogens standard, other governmental bodies and private groups—including the U.S. Environmental Pro-

From Frances M. Lynn, "The Interplay of Science and Values in Assessing and Regulating Environmental Risks," *Science, Technology, Human Values*, Vol. 11, pp. 40-50. Copyright © 1986 by the Massachusetts Institute of Technology and the President and Fellows of Harvard College. Reprinted with permission of John Wiley & Sons, Inc.

tection Agency (1985), the White House Office of Science and Technology Policy (1985), the State of California (1982), the National Academy of Sciences (1983), and the U.S. Department of Health and Human Services (1985)—have issued documents with the hope of affecting the way cancer risks are assessed and regulated.

Most of these reports have adopted William Lowrance's division of the field of risk into two phases: risk assessment and risk management.[2] Lowrance characterized the first phase, risk assessment, where one estimates the health effects that varying doses of a substance pose, as an objective pursuit with decisions and recommendations most appropriately made by scientists. Lowrance viewed the second phase, risk management, as being more value-laden, involving trade-offs between health risks and ethical, economic and other social considerations. In risk management, Lowrance saw a role for participation in decisionmaking by the non-expert.

In 1981, the National Academy of Sciences (NAS), in response to a directive from the Congress, sponsored another study of risk, convening the Committee on the Institutional Means for the Assessment of Risk to Public Health. This Committee had three primary objectives: to assess the merits of separating the analytic functions of developing risk assessments from the regulatory functions of making policy decisions; to consider the feasibility of designating a single organization to do risk assessments for all regulatory agencies; and to consider the feasibility of developing uniform risk assessment guidelines for use by all regulatory agencies.[3]

Project Director Lawrence McCray, in his working paper for the NAS Committee, labeled as "naive" the underlying premise that "matters of science" could be segregated from "matters of value" and "left to an organization primarily responsive to scientific authority."[4] In fact, the Committee's final report suggested that there were multiple places in risk assessments where risk to human health could only be inferred. In those situations, the NAS Committee commented "how difficult it is to disentangle the mixture of fact, experience (often called intuition), and personal values,"[5] and it concluded that throughout the process of risk assessment it was possible to make choices among assumptions which would increase the likelihood that a substance would be judged to be a significant risk to human health.[6] The Committee recommended

establishing a board of risk assessment which would make explicit "underlying assumption and policy ramifications" of the different choices which face scientists who perform a risk assessment.[7]

The research on which this paper is based, while conceived and executed before the National Academy of Sciences' report on risk assessment, is an empirical complement. The research considers non-scientific influences on scientists' selection of assumptions that form the basis for quantitative risk assessment and risk–benefit analysis.

Empirical Findings

The study confirmed the initial hypotheses that there were links between political values, place of employment, and scientific beliefs. Even after controlling for the influence of such standard demographic variables as age, sex, region, religion, and family background, scientists employed by industry tended to be politically and socially more conservative than government and university scientists. They chose scientific assumptions that decreased the likelihood that a substance would be deemed a risk to human health and increased the likelihood that a higher level of exposure would be accepted as safe. Government scientists were the most liberal politically and most protective in choosing among scientific assumptions. University scientists fell in between their governmental and industrial colleagues.

Perceptions of the Risks Society Faces

The respondents were asked questions that attempted to tap their general perceptions about the risks of technology as well as what they considered to be appropriate degrees of regulation. One such question was adopted from a Louis Harris poll "Risk in a Complex Society."[8] The question asked whether the respondents felt that the "risks associated with advanced technology have been exaggerated by events such as Three Mile Island and Love Canal."

Figure 1 shows how occupational health scientists interviewed for the study responded to that question. The proportion of industry scientists who supported this statement (82%) is almost identical to that of the sample of corporate executives interviewed by Harris. In the Harris survey,

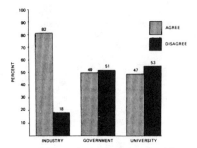

Figure 1. Percent who believed that the risks were exaggerated by TMI.

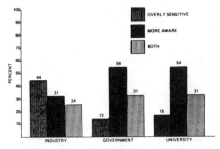

Figure 2. Feelings about American society's attitudes toward risks.

88% of the corporate executives agreed with the statement. Government and university occupational health scientists were more evenly divided in their response—echoing what Harris found when he asked the question of members of Congress, regulators, and the general public.

In another question taken from the Harris poll, respondents were asked whether

> American society is becoming overly sensitive to risk, and that we now expect to be sheltered from almost all dangers . . . [or] . . . simply becoming more aware of risks and starting to take realistic precautions.

In the Harris poll, corporate leaders were four times more likely than either the public or regulators, and three times more likely than members of Congress, to characterize American society as "overly sensitive to risk and wanting to be protected from nearly all dangers." In this study of industrial hygienists and physicians, those working for industry were three times more likely than government and university scientists to believe that Americans are overly sensitive to risk and want to be protected from nearly all dangers (Figure 2).

Respondents were also asked to agree or disagree with the statement "society has only perceived the tip of the iceberg with regard to the risk associated with modern technology." Sixty-eight percent of the government and university occupational health scientists agreed with this statement, compared to thirty-two percent who worked in industry.

No Anti-Regulation

Although they disagreed about the extent of risk facing society, those interviewed for this study, including those working for industry, were not necessarily anti-regulatory. Although the majority of industry scientists were Republicans (see Figure 3), had voted for President Reagan (74%), and were self-identified as conservative (56%), they expressed surprise at the Reagan Administration's vehement attacks on environmental regulation. When read a list of different types of environmental regulations (e.g., air, water, consumer products) and asked whether the regulations should be made "more strict," "less strict," or "kept the same," very few industry respondents wanted the regulations weakened.

On the other hand, very few wanted them strengthened. For example, when asked about reg-

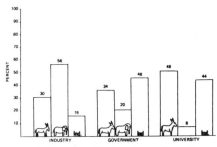

Figure 3. Party identification of respondents (Democrat, Republican, or Independent).

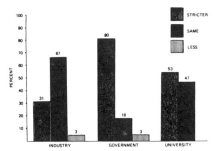

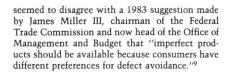

Figure 4. Percent who believed that regulations to protect employees from health risks like cancer should be stricter, be more lenient, or remain the same.

ulations to protect employees from working conditions that cause health risks like cancer, the majority of industry scientists (67%) wanted the regulations kept the same. This finding contrasts with the responses of government scientists, 80% of whom wanted the regulations made stricter. Academic opinion was evenly divided between wanting the regulations made more strict or keeping them as is (Figure 4).

The dominant sentiment across all institutional settings, however, was that a minimum level of safety had to be maintained. Majorities in all three subsamples (Figure 5) disagreed with the question taken from the Harris poll, which asked whether "a consumer should be allowed to choose between a very safe product at a higher price and the same product at a lower price without safety equipment." By inference, respondents

seemed to disagree with a 1983 suggestion made by James Miller III, chairman of the Federal Trade Commission and now head of the Office of Management and Budget that "imperfect products should be available because consumers have different preferences for defect avoidance."[9]

Attitudes Toward Cost–Benefit Analysis

Cost–benefit analysis, a major proposal for regulatory reform, was most strongly supported by industry scientists (Figure 6). Proponents view cost–benefit analysis and its cousin, risk–benefit analysis, as means by which to make environmental decisionmaking more systematic.[10] Critics challenge the use of cost–benefit analysis, suggesting that the technique has major methodological flaws and has imbedded within it philosophically conservative assumptions about issues of distribution, equity, and individual rights.[11]

The response of the sample to questions that probed the basis of cost–benefit analysis suggest the technique is not well understood. For, although 71% of the industry sample supported the use of cost–benefit analysis (Figure 6), only 52% agreed with the statement that "society must attempt to place an economic value on human life in order to allocate scarce resources."

When presented with the dominant methods currently used to value life in cost–benefit analysis (human capital, willingness-to-pay, and wage differentials), almost half of the sample was dissatisfied with all three options (Table 1). In fact, only 5% of the total sample, including 5% of industry scientists, supported the method currently

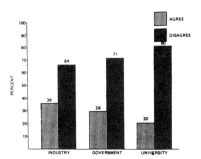

Figure 5. Attitudes toward consumer choices between price and safety.

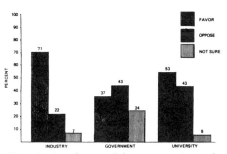

Figure 6. Attitudes toward the government's use of cost-benefit analysis.

Table 1. Attitudes toward dominant methods used by economists to value life. Respondents were asked the following question: "A number of economists think that ultimately one must place a value on human life, that is, decide how much money society is prepared to invest in order to prevent one additional death or save one additional life year. Three methods are currently being used by economists. If you had to choose a technique for valuing life, which would you select? (A) Compute the amount of earnings that would be lost in the case of premature death or disability and equate this with the value of life/disability (HUMAN CAPITAL APPROACH); (B) Ask individuals how much they would be willing to pay to reduce the probability of death or disability (WILLINGNESS-TO-PAY APPROACH); or (C) Analyze wage differentials in occupations involving varying risk of death or injury and use wage rate differentials as reflections of societal willingness-to-pay for decreases in risk (WAGE DIFFERENTIALS)."

	Human Capital	Willing-ness to pay	Wage Differ-entials	None
Industry N = 42	38%	17%	5%	40%
Government N = 41	32%	17%	5%	46%
University N = 34	9%	26%	6%	59%
TOTAL N = 117	27% (32)	20% (23)	5% (6)	47% (56)

popular among economists, using wage differentials (i.e., hazard pay) as proxies for the value that people place on measures to reduce risks of injury or death.[12] The wage differential method uses regression analysis to measure job earnings against a measure of the risk level of each job, holding constant other variables that also influence variations in observed earnings. Studies using this technique have yielded estimates of life values ranging from $300,000 to $35 million.

This research attempted to involve the scientists in a willingness-to-pay exercise. The willingness-to-pay approach is another technique currently popular with economists as a means to value life. Respondents were asked to select an acceptable level of risk, stated in an annual probability of death. They were next asked what salary increase would make them accept a job with a higher probability of death. Many refused to participate because they found such an exercise odious. Some wanted a list of common risks and

their probabilities of death in order to make comparisons. But many others said that given their existing income, they would never have to make such choices and would not now.

Critics of the willingness-to-pay approach question the technique's assumption that workers possess accurate knowledge of risks and can readily move to jobs posing lower risks.[13] Critics also claim that the technique ignores existing income distributions. The rich will pay more (or earn less) to reduce the risk of their death.[14]

Even those in the sample who generally favored the use of cost–benefit analysis did not advocate it as the deciding factor in standard setting. Ninety-eight percent of the entire sample viewed cost–benefit analysis as a "decision tool," not a "decision rule." Moreover, majorities in all employment categories in the sample (including 89% of industry scientists) supported the "public policy goal of decreasing cancer risks" even if it "caused the average price of goods and services to increase" (Figure 7). Similarly, majorities "supported the public policy goal of decreasing cancer risks . . . [even if it] . . . caused some factories to close down and increased unemployment."

Given the lack of support for the dominant techniques used to value life and a willingness to accept price rises for prevention of disease, why did respondents tend to support cost–benefit analysis? For some, support may be symbolic of the desire to lessen regulatory burdens on business. But for others, support may be a part of a hope that a technique can be found to make environmental decisionmaking easier. In this sense, cost–benefit analysis and risk assessment share a common attribute. Both are expected to provide

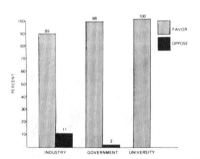

Figure 7. Attitudes toward preventing cancer at the risk of rise in prices.

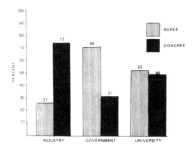

Figure 8. Attitudes toward using animal data to identify risks to people.

objective answers to uncertain and value-laden processes.

Quantitative Risk Assessment

The National Academy of Sciences in its 1983 report, *Risk Assessment in the Federal Government*, characterized risk assessment as the use of a "factual basis to define the health effects of exposure to individuals and populations to hazardous materials and situations."[15] The NAS viewed risk assessment as both "quantitative and qualitative" and involving "the interplay of science and policy." The NAS identified close to fifty areas in a risk assessment where a scientist or risk assessor must make choices among "several scientifically plausible options" in which "policy considerations inevitably affect and perhaps determine, some of the choices."[16]

Figure 8 shows this sample's response to one of those inference points: using animal data to predict risks for humans. Respondents were asked whether they agreed or disagreed that "a substance which is shown conclusively to cause tumors in experimental animals should be considered a carcinogen, thereby posing a risk to humans." The majority of government (69%) and university scientists (52%) agreed with this statement, while only 27% of the industry sample agreed. The National Academy of Sciences feels that

> the inference that results from animal tests are applicable to humans is fundamental to toxicological research; this premise underlies much of experimental biology and is logically extended to

the experimental observation of carcinogenic effects.[17]

A similar question is whether or not threshold levels exist for carcinogens below which there are no negative effects. A threshold model for carcinogenesis assumes that there is a dose below which cellular or tissue damage does not occur. Under this model, one assumes that the body has mechanisms that withstand toxic events at low doses. A linear model suggests, especially in the case of carcinogens, that a single interaction with a single cell can trigger a toxic reaction. The National Academy of Sciences Committee on Risk Assessment concluded that there was no conclusive biological evidence to support either type of model.[18] The regulatory policy implications of support for the existence of thresholds is viewed as less protective of public health. The State of California,[19] as well as the Office of Science and Technology Policy,[20] rejected the concept of thresholds for carcinogens in their guidelines.

As in the choice of using animal data to identify cancer risks for humans, the occupational health scientists working in industry held views about thresholds that differed substantially from those of government scientists. Eighty percent of the industry scientists interviewed agreed that thresholds exist for carcinogens, compared to 37% of government employees (Figure 9). Noteworthy are the responses of academics, the majority of whom supported the existence of thresholds. Among academics, age made a difference in attitudes; older academics were more likely to believe in thresholds than younger ones. A likely explanation for this difference is that when older academics entered the field of

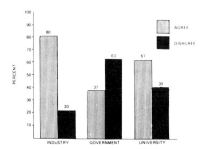

Figure 9. Attitudes toward the existence of thresholds for carcinogens.

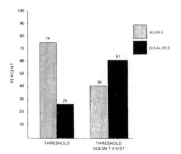

Figure 10. The relationship between belief in a threshold to attitudes about whether TMI exaggerated the risks.

occupational and environmental health in the late 1930s and 1940s, levels of exposure were high and scientific recommendations seemed clear. The older academics may have believed that government policy of the 1970s was becoming overprotective.

Figures 10 and 11 and Tables 2 and 3 show that the samples' beliefs toward the existence of thresholds correlate positively with social and political attitudes reported earlier in this article. The key finding of these data is that support for the existence of thresholds is associated with conservative political attitudes and with perceptions that suggest that American society is overly sensitive and overreacting to environmental risks. Similarly, those who question the use of animal data to predict carcinogenesis in humans are more likely to hold conservative political attitudes and believe that Americans are too risk adverse.

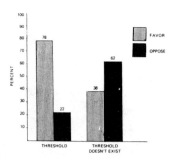

Figure 11. Attitudes toward the existence of a threshold and the government's use of cost-benefit analysis.

Table 2. The relationship between attitudes toward the existence of thresholds and the respondent's vote in the 1980 Presidential election ($p < 0.02$; N = 75).

Attitudes about Thresholds	Vote in 1980 Presidential Election		Total
	Carter	Reagan	
Thresholds exist	36% (18)	63% (31)	99% (49)
Thresholds don't exist	69% (18)	30% (8)	99% (26)
Total			

For instance, 74% of those who believe in thresholds also believe that the reactions to TMI have exaggerated the risks associated with advanced technology. By contrast, only 39% of those who question the existence of thresholds believe that the risks of advanced technology have been exaggerated by Three Mile Island (Figure 10).

A similar pattern held on the issue of risk sensitivity. Fifty-seven percent of those who believe in thresholds also believe that "Americans are overly sensitive to risk and [want] to be protected from all dangers." Only 16% of those who question the existence of thresholds for carcinogens believe that Americans are overly sensitive to risk.

Belief in the existence of thresholds correlates with voting in the 1980 Presidential election (Table 2) and self-identification as conservative and Republican. Support for the existence of thresholds for carcinogens is also linked to support for the use of cost-benefit analysis (Figure 11) as well as to a decreased willingness to strengthen environmental regulations (Table 3). In sum, in areas of science where there is no data to distinguish choices of models or assumptions, scientific choices correlate highly with personal political

Table 3. The relationship between attitudes toward the existence of thresholds and the regulations to protect employees from cancer should be made more strict or kept the same ($p < 00$; N = 86).

Attitudes about Thresholds	Regulations to Protect Employees		Totals
	More Strict	Kept Same	
Thresholds exist	43%	56%	99% (53)
Thresholds don't exist	75%	25%	100% (33)

beliefs. The policy implications of these findings are treated in the final section of this article.

Policy Implications

The idea for this study grew from the debates over OSHA's attempt to adopt a generic method to identify and classify carcinogens. OSHA's was the first in a series of continuing efforts by both public and private bodies to promulgate guidelines for identifying and assessing cancer risks. In recent years, the debate over the use of a linear dose–response model and the role for animal data has been joined by issues such as the incorporation of pharmokinetic data, differentiation among genotoxic and non-genotoxic data, the role given to different routes of exposure or to tumor sites in animals not found in humans, and whether to use "best estimates" or "worse case" characterizations of data.

A reading of the record in the OSHA hearings as well as of contemporaneous articles in scientific journals suggests a lack of consensus on the methods and models in the rapidly emerging field of carcinogenic risk assessment. The issues seemed to fall into the category of "trans-science," a term that Alvin Weinberg used in a 1972 article in the journal *Minerva*.[21] Weinberg cited the determination of the biological effect of low-level radiation insults as an example of a trans-scientific issue. He suggested that the argument about low-level radiation insults would have been far more sensible had it been "admitted at the onset that this was a question which went beyond science. The matter could have been dealt with initially on moral or aesthetic grounds."

Weinberg's observations in the early 1970s seemed to go unnoticed in much of the debate surrounding the OSHA standard and ensuing discussions of assessing the risks of cancer. As late as 1983, EPA Administrator William Ruckelshaus was reiterating the distinction between risk assessment and risk management, saying in a speech before the National Academy of Sciences that

> Nothing will erode public confidence faster than the suspicion that policy considerations have been allowed to influence the assessment of risk.[22]

A year later, however, in a February 1984 speech at Princeton University, Ruckelshaus qualified his position by saying that he had found that separating the assessment of risk from its

> management is rather more difficult to accomplish in practice . . . values, which are supposed to be safely sequestered in risk management, also appear as important influences on the outcome of risk assessments.[23]

Nonetheless, Ruckelshaus's qualification seemed to fall on deaf ears, for on 4 January 1985 the White House issued Executive Order 12498 which stated that risk assessments are to be "scientifically objective."

The results of the study on which this article is based call into question the characterization of risk assessment as "objective." The results suggest that under conditions of scientific uncertainty, regulatory policy implications either consciously or unconsciously influence the models, assumptions and theories that scientists' choose.

U.S. District Court Judge David L. Bazelon in a 1979 speech, "Risk and Responsibility," warned that

> in reaction to the public's often emotional response to risk, scientists are tempted to disguise controversial values decisions in the cloak of scientific objectivity, obscuring those decisions from political accountability.[24]

Currently, American industry is seeking to create and lodge increasing decisionmaking responsibility in science advisory panels. The most public of these efforts was a 1983 proposal by the American Industrial Health Council (AIHC), an association of over 90 different companies and trade associations formed in reaction to OSHA's cancer proposal, to establish a Central Board of Scientific Risk Analysis under the National Academy of Sciences to review regulatory agencies' risk assessments. A bill to accomplish this was introduced by Representative James Martin (R–North Carolina) and was viewed by the AIHC as a means of getting "statutory recognition of good science" and part of the AIHC's plan to "spearhead efforts to ensure distinction between risk assessment and risk management."[25]

Representative Martin withdrew his bill in the spring of 1984. It had been criticized not only by environmental groups but also by professional organizations such as the American Chemical Society and by prominent scientists. Epidemiologist Alice Whitmore, in an article in the *Journal of the Society for Risk Analysis*, argued that attempts to view toxicant risk analysis as involving two stages (risk assessment and risk management) with risk assessment relying on scientific activity and scientific judgment . . . [was] . . . an erroneous description of reality and an unattainable goal for the regulatory process.[26]

Her research suggested that values unavoidably enter virtually every aspect of risk analysis. Whitmore contended that

creating a central authoritative panel of distinguised scientists who will resolve on a case-by-case basis, complex or difficult issues for regulatory agencies . . . would move the scientists from the frying pan into the fire . . . [and] . . . would ensure that a scientist's values would drive the decision.[27]

The potential danger of these boards and panels, especially in areas with pervasive uncertainties such as quantitative risk assessment, is that scientists alone will make decisions with important political and ethical implications for the protection of human health. The question is whether scientists are the only ones that should be involved.

One could argue that the most appropriate role for the scientists in this situation would be to self-consciously provide decisionmakers and the public with as much information as possible about the uncertainties in his or her work. Social scientists and ethicists could be involved in analyzing which, if any, social, ethical and political implications flow from selecting one assumption, model or theory instead of another.

This will mean that a new type of debate will be occurring in policy discussions, one which is more conscious of those places in the scientific process where non-scientific values play a role and hard political choices must be made. This will be to the benefit of science for it may avoid the spectacle of the dueling scientist and place the very difficult decision of degrees of protection and the acceptability of a risk into the political arena, where, in a democracy, it belongs.

Appendix

This appendix focuses on the choice, construction, and evaluation of the research instrument. It also describes the sampling process and data analysis techniques.

The research instrument used was an interview pre-tested and conducted in person by the author. The decision to conduct interviews as opposed to a mailed questionnaire, and hence a larger sample, was made primarily because of the sensitivity and relative newness of the subject matter under investigation, and because of a desire to have an explanatory richness difficult to obtain through the questionnaire process. Sensitive questions included probing institutional constraints and ethical dilemmas which arise in the process of an occupational health professional's job. In the case of issues which involved scientific uncertainty and/or controversy such as the existence of thresholds and the use of cost-benefit analysis, the interview format offered the potential for probing explanations and possibly a better understanding of the basis for attitudes.

Over half of the interview items came from other studies of risk. The main source of these questions was from a study, "Risk in a Complex Society," conducted by the Louis Harris survey organization for Marsh and McLennan, Inc., the world's largest insurance broker. The survey, the most expensive ever conducted by the Harris organization, was administered in 1980. A second source of questions came from a study, "Public and Worker Attitudes Toward Carcinogens and Cancer Risk," prepared for Shell Oil by Cambridge Reports.

One hundred thirty-six randomly-selected, in-person interviews were conducted in the New York and Cincinnati metropolitan areas and the Research Triangle and Triad of North Carolina. All geographic areas contain a sufficient number of academic, government and industrial institutions to provide an adequate sampling frame.

An effort was made to make the selection process replicable. Names were selected from the main professional organizations. For industrial hygienists, these groups included the American Industrial Hygiene Association (AIHA), the American Conference on Governmental and Industrial Hygienists (ACGIH), and the American Academy of Industrial Hygiene (AAIH). Within occupational medicine there is no one or even two organizations to which all physicians, regardless of employment, belong. Physicians working for industry, but not for academia or the government, belong to the American Occupational Medicine Association (AOMA). The industry sample, therefore, was drawn from the membership rosters of AOMA. The department heads of university-based occupational health programs supplied the names of academic physicians. Heads of government agencies likewise advised on government physicians.

The sampling frame was defined by zip codes, stratified by institutional setting and profession (industrial hygiene or occupational medicine), and then randomly selected. In all but two categories (industrial and academic physicians), the response from the initial postcard request ranged from 75% to 85%. Follow-up calls to physicians in industry and academia were successful in filling quotas. These are unusually high response rates and can probably be attributed to the salience of the topic and the specialized nature of the sample. Several respondents said that they were intrigued by the topic and felt that they could learn something from the interview. The sample was predominantly white (98%), male (88%) and Protestant (56%).

The data analyzed was categorical (e.g., information measured on nominal or ordinal scales or grouped continuous data). Statistics used to analyze the data included frequencies, chi-squares and weighted least-squares, an application of the general linear model to categorical data. In the weighted least-squares technique, one looks at variations in cell probabilities and models hypothetical regression lines for associations or interactions among variables. One uses the goodness-of-fit chi-square statistic to compare expected and observed frequencies, asking the question whether "the departures between observed and expected values . . . [can] . . . reasonably be attributed to chance or . . . [whether] . . . they are so large that the model itself seems wrong?"[28]

Initial contingency tables showed extremely strong statistical significance between institutional affiliation and a wide variety of dependent variables. Methodologist Hubert Blalock feels that we may be saying "quite a bit when we can establish significance with small samples" because small samples require a "much more striking relationship in order to obtain significance."[29]

In addition to institutional affiliation, controls were run for the following variables: age, region, religion and father's education. Age was the only variable which appeared to make a substantive difference on the effect of institutional affiliation. Age did not prove to be statistically significant in altering the effect of employment setting.

An unanticipated result of doing personal interviews was the opportunity, on a limited basis, to experiment with a more interactive questioning mode. In the last set of interviews, respondents were given the option of filling out the fixed choice questions themselves. This technique permitted more time for open-ended questions and probes. In at least six interviews involving research scientists, the interviewees were asked to reflect on the process by which he or she made a hazard determination and to identify those points in the process where professional and/or personal judgment, as opposed to scientific certainty, were involved. The interviewees seemed to welcome the opportunity to reflect on the research process. The role of the interviewer was to keep the respondent on as straight a path as possible and to question constantly the basis for decisions. This is a fruitful method to be used in research of this type.

Notes

1. U.S. Department of Labor Occupational Safety and Health Administration, Identification, Classification and Regulation of Potential Carcinogins Federal Register, Volume 45, No. 15 Book 2, 1980.

2. William W. Lowrance, Of Acceptable Risk: Science and the Determination of Safety (Los Altos, CA: William Kaufman, 1976).

3. National Academy of Sciences, Risk Assessment in the Federal Government (Washington, DC: National Academy Press, 1983).

4. Lawrence McCray, An Anatomy of Risk Assessment: Scientific and Extra-Scientific Components in the Assessment of Scientific Data on Cancer Risks, Working Paper for the National Academy of Sciences Committee on the Institutional Means for Assessment of Risks to Public Health (Washington, DC: National Academy Press, 1983), p. 13.

5. National Academy of Sciences, op. cit., p. 36.

6. Ibid., p. 34.

7. Ibid., p. 171.

8. Louis Harris and Associates, Risk in a Complex Society (New York: Marsh and McLennan Companies, 1980).

9. Mark Green, "The Gang that Can't Regulate," The New Republic, Volume 188, (1984): 14–17.

10. C. Starr, Science, Volume 165, Number 3899 (1969); Ezra J. Mishan, Cost–Benefit Analysis (New York: Praeger, 1976); Edith Stokey and Richard Zeckhauser, A Primer for Policy Analysis (New York: W.W. Norton and Co., 1978); Richard Zeckhauser, "Procedures for Valuing Lives," Public Policy, Number 23, (1975): 419–462.

11. Lawrence H. Tribe, "Policy Science: Analysis or

Ideology?" *Philosophy and Public Affairs*, Volume 2, (1972): 66–110; Baruch Fischhoff, "Cost–Benefit Analysis and the Art of Motorcycle Maintenance," *Policy Sciences*, Volume 8, (1977): 188–202; Nicholas Ashford, "The Usefulness of Cost–Benefit Analysis in Decisions Concerning Health, Safety, and the Environment," *Annals of the New York Academy of Sciences*, Volume 363, 1980; Michael S. Baram, "Cost–Benefit Analysis: An Inadequate Basis for Health Safety and Environmental Regulatory Decision Making," *Ecology Law Quarterly*, Volume 8, (1980): 474–531; Marguerite Connerton and Mark MacCarthy, *Cost–Benefit Analysis and Regulation* (Washington, DC: National Policy Exchange, 1982).

12. Robert Smith, *The Occupational Safety and Health Act* (Washington, DC: American Enterprise Institute, 1976); Richard Thaler, and Sherwin Rosen, "The Value of Saving a Life: Evidence from the Labor Market," in Nestor Terleckyi, ed., *Household Production and Consumption* (New York: Pergamon Press, 1976); Kip Viscusi, "Labor Market Valuations of Life and Limb: Empirical Evidence and Policy Implication," *Public Policy* (Summer, 1978): 369–372.

13. David Zimmerman, "Coercive Wage Offers," *Philosophy and Public Affairs*, Volume 10, (1981): 121–145.

14. Thomas C. Schelling, "The Life You Save May Be Your Own," in S.B. Chase, ed., *Problems in Public Expenditure Analysis* (Washington, DC: Brookings Institute, 1968).

15. National Academy of Sciences, *op. cit.*, p. 3.

16. *Ibid.*, p. 28 and p. 33.

17. *Ibid.*, p. 22.

18. *Ibid.*, p. 25.

19. State of California, Department of Health Services, Health and Welfare Agency, *Carcinogen Identification Policy: A Statement of Science as a Basis of Policy* (1982): 19.

20. Office of Science and Technology Policy, Executive Office of the President, *Chemical Carcinogens: A Review of the Science and Its Associated Principles*, Federal Register, Volume 50, Number 50 (1985).

21. Alvin Weinberg, "Science and Trans-Science," *Minerva*, Volume 10, (1972): 209–222.

22. William Ruckelshaus, "Science, Risk and Public Policy," *Science*, Volume 221, (1982): 1026–1028.

23. William Ruckelshaus, "Risk in a Free Society," speech given at Princeton University, 18 February 1984, mimeo.

24. David Bazelon, "Risk and Responsibility," *Science* Volume 205, (1979): 277–280.

25. American Industrial Health Council, *Report to the Membership*, Scarsdale, NY, 1983.

26. Alice Whitmore, "Facts and Values in Risk Analysis for Environmental Toxicants," *Risk Analysis*, Volume 3, (1983): 23–33.

27. *Ibid.*, p. 32.

28. H.T. Reynolds, *Analysis of Nominal Data* (Beverly Hills, CA: Sage Publications, 1977), p. 58.

29. Hubert L. Blalock, *Social Statistics* (New York: McGraw-Hill Book Co., 1960), p. 227.

16

Policy Research as Social Science
Outflanking the Value Dilemma

Laurence Chalip

When social scientists first sought to characterize social inquiry as science, they grew concerned that their objectivity would be compromised by involvement in policy issues. Ever since, the tension between objectivity and relevance--the value dilemma--has vexed social scientists who seek to make their work pertinent to policy (cf. Foss, 1977). The discussion generated by that dilemma has been so protracted that Homans (1978) recently characterized it as "a pretty nearly dead horse" (p. 530).

But it is far from that. As this analysis shows, the dilemma flourishes. The dilemma continues to wield a degenerative influence on relations between policy research and mainstream social science. This analysis outlines the scope of that influence, examines its sources, and scrutinizes its premises. Whereas previous discussion has taken its momentum from the philosophy of science and/or the sociology of knowledge, this analysis draws heavily on empirical findings from the history, sociology and psychology of science. It suggests that mainstream social science will benefit from a closer interplay with policy research than it now obtains.

Throughout the following analysis, policy research is taken to include the common types of social research for policy purposes: opinion research, needs assessment, evaluation research, impact assessment, and social experimentation. Policy research also includes research for purposes of elaborating models of policy formation, implementation or impact.

This analysis follows tradition by distinguishing "positive" discourse from "normative" discourse. The former refers to discussions of fact; the latter refers to contention about values.

Scope of the Dilemma

As the policy sciences took shape, it was hoped that the interdisciplinary nature of policy issues would provide a focus around which the social sciences could find common ground and a new integration (cf. Lasswell, 1951). Subsequently, the consensus emerged that policy research could merely provide an arena for multidisciplinary discussion. Hopes for integration were replaced by expectations for cross-disciplinary communication (cf. Charlesworth, 1972). More recently, even those expectations suffer as policy science develops research paradigms which are defined independently from mainstream social science. A study of 120 social policy research projects finds that discipline-oriented social scientists rarely communicate effectively with policy-oriented social scientists, even when they are working on the same project or problem (Van de Vall & Bolas, 1981). The emerging view among academic social scientists holds that social research for policy is needed but should be done primarily by social scientists who are apart from the academic community (Ford, 1977).

From Laurence Chalip, "Policy Research as Social Science: Outflanking the Value Dilemma," *Policy Studies Review*, Vol. 5, pp. 287-308. Copyright © 1985 by the Policy Studies Organization. Reprinted by permission.

Policy research cannot provide an arena for integrative communication between the social sciences if policy scientists become dissociated from other social scientists. The consequences of similar dissociation in psychology (Barlow, 1981), urban sociology (Kierman, 1983), and organization development (Porras & Berg, 1978) show that social science and policy will be mutually impoverished if dissociation becomes institutionalized. Policy research would come to lack theoretical insight, and social theory would lose a significant source of feedback.

Declining prospects for a symbiotic relationship between academic social science and its policy-oriented analogue have not gone unchallenged. A succession of monographs has attempted to retrieve that relationship by characterizing the form it should ideally take (e.g., Bailey, 1980; Fay, 1975; Fischer, 1980; Gastil, 1977; Goodwin, 1975; MacRae, 1976; Rein, 1976). These monographs are linked by their attempts to delimit appropriate roles for the normative issues at stake in policy research contexts. Yet, despite this common thread, analysts have advocated roles which differ significantly in the intimacy of association to be allowed between normative and positive realms.

Bailey (1980) contends that the enlightenment value of social research need not be compromised by the normative nature of policymaking. Social research informs normative political discourse by clarifying issues of fact. While social problem solving is enlightened by social research, normative issues need not compromise the integrity of social research.

Gastil (1977) and MacRae (1976) concur that social research can inform policymaking, but they contend that the enlightenment value of social research requires parallel, though independent, rational discourse in normative and positive realms. Their models take the premise that normative and positive issues can be separately framed and subsequently argued in parallel: normative debate constituting a realm of rational political discourse, and positive debate occurring within the realm of social scientific discourse. Issues of fact settled through such social scientific discourse afford information which decisionmakers can use to effectuate the goals they have set via rational normative discourse. Reciprocally, the issues at stake in normative realms may direct the focus of some positive social research.

Fischer (1980) and Rein (1976) concur that positive and normative issues are conceptually distinct, but they contend that the two interact. Facts are construed by interpretations which are themselves guided by implicit values; values change as new facts must be accommodated. Given the interaction, they contend, it is misleading to argue facts and values independently. The structure of interaction between positive and normative discourse needs to be understood so that issues of fact and value do not become distorted by artificial separation. Since the interaction is inescapable, it needs to be delineated in both political and academic realms of discourse.

Fay (1975) and Goodwin (1975) concur that facts and values interact, but they conclude that the interaction can catalyze a rapid advance of social knowledge. Given the interaction, they argue, it follows that social issues can serve as signposts to inadequacies in current understandings of social fact. Normative discourse can inform social scientific discourse no less than social scientific discourse can inform normative discourse.

Efforts to reunite policy research with mainstream social science have been resisted by social scientists who seek to retain traditional canons of value freedom. Weiss (1977) summarizes their objections as five propositions: (1) policy research is not directed at the elaboration of social theory; (2) the discipline will be distorted by the political agendas of those who control funding; (3) social scientists will become the lackeys of government; (4) social science will become discredited by overstating its state of knowledge; (5) social scientists will lose their objectivity by becoming involved in value-laden policy issues. Cochrane (1980) discusses political constraints on policy research, such as client-oriented problem definition, time limits for research completion, and need for clear relevance to implementation. He contends that these constraints necessarily distinguish academic social science from policy research. Lindblom and Cohen (1979) stress that social problem solving is embedded in political constructions of reality which require policy research to originate from a base of common sense, rather than from mainstream social scientific insight. Scott and Shore (1979) contend that social science and policy are independent realms because political processes are not designed to incorporate rational scientific planning. Rule (1978) asserts that policy research is inherently "an act of political partisanship" (p. 25). He suggests that social knowledge will rarely be useful because conflicts over allocations of wealth, privilege, or power inhere in most problems policy scientists study. He sees policy issues as contests between interests rather than facts.

Meanwhile, critics of social science have seemingly finessed the issue altogether. They have asserted the uselessness of extant social theory (Mazur, 1968), the obfuscatory nature of social research (Andreski, 1972), the impossibility of predictive social theory (Matson, 1964), the impossibility of generalized objective social knowledge (Gergen, 1982), or the common-sense nature of social science explanation (Schrag, 1983). Taking these criticisms to their logical conclusion, Banfield (1980) characterizes social science as adept at problem creation but useless for problem solution. If the critics are to be believed, we need not be concerned about the relationship between social science and public policy because social science is unlikely to prove useful.

My analysis rejects trivializations of the scientific stature or the contributions of social science. In-principle objections to the possibility of social knowledge run aground on the narrowness of objectors' criteria for science (Glymour, 1983), on fallacious comparisons between social and natural science (Machlup, 1961), and on the unanticipated inventiveness of social science methodologists (Gadourek, 1977). It is simply not the case that social knowledge is inherently common-sensical (Collins, 1982). Nor is it the case that social science fails to contribute to policy (Knorr, 1977).

Nonetheless, relations between policy research and academic social science are, as we have seen, problematic. To better understand impediments to their integrative association, we next examine the analogies and resultant prestige hierarchies which fashion the relationship between them.

Sources of the Dilemma

Contemporary academic parlance differentiates "applied" research from "basic" research. It is striking that the distinction endures, since it fails to withstand conceptual analysis (e.g., Reagan, 1967). When specific research is to be distinguished as "basic" or "applied," scientists may disagree even among themselves about which category is appropriate for a particular instance (Barber, 1952). Scientists' criteria for demarcating the two categories have been found to shift substantially when examined across time and disciplines (Gieryn, 1983).

The ephemeral but tenacious character of the applied/basic dichotomy results from its fundamentally social function. The distinction stratifies researchers into prestige hierarchies. Researchers who can claim their work to be "basic" attain greater prestige than do those whose work is labeled "applied." Snow (1963) describes the attitude of research scientists at Cambridge:

> We prided ourselves that the science we were doing could not, in any conceivable circumstances have any practical use. The more firmly one could make that claim, the more superior one felt. (p. 36)

As MacRae (1976) observes, the impact on policy research is self-evident:

> As applied, rather than fundamental work, it eludes the attention which the prestige system directs to fundamental discoveries. (p. 18)

The lesser prestige accorded to policy research is both a cause and a consequence of concomitant patterns of information exchange and peer recognition. The prestige system within science creates a self-reinforcing hierarchy. Research is noted, heeded and discussed in proportion to the prestige of the responsible scientists and institutions. This attention reinforces the prestige of those scientists and institutions (Cole & Cole, 1973). Scientists who seek to have their work taken seriously by their peers dare not have that work associated with low prestige endeavors. This is clearly why academic social scientists are distancing themselves from their policy-oriented colleagues. Social scientists within the academic community have remained reticent to forge even indirect ties to policymakers (Caplan, Morrison & Stambaugh, 1975). Meanwhile, communication and peer prestige obstacles impede the organization of effective and enduring teams of policy-oriented social scientists (Orlans, 1972, especially pp. 75-76).

Social scientists who eschew relevance do so on the grounds that elaboration of social theory is the paramount goal of social research. For example, a popular textbook on social research methods claims:

> Scientific research never has the purpose of solving human and social problems, making decisions, and taking action. The researcher is preoccupied with, and should be preoccupied with, variables and their relations. He should never be required to think about or to spell out the implications of what he has done. (Kerlinger, 1979, p. 289)

Elaboration of theory is said to be more "basic" than social problem solving because problem solving requires good theory, whereas theories will not be improved as a consequence of research which aims to relieve social problems. This position has advocates throughout the social sciences.

From anthropology:

> I consider the development of fundamental science, whether of human relations or of anything else, a different matter than the solution of pragmatic problems. The practical problems can no doubt be solved more wisely if there exists genuine science to draw on. But science as science will not develop better or faster for having its pursuit mixed with problems of application. (Kroeber, 1959, p. 291)

From psychology:

> [Psychologists] can be most useful to society by staying in their laboratories and libraries, there to remain until they can come forth with reliable predictions and well-tested applications. (Pratt, 1939, p. 179)

From political science:

> If we are to make sense of policy analysis, it would be well to conceive of it as applied social science. And it would be even better to remember that it is the findings of a theoretical science that are to be applied. (Landau, 1977, p. 425)

From sociology:

> I take for granted that a fundamental difference exists between social problems and sociological problems analagous to the difference between problems of electrical or mechanical engineering and those of theoretical physics. (Znaniecki, 1952, p. 79)

The engineering analogy is so prevalent that many policy scientists adopt it uncritically, even though it legitimizes the dissociation of policy science from mainstream social science. For example, Reynolds (1975) gives the following definition:

> Policy science is that form of inquiry which seeks to produce empirical knowledge which, in respect to a policy problem, would be *functionally equivalent* to that offered jointly by the relevant science and its engineering application, but, which, at the same time would not require the creation of intellectual structures which have the same *cognitive status* as scientific theories and their engineering derivatives. (p. 5, emphasis in original)

The engineering analogy has its source in the positivist tradition that science can never include normative concerns. If science requires independence from normative issues, then it is clear why theory informs policy, but not the reverse. Policy implicates values and must therefore be outside the realm of science. As Bierstedt (1948) put it:

> [Social science] is a science or it is nothing. And in order to be a science it must diligently avoid all pronouncements of an ethical character. As a science it cannot answer questions of value. It can have no traffic with normative statements because there is no logic of the normative. (p. 310)

However, the engineering model has a challenger. Taking medical science as the appropriate analogue, advocates of a "clinical" model contend that "basic" and "applied" social research are more complementary than advocates of the engineering model are aware. Leighton (1946) summarizes the reasoning:

> ... [A]pplied social sciences can well be the meeting place of both science and practice as in clinical research. Participation in administrative programs through planning, execution and follow-up observation often presents a unique opportunity for careful compilation of data and for a degree of experimentation that is not possible elsewhere. It may be that under such

circumstances discoveries regarding the nature of society and culture can be made .... Moreover, social theories can be reduced to working hypotheses leading to predictions that are testable by the observation of subsequent events. Through such a series of steps, science as well as the techniques of application should advance. (p. 668)

The next sections measure the relative fit of clinical and engineering models to the historical relationship between science, values and practice.

Clinical versus Engineering Models

Natural Science. The clinical model predicts that some, but not necessarily all, scientific advances result from real world needs and applications. This prediction finds support in several historical studies which trace theoretical insights to research which was initiated for industrial or policy purposes. For example, Cardwell (1971) finds that solutions to problems in steam technology for industry had significant impact on the development of physical theories about heat, energy and thermodynamics. Significantly, that knowledge later came to be regarded as "basic" rather than "applied." Similarly, Tobey (1976) shows that the science of ecology had its genesis in the attempt by Nebraska scientists to control vegetation changes on American prairies. Bernal (1957) observes that, since ancient times, communication between craftsmen and scholars has lead to simultaneous advances in science and technology.

Discovery may be better served, however, when the roles of craftsman and scholar are combined. Ben-David (1960) finds that the founders of bacteriology and psychoanalysis achieved their new formulations because they were interested in practical applications. The role of practitioner made them aware of innovative ways to organize their field's knowledge. Their innovations resulted in unexpected but fruitful directions for research. There are corroborative examples. James Joule's contributions to the theory of energy conservation were a consequence of his attempt to obtain electrical power from batteries (Forrester, 1975). Rankine helped introduce the entropy function into thermodynamics because he sought to improve the efficiency of steam engines (Hutchison, 1981).

Although the clearest examples of feedback from applications to "basic" scientific knowledge are well studied historical cases, it is increasingly clear that the feedback also operates in contemporary science. For example, it has been "applied" work which has created many of the new disciplines of science which are coming to be regarded as "basic," such as fusion oriented plasma physics and chemical carcinogenesis (van den Daele, Krohn & Weingart, 1977). Furthermore, scientists who are most effective rarely restrict their work to "applied" or "pure" science, but are often concerned with both (Pelz & Andrews, 1966). A dual orientation seems to sensitize them to symbioses between practical and theoretical interests.

The symbioses occur because practical concerns provide a focus for innovative insight and integrative synthesis. Gordon and Marquis (1966) find that scientists frequently rate research from applied settings (e.g., hospitals) as more innovative than research from theory-oriented settings (e.g., universities). Gordon and Marquis show that applied settings are particularly receptive to innovative work because the visibility of practical consequences is higher there than elsewhere. As a result, scientists in those settings have unique latitude to attempt cross-paradigmatic fertilization and methodological invention. The real-world orientation of their institutions circumvents the limitations of paradigmatic presuppositions.

Practical problems also provide the scientist with metaphors for issues of importance to the elaboration of theory. Royce (1978) shows that metaphoric thinking complements rational and empirical thought by facilitating intuition and symbolization. Metaphor and analogy can be significant components of scientists' thinking. They can guide speculation about the consequences of practical action. For example, Wertheimer (1959) finds that relativity formulations were partly the result of if-then puzzles which Einstein posed himself about actions on the world.

Social Science. The review so far demonstrates that the engineering model does not fit the facts of natural science as well as does the clinical model. This is significant because social scientists who propound an engineering model do so on the grounds that it best describes the situation in natural science (e.g., Reynolds, 1975). Nevertheless, proponents of an engineering model might still contend that in the social sciences there is no feedback from practice to theory. For instance, Coser (1969) asserts "... the majority of those men who, in their day, worked on 'relevant issues' remain of interest, at best, to specialized historians of ideas" (p. 132).

It is surprising that an American sociologist makes this claim. The early preeminence of the Chicago School, one of the most influential sociology departments in America, was a direct consequence of faculty and student fascination with policy research and policymaking (Carey, 1975). And the catalytic effect of practical concerns has not been unique to the Chicago School. Rossi (1981) cites four compelling cases: Sewell's work on status attainment began as an attempt to forecast demand for higher education in Wisconsin; studies of occupational prestige originated from the military's desire to find ways to retain its scientists; Lazarsfeld's work on personal influence stemmed from the efforts by *True Story* magazine's publisher to convince advertisers that the magazine reached opinion leaders among housewives; community studies were initiated to determine the impacts of social and technological change on American life. Furthermore, Rossi observes that 19 of the 31 presidents of the American Sociological Association between 1950 and 1981 did substantial quantities of social research which had an immediate practical focus. He explains the apparent contradiction between this fact and the prevalent notion that "applied" work is an intellectual dead end:

> Most interesting and revealing in light of the earlier discussion about the lower esteem accorded applied work is that so many of the presidents are not remembered generally as applied social researchers because over time some of their most important applied research has been redefined as basic work in what appears to be an Orwellian exercise in rewriting history. (pp. 453-454)

Sociology is not the only social science to reexamine its history and discover that "basic" and "applied" research are symbiotic. Foster (1969, pp. 144-150) observes that anthropologists' concerns with problems of colonial administration and economic development gave birth to acculturation studies, economic anthropology, and cross-cultural psychology. Miller (1983) points out that practical need provided the impetus behind psychological research into information overload, selective attention, and information processing. Currently, Miller says, clinical observation of the relations between stress and disease has stimulated new laboratory research into the relations between coping, conflict, illness and discrimination. Rogers and Leonard-Barton (1978) find that market researchers have made substantial contributions to the study of attitude formation, to conceptions of innovation diffusion, and to understanding of impediments to and facilitators of behavior change. Ferber and Hirsch (1978) show that social experiments on income maintenance, supported work, health insurance, electricity rate variation, and housing allowances provide substantive information about the magnitude of effects and about the conditions under which particular economic theories secure or forfeit their validity.

The need for practical knowledge has also contributed to development of new social research methods. Examples include: sociometry, multidimensional scaling, group interviewing, field experimentation, qualitative research, and attitude surveys (Rogers & Leonard-Barton, 1978; Rossi, 1981).

The apparent connection between need-to-know and the advancement of social theory and method is consistent with Deutsch, Platt and Senghaas's (1971) finding that practical demands or conflicts have generated most of the significant social scientific advances of this century. Deutsch et al. identify and analyze 62 major social scientific advances from 1900 to 1965. The overwhelming majority are found to originate from innovative, interdisciplinary environments which are vigorously concerned with practical affairs. Furthermore, the percentage of advances originating from settings of this kind has been increasing.

Policy scientists are becoming cognizant of their own contributions to social theory. In a recent review, Hansen (1983) discovers that policy research is advancing theories of political economy and organizational decisionmaking. She also notes that policy failures have helped to pinpoint weaknesses in extant social theory, and that needs for improved policy information are prompting creation of new research tools. Krimsky (1984) finds that the "folk wisdom" encountered in real-world policy research helps social scientists to see beyond paradigmatic blinders. Joshi (1982) demonstrates that development research for Third World countries can provide opportunities which are uniquely suited to elaboration of theories about the relations between human behavior, institutions of socialization, and economic organization.

Implications. It is clear that the clinical model is more tenable than is the engineering model. But that does not imply that all research which has a practical focus impinges upon theory. Nor does it imply that social research which lacks an immediate practical focus is unsuited to advancement of social theory. Either implication would misrepresent the complexity of relations between science and practice. The point is simply that social scientific advance and policy research are complementary enterprises. Indeed, there is every reason to conclude that their integration is optimal for both.

However, integration of policy research with mainstream social science requires policy scientists to recognize themselves as social scientists whose work is worthy of status commensurate with that of other social scientists. That recognition, in turn, requires policy scientists to clarify the role of normative issues in their research. As we have seen, feedback from policy research to social theory implicates values. We turn next to an examination of the relation between values and social knowledge.

The Place of Values

The Value Dispute. Dispute over the appropriate role of values in science has assumed that value freedom is, in fact, a scientific norm. Advocates (e.g., Hall, 1956) take norms of value freedom to be the fountainhead of modern science; whereas critics contend that value freedom is an historical accident (Uberoi, 1978), a reinforcer of Protestant values

(Sampson, 1978), or a mask for the production of ideology (Samelson, 1974). Both sides assume that scientists--at least prestigious scientists--conduct their research in ways which are consistent with norms of value freedom. But that assumption may be unfounded.

Studies of scientists suggest that value freedom is not, in fact, a functioning norm of their work. Research decisions are typically influenced by such purposes of the scientist as personal preferences, publication objectives, grant considerations, and methodological skill (Platt, 1976). Theories are sometimes accorded credence for ideological rather than empirical reasons (Richardson, 1984). Scientists are rarely as open-minded, objective or rational as norms of value freedom would require (Mahoney, 1979).

Even more disconcerting are findings that natural scientists who are most highly regarded are also those who most readily admit extra-rational criteria. Hill (1974) finds that scientists rated as most successful by their colleagues stress creativity, flexibility, and compromise over objectivity; while scientists deemed less successful emphasize objectivity over creativity and compromise. Mitroff (1974) interviewed 40 NASA scientists and finds them to be highly committed to personal hypotheses. They feel that their good ideas should not be easily lost to apparent refutation. Moreover, the scientists most committed to this view are rated by their peers as the most prominent and successful.

These studies show that natural scientists admit criteria into their science which norms of value freedom would not permit. Studies of leading social scientists find that normative commitments also operate in social scientific research. Morawski (1982) reviewed the utopian writings of G. Stanley Hall, William McDougal, Hugo Munsterberg, and John B. Watson. He finds a consistent relationship between their utopian visions and their subsequent research and theories. Hannush (1983) studied the lives and writings of B.F. Skinner and John B. Watson. He finds that both gave regular lip service to canons of value freedom; but across more than 20 categories, he finds convergence between their personal values, their stated sociocultural preferences, and their research and theories.

The consistency between personal values and scientific research may be due to the thematic character that human lives take on when they are productive. Life history research shows that lives become organized around themes which give shape, meaning and continuity to ongoing work (Csikszentmihalyi & Beattie, 1979). These themes are organized around a central problem which has attained personal meaning from the interaction of life events and family circumstances. Given the thematic character of productive lives, the scientist who embraces value neutrality may forfeit the very concerns giving coherence, purpose and creativity to his work.

But the admission of values into science is not unproblematic. Experimenter bias can predetermine the outcomes of research (Rosenthal, 1966). Strong opinions may lead to selective attention to confirmatory data (Lord, Ross & Lepper, 1979). Indeed, social studies of science are frequently justified on the grounds that they can sensitize scientists to these biasing effects of value premises, thus helping them to free themselves from those effects. A currently emerging position concedes that values enter into scientific work, but contends that scientists should transcend their values by becoming aware of them and then suspending them (e.g., Papineau, 1978). Value freedom becomes value neutrality.

If good scientists are value neutral, it is argued, good science will lead to conclusions on which scientists concur, even when policy decisions are at stake. The value neutralist position holds that we can agree on the facts before us because we are not blinded by confounding values. Thus, policy scientists who seek to make policy research value neutral seek also to shun dissensus. Zeisel's (1982b) recent closing comments on his debate with Rossi, Berk and Lenihan (1982) provide a case in point. In a critique of Rossi, Berk and Lenihan's conclusion that income maintenance programs can reduce prisoner recidivism, Zeisel (1982a) reexamines their data and suggests that income maintenance programs provide little benefit. Rossi, Berk and Lenihan (1982) rejoin that when their data are considered in conjunction with data from a pilot study, their conclusion that a benefit exists is warranted. Despite the substantive, methodological and empirical issues which clearly remain unresolved, Zeisel (1982b) then responds that controversies of this sort are bad for social science, and that both sides probably agree that a beneficial income maintenance program might be found, even if it has not been found yet. What is astonishing about this conclusion is that it glosses over the scientific issues, while favoring a contrived consensus.

Conclusions of this sort result from fears that controversy compromises the integrity of research findings, and that disputes between scientists implicate values in a way which is synonymous with bad science. It is these fears which have lead policy scientists to develop logical (Adelman & Mumpower, 1979), dialectical (Mitroff, 1983), and decision analytic (Hammond & Adelman, 1976) tools by which policy researchers might circumvent controversy. As useful as these tools are, the underlying premise that consensus is the *sine qua non* of science reinforces the notion that values must be excluded from scientific discourse.

The next two subsections weight the utility of consensus and value neutrality. First, the roles of bias in research are examined; then, the functions of controversy are surveyed.

The Roles of Bias. The preceding discussion observes that researchers' values can predispose their work to confirmatory findings. Objectors to value committed research stress that scientists should be prepared to refute, rather than merely to confirm, positions they hold. However, research biases have their uses in the long-run advance of knowledge.

Empirical investigations of research processes show that the elaboration of knowledge is more complex than strict falsificationists have realized. Experimental studies of research procedures find that confirmatory work is necessary before it becomes effective to subject theories to strong risks of refutation (Mynatt, Doherty & Tweney, 1978). If comparison or synthesis of opposing hypotheses is to be accomplished, there must first have been sufficient empirical elaboration of the underlying theoretical alternatives to highlight relevant strengths, weaknesses, commonalities and points of contrast. Confirmatory research thus aids the advance of knowledge by clarifying the bases along which competing hypotheses are fruitfully contrasted or synthesized (Tweney, Doherty, Worner, Pliske, Mynatt, Gross & Arkkelin, 1980).

The significance of these findings is illustrated by historical study of avowedly successful scientific inquiries. For example, Rudwick (1974) examines the debate among geologists over the origins of three naturally occurring "roads" in Scotland. At the debate's onset in the early nineteenth century several incompatible theories were advanced to explain the roads. Each theory was tenaciously held by its proponents. The resulting disputes lead to continuing confirmatory research by each side. However, accumulation of new data on each side pointed the way to necessary modifications of the opposing theories. Those modifications, in turn, provided the basis for synthesis of contrary views into a new explanation which has stood for more than a century. Iltis (1973) shows that a similar sequence of confirmatory research, theory comparison, and theory synthesis laid the foundations of pre-relativistic physics.

These studies make the point that scientific knowledge is forthcoming when communities of competing ideas are forced over time to accommodate to one another's accumulating evidence. The clear implication is that values held by individual social scientists pose less threat to social scientific objectivity than would value consensus within the community of social scientists. One benefit of contrasted values is that the contrast provides a necessary basis for elaborating alternative hypotheses. Elaboration of those alternatives is necessary for subsequent convergence to adequate comprehension. That is why Horowitz and Katz (1975) can trace American policy failures in Viet Nam to the unwillingness of Pentagon social scientists to entertain alternative value premises. Value neutralism became a pretext for value consensus.

There are further limitations to value neutralism. Perhaps the most potent is that value neutral research injects distortions of its own. For example, subjects sometimes provide inadequate or inaccurate information because value neutral social scientists make them feel dependent or socially distant (Argyris, 1968; Jourard & Kormann, 1968). In more extreme instances, subjects have stymied research by refusing to permit studies which they felt could benefit no one but social scientists (New & Hassler, 1973; Vargus, 1971). Even where access has been available, research has been spoiled by subjects' frustrations with value neutralism. Proshansky (1972) paraphrases two administrators of public agencies:

> Too often you people come in not as problem oriented research-
> ers but academic purists more interested in searching and test-
> ing what is important for your theory than for the problem
> itself. But what really gripes me is that there is no long-run
> commitment. You can't come in, have your fun, and then leave--
> and then expect us to welcome you back, particularly after you
> have left a mess. (p. 212)

There are, then, at least two ways in which value neutralism distorts social knowledge: it can incline subjects to provide misleading data, and it can cause selective data mortality.

Bredemeier (1973) argues that distortions will be minimized if social phenomena are studied by social scientists who, among themselves, differ in their value commitments. He contends that opposing teams of value committed researchers should obtain complementary data. Since subjects will have differing stakes and viewpoints, the information they provide will be differently skewed by their biases, secrets, and selective presentations. Depending on its particular value commitments, each research team will be able to coax forth different information and perspectives. By contrasting the varying perspectives, Bredemeier says, social scientists can triangulate toward an adequate comprehension. Johnson (1975) makes a similar point. He observes that social science data are shaped by the role relations between social scientists and their subjects. He recommends that data be obtained by social scientists who take a variety of roles relative to their subjects. In other words, Bredemeier and Johnson point out that robust social knowledge results from triangulation by a community of fallible scientists rather than from the objectivity of value neutral individuals. They suggest that value committed social research is not merely OK, but is in fact essential to the social scientific enterprise.

The significance of this suggestion is furthered by a substantial body of psychological research which questions the feasibility of value neutrality. Klausner (1968) finds that social scientists' metaphoric thinking injects the valuative connotations of the metaphors, thereby impacting the scientists' attitudes toward their subject matter. Attitudes, themselves, turn out to be a complex interaction between the facts believed about a topic and the values attached to the component facts (Fishbein, 1963). Sperry (1983) contends that the interaction between facts and values is inherent in brain activity, because the human mind is goal oriented, while values are goal dependent. Since facts impact goal perceptions, and goal perceptions construe facts, facts and values are neurologically intertwined. Kohler (1936) reaches a similar conclusion from the standpoint of gestalt theory. Values provide the "ground" on which facts are perceived as "figure," and vice versa. For Kohler, facts and values are perceptually interdependent. Experimental and clinical research confirm that cognition and emotion are codeterminant processes (Greenberg & Safran, 1984). For social scientists, the significance of this codetermination is reflected in Powdermaker's (1966) telling observation about her sole unsuccessful study:

> Hollywood was the only field experience in which I made no notes of my personal reactions. This in itself is significant. I was not the functioning, feeling as well as thinking, human being that I was in other field research. Feelings were muted. I saw myself as an objective social scientist. (p. 211)

We conclude, then, that value neutralism stunts the growth of scientific knowledge by restricting the range of permissible routes to information, and by constraining the scope of scientific deliberation. Robust social theory is the product of a many-valued community of scholars who both think and feel.

The Functions of Controversy. We have noted that some social scientists object to the value-tinted debates which policy research sometimes generates among scientists (e.g., Hammond & Adelman, 1976; Zeisel, 1982b). This contrasts with the view that failure to admit valuative dispute leads to bad social inquiry and correspondingly misguided policy (e.g., Tribe, 1973).

Elsewhere in science, value-tinted controversy has assisted the advance of knowledge. For example, quantum physics emerged, in part, as a hostile reaction to the determinist ideology of Weimar culture (Forman, 1971); statistics developed as a means to demonstrate eugenic principles (Cowan, 1972); and much of our knowledge about cerebral anatomy resulted from extended controversy over the social programs advocated by 19th century phrenologists (Shapin, 1979). This latter case is particularly instructive because a flurry of research was generated by debates over the validity of theories by which phrenologists' social policies were defended or opposed. That research eventuated in a corpus of knowledge about the brain which is today regarded as "value free." Shapin summarizes the implication:

> Science does not guarantee its growth towards esoteric naturalism by systematically immunising [sic] itself from the action of social interests. Rather, it may be the action of conflicting social interests, and actors' ability to assign ideological concerns to knowledge claims, which provide a significant push towards

the development of increasingly naturalistic forms. It is when the "pressure is on" that knowledge develops most intensely in these directions. Hence, social conflict and ideological considerations may be seen as an important element in the development of bodies of knowledge valued as "interest-free," rather than as a feature of the environment which retards such development. (p. 171)

These benefits of controversy are consistent with sociological and psychological findings. Studies of communication networks find that differences in values, attitudes, and beliefs improve the potential for information exchange (Rogers & Kincaid, 1981, especially pp. 129-131). Controversy prompts fact seeking (Lowry & Johnson, 1981) and leads to more accurate understanding of viewpoints which differ from one's own (Tjosvold & Johnson, 1977). As a result, scientific knowledge emerges as the consequence of clashes between competing perspectives (e.g., Iltis, 1973; Rudwick, 1974), but not when consensus is forced (E.g., Medvedev, 1969; Shinn, 1980).

Robust social theory is the product of a many-valued community of scholars because controversy aids, rather than hinders, scientific pursuits of knowledge. This applies no less to policy research than it does to other channels of social scientific inquiry. A vivid illustration is provided by content analysis of social problem research taken from the past four decades (Gregg, Preston, Geist & Caplan, 1979). Studies of rape, suicide, delinquency, job dissatisfaction, substance abuse, and race relations were coded for attributions about each problem's causes. The three attributional categories coded were: person (e.g., personality, strength of will), milieu (e.g., family, peer group), and system (e.g., social stratification, institutions). An adequate examination of each problem requires balance and integration of these explanatory levels. However, four of the six problem areas analyzed show an overwhelming predominance of person blame. Rape and race relations are the only two topics in which explanations tend toward a balance among the three levels. Significantly, these are the only two areas "... in which there are organized social movements and organized, politicized constituency groups within the research community" (p. 51). Value committed social scientists have helped provide a balanced representation of these two social problems. If we are to prevent myopic misunderstanding of policy issues, social inquiry must admit value-tinted controversy.

Implications. Triangulation requires that several positions have been elaborated. It is insufficient to consider only those perspectives which obtain easy access to a community of social scientists. The presuppositions which are shared by social scientists can themselves become a source of disabling bias. Debate, cross-disciplinary fertilization, and input by persons outside the social scientific community are required.

The admission of normative discourse into social scientific processes does not imply, however, that positive and normative discourse are equivalent. The utility of triangulation lies, in part, in its capacity to aid the disentangling and investigation of normative and positive suppositions. The interrelations between theory and value are more readily identified as perspectives clash and accommodate. In the process, the subterfuges of pseudoscience are exposed.

This conclusion resonates well with the contention that one task of policy research is to analyze the structure of interaction between positive and normative discourse (e.g., Rein, 1976; Fischer, 1980). Disentangling normative from positive suppositions requires more than mere labeling of particular assertions as one or the other. It is necessary to clarify the ways these frame each other.

Some have argued further that more ambitious analysis of the interaction can provide a useful guide for necessary elaborations of social theory (e.g., Fay, 1975; Goodwin, 1975). Policy research becomes a social scientific vehicle *par excellence* because normative concerns make social theories self-reflexive. Not only is each social theory part of the social system it seeks to describe, but the interactions between our theories and our values can generate changes in the phenomena from which our theories are constructed. By seeking to understand the system, we change it; by attempting to change the system, we come to understand it better. The next section examines the tenability of this position.

Self-reflexive Social Theory

Social theories become self-reflexive because they are embedded in the phenomena they represent and simultaneously serve as sources of insight into means by which those phenomena may be improved. Social scientists have long been aware of the conundrum. Mead (1899) summarized it before the turn of the century:

> In the physical world we regard ourselves as standing in some degree outside the forces at work, and thus avoid the difficulty of harmonizing the feeling of human initiative with the recognition of series which are necessarily determined. In society we are the forces being investigated, and if we advance beyond the mere description of the phenomena of the social world to the attempt at reform, we seem to involve the possibility of changing what at the same time we assume to be necessarily fixed. (pp. 370-371)

A substantial literature has developed around the finding that social predictions are sometimes self-fulfilling or self-defeating (see Henshel, 1978 for a review). This self-reflexive feature of social prediction is significant because it poses a challenge to the objectivity of social knowledge. If our theories yield predictions which are true or false simply because we possess them, then social reality takes on an arbitrariness which seems to defy investigation, and to mock rational planning. What we know or think we know changes the system we seek to understand.

Reflexivity is amplified by the counterintuitive impact theories can have. The policies they indicate frequently lead to unexpected consequences or to impacts which are far less substantial than either the theories or their laboratory data would predict (Sieber, 1981). More confusing still, once-valid generalizations sometimes decay (Cronbach, 1975). These phenomena have been attributed to the interconnected and multiply determined properties of social events (e.g., Forrester, 1971). Social policies trigger systemic feedback which changes the system our theories initially represented.

These consequences of self-reflexiveness are characteristic of self-restructuring systems. It has been shown that such systems are most parsimoniously described by the rules of elemental interactions which generate structural change (Ulam, 1962). Descriptions built from the patterns of particular system states require substantially more information. In other words, these systems are best comprehended via theories which describe dynamic processes rather than stasis. Self-restructuring is not a nuisance. It is a feature of social phenomena which warrants singular attention.

That requires us to capture the creative, transformative impact of human self-understanding and consequent human action, while we simultaneously delineate the paths by which understanding and action ramify-- both proximally and distally. It requires that we determine how alternatives are chosen, why particular means to preferred alternatives are selected, and how consequences--both intended and unintended--are or are not fed back into ongoing decision processes. Theories which incorporate their own self-reflexivity will develop from study of the interactions among ideas, intentions, deeds, values, and information. These are, after all, both cause and consequence of self-reflexiveness.

Given this conception, policy formation, elaboration and implementation present themselves as topics by which social phenomena are profitably studied--not merely by social scientists who envision themselves as outside the system--but also by social scientists who seek to understand their own impacts as part of the system. By studying attempts at change or stabilization, we illuminate forces which hold elements in place while giving new structure to others. Self-altering prophecies and unintended consequences become the kinds of anomaly which impel the advance of knowledge. Sieber (1981) illustrates resultant benefits by showing how policy research illuminates forces which bear implication for social theory.

In order to better understand the functions and limitations of social theory reflexivity, we can exploit the feedback between our conceptions and their consequences. By attempting to maximize the effect of feedback, we place ourselves in the most opportune position to study the impacts we make as part of the system we study. This requires that our data and theories be fed back to our subjects, and that their short-term and long-term responses be incorporated into our analyses. Goodwin (1975) comments:

> This confrontation can have an emotional impact upon participants affecting their views of the world and thereby their subsequent actions. The new actions can be used to test the old predictions made, while continuing historical analysis can trace the significance of events not considered by the scientific models, and so on. [This procedure] as an ongoing activity advances knowledge while potentially advancing the solution of social problems. (p. 58)

By exploiting the advantages of reflexivity, we transcend the objective/ critical dualism.

When similar procedures have been implemented, whether by intent or accident, their worth has been demonstrated. Maquet (1964) observes that biases in anthropological knowledge about Africa have been reduced as a consequence of African critiques. Maruyama (1969) finds that unique research questions and unusual interpretive insights result from inclusion of untrained researchers who have been recruited from the group under study. Ackoff (1970) reports that by incorporating ghetto residents into the research process, his department obtained access to data which would otherwise have been lost. Psychologists find that discussing data interpretations with the persons they study improves the ease of quality of research (e.g., Chavis, Stucky & Wandersman, 1983). These benefits are convergent with experimental work showing that participants are frequently better able than observers to construct accurate explanations, because participants are more aware of their own concerns and the experiences which generated them (e.g., Monson & Snyder, 1977).

This is not to suggest that researchers should take participants' explanations at face value. Rather, it is to point out that participants' understandings provide an additionally useful starting point for triangulation. Nor is it to suggest that social scientific advance results solely from field research. Properly integrated into processes of triangulation, field and laboratory are complementary (Dipboye & Flanagan, 1979; Lavine, 1953). Robust social theory is built with insights from social scientists and subject, from laboratory and field.

Conclusions

We have covered a great deal of ground, and for good reason. The value dilemma derives from our core conceptions of science and our resulting self-conceptions as social scientists. Despite indications that the dilemma is needless, it persists. It persists because our prevailing self-image as social scientists has been misconceived. A bolder and more accurate conception is possible.

There are sound reasons to conclude that policy research can provide an integrative, interdisciplinary focus for the advance of social theory. This is not to say that all policy research will contribute to theory, nor that all theories can benefit from policy research. Nevertheless, symbiotic relations between social theory and policy would be congruent with the social, psychological and historical facts of scientific advance. Some social scientists have already discovered firsthand the advantages that symbioses provide. They report that antagonisms between schools of social science thought resolve into complementarities (e.g., Bataille & Clanet, 1981; Friedrichs, 1972).

However, full exploitation of symbioses requires that we comprehend the place of normative discourse in social science. It is useful to retain the analytic distinction between positive and normative realms. Nevertheless, positive and normative discourse give shape to one another. Social phenomena are resultantly self-restructuring, and our theories are consequently self-reflexive. As we have seen, this interdependence of positive and normative suppositions provides a fulcrum for the advance of social theory.

We find, then, that the positive and the normative are ontologically coupled, but analytically divisible. Each stands out in separate relief only as a consequence of disputation within a heterogeneous community of social scientists who are willing to both think and feel.

REFERENCES

Ackoff, R.L. (1970). A black ghetto's research on a university. *Operations Research, 18*, 761-771.

Adelman, L., & Mumpower, J. (1979). The analysis of expert judgement. *Technological Forecasting and Social Change, 15*, 191-204.

Andreski, S. (1972). *Social sciences as sorcery*. London: Andre Deutsch.

Argyris, C. (1968). Some unintended consequences of rigorous research. *Psychological Bulletin, 70*, 185-197.

Bailey, J. (1980). *Ideas and intervention: Social theory for practice*. London: Routledge and Kegan Paul.

Banfield, E.C. (1980). Policy science as metaphysical madness. In R.A. Goldwin (Ed.), *Bureaucrats, policy analysts, statesmen: Who leads?* Washington, DC: American Enterprise Institute.

Barber, B. (1952). *Science and social order*. New York: The Free Press.

Barlow, D.H. (1981). On the relation of clinical research to clinical practice: Current issues, new directions. *Journal of Consulting and Clinical Psychology, 49*, 147-155.

Bataille, M., & Clanet, C. (1981). Elements contributing to a theory and a methodology of action-research in education. *International Journal of Behavioral Development, 4*, 271-291.

Ben-David, J. (1960). Roles and innovations in medicine. *American Journal of Sociology, 65*, 557-568.

Bernal, J.D. (1957). *Science in history* (2nd ed.). London: C.A. Watts.

Bierstedt, R. (1948). Social science and social policy. *American Association of University Professors Bulletin, 34*, 310-319.

Bredemeier, H.C. (1973). On the complementarity of "partisan" and "objective" research. *American Behavioral Scientist, 17*, 125-143.

Caplan, N., Morrison, A., & Stambaugh, R. (1975). *The use of social science knowledge in policy decisions at the national level*. Ann Arbor, MI: University of Michigan Institute for Social Research.

Cardwell, D. (1971). *From Watt to Clausius*. London: Heinemann.

Carey, J.T. (1975). *Sociology and public affairs: The Chicago school*. Beverly Hills, Ca: Sage.

Charlesworth, J.C. (Ed.). (1972). *Integration of the social sciences through policy analysis*. Philadelphia, PA: American Academy of Political and Social Science.

Chavis, D.M., Stucky, P.E., & Wandersman, A. (1983). Returning basic research to the community: A relationship between scientist and citizen. *American Psychologist, 38*, 424-434.

Cochrane, G. (1980). Policy studies and anthropology. *Current Anthropology, 21*, 445-458.

Cole, J.R., & Cole, S. (1973). *Social stratification in science*. Chicago, IL: University of Chicago Press.

Collins, R. (1982). *Sociological insight: An introduction to non-obvious sociology*. New York, NY: Oxford University Press.

Coser, L.A. (1969). Letter to a young sociologist. *Sociological Inquiry, 39*, 131-138.

Cowan, R.S. (1972). Francis Galton's statistical ideas: The influence of eugenics. *Isis, 63*, 509-528.

Cronbach, L.J. (1975). Beyond the two disciplines of scientific psychology. *American Psychologist, 30*, 116-127.

Csikszentmihalyi, M., & Beattie, O.V. (1979). Life themes: A theoretical and empirical exploration of their origins and effects. *Journal of Humanistic Psychology, 19*(1), 46-63.

Deutsch, K.W., Platt, J., & Senghaas, D. (1971). Conditions favoring major advances in social science. *Science, 171*, 450-459.

Dipboye, R.L., & Flanagan, M.F. (1979). Research settings in industrial psychology and organizational psychology: Are findings in the field more generalizable than in the laboratory? *American Psychologist, 34*, 141-150.

Fay, B. (1975). *Social theory and political practice*. London: George, Allen & Unwin.

Ferber, R., & Hirsch, W.Z. (1978). Social experimentation and economic policy: A survey. *Journal of Economic Literature, 16*, 1379-1414.

Fischer, F. (1980). *Politics, values, and public policy: The problem of methodology*. Boulder, CO: Westview Press.

Fishbein, M. (1973). An investigation of the relationship between beliefs about an object and the attitude toward that object. *Human Relations, 16*, 233-239.

Ford, T.R. (1977). The production of knowledge for public use. *Social Forces, 56*, 504-518.

Forman, P. (1971). Weimar culture, causality and quantum theory, 1918-1927. *Historical Studies in the Physical Sciences, 3*, 1-115.

Forrester, J. (1971). Counterintuitive behavior of social systems. *Theory and Decision, 2*, 109-140.

Forrester, J. (1975). Chemistry and the conservation of energy: The work of James Prescott Joule. *Studies in History and Philosophy of Science, 6*, 273-313.

Foss, D.C. (1977). *The value controversy in sociology*. San Francisco, CA: Jossey-Bass.

Foster, G.M. (1969). *Applied anthropology*. Boston, MA: Little, Brown.

Friedrichs, R.W. (1972). Dialectical sociology: Toward a resolution of the current "crisis" in Western sociology. *British Journal of Sociology, 23*, 263-274.

Gadourek, I. (1977). The impact of technology and the growth of knowledge upon some current pitfalls of the methodology of sociology. *Methodology and Science, 10*, 222-239.

Gastil, R.D. (1977). *Social humanities*. San Francisco, CA: Jossey-Bass.

Gergen, K.J. (1982). *Toward transformation in social knowledge*. New York, NY: Springer-Verlag.

Gieryn, T.F. (1983). Boundary work and the demarcation of science from non-science: Strains and interests in professional ideologies of scientists. *American Sociological Review, 48*, 781-795.

Glymour, C. (1983). Social science and social physics. *Behavioral Science, 28*, 126-134.

Goodwin, L. (1975). *Can social science help resolve national problems?* New York, NY: The Free Press.

Gordon, G., & Marquis, S. (1966). Freedom, visibility of consequences and scientific innovation. *American Journal of Sociology, 72*, 195-202.

Greenberg, L.S., & Safran, J.D. (1984). Integrating affect and cognition: A perspective on the process of therapeutic change. *Cognitive Therapy and Research, 8*, 559-578.

Gregg, G., Preston, T., Geist, A., & Caplan, N. (1979). The caravan rolls on: Forty years of social problem solving. *Knowledge: Creation, Diffusion, Utilization, 1*, 31-61.

Hall, E.W. (1956). *Modern science a human values*. Princeton, NJ: D. Van Nostrand.

Hammond, K.R., & Adelman, L. (1976). Science, values and human judgement. *Science, 194*, 389-396.

Hannush, M.J. (1983). The mirage of value-neutrality in the behaviorisms of J.B. Watson and B.F. Skinner: The nature of the relationship between personal and professional value areas. *Journal of Phenomenological Psychology, 14*, 43-90.

Hansen, S.B. (1983). Public policy analysis: Some recent developments and current problems. *Policy Studies Journal, 12*, 14-42.

Henshel, R.L. (1978). Self-altering predictions. In J. Fowles (Ed.), *Handbook of futures research*. Westport, CT: Greenwood Press.

Hill, S.C. (1974). Questioning the influence of a "social system of science": A study of Australian scientists. *Social Studies of Science, 4*, 135-163.

Homans, G.C. (1978). What kind of a myth is the myth of a value-free social science? *Social Science Quarterly, 58*, 530-541.

Horowitz, I.L., & Katz, J.E. (1975). *Social science and public policy in the United States.* New York, NY: Praeger, 1975.

Hutchison, K. (1981). W.J.M. Rankine and the rise of thermodynamics. *British Journal for the History of Science, 14*, 1-26.

Iltis, C. (1973). The Leibnitzian-Newton debates: Natural philosophy and social psychology. *British Journal for the History of Science, 6*, 343-377.

Johnson, J.M. (1975). *Doing field research.* New York, NY: The Free Press.

Joshi, P.C. (1982). Perspectives in social science research: The problem of relevance or of value conflict. In Institute of Economic Growth (Ed.), *Relevance in social science research.* New Delhi: Vikas Publishing House.

Jourard, S.M., & Kormann, L.A. (1968). Getting to know the experimenter and its effect on psychological test performance. *Journal of Humanistic Psychology, 8*(2), 137-142.

Kerlinger, F.N. (1979). *Behavioral research: A conceptual approach.* New York, NY: Holt, Rinehart & Winston.

Kierman, M.J. (1983). Ideology, politics and planning: Reflections on the theory and practice of urban planning. *Environment and Planning B: Planning and Design, 10*, 71-87.

Klausner, S.Z. (1968). Choice of metaphor in behavioral research. *Methodology and Science, 1*, 69-92.

Knorr, K.D. (1977). Policymakers' use of social science knowledge: Symbolic or instrumental? In C.H. Weiss (Ed.), *Using social research in public policy making.* Lexington, MA: D.C. Heath.

Kohler, W. (1936). *The place of value in a world of facts.* New York, NY: Liveright.

Krimsky, S. (1984). Epistemic considerations and the value of folk wisdom in science and technology. *Policy Studies Review, 3*, 246-252.

Kroeber, A.L. (1959). Critical summary and commentary. In R.F. Spencer (Ed.), *Method and perspective in anthropology.* Minneapolis, MN: University of Minnesota Press.

Landau, M. (1977). The proper domain of policy analysis. *American Journal of Political Science, 21*, 423-427.

Lasswell, H.D. (1951). The policy orientation. In D. Lerner & H.D. Lasswell (Eds.), *Policy sciences.* Stanford, CA: Stanford University Press.

Lavine, T.Z. (1953). Note to naturalists on the human spirit. *Journal of Philosophy, 50*, 145-154.

Leighton, A.H. (1946). "Applied" and "pure" research. *American Anthropologist, 48*, 667-668.

Lindblom, C.E., & Cohen, D.K. (1979). *Usable knowledge: Social science and social problem solving.* New Haven, CT: Yale University Press.

Lord, C.G., Ross, L., & Lepper, M.R. (1979). Biased assimilation and attitude polarization: The effects of prior theories on subsequently considered evidence. *Journal of Personality and Social Psychology, 37*, 2098-2109.

Lowry, N., & Johnson, D.W. (1981). Effects of controversy on epistemic curiosity, achievement, and attitudes. *Journal of Social Psychology, 115*, 31-43.

Machlup, F. (1961). Are the social sciences really inferior? *Southern Economic Journal, 27*, 173-184.

MacRae, D., Jr. (1976). *The social function of social science*. New Haven, CT: Yale University Press.

Mahoney, M.J. (1979). Psychology of the scientist: An evaluative review. *Social Studies of Science, 9*, 349–375.

Maquet, J. (1964). Objectivity in anthropology. *Current Anthropology, 5*, 47–55.

Maruyama, M. (1969). Epistemology in social science research: Exploration in inculture researchers. *Dialectica, 23*, 229–280.

Matson, F.W. (1964). *The broken image*. New York, NY: George Braziller.

Mazur, A. (1968). The littlest science. *American Sociologist, 3*, 195–200.

Mead, G.H. (1899). The working hypothesis in social reform. *American Journal of Sociology, 5*, 367–371.

Medvedev, Z.A. (1969). *The rise and fall of T.D. Lysenko* (I.M. Lerner, Trans.). New York, NY: Columbia University Press.

Miller, N.E. (1983). Behavioral medicine: Symbiosis between laboratory and clinic. *Annual Review of Psychology, 34*, 1–31.

Mitroff, I.I. (1974). *The subjective side of science*. New York, NY: Elsevier.

Mitroff, I.I. (1983). Beyond experimentation: New methods for a new age. In E. Seidman (Ed.), *Handbook of Social Intervention*. Beverly Hills, CA: Sage.

Monson, T.C., & Snyder, M. (1977). Actors, observers, and the attribution process: Toward a reconceptualization. *Journal of Experimental Social Psychology, 13*, 89–111.

Morawski, J.G. (1982). Assessing psychology's moral heritage through our neglected utopias. *American Psychologist, 37*, 1082–1095.

Mynatt, C.R., Doherty, M.E., & Tweney, R.D. (1978). Consequences of confirmation and disconfirmation in a simulated research environment. *Quarterly Journal of Experimental Psychology, 30*, 395–406.

New, K.M., & Hassler, R.M. (1973). Community researchers meet community residents: Interpretation of findings. *Human Organization, 32*, 243–255.

Orlans, H. (1972). *The nonprofit research institute*. New York, NY: McGraw-Hill.

Papineau, D. (1978). *For science in the social sciences*. New York, NY: St. Martin's Press.

Pelz, D.C., & Andrews, F.M. (1966). *Scientists in organizations*. New York, NY: John Wiley & Sons.

Platt, J. (1976). *Realities of social research*. New York, NY: John Wiley & Sons.

Porras, J.I., & Berg, P.O. (1978). Evaluation methodology in organization development: an analysis and critique. *Journal of Applied Behavioral Science, 14*, 151–173.

Powdermaker, H. (1966). *Stranger and friend: the way of an anthropologist*. New York, NY: W.W. Norton.

Pratt, C.C. (1939). *The logic of modern psychology*. New York, NY: Macmillan.

Proshansky, H.M. (1972). For what are we training our graduate students? *American Psychologist, 27*, 205–212.

Reagan, M.D. (1967). Basic and applied research: A meaningful distinction? *Science, 155*, 1383–1386.

Rein, M. (1976). *Social science and public policy*. Harmondsworth: Penguin.

Reynolds, J.F.   (1975).   Policy science: A conceptual and methodological analysis. *Policy Sciences, 6*, 1-27.

Richardson, R.C.   (1984).   Biology and ideology: The interpenetration of science and values. *Philosophy of Science, 51*, 396-420.

Rogers, E., & Kincaid, D.   (1981).   *Communication networks: Toward a new paradigm for research*. New York, NY: Macmillan.

Rogers, E.M., & Leonard-Barton, D.   (1978).   Testing social theories in market settings. *American Behavioral Scientist, 21*, 479-500.

Rosenthal, R.   (1966).   *Experimenter effects in behavioral research*. New York, NY: Appleton-Century-Crofts.

Rossi, P.H.   (1981).   Postwar applied social research: Growth and opportunities. *American Behavioral Scientist, 24*, 445-461.

Rossi, P.H., Berk, R.A., & Lenihan, K.J.   (1982).   Saying it wrong with figures: A comment on Zeisel. *American Journal of Sociology, 88*, 390-393.

Royce, J.R.   (1978).   Three ways of scientific knowing and the scientific world view. *Methodology and Science, 11*, 146-164.

Rudwick, M.   (1974).   Darwin and Glen Roy: A "great failure" in scientific method? *Studies in History and Philosophy of Science, 5*, 97-185.

Rule, J.B.   (1978).   *Insight and social betterment? A preface to applied social science*. New York, NY: Oxford University Press.

Samelson, F.   (1974).   History, origin, myth and ideology. *Journal for the Theory of Social Behavior, 4*, 217-231.

Sampson, E.E.   (1978).   Scientific paradigms and social values: Wanted--A scientific revolution. *Journal of Personality and Social Psychology, 36*, 1332-1343.

Schrag,F.   (1983).   Social science and social practice. *Inquiry, 26*, 107-124.

Scott, R.A., & Shore, A.R.   (1979).   *Why sociology does not apply: A study of the use of sociology in public policy*. New York, NY: Elsevier.

Shapin, S.   (1979).   the politics of observation: Cerebral anatomy and social interests in the Edinburgh phrenology disputes. *Sociological Review Monograph, 27*, 139-178.

Shinn, T.   (1980).   Orthodoxy and innovation in science: The atomist controversy in French chemistry. *Minerva, 18*, 540-555.

Sieber, S.D.   (1981).   *Fatal remedies: The ironies of social intervention*. New York, NY: Plenum Press.

Snow, C.P.   (1963).   *The two cultures: And a second look*. New York, NY: New American Library.

Sperry, R.   (1983).   *Science and moral priority: Merging mind, brain, and human values*. New York, NY: Columbia University Press.

Tjosvold, D., & Johnson, D.W.   (1977).   Effects of controversy on perspective taking. *Journal of Educational Psychology, 69*, 679-687.

Tobey, R.   (1976).   Theoretical science and technology in American ecology. *Culture and Technology, 17*, 718-728.

Tribe, L.   (1973).   Policy science: Analysis or ideology? *Philosophy and Public Affairs, 2*, 66-110.

Tweney, R.D., Doherty, M.E., Worner, W.J., Pliske, D.B., Mynatt, C.R., Gross, K.A., & Arkkelin, D.L.   (1980).   Strategies of rule discovery in an inference task. *Quarterly Journal of Experimental Psychology, 32*, 109-123.

Uberoi, J.P.S.   (1978).   *Science and culture*. Delhi: Oxford University Press.

Ulam, S.   (1962).   On some mathematical problems connected with patterns of growth figures. *Proceedings of Symposium on Applied Mathematics, 14*, 215-224.

Van de Vall, M., & Bolas, C. (1981). A paradigm of social policy research (SPR) in advanced social systems: An empirical analysis. *Revue Internationale de Sociologie, 17*, 93-111.

Van den Daele, W., Krohn, W., & Weingart, P. (1977). The political direction of scientific development. In E. Mendelson & P. Weingart (Eds.), *The social production of scientific knowledge*. Boston, MA: D. Reidel.

Vargus, B.S. (1971). On sociological exploitation: Why the guinea pig sometimes bites. *Social Problems, 19*, 238-249.

Weiss, C.H. (1977). Introduction. In C.H. Weiss (Ed.), *Using social science research in public policy making*. Lexington, MA: D.C. Heath.

Wertheimer, M. (1959). *Productive thinking* (enlarged edition). New York, NY: Harper & Row.

Zeisel, H. (1982a). Disagreement over the evaluation of a controlled experiment. *American Journal of Sociology, 88*, 378-389.

Zeisel, H. (1982b). Hans Zeisel concludes the debate. *American Journal of Sociology, 88*, 394-396.

Znaniecki, F. (1952). Should sociologists be also philosophers of values? *Sociology and Social Research, 37*, 79-84.

This analysis owes a great deal to discussion and debate with many colleagues. Particular thanks are owed to John Bormuth, Pamela Chalip, Donald Fiske, Russel Hardin, Howard Mitzel, and William Wimsatt. Conclusions remain the responsibility of the author.

17

The Jury Is In
Use of a Modified Legal Model for
School Program Evaluation

Kit C. Wood, Sarah E. Peterson,
James S. DeGracie, and James K. Zaharis

The Judicial Evaluation Model or the Adversary Model of Evaluation
has been used in a number of educational settings. This article
examines the use by a local education agency of a modified judiciary
model: the Advocacy-Judiciary Model. The model was used to investigate programs specifically directed toward the academic needs of
the gifted and talented student population. This article presents the
development of the model as well as the results of using the model
in a local school setting.

School districts are constantly faced
with the need for periodic review and
evaluation of their existing programs.
This process has taken a greater importance in the current age of accountability
and quality control. In many cases, traditional program evaluation and data collection procedures are adequate for the
purpose. However, in some instances, a
broader base of information is needed, not
only for evaluating an educational program, but also for dealing with politically
sensitive issues involving such a program.

A case in point was the recent evaluation of the program for gifted students in
the Mesa (Arizona) Public Schools. Because the program had grown and diver-
sified rapidly, a thorough evaluation was
needed as a basis for deciding the future
of the program. However, because the
program was also a politically sensitive
issue in the district, we believed that future program decisions that were to affect
the gifted students would be better sup-

ported if representatives from the schools
and the community were included in the
evaluation process. Therefore, it was necessary to develop or adapt a form of evaluation that would include input from a
variety of sources. This article describes
the development and use of a modified
judiciary model employed in the evaluation of our gifted program.

The Program

The Mesa Public Schools System has
attempted to meet the needs of intellectually gifted and high-achieving students
through two separate programs: (a) the
Extended Learning Program (ELP) for the
intellectually gifted (identified on the basis of IQ scores), and (b) the Accelerated
Learning Program (ALP) for the high-
achieving student (identified on the basis
of achievement scores). Traditionally,
ELP students have been pulled out of their
regular classroom one day a week to participate in ELP enrichment activities,

From Kit C. Wood, Sarah E. Peterson, James S. DeGracie, and James K. Zaharis, "The Jury Is In:
Use of a Modified Legal Model for School Program Evaluation," *Educational Evaluation and Policy
Analysis,* Vol. 8, pp. 309-315. Copyright © 1986 by the American Educational Research Association.
Reprinted by permission.

whereas ALP students have been accommodated through individualized and small group instruction, usually involving ability grouping in the regular classroom.

Due to varying philosophical beliefs of school leaders, as well as differing needs of individual school populations, a pilot program for ELP and ALP students was implemented in two of Mesa's elementary schools in 1983–84. At these schools, ELP and ALP students were grouped together in a self-contained classroom at each grade level. An ELP resource teacher served each school half time by providing in-service training to the classroom teachers, conducting enrichment activities in the classroom, and so on. In 1984–85, a second pilot program was implemented in two additional elementary schools. The second pilot was similar, but ELP students were also pulled out of their ELP/ALP classroom twice a week to participate in enrichment classes conducted by the ELP resource teacher.

In addition to these two pilot programs, a third pilot, based on Renzulli's model (Renzulli, Reis, & Smith, 1981), was implemented at one elementary school. In this program, gifted students were selected on the basis of above average general abilities, high levels of task commitment, and high levels of creativity; selected students were included in a talent pool to receive differentiated levels of service.

The three pilot programs, as well as the traditional ELP/ALP program (nonpilot) in the other elementary schools, served as the focus of our evaluation.

The Model

The Advocacy-Judiciary Model (AJM) was chosen as the evaluation method for examining the ELP/ALP programs. This model was adapted from the adversary proceeding proposed by Owens (1973), the judicial evaluation model implemented by Wolf (1975), and the National Institute of Education's national adversary hearings on minimum competency testing (Madaus, 1981, 1982; Popham, 1981, 1982; Thurston & House, 1981). Although the AJM incorporated elements from previous research, there were several modifications applied to the Mesa Public Schools framework. Owens supported this process

of adjustment and school district customization and encouraged that judiciary strategies "...be creatively applied to other educational decision-making situations..." (p. 304).

Like the former models, the AJM incorporated the legal component of hearings using witnesses, testimony, and a jury. Unlike the former models, there was no adversarial element where competitive teams vied to win their case. There were two major reasons for omitting the adversarial component: (a) we did not want the outcome of this process to rest on the individual dynamism of well-versed orators, and (b) we wanted to protect against harmful effects on the existing school climate. This variation from previous models eliminated cross-examination of witnesses and the need to rule on the admissibility of testimony. All testimony was received as acceptable.

Our first reason for eliminating the adversarial approach was supported by Popham and Carlson (1977), who participated in an adversarial evaluation of the Hawaii 3-on-2 program. A number of drawbacks to using the adversary method in education were cited, with imbalance in the skills of the proponents ranking number one. Basing educational decisions that will affect many students on the individual skills of team members is a questionable practice. There is danger in allowing the rhetoric and eloquence of well-practiced witnesses to sway the judgment of the jury, especially considering that the most substantial viewpoints may not be expressed and supported by those with the most powerful formal delivery.

Although the AJM did allow differences in skills of the advocates to surface during the hearings, balancing checks were placed as safeguards against overriding personal influence. First of all, the jury was acting in an advisory capacity; it was not rendering decisions. The jury's responsibility was to submit recommendations for program improvement based on a variety of information. Also, the jury was under no obligation to accept or reject all presented information and could exercise the prerogative to partially support or oppose program components. In other words, the jury's purpose was not to decide in favor of one specific program over another, nor was it required to recommend a particular program in its current status. Indeed, in the final document, no one program was specifically endorsed. The jury's recommendations were a combination of the perceived strengths from each of the district's programs.

A second protection from individual effects was that information from the hearings did not constitute the sum total of available resources. In addition to the hearings, each jury member was required to make a minimum of four visitations—at least two to the pilot schools and two to the nonpilot schools. Attitudinal surveys were developed and disseminated to students, teachers, administrators, and parents at the pilot and nonpilot schools, and a cost analysis was performed to determine the cost effectiveness of each program. Finally, student achievement factors, as measured by several different tests, were included in the total package of information gathered.

Our second reason for omitting the adversarial component—protection against harmful effects on school climate—was based on accounts from previous evaluation processes that had followed the judicial approach (Owens, 1973, p. 303). In reviewing these accounts, it became apparent that the presence of both advocacy and adversary teams advanced the potential for divisiveness and conflict. As alternative arguments and defenses were presented, the tension of the win-lose situation increased. At times the emphasis on confrontation led to "a sharpening of issues possibly to the point of distortion" (Arnstein, 1975, p. 189). The adversary model offers more opportunity for distortion, a highly undesirable situation when making program decisions that will affect the lives of students.

The general consensus was that the adversary procedure would not lead to productive outcomes in the educational setting and might result in divisiveness, antagonism, and other negative consequences. If the adversary principle had remained in the model, the assignment or selection of teams undoubtedly would have generated discontent concerning team members' skills and program preferences. There was no way to anticipate the negative impact this adversarial approach could have imposed on the school system and surrounding community. The process of exploring and understanding the strengths and weaknesses of the separate programs would have been undermined from the start.

In approaching a decisionmaking process, careful consideration must be given to the population that will be affected, as well as to the information base from which direction will be sought. When the decision at stake is of a highly political nature and there are powerful supporting advocacy groups, these considerations become even more important. Quantitative information alone will not suffice as a basis for decisionmaking. The spread of the information base and human responses must be broadened by including human input from firsthand experience and judgment; hence, a decision was made to incorporate the AJM, along with more traditional data gathering procedures, in the evaluation and review of the gifted program.

The Process

Once the decision was made to employ the AJM, an 11-member jury was selected from among district personnel and the community. Jury members included an assistant superintendent, three principals (nonparticipating schools), a school psychologist, three parents (two with children in the ELP program and one with a child in the ALP program, none of whom attended participating schools), a basic skills resource teacher, a regular classroom teacher, and a Governing Board member. The director of the ELP program served as the judge at the hearings, and the director of the research department directed the entire evaluation process, including the hearings and all of the data collection procedures. Witnesses consisted of four different advocacy teams representing each of the district's programs. Each team included a school principal and an ELP resource teacher.

An initial outline of procedures included the following: three hearings before the jury; administration of surveys to parents, teachers, and students; visitations by jury members to the pilot and traditional schools; working meetings of the jury; analysis of available student achievement data, a cost analysis of the program; and a final meeting to present the jury's documented findings and recommendations.

The initial gathering of the jury was at the first hearing. Jury members sat in a semicircle on an elevated platform in the school district board room while witnesses presented testimony from a stand placed before the jury. This was the setting for each hearing.

Originally, the first hearing was intended to be strictly informational, with no biases or partiality expressed by the advocates. Yet although fundamental information was provided, presentations were not delivered without some stated selling points. From the onset, each advocacy team described its program's merits within the context of its school's special need for those particular benefits.

Following the first hearing, jury members planned visitations to the pilot and nonpilot schools. A few visitations were carried out by pairs of jurors; however, the majority were conducted individually. Of particular interest was the eagerness with which students and teachers sought opportunities to share their projects and activities with jury members. Contrary to the original intention of observing unobtrusively, the jurors occasionally found themselves drawn into a teacher's enthusiastic explanation of a program designed to meet specialized student needs. Meanwhile, the students were enthusiastic about the opportunity to display and explain their work. The advocacy process was clearly operating.

Overall, the jurors were positive about the inclusion of school visitations in the AJM. They agreed that actual observations added meaning to the program content in the first hearing. One factor the jurors found frustrating was the short period of time they had to observe each program. Although they believed the observations were useful, they were barely able to scratch the surface as far as program content, structure, and implementation were concerned.

The second hearing was the prime advocacy event, with each advocacy team presenting the most positive aspects of the program. Their cases were based on the practical aspects of how to best serve the needs of their gifted and high-achieving students, considering the available resources and unique circumstances at each school. No team sought to impose or mandate their particular program for the entire school district. Rather, they believed their programs worked well at their schools and had the potential to be used at other schools.

Following the second hearing, surveys were distributed to teachers, students, and parents at pilot and nonpilot schools. These surveys, coded according to program and respondent type, gathered information concerning perceptions of the effectiveness of existing programs and practices, along with suggestions for improvement. An additional questionnaire, sent to principals and teachers at pilot and nonpilot schools, was used to gather data on the amount of instruction and kinds of services provided to intellectually gifted and high-achieving students at the various schools.

Before the third hearing the jury held its first working meeting, one of six such gatherings. The goals of this meeting were to (a) allow jury members of share information they had gathered, (b) share information collected by the department of research and evaluation, and (c) develop specific questions to ask the advocacy teams at the third hearing.

It was at this working meeting that the AJM started to advance as an evaluation process from which recommendations were to evolve. Jury members were cautious at first and talk was scattered, because this process of program evaluation was so new and without precedent in any of the members' experience. They were confused about their purpose and the expected outcomes of their efforts. Through a rather lengthy discussion and sharing of interpretations, the jury was able to clarify and state its particular role in the evaluation process.

Once their mission and work had been defined to everyone's satisfaction, the meeting continued in round robin fashion. Jury members took turns sharing their perceptions and opinions on the merits and demerits of the different programs they had observed, the information received so far, and gifted education in general. Thus, jurors had an opportunity to learn of each other's viewpoints and to develop some unity as a group.

An interesting point is the flexibility demonstrated by the jury from the start. The first working meeting lasted a long time and jury members were tired, yet since they had not determined the questions to be asked of the advocacy teams at the third hearing, they planned a second working meeting to develop the questions. This initial display of adaptability in scheduling helped further solidify and commit the jury to the evaluation cause.

The third hearing began with the presentation by a parent of a different model of gifted education that focused on the formation of a special school for intellectually gifted and high-achieving students. The original design for the evaluation model had provided for advocacy of additional programs by other concerned citizens. Following this presentation, advocacy teams from the pilot and nonpilot programs were questioned before the jury. Since the teams had been notified of the specific questions to be asked, their defenses were well prepared and delivered.

Following this third hearing, the jury began a series of working meetings, called draft meetings, to compile and finalize their recommendations. Once again, jury members remained flexible and willing to commit themselves to additional meetings.

The first task of the jury was to develop a statement of philosophy in relation to intellectually gifted and high-achieving students. Next, differences between the social and academic needs of intellectually gifted and high-achieving students were addressed. Then specific program recommendations for intellectually gifted and high-achieving students were outlined. Finally, a document was compiled that included these specified components. A second document containing the jury's assessment of the pilot and nonpilot programs was also completed.

The draft meetings were intense sessions during which diverse perspectives and interpretations surfaced. At times, not all jury members could agree. Sometimes compromises were reached as a few words were juggled here and there; occasionally one or two members willingly bowed to the vote of the remaining majority; and, in a limited number of in-stances, a member strongly disagreed with the majority and requested that a dissenting viewpoint be attached to the final document. But the jury came together as a unit, and, although members did not agree on all issues, they definitely were pleased with the outcome of their labors. They believed in the document and supported it. The jury's trial was to be the final recommendations meeting.

A concise presentation of the jury's statement of philosophy and separate recommendations for intellectually gifted and high-achieving students opened the recommendations meeting. Following this presentation, members of the advocacy teams and audience were permitted to ask the jury questions. At the close the audience commended and applauded the jury for the fine outcome of its efforts and the long hours members had contributed to the process. The recommendations had been well received, and the jury's trial had been brief.

The Verdict

The AJM of program evaluation has been developed and successfully implemented. Based on the results of this initial attempt to incorporate the process into a school district setting, evidence now exists to support its use in other educational systems.

Based on our results, we urge using the strict advocacy approach when judicial proceedings are employed within the public school setting. In addition to being sensitive to the special environment of schools, people must exercise caution in designing evaluation processes and take full consideration of possible negative and positive results.

We also encourage that the jury be commissioned and charged only with producing recommendations. If the jury is to submit recommendations rather than render decisions, then the jury (along with the advocacy teams and other interested parties) is taking on a less burdensome and implicating posture. Actual program decisions rightfully belong with those who will be held most accountable; however, a wise administration will not ignore the results of the invested labors of its dedicated employees and community members.

Perhaps the greatest strength of the AJM was the representation of all groups that would be implementing results or affected by the outcomes of the procedure. Broad human involvement becomes even more important when dealing with politically sensitive issues as in the case of our gifted program. The AJM also provided for a broader data base than what is available from more traditional processes. By incorporating a variety of techniques such as surveys, visitations, hearings, and working meetings, a wider understanding of actual program strengths and weaknesses was gained, thus improving the quality of our decisions and subsequent actions. In addition to being an evaluation technique, the AJM is a viable process for arriving at a political consensus.

Is anything lost in applying the AJM? Cost could be a limiting factor, although this was not a consideration in the Mesa Public Schools. With a research and evaluation department in the district, undertaking this project simply involved the assignment of staff to various tasks. Other school systems lacking these resources might find cost to be a clearly limiting factor, yet the people most actively involved in the AJM were the jury and advocacy teams selected from district personnel and community members. Their services were freely given, and tremendous appreciation was expressed for their commitment and support. Obviously, the selection of qualified, interested jurors is of paramount importance. Other school districts seeking to implement this model will want to place a strong initial emphasis on securing dedicated and committed jury members.

The fact that the judiciary approach to evaluation is time-consuming could be another limiting factor. Preparation for the hearings, working meetings, and survey administration, as well as the hours consumed by the actual meetings and school visitations, represented an enormous investment of time. In addition, the process was long. This particular program evaluation spanned more than 6 months. Because of the great investment of time, we suggest that measured consideration be given to the selection of issues evaluated by this model. Many, if not most,

issues will be more efficiently evaluated in a more conventional manner.

The most noticeable weakness in the model was the failure to gather together the jury members at the onset of the entire process. They were individually advised about their role and responsibilities, and as a group they were charged by the Assistant Superintendent with the mission of producing program recommendations at the first hearing. However, a circulated list of jury members served as their only introduction to one another. Indeed, other than those previously acquainted, jury members were not personally introduced to each other in a small group setting until after the second hearing. At the first working meeting, confusion about the jury's purpose had to be clarified and agreed upon before serious work could begin. Also, because the jury did not meet until well into the process, group cohesion was slow to develop. We recommend that more adequate in-service training of the jury be undertaken at the onset. Effectiveness is enhanced if those most centrally involved in a process are apprised of the purposes and goals from the beginning, especially when the process is new and unique.

Certainly the AJM has potential for use in other educational settings. The nature of the program and the issues at stake are primary determining factors in a school system's attempt to incorporate this evaluation method. The process is long, and time commitment from school personnel and community members is necessary. Yet, these are not unreasonable sacrifices if a particular program warrants this kind of time and attention. In the Mesa Public Schools, we believed the complex effort was needed to arrive at a quality program and to deal with politically intertwined issues.

The Sentence

As the Superintendent of the Mesa Public Schools, I am faced with making program choices. To make intelligent decisions concerning these program choices, I must have the best possible information. At times, however, I am faced with a number of challenges in obtaining such information. Some areas are extremely controversial and/or political. In other situations the available information yields input concerning only test scores or attitudes.

I believed strongly that the investigation of the gifted program in the district was a controversial and political program decision. To get the very best possible information, our research and evaluation department had to come up with a method of evaluation that would address both potential problem areas: that of political issues and that of gathering all the information needed to make an intelligent decision. I totally concur with the "verdict" that the advocacy-judiciary process was extremely time-consuming. However, in this case it was worth the effort for us to receive information needed to make our decisions concerning the gifted programs. We accepted the jury's recommendations in total and subsequently submitted their recommendations to the Board of Education, who in turn completely accepted the jury recommendations.

The reader may question whether this "experiment" is, in fact, successful since no specific criteria or a priori standards were set down to judge its success. However, I challenge that view. It is true that there was no single outcome variable set down to measure the success of the implementation of the AJM in our local setting. However, I view this in a procedural justice framework as opposed to a procedural law framework. That is, I strongly feel that justice is served when all of the evidence is brought to bear on a specific problem and when this evidence feeds into a process so that it can be judged on its merits and make an impact on the final decision. I strongly feel that this was the case in the implementation of the AJM in our school district. Classical evaluation techniques were used to augment the advocacy information presented, and the jury, made up of a cross-section of the local educational community, sat in judgment of this evidence. I feel that the true measure of its success was the acceptance of the final jury recommendation by all concerned.

My final sentence is that this type of model, with slight modifications, will again be used in the Mesa Public Schools when the programs to be evaluated are such that its use is warranted. Furthermore, I challenge educational evaluators to develop other systems that can be used in local education agencies when they are faced with these types of problems.

References

ARNSTEIN, G. (1975). Trial by jury: A new evaluation method—II the outcome. *Phi Delta Kappan, 57,* 188–190.

MADAUS, G. F. (1981). NIE clarification hearing: The negative team's case. *Phi Delta Kappan, 63,* 92–94.

MADAUS, G. F. (1982). The clarification hearing: A personal view of the process. *Educational Researcher, 4,* 6–11.

OWENS, T. R. (1973). Educational evaluation by adversary proceeding. In E. R. House (Ed.), *School evaluation: The politics and process.* Berkeley: McCutchan.

POPHAM, W. J. (1981). The case for minimum competency testing. *Phi Delta Kappan, 63,* 89–91.

POPHAM, W. J. (1982). Melvin Belli beware. *Educational Researcher, 5,* 11–15.

POPHAM, W. J., & CARLSON D. (1977). Deep dark defects of the advisory evaluation model. *Educational Researcher, 6,* 3–6.

RENZULLI, J. S., REIS, S. M., & SMITH, L. H. (1981). The revolving-door model: A new way of identifying the gifted. *Phi Delta Kappan, 63,* 648–649.

THURSTON, P., & HOUSE, E. R. (1981). The NIE advisory hearing on minimum competency testing. *Phi Delta Kappan, 63,* 87–89.

WOLF, R. L. (1975). Trial by jury: A new evaluation method—I the process. *Phi Delta Kappan, 57,* 185–187.

Authors

KIT C. WOOD, Assistant Principal, Deer Valley Public Schools, 20402 N. 15th Avenue, Phonix, AZ 85207. *Specialization:* Educational administration.

SARAH E. PETERSON, Assistant Professor, Indiana University at Fort Wayne, Division of Education, 2101 Coliseum Blvd., Fort Wayne, IN 46805. *Specializations:* Educational research and evaluation.

JAMES S. DEGRACIE, Director, Research & Evaluation, Mesa Public Schools, 549 N. Stapley Dr., Mesa, AZ 85203-7297. *Specialization:* Educational evaluation.

JAMES K. ZAHARIS, Superintendent, Mesa Public Schools, 549 N. Stapley Dr., Mesa, AZ 85203-7297. *Specialization:* Educational administration.

18

Mediating Science-Intensive Policy Disputes

Connie P. Ozawa and Lawrence Susskind

Abstract *Public policy disputes involving complex scientific issues usually entail conflicts not only over those scientific issues, but also over the distribution of gains and losses. The presence of scientific or technical dimensions to a dispute should not be allowed to mask underlying distributional considerations. On the other hand, science-intensive disputes require special attention. Merely resolving distributional conflicts without incorporating the best scientific judgment will produce unwise and potentially dangerous results. The usual adversarial approach that characterizes the handling of such disputes by agencies and courts is less than ideal for creating an understanding of scientific evidence or the resolution of scientific differences. A process of mediation, already applied in a number of significant cases, offers strong promise as a superior approach.*

Public policy disputes revolving around ambiguous or contradictory scientific or technical information are puzzling in several respects. These disputes characteristically involve both scientific analysis and political considerations, both essential for designing realistic policy. Achieving a balance between scientific and political concerns is extremely difficult. Sometimes, scientific advice is reduced to an instrument for legitimating political demands. Scientific analysis, in turn can distort policy disputes by masking, beneath a veneer of technical rationality, underlying concerns over the distribution of costs and benefits. The problem is, how shall we attain the proper balance?

In 1974, the Occupational Safety and Health Administration (OSHA) held hearings to solicit public comments on a proposed permanent safety standard for workers involved in the production

This paper was presented at the annual meeting of the Association for Public Policy Analysis and Management, New Orleans, October 18–20, 1984.

of vinyl chloride monomer (VCM) and polyvinyl chloride (PVC).[1] Both products are suspected carcinogens. Predictably, the industry opposed a "no detectable level" standard (zero parts per million parts air); not surprisingly such a standard was supported by labor unions, public health groups, and OSHA staff. Those who spoke for industry contended that health and safety levels in the workplace ought to be set relative to the actual benefits of production. According to industry experts, the cost of meeting the proposed standards would cause many plants to close and would result in the loss of 1.7 to 2.2 million jobs; the proposed standards, they asserted, were clearly too stringent. Industry's scientific witnesses argued for maximum exposure limits in the range of 20 to 40 parts per million. Supporters of the zero standard countered that if plastic could not be produced safely (in other words, by meeting the proposed standards), it should be phased out. They argued that safe substitutes should be the goal—and that the health and welfare of workers should not be sacrificed.

Advocates on all sides bolstered their positions by citing available scientific evidence. Industry scientists noted that studies by the Dow Chemical Company showed no increase in mortality rates among workers exposed to less than 200 parts per million during an 8-hour day. Moreover, they contended that the epidemiological evidence indicated that the incidence of angiosarcoma of the liver, the primary disease associated with vinyl chloride at that point, occurred primarily among reactor cleaners, who comprised only a small percentage of workers in the industry.

Supporters of the proposed zero standard argued that the lack of data on the effects of varying exposure levels precluded reliable epidemiological studies. Since no animal or human studies were available at exposures below 50 parts per million, a level at which carcinogenicity had been detected, they argued that only a "no detectable level" standard would guarantee an adequate margin of safety. Hence, scientific testimony was utilized to support two contradictory policy positions.

In a similar conflict, the Environmental Protection Agency (EPA), acting under a court order ensuing from a suit by the National Resources Defense Council, promulgated regulations restricting the use of lead additives in gasoline.[2] Under the 1970 Amendments to the Clean Air Act, EPA was required to control the major sources of ambient lead, a pollutant identified by EPA as a health risk. Section 211 of the Act specifically authorized EPA to regulate fuel additives. Accordingly, EPA proposed to phase down the use of lead additives to achieve ambient lead levels adequate to protect what EPA considered the most susceptible populations, which included young children and traffic policemen.

A number of gasoline and chemical manufacturers challenged EPA's proposed regulations. EPA's actions, they claimed, were not supported by available scientific evidence. They contested the prevalence of elevated blood lead levels among the general public, the extent to which automobile lead emission products are absorbed into the body, and the degree to which airborne lead mixes with dust and poses a health threat to children. If EPA's regulations were upheld, according to these petitioners, they would suffer substantial commercial losses.

The petitioners vigorously contested the scientific basis of the regulations. In a majority decision, the U.S. Circuit Court of Appeals, District of Columbia, found that this disagreement was not surprising given the uncertain nature of the scientific information. Nonetheless, the Court sustained the Agency's prerogative to make policy judgments in the face of conflicting and inconclusive evidence for the purpose of instituting preventive regulations.[3]

As these two cases illustrate, contending interests frequently seek to manipulate scientific advice to provide a rationale for the decision they prefer. This most often occurs when scientists disagree.[4] Disagreement can arise at two key points in a policy debate. As in the vinyl chloride case, scientists may disagree on the significance or implications of available scientific evidence; or, as the airborne lead case illustrates, scientists may disagree on the scientific evidence itself. Rather than dealing with these disagreements, decision makers operating through existing dispute resolution mechanisms commonly gloss over them and focus instead on the importance of constitutional guarantees.

Failure to deal directly with conflicting scientific advice frustrates scientists and diminishes the public's faith in scientific expertise. Moreover, the decisions may be politically palatable, but scientifically unwise. FDA's approval of saccharin, for instance, was a scientifically unwise decision, in light of its ban on cyclamates, which are now generally thought to be less harmful than saccharin. The approval of saccharin appeared to undermine agency credibility.

Recent efforts to deal more effectively with science–intensive policy disputes date back to 1967 when one observer proposed a "science court."[5] Numerous variations on the science court idea have been suggested; most presume that the key to making wise decisions in science-intensive policy disputes is to have scientists first address "science questions" and to have decision makers then act on "policy questions." Since controversy appears to escalate when experts admit their differences publicly, proponents of the science-court approach suggest that a consensus on the scientific components of a dispute ought to precede any analysis of political choices. Indeed, the advocates of such thinking assert that scientists ought to reach a consensus on scientific issues without interference from non-expert participants.[6] In sum, science court proponents advocate separating "fact" and "value" questions, a task they view as difficult but not impossible.

While it is important to distinguish between disagreements over scientific evidence and disagreements over the implications of such information, making this distinction only partially addresses the troublesome aspects of incorporating scientific advice into policymaking. As we shall presently point out, scientific investigations often produce varying results depending on the institutional environments in which they are undertaken and the political orientation of the investigators.

We are not the first to express skepticism about the possibility of separating "fact" and "value" components of policy choices. Harvey Brooks has argued that science-intensive policy disputes demand a greater recognition of the "non-technical values and preferences that affect both the selection of evidence and its interpretation by all participants, both laypersons and experts."[7] Other writers state more pointedly that scientific findings are not pure "fact"; scientific and technical analyses are not devoid of value biases.[8]

While underscoring the complexity of folding scientific advice into policymaking, our objective here is to propose a framework for making decisions that are sound in both political and scientific terms.

THE RELATIONSHIP AMONG POLICY ACTORS Disputes that entail the use of scientific evidence typically involve three sets of actors: individuals and groups likely to receive the benefits or bear the costs of a particular policy decision (affected interests); elected or appointed officials with decision-making authority (decision makers); and technical experts called upon to provide relevant technical expertise (scientists). In practice, these three sets of actors are rarely mutually exclusive: Public officials commonly hold allegiances to agencies with a stake in decisions, that is, they are "affected interests"; scientific advisors may be linked to an "affected interest," most conspicuously through the sources of their research funding; and individuals who are likely to be directly affected by a policy decision as well as public officials engaged in the debate may also be professionals with relevant expertise. Although the precise relationship among these three sets of policy actors is dependent on the affiliations of the individuals involved, certain generalizations can be made about the interactions among them.

In the formulation of mechanisms for the resolution of disputes, it is usually assumed that scientific experts stand apart from the "political" arena in which decision makers and affected interests operate. According to this view, scientists work within the protective insulation of their expertise, seeking to establish scientific "facts." On the basis of such "facts" they inform decision makers and affected interests about the outcomes associated with various policy options. By definition, such advice is presumed to be rationally sound and "apolitical."

Under such a model, decision makers are influenced directly by both technical and political exigencies. In some circumstances, therefore, political objectives can prevail as easily as technical ones. Several authors have observed that decision makers (and affected interests) tend to place especially heavy weight on scientific advice when it happens to support a decision they prefer on other grounds, and that they tend to place little weight on such advice when it conflicts with their political preferences. According to one former senate leader, he and other congressional leaders were well aware that scientists were skeptical of the idea that some threshold level existed, below which a given air pollutant could be said to offer no carcinogenic threat; yet despite that awareness the leaders continued to advocate federal legislation that presumed the feasibility of a "no threat" standard.[9] Behind that position was the political judgment that such a standard was the one most likely to win legislative support. Decision makers also find it easier to justify relying on political factors when scientific evidence fails to point to a firm conclusion, or when the implications of the evidence are in dispute. Such judgments have been upheld by the courts in several important instances.[10]

WHY SCIENTISTS DISAGREE   Because cases in which scientists disagree offer the greatest latitude for discussion based on political factors, it is important to understand the underlying causes of such disagreements.

Miscommunication   Some observers have suggested that scientists do not always disagree when the public thinks they do.[12] There are at least two explanations for the illusion of controversy. First, the intentional use of certain rhetorical devices may cause confusion. Second, the scientists involved may be addressing essentially different issues. In neither case is there what we would call a "substantive" conflict.

One author described how scientists have used rhetorical devices to sway public opinion in the nuclear power and fluoridation debates. Scientists on both sides frequently resorted to phrases such as, "There is no evidence to show that analysis is unhelpful, either because data are lacking or the available data are inconclusive." Scientists who support one of the options despite the absence of scientific evidence have been known to make such statements in order to disparage contending positions. A lay audience that hears opposing scientists use such language might easily infer that a "scientific" disagreement existed. Thus, while scientists may actually agree that no conclusive evidence to support either scientific claim is available, their public statements sound like they disagree about the facts.

Scientists may also cause some confusion by presenting the same facts in different ways. Harvey Brooks describes such a case, referring to the debate over the effects of nuclear fallout that preceded the adoption of the 1963 test ban treaty:

> Those [scientists] who favored testing expressed health dangers in terms of the increased chances of cancer for an individual exposed to fallout. Expressed as a fraction, such increases were miniscule. The critics of testing, however, often expressed the identical facts in terms of actual deaths that would occur worldwide within a period of 50 years . . . as a result of current fallout. Some figures were very high.[14]

The scientists were not actually disputing the facts. They were simply using different forms of measurement to translate statistical estimates into concepts they hoped would reasonate with their listeners. The different presentations, however, were intentionally designed to pull public opinion in contrary directions.

The case involving pollution standards for vinyl chloride provides another example of an instance in which scientific disagreement did not exist even though scientists were at odds. Pro-standards scientists stressed one set of concerns, industry scientists another. Proponents for the standard emphasized the toxicity of exposure, while industry scientists focused their testimony on the long-term effects of exposure upon death rates. If asked outright, it is likely that neither group would have challenged the validity of the other's arguments. In their testimonies, however, each side emphasized those aspects of the issues that best supported their own policy positions.

Differences in the Design of Inquiries   Other observers have concluded that scientists disagree because of the different ways in which they organize their research. Although the "scientific method" is widely accepted as a technique for testing the validity of a given proposition, it has become increasingly apparent that the method entails inescapable elements of subjectivity. Any research design, for instance, requires the framing of hypotheses, the specification of assumptions, and the selection of data; and each of these offers scientists an opportunity for the exercise of choice.

Consider the choice of data. Scientists attempting to answer the same questions can reach contradictory conclusions if they rely on different data sets. For example, in a report by the Committee on the Biological Effects of Ionizing Radiation of the National Research Council, a dissenting opinion noted a disconcerting discrepancy between findings, depending on whether one particular source study was included in the data base.[16] In the fluoride controversy, scientists routinely dismissed as invalid data that did not support their hypothesis.[17]

Consider, too, the simplifying assumptions that are a part of any study design. Any scientific inquiry rests on a set of operating assumptions aimed at simplifying reality. Such assumptions cannot be validated prior to (or even subsequent to) a particular inquiry. They rest squarely on the judgment of the individual investigator, and are often based on the prevailing logic in a particular academic discipline.

For example, in predictive analysis, assumptions must be made regarding future conditions within a system under study. One author cited a case in which two scientists, asked to predict the number of cancer cases per year likely to result from radiation exposure to nuclear power, gave responses that differed by an order of 10^6.[18] Upon closer examination, it became clear that the two had grounded their predictions on one powerfully different assumption—their estimate of the radiation level to which the population is normally exposed. One scientist based his calculation on what he thought the maximum allowable exposure level ought to be, while the other used estimated actual average exposure. While neither was "right" or "wrong," their estimates about the impact of nuclear power facilities critically hinged on an assumption that had no scientific base. Without the disclosure of such an underlying assumption, the lay public would be confused by the apparent disagreement between these two scientists.

Consider, finally, how hypotheses are formulated. Some observers have concluded that scientists called upon for advice often focus on different questions. As Thomas Kuhn has explained, "scientific knowledge" is built upon shared beliefs in certain untested axioms.[19] Scientists trained within a given "paradigm" tend to frame research questions in a manner that reflects their "school of thought." As a result, scientists with different ideologies examining the same issue (even using the same data) may arrive at contrary conclusions. Although they are not in agreement, neither are they actually disagreeing. More precisely, they are talking past each other. For example, an engineer evaluating highway options will choose the alternative most likely to increase the flow of traffic, while an ecologist or an economist will pick a different "best" option. In many instances, they will know that they disagree, but will prefer to avoid analyzing why they disagree and explaining how to pool their knowledge.

Errors in the Inquiry Sometimes scientists present conflicting evidence or support opposing views because one or both have erred. Erroneous scientific findings can easily spark policy debates. At one juncture in the debate over the toxicity of "Agent Orange," for example, a study which suggested that the chemical might lead to malformations and tumors was found to be seriously flawed. As it happened, subsequent work confirmed the results of the flawed study. Yet it was that study which helped mobilize the groups on both sides of the debate.[20]

Differences in Interpretation of Findings Even if two scientists agree upon the validity of a given body of evidence, they might disagree on how to interpret the evidence.[21] For instance, the existence of a geological fault line in an area that has not experienced perceptible tremors in 40,000 years may be interpreted to signal two contradictory futures. One geologist may read the finding to indicate that a future earthquake in the area is highly unlikely, while a colleague may conclude that the existence of the fault line indicates significant potential for an earthquake.

Uncertainty represents perhaps the major interpretive hurdle for scientists, especially those working at the frontiers of a scientific field of knowledge. In many situations, analysts are constrained by methodological barriers and are forced to make estimates of some sort—the accuracy of which cannot be ascertained. When testing for adverse health effects in chemicals, for instance, experimenters commonly use high doses in an effort to estimate the effects of much lower levels of exposure. Similarly, experimenters commonly use the results of tests on laboratory animals as a substitute for epidemiological studies. The decision whether to accept such results as a basis for determining the actual effects of some given hazard is not often subject to scientific determination.

Uncertainty provided the basis for the petitioners' appeal of EPA's decision to reduce lead additives in gasoline. Because of the many channels by which lead can enter the body, because of the wide variations in the amount of ambient lead found in different sectors of the population, and because of the lack of data pertaining to the effect of lead on those exposed to it, scientists reached a legitimate disagreement over whether lead additive reductions would improve the health of the population.

For many scientists, the temptation to offer prescriptive advice is nearly irresistible. In addition, many policymakers seem to feel cheated if their scientific advisors stop short of offering policy recommendations. Yet, the question, "Does substance X induce cancer in laboratory animals?" is quite different in character from the question "Should substance X be banned from human use?" The first is within the legitimate realm of the scientists; the second is not. Their opinions about what ought to be done are no more scientific than those of nonscientists. Consequently, when scientists disagree about what ought to be done on a particular policy issue, the disagreement is more likely to be based on politics than on science.

RESOLVING SCIENCE-INTENSIVE POLICY DISPUTES

Policy disputes that entail considerable scientific controls are commonly handled through administrative action or judicial review. Federal legislation such as the National Environmental Policy Act and the Administrative Procedure Act, along with special provisions of specific laws, mandate opportunities for review and comment by affected interests; similar provisions are found in the legislation of the various states. Federal agencies proposing new regulations, for instance, are required to publish a notice of their intended rulemaking in the Federal Register, to promulgate a draft of regulations they are contemplating, and to receive and respond to written comments from interested parties. When regulations are challenged by a force with sufficient political clout and economic strength, public hearings are usually arranged to provide an opportunity for a public airing of the debate. Typically in science-intensive disputes, groups opposing the new regulations will present evidence that appears to contradict or cast doubt on the scientific basis for the proposed rules. Often without attempting to reconcile such discrepancies, the appropriate elected or appointed decision makers act on the proposal, usually approving the version proposed by agency staff.

Parties dissatisfied with the decisions of the agency can appeal to the courts. Rarely, however, do the courts have sufficient resources or expertise to conduct their own independent inquiry into the scientific aspects of a dispute. In fact, some legal scholars warn that the courts lack a public mandate to do so.[22] As a result, courts tend to restrict themselves to taking a "hard look" at the evidence submitted in order to determine whether or not a decision maker (or agency) has acted in a fashion consistent with existing statutory requirements. In short, the judiciary does not attempt to adjudicate scientific disputes.

Given the inadequacies of existing mechanisms for the resolution of disputes, various innovations have been proposed from time to time. Among these are various forms of the science court, scientific panels, and consensus-finding conferences.[23]

The science court concept extends the adversarial nature of the American legal system, involving scientists who espouse contradictory views in an adjudicatory process. Although its numerous variations differ in details, the science court idea revolves on an especially qualified judge or panel of judges who listen to prepared arguments of opposing "advocate scientists" and then come to conclusions on the basis of their own expertise. The authoritativeness of the court's findings derives primarily from the scientific reputations of the participating judges.

Scientific panels are structured less formally than science courts. They are akin to other appointed committees with members who are highly regarded in their fields. The panel reviews all available scientific evidence pertinent to a policy dispute and then issues a report and recommendations. The reports of such panels usually reflect at least a limited consensus among the members.

Consensus-finding conferences bring together scientists from diverse perspectives to discuss a disputed issue. The group can be divided into special workshops or subcommittees to examine relevant questions in detail. Through the course of the discussions, the experts seek to establish points of agreement and those on which further study is necessary. Like the science court and scientific panels, consensus-finding conferences allow scientists to communicate directly, thereby avoiding the intervention of attorneys.

Although each of these proposals has some appeal under the proper circumstances, they also suffer from fundamental shortcomings. One of the most common concerns about the science court is that the adversarial character and formalistic nature of its proceedings and the formalistic rules of conduct it engenders are antithetical to the conduct of "good science."[24] Expert panels often lack credibility in the eyes of the public, especially because of a suspicion that the deck has been stacked. And consensus-finding conferences suffer from the fact that, lacking authority, they may achieve little more than setting the stage for a court battle.[25]

It is worth noting that all three mechanisms presume that scientists can best contribute to the resolution of policy disputes by operating independently of the affected interests and the decisionmakers. Our earlier analysis suggests a separation may be unjustified, unwise and undesirable. As was observed earlier, differences in scientific judgments often arise from factors that are not "scientific" in character, such as differences in hypotheses and in simplifying assumptions. Isolating the scientists does little to educate decisionmakers and affected interests regarding the underlying factors that may have been responsible for the differences among the scientists.

MEDIATION OF SCIENCE-INTENSIVE DISPUTES Mediation, in our view, offers a greater opportunity for constructive interaction among scientists, affected interests, and decision makers. The flexibility of the mediation process allows the values and interests of each group to be expressed at appropriate moments during the fact-finding process. Mediation allows the distribution of costs and benefits to be woven into the process of analysis. Moreover, the credibility of the process derives less from the pre-established reputations of the participants than from the success of the process itself.

Several studies describe the application of mediation to public policy disputes; some providing case studies[26] and others more theoretical discussions.[27] We will sketch only the more prominent features of mediation, especially those that indicate its applicability to policy disputes that entail substantial scientific considerations.

Mediation is a voluntary process distinguished from simple ne-gotiation by the inclusion of a nonpartisan facilitator who serves at the pleasure of the disputants. A mediator is responsible not only for tending to the more mechanical aspects of negotiation such as scheduling meetings and keeping records, but also for more substantive functions such as ensuring a common under-standing of technical points among all participants, suggesting courses of action for helping to resolve disputed points, and pro-posing alternative formulations of agreements. In disputes of the kind considered here, participants might include government agencies, special interest groups, and private individuals, along with their respective scientific advisors.

A number of techniques routinely employed during mediation may be particularly well suited for resolving science–intensive disputes. These include information sharing, joint factfinding, and collaborative model building.

Information Sharing
Information is the key to scientific analysis. Theoretically, the more information an analyst is able to incorporate, the more com-pelling his or her work should be. In the community of scientists, information is presumed to be socialized.[28] That is, scientists readily share new-found knowledge with their colleagues to further the search for scientific truths. This is in contrast to adversarial ap-proaches to dispute resolution, which encourage the withholding of information helpful to an adversary's case. In contrast, some observers have suggested that mediation creates a setting especially conducive to the scientist's information-sharing norms.[29] While disputants in adjudicatory proceedings see every non-supportive piece of information as a threat to their claims, participants in a mediation process are encouraged to see information as a means of opening up new possibilities for dealing with differences.

Moreover, in mediation, any effort to suppress information carries with it the possibility of being discovered, resulting in a subsequent loss of credibility. As mediation unfolds, the participants usually become more reluctant to risk the success of the effort for the uncertain gain associated with suppressing information.

Mediation also has the virtue of placing the decision makers in any dispute in a participating role. In adversary proceedings, the decision-makers remain aloof, hearing the claims of the contending parties and having relatively little influence over the type and format of the information presented. As a participant in mediation, decision makers can demand and receive information in whatever form they feel best highlights the contradictory claims put forth by affected interests. Their understanding of critical issues will likely result in better-grounded policy decisions.

Joint-Factfinding   Mediation can easily accommodate joint factfinding if the participants so desire. The participants can jointly frame the research questions, specify the method of inquiry, select the researchers, and monitor the work, injecting their concerns at every appropriate point. If the parties to a dispute make these decisions collectively and debate the possible alternatives before an analysis is completed, they are less likely to reject the scientific findings that emerge. Their understanding of technical aspects of the issue is also likely to improve through such an exercise.

One vehicle for joint factfinding is the collaborative building of forecasting models. Science-intensive disputes frequently revolve around projections of the likely consequences of proposed actions. When more than one forecasting model is possible, competing parties usually subscribe to the one that best supports their claims.

Every modelling effort incorporates some value-bound assumption such as the specifications of sub-system boundaries, the level of sub-system complexity, the extent to which historical data can be used to describe future circumstances, and the relative importance of forces and factors external to the model. Mediation can provide a means of disengaging each party from its preferred models and encouraging a collaboration that forces a discussion of those assumptions. If the parties to a technical dispute can develop a model that incorporates key assumptions acceptable to all of them, they are more likely to produce a prediction that none can easily dismiss. The deceptive shield that technical analysis sometimes offers to affected interests wishing to disguise the self-serving nature of their position is torn away. An example from the Law of the Sea negotiations illustrates.

One sticky impasse in the negotiations concerned the allocation of profits from mining manganese modules in the ocean floor. Predictably, representatives from developing countries and countries without mining interests supported financing schemes that would tax miners heavily for mining rights in international waters. Delegates from countries with mining interests favored lower payments. A computer model was developed under conditions that led the participants to see it as nonpartisan. The model provided a means of testing various allocation plans based on a wide range of assumptions about future costs and prices. Delegates took turns trying out their financing proposals to determine what their consequences would be under the conditions they considered most likely. Because the structure of the model was perceived as neutral with regard to the interests of the various parties, the representatives felt no loss of face in revising their financial demands in accordance with the results of the model.

Why was this particular model perceived as nonpartisan within the negotiation setting? There were several reasons.[30] First, although the model was created by a team of American academic researchers at M.I.T., with funding from a U.S. government agency, the project was undertaken without direct reference to the Law of the Sea negotiations. Second, the various key estimates, such as research and development costs, operating costs and capital investment requirements were established independently by those who had designed the model. Moreover, those who used the model were free to substitute their own assumptions if they preferred. Fourth, the model had been critically reviewed at two conferences attended by American academics, technical representatives of the mining consortia and government scientists, and had been revised thereafter in response to points raised in the conferences. At those meetings, little reference had been made to the Law of the Sea negotiations. Finally, the fact that the model's early findings failed to give clear support to the position of any particular delegation at the negotiations seemed to enhance its credibility.

Models can be used to facilitate a settlement as long as the model structure is perceived as neutral with respect to the interests of the parties involved. Although in the Law of the Sea example the model's nonpartisanship was achieved by happenstance, a perception of nonpartisanship has been established in other cases through the collaboration of the participants.[31]

Creating and using a model in this way represents a form of mediation. The process provides a favorable climate for joint fact-finding and collaborative model building because disputants deal with each other face-to-face. Decision makers and representatives of affected interests, constantly drawing on the scientists, are able to remain at the helm of the dispute, injecting their own value preferences when value judgments are required and gaining a clearer understanding of the variations that are produced by changes in the scientific analyses. The participation of affected interests and scientists facilitates debate over the values and distributional concerns at every stage of the dispute, from the specification of assumptions to the final prescriptive judgments. Most importantly, decision makers gain a more accurate understanding of the political nature of technical advice.

ROLE OF THE MEDIATOR Although the role of the mediator has been variously conceived and contested,[32] a process in which the mediator assumes an activist role offers special promise for "keeping the negotiators honest." As long as mediators can remain aloof from judging whether any given distribution of costs and benefits is superior to any other, they can retain sufficient distance from the debate to perform a critical nonpartisan role. A mediator can ensure that information is conveyed in a language that is readily comprehensible to all the participants, and that technical assistance is made available to all. By meeting with parties in private sessions, the mediator can ascertain whether the participants share a common understanding of key technical points. If not, the mediator can take steps to remedy the discrepancies; for instance, in a negotiation involving the conversion to coal of an oil-fired electric generating plant in Massachusetts,[33] the mediator organized training sessions to educate the participants in the more technical aspects of the dispute. In short, as a guardian of the process, a mediator can intervene to correct miscommunications, to clarify ambiguous messages, and to challenge deceptive communications. Also, a mediator can point out when differences in interpretations have arisen and when participants are making prescriptive rather than descriptive statements.

THE NEW YORK CITY DIOXIN DISPUTE Illustrative of the mediator's role was the handling of a 1984 dispute over the building of a series of refuse plants in New York City. At the request of the New York City Sanitation Department, the New York Academy of Sciences organized a meeting of the parties concerned about the city's proposal to build a series of such plants. It was clear that some such alternative to landfill would soon be needed to handle the 20,000 tons per day of trash that the city produces. Residents of Brooklyn, living near the site of the first proposed facility, had grown increasingly alarmed about the health risks posed by the plan. Barry Commoner, a noted environmentalist and Professor at Queens College, issued several reports criticizing the city for underestimating the dioxin risks likely to be created by such facilities.[34] While the leaders of the Academy were not willing to assemble a blue ribbon committee of scientists to determine the "true" level of risk associated with the proposed plants, they were willing to organize and host a mediation effort.

On December 18, 1984, 55 men and women gathered at the Academy's mid-Manhattan offices. Most of the members of the city's Board of Estimate—the elected council of the city, charged with making the decision whether to adopt the program—were represented. Approximately 30 neighborhood and environmental groups, including a heavy concentration from Brooklyn, were in attendance. With the help of a mediator, national experts were present who could address various key issues; the engineering of resource recovery plants; the epidemiology of the health risks associated with dioxin emissions; and the physics of mass burning of municipal trash. The mediator worked with the Academy staff to assemble and summarize all the relevant technical documents, including the environmental impact and risk assessments prepared by the city and its consultants.[35] He organized and moderated the panels of engineers and scientists. The Academy staff worked with the Board of Estimate to ensure that all their questions and concerns were addressed by the panel. Open discussion followed each panel session. Throughout, the mediator maintained a visual record of the key points made and highlighted the points of agreement and disagreement at the conclusion of each section of the program. The session lasted almost nine hours. By the time it ended, the sources of scientific and technical disagreement had been clarified and the policy makers felt better equipped to move ahead.

The most telling disagreement was over the estimation of risks associated with the resource recovery technology selected by the city. This disagreement stemmed in part from gaps in the basic research in the field. It also grew out of the fact that there are competing theories of the combustion process; some experts assume that dioxins are a normal byproduct of the burning of municipal waste, while others assume that dioxin only occurs when the burning process is not managed properly. A third source of disagreement was the reliability of various pollution control devices and strategies. Finally, the disagreements were also traced to substantial uncertainty surrounding the estimates of the threat to human health, which had been calculated by scaling up the results of laboratory tests on rats.

The most significant source of controversy, however, resulted from neither the scientific, engineering, or epidemiological differences mentioned above. The primary source of disagreement hinged, it turned out, on Professor Commoner's use of a "worst case" scenario. It soon became clear that what had been thought of as a fundamental disagreement regarding the facts, or the basic science, was in reality a disagreement over the appropriate method of analysis.

While the sessions were somewhat heated, the debate proceeded in an orderly fashion. The scientists were urged by the mediator to present their ideas and findings in language understandable to the representatives of the Board of Estimate.

After considering what it heard at the session sponsored by the Academy, the Board decided to proceed with a full assessment of the impact of a city-wide system of trash-to-energy plants. By that time, they had a better grasp of the sources of risk. The interest groups in attendance understood why and how the decision makers had reached their conclusions. The scientific and technical discourse had, with the help of the mediator and the Academy staff, provided a common basis for decision making, one shared by elected officials and interest group representatives.

THE PROMISE OF MEDIATION Mechanisms that seek to resolve disagreements among scientists by separating them from decision makers and affected interests are undesirable because they place power in the hands of the scientists to which they are not entitled. Many steps within the analytic process require judgments that rest on subjective considerations and individual values. Allowing scientists to select the "one best answer" to what appears to be purely technical aspects of a policy dispute, gives responsibility to an elite corps who are in no way accountable to the public.

Mediation is one method of resolving disputes that casts the scientists in an appropriate role in relation to decision makers and affected interests. Techniques available in a mediation context directly confront value-bound components of scientific analysis, which we suggest lie at the root of conflicting scientific testimony. By revealing the basis of disagreement among scientists when disagreement appears to exist, mediation may help to clarify the power and the limitations of scientific analysis.

The success of a mediation process, however, depends on a number of issues.

The first requirement for success is appropriate representation. Mediation should only proceed if all the key interests are adequately represented. Without the participation of every party that has the political or economic power to block resolution, the process will not succeed.

Moreover, mediation is dependent on the willing participation of all the relevant parties. Since the participants do not surrender their legal rights to resort to the adversarial approach, efforts at coercing the parties into mediation have their distinct limits.

Mediation has been applied in a number of environmental disputes over the past decade or so.[36] Several mediation experiments have also been conducted, aimed at resolving intergovernmental policy conflicts.[37] Federal agencies have begun to take an interest in mediated rulemaking. In fact, the Environmental Protection Agency recently completed several exercises of this sort.[38] Many of these mediation projects have involved a substantial amount of hotly contested, highly technical information. Most have also involved heated emotions tied to distributional issues. Mediation has a long way to go before it will become commonplace, but as the costs of the existing adversarial approaches become more widely recognized, the demand for more effective methods may well intensify.

CONNIE P. OZAWA is a Doctoral Candidate in the Department of Urban Studies and Planning at the Massachusetts Institute of Technology.

LAWRENCE SUSSKIND is a Professor of Urban Studies and Planning, at the Massachusetts Institute of Technology and Executive Director, Program on Negotiation at Harvard Law School.

NOTES   1. Michael Brown, "Setting Occupational Health Standards: The Vinyl Chloride Case," in Dorothy Nelkin, ed., *Controversy*, (Beverly Hills, CA: Sage Publications, Inc., 1984), pp. 125–142.

2. Phillip Boffey, *The Brain of America: An Inquiry Into the Politics of Science*, (New York: McGraw Hill, 1975) pp. 229–244.

3. *Ethyl Corporation v. EPA*, 541 F.2d (D.C. Circuit, 1976).

4. See Yahron Ezrahi, "Utopian and Pragmatic Rationalism: The Political Context of Scientific Advice," *Minerva*, 18 (1980): 111–131; and Dorothy Nelkin, "The Political Impact of Technical Expertise," *Social Studies of Science*, 5 (1975): 35–54.

5. Arthur Kantrowitz, "Proposal for an Institution for Scientific Judgment," *Science*, (156)33776 (May 12, 1967): 763–764.

6. See, for example, Allan Mazur, "Science Courts." *Minerva* (15)3 (Spring 1977): 1–4; J. D. Nyhart and Milton M. Carron, eds., *Law and Science in Collaboration*, (Lexington, MA: Lexington Books, 1983); and Milton Wessel, *Science and Con-Science*, (New York: Columbia University Press): p. 49.

7. Harvey Brooks, "The Resolution of Technically Intensive Public Policy Disputes," *Science, Technology, and Human Values*, (9)1 (Winter, 1984): p. 49.

8. For example, Nelkin, 1984, pp. 16–19; and Briane Wynne, *Rationality and Ritual: The Windscale Inquiry and Nuclear Decisions in Britain*, (England: The British Society for the History of Science, 1982).

9. H. Shep Melnick, *Regulation and the Courts: The Case of the Clean Air Act*, (Washington, D.C.: The Brookings Institute, 1983), p. 253.

10. See *Industrial Union. AFL-CIO v. Hodason*, 162 U.S. Appl. D.C. 331, 499 F.2d 467 (1974); and *South Terminal Corporation v. EPA*, 504 F.2d 646 (1st circuit, 1974).

11. Among others, see Lawrence Bacow, "The Technical and Judgmental Dimensions of Impact Assessment," *Environmental Impact Assessment Review*, (1)2 (June 1980): 109–124; Stephen Kelman, *Regulating America, Regulating Sweden*, (Cambridge, MA: M.I.T. Press, 1981): and Helen Longino, "Beyond 'Bad' Science: Skeptical Reflections on the Value-Freedom of Scientific Inquiry," *Science, Technology, and Human Values*, (8)1 (Winter 1983): 7–17.

12. Brooks; and Allan Mazur, "Disputes Between Experts," *Minerva*, (11) (1973): 243–262.

13. Mazur, 1973, p. 249.

14. Brooks, p. 39.

15. For an illustrated discussion of these non-objective judgments, see Lawrence Susskind and Louise Dunlap, "The Importance of Non-Objective Judgments in Environmental Impact Assessment," *Environmental Impact Assessment Review*, (2)4 (December 1981): 335–366.

16. National Research Council, Committee on the Biological Effects of Ionizing Radiations, *The Effect on Populations of Exposure to Low Levels of Ionizing Radiation: 1980* (Washington, D.C.: National Academy Press, 1980), p. 262.

17. Mazur, 1973, pp. 254–255.

18. Ibid., pp. 249–250.

19. Thomas Kuhn, *The Structure of Scientific Revolutions*, (Berkeley, CA: University of California Press, 1967).

20. Wessel, pp. 151–152.

21. Mazur, 1973, pp. 255–256.

22. See, for example, David Bazelon, "Science and Uncertainty: A Jurist's View," *Harvard Environmental Law Review* (5)2 (1981): 209–215; and Thomas O. McGarity, "Judicial Review of Scientific Rulemaking," *Science Technology, and Human Values*, (9)1 (Winter 1984): 97–106.

23. See Mazur, 1977; Nyhart and Carrow; and Wessel.

24. Nancy Ellen Abrahms and R. Stephen Berry, "Mediation: A Better Alternative to Science Courts," *Bulletin of the Atomic Scientists*, 33 (April 1977): 50–53.

25. See Wessel.

26. See R. B. Goldman, *Roundtable Justice: Case Studies in Conflict Resolution*, (Boulder, CO: Westview Press, 1980); Lawrence Susskind, Lawrence Bacow, and Michael Wheeler, eds., *Resolving Environmental Regulatory Disputes* (Cambridge, MA: Schenkman Publishing Company, 1983); Lawrence Bacow and Michael Wheeler, *Environmental Dispute Resolution* (New York: Plenum Press, 1984); and Allan Labot, *Settling*

Things: Six Case Studies in Environmental Mediation, (Washington, D.C.: The Conservation Foundation, 1–95).

27. Thomas Colosi, "Negotiation in the Public and Private Sectors," *American Behavioral Scientist,* (27)2 (November/December 1983): 229–253; and Lawrence Susskind and Connie Ozawa, "Mediated Negotiation in the Public Sector: Mediator Accountability and the Public Interest Problem," *American Behavioral Scientist,* (27)2 (November/December 1983): 255–276.

28. Michael Polanyi, "The Republic of Science: Its Political and Economic Theory," *Minerva* 1 (Autumn 1962): 54–73.

29. See Susskind, Bacow, and Wheeler; Bacow and Wheeler.

30. James K. Sebenius, "The Computer as Mediator: Law of the Sea and Beyond," *Journal of Policy Analysis and Management* (1)1 (Fall 1981): 77–95.

31. See descriptions of collaborative model building in mediated cases in Goldmann.

32. A well-articulated debate over the role of mediation can be found in the following set of three articles: J. P. McCrory, "Environmental Mediator—Another Piece of the Puzzle," *Vermont Law Review* (6)1 (Spring 1981): 49–84; J. B. Stulberg, "The Theory and Practice of Mediation: A Reply to Professor Susskind," *Vermont Law Review* (6)1 (Spring 1981): 85–117; and Lawrence Susskind, "Environmental Mediation and the Accountability Problem," *Vermont Law Review,* (6)1 (Spring 1981): 1–47.

33. See H. Burgess and D. Smith, "Brayton Point Coal Conversion," in Susskind, Bacow, and Wheeler, pp. 122–155.

34. Barry Commoner, Karen Shapiro and Thomas Webster in *"Environmental and Economic Analysis of Alternative Municipal Solid Waste Disposal Techniques,"* (Flushing, NY: Center for The Biology of Natural Systems, Queens College, CUNY, 1982).

35. Fred Hart, Environmental Impact Statement.

36. Goldmann; Talbot; Susskind, Bacow and Wheeler; Bacow and Wheeler.

37. Nancy A. Huelsberg and William F. Lincoln (Eds.), *Successful Negotiating In Local Government,* (Washington, DC: International City Managers Association, 1985).

38. Lawrence Susskind and Gerald McMahon, "The Theory and Practice of Negotiated Rulemaking," *Journal of Regulation,* Yale Law School, forthcoming.

19

Market Justice, Political Justice

Robert E. Lane

The defense of capitalism in America is rooted in a preference for the market's justice of earned deserts over the justices of equality and need associated with the polity. These preferences have structural roots in the way governments and markets serve different values and purposes, satisfy wants, focus on fairness or justice, enlist causal attributions, distribute or redistribute income, are limited by rights, and seem to offer either harmony or conflict of interest. Some of these "structural" differences, however, are themselves perceptual, and corrected by changed perceptions of the productivity of government and of our historic predecessors, and by a community point of view involving changed accounting systems, as well as by policies of full employment rather than guaranteed incomes. With few institutional changes, these altered perceptions may partially restore political justice to favor.

"Without some very considerable surge of moral anger . . . [political and social] changes do not occur" (Moore, 1978, p. 459). To account for "moral anger" is to contribute to our understanding of popular turbulence—or, more likely, to our understanding of "the cankers of a calm world and a long peace."

Our concern is with the American sense of justice and injustice regarding the distribution of valued goods by markets and democratic politics—how they compare with each other, and what structural and ideological factors explain the apparent preference for market justice over political justice. Inasmuch as the following analysis makes certain assumptions on contested issues, we turn to these first. For our purposes a standard definition of the market will do: it is the device for coordinating an economy by prices largely determined by relatively free, competitive transactions among firms guided by anticipated profits (Lane, 1978a, p. 4; Lindblom, 1977; Weber, 1947, pp. 179-83). Similarly, democratic politics embraces

standard elements: competitive elections, a legitimate opposition, a relatively free (officially uncensored) press, and protection of minority rights. The relation between these two institutions offers more difficulty. While for certain purposes it is desirable to emphasize their close interrelation, for the purposes at hand it is desirable, and equally legitimate, to regard them as separable and alternative methods of coordinating production and distributing goods; neither is merely the disguised servant of the other. The public regularly makes this distinction: functions belong either to "business" or to "government," albeit with some confusion and overlap (Lipset and Schneider, 1983; McClosky and Zaller, 1985).

We assume that the perceptions and values we encounter and their institutional and material bases have reciprocal influences. Whereas the sociology of knowledge, like its Marxist origins, closely ties beliefs and values to their parent institutions and social locations (Mannheim, 1949), we follow a Parsonian (1951) and Weberian (1947) analysis, loosening

From Robert E. Lane, "Market Justice, Political Justice," *American Political Science Review*, Vol. 80, pp. 383-402. Copyright © 1986 by the American Political Science Association. Reprinted by permission.

these ties. Thus, in the analysis of structural roots we show the influence of social structures on perceptions, while in discussing perceptual changes we rely on the independent effects of perceptions on the interpretation of structures. We return to this problem later.

Popular perceptions of justice are related to, but distinct from, philosophical conceptions of justice. They are related in the sense that most philosophical treatments regard people's sense of justice as relevant, but certain treatments—such as Ross's (1939, p. 2) reliance on "a large body of beliefs and convictions," or J. S. Mill's (1910, p. 49) use of "the social feeling," or Edmund Cahn's (1964, p. 25) reliance on the "predisposition (of) . . . the human animal . . . to fight injustice"—are misleading, for they fail to preserve sufficiently the distinction between philosophical justice and the public's sense of injustice. In rejecting that tradition we take the further step of assuming, like others (e.g., Deutsch, 1975; Harman, 1983; Kaufman, 1973; Sidorsky, 1983), that conceptions of justice are partially dependent upon other goals simultaneously pursued, and upon institutional settings. There is evidence that the public follows this course (Barrett-Howard and Tyler, forthcoming; Hochschild, 1981), denying the universal applicability of such formulations of justice as those recently put forward by Rawls (1971), Nozick (1974), and Ackerman (1980).

Our aim is not to clarify philosophical justice; we do attempt to illuminate concepts of the legitimacy of markets and politics, to contribute to an understanding of the forces of social change, and above all, to help explain the tenacious hold of market capitalism on the public mind. There is an irony in the public's justice-based defense of the market, for that is the very point where many commentators have found it weakest (e.g., Rawls, 1971). It is uncertain whether this defense represents a social lag, a "contradiction" between institutions and perceptions, or, as we shall argue and then modify, a structurally induced perception based on the functioning of the market and its political alternatives.

Finally, the analysis helps to explain a historical anomaly, as well as a current situation. In his study, *The Pursuit of Equality in American History*, J. R. Pole (1978, p. xi) puzzles over the focus on political equality and the lack of attention to "such questions as the redistribution of wealth or an effective re-examination of the criteria by which economic rewards are allocated." The puzzle is made greater by the increasing economic inequality over most of this period (Williamson and Lindert, 1980). Two points are in order: (1) American concepts of justice were never predominantly directed toward equality of condition (Tocqueville, 1945, vol. 1, p. 51, but see vol. 2, p. 94; Potter, 1954); hence, sentiments of justice took other forms; and (2) for reasons we shall explain, Americans tend to prefer market methods to political methods.

Origins and Elements of a Sense of Injustice

Certain perceptions and beliefs favor the translation of deprivation into an "injustice." The minimum condition seems to be that people want something they do not have, and believe they deserve it (Crosby, 1982, chs. 1–2; Runciman, 1966). It is the genius of the market to stimulate wants without at the same time stimulating a sense of deserving more than one gets. Comparing oneself or one's group with some better-off relevant person or group, especially a member of an "in-group," makes deserving more salient, but in the market comparisons of this kind encourage effort and not an acute sense of injustice. Expectations are important, for both past expectations that by now one would possess some good and expectations that one will in the future possess that good affect justice sentiments. For the lay person, as for the philosopher, the sense of feasibility implied by these expectations influences justice sentiments (Galston, 1980, p. 110; Moore, 1978, ch. 14). As we shall see, the belief that the market follows natural laws makes market outcomes seem more inevitable than political outcomes. Finally, if one believes that outcomes are attributable to one's own acts—that the self is to be credited or blamed for one's own fate —one does not invoke justice sentiments. Again, this sense of controlling one's own destiny in the market, but not in politics, leads to more of a sense of political injustice than of market injustice.

Conceptually, the problems of a sense of distributive justice may be expressed in a question:

Who distributes what to whom, in virtue of what criterial characteristics, by what procedures, with what distributive outcomes?

Employing this conceptual formula, we turn to a brief analysis of these six terms, comparing their market and political expressions.

American Perceptions of Market and Political Justice

Agent (who distributes). Although in the 1980s about three-quarters of the public agreed both that government favored "a few big interests" at the expense of the "benefit of all the people" and that business pursued "profits" at the expense of "the interests of the public" (surveys reported in Lipset and Schneider, 1983, pp. 17, 183), there is a difference in the legitimacy attached to these two perceived biases. As we shall see, it is more legitimate, and publicly beneficial, for business to pursue profits than for government to cater to the interests of "a few big interests." That difference is brought out in answers to questions on the fairness of the two systems. Answering a series of questions about the fairness of the American free enterprise system, very large majorities of national samples in 1958 and 1977 held that the free enterprise system is "fair and wise" (82%), "gives everyone a fair chance" (65%), and that it is a "fair and efficient system" (63%) (McClosky and Zaller, 1985, ch. 5). In contrast, in 1980 large majorities believed that "the government is pretty much run by a few big interests looking out for themselves" (70%), and that "you cannot trust the government to do what is right" most of the time (73%) (Center for Political Studies, in Lipset and Schneider, 1983, p. 17). The market is thought to be "fair and wise," but not the government.

Goods. People tend to exclude collective goods when thinking about their standard of living; thus, a large category of governmental distributions is omitted from justice calculations (Compton Advertising, Inc., 1975). Furthermore, although people seek and demand certain kinds of government payments, especially when they are in need, they prefer market income to transfer payments. In spite of Rawls's (1971, p. 440) belief that self-esteem, "perhaps the most important primary good," is distributed by government in the form of political rights, in fact it is the market (and small primary groups) that confers self-esteem (Lane, 1982). Finally, the government, through its police and courts, is seen as an agent of punishment as much as a distributor of goods, even though in concrete forms the services of the welfare state are often appreciated. Thinking concretely, the public appreciates these services; thinking generally, the public tends to derogate them as inefficient and wasteful (Katz, Gutek, Kahn, and Barton, 1975; Lipset and Schneider, 1983). Where benefits are thus discounted (at least in general) and punishments counted, any distributor of "goods" will suffer perceptions of injustice.

To whom. In assessing the market, the public tends to think only of those who are in the market, and more particularly of the full-time employed, forgetting the unemployed and the part-time employed. Reporting on this tendency, Lee Rainwater (1974, p. 166) suggests that "unemployment is the major factor responsible for a divergence in [actual] relative income shares from the shares our respondents judge to be fair." But the unemployed and the poor who are not in the labor market are justice problems for the government, and are perceived to be such (Hochschild, 1981; Rainwater, 1974). Beyond this, other data suggest that the American public tends, more than other publics, to define disadvantages in racial terms—therefore more suitable for political action—than in economic terms, where market justice would seem to be more relevant (Jennings, 1983). Defining the unemployed out of the market and injustice more as a matter of race than income tends to politicize the sense of injustice.

Criteria. As Hochschild (1981) has pointed out, people tend to apply the patently inegalitarian criteria of earned deserts to the market, and, with some anguish and ambivalence, the criteria of equality and need to the polity. Except for political resources, "the idea of essentially equal distribution of resources does not seem attractive to most people" (Rainwater, 1974, p. 168; see also Lane, 1959). One reason for this is the belief that the criteria of earned deserts enhances productivity, whereas the criteria of equality and need do not (see below). Preferring the market's criteria of earned deserts over the criteria of equality and need associated with the polity, the public tends to favor market justice over political justice.

Procedures. For the market to be considered fair, two related procedural requirements must be met: there must be

perceived openness, if not equality, of opportunity, and the market must be considered responsive to effort—to hard work. For the polity to be considered procedurally fair, there must be "adherence to a general norm of political equality," at least among groups if not among individuals (Verba and Orren, 1985, p. 214), and one must believe that the government is responsive to one's influence. By and large, the market passes the test but the polity does not. Over the 1970s, about 65% of the public believed that "hard work is most important in getting ahead," while most of the time fewer than 10% held that "luck or help from others is most important" (NORC, 1981). In 1984 more than 85% of the public believed that: "America has an open society. What one achieves in life no longer depends on one's family background, but on the abilities one has and the education one acquires" (NORC, 1984). In contrast, a cross section of leaders rejected the view that there is equality of influence in the United States (Verba and Orren, 1985, ch. 9), and about half of the public has believed for over a decade that "public officials don't care much about what people like me think" (Miller, Miller, and Schneider, 1980, Table 4.7; Lipset and Schneider, 1983, p. 22). These interpretations are confirmed by direct questions on procedural fairness: Only about a quarter of a sample of 300 adult Chicagoans thought that the procedures used to decide tax levels were fair, and only two-fifths thought that procedures used to allocate benefits were fair (Tyler, Rasinski, and McGraw, forthcoming).

Outcomes. The crucial question, of course, is whether, in the end, people think that they get what they deserve. As we mentioned, a sense of deservedness is central to the concept of justice, at least among the lay public, if not always among philosophers (e.g., Rawls, 1971, p. 311; but see Rescher, 1966, p. 48). What is striking about the survey material is the high proportion of people who believe they do get about what they deserve. For example, in a small study comparing British and American adults in London and New Haven, 62% of the Americans stated that they "personally have the standard of living that [they] feel they deserve" (Perkins and Bell, 1980, p. 81). In a larger study of 400 employed men and women (including housewives), both men and women in high- as well as low-prestige jobs (almost equally in both cases) scored high on a "deservedness scale"—i.e., "they feel that they are receiving approximately what they deserve and what they expected to receive" (Crosby, 1982, p. 64). The unemployed are different only in a modest degree (Schlozman and Verba, 1979, p. 141). These judgments of the fairness of the market do not extend to the way others are treated (e.g., women referring to other women, the public referring to "most people"), but since correcting injustice to others implies political means, at that point we enter the political arena.

While similar questions on the fairness of the benefits one receives from government and the taxes one pays do not reveal "moral outrage," they do reveal a much lower sense of fairness than these studies of market fairness show. For example, compared with almost two-thirds of the New Haven sample reporting they received the incomes they deserved, only a little over a third of the Chicago sample thought that the taxes they paid and the benefits they received from economic policies were fair (Tyler et al., forthcoming). Similarly, in a comparison of leaders' assessment of income and assessment of political influence, political justice is considered less fair than market justice. When asked to construct a preferred income distribution among occupations, leaders of various social groups (labor, business, blacks, feminists, etc.) rank occupations by income in the same order in which these occupations are currently paid, and place themselves at approximately the same ordinal position as the one they now occupy. However, when they are asked to order a preferred distribution of political influence they radically revise what they perceive to be the current distribution in such a way that their own group's position is much improved. That is, people generally are seen to get about the relative magnitude of income they deserve in the market, but, given the norm of equal (group) influence mentioned above, other groups, but not one's own, are seen to have more influence than they deserve (Verba and Orren, 1985, chs. 8–9).

On balance, therefore, it seems that the public tends to believe that the market system is a more fair agent than the political system. People tend to include the problem cases in the political domain and exclude them from the market. They ignore many of the public benefits and, with certain exceptions, prefer market goods to political goods. They prefer the market's criteria of earned deserts to the polity's criteria of equality and need, and believe that market procedures are more fair than political procedures. They are satisfied that they receive what they deserve in the market, but much less satisfied with what they receive in the polity. By a different measure, they are much more satisfied with the general income distribution among occupations than with the distribution of influence among social groups in the polity.

There is a "deep structure" to these assessments residing in the very way these institutions distribute their goods, but, as we shall see, this "deep structure" is also partly a matter of perception.

Market and Political Invitations to Justice Complaints

Because their functions and responsibilities differ, our two institutions invite justice complaints in different ways. They differ in four ways. The first difference is in the way they enlist and frustrate individual beliefs, preferences, and levels of assessment. Among the many such beliefs and preferences—e.g., the goodness of human nature, the sources of authority, the reliability of various kinds of knowledge, and the unity or diversity of mankind (Lane, 1972, ch. 10)—we focus on four: dominant values, satisfaction of wants, preferred justice criteria, and level of assessment (process or outcome). Second, the perceived causes of agency allocations differ, relying on external circumstances in some cases and on the dispositions and values of the allocators in others. Here we focus on a systematic difference: firms are thought to be bound by circumstantial necessities, but governments are thought to be free to follow political discretion. Third, the justice process is rarely free from constraints, such as lack of resources or authority, legal limits, force majeure, and so forth. We will focus on two such constraints: the disadvantage of coming second in a distributive sequence, and the constitutional constraints imposed by rights. Finally, the perceived harmony or conflict of interests involved in market and political distributions alters perceptions of justice; we explicate these perceptions in terms of class conflict, the uses of profits, and competition.

Structured Differences in Individual Preferences and Levels of Assessment

Purposes and values. As mentioned, both philosophical discussion and research evidence point to the selection of justice formulae in order to serve other values (production, solidarity, personal development, and so forth). Thus the perceived purposes of our two institutions and the values they enlist affect the selection of justice principles. There are times, of course, when the nonmaterial purposes of government are ascendant, as in the case of war or when freedom is threatened, but for most people most of the time earning a living and related material values take precedence. In assessing public policy, for example, three times as many Americans give priority to policies promoting income stability and growth compared to policies promoting freedom, "more say in government," or other values (Inglehart, 1981). In that limited sense there are three times as many materialists as "postmaterialists" in America. Justice concerns may be important, but, as mentioned, people favor the justice of earned deserts—partly because that form of justice is thought to promote higher productivity and income, that is, material values. Furthermore, the market is conceived to be the agent of productivity, while politics is thought to be a burden on productivity, indeed, government is blamed more than the market for failures of the productive mechanism (Katona and Strumpel, 1978, p. 43). A justice system that encourages productivity and that produces income is therefore better than one that, at best, merely redistributes it.

Satisfaction of wants: individual or collective. Both markets and polities are want-satisfying mechanisms, the distinction being that markets satisfy wants individually, while polities satisfy collective wants, or, at least, wants grouped by categories (whose members, of course, individually may want what is offered). While the equal treatment associated with public goods appeals to some senses of justice, in general people prefer to tailor the satisfaction of their wants to their own particular tastes, something they can do in the market but not easily in their dealings with government. If they have the money they can buy the kinds of cars they want, but they cannot order the kind of road system they want. Therefore, the political method of collective satisfaction of wants creates more claims of injustice than does the market method of individual satisfaction of wants.

The distinction may be clarified by a contrast between two concepts of equality suggested by Douglas Rae (1981, ch. 5). *Lot-regarding* equality is achieved for a group whose members have identical goods such that each is indifferent to whose bundle he may have. *Person-regarding* equality is achieved when each person in a group has equal fungible resources to begin with, and with these acquires goods which leave him as well satisfied as every other person, tested by the availability of exchange among group members to the point where no further trades are desired. Notice that both equalities are "fair" in the sense that in both each person is treated identically, but the second is more satisfying to the group members.

Lot-regarding equality may be achieved by the public provision of, say, (1) a *rule* against smoking applying equally to smokers and non-smokers; (2) the provision of *collective goods*, e.g., public parks equally available to the well and the bedridden; or (3) equal allotments of *goods in kind*, e.g., food stamps for the urban hungry and for the farmer growing his own food. While such rules and offerings are fair in one sense, the smoker, the bedridden, and the farmer may complain that in another, important, sense they are unjust. The public method of allotment contrasts with the market's method of monetary rewards and transactions that permit individuated satisfaction of tastes.

The flaw in this analysis, of course, is that the market generates enormous inequalities of income, permitting some to satisfy a wide variety of individuated tastes and others to satisfy almost none. This argument will count heavily with egalitarians, but most members of the public "do not find gross inequity in the way income is [now] distributed" (Rainwater, 1974, p. 166). For many, including many of the relatively poor, market processes without equality will seem fairer than government-induced equality without market processes.

Justice criteria: the polity's reversal of earned deserts. Most people exhibit very considerable sympathy with those who are poor, handicapped, or unemployed through no fault of their own. But how can people be sure that such government beneficiaries are, indeed, without fault of their own? The "just world" syndrome (a tendency to justify all distributions) leads people to "blame the victim" (Lerner, 1980), and that corresponds with the favored justice of earned deserts. The confluence of sentiments of sympathy with sentiments favoring the justice of deserts is painful. Lee Rainwater (1974, p. 180), on the basis of extensive interviews, finds this pain stemming from the opposition of two principles: "Opposed to the principle that no one should live on so little money is the principle that everyone should have to work for what he gets." Transfer payments to relieve poverty present the public with the most acute difficulties in assessing justice, difficulties reflected in the lower evaluation of political justice than market justice.

The justice of taxes, especially progressive income taxes, is even harder to assess. For purposes of contrast we will compare four tax-related experiences and perceptions with partially comparable market experiences and perceptions. (1) People are often uncertain whether others similarly situated are paying the same amount of taxes as they do—the greatest single source of tax cheating (Lewis, 1982, ch. 8). At the same time, people either assume that others in the market pay the same price, or, if they pay less, that they are model consumers rather than cheaters ("I can get it for you wholesale"). (2) Tax payments are compulsory, market payments are regarded as voluntary. (3) The benefits of paying taxes are delayed, often obscure, and sometimes regarded with hostility (as when a pacifist pays for the defense appropriations he abhors). But market payments for goods and services are inevitably for something one wants, the yield in utility of which is visible and usually immediate. Finally, and most importantly in this analysis, (4) payment of taxes proportional to what is regarded as one's contribution to productivity reverses the normal interpretation of the justice of earned deserts: while in the market one is rewarded for such contributions, in the polity one is penalized. This seems unfair.

Level of assessment: fairness versus justice. Philosophers distinguish between *fairness,* as a method of, or criterion for, allocation, and *justice,* as the outcome of the allocation process (Feinberg, 1973, p. 117; Rescher, 1966, p. 90; but see Hart, 1961, p. 154). But there are times when justice may be defined by the outcome of fair procedures. Thus Rawls's (1971, p. 86) "pure procedural justice" refers, it seems, to market justice, where "there is a correct or fair procedure such that the outcome is likewise correct or fair, whatever it is, provided that the procedure has been properly followed." Rawls grounds his general theory in the rationality of persons in the original position, but there is another interpretation.

The psychologist Philip Brickman asked his subjects to allocate certain scarce goods fairly, but after they had done so they were dissatisfied with the shape of the resulting distribution, finding it too inegalitarian. In their own views, fairness did not produce justice. As Brickman and his associates say, "Even if all groups, as well as individuals, receive what their aggregate merits appear to deserve, the distribution of rewards in a system as a whole can be judged unfair" (Brickman, Folger, Goode, and Schul, 1981, pp. 174–75). Brickman also tested Rawls's hypothesis regarding decisions on distributional arrangements by persons in

the original position. He found that people who did not know their own abilities in a certain situation—one in which those abilities would later earn them benefits— were more egalitarian in their preferences for distributional methods than those who knew they had great abilities. But beyond that, Brickman also found that both those who knew their own abilities and those who did not were more egalitarian when asked to plan a distributional system than when they were asked to decide on fair methods of allocation. Thus, while confirming Rawls's hypothesis regarding the greater egalitarianism of those behind a veil of ignorance, Brickman suggests that part of the egalitarian effect of the original position stems from the difference between looking at outcomes in contrast to looking at distributional criteria (Brickman, 1977).

The relevance to market and political justice both of this distinction between fairness and justice and of Brickman's experiments and hypothesis is plain. The market leads people to think about processes of allocation and deserts, whereas politics leads people to think about outcomes of allocation—the overall shape of a distribution where concepts of equality are more salient. This is true in part because the market has no machinery for adjusting outcomes, or even the conceptual apparatus for thinking about them, except as they emerge from market processes; as in Rawls's idea of "pure procedural justice," the market is a domain of transactions that sum to an unplanned distribution. But politics has machinery in its tax and transfer payment mechanisms for adjusting outcomes, and even the most casual political thinking must turn to questions of the poor and the rich, deprived groups and privileged ones. In politics everyone is to some extent forced to consider societal arrangements, in which other people's claims must be considered along with one's own. This is the very heart of the method of philosophical justice, in which, assuming reason, each person's claim must be treated as having a worth equal to another person's similar claim. Reason is defined as the process that recognizes identical instances as such, without regard for "accidental" personal differences (Hare, 1963).

Hochschild's (1981) important discovery of public "ambivalence" flowing from a tendency to employ a justice of deserts in the economic domain and, on occasion, the justices of need and equality in the political domain, can now be understood as more than a simple application of different social norms to the two different domains. In their discussion of fairness in the economic domain; people were looking at the process of allocation—the fairness of individual payments, or Brickman's "micro-justice." In their discussion of political justice, however, they were led by the perspective of that domain to consider the shape of outcomes—of social rather than individual justice, or Brickman's "macro-justice." Hence the confusion and ambivalence.

The consequence of this difference in perspective is a kind of asymmetry in the way procedures and outcomes are perceived in the market and in politics. While it is the case that market procedures are, in practice, considered more fair than political procedures, at an abstract level both procedures are considered fair in their respective domains. The main difference between them lies in the fact that the market escapes criticisms for unjust outcomes if it adheres faithfully to its criteria of allocation (contribution to productivity), because people apply to it the criteria of Rawls's pure procedural justice. But the polity does not escape such criticism. A fair procedure is sufficient justification in the market, but not in the polity. More than that, the polity may be called upon to redistribute (see below) what the market "fairly" distributed in the first place, for, from a political perspective, the outcome of that "fairness" is seen to be unjust, making the polity doubly vulnerable to allegations of both unfairness and injustice.

The Causes of Agency Behavior

Market necessity, individual responsibility, and government discretion. Interpreting the causes of an event exercises a powerful influence on the sense of grievance and, usually, though not necessarily, on the sense of injustice. Where the agent intended to inflict pain the sense of grievance and injustice are most acute; where the agent did not intend to inflict pain, but might have avoided it and did not, our sense of grievance and injustice is severe but less acute; where the agent did not intend and could not avoid the pain inflicted, we may feel grieved, but do not feel that an injustice has been done (Utne and Kidd, 1980). This gradation is securely lodged in our concepts of responsibility (Heider, 1958).

Consider now the way in which people interpret the causes of market and political outcomes. In the market people offer two kinds of attributions, both of them exculpating the market from injustice. On the one hand, people believe, with some room for difference (Lipset and Schneider, 1983, pp. 176–83) that a firm must do what it does do, constrained as it is by competition and the laws of supply and demand. If a firm pays more than market wages it risks bankruptcy. The firm cannot avoid inflicting pain. On the other hand, laymen, like economists, read backwards from rewards, a person's level of pay, to discover the source in his contribution to productivity—a doctrine of "revealed contribution" similar to the economist's concept of "revealed preference." Noone knows what his contribution is worth until he sees what he gets; there is no opportunity for discrepancy between worth and reward, no way in which a hypothesis about a person's worth can be falsified. Thus, by the magic of the market, a person gets what he deserves and a firm must pay what it pays. These two forms of attribution require a person to believe that if he is unemployed it is through some discretionary act of his own, but that if a firm lays him off it is because it could not do otherwise. No system could develop a more elegant device for avoiding attributions of injustice to the rewards and punishments it distributes.

In contrast, benefits received from government are not considered to be the inevitable and precise measure of some previous contribution or status or need; they are perceived to be the consequence of a partisan dispute in which one group won over another group—e.g., labor over managers and owners, dairy interests over the weaker spokesmen for consumers. What is revealed, or so it is said, is political muscle, which until might is converted into right affords only small purchase for a belief that justice has been done. The polity is, therefore, more vulnerable to claims of unjust allocations.

This distinction in vulnerability to claims of injustice is related to the general belief that in both the market and the polity people are animated by self-interest (Lipset and Schneider, 1983, p. 169). In the market, however, self-interest is thought to be both fruitful for the common good and policed by competition, while in the polity self-interest is seen as neither fruitful nor properly constrained. Unwilling to criticize the system of democracy, the public levels its criticisms at the political leaders: "[In recent decades] Americans continued to say that they were proud of our system of government. Their lack of confidence was clearly directed at the people running those institutions" (Lipset and Schneider, 1983, p. 309). Combining a perception of insufficiently constrained self-interest with the belief that politicians hold discretionary powers in allocating benefits and costs, the public is inevitably suspicious of the fairness of the resulting outcomes.

Constraints

Sequence: distribution versus redistribution. We turn to popular responses to an initial distribution of resources and compare them with the responses to a change in that distribution, a redistribution (Jouvenel, 1951). Consider first the concept so dear to the heart of economists, Pareto optimality, which says that, given the proscription against comparing interpersonal utilities, a situation is just when no transfers can be made that improve the lot, however small, of any one person without diminishing the lot, however large, of any other. By this reasoning, before the cake is divided all distributions are just; after it has been divided no further distributions are just. The market divides the cake in the first place; the government must then alter that distribution and, by Pareto optimality reasoning, nothing the government can do is just. The world pays little attention to Pareto optimality, but the point illustrates the problem of changing any distribution, for that involves taking something away from someone in order to give it to someone else.

The justices of need and equality seem to justify a process of redistribution. But how can they justify taking from an individual who has done nothing to deserve the punishment inflicted on him? As we have seen, the justice of earned deserts finds this taking a grave injustice, and that injustice occurs because the government comes second in the distribution process.

The asymmetry of the public's attitude toward giving and taking in redistribution is revealed in attitudes toward income floors and ceilings: in one survey ony 9% of the public favored a ceiling on incomes, while 32% favored a guaranteed minimum income and 81% favored guaranteed jobs so that people could earn a decent income (Verba and Orren, 1985, p. 81). Assuming tax and transfer methods, one might say that facilitating *earning* is best, *giving* to the truly needy is acceptable, but *taking*, even from the rich, is bad. Redistribution implies little earning, and both giving and taking.

Trespassing on rights by government and business. From their reserve of sovereignty the people have granted government certain powers which, if they are exceeded, lead to claims of injustice. These boundaries of legitimate governmental action are marked by rights, among which are the rights to property and contract. While it is certainly the case that corporations are granted their special rights by the statè, business in general has not been granted its powers from any source. Rather, it seems, business powers derive, without such a grant, from the same reserved powers that serve as the source of governmental powers. Government, therefore, is more subject to claims of trespass than is business, and, being subject to such claims, more vulnerable to cries of injustice.

Harmony and Conflict of Interest

The problem of distributive justice arises only when there is a conflict of interest; it is moot when there is a harmony of interest (Barry, 1973, p. 15). Of course, businessmen and candidates for jobs know that they are in conflict with others, but the crucial question is the one that Marx (and others) identified: Is there a basic conflict of interests between owners and workers, management and labor? The answer to this question turns on whether one considers periodic pay disputes as "basic," or only as quarrels among allies in the productive process. Following that answer is the further question of the expression of such conflict as there may be in the economic and political domains. We examine these questions in three parts: class conflict, the uses of profits, and the nature of competition.

Class conflict. Of a national sample of Americans asked in the period 1975–1977

whether workers and management (1) "have conflicting interests and are natural enemies," or (2) "share the same interests in the long run," only 13% thought that workers and management have conflicting interests, while about two-thirds agreed that they have "the same interests in the long run" (McClosky and Zaller, 1985, Table 6-4). A different study with a comparable question (without reference to "natural enemies") conducted at the same time also showed about two-thirds holding that management and workers have "basically the same interests," but this time about a third held that they were "basically opposed." Moreover, this second study showed a declining relation between a belief in "basic opposition" and occupational level, such that by 1975 professional and managerial employees were scarcely different in this respect from blue collar workers (Schlozman and Verba, 1979, pp. 125, 130). Without a sense of class conflict the problem of justice between social classes is, as we have said, not a major issue.

But why does this weak or absent sense of class conflict and declining class division not also reduce the perception of conflict in politics? Some of the conditions for de-emphasizing class conflict in politics certainly exist. The two main parties have, over the years, followed the lines indicated: in the 1970s and early 1980s there has been very little difference in the class composition of the voters for the two main American parties (Ladd and Hadley, 1976; but see Pomper, 1985, p. 67). But it cannot be said that political conflicts have declined in intensity, for a variety of other issues—the Vietnam war, the Central American engagements, defense policy, prayer in the schools, racial issues—has kept the political conflict boiling. Structurally, then, the low sense of class conflict and apparently declining class divisions of the American public express themselves in a low sense of worker-management conflict in economic matters, where other issues are irrelevant, but not in a comparably low sense of political conflict, where other issues have become salient.

Profits. The idea of a harmony of interest is contained in market theory: as businesses prosper—that is, as they make larger profits—everyone prospers. Behind this thesis is the assumption, not that profits are deserved—though that will be said, for it is an economic theory and not a justice theory—but rather that profits are fruitful for the system: (1) they spur businessmen to greater effort, and (2) they are reinvested in the system, fructifying the economy. The harmony of interest lies, then, in the belief that "surplus value," to use an unfriendly term, goes back into the economy as the source of future prosperity, which, in turn, will benefit all, even if it is allocated quite unequally. The alternative theory, of course, is that surplus value—profits—goes to make the rich richer and does nothing for the ordinary person; in this version, all would be better off if smaller profits remained after earnings were distributed as wages and lower prices. There is evidence that the public is divided on this point (Lipset and Schneider, 1983, pp. 176-83), but the weight of the evidence lies with the harmony theory: profits are legitimate, both as earned income for owners, and—what is at stake here—as the source of "good times" and future income for workers.

Four different kinds of evidence may be cited. (1) Among the research findings are those from coded answers to open-ended questions showing that of those with opinions, two-thirds believed that profits were reinvested, and a large majority believed that a rise in profits meant "the good life" (Compton Advertising, Inc., 1975, questions 13a-13c). In answer to direct survey questions, twice as many respondents believed that "if business is allowed to make as much as it can . . . everyone profits in the long run" as

believed that "the workers get less." The profit motive is thought by most people to be the cause of "higher productivity and investment" (McClosky and Zaller, 1985, Table 4-5). (2) A computer simulation of various labor strategies under circumstances in which profits might be used for owner consumption or for reinvestment found that the most advantageous strategy is not to maximize demands but to moderate them (Przeworski, 1980). (3) Studying labor union responses in Germany just prior to World War I, Barrington Moore (1978, p. 220) found that union discipline and restraint "received considerable support from the awareness that in the end jobs depended on the prosperity of German Industry." Finally, (4) the idea that profits are the source of benefits for all is supported by the overwhelming endorsement of the "free enterprise system" that embraces this tenet among its principles (Harris Survey, in Lipset and Schneider, 1983, p. 286). From such evidence it seems fair to say that people generally regard differences of opinion on the use of profits as family quarrels, and not as basic conflicts.

Skipping over the many objective reasons for public uncertainty on the uses of profits (ignorance of the meaning of the term, possible owners' uses for their own consumption, investment overseas or in nonproductive but lucrative instruments, concealment), let us examine one of the justice implications of this harmonic interpretation of the system. It is just for an owner, say, to take $100 from what may be interpreted as a common fund, when each employee takes, say, only $10. In the harmonic view, the owner is justified in an income ten times that of his employees, on the grounds that if he should invest, say, half of that in the firm—still living five times as well as his employees, given the non-progressive tax system—the employees' wages might rise to $12 in a future year. Meanwhile, the owner's income might fairly rise to $125, slightly increasing the inegalitarian ratio and substantially increasing the absolute difference. Thus, the belief that (a) profits will be reinvested, and (b) the benefits of reinvestment will return to the employees is, in this case, a powerful argument for inequality of income.

Where lie the deserts in this case? Assuming that the owner's rate of return was average, his claim for a reward for skill is minimal. His claim that he deserves the income for "waiting"—Marshall's (1938) argument, now obsolete (Robinson, 1958, p. 394)—is matched by the employee's claim to have waited just as long.

But even if there were a justification for increased gain on the part of the owner, what would justify the employees' higher salary in later years? It seems more realistic to waive all efforts to ground these outcomes in the justice of deserts, and to recognize the play of a self-interest justified only by the recognition by all parties of certain rules of the game—certain procedural requirements within which hedonistic motives are allowed because, shall we say, of the harmony of interest involved. In this sense, then, harmony of interest takes the place of justice, and claims of justice will be muted.

These considerations overflow into the political domain in several ways. In the first place, it has been said that "government policy favoring business is seen [by the public] not as a response to the special interests of business but as a policy that serves the economy more generally" (Verba and Orren, 1985, p. 216). Moreover, anything that makes the "business climate" unfavorable, as businessmen see it, is thought to reduce investment and increase unemployment, "the fiendishly clever" device that Lindblom (1982, p. 324) says imprisons us in a market society. In this context political justice is seen to be served by catering to market justice. Second, confidence in the free enterprise system stifles political reform,

for the public strongly opposes at least two of the ways to alter the flow of profits: they do not want (by 73% to 13%) limits on profits (McClosky and Zaller, 1985, Table 6-2); and they oppose nationalization of industry even more strongly (Lipset and Schneider, 1983, pp. 265–69). One can imagine, indeed, that the fear of government intervention (in these, but not necessarily in more limited ways) is a source as well as a consequence of the more hopeful view of the harmony in the economic system, a kind of backflow following the overflow we mentioned.

But these limits on government do not lead to exculpation of the government for any injustices perceived in the market; in the end, the responsibility for rectifying any injustices of the economic system lies not with the market, but with the government. Rainwater (1974, pp. 180, 186) says of his respondents that "they look to government as the mechanism for developing policies for this improvement [in the fairness of the system] and then enforcing it," but that "they do so without conviction, because it is hard to imagine how the desirable end result . . . might be accomplished." Bricks without straw, ends without means, injustice lodged at the door of the government without any approved policy for rectifying it.

Almost as many Americans name politicians as being unfairly advantaged as name the rich and big business (Jennings, 1983). One reason for this attitude toward politicians may be that, in contrast to the belief that employees benefit from owners' profits, people not only believe high politicians' salaries do not benefit them, but that these salaries come from their own tax payments. There is no harmonic device here, but there is a conflict of interest.

Competition. In both markets and politics people welcome competition: power checking power, firm competing with firm, party with party, and indeed government and business checking each other. Members of the public "distrust power and its potential for abuse in any setting, public or private . . . [although] most Americans are more fearful of state power than of business power" (Lipset and Schneider, 1983, pp. 256–59). But there is a fundamental difference in the structure of the competition between firms and that of the competition between parties that makes market competition, at least for commodities, seem more benign than political competition. In the commodity market, the consumer is not a competitor, but an interested and favored third party. Not being a member of the competing firms, he has everything to gain from their competition, no matter who wins. In electoral competition, on the other hand, the citizen is a participant in the conflict; thus, like an owner of an enterprise, he can expect to win those things for which he voted only if his side wins. In the commodity market all consumers gain something from the competition, no matter who wins a greater share of the market, but in political competition, if it is closely contested, only a little over half the citizenry gains its partisan objectives.

Put differently, for third parties—like consumers in the market—competition is always a positive sum game, while in politics it is a zero sum game. Positive sum games permit greater harmony (indeed, they permit Pareto optimality), while zero sum games are patently antagonistic.

For the ordinary person the labor market is quite another matter, yet competition there occurs (as we have seen) within a general agreement about the hierarchy of income. There is, however, no such agreed upon hierarchy of political influence, in which each group would leap over the others and place itself at the top (Verba and Orren, 1985, ch. 9). Unlike competition for income, competition for

influence takes place without any consensus as to who should have what, and is therefore bound to be more antagonistic in nature.

There is a more fundamental reason for these different assessments of justice in the very concept of conflict in the two domains. As suggested above, the market can claim that, in some sense, when one person gains something others gain something too. In this fashion economists from Adam Smith on have been able to claim— and a large section of the American public to accept—the idea of a harmony of interest. Democratic theory and its popular interpretations are less happily endowed. Except for Rousseau—and he only by assuming people abandoned their particular interests—democratic theory has located the harmony of interest in the preservation of a framework within which an accepted conflict of interest takes place. The "harmony" does not arise from the reciprocal advantages which each party to the conflict receives from the other's advantage, as in the market, but rather from an exterior, partially removed, joint advantage in maintaining that conflict in peace, if not in actual harmony. Democratic theory assumes a conflict of interests and seeks to channel it, while market theory assumes that underlying the conflict is a harmony of interests. Since questions of justice arise only in situations of conflict, the acute sense of conflict that is present in politics but not in markets stimulates the justice nerve with greater force and arouses sensitivity to political injustice.

Summary and Implications for Political Economy and Justice

The public is endowed with an active sense of justice, a sense that has been said to be "the basic template for organizing one's view of the world" (Lerner, 1981, p. 23). This sense of justice seems to influence judgments of candidates more than does perceived self-interest (Tyler et al., forthcoming); it is employed in interpersonal relations (Lerner, 1981; Mikula, 1980), and in appraising the police (Tyler & Folger, 1980), the courts (Sarat, 1977; Thibaut and Walker, 1975, Tyler, 1984), and not least, market processes (Curtin, 1977; Hochschild, 1981; Rainwater, 1974; Tyler and Caine, 1981). However, partly for the reasons given and partly because the market has been an enormously fruitful device for generating wealth and relieving poverty, the public favors the market.

What happens in a political economy in which the market is regarded as "fair and wise" and political practices, at least, are regarded as neither? In such a society, however much people sympathize with the unemployed, the handicapped, and even children, they will regard these nonproductive others as externalities, for in the market they are undeserving. People tend to prefer somewhat more egalitarian outcomes than the market provides, but their love of market methods inhibits them from advocating any solutions that seem to frustrate these methods. Even where the market's methods are thought to be unfair to certain groups, such as blacks or women, the intrusion of the government into the sacred market precincts is often regarded with suspicion, for the government's program of rectification trespasses on the evaluation of persons by the market's process of revealed contribution. Where government purposes are approved, their implementation is stifled, at least partly because such implementation violates market fairness norms. Belief in these norms weakens the belief, say, that a worker's child does not have a fair chance at success (Schlozman and Verba, 1979, p. 110), as well as a veridical perception of one's own life chances. Astigmatism of this sort also weakens collective effort, through unions and labor parties, to alter life chances. Minimal government is assured and people are

endowed with more commodities and fewer collective goods. The dynamism of history is confined to market dynamics—technical and material, but not ethical. In an imperfect world, employing imperfect mechanisms to achieve these flawed results may be the best we can do, but to give up so easily is contrary to people's belief in their capacity to control their own destinies.

Perceptions and Structures

We have argued that the preference for market justice over political justice has deep structural roots in the purposes and values of the two institutions, in the way they satisfy wants, in their differential employment of justice criteria, and in the levels of popular justice assessments in the two domains. We have seen how the attributions of causes, how the differences between initial distribution and redistribution, and how the application of rights differentially affect justice claims. The perceived harmony of interest in the market was contrasted with the perception of conflict in politics. While these structural effects are indeed significant, at an even deeper level they are themselves partly perceptual, ideological. That is, social structures are vulnerable to variable "definitions of the situation" (Magnusson, 1981; Mischel, 1968), to the "social construction of reality" (Berger and Luckman, 1967)—in short, to ideology (Geertz, 1964; Lane, 1962). Ideologies are, on the one hand, the joint products of both culture and what people bring to an interpretation, and on the other, "structures"—or what may be said to be "objectively" there—of dispositions and circumstances, of culture and science (Kardiner, Linton, DuBois, and West, 1945, p. 34; Nisbett and Ross, 1980). While interpretations of justice, as parts of ideologies, are more cultural and dispositional than other parts, they take their cues from perceptions of circumstances. They are not given in a situation; they are constructions placed upon situations.

At least three kinds of current evidence support the independence of perceptions (including what we shall call "the community point of view") from structural determination and from perceived material self-interest: (1) research showing that concepts of justice are only loosely related to perceptions of self-interest (e.g., Tyler et al., forthcoming); (2) research showing that people seem to vote more according to national news of unemployment and inflation than according to their own perceived benefits and burdens (Kiewiet, 1983; Kinder and Kiewiet, 1979); and (3) research documenting what we have called "sociological release" (Lane, 1978b). On this last point, it has been found that it is their ideologies, quite independent of their relative incomes, that determine people's attitudes toward income distribution and their perceptions of social advantage and disadvantage (Jennings, 1983; Verba and Orren, 1985, p. 180). Like Mannheim's (1949) intellectuals, people have already been partially liberated from the perspectives of their social positions, and therefore from structural determination.

Without greatly modifying (except for a change in policy emphasis) the institutions that have served us reasonably well, without weakening the justice of earned deserts that is both ethically honorable and psychologically rooted in our desire to be the cause of our fate, and without going against the grain by undermining materialist values, can we reconceptualize social structures to offer a different, and, I think, more veridical construction of reality? We focus on two reconceptualizations: (1) contributions to production, often slighted by egalitarian socialists (e.g., Harrington, 1973) and by philosophers of justice (see comments by Galston, 1980, p. 223; Rescher, 1966, p. 89), and (2) taking a community point of view.

Contributions to production. (1) Instead of being based on personhood, or on the idea that we deserve equal concern from government because we are "human beings with the capacity to make plans and give justice" (Dworkin, 1977, p. 82), public justice might be based on the idea that we all contribute to society—not, it is true, that we contribute equally, but that we all contribute something. In a full employment society (this is the policy change), the problem of deserts is partially solved: while children and the handicapped are embraced by an unambiguous justice of need, everyone else—including those contributing to child care in the home—is embraced by a justice of earned deserts. Although difficult to achieve, a full employment society is not impossible (viz. Sweden) and it is better than guaranteed incomes which both erode work efforts (Danziger and Associates, 1981) and violate the justice of earned deserts. We may keep the market's preferred "fair wage" measured by private net marginal productivity (provided this productivity is everywhere equal, and equal to social net marginal productivity [Pigou, 1949, pp. 549-50; but see Thurow, 1973, pp. 70-73]), and publicly supplement the incomes of those who are below some minimal standard of living. Since people's unfavorable assessments of welfare payments are based on the suspicion that the payees are not trying to earn, rather than that they are not actually "earning," their incomes, supplementary benefits escape popular obloquy. And with this change come some of the benefits of the republican ideal: we are all members of the Republic because we all contribute to it.

(2) Employing the justices of equality and need in its educational and health policies, the government creates human capital that promotes productivity quite as efficiently as does physical capital. Thus, the justices of equality and need can also add to productivity. By these and other means the government creates

wealth, and does not merely redistribute it. As a producer, government may fairly claim its own income by the justice of earned deserts.

(3) To accept the market's criteria of "contribution to production" is to ignore history, the history of the many previous contributions to productivity that make possible the current high level of payments to members of affluent societies. If we are pygmies standing on the shoulders of giants, what is owed to the pygmies and what to the giants, or to the giants' inheritors, society? Without a method and without consideration of incentive effects, Hobhouse's (1922, pp. 161–63) argument along these lines remains barren, but it has far-reaching implications that deserve attention: wages, interest, and profits owe so much to society that their allotments by the market are arbitrary, because they do not accurately reflect contributions to productivity. Social benefits, then, may be seen as society's return to individuals of its inherited contribution to productivity. Taxes may be seen as payment to society for its trusteeship of the giants' past contribution.

(4) By one set of calculations, the market rewards people as much on the basis of luck and chance as on the basis of performance (Jencks, 1973). As a kind of Darwinian device, the market's reward to chance factors does not alter its productive efficiency, nor the fruitfulness of its incentives, but it does alter its justice— and therefore the injustice of "taking" mentioned earlier. This consideration relaxes the relationship between justice and productivity that forms one basis for the preference of the market's justice of earned deserts.

The community point of view. Without giving up their cherished individualism, people can take a community point of view with at least six relevant effects. (1) As we have seen, viewing the world from the bottom up, people see processes rather than outcomes, emphasizing individual deserts rather than the overall shape of a resulting distribution. The community point of view restores a more egalitarian attention to distribution.

(2) Government, market, and other partial accounting systems are always incomplete from the community point of view, for there are always costs and benefits representing externalities for the unit involved: governments issue regulations for which firms pay the administrative costs; firms profit from relocations, pollution, and possibly unemployment, for which communities bear the costs; government policies have unintended effects for which "community impact," "family impact," and other impact studies are commissioned. In some sense these represent "injustices," that is, undeserved or unmerited benefits and burdens. While economic rent and windfall profits and their opposites are inevitable, accounting systems that embrace these externalities (e.g., Bauer and Fenn, 1972; Schultze, 1977; Sheldon and Moore, 1968; Terleckyj, 1975) reveal the deficiencies of market and governmental accounting by incorporating more of the community point of view. Inevitably, the preference for market justice and the concept of earned deserts is affected by the changed perspective.

(4) The segmented accounting systems of individuals, like those of the market and government, distort perceptions affecting justice assessments. For example, popular perceptions of government discretion, and therefore of unconstrained bias, often rest on the failure to see the necessity of government tradeoffs, especially, but not solely, in terms of the logic of taxes, expenditures, and deficits, leading to a "something for nothing" mentality (Sears and Citrin, 1982). In a segmented accounting system it is "costless" to want everything and to see injustice in any denial. The community point of view

asks the public to internalize these choices: "What am I willing to give up for the policies and services desired?" Thus some of the constraints seen to apply to firms in the market are also seen to apply to government choices, and governments may be perceived as applying justice with less freely available discretion.

(5) The market's advantage over the polity seems to lie in its solution to the problem of free riders pursuing "the logic of collective action" (Olson, 1971)—a moral problem as well as an economic one. But introduce any common good, such as clean air or a healthy and safe environment, and market forces lead to a less felicitous solution, sometimes called "the tragedy of the commons" (Hardin, 1968), collectivizing injustice as well as impoverishment. While the community point of view seems to rely on moral incentives, in the tragedy of the commons it enlists material incentives and the value of productivity discussed above. Indeed, in the tragedy of the commons, market calculations of individually earned deserts lead to lower productivity.

(6) From the community point of view political conflicts are like labor-management quarrels over the disposition of profits: they are frankly quarrels. As in the harmonic view of the market, benefits to others are also, if in lesser degree, benefits to the self, partly because of the market itself: the grocer, made unhappy by the taxes he pays to support welfare, is happy to receive the custom of his welfare clients. The community point of view makes the connection.

Without entering here into the crucial economic implications of these changes in perception, it is clear that reinterpreting productivity and looking at the world from a community point of view somewhat erode the structural advantages of market justice over political justice; these perspectives represent counterweights in the scales of justice now so unevenly tilted against political justice in favor of market justice.

Note

An earlier version of this paper was delivered as the inaugural Hugo Wolfsohn Memorial Lecture, May 1, 1985, Melbourne, Australia. I wish to thank the History of Ideas Unit, Research School of Social Sciences, Australian National University, for hospitality while I prepared this paper, and the Institution for Social and Policy Studies, Yale University, for its continuing generous support.

References

Ackerman, Bruce A. 1980. *Social Justice in the Liberal State.* New Haven: Yale University Press.
Barrett-Howard, Edith, and Tom R. Tyler. Forthcoming. Procedural Justice as a Criterion in Allocation Decisions. *Journal of Personality and Social Psychology.*
Barry, Brian. 1973. *The Liberal Theory of Justice.* Oxford: Clarendon.
Bauer, Raymond A., and Dan H. Fenn, Jr. 1972. *The Corporate Social Audit.* New York: Russell Sage.
Berger, Peter L., and Thomas Luckman. 1967. *The Social Construction of Reality.* Garden City, NY: Doubleday, Anchor.
Brickman, Philip. 1977. Preference for Inequality. *Sociometry,* 40:303–10.
Brickman, Philip, Robert Folger, Erica Goode, and Yaacov Schul. 1981. Microjustice and Macrojustice. In Melvin J. Lerner and Sally C. Lerner, eds., *The Justice Motive in Social Behavior.* New York: Plenum.
Cahn, Edmond N. 1964. *The Sense of Injustice.* Bloomington: Indiana University Press. (Originally published in 1949.)
Compton Advertising, Inc. 1975. *National Survey of the U.S. Economic System: A Study of Public Understanding and Attitudes.* New York: Compton.
Crosby, Faye J. 1982. *Relative Deprivation and Working Women.* New York: Oxford University Press.
Curtin, Richard T. 1977. *Income Equity Among U.S. Workers: The Bases and Consequences of Deprivation.* New York: Praeger.
Danziger, Sheldon, and Associates. 1981. How Income Transfer Payments Affect Work, Savings, and Income Distribution: A Critical Review. *Journal of Economic Literature,* 19: 975–1028.
Deutsch, Morton. 1975. Equity, Equality, and Need: What Determines Which Value Will Be Used as the Basis of Distributive Justice? *Journal of Social Issues,* 31:139–49.
Dworkin, Ronald. 1977. *Taking Rights Seriously.* Cambridge, MA: Harvard University Press.
Feinberg, Joel. 1973. *Social Philosophy.* Englewood Cliffs, NJ: Prentice-Hall.

Galston, William A. 1980. *Justice and the Human Good.* Chicago: University of Chicago Press.

Geertz, Clifford. 1964. Ideology as a Cultural System. In David Apter, ed., *Ideology and Discontent.* New York: Free Press.

Hardin, Garrett R. 1968. The Tragedy of the Commons. *Science,* 162:1243–48.

Hare, Richard Mervyn. 1963. *Freedom and Reason.* Oxford: Oxford University Press.

Harman, Gilbert. 1983. Justice and Moral Bargaining. *Social Philosophy and Policy,* 1:114–31.

Harrington, Michael. 1973. *Socialism.* New York: Bantam.

Hart, H. L. A. 1961. *The Concept of Law.* Oxford: Clarendon Press.

Heider, Fritz. 1958. *The Psychology of Interpersonal Relations.* New York: Wiley.

Hobhouse, Leanard Trelawney. 1922. *The Elements of Social Justice.* London: Allen & Unwin.

Hochschild, Jennifer L. 1981. *What's Fair? American Beliefs about Distributive Justice.* Cambridge, MA: Harvard University Press.

Inglehart, Ronald. 1981. Post-Materialism in an Environment of Insecurity. *American Political Science Review,* 75:880–900.

Jencks, Christopher. 1973. *Inequality: A Reassessment of the Effect of Family and Schooling in America.* New York: Harper, Colophon Books.

Jennings, M. Kent. 1983. Trends in the Perception of Social Injustice. Presented at the annual meeting of the International Society of Political Psychology, Oxford.

Jouvenel, Bertrand de. 1951. *The Ethics of Redistribution.* Cambridge: Cambridge University Press.

Kardiner, Abram, Ralph Linton, Cora DuBois, and James West. 1945. *The Psychological Frontiers of Society.* New York: Columbia University Press.

Katona, George, and Burkhard Strumpel. 1978. *A New Economic Era.* New York: Elsevier North Holland.

Katz, Daniel, Barbara A. Gutek, Robert L. Kahn, and Eugenia Barton. 1975. *Bureaucratic Encounters: A Pilot Study in the Evaluation of Government Services.* Ann Arbor, MI: Institute for Social Research.

Kaufman, Walter. 1973. *Without Guilt and Justice: From Decidophobia to Autonomy.* New York: Wyden.

Kiewiet, Roderick D. 1983. *Macroeconomics and Micropolitics: The Electoral Effects of Economic Issues.* Chicago: University of Chicago Press.

Kinder, Donald R., and Roderick D. Kiewiet. 1979. Economic Discontent and Political Behavior: The Role of Personal Grievances and Collective Economic Judgements in Congressional Elections. *American Journal of Political Science,* 23: 495–527.

Ladd, Everett C., and Charles D. Hadley. 1976. *Political Parties and Political Issues.* Beverly

Hills, CA: Sage.

Lane, Robert E. 1959. The Fear of Equality. *American Political Science Review,* 53:35–51.

Lane, Robert E. 1962. *Political Ideology: Why the American Common Man Believes What He Does.* New York: Free Press.

Lane, Robert E. 1972. *Political Man.* New York: Free Press.

Lane, Robert E. 1978a. Autonomy, Felicity, Futility: The Effects of the Market Economy on Political Personality. *Journal of Politics,* 40:2–24.

Lane, Robert E. 1978b. Interpersonal Relations and Leadership in a "Cold Society." *Comparative Politics,* 10:443–59.

Lane, Robert E. 1982. Government and Self-Esteem. *Political Theory,* 10:5–31.

Lerner, Melvin J. 1980. *The Belief in a Just World: A Fundamental Delusion.* New York: Plenum.

Lerner, Melvin J. 1981. The Justice Motive in Human Relations. In Melvin J. Lerner and Sally C. Lerner, eds., *The Justice Motive in Social Behavior.* New York: Plenum.

Lewis, Alan. 1982. *The Psychology of Taxation.* New York: St. Martin's Press.

Lindblom, Charles E. 1977. *Politics and Markets: The World's Politico-Economic Systems.* New York: Basic Books.

Lindblom, Charles E. 1982. The Market as Prison. *Journal of Politics,* 44:324–36.

Lipset, Seymour Martin, and William Schneider. 1983. *The Confidence Gap: Business, Labor, and Government in the Public Mind.* New York: Free Press.

Magnusson, David, ed. 1981. *Toward a Psychology of Situations.* Hillsdale, NJ: Erlbaum.

Mannheim, Karl. 1949. *Ideology and Utopia.* Trans. Lovis Wirth and Edward Shils. New York: Harcourt, Brace.

Marshall, Alfred. 1938. *Principles of Economics,* 8th ed. London: Macmillan.

McClosky, Herbert, and John Zaller, 1985. *The American Ethos: Public Attitudes Toward Capitalism and Democracy.* Cambridge, MA: Harvard University Press.

Mikula, Gerold, ed. 1980. *Justice and Social Interactions: Experimental and Theoretical Contributions from Psychological Research.* Bern: Huber.

Mill, John Stuart. 1910. *Utilitarianism.* In *Utilitarianism, Liberty, and Representative Government.* London: Dent.

Miller, Warren E., Arthur H. Miller, and Edward J. Schneider. 1980. *American National Election Data Sourcebook, 1952–1978.* Cambridge, MA: Harvard University Press.

Mischel, Walter. 1968. *Personality and Assessment.* New York: Wiley.

Moore, Barrington, Jr. 1978. *Injustice: The Social Bases of Obedience and Revolt.* New York: Macmillan.

Nisbett, Richard, and Lee Ross. 1980. *Human*

Inference: Strategies and Shortcomings of Social Judgement. Englewood Cliffs, NJ: Prentice-Hall.

NORC (National Opinion Research Center) Survey. 1981. Public Opinion, 4(Aug./Sept.):27.

NORC 1984. Public Opinion, 17(Oct./Nov.):30.

Nozick, Robert. 1974. Anarchy, State, and Utopia. New York: Basic Books.

Olson, Mancur. 1971. The Logic of Collective Action, rev. ed. Cambridge, MA: Harvard University Press.

Parsons, Talcott. 1951. The Social System. Glencoe, IL: Free Press.

Perkins, Wesley H., and Wendell Bell. 1980. Alienation and Social Justice in England and the United States: The Polity and the Economy. Vol. 3 of Comparative Social Research. Greenwich, CT: JAI Press.

Pigou, Arthur C. 1949. The Economics of Welfare, 4th ed. London: Macmillan.

Pole, J. R. 1978. The Pursuit of Equality in American History. Berkeley, CA: University of California Press.

Pomper, Gerald M. 1985. The Presidential Election. In Gerald M. Pomper, ed., The Election of 1984. Chatham, NJ: Chatham.

Potter, David M. 1954. People of Plenty: Economic Abundance and the American Character. Chicago: University of Chicago Press.

Przeworski, Adam. 1980. Material Bases of Consent: Economics and Politics in a Hegemonic System. In Maurice Zeitlin, ed., Political Power and Social Theory. Vol. 1. Greenwich, CT: JAI Press.

Rae, Douglas. 1981. Equalities. Cambridge, MA: Harvard University Press.

Rainwater, Lee. 1974. What Money Buys: Inequality and the Social Meaning of Income. New York: Basic Books.

Rawls, John. 1971. A Theory of Justice. Cambridge, MA: Harvard University Press.

Rescher, Nicholas. 1966. Distributive Justice: A Constructive Critique of the Utilitarian Theory of Distribution. Indianapolis: Bobbs-Merrill.

Robinson, Joan. 1958. The Accumulation of Capital. London: Macmillan.

Ross, W. David. 1939. Foundations of Ethics. Oxford: Clarendon Press.

Runciman, W. G. 1966. Relative Deprivation and Social Justice. Berkeley, CA: University of California Press.

Sarat, Austin. 1977. Studying American Legal Culture: An Assessment of Survey Evidence. Law and Society Review, 11:427–88.

Schlozman, Kay L., and Sidney Verba. 1979. Injury to Insult: Unemployment, Class, and Political Response. Cambridge, MA: Harvard University Press.

Schultze, Charles L. 1977. The Public Use of Private Interest. Washington, D.C.: Brookings.

Sears, David O., and Jack Citrin. 1982. Tax Revolt: Something for Nothing in California. Cambridge, MA: Harvard University Press.

Sheldon, Eleanor B., and Wilbert E. Moore, eds. 1968. Indicators of Social Change: Concepts and Measurements. New York: Russell Sage.

Sidorsky, David. 1983. Contextualization, Pluralism, and Distributive Justice. Social Philosophy and Policy, 1:172–95.

Terleckyj, Nestor E. 1975. Improvements in the Quality of Life: Estimates of Possibilities in the United States, 1974–1983. Washington, D.C.: National Planning Association.

Thibaut, John, and Laurens Walker. 1975. Procedural Justice: A Psychological Analysis. Hillsdale, NJ: Erlbaum.

Thurow, Lester. 1973. Toward a Definition of Economic Justice. The Public Interest, no. 31: 56–80.

Tocqueville, Alexis de. 1945. Democracy in America. 2 vols. Trans. H. Reeve; ed. Phillips Bradley. New York: Knopf.

Tyler, Tom R. 1984. The Role of Perceived Injustice in Defendants' Evaluations of Their Courtroom Experience. Law and Society Review, 18:51–74.

Tyler, Tom R., and Andrew Caine. 1981. The Influence of Outcomes and Procedures on Satisfaction with Formal Leaders. Journal of Personality and Social Psychology, 41:642–55.

Tyler, Tom R., and Robert Folger. 1980. Distributional and Procedural Aspects of Satisfaction with Citizen-Police Encounters. Basic and Applied Social Psychology, 1:281–92.

Tyler, Tom R., Kenneth Rasinski, and Kathleen McGraw. Forthcoming. The Influence of Perceived Injustice on the Endorsement of Political Leaders. Journal of Applied and Social Psychology.

Utne, Mary K., and Robert E. Kidd. 1980. Equity and Attribution. In Gerold Mikula, ed., Justice and Social Interaction: Experimental and Theoretical Contributions from Psychological Research. Bern: Huber.

Verba, Sidney, and Gary R. Orren. 1985. Equality in America: The View from the Top. Cambridge, MA: Harvard University Press.

Weber, Max. 1947. The Theory of Social and Economic Organizations. Trans. T. Parsons. New York: Oxford University Press.

Williamson, Jeffrey G., and Peter H. Lindert. 1980. American Inequality: A Macroeconomic History. New York: Academic Press.

Robert E. Lane is Professor Emeritus of Political Science, Yale University, New Haven, CT 06520.

20

Alternative Systems of Ethics and Their Application to Education and Evaluation

Mary Anne Bunda

ABSTRACT

Three schools of moral thought are presented to illustrate differences in moral reasoning and the assignment of value claims. Several educational program alternatives are used as illustrations of moral reasoning within and across the schools of thought. Finally, the schools of moral thought are used in a discussion of evaluation practice. Good practice in the current evaluation literature is shown to be a blend of the three schools of thought.

Consideration of moral issues or moral dilemmas has often been treated by considering cases of conflict and analyzing the alternative action options within the cases. This paper takes a different strategy in the analysis of ethical issues. A discussion will be presented of three schools of moral philosophy. Each of these schools will then be used in a discussion of educational programming and evaluation. The purpose of the discussion using these various rubrics is to show that often the starting point and the reasoning in moral dilemmas are different. Although a particular action might be considered either right or wrong by several schools of moral thought, the reasons for assigning the value claim can be different. In the application of the various schools in the educational arena, three different program alternatives will be discussed. In the final section of the paper, three aspects of evaluation will be used to illustrate the reasoning used by the three schools of moral philosophy. In each section, the value claims and reasoning used clarify the programs.

Clarification of value claims made about programs and policies is particularly important today. The contemporary problem in most public institutions seems to be how more and better service can be provided with fewer resources. In some cases, the services that are provided are targeted to small parts of the total clientele of the institution. The value of the claims for special services is rarely discussed. Rather, the evalua-tion literature concentrates on the extent to which the service was delivered and the program met its ends. Rarely are the problems of competing services focused upon.

There are two possible causes for the lack of inquiry into claims for competing services. One may be the explanation given by Goodman: "Many of us want things that we will not accept as contradictory: a clean environment and full employment; meaningful work and college tuition; social justice and a balanced budget" (1979, p. 21). In other words, we are reluctant to investigate the competition for resources and programs because we might find that services provided to meet one set of goals necessarily reduce the probability of achieving another set of goals. Rather than setting the goals against each other, we simply argue which program is achieving its own ends most efficiently. Thus, we avoid the question of resolving the competing goals.

A second explanation for our imprecise treatment of competing value claims has been offered by Fullin-wider (1980). He pointed out that earlier patterns of service or lack of service to special groups were so egregiously offensive that people could unite in condemning them without being forced to precisely formulate the principles upon which their condemnation rested. Now, however, the patterns of service and proposed solutions to problems cause controversies. These controversies often force us "to notice that at

The work reported herein was supported in part by the Evaluation Network and the National Institute of Education through Contract No. 400-80-0105 with the Northwest Regional Educational Laboratory. It does not necessarily reflect the view of any of the three agencies, however, and no endorsements should be inferred.

The author is indebted to many colleagues who reviewed previous drafts of this paper.

Requests for reprints should be sent to Mary Anne Bunda, The Evaluation Center, Western Michigan University, Kalamazoo, MI 49008.

the level of deepest principles there might be considerable disagreement among us and deep puzzlement about how to resolve those differences" (p. 8).

The need for analysis of the moral principles upon which choices are made can be defended, then, on two bases. *First,* the principles allow for analysis of one program versus another at the goal level rather than at the operational level. Thus, they allow choices to be made by setting priorities among the principles. *Second,* analysis of the moral principles clarifies the purpose of the services provided. If disagreements about competing services exist because of "basic principles," it is our task to explicate those differences to the client.

The level of basic principles I'm suggesting is found in systems of moral philosophy that help us explain what is good. Moral philosophy should help us to develop ways in which we should behave as professionals. For the educational evaluator, there are two realms of professional practice that must be considered: the oughts of the educator and the oughts of the evaluator. Most discussions of good professional practice list dos and don'ts from a methodological viewpoint of research evidence. Let me suggest that moral philosophy can also be used to generate lists of dos and don'ts. However, rather than generate those lists here, let us investigate how alternative lists might develop.

MORAL PHILOSOPHY

Three different positions in moral philosophy will be discussed in this section. Each of the positions has been selected because of the approach that is taken in first principles. It should be noted that, for the sake of simplicity, a position will not be described in its total complexity, using all of the various philosophers who have contributed to its development. The three positions used will be utilitarianism, a rights-based theory, and a duty-based theory.

The utilitarians are often called *teleological moralists* in that they claim an action is right only if it leads to the best possible consequences and is wrong if otherwise. The rights-based theory and duty-based theory, often called *deontological,* contend that there are other considerations besides consequences that must be accounted for. In fact, in some cases, the claim for action may be so strong that consequences are disregarded. Consequently, the positions differ in the extent to which the goodness of an action depends upon the consequences of that action. Additionally, they differ with respect to the role reason plays in the determination of the goodness of an action. In utilitarianism, reason is used in each moral judgment. In deontological theories, reason and experience aid in the development of a morally developed person, but they are not the focus of each moral judgment. The essential differences, however, are exhibited in the extent to which consequences of an action are considered and in rules for handling competing principles in a situation. The points of contrast are more important for the purposes of this paper than is complete understanding of the nuances of each system. Within any one of the systems described, there are various positions, some of which tend to shade and blur the lines of distinction.

Utilitarianism

Although the first expository pieces on utilitarianism were written by Jeremy Bentham (1748–1832), John Stuart Mill (1806–1873) is generally regarded as responsible for its major exposition (Beauchamp,

1982; Hudson, 1980). Under this rubric, an action is correct if it provides the greatest good, happiness, or satisfaction to the greatest number. This is called the *principle of utility.* Happiness in this case is the aggregate of happiness over a defined group. In consideration of the distribution of happiness to members of the group, Bentham formulated the proposition that each person counts as one and no one is to count for more than one. This principle is referred to as *impartial benevolence.* Impartial benevolence forces the individual considering alternative moral choices to look objectively at all of the consequences of each of the actions and not to concentrate only on himself or herself or individuals in whom he or she is interested. The group being considered, however, can vary from one decision maker to another. One person may consider all human beings; one, a nation state; and one, perhaps, a corporation. However, although each person in the aggregate counts as one in the determination of the consequent happiness of an action, it doesn't follow that each person's happiness will be equal in the end.

The principle of utility, upon which actions are judged, requires only that the aggregate good of one action be quantitatively or qualitatively better than another action. That is, more people may have the same level of happiness, more happiness may accrue to the same number of people, or the kind of happiness or satisfaction experienced by a group may be qualitatively changed by a good action. A judgment then, concerning the correctness of action alternatives, requires the agent to hypothesize the consequences of the alternatives available, to quantify the effects of those alternative actions on the members of the group (both positive and negative effects), and then to aggregate the quantification across the members of the group. That action is correct which results in the greatest aggregate increase in positive effects.

Utilitarianism has been criticized because it can lead to injustice, especially to unjust social distributions (Beauchamp, 1982). However, it should be noted that the distribution of happiness or benefits is not the essential feature of the determination of goodness. Rather, the aggregate good of the consequence of the action is critical. In writing about distribution of the means to happiness, as opposed to happiness as a consequence, Sidgwich (1970) has said

> If more happiness on the whole is produced by giving the same means of happiness to B rather than to A, it is an obvious and incontrovertible deduction from the utilitarian principle that it ought to be given to B whatever inequality in distribution of the *means* to happiness this may involve. (p. 43)

A second criticism of utilitarianism concerns the quantification of good and its aggregation over a group. Utilitarians argue among themselves regarding the appropriate definition of happiness. Even if they use the same definition, two utilitarians could come to different courses of action because of different data sets and experiential backgrounds when hypothesizing the effects of a particular action. Yet, the utilitarians would counter that the important thing, morally speaking, is that an agent attempt to determine the consequences of an action and then seriously pursue that course.

Some utilitarians go beyond judgment of the consequences of each act and say that it is possible to formulate rules as to what is desirable or undesirable. These authors (e.g., R. B. Brandt) are referred to as *Rule Utilitarians* as opposed to *Act Utilitarians* (e.g., J. J. C. Smart). Rules are justified when they would maximize the common good if individuals conformed to them. This distinction is made here because of the similarity on one level between Rule Utilitarians and the deontological positions described later. Both would posit a set of rules or duties, yet only the Rule Utilitarian would be subordinate to, or determine all rules by, that which maximizes the common good. Hence, in situations in which, on the face of it, rules or principles seem to conflict, the Rule Utilitarian has a method for resolving the conflict, which the deontologist might not.

Duty-Based Theories
Deontological systems of moral philosophy differ from teleological systems primarily in the extent to which the sole consideration of the consequences of the action determine its rightness or wrongness. Rules of behavior can be apprehended by a morally developed person as good in and of themselves. Right carries with it a sense of duty, and this in itself is the reason for behaving rightly apart from the consequences of the behavior. In the writings of Kant, these maxims of behavior are called *categorical imperatives*. Kant also suggested that the categorical imperatives that form morality have the characteristic of universality; that is, they are always applicable in relevantly

similar cases. This opens the duty-based philosophers to two major criticisms – the problem of conflicting rules and the problem of exceptions to rules.

These problems were dealt with by Sir David Ross with his system of prima facie obligations and rule-utilitarianism. Any of the codes of behavior are called obligations or duties, and not rules, so that in a situation where two are in conflict, the more important obligations can be followed. It also allows for the possibility of the correctness of breaking one obligation in order to maximize human happiness. However, each of the obligations is independently grounded. Ross's (1970) list of duties includes

1. Duties that result from previous actions,
   a. from promises either implicit or explicit and
   b. from previous wrongful acts. These are called duties of *fidelity* and duties of *reparation*.

2. Duties that result from services given by other individuals. These are called duties of *gratitude*.

3. Duties that result from the fact or possibility that happiness is not distributed in accordance with the merits of persons. These are called duties of *justice*.

4. Duties that require the conditions of others be made better. These are called duties of *beneficence*.

5. Duties to improve our own condition of virtue or intelligence. These are called duties of *self-improvement*.

6. Duties not to harm others. These are called *nonmaleficence*.

It should be noted that the duties of beneficence and the duties of nonmaleficence (which are more stringent than beneficence) are both principles to which Rule Utilitarians could subscribe. Thus, we see a charge leveled at deontologists by utilitarians in which they show covert consequential appeals. As duty-based theories moved from Kant, who contended that the rightness of an action could be determined independent of consequences, to Ross, who admits that consequences are relevant to moral judgments, although not the sole consideration, utilitarians could charge that the justification for the rightness of an action was a covert appeal to ends.

A second criticism of duty-based theories comes from the number of duties posited. Unlike utilitarianism, with the single principle of utility, duty-based theories have multiple principles. Thus, there is a possibility for duties to conflict in any one situation. And, without the underlying principle of utility, there is no easy way to show which principle or duty is most relevant or most important in a given situation. The duty-based theorists don't have a single or hierarchical set of values that should be considered; rather it is a cluster of values that people should bear in mind when they approach a problem. Even if duty-based philosophers did have a single hierarchy of duties, different actions could be recommended simply because the situation was diagnosed differently. The facts of the situation have to be recognized before the principles can be applied (M. Pritchard, personal communication, November 1982).

The principles in a duty-based system such as Ross's hinge on a morally developed person's recognizing that these principles should be followed simply because they are right and not out of the sole motive that the consequences of the behavior will improve that individual's or someone else's condition. However, principles of moral behavior can also come from the rights of others, as in the deontological systems discussed next.

Rights-Based Theories

The second deontological system to be discussed is one that describes principles of behavior in terms of individual rights rather than obligations. The moral basis for obligations comes from others; that is, rights and obligations are logically correlative. One person's right implies another person's obligation to refrain from some behavior or to act in some way to benefit the first person. Similarly, all obligations imply some rights. There is some controversy in the literature whether rights are generated from obligations or obligations generated from rights (Beauchamp, 1982).

Systems that have as their first principles the rights of individuals make careful differentiation between moral rights and legal rights. Moral rights do not require a referent in a legal code. There are some differences among authors in this system as to which rights are fundamental and which are derivative. Although such items as life, liberty, and equality have claims as rights, some people have suggested that the right to food is a valid moral right (Gorovitz, 1977). Thus, there are a number of different positions that could have served as examples in this area. John Rawls was selected because of the use of his writing in the evaluation literature.

Rights-based deontological theories take exception with utilitarianism in two special ways. *First,* some branches of utilitarianism consider the aggregated to be all sensing species. However, rights-based theories posit human beings to be qualitatively different from animals. Thus, from Kant onward these theories have held the rights of humans to dignity and autonomy. *Second,* violations of the principles of justice that are allowed under utilitarianism led to the development of Rawls's (1971) *justice as fairness* theory.

Rawls begins from the Kantian conception of equality. He suggests that if individuals were forced to form a social contract under a "veil of ignorance," principles of justice would emerge. That is, if bargains had to be struck, and no one knew either his or her position in society or his or her special talents, two principles of justice would be unanimously agreed upon:

First: each person is to have an equal right to the most extensive basic liberty compatible with a similar liberty of others.

Second: social and economic inequalities are to be arranged so that they are both (a) reasonably expected to be to everyone's advantage, and (b) attached to positions and offices open to all. (Rawls, 1971, p. 60)

The principles of justice are arranged by Rawls in serial order. First a justice system must have equality of liberty. But, if social or economic inequalities are to exist, then all must be advantaged by them. This is in contrast with the utilitarian position that would support moving some people to a slightly disadvantageous position so that others could gain considerable ground, thus improving the aggregate good. The second principle should not be viewed as a principle of redress. It does not specify that the least advantaged should always gain more. It merely suggests that if inequalities are to exist, all must benefit from these inequalities. In further development of the second principle, Rawls goes on to say that inequalities would be justifiable only if they most enhanced the position of the least advantaged.

TABLE 1
Summary of Moral Positions

Philosophical School	Criteria for Action	Focus of Moral Decision	Options for Agent
Utilitarians	Aggregate common good	Consequences of alternative action.	Definition of group
Duty-Based	Duties of behavior e.g., fidelity, gratitude, justice	Relevant duties in the situation	Most relevant duty
Rights-Based	Rights of individuals, e.g., dignity, liberty	Relevant rights of individuals affected by actions	Principle II in Rawls

Thus, the first criterion for morally correct actions is the result of federal or state law in most instances. The Second, if inequalities, either social or economic, are to exist, they must benefit the most disadvantaged the most, or at least benefit all equally.

Summary

While there certainly are more variations in moral philosophy, this trio is likely to serve as an interesting set through which to view educational programs and educational evaluation. In summary, then, as can be seen in Table 1, utilitarians focus on the consequences of an action and use the criterion of aggregate good. The two deontological systems, although they consider consequences, do not focus solely on them. Rather, they focus on the relevant principles in a situation. In these systems, moral behavior is seen as an end in and of itself and not solely as a means to an end.

EDUCATIONAL PROGRAMMING

Several classes of educational programming will be discussed because they are prevalent in schools and are the result of federal or state law in most instances. The implementation of these programs will be discussed within the context of the moral decisions made by hypothetical educators from each of the three schools presented. The justifications and reasoning will be drawn from the simple descriptions presented. Four caveats concerning the justification should be given at this point.

First, the facts of the case must be stipulated. Some of the examples are programs mandated by law, but they will be considered as options for school people. Additionally, the outcomes of all of the hypothetical programs will be necessarily presented. These outcomes must be accepted as representing the facts of the case. *Second,* the reasoning processes of real individuals who represent these points of view could achieve different conclusions. The conclusion with respect to each of the programs is less important for the purposes of this paper than the focus and process used by each system. *Third,* an assessment of moral justification is a different matter than the assertion that an action is morally required (Beauchamp, 1982, p. 212). This issue of moral requirement will not be discussed. And, *fourth,* it is an open question whether there would be a clear causal relationship between a single moral philosophy and the actions of an educational institution.

All of the other factors that color the decision-making process will not be considered. Moreover, in real life, a blend of various philosophies probably is more prevalent than the simple forms being used in this discussion. Surely, in some cases, all of the moral theories would agree on a single action, albeit arriving at the decision from different first principles.

The cases presented next are situations of choice. Although two of the programs are federally mandated, the decision to offer them will be considered unbound. The focus, then, of the discussion will surround the moral justification of such programs.

ESEA Title I

Let us consider first a program designed to counter the social and economic disadvantages of the home environments of some children. Although the specifics of any one program may differ from district to district, let us stipulate for the hypothetical moral decision maker certain features of the ends and means, in other words, the facts of the situation. Title I programs provide special (additional) education in the basic skills to children from disadvantaged homes. The results of the program are that these children perform as well as children from homes that are advantaged in the economic sense. Let us suppose, however, that the district that offers this program must cut its science enrichment program. I am presuming that at budgeting time all of the programs of the school have been put in priority order, and these two programs are head to head. The decision for the hypothetical decision maker, then, is to determine which program is preferable on moral grounds.

The first task of the utilitarian is to define the group who will be considered the aggregate. The second task is to hypothesize the effects of each of the options on that group. Suppose that the decision maker decides to use the school population as the group. In this situation, one may decide that additional understanding of science does not outweigh basic-skill improvement. Under this line of reasoning, the benefits that accrue to the children and the school district under a Title I program are seen as more important. Some of the rationale might include easier programming at the high school level; that is, children are more homogeneous in terms of both their basic skills and science achievement, so that high school programming is presented in a narrow band (an economical band) of options. A second rationale might be at the basic-skill improvement level; although it has happened to only a small part of the group, indeed it has facilitated the entire group in terms of the speed with which other material can be presented. On the other hand, the science program would not facilitate learning in the other areas. Although all children would benefit from the science instruction, no benefits in other curricular areas are seen.

Suppose, however, that the utilitarian were to select the nation as a whole as the aggregate to be used in the decision. The reason for the selection could be that schools have a responsibility to the nation or it might be that our society is so mobile that program decision makers in any district must consider the consequences for all districts. Whatever the reason for the selection of the aggregate definition, the decision maker is now faced with hypothesizing the effects of the two programs on the citizenry of the nation as a whole. With this definition of aggregate, the situation is changed. Here, the decision maker might say that the need for science and technology at the national level is so great that the district must balance slightly depressed achievement scores of part of its school-age population in order to increase the probability that some students will achieve well in science. That is, the greatest common good is served by exposing all children to science and dealing with the program of basic skills throughout the child's school career rather than investing in programs at the beginning of an elementary experience. So, we see that a utilitarian could come to two different decisions based upon the aggregate selected. However, in each case, the consequences of the program are the focus of the decision, and, within each aggregate, each individual is considered with impartial benevolence. That is, once the aggregate has been defined, the effects of the action, both positive and negative, must be considered on each individual equally.

If the decision were to be made by the hypothetical person using a rights-based theory, he or she might rely on the counsel of Rawls (1971). In discussing the difference principle (the second principle), Rawls shows how it is similar to and yet different from a principle of redress. In pursuit of the principle of redress, he suggests that "greater resources might be spent on the education of the less rather than the more intelligent, at least over a certain time of life, say the earlier years of school" (p. 100). This rationale is based on improving the long-term standard of living of these individuals—not only their economic well being, but also their ability to participate in the culture. He does not suggest, however, that the second principle is equal to a principle of redress, with which all handicaps are evened out. However, let us suppose that the decision maker in this case sees the effect of the science enrichment program as having no redressive effects, but rather as simply enhancing some students and further separating students. Additionally, in balancing the principles of rights in the two situations, he or she decides that the compelling rights are those of the disadvantaged. The morally justifiable decision then would be to offer the Title I program.

The duty-based decision maker makes a different analysis of the situation. The situation must be investigated as to which principles are relevant; and, if obligations are in conflict, the most important principle must be followed. Suppose that, in an analysis, the science program seems to be compelling from the principle of self-improvement and beneficence. On the other hand, the Title I program is seen as having as its basis the duties of reparation and nonmaleficence, that is, withholding Title I does real harm to students in their later school careers. If this is the analysis, the Title I program is offered because the more stringent duties are seen as relevant to the situation. But note that a Rule Utilitarian might come to the same conclusion, because nonmaleficence is a utilitarian rule

PL 94-142

The complexity of the facts surrounding mainstreaming are greatly reduced in this situation. Let us stipulate that the mainstreaming law has as its means placing children in a "least restricted environment," in other words, one in which they are integrated with the general population of learners in the schools. The ends of the program are social integration of handicapped students and intellectual functioning at the highest level possible for each student. Suppose that the competing alternative action for the district is self-contained classrooms, either within the district or via cooperation between districts, to create homogeneous classrooms by handicap type.

In this instance, let us consider that the utilitarian-oriented decision maker considers only the school as the aggregate for which the ends of both of the options must be considered. In the case of enacting full mainstreaming, he or she sees effects on students and staff. The students, on the average, receive slightly less instruction because of time and resources spent to accommodate special needs of individuals. Thus, overall achievement declines.

However, students do gain substantially in the affective area. Special students have substantial increases in their self-concept over self-contained programs, and typical students become more open to individual talents in all people. The staff, on the other hand, have much higher morale in the case of the self-contained programs. Suppose that the hypothesized result of full mainstreaming was high stress due to unusual pressures on all teachers. Stress symptoms of absenteeism are predicted. This analysis of the case would force the utilitarian to balance large gains for the students in the affective area against small losses in the cognitive area for students and large staff losses in the affective area. The focus of the decision then would be on the relative merits for the whole school of the gains in positive affect. Let me suggest that the utilitarian might decide that the balance was tipped in the direction of the self-contained program.

The rights-based decision maker might analyze this situation as a case in which Rawls's first principle should be used. That is that the mainstreaming act simply gives to handicapped students the same basic liberty within the school setting that all other children have. Without certain environmental changes in the classroom, these children are deprived of their basic right to equality. In this analysis of the case, the competing consequences of the two programs are not considered, because the second program restricts liberty. Or more strongly, the second program is unjust and, hence, morally indefensible.

The duty-based decision maker might also analyze the situation as one in which the principles or obligations of justice apply. However, if he or she were to use Ross's description of justice in which the fact or possibility of happiness must be distributed in accordance with the merits of a person, then the two programs must be viewed with respect to the way in which they define *merit* of a person. In this situation, the decision maker might decide that the school cannot include the handicap per se as part of the merit consideration for program entry. Further, one might reason that the self-contained program is unjust from an educational point of view because it uses an accidental characteristic of students to make substantial educational decisions.

Advanced Placement Courses
In this situation, suppose that the decision makers from the various schools of moral philosophy are sitting on a building planning committee. A decision has to be made to provide facilities for various vocational training programs or to install special laboratories and equipment for advanced placement courses. The design of the building would, of course, carry with it subsequent differences in staffing patterns and program offerings. In one case, various introductory courses in clerical and skill vocations can be offered to the general high school population. In the other case, advanced work in chemistry, physics, and computer science can be provided to the collegebound.

The facts of the situation for the utilitarian require the hypothesized ends of each program to be in the common good. The aggregate selected is the state as a whole. The vocational facilities would provide entry-level skills for a large number of students, thus enhancing the employability of the students and increasing social welfare. The programs, however, would not remove the necessity for training in the private sector. Specific job-related skills would still have to be learned on the job, due to the general nature of the vocational training provided. Additionally, some students would not use the skills in these programs, because they were college bound. On the other hand, the special facilities would allow the advanced placement students to proceed through college in a more efficient manner, thus providing educational benefits to these students in a much less costly environment. The citizens of the state would achieve the same level of science achievement for a much smaller tax expenditure.

The analysis, then, is that the labs should be installed, because the cost of high school facilities and staff is much less to the public than college facilities, and vocational training can be carried on by the private sector.

The rights-based theorist might apply Rawl's difference principle. The facts of the situation are that, in one case, more resources are being channeled to the more intelligent than in the other. The decision, however, is not clearly in favor of the vocational programs. The ends of the two programs must be compared in terms of which finally would improve the long-term expectation of the least endowed. Rawls has suggested that this end might be attained by "giving more attention to the better endowed" (1971, p. 102). In other words, the long-term effects of each of the facilities must by hypothesized. If the decision maker sees that the labs would lead to early development of creative scientists, who in the end will improve the quality of life of all individuals, then the science labs should be installed. If, on the other hand, the science labs would differentially benefit the gifted, who in turn are not likely to benefit the common good, and the installation of the vocational facilities would differentially enhance students at the lower end of the academic potential pool, then this decision would go in the opposite direction. In this analysis of the case, the vocational facility should be installed. Whatever the final choice, however, the focus of the selection is the long-term effects on the least advantaged part of the population. But rationales for both options can be built using Rawls.

The duty-based theorist might also analyze the situation as one in which the duties of justice are important. Suppose, however, that additionally the duty of fidelity is seen on the side of the vocational program. In this analysis of the situation, one might suppose that each option is equally just. That is, the facilities are useful to students in accordance with their merit. However, the duties of fidelity require that the school prepare students to enter postsecondary environments. With advanced placement (AP) labs, students are more than prepared to enter college. In fact, the high school goes beyond entry-level skills. On the other hand, the vocational facilities allow individuals to enter the job market with saleable skills. Withholding either of the programs would cause harm. The question, then, centers around what kind of harm and to whom and what the past wrongs in the area are. In this case, suppose that the duty of fidelity is seen as the overriding concern. The promise of the school to prepare a student for postsecondary society is seen as essential. On the balance, the vocational facility keeps that promise, whereas the AP lab goes beyond the promise for some people. If this principle were used, the vocational facility would be selected.

TABLE 2
SUMMARY OF APPLICATIONS OF MORAL POSITIONS IN EDUCATION

Educational Program	Alternative Program	Critical Feature of Means	Critical Feature of Ends	Critical Feature of Contrast
ESEA I	Science enrichment	Extra programming for children because of parents' economic status.	Children achieve at expected level for their grade.	Extra attention to lower end of ability, causing middle and upper ranges to suffer.
PL 94-142	Self-contained classrooms or buildings	Program delivered to children in "least restricted environment."	Child not isolated, performing at best level. Staff must accommodate groups they are not prepared for.	Barriers in environment removed; more heterogeneity of students.
Advanced Placement Courses	Vocational courses	Small groups of H.S. students receive special academic preparation.	Students enter college with special preparation.	Extra expenditure goes to most advantaged.

Summary

In the analyses just given, the decisions regarding the options differed for each of the schools of ethics (see Table 2 for a summary). Two key features of the analyses should be noted. In each case, the programs under discussion were compared with one particular option. If the alternative course of action were changed, the decisions relative to the three programs might very well change. Additionally, in each analysis, lines of reasoning were followed that could vary within utilitarianism or rights-based or duty-based theories. The analysis of the case and the application of principles could be different with a different hypothetical decision maker. What would not change, however, is the focus of the discussion. The critical comparison among the three schools of ethics, then, is how they focus ethical decision making. Utilitarians concentrate on the consequences of the action in terms of the aggregate common good with impartial benevolence toward individuals. Rights-based theories concentrate on the rights of the individuals involved. In Rawlsian theory, the least advantaged are given special consideration. Duty-based theorists look at other responsibilities of the moral person and do not consider only the consequences of a particular set of action options. Most educators probably use a blend of the systems when justifying a program's existence, using principles from more than one system as a rationale for offering the program. Problems would be encountered only when one set of principles prescribed one action and another set a different act.

EDUCATIONAL EVALUATION

The blending of principles from the three schools of moral philosophy is evident in the writings in evaluation. In a review of the professional writing in the area, one is likely to encounter terms that have to do with the consequences of a program, the rights of individuals, and the duty of the evaluator. When considering ethics in evaluation, authors take either narrow or broad definitions of the term *ethics*. Although consideration of a specific aspect of evaluation could help bring to bear methodological solutions to that issue (see Boruch, 1972; or Boruch, 1982), it does not ask first-principle questions.

Let us consider first some principles that have been developed by individual authors in the area of evaluation. Sieber (1980) analyzed the principles of the National Commission for the Protection of Human Subjects of Biomedical and Behavioral Research—beneficence, respect, and justice—and came up with eight principles of action. Notice that the commission principles can be interpreted as either the rights of the subjects or the duties of the researcher-evaluator—an example of the correlative thesis. In Sieber's analysis, the beneficence principle serves as the basis for deducing the principles of usefulness in evaluation and the responsibility to look at the consequences of a mode of evaluation. In fact, four of the five principles Sieber developed from beneficence are consequential in nature, which is not surprising, because beneficence is defined as the "avoidance of unnecessary harm and the maximization of good outcomes" (Sieber, 1980, p. 54). This definition is a combination of Ross's beneficence and nonmaleficence, which would be considered rule-utilitarian in nature. The other principles of evaluator ethics presented are deductions from the rights of individuals in the study. In addition to the deduction of modes of behavior for the evaluation, Sieber also came to the conclusion that an ethical evaluation is one in which there is little or no role conflict. "The hallmark of being ethical in program evaluation research is planning so that the context of evaluation does not produce ethical dilemmas" (Sieber, 1980, p. 58). Her conclusion that dilemmas must be avoided by planning is counter to some contentions that it is through conflict that change results. Nisbet (1971) contended that it is only through ethical conflicts that institutions change. He asserted that conflict and competition in institutions reflect the minds and moral aspirations of the persons concerned. Pritchard (personal communication, 1982) suggested that, in anticipating dilemmas, we can also bring about change. The anticipation of the dilemma provides an opportunity for consideration of the issues under less stressful circumstances than waiting for the dilemma to be encountered without planning.

Another author who has added to the discussion of ethics in evaluation using a broad framework is Ernest House. The writings of House are different from others in that he generally used Rawls in his discussion of justice and bases his principles of ethical action on Rawlsian justice as fairness and social contract theory. House (1980) suggested that there are four values that serve as the moral basis of evaluation: "moral equality, moral autonomy, impartiality, and reciprocity" (p. 189). He suggested that these principles are rooted in the principles of liberalism and the right of individuals to choose. Let me suggest that they can also be considered as a rights-based system or theoretical framework. In this analysis, three of them have counterparts in philosophy—moral equality is the same as Rawls's first principle; moral autonomy is a characteristic of deontological theories such as Kant's (Dworkin, 1978); and impartiality is similar to impartial benevolence, that is, each person or interest counts as one and only one. Thus, House blended the systems of moral philosophy in his values for evaluation.

Both House and Sieber also suggested that evaluators should have professional ethics, not only with respect to the way individuals are treated within an evaluation, but also with respect to the fact that a contract signed by both evaluator and client is a sign of ethical evaluator conduct. The rationale for the suggestion from Sieber lies in the role clarification that a contract can provide, and House finds the need for it in social contract theory.

The issue of the need for an evaluation contract is also raised by the standards written by the Joint Committee on Standards for Educational Evaluation (1981). During the last 5 years, many professional organizations have been concerned with the ethical activities of evaluators. Two sets of standards of evaluation practice have been published (Evaluation Research Society and Joint Committee). Although the number of standards in each differ, and the organization is slightly different, Stufflebeam (1982) has shown that there is a high degree of agreement in the concepts covered. In each of these sets, a section has been devoted to ethics.

In the Joint Committee standards, the area of propriety deals mainly with the interactions among the evaluator, the public, and the individuals who provide data in the study. Under the propriety area, the standards are formal obligation (providing a contract), conflict of interest, full and frank disclosure, the public's right to know, rights of human subjects, human interactions, balanced reporting, and fiscal responsibility. The other major sections are utility, feasibility, and accuracy. Thus, it can be seen that the Joint Committee (1981) standards are also a blend of the three schools of moral philosophy—utilitarianism (e.g., standard A8 Evaluation Impact), rights-based theory (e.g., standard C5 Rights of Human Subjects), and duty-based theory, (e.g., standard C3 Full and Frank Disclosure). In the preceding sentence, notice that one of the examples is taken from section A of the standards, or the utility, not the propriety, section. Let me suggest that, in a broad sense, all 55 of the standards represent what is meant by good, moral, or ethical evaluator behavior. The maxims contained in both lists that require evaluators to collect valid information and produce reports that are timely define good evaluator behavior just as much as the requirement to treat individuals with dignity. Because the standards presented are also a blend of the three schools of philosophy, one might guess that evaluators are used to using as rationales for behavior principles that can be deduced from all of the moral philosophies. In most cases, one would suppose that evaluators and clients could agree on actions with multiple justifications. Conflicts would develop when the various schools suggested alternative actions as the morally preferable routes.

Rather than categorize the sets of standards into the three schools of philosophy or introduce morally required actions based upon any of the schools, let me suggest some morally justifiable actions that are consequences of the first principles of the three schools of moral philosophy in terms of three aspects of evaluation. Let me submit that, whatever else an evaluator might do, three items are critical to the operation of an evaluation and can be related to a moral stance.

First, the definition of what is good in the program is the way in which goodness becomes operational in a particular case. How does an evaluator begin to put out a net to capture what the meaning of good is? For the utilitarian, the matter is quite simple on one level. Goodness means increasing the happiness of the aggregate. However, this statement has two major issues in it. *First,* what is the appropriate unit that should be considered the aggregate? Is it a particular project site or the program as a whole? *Second,* there is a problem in the quantification of effects, both negative and positive, followed by balancing the relative importance of each of those effects when the aggregation is made. However, aggregating those effects is simply a weighting problem because of the value of the effects and not because of what individual received those effects. The Rawlsian rights-based theorist would have this second sort of problem. Under the difference principle, one would have to define who was receiving what sort of effect in order to make a judgment. However, this is serially less important than the first principle of equality of liberty. Both the duty-based theorist and the rights-based theorist would be required to formulate a definition of a good program that was not solely based on its consequences.

The other principles applied to a particular instance would, no doubt, depend on the program. However, there would have to be some aspect of the program that was viewed as a moral requirement. The evaluation, then, would focus upon whether or not this part of the program happened. As noted, the goals of various educational programs are viewed very differently by rights-based and duty-based agents. I'm not suggesting that evaluators who are fundamentally from these schools would not collect data on effects; rather, I believe that these evaluators would limit the scope of decisions that might be made. The situation might be even more strongly stated by saying that termination of the program would not be considered.

The *second* feature of evaluation that shall be considered is its focusing aspect. Focusing takes place between the initial contact with the client and a complete specification of the design. It is an iterative phase of evaluation work, characterized by several large decisions and thousands of small ones. During the focusing stage, the utilitarian would be sure that interests of the group were presented in proportion to their numbers in the aggregate. The Rawlsian, on the other hand, would be likely to check out the equal liberty of those involved. If the system were shown to have

violated the first principle, then the difference principle would take over, and representation of points of view and value do not necessarily reflect proportionate numbers in the group. The utilitarian would be likely to seek out a comparative progam to use in the evaluation, whereas comparisons might not be necessary for the duty-based evaluator. Evaluators are often cautioned to be sure to reflect the multiple audiences and perspectives when designing an evaluation. Let me submit that they might also want consciously to reflect multiple perspectives on what is good, so that an evaluator could use all of the techniques in the second row of Table 3. Multiple perspectives need not come from specific individuals involved in the project or program. Rather, they could flow from the various bases that might be used to judge the program and the evaluation.

Third, let us consider what the evaluator is likely to do with the report. Although report distribution would likely be covered in the contract, actions during and after the contract signing would probably be different. The utilitarian evaluator would likely sign a contract making the program manager or funding agent the prime recipient of the report. Thus, he or she would be trying to maximize the good use of the report by putting it into the hands of the powerful. The only reason for giving the report to other individuals would be to assure that the aggregate good would be increased. For instance, in cases where a manager was misrepresenting the report to the press, the evaluator would be morally justified in leaking the report *only* if the misrepresentation were actually cutting off good services from people or intentionally promoting bad practices.

The Rawlsian evaluator, however, would be more likely to negotiate a contract allowing the report to be

TABLE 3
POSSIBLE JUSTIFIABLE EVALUATOR ACTIONS

	Utilitarian	Rights-based	Duty-based
Good of Program	Aggregate goodness across individuals.	Principle I requires equality, but, if inequality exists, it must be used in a certain distribution.	Consequences of the program must be tempered by judgments of the operations.
Focus	1. Ends of the program central.	1. Seek out views of least powerful.	1. Both means and ends become the focus of the evaluation.
	2. Comparative "good" of program assessed.	2. Effects of program on various types of students investigated and coded by student type.	2. Comparative information not necessarily valuable.
Report	Report goes to decision makers; only if common good is not served is it leaked.	Powerless groups get information.	Duty to provide information to client overridden by many different duties.

put into the hands of less powerful persons and decision makers. Thus, the distributional pattern of the report would probably be broader than in the utilitarian case. Last, the duty-based theories have more than simply the principle of utility, which can be used to give the report to nonclient groups. For instance, the principle of self-improvement could be seen as relevant and the report printed in a journal afterward. The duty-based evaluator might see the report as more his or her own property than that of the clients.

In summary then, evaluators could develop very different modes of behavior within any one of these schools of thought that would be difficult to justify within the others. However, let me reiterate that the vast majority of actions and tasks performed by an evaluation specialist are probably justifiable across all three schools. Current writing in the area of codes of conduct for evaluators seems to be heavily influenced

by utilitarian definitions of good. This is not surprising, because most public policy is determined on utilitarian grounds (Beauchamp, 1982). However, because utilitarianism can lead to injustice, the counterinfluence of rights and duty theories, particularly in the case of human subjects, can be seen. The proposition presented above is that the central concern should be understanding the principles on which actions are based and resolving the conflict.

I'm not sure that individual evaluators or clients could determine which of the schools of morality best reflected their personal codes of conduct. However, not being able to self-report a complex set of beliefs doesn't mean that the belief structure doesn't impact on professional behavior. Our task is to be sure we can communicate about the analysis of the facts of the situation and how moral principles are applied to those situations.

REFERENCES

BEAUCHAMP, T. L. (1982). *Philosophical ethics.* New York: McGraw-Hill.

BORUCH, R. F. (1972). Relations among statistical methods for assuring confidentiality of social research data. *Social Science Research, 1,* 403–414.

BORUCH, R. F. (1982). Methods for resolving privacy problems in social research. In T. L. Beauchamp, R. R. Faden, R. J. Wallace, Jr., & L. Walters (Eds.), *Ethical issues in social science research* (pp. 292–314). Baltimore: Johns Hopkins University Press.

DWORKIN, G. (1978). Moral autonomy. In H. T. Engelhardt, Jr. & D. Callahan (Eds.), *Moral science and sociality* (pp. 156–171). Hastings-on-Hudson, NY: The Hastings Center.

FULLINWIDER, R. K. (1980). *The reverse discrimination controversy.* Totowa, NJ: Rowman & Littlefield.

GOODMAN, E. (1979). *Close to home.* New York: Simon and Schuster.

GOROVITZ, S. (1977). Bigotry, loyalty, and malnutrition. In P. G. Bown & H. Shue (Eds.), *Food policy: The responsibility of the United States in the life and death choices.* New York: Free Press.

HOUSE, E. R. (1980). *Evaluating with validity.* Beverly Hills, CA: Sage Publications.

HUDSON, W. D. (1980). *A century of moral philosophy.* New York: St. Martin's Press.

JOINT COMMITTEE ON STANDARDS FOR EDUCATIONAL EVALUATION. (1981). *Standards for evaluations of educational programs, projects and materials.* New York: McGraw-Hill.

NISBET, R. (1971). The impact of technology on ethical decision-making. In J. D. Douglas (Ed.), *The technological threat* (pp. 39–55). Englewood Cliffs, NJ: Prentice-Hall.

RAWLS, J. (1971). *A theory of justice.* Cambridge, MA: Harvard University Press.

SIDGWICH, H. (1970). Utilitarian morality. In B. A. Brody (Ed.), *Moral rules and particular circumstances* (pp. 37–63). Englewood Cliffs, NJ: Prentice-Hall.

SIEBER, J. E. (1980). Being ethical: Professional and personal decisions in program evaluation. In R. Perloff & E. Perloff (Eds.), Values, ethics, and standards [Special issue]. *New Directions for Program Evaluation 7,* 51–63.

STUFFLEBEAM, D. L. (1982, October). *An examination of the overlap between the ERS and Joint Committee standards.* Paper presented at the Annual Meeting of the Evaluation Network, Baltimore, MD.

BIBLIOGRAPHY

ARTHUR, J. (Ed.). (1981). *Morality and moral controversies.* Englewood Cliffs, NJ: Prentice-Hall.

BRODY, B. A. (Ed.). (1970). *Moral rules and particular circumstances.* Englewood Cliffs, NJ: Prentice-Hall.

BROUDY, H. S. (1972). *The real world of the public schools.* New York: Harcourt Brace Jovanovich.

BROUDY, H. S. (1981). *Truth and credibility: The citizen's dilemma.* New York: Longman.

BROUDY, H. S., ENNIS, R. H., & KRIMERMAN, L. I. (Eds.). (1973). *Philosophy of educational research.* New York: John Wiley.

DENZIN, N. K. (1970). *The research act.* Chicago: Aldine.

DOUGLAS, J. D. (Ed.). (1971). *The technological threat.* Englewood Cliffs, NJ: Prentice-Hall.

FRANKENA, W. K. (1963). *Ethics.* Englewood Cliffs, NJ: Prentice-Hall.

FRANKENA, W. K. (1980). *Thinking about morality*. Ann Arbor, MI: The University of Michigan Press.

GIDEONSE, H. D., KOFF, R., & SCHWAB, J. J. (Eds.) (1980). *Values, inquiry and education* (CSE Monograph Series in Evaluation No. 9). Los Angeles: University of California at Los Angeles.

GOODPASTER, K. E. (1976). *Perspectives on morality essays by William K. Frankena*. Notre Dame, IN: University of Notre Dame Press.

GORDON, S. (1980). *Welfare, justice and freedom*. New York: Columbia University Press.

HAMPSHIRE, S. (1978). *Public and private morality*. London: Cambridge University Press.

LIEBERMAN, A., & McLAUGHLIN, M. W. (Eds.). (1982). Policy making in education. *The eighty-first yearbook of the national society for the study of education, Part I*. Chicago: The University of Chicago Press.

PASSOW, A. H. (Ed.). (1979). The gifted and the talented: Their education and development. *The seventy-eighth yearbook of the national society for the study of education, Part I*. Chicago: The University of Chicago Press.

PERLOFF, R., & PERLOFF, E. (Eds.). (1980). Values, ethics, and standards [Special issue]. *New Directions for Program Evaluation*, 7.

RAWLS, J. (1971). *A theory of justice*. Cambridge, MA· Harvard University Press.

ROSS, D. (1970). What makes right acts right? In B. A. Brody (Ed.), *Moral rules and particular circumstances* (pp. 63–95). Englewood Cliffs, NJ: Prentice-Hall.

SCRIBNER, J. D. (Ed.). (1977). The politics of education. *Seventy-sixth yearbook of the national society for the study of education, Part II*. Chicago: The University of Chicago Press.

SOLTIS, J. F. (Ed.) (1981). Philosophy and education. *Eightieth yearbook of the national society for the study of education, Part I*. Chicago: The University of Chicago Press.

STROH, G. W. (1979). *American ethical thought*. Chicago: Nelson-Hall.

YANKELOVICH, P. (1981). *New rules*. New York: Random House.

PART V

EDITORS' COMMENTS
Knowledge Construction

Evaluation has entered a postpositivist era in which no single epistemology enjoys a consensus of support. Instead, our understanding of knowledge construction is in a state of productive debate. The articles reprinted in this section represent a summary of current thinking, and a cross-section of possible new directions for understanding knowledge construction. The section begins with an article by Phillips (1985) that summarizes the epistemological dilemmas that confronted positivism, which in turn must be confronted by any candidate for a new theory of knowledge construction. Next, Cronbach (1985) provides the wise council of an evaluator who has long been at the center of arguments about knowledge construction. Over the years, he has grown ever more skeptical of the ability of social sciences to produce scientific theories and knowledge in the manner of the physical sciences. Instead, he asks us to think of social science as more akin to architecture, music, and philosophy than to physics, chemistry, or biology. Lincoln and Guba (1986) would be sympathetic with much of Cronbach's thinking because it is consistent with the naturalistic paradigm they propose. Lincoln and Guba have described this paradigm before (1985; Guba & Lincoln, 1981) and have argued that it should be "the paradigm of choice" for social inquiry (Lincoln & Guba, 1985, p. 68). In the article reprinted in this volume, Lincoln and Guba review criteria of trustworthiness and authenticity for judging whether or not naturalistic inquiry is rigorous.

Other authors are less sure that we know which inquiry paradigm should replace logical positivism. Both Lather (1986) and Cook (1985) respond to postpositivism with different variants to the assertion that since no single paradigm can be shown to be correct, research ought to "move in many different and, indeed, contradictory directions." Lather's (1986) "research as praxis" is committed both to novel ways of knowing and to the establishment of a just social order. Cook's (1985) "critical multiplism" embraces multiplicity of theory and method in social science. But his emphasis on criticism is drawn less from the "critical theory" used by Lather than from the common sense notion that it is useful to locate and minimize sources of constant bias in the design of research. The thrust of both these authors is best captured by Lather's (1986) remark that "rather than establishing a new orthodoxy, we need to experiment, document, and share our efforts" (p. 272). This section concludes with an article by Kelly (1986) that compares several of the emerging epistemological stances in evaluation research. Her examination of Cook, Lincoln and Guba, and others reveals both differences and commonalities.

REFERENCES

Guba, E. G., & Lincoln, Y. S. (1981). *Effective evaluation: Improving the usefulness of evaluation results through responsive and naturalistic approaches.* San Francisco: Jossey-Bass.

Lincoln, Y. S., & Guba, E. G. (1985). *Naturalistic inquiry.* Newbury Park, CA: Sage.

21

On What Scientists Know, and How They Know It

D. C. Phillips

In the opening speech of Shakespeare's *King Henry the Fifth*, the issue is raised of whether the stirring and heroic events of that monarch's reign could be adequately conveyed with the meager resources of the Globe Theater:

> Can this cockpit hold
> The vasty fields of France? Or may we cram
> Within this wooden O the very casques
> That did affright the air at Agincourt?

The answer, of course, was a qualified "yes." A parallel question— hopefully with the same answer—may be raised about the present enterprise: Can a single chapter, limited with respect to the number of pages available, present an adequate account of the contemporary debates about the nature of scientific knowledge? For there can be little doubt that momentous events have taken place here as well; there have been intellectual Agincourts aplenty that have laid waste to many long-standing beliefs about the nature of science. The literature is voluminous, and there are great subtlety and depth to many of the contributions. So, at the outset of any attempt to give an overview or an interpretation of what has been happening, it is wise to follow the bard's example and to seek pardon for daring to "bring forth so great an object."

The Centrality of Science

During the last few centuries of Western intellectual history,

I thank Harris Cooper, Robert Ennis, Rob Orton, Harvey Siegel, and Lynda Stone for their comments on the penultimate draft.

Phillips, D.C. "On What Scientists Know and How They Know It," in *Learning and Teaching the Ways of Knowing*, ed. Elliot Eisner, Eighty-fourth Yearbook of the National Society for the Study of Education, Part 2 (Chicago: University of Chicago Press, 1985)

educated people typically have held an exalted view of science.[1] Together with mathematics, it has stood as the model of what a body of knowledge ought to be. In epistemological discussions in philosophy, it has been taken as an important case of "justified true belief." John Dewey wrote of science as "authorized conviction," and he said that "without initiation into the scientific spirit one is not in possession of the best tools which humanity has so far devised for effectively directed reflection."[2] Researchers in a variety of fields, ranging from history to psychology and sociology, have felt apologetic if their disciplines have fallen short of the ideals derived from physical science; they have engaged in the quest for laws and theories with vigor but without resounding success. In the field of education, curriculum theorists have often considered science to be one of the "basics," and since the time of Herbert Spencer it has been regarded as an important component of a liberal (or liberating) education. Plato, of course, thought of science as inferior to mathematics and philosophy because it dealt with the changing and hence unreal world of sense-experience, but Plato was not speaking for epistemologists of the nineteenth and twentieth centuries. The etymology of the word "science" reveals all; Jacob Bronowski writes that "we are a scientific civilization: that means, a civilization in which knowledge and its integrity are crucial. Science is only a Latin word for knowledge."[3]

During the last three decades this epistemological status of science has come into question. Not that there was a scarcity of serious questions earlier. In some ways John Dewey pointed the direction that later inquiry was to follow. For those who paid attention, he clearly raised the issue of how our various knowledge claims were warranted, and he suggested that there was no difference in principle between the warranting of scientific and other types of claims (including aesthetic and moral ones). But, for a variety of reasons, his work did not inspire more than a handful of those at the cutting edge of the philosophy of science during the 1950s and 1960s. For some, the landmark was the translation into English of Popper's *Logic of Scientific Discovery* in 1957. Here the message was clear—scientific knowledge claims can never be proven or fully justified, they can only be refuted. For others, the turning point was less sharply demarcated, and was constituted by the gradual erosion in the credibility of logical positivism—the position that seemed to be the foundation for the traditional view of the epistemology of science. Others were finally shaken by Kuhn's *The Structure of Scientific Revolutions* in 1962, or by the work of Lakatos or Feyerabend a little later. By the mid 1970s, the "rationality of science" had become a major issue, and the literature now has grown to mammoth proportions. Newton-Smith has summarized the situation well:

> The scientific community sees itself as the very paradigm of institutionalized rationality. It is taken to be in possession of something, the scientific method, which generates a "logic of justification.". . . For Feyerabend, Kuhn, and others, not only does scientific practice not live up to the image the community projects, it could not do so. For that image, it is said, embodies untenable assumptions concerning the objectivity of truth, the role of evidence and the invariance of meanings.[4]

Where do we stand today? How are scientific claims warranted? What rational grounds, if any, are there for a person to assent to the doctrines of modern science? Should workers in other disciplines strive to make them more like science? Or should people working in the sciences finally capitulate and acknowledge that, epistemologically speaking, their knowledge claims are no more secure than those put forward elsewhere?

Headway can be made with respect to these important questions by focusing on the insights that have been achieved over the past twenty years in philosophy of science. And the discussion of these insights can be grouped conveniently under the following headings: (a) Is observation in any sense foundational in science? (b) Are theories generated from, or determined by, evidence? (c) Is rational justification of knowledge claims possible? (d) Is justification necessarily relative to a framework? (e) Is there a difference in kind between natural and social science?

The Role of Observation

In the account of science given in textbooks for most of the century—an account supported to some degree by the philosophy of logical positivism—observation played a key role. There is little point in reviewing in detail the historical steps through which this "received view" decayed; it is sufficient to say that it is now widely regarded as untenable to hold that scientific theories are built up from a foundation of secure, unquestionable, objective, and theory-neutral observation.

Nor do any convincing grounds remain for believing that scientific theories, wherever they come from, can, after their production or invention, be reduced to a set of neutral "observation statements."

The two viewpoints that are rejected here are related, but they are not identical. The first view focuses upon the *production* of theories, while the second deals with the *logical status* of theories however they are produced. But taken together, the rejections of both theses have seemed to some writers to lead to a conundrum: science apparently is a body of knowledge about the sensible world, yet if observation plays no central role either in the production or in establishing the logical status of this knowledge, how can science be about the real world? In recent years there are many who have taken this slippery argument seriously; they have held that science has no objective basis whatsoever, it is merely one ideology or world view among many, but it has no special status or rationale warranting special respect. However, a good case can be made that the conundrum is overstated; it is not that observation plays no role at all, but that its role is not *foundational* in the sense (or senses) understood in earlier decades. Nor does it follow that science is ideological, or that it is a matter of whim. What, then, are the insights that have been attained about observation, and what is the new understanding of the role that can be ascribed to it?

To start with the rejection of the view that scientific theories are produced from an objective observational base, the work that immediately comes to mind here is that of N. R. Hanson. His discussion of the theory-laden nature of observation in his *Patterns of Discovery* (1958) has won the status of a classic.[5] He was not the first to say the things he did; several years earlier, in *Philosophical Investigations*, Wittgenstein even used one of the same diagrams to make the same point, and earlier still John Dewey realized that perception was not "neutral" but that knowledge and intelligence operated so as to influence it—"judgment is employed in the perception; otherwise the perception is mere sensory excitation. . . ."[6] But, for whatever reason, it was Hanson rather than these others who finally fixed the idea in contemporary consciousness.

Hanson's thesis may be stated in one sentence: "The theory, hypothesis, framework, or background knowledge held by an investigator can strongly influence what is observed." Or, in his own words, "there is more to seeing than meets the eyeball."[7] Thus, in a famous psychological experiment, slides were made from cards selected from a deck, and these were projected for very short periods onto a screen in front of various observers. The slides were all correctly identified, except for one that was a trick slide where the card was given the wrong color (for example, a black six of hearts). Most commonly the observers in the experiment saw this trick slide as a blur, or they misidentified the suit of the card. A Hansonian interpretation of this is that the observers' background knowledge (cards in the suit of hearts are red in color) influences their perception. There is some sort of interaction with the sensory data received from the slide, so that the final result is that the observers actually *see* a blur. There have been other psychological experiments in which people looking at slides of drawings saw different things depending on what particular theories they were armed with.

Until recently there has been little dispute about the truth of Hanson's thesis. Philosophers of science as diverse as Hempel, Popper, Scheffler, and Kuhn have accepted it. Recently, however, Jerry Fodor has begun to swim against the tide by arguing that indeed there are some observations, important for science, that are theory-neutral.[8] Putting this to one side, however, for some time there has been dispute about the *significance* of the thesis. A passage from Kuhn nicely expresses this; he is discussing several scientists who were looking at the same phenomenon but from the perspective of different background theories, and the Hansonian issue arises as to whether they therefore were seeing different things:

Do we, however, really need to describe what separates Galileo from Aristotle, or Lavoisier from Priestley, as a transformation of vision? Did these men really *see* different things when *looking at* the same sorts of objects? . . . Those questions can no longer be postponed.[9]

One thing does seem clear: Hanson's thesis successfully undermines crude forms of empiricism and positivism, that is, those philosophical positions that suggest knowledge is built up from a neutral or objective observational base. For, according to Hanson, there is no such theory-neutral base. There has been no lack of writers, inspired by Hanson, who are willing to spell all this out. Thus, the neo-Marxist philosopher of education Kevin Harris, in his *Education and Knowledge* (1979), assumes all empiricists are crude, and he writes:

The empiricist observes, collects, and infers. He goes out into the world and collects his data or his facts diligently, he puts them together and analyzes them, and then he draws out relations between them.[10]

It is, then, an easy matter for Harris to show (correctly) that "most of the problems with this approach come in the first step," for the observation and collection of "facts" are of course theory-laden.

At this point the discussion needs to turn, to focus upon the second role ascribed to observation. For what is overlooked by Harris, and by others who also wish to destroy the credibility of empiricism in a similar way, is that modern forms of empiricism do not talk of the *origins* of knowledge but of its *validation* or *justification*.[11] This is an entirely different matter, where the theory-ladenness of observation presents no problem. Indeed, it can be argued that here Hanson is a blessing; for in order to test or validate a theory one *must* use that theory's "way of seeing the world." For instance, when examining Freudian theory to see if it is warranted, one must use Freud's categories to deduce tests—it is illicit to use Skinnerian categories (except, of course, for a test of Skinner, or for a comparative test of the two theories, but in this latter case one would still have to use Freud as well). Neither does it follow from the truth of Hanson's thesis (if, indeed, it is true) that the very possibility has disappeared of running objective tests of a scientific theory. For no reason has been offered to support the view that because a theory is being worked with, and because, therefore, the observer will be influenced to see the world via the categories contained in the theory, then the world is thereby bound to *confirm* that theory. Israel Scheffler has put the point clearly:

What is the upshot? There is no evidence for a general incapacity to learn from contrary observations, no proof of a preestablished harmony between what we believe and what we see. . . . Our categorizations and expectations guide by orienting us selectively toward the future; they set us, in particular, to perceive in certain ways and not in others. Yet they do not blind us to the unforeseen. They allow us to recognize what fails to match anticipation.[12]

There is a crucial difference between the thesis advanced here about the role of observation in testing, and a notorious view (referred to earlier) that was held by some of the logical positivists of past decades concerning "observation sentences" or "protocol sentences" (such as "red here now"). In holding that observation can still play an important role in the testing or justification of scientific knowledge claims, despite its theory-laden nature, it is not being held that scientific theories can be reduced to—that is, translated into—statements fully in observational terms. Indeed, a multitude of critics of logical positivism have driven home the point that the theoretical concepts of science have meanings that transcend definition in observational terms. Thus there are few today who would endorse the quest of yesteryear of Rudolf Carnap, who stated the theme of his first major book as follows: "The main problem concerns the possibility of the rational reconstruction of the concepts of all fields of knowledge on the basis of concepts that refer to the immediately given" (immediately given, that is, in experience such as observation).[13] Nor would many now endorse the program of P. W. Bridgman and the operationists, a program that had at its heart the belief that the meaning of any scientific construct or variable is given by the specification of the "activities or operations" necessary to measure it.[14]

But here another conundrum arises. On one hand it has just been argued that theory-laden observation can be efficacious in testing a scientist's knowledge claims. On the other hand, if these claims cannot be translated fully into observational terms, then it would seem to follow that any test that was conducted would not be absolutely authoritative. A theory that does not necessitate a precise set of observational consequences can never be decisively probed by any test, for there must always be some leeway or looseness that could allow the scientist to argue that the theory somehow was compatible with the test results (whatever they were). How, then, can it be argued that observation plays any worthwhile role in testing?

In effect, this query is a narrower version of a larger general question: In what ways are scientific theories related to evidence? It is to this that the discussion must turn.

Theory and Evidence

In the past few decades a whole host of problems concerning the relation between scientific theories and evidence have come to light. The overall effect of these has been to cement in place the view that theories are *underdetermined* by evidence. That is, whatever evidence is available, a variety of theories can exist that are compatible with it. Furthermore, as new evidence accumulates, there is a variety of ways in which every one of these competing theories could be adjusted in order to take account of the new material. No *specific* change in any theory is necessitated by new evidence; all that new evidence necessitates is that some accommodation be made somewhere. In the light of all this, there is little wonder that the rationality of science has become a topic of importance—what grounds are there for believing that any scientific theory is warranted, when the available evidence can also be used to support a host of rival theories? While this problem is a serious one, it will be argued that there are no grounds for despair.[15]

Because the developments that have led in this direction are numerous, and because they tend to overlap and partially reinforce each other, it is difficult to organize a clear discussion. The simplest procedure is to enumerate the points:

1. It has been recognized, at least since the time of David Hume in the eighteenth century, that there is a problem with the inductive support of scientific theories. A finite amount of evidence, for example, that all swans that have so far been observed are white does not, in logic, establish the claim that *all* swans are white. This is an inductive inference, and by definition the conclusion goes beyond the evidence provided—a finite number of observations on swans does not firmly establish anything about all swans. And although at first sight it seems reasonable to claim that the finite evidence makes the inductive inference probable, it is not clear how to calculate the precise degree of probability, nor is it clear that this does not beg the whole question. For the heart of the problem of induction lies in whether we have sound reason to believe that evidence about the past can throw any light at all on the future. (It would help if we could establish that nature was regular; but of course this principle itself would be a product of induction, so there is no succor here.) This "problem of induction" has been seen as a blot on the escutcheon of science (and of philosophy) for over two centuries.

2. With the questioning of the tenets of logical positivism over the past few decades,[16] it has been generally recognized, as discussed earlier, that the theoretical terms of science cannot have their meanings rigidly defined in observational or operational terms. Instead, theoretical terms gain their meaning from the network of relationships that tie them in with other terms in a theory. A scientific theory is a whole, it is an entity made up of interconnected parts, and as a whole it is

testable. Data can be fed in, providing that the net as a whole has some link with the observable or measurable realm—it was a mistake to believe that every individual theoretical term had to be so definable. Indeed, the image of a theory as net has gained great currency; even the partly reformed positivist Carl Hempel expressed it well:

A scientific theory might therefore be likened to a complex spatial network: its terms are represented by the knots, while the threads connecting the latter correspond, in part, to the definitions and, in part, to the fundamental and derivative hypotheses included in the theory. The whole system floats, as it were, above the plane of observation and is anchored to it by rules of interpretation. These might be viewed as strings which are not part of the network but link certain points of the latter with specific places in the plane of observation.[17]

Now, the network analogy leads directly to the so-called Duhem-Quine thesis: evidence does not impinge on any particular individual item or theoretical element in science, it impinges on the whole net.[18] According to Duhem and Quine, it is the theory as a whole, as a single complex entity, that interfaces with evidence. The theoretical elements are not isolable, they always travel with the other items in the net. And so it is as an interrelated whole that they face up to the test of experience. Consequently, if a piece of recalcitrant evidence emerges, it can be accommodated by any of a variety of changes or modifications to various parts of the network; one scientist may want to change one part of the theoretical net, while another may advocate that changes be made elsewhere—it is always possible, by making sufficient changes in other parts, to preserve a favored portion of the net that might, at first, seem to have been thrown into question by the new evidence. Of course, the ease with which various parts of the network can be preserved may vary; in order to save one favored portion, quite severe changes may have to be made elsewhere—the tradeoffs involved might be quite difficult ones to make. But the point is that theoretical changes and developments in science are not *necessitated* by the evidence; scientists are free to use their judgment and their creativity. (The point being made here parallels the one made earlier during the discussion of the underdetermination of theories.) It would be a mistake to interpret this as indicating that scientific theories are a matter of mere whim or individual taste; to stress that individual judgment is required is not to throw away all standards, it is just to stress that decisions cannot be made in any mechanical way. However, contemporary philosophers of science generally recognize that not all "nonmechanical" decisions are equally sound, and one of the current unresolved issues is the precise delineation of the rational constraints that operate on scientific judgment.[19]

3. A number of issues have arisen which together make a similar point about testing. There is no mechanical procedure by which a given portion of a theoretical network in science can be put to decisive test. A scientist can use a theory, or part of a theory, to deduce a prediction that if X is done, then Y should result. But if this test is carried out, and Y does not result, there are many ways the new evidence can be accommodated; similarly, if Y does result, then there are various ways in which this can be accounted for. Again, a challenge for professional judgment.

For one thing, in striking contrast to older views of "scientific method," it is now accepted that it is legitimate to "save" or "repair" a theory that appears to have failed a test by introducing an *ad hoc* hypothesis. The "new" philosophers of science, led by Lakatos and Feyerabend, have provided many detailed historical case studies which give a quite realistic picture of how science has actually been carried out by successful scientists; and it is clear from this work that the use of *ad hoc* hypotheses is not uncommon and, furthermore, that often it has turned out to be fruitful. Feyerabend made the point strongly:

The idea of a method that contains firm, unchanging, and absolutely binding principles for conducting the business of science gets into considerable difficulty when confronted with the results of historical research. We find, then, that there is not a single rule, however plausible, and however firmly grounded in epistemology, that is not violated at some time or other. It becomes evident that such violations are not accidental events. . . . On the contrary, we see they are necessary for progress. . . . More specifically, the following can be shown: considering any rule, however "fundamental," there are always circumstances when it is advisable not only to ignore the rule, but to adopt its opposite.[20]

Most philosophers of science regard Feyerabend's "anarchistic" position as too strong; and again an unresolved issue is the nature of the restraints on the use of *ad hoc* hypotheses.

Another insight concerns the use of "auxiliary" premises in the making of scientific predictions. The point here is that no test consequences follow from an isolated theory; in order to put a theory to a test some chain of reasoning has to be followed, and data and information from other branches of science—as well as from common sense, mathematics, and so forth—have to be used. (Typically measurements are made, using instruments that were designed on the basis of a host of other theories; and calculations are performed, using formulae drawn from many areas of science and mathematics.) Hempel has a striking example:[21] Semmelweis, the nineteenth-century physician who realized (before the development of the germ theory of disease) that "childbed fever" was a type of blood poisoning, deduced that if the physicians in his hospital washed their hands before attending to patients giving birth, then the patients would not get infected. He chose to use chlorinated lime as the cleansing fluid. And his test was successful—incidence of the usually fatal fever dropped dramatically. It is clear here that as well as the theory under test (that fever was caused by infection of the bloodstream of the patients), Semmelweis was making other (auxiliary) assumptions—that washing the hands of doctors would be efficacious, that chlorinated lime would do the job, and so forth. If the test had failed, if the patients still became infected, he might have rejected his theory as being incorrect when in fact it may have been one of the auxiliaries that was to blame (for example, the chlorinated lime might have been too weak). So, to generalize the point, if a test is failed it is a matter of judgment whether to blame the theory or to "pass the buck" to one of the everpresent auxiliary assumptions.

Another problem arises if the test has positive results. For as a point of logic, the positive result does not give unequivocal support to the theory or hypothesis under test; the form of inference involved is "affirming the consequent," which is fallacious.[22] If from some theory T it is deduced that some consequence C will follow under certain conditions, and if the test is carried out and C is found to occur, it cannot be concluded that therefore T is true:

$$\frac{\text{If } T \text{ then } C}{\text{Therefore } T}$$

388   **KNOWLEDGE CONSTRUCTION**

Which is not valid. (Consider "If it is raining then it is cloudy; it is cloudy; therefore it is raining.")[23]

Karl Popper concluded, after reflecting on these matters, that although a scientific theory or hypothesis cannot be proven, it *can* be decisively refuted—one negative result can show that a theory is untenable. The logical form involved here would be "modus tollens," which is valid:

$$\text{If } T \text{ then } C$$
$$\text{Not } C$$

$$\text{Therefore, not } T$$

Thus, "If it is raining then it is cloudy; it is not cloudy; therefore it is not raining," which is logically unassailable. This Popperian "naive falsificationism," however, will not do as an account of the logic of scientific testing. (Popper has denied that he is "naive" in this sense.) For once it is recognized that, in carrying out the test, the scientist has made use of auxiliary premises or assumptions, then the negative test results can always be evaded by ascribing the blame onto one of these, or even by introducing some new *ad hoc* assumption. Schematically:

$$\text{If } T \text{ (and given auxiliary } A \text{ etc.), then } C$$
$$\text{Not } C$$

$$\text{Therefore, either not } T \text{ or not } A \text{ (etc.)}$$

Which again is perfectly valid. So, sadly, a scientific hypothesis or theory can neither be disproven, nor proven, by means of tests!

A final group of problems concerning testing has given substance to the suggestion that it cannot be judged, in isolation from the corpus of scientific theory as a whole, whether or not a piece of evidence offers support for a particular theory or hypothesis. It is not necessary to pursue at great length Hempel's "raven paradox" or Goodman's "grue and bleen paradox";[24] suffice it to state that because scientific theories are underdetermined by evidence, any single piece of evidence—any observation—may in principle support a range of theoretical statements, no matter how fanciful. (Goodman's example shows that the observation that emeralds are green may also be taken to support another theory that they are "grue," that is, green up to a certain date and blue after that!) In order to judge what the evidence can most reasonably be interpreted as supporting, it seems as if other theories must be drawn upon. (For instance, in Goodman's example, there are theories about the chemical constituents of emeralds, and theories about how the color is caused by these constituents, and it is these other theories that make the grue hypothesis unlikely—greenness is too well "embedded" a concept to be bypassed so frivolously.) But again, it is all a matter of judgment, and there is no routine or mechanical procedure a scientist can follow to link his or her evidence to the theories that are under investigation.

Rational Justification

Each of the points discussed above highlights, in its own way, the same fundamental issue: in what sense is the knowledge embodied in the sciences rationally justified or warranted? For scientific knowledge is not based, in any logically compelling sense, on observation; neither do tests absolutely confirm nor absolutely refute it. It seems that, on the basis of any body of evidence, a host of rival theories could be advanced, and the accumulation of further evidence does not compellingly disqualify any of these.

At first this situation seems shocking, but calm reflection puts the matter in a different light. It has long been realized that scientific knowledge is fallible; scientists seek the truth and often think they have found it, but when pushed they usually concede that one day they may be shown to be wrong—the tide of opinion, and of evidence, may turn against them. Thus, Newtonian physics prevailed for several centuries, but eventually it succumbed to Einstein;[25] in its turn, Einsteinian physics has started to develop flaws that some believe signal its imminent overthrow. Science moves, as the title of one of Popper's books so elegantly puts it, by "conjectures and refutations," with the caveat that refutations, as well as conjectures, are only tentative. Contemporary philosophy of science merely shows some of the logical and epistemological reasons why this must always be so.

But there is a point of deeper significance, a point which shows why philosophy of science has been a central area in philosophy in recent decades. The developments in philosophy of science that have been outlined have led to the abandonment (in many quarters) of justificationist or foundationalist epistemologies. These epistemologies—and all traditional schools of thought fit under these headings—worked on the supposition that we accept items of knowledge because they are soundly based. Thus, empiricists claimed that knowledge claims were soundly based if they were based on experience, while rationalists claimed that knowledge was soundly based when supported by the "light of reason." Knowledge, in other words, was identified with authority, either the authority of experience or that of reason.

The new epistemologies are nonjustificationist or nonfoundationalist in character, although the term "nonjustificationist" is somewhat misleading. People who adhere to this position still seek justified belief; the point is that they no longer hold that beliefs can be *absolutely* justified in the sense of being proven or being based upon unquestionable foundations. Walter Weimer has expressed it well:

Knowledge claims must be defended, to be sure; however the defense of such a claim is not an attempt to prove it, but rather the marshalling of "good reasons" in its behalf. . . . The only way to defend fallible knowledge claims is by marshalling other fallible knowledge claims—such as the best contingent theories that we possess. There are no "ultimate" sources of knowledge or epistemological authorities.[26]

There is a metaphor that has been used by philosophers of science and by scientists for half a century that nicely captures this. The scientist is like an explorer crossing a wide expanse of water on a rotting ship. The worst plank is chosen and replaced by a little lumber found in the hold, but during the process the explorer has to place full weight on the other and hopefully less rotten planks; after one plank is replaced, it can bear the weight while another board is thrown away and replaced, but all the while the new planks are themselves rotting! An exciting situation; no wonder scientists have been regarded as paragons of intellectual virtue.

A further point can be illustrated using this metaphor. The rationality of the scientist's endeavors cannot be judged by examining what is happening at any instant (tearing out a plank in mid-ocean is not always a good idea); rather, what happens over time has to be considered (whether or not the ship is progressively made more seaworthy). Stephen Toulmin has endorsed the view that a person's rationality is displayed in how his or her beliefs change in the face of new evidence or experience.[27] Imre Lakatos also developed his "methodology of scientific research programs" to deal with this sort of situation; he stressed that there is no "instant rationality."[28] A scientist is free to make the best adjustments to a theory that he or she can—by abandoning an auxiliary assumption, by adding an *ad hoc* ingredient, or even by just ignoring temporarily the embarrassing evidence. The crucial thing is whether such changes make the theory or research program more progressive, in the sense that it is now able to predict and explain phenomena that previously it could not deal with. Lakatos wrote:

> . . . the idea of instant rationality can be seen to be utopian. But this utopian idea is the hallmark of most brands of epistemology. Justificationists wanted scientific theories to be proved even before they were published; probabilists hoped a machine could flash up instantly the value (degree of confirmation) of a theory, given the evidence; naive falsificationists hoped that elimination at least was the instant result of the verdict of *experiment*. I hope I have shown that *all these theories of instant rationality—and instant learning—fail*. . . . Rationality works much slower than most people tend to think, and, even then, fallibly.[29]

Unfortunately, rotting planks are not the only hazard facing the ship of science. The shoal of relativism will have to be traversed during the next stage of the journey.

Relativism and "Good Reasons"

The position that was advanced in the previous section seems reasonable: a scientist defends a knowledge claim by making the best case that is possible—by marshalling good arguments, relevant observations, solid experimental results, and so forth. And, where necessary, the scientist makes adjustments to the "web of science" (or to the "scientific research program") in the way that seems most appropriate and fruitful. But by what criteria are these things to be judged? On what grounds can it be decided that indeed the arguments are cogent, that the evidence is relevant, and that the results are solid? For we have seen that the case can be made that these things are not clear-cut—they are matters of professional judgment, and there can be disagreements. And it is here that the work of Thomas S. Kuhn becomes especially relevant.

Kuhn's book, *The Structure of Scientific Revolutions*, has meant many different things to many different people, but undoubtedly one of its chief "messages" has been the importance of the framework or paradigm in the context of which the scientist's work takes place. Even most of those who regard Kuhn's work as flawed, and who see his notion of "scientific paradigms" as being so vague as to be almost worthless, are forced to acknowledge that scientists do work within the context of sets of theories and assumptions that play an important role in shaping the direction and form that their work takes. Thus, a Freudian psychologist will work with the concepts and methods of that theoretical framework, and will tackle problems that appear to be important from that perspective. And the radical behaviorist will work within a different framework. Kuhn, of course, goes further than this, and he argues that rival paradigms are incommensurable—scientists in each will not be able to engage in rational dialogue across the boundary, for their concepts are different, their problems are different, and even the rules and criteria by which they make judgments are different. Scientists in different paradigms, according to Kuhn, live and work "in different worlds."[30]

Whether or not one goes the whole distance with Kuhn, there seems to be a problem here concerning the rational or at least the objective status of scientific knowledge. For if the pursuit of science involves the assessing of "best arguments," and if the scientist's criteria are greatly influenced by the framework in which he or she is housed, then it cannot be argued that the arguments advanced by a scientist from one frame are better (or "truer") than those put forward by someone from a different frame, for there are no framework-independent criteria (that is, no "absolute" or "external" criteria) by which to decide between the two cases. Once again, the claim of science to have solid knowledge seems to be overstated. The best that can be claimed, it appears, is that *relative to a given framework or paradigm*, a particular argument or a particular knowledge claim is well warranted. The argument has, indeed, led to the ship running aground on relativistic shores.[31]

Fortunately the whole train of argument is dubious, although a great deal of ink has been spilled over it in the past two decades. The crucial issue is whether Kuhn's incommensurability thesis is accepted; for if so—if two paradigms or frameworks are so disparate that rational discussion (and particularly the giving and receiving of sharp and cogent criticism) is impossible—then the relativistic conclusion is bound to be reached. If the thesis is rejected, and as will be indicated shortly there are good reasons to believe that it should be, then although it still has to be acknowledged that scientists work within frameworks it no longer follows that they cannot engage in rational discourse with each other. And if rational discourse is possible, then in principle there is no insurmountable obstacle to the making of defensible interparadigmatic judgments about which knowledge claims are the best-supported ones. There still is no mechanical procedure available for doing this, of course, but rationality has never been appropriately conceived as a mechanical process.

There have been many lines of attack on Kuhn's incommensurability thesis.[32] Scheffler has argued that because two scientists differ in the paradigms to which they adhere (and because, therefore, they differ with respect to their "first order" concepts and criteria and so on), it does not follow that they disagree at higher or deeper levels of abstraction (the "second order" level) about the basic criteria that are to be used in judging the merits of scientific work. There is, according to this view, no breakdown in communication at the really fundamental levels.[33] Toulmin has stressed that although two paradigms may differ with respect to many important items (witness Newtonian and Einsteinian physics), there will be many items that they possess in common (both Einstein and Newton accepted much of the corpus of physics, and of mathematics and logic). These common ingredients ensure that the paradigms overlap, rather than being incommensurable, and the channel for communication is left open.[34] Still other writers have attacked the theory of meaning that lies at the heart of much thinking about incommensurability and relativism—the theory, sometimes called semantic holism, that if a term (for example, energy) is embedded in several different theories or paradigms, then its meaning in all of these cases will be quite different because meaning is determined by the whole "web" in which the term is located. (It is interesting to note that this theory of meaning is one that has come down from the positivists and their view of scientific theories as networks; many contemporary relativists who accept this theory are fond of saying that there was nothing they admired about the positivists.)[35] Much of Newton-Smith's book, *The Rationality of Science*, to mention only one recent source, is devoted to a discussion of this theory of meaning, which he calls "radical meaning variance."

He points, *inter alia*, to a consequence of the theory that has been widely recognized: rival paradigms cannot be incompatible if the meanings of their terms are different. In other words, if paradigms are incommensurable, a person is free to accept every one of them.

The meaning of a theoretical term was said to be determined by the entire set of sentences within the theory containing the term. Consequently any change in the postulates containing a given theoretical term was claimed to bring a change in the meaning of that term. Thus, if Einstein and Newton discourse about mass, force and all that, they fail to disagree. They are simply equivocating. On this account of the matter the assertion by the Newtonian "Mass is invariant" and the assertion by the Einsteinian "Mass is not invariant" are not logically incompatible, as the meaning of "mass" is not constant across the theories.[36]

This leads directly to another important point about relativism. In practice no one can consistently lead a life in strict adherence to the relativist position, for it is self-defeating. Relativists hold that their viewpoint is true, that is, true for everyone, and not just for them. And no relativistic professor would accept the argument from a student who had turned in an incorrect or faulty piece of work that "it is only faulty or incorrect for you, Professor, but for me, from my perspective, it is sound." It is apparent that the making of corrections, and the detection of error, disappear as options for the consistent relativist. Certainly there are few scientists who would be prepared to be so charitable to their rivals as to forego the right to offer criticisms in the course of day-to-day professional activity. On the contrary, on all sides in science there is commitment to truth as a *regulative ideal* (as Popper and others have termed it); scientists try to determine the truth and to hold true beliefs—their disputes are about whose views *are* true, or are *best regarded* as being true. Toulmin sums up a recent brief discussion of some of these issues pertaining to relativism with the words "It is hard to see how Kuhn can ultimately hold his critics at bay." [37]

Insights into Social Science

The points that have been made thus far pertain to the epistemology of science in general. Indeed, they may well apply to all forms of knowledge—that is, to all forms of belief that are justified or warranted by appeal to some kind of evidence (although, of course, to the nonjustificationist or nonfoundationalist there is no favored *kind* of evidence). It is to be supposed that the points also apply to the social sciences, and not just to the physical sciences that customarily provide the examples that philosophers are wont to ponder over. The social sciences, of course, have less remarkable achievements to point to than the physical sciences, and it is sometimes stated that developmentally they are on a par with physics just before the time of Newton and Boyle. Nevertheless, it can be said, epistemologically they are rather similar—the relationship between the evidence that is appealed to, and the knowledge claims that are made, is the same.

There is, however, one vital difference between these two areas of science. In physics, typically what is being studied is the behavior of some entity or system that is not sentient; a satisfactory explanation points to the causes that influence the behavior under investigation, and the resulting physical knowledge is codified in the form of laws and theories. In the social sciences the situation is different; humans are sentient—they act for reasons and motives, they react not to the features of their environments but to their interpretations or under-standings of these features. While this viewpoint has never won dominance among social scientists in the United States, it has been fairly commonplace among philosophers and philosophically oriented social scientists on the Continent. Thus, late last century Wilhelm Dilthey wrote:

We explain nature, but we understand mental life. . . . This means that the methods of studying mental life, history and society differ greatly from those used to acquire knowledge of nature.[38]

Later, Wittgenstein drew a distinction between behavior and action (roughly, human action is bodily movement or behavior "plus" some ingredient such as meaning). In recent times the philosopher Michael Simon has claimed that action is an "irreducible category";[39] and Macdonald and Pettit, echoing the sentiments of Peter Winch in his famous *The Idea of a Social Science*, have written (in a passage where they unfortunately use "human behavior" to refer to what others have called "human action"):

Social science, insofar as its concern is the explanation of human behavior, begins to look like a discipline which belongs with the humanities rather than the sciences. Social history, social anthropology, and social psychology, are attempts to do with art what is done crassly by common sense.[40]

It is not appropriate to pursue the details of this work, or the way in which philosophical "theory of action" has developed over the last few decades. Suffice it to say that a moral can be drawn that is similar to the one that was drawn at several places in the earlier discussion: pursuing an understanding of our fellow humans, like pursuing understanding of the physical universe, involves the making of reasoned judgments by researchers—there is no mechanical method or process by which such understanding can be generated, nor any mechanical process by which conclusions can be substantiated. There may well be constraints determining the range of reasoned judgments that are entertained, but this issue lies unresolved.

Conclusion, and Some Final Remarks on Education

The psychologist, educationist, and philosopher Donald Campbell has written a passage that captures well the themes that have been covered in the present essay:

Nonlaboratory social science is precariously scientific at best. But even for the strongest sciences, the theories believed to be true are radically underjustified and have, at most, the status of "better than" rather than the status of "proven." All commonsense and scientific knowledge is presumptive. In any setting in which we seem to gain new knowledge, we do so at the expense of many presumptions. . . . Single presumptions or small subsets can in turn be probed, but the total set of presumptions is not of demonstrable validity, is radically underjustified. Such are the pessimistic conclusions of the most modern developments in the philosophy of science.[41]

All of which is true, and in the face of which some have lost heart. But Campbell has not lost his nerve, nor lapsed into despair or apathy or succumbed into the mire of relativism. And neither should the rest of us. To use Dewey's expression, who can doubt the importance of seeking "authorized conviction," even if the quest is less straight-forward than it might have appeared in the heyday of positivism?

However, while the scientist need not lose heart, what about the science educator? If it is difficult, although possible, for the trained scientist to come to grips with the new epistemology—to learn that establishing a claim is a matter of building a strong case by making the best professional judgments one can—will it even be *possible* for the science student? Experience throughout the century has shown how nearly impossible it has been to teach the scientific method (whatever it was conceived to be), and to teach a deep understanding of science, to the general student. The post-Sputnik science curricula of the 1960s ran into trouble on this score, despite the many innovative exercises and examples that were woven into their materials. Earlier still, Dewey recognized the problem, but he also exposed the deficiencies in sticking to the easier path of just teaching the "facts of science" as they appear at the moment. There was little merit, he argued, in having students "copy at long range and secondhand the results which scientific men have reached"; this way students merely "learn a 'science' instead of learning the scientific way of treating the familiar material of ordinary experience." He poked gentle fun at the mindlessness of traditional science teaching: "There is sometimes a ritual of laboratory instruction as well as of heathen religion." [42] Of course, the new epistemology would have the scientist, at whatever level of expertise, avoid ritual and engage instead in *thinking*. Again, Dewey summarized it with words that have weathered the years well:

The method of science engrained through education in habit means emancipation from rule of thumb and from the routine generated by rule of thumb procedure. . . . It means reason operates within experience, not beyond it, to give it an intelligent or reasonable quality. Science . . . changes the idea and the operation of reason. [43]

For Dewey, an epistemology had become an educational method. We could do worse than follow his lead.

FOOTNOTES

1. This is not to deny that there has been a degree of social schizophrenia about science—after all, the deranged scientist has been a common cultural symbol. But few if any epistemologies have been based on this model.

2. John Dewey, *Democracy and Education* (New York: Free Press, 1966), p. 189.

3. Jacob Bronowski, *The Ascent of Man* (Boston: Little, Brown, and Co., 1973), p. 437.

4. W. H. Newton-Smith, *The Rationality of Science* (Boston and London: Routledge and Kegan Paul, 1981), pp. 1-2.

5. Norwood R. Hanson, *Patterns of Discovery* (Cambridge, England: Cambridge University Press, 1958).

6. Dewey, *Democracy and Education*, p. 143.

7. Hanson, *Patterns of Discovery*, p. 7.

8. Jerry Fodor, "Observation Reconsidered," *Philosophy of Science* 51, no. 1 (March 1984): 23-43.

9. Thomas S. Kuhn, *The Structure of Scientific Revolutions* (Chicago: University of Chicago Press, 1962), p. 119.

10. Kevin Harris, *Education and Knowledge* (London: Routledge and Kegan Paul, 1979), p. 5.

11. A variety of perspectives on modern empiricism is presented in Harold Morick, ed., *Challenges to Empiricism* (Indianapolis: Hackett Publishing, 1980).

12. Israel Scheffler, *Science and Subjectivity* (New York: Bobbs-Merrill, 1967), p. 44.

13. Rudolf Carnap, *The Logical Structure of the World* (Berkeley: University of California Press, 1969), Preface, p. v. This book was first published in 1928; Carnap later softened his views.

14. Percy W. Bridgman, *The Logic of Modern Physics* (New York: Macmillan, 1927), p. 34.

15. For discussion of some issues, and a suggested solution to the problems, see Clark N. Glymour, *Theory and Evidence* (Princeton, N.J.: Princeton University Press, 1980).

16. For a discussion of the strengths and weaknesses of positivism as an approach to science, see Denis C. Phillips, "After the Wake: Postpositivistic Educational Thought," *Educational Researcher* 12 (May 1983): 4-12.

17. Carl Hempel, *Fundamentals of Concept Formation in Empirical Science* (Chicago: University of Chicago Press, 1952), p. 36.

18. So named for the turn-of-the-century continental physicist-philosopher Pierre Duhem and the contemporary Harvard philosopher W. V. O. Quine, who both developed forms of this thesis.

19. For example, see Harvey Siegel, "Brown on Epistemology and the New Philosophy of Science," *Synthese* 56(1983): 61-89.

20. Paul Feyerabend, "Against Method," in *Analyses of Theories and Methods of Physics and Psychology*, ed. Michael Radner and Stephen Winokur, Minnesota Studies in the Philosophy of Science, vol. IV (Minneapolis: University of Minnesota Press, 1970), pp. 21-22.

21. Carl Hempel, *Philosophy of Natural Science* (Englewood Cliffs, N.J.: Prentice-Hall, 1966), chaps. 2, 3.

22. But see Glymour, *Theory and Evidence*, where he offers a "bootstrapping" theory of how evidence can be used to confirm a theory.

23. Jum Nunnally has a nice psychometrically oriented example involving a hypothetical theory relating anxiety and stress. See his *Psychometric Theory*, 2d ed. (New York: McGraw-Hill, 1978), p. 104.

24. A readable discussion of both of these can be found in Karel Lambert and Gordon Brittan, *An Introduction to the Philosophy of Science* (Englewood Cliffs, N.J.: Prentice-Hall, 1970), chap. 4.

25. Of course, Newtonian physics lives on as a very useful approximation, and the same fate may befall Einstein's work; "overthrow" in science does not always mean complete abandonment.

26. Walter B. Weimer, *Notes on the Methodology of Scientific Research* (Hillsdale, N.J.: Lawrence Erlbaum Associates, 1979), p. 41.

27. See the opening quotation in Stephen Toulmin, *Human Understanding* (Princeton, N.J.: Princeton University Press, 1972).

28. For discussion of Lakatos, and applications to education, see Denis C. Phillips, "Post-Kuhnian Reflections on Educational Research," in *Philosophy and Education*, ed. Jonas Soltis, Eightieth Yearbook of the National Society for the Study of Education, Part 1 (Chicago: University of Chicago Press, 1981).

29. Imre Lakatos and Alan Musgrave, eds., *Criticism and the Growth of Knowledge* (Cambridge, England: Cambridge University Press, 1972), p. 174.

30. Kuhn, *The Structure of Scientific Revolutions*, chap. 10. For further discussion of the issues raised here, see Denis C. Phillips, "Post-Kuhnian Reflections on Educational Research," and the papers in Lakatos and Musgrave, *Criticism and the Growth of Knowledge*.

31. Maurice Mandelbaum distinguishes three types of relativism in his Subjective, Objective, and Conceptual Relativisms," *The Monist* 62 (October 1979): 403-28.

32. For a good overall view, see Harvey Siegel, "Objectivity, Rationality, Incommensurability, and More," *British Journal for the Philosophy of Science* 31 (December 1980): 359-75.

33. Scheffler, *Science and Subjectivity*, pp. 81-83.

34. Toulmin, *Human Understanding*, pp. 123-24.

35. For examples of the mistakes made by critics of positivism, see Phillips, "After the Wake," and the reply by Elliot Eisner in the same issue of *Educational Researcher*.

36. Newton-Smith, *The Rationality of Science*, p. 11.

37. Stephen Toulmin, "From Form to Function: Philosophy and History of Science in the 1950s and Now," *Daedalus* 106 (Summer 1977): 156.

38. Wilhelm Dilthey, in *Dilthey: Selected Writings*, ed. Hans P. Rickman (Cambridge, England: Cambridge University Press, 1976), p. 89.

39. Michael A. Simon, *Understanding Human Action* (Albany, N.Y.: State University of New York Press, 1982).

40. Graham Macdonald and Philip Pettit, *Semantics and Social Science* (London: Routledge and Kegan Paul, 1981), p. 104.

41. Donald T. Campbell, "Qualitative Knowing and Action Research," in *The Social Contexts of Method*, ed. Michael Brenner, Peter Marsh, and Marylin Brenner (New York: St. Martin's Press, 1978), p. 185.

42. Dewey, *Democracy and Education*, pp. 220-22.

43. Ibid., p. 225.

22

Social Inquiry by and for Earthlings

Lee J. Cronbach

Philosophers' "rational reconstruction" has created a legend of science as a transcendental activity, one that could best be conducted by sending teams of observers to hover over Earth.[1] Standing highest on the scale of being, said Kant, are "the most sublime classes of rational creatures, which inhabit Jupiter and Saturn" (see Toulmin & Goodfield 1965, 99); there, if anywhere, must the idealized scientist dwell. Saturn's inhabitants are not bent on exploiting Earth's resources, nor is their quest primarily for knowledge useful on Saturn. Hermann Hesse caught their spirit in his Bead Game: Ingenuity is testimony to one's own excellence and, like other art forms, an expression of reverence.

Because observations unordered cannot be an object of contemplation, an integrative story is the most valued product of science. Saturnians cherish retellings that capture most of what observers have reported and that can make sense of (or, better, foretell) observations yet to be made. The stories that have commanded greatest respect have always been incomplete, some of them have been contradicted by new observations, and there is always the possibility that some genius will rearrange a collage of peephole visions into a graceful gestalt. Saturnians therefore do not expect the Bead Game to end at some moment when clarion certainty is proclaimed.

But Beadmasters do have faith that the universe will yield its secrets to scientific method, as the bandits' cave was attuned to "Open Sesame!" Beings from Jupiter as well as Saturn might begin to play the Bead Game. Learning from the responses and rebuffs of Nature, these new players would become better and better at the game. If Jupiter's Beadmasters should happen to make Earth the object of inquiry, say the Saturnians, then their evolving model and the Saturnian model must come closer and closer to agreement.

Two atoms of hydrogen combine with one of oxygen. Attraction is inversely proportional to the square of distance. A Beadmaster believes that such statements would be supported if a time machine enabled us to observe the world of a million years ago or of a million years hence. That is why investigators from Jupiter, in another eon, can be expected to converge on Saturnian chemistry and celestial mechanics. For Saturnians, then, time has a boundless horizon. A line of inquiry started in one generation can be advanced endlessly. The cost of studying events that are rare or buried in noise can be spread over millennia by the patient Saturnian community.

Saturnians, with their timeless perspective, do not discount the future; a similar patience among earthly students of society would be irresponsible. Faith that solid theories will evolve in some future century, from whatever we now report, is insufficient to justify large investments in the many social science disciplines. Resources for social inquiry are necessarily limited, hence policies for deploying them are required. What should members of our disciplines be trying to accomplish, if the Saturnian ideal is not the appropriate one? The community needs and will continue to need richer ideas about ability, aging, aggression, attitudes, and all other topics in the *International Encyclopaedia of the Social Sciences,* and we should favor studies that promise to shed light on these topics for our generation and the next.

In saying this, I do not place a premium on ad hoc "applied" research. Challenges to social thought and practice, and new proposals, can arise from inquiry of almost any kind, from piecemeal technology to abstract philosophizing. Quite "basic" inquiries can alter thought about man and society—the work of Harlow and of von Neumann come to mind as examples. Targeted policy research does the same. Instead of "answering" the practical question toward which it was pointed, the targeted study usually contributes primarily by changing perceptions of a broad topic, according to recent studies of utilization (Weiss 1977). A good example is the origin of a social psychology of the workplace in the Hawthorne research, which began as an attempt at psychotechnology, an example to which I shall return.

WHY SATURNIAN IDEALS DO NOT SUIT SOCIAL INQUIRY

A "social physics" is an unlikely development. The Pill dates back less than one generation; widespread advanced education of women dates back less than two; about four generations back, in Western democracies, free public education spread; five generations back, the Industrial Revolution. Such rapid change severely limits generalization about social structures and relationships.

Much of the similarity in persons' actions comes from shared experiences, and customary behavior (hence an institution) is modified by a process of contagious reinterpretation of roles and goals. Traditional natural science encounters no irregularities of this character. Although particles are attracted to other particles, they don't fall in love. Within a troop of baboons, correlated changes in perception do account for the change in females' response to an aging male; but that is no counterpart of the way a culture uses language to define appropriate objects for sexual love. To explain conduct, a phenomenology—especially an appreciation of the nouns and verbs our subjects call upon to organize experience—is indispensable (see especially Geertz 1983, 58–68, on changes from culture to culture in the concept of "person" or "self").

The astronomer and zoologist do not talk to stars and starfish, so they can expect the same processes to operate before and after they produce a theory. Humans who investigate human affairs cannot pretend to be bystanders; social institutions and actions are notoriously reactive to the scribbler in the garret or at court (Gergen 1982). Social scientists define many of the terms by which community affairs are regulated. Census tabulations, for example, determine how much influence citizens of different backgrounds will have; introducing a census category such as "Hispanic-American" fosters political coalitions and conflicts that otherwise might never have been.

An Ideal in Personality Research

Today's widespread dissatisfaction within the social science community (Kruskal 1982) derives in large measure from our positivistic heritage and the consequent idolization of formal theory. It comes also from the fact that any stone can make a wrecking ball whereas well-shaped building stones are hard to come by. For us to place an exaggerated valuation on rigor and on "theory-choice" can be self-defeating (Merton 1975).

In the 1950s, a serious effort was made to bring rigorous evaluation to interpretations of psychological tests, particularly personality tests. Paul Meehl and I described how this rigor could be achieved in the light of philosophy of science as it stood just before Popper took over the lead (Cronbach & Meehl 1955).[2] Despite some complaint that our paper was insufficiently positivistic, its notion of "construct validation" has been popular and the ideals are still being relayed to fledgling researchers. Useful though the formulation was and in some ways still is, this movement has had a repressive effect.

The call for validation originated in an attempt at professional self-regulation, an attempt to bring to testing criticism stern enough to keep users aware of limitations yet gentle enough to encourage innovation in technique and theory. Our advice was upbeat: Sound ideas survive validation and the others are kept out of print, so each year's interpretations are sure to be better. Our paper even spoke cheerfully of the cloudy notions out of which orderly theories crystallize. Taken as a whole, however, the paper devalued conjectural interpretations. Some of our contemporaries went further, writing that a research report should be denied publication unless the test of a prespecified formal hypothesis implied a risk of type 1 error less than .001.

Unfortunately, the more explicit a proposition and the more rigorous the investigation of it, the more likely it is to be disconfirmed. Personality research in particular is now demoralized (Fiske 1974; Rorer & Widiger 1983). In the two decades prior to the enshrinement of construct validation, many personality variables had been conceived and means of measuring them proposed. After 1955, hardly anyone tilled those potentially fertile fields. A program of validation for any one construct could require at least a lifetime's work, so almost no one attempted it. Sustained cooperative concentration on some limited aspect of personality could shorten the work, but such effort is rare. "Motivation to achieve" is perhaps unique in having a fifty-year history of progressive elucidation by a community of scholars, yet that program of work examined just a tiny corner of the Murray system of concepts.

When each construct (and each proposed indicator of it) is expected to justify its existence from the outset by successfully predicting novel observations, ideas face an up-or-out decision much too early. Progress requires that we respect poorly formed and even "untestable" ideas. Open-mindedness can be carried too far, of course; a possible truth is a possible falsehood. The judgment that an idea may be viable should nonetheless be granted generously. We should be stern only where it would cost us much to be wrong (Putnam 1978, 90).

Not infrequently, a candidate notion in physical theory receives sympathetic attention for decades before it is stated in a defensible manner. Thus the most basic aspects of atomic theory were in dispute from 1800 to 1860. According to Glymour (1980b), Dalton's initial reports just after 1800 were "vague" and "conjectural" in places and incompatible with the contemporary data of Gay-Lussac on gases. Worse, Dalton put forward a calculus for determining atomic weights that was "wonderfully appealing . . . also plainly unsatisfactory." From 1826 to 1837, the prestigious M. Dumas published "apparently devastating criticisms"; yet the community persevered. During half a century, the arguments of the leading chemists ranged from tough-mindedness to open-mindedness to special pleading. Each investigator had his own list of atomic weights, accepting from a neighbor only procedures and results that advanced his preferred scheme. Somehow the chemists managed to encourage each other, through their years of disharmony, to stay with the puzzle.

Explanations for Capacities

Before looking further at typical social inquiry, I note that the Saturnian ideal probably does apply to the study of "capacities." Capacities are described in propositions about the conductivity of wires of various composition, for example, and in statements about the number of bits that can be held in short-term memory. A physical law is typically a statement of a capacity, dividing possibility from impossibilities. The gas law tells what volume a mole of a gas can (and must) occupy at a specified temperature and pressure. Capacities are the prime source of the "puzzles" to which Kuhnian normal science attends.

For scientists seeking to explain a capacity, the question is, How could this have come about? (Toulmin 1972). Why must it be this amount of hydrogen that combines with one mole of oxygen and not some other? Why must the ratio of round to wrinkled peas be three to one? Such a definite, solidly confirmed phenomenon should be explainable. One reason for the chemists' six decades of concentration on atomic weights was that the law of definite proportions described capacities that clamored for explication. Similarly, Toulmin tells how provocative for the science of optics was the discovery that Iceland spar produces a double image. There was nothing inherently or practically important about Iceland spar; its importance was that it posed a sharp challenge within the theory of its time.

Manicas (1982) foresees that part of psychology can become a hard science about capacities. Behavioral capacities, he suggests, can be explained in terms of physiology, and on this biological frontier, Saturnian ideals should apply. Physiology can in principle explain how this or that action is possible. Perhaps we have been insufficiently attentive to capacities of experiential or social origin. The German postwar economic miracle, the musical prodigy, the society without an incest taboo, the fakir on his bed of nails—these are capacities for which it seems reasonable to seek nonphysiological explanations.

Scientists often uncover an unrecognized capacity by establishing exceptional conditions: pure substances or strains, high temperatures, massive doses, extensive practice, and the like. Sometimes what has been thought impossible is brought about; thus what were once "inert gases" have been caused to enter chemical reactions. Akin to the Iceland-spar observation is the discovery of Hatano and Osawa (1983) that abacus experts remember very much longer digit strings than ordinary students can retain. (The experts store a visual-kinesthetic representation that is more efficient than auditory storage.)

Insofar as social scientists seek to account for capacities, they will combine historical research with retroduction and rational analysis. They can add manipulation and contemporary observation when the phenomenon recurs naturally or can be induced. One excellent example in psychology is the work by Simon (1979) and others on the skill of chessmasters. A bit less theoretical and less experimental is the political scientists' postmortem analysis of a pre-election survey that is contradicted by the actual vote. An explanation is likely to be time-and-place-bound; prediction of recurrence is not necessary.

Intriguing through the study of capacities may be, it is not the main business of social inquiry. The main thrust of inquiry has to concern itself with what people and institutions typically do and with how change occurs. With reference to abilities, aging, and so on, we can record single case histories or we can compile distributions of variables and changes in the distributions and the conditions associated with the variation. The information is thus idiosyncratic or probabilistic, and explanations must be correspondingly loose or underjustified.

LEVELS OF SOCIAL KNOWLEDGE

Social inquirers might seek knowledge of four types—descriptive and historical reports, concepts, generalized propositions, and systematic explanations. We are well able to produce the first two, and they should not be undervalued.

Historical Knowledge

To most present-tense questions about everyday behavior and society, a Saturnian study of Earth in 1800 would have given an answer different from that of a Jovian study in year 2000. Here are examples:

In a certain polity, what kinds of persons have disproportionate influence on governmental policy?

What are the "developmental tasks" whose successful accomplishment near such and such age is associated with mental health?

Among American adults of similar age and income, what distinguishes those who save money from those who go into debt?

These local correlational questions are nontrivial. They are important for self-understanding, for evaluation of the society, and for suggesting how an individual or institution might intervene to some advantage.

The answers are historical findings. Each question could have been stated for an earlier year and studied by traditional historical method. The questions are no less historical for being studied in real time, because the answers are properly put in the past tense. To report on last week's data in the present tense is to assert: "I believe that today's situation differs in no important way from the situation observed."

Concepts

Investigators attempt to extend historical reports into propositions, and understanding is often identified with the number and power of the propositions. I would stress, however, the benefit that concepts confer when we are not prepared to specify their interconnections or even to define them sharply. A concept captures a line of thought and by its very existence points to an aspect of events that some thinker has considered important. The armatures of the research questions posed above are concepts: "influences," "developmental tasks," "saving." Concepts suggest first-order questions to investigate and aspects of a situation to be observed or put under research control. A concept such as "electricity" or "social class" has value even when, in its early days, it is a place marker for a possible building site rather than the keystone of a theoretical arch.

Generalizations

A general proposition links concept words in a present-tense sentence (or, in specifically historical scholarship, the past tense). Corresponding to the questions above are these beliefs, all of them important as sources of understanding and as heuristics:

> In a democracy, equal eligibility to vote does not imply equal influence.

> In any culture, mental health is conditioned in part by some set of accomplishments the culture expects at a given age.

> Economic behavior is conditioned by subcultural influences and personal psychological history.

Such propositions can be loosely knitted into networks, but for this discussion, single sentences can represent types of theory. A present-tense proposition in social science is unlikely to be at once definite, general, and dependable (Thorngate 1976).

Klein (1983) set out to persuade a nonspecialist academic audience that economists command lawlike knowledge. He offered many examples but went on to say that some of the propositions are no more than truisms arising from definitions or assumptions—mathematical idealizations rather than substantive summaries. Propositions such as the law of supply and demand describe, at best, "tendencies that prevail in the long run," Klein said. Because of inelasticity and restraints on trade, the variables can move contrary to the law—for a certain commodity, in a certain market, for some period of time. Because the average of trends across commodities or decades is fairly consistent with the law, it can be a point of departure for thinking. The escape clause "in the long run," however, makes the proposition incapable of falsification, so it is not the stuff of Saturnian theory.

Can We Hope for Theory?

Our propositional knowledge, such as it is, consists almost wholly of statistical associations found in a certain range of contexts; the range of our evidence is far less than the reach of almost all our propositions. It is doubtful that we will have explanatory networks of significant scope, at least during our era (this remark echoes Meehl 1978, 829; see also Putnam 1978, 62–66).

Putnam (1978) argues that realism is an empirical hypothesis, one that can be defended if we observe that a science converges. It has been traditional to assert that because convergence has occurred in physics and biology, similar convergence will occur in social science. That extrapolation one is free to believe or disbelieve. In my opinion, social science is cumulative, not in possessing ever-more-refined answers about fixed questions, but in possessing an ever-richer repertoire of questions.

The Difficulty of Bounding Generalizations

Saturnian science constructs if-then statements about a system, that is, about a set of objects so bounded that the objects move and metamorphose in essentially the same manner no matter what is going on outside the system. The challenge is to devise or discover boundaries across which transactions are few or effectively constant. When Darwin began on Galapagos he bagged finches and described each one without recording where the capture was made. He made no progress in explaining the variety of finches as long as he regarded the entire archipelago as a system. The hunch that the islands had distinct populations led him to keep records of locale. He might never have achieved his great synthesis had he not stumbled upon a natural laboratory where life on one island proceeds indepedent of life on the next. On the mainland, the greater number of competing populations and their overlapping ranges obscure the patterning of the distribution.

An object of social inquiry is more like the mainland than like one of Darwin's island. The economy, the family, and the ideology of Middletown change because dollars, people, and messages zip across town lines and state lines and even across oceans. Our norms, regression coefficients, and so on, describe how often persons or other objects in a named category make a kind of response under incompletely specified conditions. The category rarely represents a system. An experimenter tries to wall off a subsystem and is likely to ignore the larger system when he puts his conclusion into words. Actually, the so-called independent variable is the conjunction of the manipulated variable with all the other features of the system.

Brownell and Moser (1949) conducted a particularly admirable educational experiment in which it might seem as if each classroom was a system and the teaching method the independent variable, but that view is naive (as they showed). Brownell and Moser randomly assigned dozens of third-grade classrooms to four specified methods of teaching subtraction. The borrowing technique, taught meaningfully, was far superior to the alternatives. The substantial residual variance was largely explained by pupils' past history. Only the pupils whose earlier teachers had stressed meanings profited from the meaningful lessons on borrowing. Pupils whose past teachers had emphasized practice (and ignored meaning) succeeded with rote instruction and not with explanatory instruction; these pupils could make nothing of the explanations. The question initially posed, "Which subtraction lessons produce the best outcome?" was unanswerable. The combination of subtraction technique and teaching technique and pupils' past history was what mattered.

Social scientists have overemphasized the kind of quantitative summary that is contingent on a time-bound mix of events in the sample. The only way to give a magnitude for "effect size" in the Brownell study was to average over the distribution of pupil histories. Whether a similar result will be found in another place and time depends on the larger system that influences the instructional style of primary teachers. With probabilistic information, we can identify only a part of a sufficient condition for an outcome (Mackie 1974). No matter how much information on contingencies is compiled, the summary is likely to remain inexact and the fully sufficient explanation beyond reach. (Physics is less troubled by its probabilistic events than we are; a tiny amount of matter consists of a great number of particles or microfields; hence at a very low level of aggregation, probabilities approach 1.00 or .00.)

Evaluating Direct Conclusions

Information collected by specific procedures in specific places leads to statements of three types: about *uto*, *UTO*, and **UTO*. The symbols *U*, *T*, and *O* refer to aspects of the study plan *UTO*—respectively, to the sort of unit-treatment combination identified as the target and the proposed operations for observing and for processing data (Cronbach 1982). The units are from a certain time and place, hence variation associated with the setting or cultural-context is confounded with choice of units. The investigator recruits subjects, observes them under chosen circumstances (perhaps specially created), and records and tabulates what happens; this generates a particular *uto* combination. She may report on *uto* or she may generalize to the class *UTO*, but she and those who follow her will almost always extrapolate to a domain **UTO* that differs from *UTO*.

Any investigation is first of all a case study. The historical record on *uto*—of what was done to produce data and of the data themselves—is noninferential; there is no issue of sampling error or of bias in the experimenter's perception or of the "meaning" of the facts. The only inference stems from the reader's need to assume that the investigator did not lie and did not suppress information she knew would change the story.

The *u* of the study are a subset of the population *U* identified for investigation. The units may be, for example, individuals, families, clinics, communities. Likewise, because the plan for observing and analyzing (*O*) is capable of being carried out in many ways, the actual procedures (*o*) are to be regarded as an unsystematic sample of the observations, codings, and so on, that would be consistent with the plan. The conditions to which a given subject is exposed constitute a realization *t* of treatment plan *T*. That plan specifies much, but by no means all, of what will be done. In psychotherapy of a stated kind, for example, the treatment events vary from person to person; each realization is a sample of what the treatment description implies.

Accepting a Claim to Reproducibility

The actual *uto* is thus one among the many on which investigators supplied the plan *UTO* might have reported. Typically an investigator generalizes, claiming that the findings in her *uto* would have appeared (within a stated margin of error) in other studies under the plan. The plan *UTO* constitutes the more or less operational definition needed to guide a replicator. The firmer the plan, the greater the reproducibility of both procedures and (uninterpreted) findings.

Any reader accepting the generalization to *UTO* relies on many assumptions, usually tacit ones. Acceptance implies confidence, for example, that the sampling plan for *U* was carried out so that *u* fits the statistical model. Thus if twenty-five students were taught by the same teacher, and the analyst based the error estimate on an *N* of twenty-five, she has assumed that the teacher does not matter, that the variability of scores would be the same if the twenty-five students had come from twenty-five classes. Another assumption is that the particular observers gave much the same data as other representatives of the class *O* would have given; controls such as blind scoring make that assumption more credible. Essentially, acceptance of the argument leading from *uto* to *UTO* rests on a thought experiment. When the reader imagines a contemporary and entirely independent replication guided only by the verbal specification of *UTO*, does he expect it to yield essentially the same regression coefficient or effect size or other result?

A principal advantage of the social sciences and history over other sources of social ideas is the reproducibility that reports at the operational levels *uto* and *UTO* can claim. A discipline learns a great deal about how to make studies reproducible, hence about how to anticipate whether a study will be reproducible. The limitations of particular techniques are searched out and controls are devised; a technology of investigation develops. When observations are guided by such expertise, a contradictory outcome in a companion study is as enlightening as a confirmation, if not more so.

EXTRAPOLATIONS AND THEIR ACCEPTANCE

Ellipsis and abstraction are necessary for communication, so a finding is almost never reported in the operational language of *UTO*. A broader statement is made: "Meaningful instruction produced better performance of subtraction than rote instruction." The user of the information goes further, shifting to the present tense and possibly ignoring specifics, as in "Meaningful instruction works better than rote." Any proposition that is not explicitly about the historical *uto* or the *UTO* it sampled refers to a **UTO*; the asterisk indicates a change in *U*, *T*, and/or *O*. The proposition about **UTO* is in effect an extrapolation, a prediction about what will be observed in a study where the subjects or operations depart in some respects from those of the original study.

In a clinical judgment where a probabilistic finding about a class of persons is brought to bear on a new case, **UTO* is narrower than the original *UTO*. One way to reduce inferential risk is to collect data in the immediate local situation. The physician, knowing that drug X often cures disease Y, takes that generalization as a fallible prior for the next case; he finds both the "go" and "no go" decisions defensible, and when he opts to use the drug, he monitors closely the response of the particular patient. The virtues of such efforts are unquestionable; the chief perplexity is just how much to invest in close-coupled monitoring of a given application.

Often the risk of generalization and abstraction simply has to be taken. A particularly common form of ellipsis is to say that the treatment had such and such effect. The asymmetric emphasis on the treatment as the cause, rather than on the combination of treatment, units, setting, and so on, arises from the intent of social scientists to aid in the manipulation of human affairs (Cook & Campbell

1979, 25–28). The elliptical conclusion becomes even less replicable and harder to justify when a generic treatment name is substituted for the specification of T and the description of t; yet only a statement at the conceptual level can guide further inquiry or practical actions.

The Brownell-Moser lesson materials were particular, and no logic warrants extrapolating to other materials on subtraction or to other topics in arithmetic; but the label "meaningful" does point to a characteristic of stimuli that often has made a difference. The concept "meaningful" obviously is crude. Psychologists have done a great deal to sharpen it as it applies to syllables and word strings, and someday its application to lessons will be elaborated. Documenting just which lesson plans or, better, lesson realizations have led to the positive result in any one study is a starting point for that elaboration.

An investigation carried out under reproducible but highly specific conditions is not usually of great value in itself. It is in combining with other reports and with beliefs from other sources, into interpretations mediated by concepts, that a finding is helpful (Lindblom & Cohen 1979; Geertz 1983; Mook 1983). Nearly every reader of social research uses the original accounts and the secondary accounts for "enlightenment" (Weiss 1977). Though a study of a social service may have been motivated by uncertainties about its adequacy, only its operators are likely to fixate on information specific to it. Policymakers use each month's news from research primarily to reshape their broad perspectives and to note factors to bear in mind in the future. Likewise, a psychology textbook is mainly extrapolation from the corpus of research. In writing such a book, I look for concepts and questions that students will find useful in future contexts; the specifics of a study come in, not for their own sake, but to "vivify" the point (Gergen 1982).

The Role of Beliefs

The grounds for accepting or doubting a proposition about *UTO* are primarily methodological. The grounds for accepting a proposition about **UTO* are primarily substantive. That is, one judges whether the changes from *UTO* to **UTO* matter. Where data are projected to conditions not yet observed, readers must be skeptical if the model neglects a variable they consider relevant.

Coleman, Hoffer, and Kilgore (1982) allegedly found private schools more effective than public schools (according to certain measures on a certain sample). The United States is considering policies under which more children, including more children from poorer families, would go to private schools. Is it safe to infer that more chidren would be better educated under the proposed policy? To judge that extrapolation, one must speculate about causal processes. Coleman, having some evidence that the private schools had superior discipline, gives that as a reason for their past success and future promise. A critic can respond that when a private school acquires a wide-range student body, its discipline will deteriorate (James & Levin 1983). Anyone who finds the criticism sensible must doubt Coleman's optimistic extrapolation.

Each of us decides which extrapolations to store in mind. A statement is accepted to the degree that it and the accompanying explanation are compatible with the hearer's store of beliefs. Rationalists protest this emphasis on audience response, because acceptance depends on the rhetorical skill and sometimes the prestige of advocates. "Objective" knowledge, we are told, should dominate over beliefs and impressions. The counterargument is that our general propositions are weak and our networks gappy, so a rigorous defense for an extrapolation is usually beyond reach. To deal with uncertainties, it is rational to call upon cultural tradition (Campbell 1975) and personal empathy; both are empirically grounded. Not surprisingly, undisciplined sources of belief are especially influential in personal-social areas (Lindblom & Cohen 1979).

Admitting that loose thinking is characteristic of everyday coping, can we not refuse a proposition the status of "knowledge" when a multiply anchored and convincing argument is lacking? That ideal has to be discarded. As Lakatos (1978) pointed out, "hard" scientists, to get on with their work, have to commit themselves to beliefs that reach beyond available evidence and perhaps beyond conceivable evidence. For example, Toulmin and Goodfield (1965, 264) comment that, for all we know, the value of Planck's h has been changing over time; if so, ideas about the galaxy derived from Hubble's red shift are wrong. Most of the tacit assumptions behind interpretations of physical data are derived from previous scientific findings, or at worst, the heuristic fruitfulness of an assumption has been demonstrated in many contexts. The social scientists' plight is much worse, as the underpinnings of our arguments are usually as much in question as the issues on which the research centers (Meehl 1978; Cook & Campbell 1979, 25).

Those who believe that social research is already converging counsel patience, confident that dependable theoretical networks

414 KNOWLEDGE CONSTRUCTION

will be the reward of assiduous sciencing. That pietism—the pie being in the sky by and by—does not face up to our chief mission; scholars ought to offer tenable interpretations today and tomorrow. In Mary Hesse's words,

> I suggest that the proposal of a social theory is more like the arguing of a political case than like a natural-science explanation. It should seek for and respect the facts when these are to be had, but it cannot await a possibly unattainable total explanation. It must appeal explicitly to value judgments and may properly use persuasive rhetoric. No doubt it should differ from most political argument in seeking and accounting for facts more conscientiously, and in constraining its rhetoric. . . . Here the inheritance of virtues from the natural sciences comes to the social scientist's aid, and I hope that nothing I have said will be taken to undermine these virtues. (Hesse 1978, 16)

Pluralism

No one, I think, would question the need to have a population of concepts in circulation, so that some new ideas can win adherents and enter the main stream of thought (Merton 1975; Toulmin 1972, 1981). It is reasonable for different persons to accept different interpretations, and unreasonable to hope that empirical research can (or should) resolve all the conflicts among conceptualizations. A conception that some audience finds stimulating should be entertained unless and until it is proved untenable. We allow a work of art to throw new light on events without expecting the interpretation to be the whole and only truth; indeed, we value art because its practitioners offer alternative interpretations (Putnam 1978, 87ff.). Shaffer's *Amadeus* has impact just because Shaffer violates the expectation of Mozart-the-man the audience brings to the theater. For anyone who accepts Shaffer's portrait as a possible, partial truth, the show is more than a pastime; it advances a thesis: "Goodness has nothing to do with art." Interpretations arising out of scholarship ought to be afforded the tolerance afforded to art, and fortunately they sometimes are. For example, it was as artistic portrayal that Murray's list of needs and presses made its contribution. Murray offered, not a set of propositions intended to displace all competitors, but an alternative vocabulary for talking about persons, incentives, and gratifications.

Many a realist wants concepts to name entities that exist in nature quite apart from man's construing. Social inquiry, I think, would be better off without that aspiration. To be sure, interpretations must be compatible with observations; Shaffer's story can command respect only because it is consistent with letters and other documents from Mozart's life. But when we ask our theories to "cut Nature closer to the joint," we ask too much. In physical nature, systems are disjoint; there are conspicuous gaps between galaxies, between molecules, between muons. Though carbon atoms are not the little black balls of my high-school chemistry, we have no reason to doubt that carbon enters physical events as if it consists of coherent units built round twelve or fourteen protons. Few targets of social inquiry function as lasting entities, and such entities as we have are not classifiable into categories as "real" as those for atoms and plants. There is no reason to think that any one "structure" for personality or for social groups is more real than another. Rather, alternative conceptualizations highlight particular aspects of behavior and feeling and so suit particular purposes. To speak of "the structure" of a family or a classroom is no more justified (and no less) than a sculptor's reference to "the structure" of his sitter's face.

Because their information is limited, interpreters have to rely on what Vico called *fantasia* and what the Germans called *Verstehen*. Dilthey and his colleagues were right to assign a central role to the *gestaltende Kraft* we bring to explanations. Murray's analysis of Satan (1962) is an example to set alongside Shaffer's Mozart. Concepts from psychology, glosses of theological writings in their historical context, and fantasia combine to make this an impressive *tour d'élan*.

A scholarly community has a great talent for generating plural explanations that are consistent with much the same premises. Each interested person attaches subjective probabilities to rival statements. Further inquiry, critical analysis, and debate can bring the members of the community more nearly to agreement, or can show the value of dialectical alternation. Members of a discipline identify the types of faulty extrapolation their brand of inquiry is likely to inspire and can alert their professional successors to all such lines of criticism. Each specialty knows of specific pitfalls to bear in mind; that is where the power of a discipline lies.

We can rarely see a topic in proper perspective if our inquiry employs resources from only one discipline (Toulmin, in Kasschau & Cofer 1981, 268ff.; and in Brewer & Collins 1982, 33). With regard to problems I have worked on, someone with a disciplinary base far from my own has often supplied a relevant framework my analysis had missed. Social science profits from interdisciplinary task forces or institutes and from reviews of proposals by broadly constituted study sections. We need additional mechanisms for bringing multiple perspectives to bear. How often, for example, is a paper in sociology referred by a psychologist or an economist? This is but one of many possible devices by which a person working within one speciality can develop a more profound view. Bring in anthropology, political science, or history, and a vision emerges of a powerful and constructive machinery for developing interpretations. Interdisciplinary contacts will have their greatest benefit when each participant individually makes colleagues' idioms part of his or her own thinking. Schultz quotes two apt sentences from Hayek: "Nobody can be a great economist who is only an economist. . . . An economist who is only an economist is likely to become a nuisance if not a positive danger" (in Kruskal 1982, 129).

How Narrowly Should Inquiry Be Targeted?

A recurrent issue in research planning is concentration versus diversification, standard conditions versus representative conditions, justification versus discovery.

Three Strategies

When heterogeneous situations interest us, one strategy is to draw a large and representative sample and report an overall statistic. That can be useful if we will thereafter apply the knowledge to aggregates whose makeup matches the present one. But a statistical summary may misrepresent underlying relations; recall Estes' 1956 demonstration that the composite learning curve based on a group average differs in shape from the individuals' curves. If the individual curves are similar in some respect, one can of course represent that similarity by a composite statistic; but the formula for compositing is to be determined after the common pattern is perceived. A purely statistical study is a case study manqué.

Instead of aggregating diversity, we can narrow the target, studying a more homogeneous subclass of situations. That works fine when we care about the subclass and will encounter future instances of it. The price is continued ignorance about situations outside the subclass. To limit investigation to animals of a single strain makes a study powerful and informative so long as every other strain would lead one to the same conclusion. That assumption is risky until theory is well advanced, as is demonstrated by a historic dispute among psychologists that arose when Tolman's rats at Berkeley exhibited "latent learning" and Iowa rats did not. The battle died down unresolved. When, two decades later, someone ran rats from the Iowa and Berkeley strains side by side, the data replicated the inconsistency! (Jones & Fennell 1965). Tolman would not have discovered latent learning if he had unluckily stocked his colony with the Iowa strain.

A third strategy will often be advisable, though it does not promise firm and replicable conclusions. A program of investigation can divide resources over many subcategories or small collectives, attending to them separately. The data are comparatively thin, and any contrast identified post hoc to account for variation is suspect. The rule of parsimony discourages such shredouts; when in doubt, it says, act as if the null hypothesis were true. But variation observed in shredouts is valid information at the level of local history. Even "errors of observation" are facts that have causes. It is wrong to ignore the variations and wrong to describe them in present-tense conclusions; rather, like other historical facts, they ought to be recorded as reminders of possibilities.

The Hawthorne Research

A notable example of effective investigation is found in *Management and the Worker* (Roethlisberger & Dickson 1939). Its power to stimulate is evidenced by the controversy that continues to this day (Bramel & Friend 1981, 1982; Sonnenfeld 1982). Fault-finding (in the best sense as well as the worst) is to be expected when a study deals with important matters, and that study touched a nerve.

The Western Electric investigators adopted an empirical, quantitative, experimental paradigm, yet they followed the third of my strategies.[3] They knew what factors influenced productivity (they thought) and set out to show just what level of illumination, timing of work breaks, and so on would maximize output. Worker morale turned out to be the salient influence, so much so that adverse physical conditions arranged for test purposes did not impair output. What was conceived as a study of worker-as-machine became a report on interpersonal relations.

Among many things Roethlisberger and Dickson did right, two seem most noteworthy. They modeled the situation that interested them with considerable realism, and observers remained on the scene, ready to record prespecified variables plus anything else of interest. I speak of modeling. The test room was artificial, to facilitate manipulation and observation, but a team of workers worked real shifts with real tasks over many weeks. Roethlisberger and Dickson, like Darwin, found themselves in a situation where complex processes were isolated just sufficiently for important effects to come to attention.

It is easy to imagine what could have happened if, at the outset, Western Electric had solicited bids for a project to determine the trend relating output to illumination. The successful proposal would very likely have included the test room, the programmed change in lighting, and the measurement of output. But to hold down costs and compete successfully, the bidders might have turned the execution over to machines. The inquiry can be reduced to a routine: collect volunteers, divide at random, ring the changes on illumination, keep score, fit a curve. Here, as in the actual experiment, there might have been no difference between the experimental group and the controls. We cannot believe that illumination is irrelevant to assembly work, but the automated investigation would have nothing to say about why the results defied common sense.

The Western Electric investigators were not taken aback by their no-difference result because they had left themselves open to experience. They not only kept a fine-grain, worker-by-worker record of output, but they listened to conversations and made notes on the life of the group. Their report brought the test room alive for readers, which added greatly to the acceptance of the post hoc explanation. Not everyone has agreed with that interpretation, and—significantly—it is on the basis of the detailed volume that the critics make their case for alternative readings.

The "Search" in Research

To recommend that investigators try to see what is going on must seem like a trivial restatement of the obvious. An experienced investigator might be expected to do that almost as second nature. But the apprentice is positively discouraged from wide-eyed unstructured observation, and many investigators seem never to throw away the crutches supplied in the first year of graduate school.

In the quantitative branches of social science, preoccupation with formal hypothesis testing dominates course work, the doctoral dissertation, summaries of past research, and much of methodological doctrine (e.g., Cohen 1982). In evaluation research, for example, methodological recommendations are generally tilted toward the controlled testing of prespecified hypotheses—toward the formal, the replicable, the confirmatory (Cronbach 1982). In truth, many past evaluations were influential, not because of the controls imposed by the design, but because variation that was not controlled proved informative. In randomized experiments (Brownell's among them), it often has been information from uncontrolled variables or unplanned contrasts that influenced subsequent thought.

The formalities of testing null hypotheses and fits to models are geared to justification, which is a culminating step in a scientific effort. The function is to convince oneself and others that an interpretation developed out of less formal observation and retroduction is worth taking seriously. Much investigation has to precede a formal test to reach a hypothesis that warrants such an investment. Investigators free to do so should sniff round the phenomenon and probe unsystematically for a long while before they mount a wrap-up study intended to "establish" what they have perceived.

In the social sciences, virtually any study should be exploratory, even one that centers on a fixed hypothesis. The Roethlisberger-Dickson study was, after all, confirmatory, with an excellent formal design and quantification. The famous conclusion about the social side of worker response took off at an angle oblique to the initial hypotheses when those were disconfirmed. Detective work can be equally important in studies after a hypothesis is supported, particularly in elucidating cases that depart from the main trend.

We cannot be reminded too often of the way R. A. Fisher himself treated quantitative data in an experiment within a partly social system:

> He had a fine criterion, yield of wheat in bushels per acre. He found that after he controlled variety, and fertilizer, there was considerable variation from year to year. This variation had a slow up-and-down cycle over a seventy-year period. Now Fisher set himself on the trail of the residual variation. First he studied wheat records from other sections to see if they had the trend; they did not. He considered and ruled out rainfall as an explanation. Then he started reading the records of the plots and found weeds a possible factor. He considered the nature of each species of weed and found that the response of weed varieties to rainfall and cultivation accounted for much of the cycle. But the large trends were not explained until he showed that the upsurge of weeds after 1875 coincided with a school-attendance act which removed cheap labor from the fields, and that another cycle coincided with the retirement of a superintendent who made weed removal his personal concern. (Quoted from Edwards & Cronbach 1952, 58; based on Fisher 1920)

Enriching the Record of Observation

Conventional publication of full accounts is impractical with today's research volume and today's costs. Fortunately, technology is rushing to our aid. The computer has brought us a long way forward in the distribution of files of raw quantitative data, allowing secondary analyses and meta-analyses to capitalize on the initial investment. The computer has also encouraged historians to code documentary archives for statistical analysis.

These possibilities have crept up on us; so far we have reflected very little on their strengths and limitations. I am enthusiastic about reuse of old data, having repeatedly found it a stimulating and economical way to develop new ideas and sometimes to shatter conclusions I had strongly believed (e.g., Cronbach & Webb 1975). Still, it is difficult to make sense of data that we come to from a distance. In any single structured study, descriptive information influences the interpretation of the calculated result. The currently popular meta-analysis of quantitative summaries is impoverished; to understand the material, analysts would have to go back to descriptive information (particularly, information on atypical cases).

An antidote for the decontextualization that goes with computerizing may well be found in the microfiche and similar technologies that make permanently available much qualitative information that could interest later interpreters, subject to whatever denaturing protects subjects' rights. (I do not suggest saving every scrap of paper for posterity; investigator judgment is as important here as in deciding originally what data to collect.)

CONCLUDING REMARKS

Planning inquiry cannot be the subject of prescriptions because planning is the art of recognizing tradeoffs and placing bets (Cronbach 1982). The tradeoffs have to do with the breadth of an inquiry, the time scale of the undertaking, the appeal of each rival hypothesis, the degree of control imposed on events and observers, the form the report is to take, and many other considerations (Cook & Campbell 1979). Once outright blunders in a plan for a single investigation or for a community effort have been corrected, further improvement requires giving up some desideratum. Making an investigation more reproducible, for example, narrows its scope and makes broad interpretations riskier.

The style and procedures preferred for one inquiry can be ill-suited for another topic or at another stage in the evolution of knowledge or for an investigator in different circumstances. With that caveat, I recapitulate a few preferences I have suggested: for more exploratory work, for less emphasis on the magnitude and statistical significance of "effect sizes," for more effort to record concomitant and intermediate events that help explain local variation, for more discussion of research plans and interpretations with peers having disparate backgrounds. Each piece of research should be an effort to give an unimpeachable and reasonably full account of events in a time, place, and context. Multiple interpretations of information already in hand will often be more instructive, at less cost, than additional data gathering. I have encouraged critical analysis of research methods and their further development, along with substantive criticism of extrapolations. To advocate pluralistic tolerance of alternative accounts is in no way to advocate tender-mindedness.

I have expressed doubt about professional ideals that would keep social "sciences" walled off from each other and from "non-scientific" attempts to observe, describe, and explain. We can enthusiastically endorse "Do your damnedest with your mind" without claiming that social science is the only profession approaching human affairs in that way. To grapple with loosely bounded problems—that is, with almost any problem that connects up with community concerns—we need to blur lines that separate "values" from "facts," "humanities" from "sciences," and "quantitative" from "qualitative" or "applied" from "basic" research (cf. Almond & Genco 1977; Geertz 1983; and Toulmin 1977).

If such suggestions are followed, will social knowledge "progress"? My answer is an emphatic "Yes, but. . . ." The progress will not be toward the theory of which Saturnians dream. It will be the kind of progress seen in architecture, music, and philosophy. Each of these fields has become richer in each century, the contributions of the past remaining a resource for the present. We are better off for having Descartes and Kant, Beethoven and Bartok, Piranesi and Le Corbusier. We do not store up truths or laws. What social scientists mostly harvest are additional concepts and inquiry skills, along with careful records of events observed. Rather than disparaging such inquiry as unproductive, we should cherish its power to nourish the culture. Mary Hesse put it nicely: "What progresses is the ability to use science to *learn* the environment. That learning is ever to be done afresh, day by day and generation by generation" (1978, 4; emphasis added).

Notes

1. My retelling of the legend, intended to be provocative as well as evocative, is not an entirely fair representation of the view of any philosopher living, dead, or present at this conference. In treating social inquiry, I echo many writers, notably Gergen, Meehl, Putnam, and Toulmin. I cannot hope that my arguments will be endorsed by all those I borrow from. Denis Phillips heads the list of Stanford friends to whom I am indebted for supportive suggestions and timely reproof.

2. Insofar as the paper reflected accurately the prevailing philosophy, Meehl deserves the credit. I was senior author only because Meehl wanted to encourage his student in that way. Although the metatheory of science has been greatly enriched since 1955, Meehl and I believe that the 1955 argument would stand, after some softening of language to recognize changes in rationalist thinking (see Glymour 1980a, and the appended discussion; Cronbach 1985). The more important question is whether our proximate goal should be to produce elaborated arguments of the kind to which the rationalists' criteria apply (Toulmin 1977).

3. My account confabulates Pennock's early studies on lighting with the later studies of rest pauses and incentives. The only public report of Pennock's work appears to have been that of Roethlisberger and Dickson.

References

Almond, G. A., and Genco, S. J. 1977. Clouds, clocks, and the study of politics. *World Politics* 29: 489–522.

Bramel, D., and Friend, R. 1981. Hawthorne, the myth of the docile worker, and class bias in psychology. *American Psychologist* 36: 867–78.

———. 1982. More Harvard humbug. *American Psychologist* 37: 1399–1401.

Brewer, M., and Collins, B., eds. 1982. *Scientific inquiry and the social sciences.* San Francisco: Jossey-Bass.

Brownell, W. A., and Moser, H. E. 1949. *Meaningful versus mechanical learning: A study in Grade III subtraction.* Duke University Research Studies in Education no. 8. Durham, N.C.: Duke University Press.

Campbell, D. T. 1975. On the conflicts between biological and social evolution and between psychology and moral tradition. *American Psychologist* 30: 1103–1126.

Cohen, P. 1982. To be or not to be: Control and balancing of Type I and Type II error. *Evaluation and Program Planning* 5: 247–54.

Coleman, J. S.; Hoffer, T.; and Kilgore, S. 1982. *High school achievement: Public, Catholic, and private schools compared.* New York: Basic Books.

Cook, T. D., and Campbell, D. T. 1979. *Quasi-experimentation: Design and analysis issues for field settings*. Chicago: Rand McNally.

Cronbach, L. J. 1982. *Designing evaluations of educational and social programs*. San Francisco: Jossey-Bass.

———. 1985. Construct validity after thirty years. Paper presented at the symposium "Intelligence: Measurement, Theory and Public Policy," Urbana, Illinois, 1 May.

Cronbach, L. J., and Meehl, P. E. 1955. Construct validity in psychological tests. *Psychological Bulletin* 52: 281–302.

Cronbach, L. J., and Webb, N. 1975. Between-class and within-class effects in a reported Aptitude x Treatment interaction: Reanalysis of a study by G. L. Anderson. *Journal of Educational Psychology* 67: 717–24.

Edwards, A. L., and Cronbach, L. J. 1952. Experimental design for research in psychotherapy. *Journal of Clinical Psychology* 8: 51–59.

Estes, W. K. 1956. The problem of inference from curves based on group data. *Psychological Bulletin* 53: 134–40.

Fisher, R. A. 1920. Studies in crop variation. *Journal of Agricultural Science* 11: 107–35.

Fiske, D. W. 1974. The limits of the conventional science of personality. *Journal of Personality* 42: 1–11.

Geertz, C. 1983. *Local knowledge*. New York: Basic Books.

Gergen, K. J. 1982. *Toward transformation in social knowledge*. New York: Springer-Verlag.

Glymour, C. 1980a. The good theories do. In *Construct validity in psychological measurement*, ed. A. P. Maslow and R. H. McKillip. Princeton: Educational Testing Service.

———. 1980b. *Theory and evidence*. Princeton: Princeton University Press.

Hatano, G., and Osawa, K. 1983. Digit memory of experts in abacus-derived mental computation: A further support for the "mental abacus" model. Paper presented to American Educational Research Association.

Hesse, M. 1978. Theory and value in the social sciences. In *Action and interpretation: Studies in the philosophy of the social sciences*, ed. C. Hookway and P. Pettit. Cambridge: Cambridge University Press.

James, T., and Levin, H. M., eds. 1983. *Public dollars for private schools: The case of tuition tax credits*. Philadelphia: Temple University Press.

Jones, M. B., and Fennell, R. S., III. 1965. Runway performance in two strains of rats. *Quarterly Journal of the Florida Academy of Sciences* 28: 289–96.

Kasschau, R. A., and Cofer, C. E., eds. 1981. *Psychology's second century: Enduring issues*. New York: Praeger.

Klein, L. R. 1983. Some laws of economics. *Bulletin of the American Academy of Arts and Sciences* 36: 21–45.

Kruskal, W. K., ed. 1982. *The future of the social sciences*. Chicago: University of Chicago Press.

Lakatos, I. 1978. *The methodology of scientific research programmes.* Ed. J. Worrall and G. Currie. Cambridge: Cambridge University Press.

Lindblom, C. E., and Cohen, D. K. 1979. *Usable knowledge.* New Haven: Yale University Press.

Mackie, J. L. 1974. *The cement of the universe: A study of causation.* Oxford: Clarendon Press.

Manicas, P. T. 1982. The human sciences: A radical separation of psychology and the social sciences. In *Explaining human behavior: Consciousness, human action, and social structure,* ed. P. F. Secord. Beverly Hills: Sage.

Meehl, P. E. 1978. Theoretical risks and tabular asterisks: Sir Karl, Sir Ronald, and the slow progress of soft psychology. *Journal of Consulting and Clinical Psychology* 46: 806–34.

Merton, R. K. 1975. Structural analysis in sociology. In *Approaches to the study of social structure,* ed. P. M. Blau. New York: Free Press.

Mook, D. G. 1983. In defense of external invalidity. *American Psychologist* 38: 379–87.

Murray, H. A. 1962. The personality and career of Satan. *Journal of Social Issues* 28: 36–54.

Putnam, H. 1978. *Meaning and the moral sciences.* London: Routledge and Kegan Paul.

Roethlisberger, F. J., and Dickson, W. J. 1939. *Management and the worker.* New York: Wiley.

Rorer, L. G., and Widiger, T. A. 1983. Personality structure and assessment. *Annual Review of Psychology* 34: 431–63.

Simon, H. A. 1979. *Models of thought.* New Haven: Yale University Press.

Sonnenfeld, J. 1982. Clarifying critical confusion in the Hawthorne hysteria. *American Psychologist* 37: 1397–99.

Thorngate, W. 1976. Possible limits on a science of social behavior. In *Social psychology in transition,* ed. L. H. Strickland et al. New York: Plenum.

Toulmin, S. 1972. *Human understanding.* Princeton: Princeton University Press.

———. 1977. From form to function: Philosophy and history of science in the 1950s and now. *Daedalus* 106: 143–62.

———. 1981. Evolution, adaptation, and human understanding. In *Scientific inquiry and the social sciences,* ed. M. B. Brewer and B. E. Collins, San Francisco: Jossey-Bass.

Toulmin, S., and Goodfield, J. 1965. *The discovery of time.* Chicago: University of Chicago Press.

Weiss, C. H., ed. 1977. *Using social research in public policy making.* Lexington, Mass.: D. C. Heath.

23

But Is It Rigorous?

Trustworthiness and Authenticity in Naturalistic Evaluation

Yvonna S. Lincoln and Egon G. Guba

*The emergence of a new paradigm of inquiry
(naturalistic) has, unsurprisingly enough, led to a
demand for rigorous criteria that meet traditional
standards of inquiry. Two sets are suggested, one
of which, the "trustworthiness" criteria, parallels
conventional criteria, while the second, "authenticity"
criteria, is implied directly by new paradigm
assumptions.*

Until very recently, program evaluation has been conducted almost exclusively under the assumptions of the conventional, scientific inquiry paradigm using (ideally) experimentally based methodologies and methods. Under such assumptions, a central concern for evaluation, which has been considered a variant of research and therefore subject to the same rules, has been how to maintain maximum rigor while departing from laboratory control to work in the "real" world.

The real-world conditions of social action programs have led to increasing relaxation of the rules of rigor, even to the extent of devising studies looser than quasi-experiments. Threats to rigor thus abound in

We are indebted to Judy Meloy, graduate student at Indiana University, who scoured the literature for references to fairness and who developed a working paper on which many of our ideas depend.

sections explaining how, when, and under what conditions the evaluation was conducted so that the extent of departure from desired levels of rigor might be judged. Maintaining true experimental or even quasi-experimental designs, meeting the requirements of internal and external validity, devising valid and reliable instrumentation, probabilistically and representatively selecting subjects and assigning them randomly to treatments, and other requirements of sound procedure have often been impossible to meet in the world of schools and social action. Design problems aside, the ethics of treatment given and treatment withheld poses formidable problems in a litigious society (Lincoln and Guba, 1985b).

Given the sheer technical difficulties of trying to maintain rigor and given the proliferation of evaluation reports that conclude with that ubiquitous finding, "no significant differences," is it not surprising that the demand for new evaluation forms has increased. What is surprising—for all the disappointment with experimental designs—is the *continued* demand that new models must demonstrate the ability to meet the same impossible criteria! Evaluators and clients both have placed on new-paradigm evaluation (Guba and Lincoln, 1981; Lincoln and Guba, 1985a) the expectation that naturalistic evaluations must be rigorous in the conventional sense, despite the fact that the basic paradigm undergirding the evaluation approach has shifted.

Under traditional standards for rigor (which have remained largely unmet in past evaluations), clients and program funders ask whether naturalistic evaluations are not so subjective that they cannot be trusted. They ask what roles values and multiple realities can legitimately play in evaluations and whether a different team of evaluators might not arrive at entirely different conclusions and recommendations, operating perhaps from a different set of values. Thus, the rigor question continues to plague evaluators and clients alike, and much space and energy is again consumed in the evaluation report explaining how different and distinct paradigms call forth different evaluative questions, different issues, and entirely separate and distinct criteria for determining the reliability and authenticity—as opposed to rigor—of findings and recommendations.

Rigor in the Conventional Sense

The criteria used to test rigor in the conventional, scientific paradigm are well known. They include exploring the truth value of the inquiry or evaluation (internal validity), its applicability (external validity or generalizability), its consistency (reliability or replicability), and its neutrality (objectivity). These four criteria, when fulfilled, obviate problems of confounding, atypicality, instability, and bias, respectively, and they do so, also respectively, by the techniques of controlling or randomizing possible sources of confounding, representative sampling, replication, and insulation of the investigator (Guba, 1981; Lincoln and Guba, 1985a). In fact, to use a graceful old English cliché, the criteria are honored more in the breach than in the observance; evaluation is but a special and particularly public instance of the impossibility of fulfilling such methodological requirements.

Rigor in the Naturalistic Sense: Trustworthiness and Authenticity

Ontological, epistemological, and methodological differences between the conventional and naturalistic paradigms have been explicated elsewhere (Guba and Lincoln, 1981; Lincoln and Guba, 1985a; Lincoln and Guba, 1986; Guba and Lincoln, in press). Only a brief reminder about the axioms that undergird naturalistic and responsive evaluations is given here.

The axiom concerned with the nature of reality asserts that there is no single reality on which inquiry may converge, but rather there are multiple realities that are socially constructed, and that, when known more fully, tend to produce diverging inquiry. These multiple and constructed realities cannot be studied in pieces (as variables, for example), but only holistically, since the pieces are interrelated in such a way as to influence all other pieces. Moreover, the pieces are themselves sharply influenced by the nature of the immediate context.

The axiom concerned with the nature of "truth" statements demands that inquirers abandon the assumption that enduring, context-free truth statements—generalizations—can and should be sought. Rather, it asserts that all human behavior is time- and context-bound; this boundedness suggests that inquiry is incapable of producing nomothetic knowledge but instead only idiographic "working hypotheses" that relate to a given and specific context. Applications may be possible in other contexts, but they require a detailed comparison of the receiving contexts with the "thick description" it is the naturalistic inquirer's obligation to provide for the sending context.

The axiom concerned with the explanation of action asserts, contrary to the conventional assumption of causality, that action is explainable only in terms of multiple interacting factors, events, and processes that give shape to it and are part of it. The best an inquirer can do, naturalists assert, is to establish plausible inferences about the patterns and webs of such shaping in any given evaluation. Naturalists utilize the field study in part because it is the only way in which phenomena can be studied holistically and *in situ* in those natural contexts that shape them and are shaped by them.

The axiom concerned with the nature of the inquirer-respondent relationship rejects the notion that an inquirer can maintain an objective distance from the phenomena (including human behavior) being studied, suggesting instead that the relationship is one of mutual and simultaneous influence. The interactive nature of the relationship is prized, since it is only because of this feature that inquirers and respondents may fruitfully learn together. The relationship between researcher and respondent, when properly established, is one of respectful negotiation, joint control, and reciprocal learning.

The axiom concerned with the role of values in inquiry asserts that far from being value-free, inquiry is value-bound in a number of ways. These include the values of the inquirer (especially evident in evaluation, for example, in the description and judgment of the merit or worth of an evaluand), the choice of inquiry paradigm (whether conventional or naturalistic, for example), the choice of a substantive theory to guide an inquiry (for example, different kinds of data will be collected and different interpretations made in an evaluation of new reading series, depending on whether the evaluator follows a skills or a psycholinguistic reading theory), and contextual values (the values inhering in the context, and which, in evaluation, make a remarkable difference in how evaluation findings may be accepted and used). In addition, each of these four value sources will interact with all the others to produce value resonance or dissonance. To give one example, it would be equally absurd to evaluate a skills-oriented reading series naturalistically as it would to evaluate a psycholinguistic series conventionally because of the essential mismatch in assumptions underlying the reading theories and the inquiry paradigms.

It is at once clear, as Morgan (1983) has convincingly shown, that the criteria for judging an inquiry themselves stem from the underlying paradigm. Criteria developed from conventional axioms and rationally quite appropriate to conventional studies may be quite inappropriate and even irrelevant to naturalistic studies (and vice versa). When the naturalistic axioms just outlined were proposed, there followed a demand for developing rigorous criteria uniquely suited to the naturalistic approach. Two approaches for dealing with these issues have been followed.

Parallel Criteria of Trustworthiness. The first response (Guba, 1981; Lincoln and Guba, 1985a) was to devise criteria that parallel those of the conventional paradigm: internal validity, external validity, reliability, and objectivity. Given a dearth of knowledge about how to apply rigor in the naturalistic paradigm, using the conventional criteria as analogs or metaphoric counterparts was a possible and useful place to begin. Furthermore, developing such criteria built on the two-hundred-year experience of positivist social science.

These criteria are intended to respond to four basic questions (roughly, those concerned with truth value, applicability, consistency, and neutrality), and they can also be answered within naturalism's bounds, albeit in different terms. Thus, we have suggested credibility as an analog to internal validity, transferability as an analog to external validity, dependability as an analog to reliability, and confirmability as an analog to objectivity. We shall refer to these criteria as criteria of trustworthiness (itself a parallel to the term *rigor*).

Techniques appropriate either to increase the probability that these criteria can be met or to actually test the extent to which they have been met have been reasonably well explicated, most recently in Lincoln and Guba (1985a). They include:

For credibility:

- Prolonged engagement—lengthy and intensive contact with the phenomena (or respondents) in the field to assess possible sources of distortion and especially to identify saliencies in the situation
- Persistent observation—in-depth pursuit of those elements found to be especially salient through prolonged engagement
- Triangulation (cross-checking) of data—by use of different sources, methods, and at times, different investigators
- Peer debriefing—exposing oneself to a disinterested professional peer to "keep the inquirer honest," assist in developing working hypotheses, develop and test the emerging design, and obtain emotional catharsis
- Negative case analysis—the active search for negative instances relating to developing insights and adjusting the latter continuously until no further negative instances are found; assumes an assiduous search
- Member checks—the process of continuous, informal testing of information by soliciting reactions of respondents to the investigator's reconstruction of what he or she has been told or otherwise found out and to the constructions offered by other respondents or sources, and a terminal, formal testing of the final case report with a representative sample of stakeholders.

For transferability:

- Thick descriptive data—narrative developed about the context so that judgments about the degree of fit or similarity may be made by others who may wish to apply all or part of the findings elsewhere (although it is by no means clear how "thick" a thick description needs to be, as Hamilton, personal communication, 1984, has pointed out).

For dependability and confirmability:

- An external audit requiring both the establishment of an audit trail and the carrying out of an audit by a competent external, disinterested auditor (the process is described in detail in Lincoln and Guba, 1985a). That part of the audit that examines the process results in a dependability judgment, while that part concerned with the product (data and reconstructions) results in a confirmability judgment.

While much remains to be learned about the feasibility and utility of these parallel criteria, there can be little doubt that they represent a substantial advance in thinking about the rigor issue. Nevertheless, there are some major difficulties with them that call out for their augmentation with new criteria rooted in naturalism rather than simply paralleling those rooted in positivism.

First, the parallel criteria cannot be thought of as a complete set because they deal only with issues that loom important from a positivist construction. The positivist paradigm ignores or fails to take into account precisely those problems that have most plagued evaluation practice since the mid 1960s: multiple value structures, social pluralism, conflict rather than consensus, accountability demands, and the like. Indeed, the conventional criteria refer only to methodology and ignore the influence of context. They are able to do so because by definition conventional inquiry is objective and value-free.

Second, intuitively one suspects that if the positivist paradigm did not exist, other criteria might nevertheless be generated directly from naturalist assumptions. The philosophical and technical problem might be phrased thus: Given a relativist ontology and an interactive, value-bounded epistemology, what might be the nature of the criteria that ought to characterize a naturalistic inquiry? If we reserve the term *rigor* to refer to positivism's criteria and the term *reliability* to refer to naturalism's parallel criteria, we propose the term *authenticity* to refer to these new, embedded, intrinsic naturalistic criteria.

Unique Criteria of Authenticity. We must at once disclaim having solved this problem. What follows are simply some strong suggestions that appear to be worth following up at this time. One of us (Guba, 1981) referred to the earlier attempt to devise reliability criteria as "primitive"; the present attempt is perhaps even more aboriginal. Neither have we as yet been able to generate distinct techniques to test a given study for adherence to these criteria. The reader should therefore regard our discussion as speculative and, we hope, heuristic. We have been able to develop our ideas of the first criterion, fairness, in more detail than the other four; its longer discussion ought not to be understood as meaning, however, that fairness is very much more important than the others.

Fairness. If inquiry is value-bound, and if evaluators confront a situation of value-pluralism, it must be the case that different constructions will emerge from persons and groups with differing value systems. The task of the evaluation team is to expose and explicate these several, possibly conflicting, constructions and value structures (and of course, the evaluators themselves operate from some value framework).

Given all these differing constructions, and the conflicts that will almost certainly be generated from them by virtue of their being rooted in value differences, what can an evaluator do to ensure that they are presented, clarified, and honored in a balanced, even-handed way, a way that the several parties would agree is balanced and even-handed? How do evaluators go about their tasks in such a way that can, while not guaranteeing balance (since nothing can), at least enhance the probability that balance will be well approximated?

If every evaluation or inquiry serves some social agenda (and it invariably does), how can one conduct an evaluation to avoid, at least probabilistically, the possibility that certain values will be diminished (and their holders exploited) while others will be enhanced (and their holders advantaged)? The problem is that of trying to avoid empowering at the expense of impoverishing; all stakeholders should be empowered in some fashion at the conclusion of an evaluation, and all ideologies should have an equal chance of expression in the process of negotiating recommendations.

Fairness may be defined as a balanced view that presents all constructions and the values that undergird them. Achieving fairness may be accomplished by means of a two-part process. The first step in the provision of fairness or justice is the ascertaining and presentation of different value and belief systems represented by conflict over issues. Determination of the actual belief system that undergirds a position on any given issue is not always an easy task, but exploration of values when clear conflict is evident should be part of the data-gathering and data-analysis processes (especially during, for instance, the content analysis of individual interviews).

The second step in achieving the fairness criterion is the negotiation of recommendations and subsequent action, carried out with stakeholding groups or their representatives at the conclusion of the data-gathering, analysis, and interpretation stage of evaluation effort. These three stages are in any event simultaneous and interactive within the naturalistic paradigm. Negotiation has as its basis constant collaboration in the evaluative effort by all stakeholders; this involvement is continuous, fully informed (in the consensual sense), and operates between true peers. The agenda for this negotiation (the logical and inescapable conclusion of a true collaborative evaluation process), having been determined and bounded by all stakeholding groups, must be deliberated and resolved according to rules of fairness. Among the rules that can be specified, the following seem to be absolute minimum.

1. Negotiations must have the following characteristics:
   a. It must be open, that is, carried out in full view of the parties or their representatives with no closed sessions, secret codicils, or the like permitted.
   b. It must be carried out by equally skilled bargainers. In the real world it will almost always be the case that one or another group of bargainers will be the more skillful, but at

least each side must have access to bargainers of equal skill, whether they choose to use them or not. In some instances, the evaluator may have to act not only as mediator but as educator of those less skilled bargaining parties, offering additional advice and counsel that enhances their understanding of broader issues in the process of negotiation. We are aware that this comes close to an advocacy role, but we have already presumed that one task of the evaluator is to empower previously impoverished bargainers; this role should probably not cease at the negotiation stage of the evaluation.

  c. It must be carried out from equal positions of power. The power must be equal not only in principle but also in practice; the power to sue a large corporation in principle is very different from the power to sue it in practice, given the great disparity of resources, risk, and other factors, including, of course, more skillful and resource-heavy bargainers.

  d. It must be carried out under circumstances that allow all sides to possess equally complete information. There is no such animal, of course, as "complete information," but each side should have the same information, together with assistance as needed to be able to come to an equal understanding of it. Low levels of understanding are tantamount to lack of information.

  e. It must focus on all matters known to be relevant.

  f. It must be carried out in accordance with rules that were themselves the product of a pre-negotiation.

2. Fairness requires the availability of appellate mechanisms should one or another party believe that the rules are not being observed by some. These mechanisms are another of the products of the pre-negotiation process.

3. Fairness requires fully informed consent with respect to any evaluation procedures (see Lincoln and Guba, 1985a, and Lincoln and Guba, 1985b). This consent is obtained not only prior to an evaluation effort but is continually renegotiated and reaffirmed (formally with consent forms and informally through the establishment and maintenance of trust and integrity between parties to the evaluation) as the design unfolds, new data are found, new constructions are made, and new contingencies are faced by all parties.

4. Finally, fairness requires the constant use of the member-check process, defined earlier, which includes calls for comments on fairness, and which is utilized both during and after the inquiry process itself (in the data collection-analysis-construction stage and later when case studies are being developed). Vigilant and

assiduous use of member-checking should build confidence in individuals and groups and should lead to a pervasive judgment about the extent to which fairness exists.

Fairness as a criterion of adequacy for naturalistic evaluation is less ambiguous than the following four, and more is known about how to achieve it. It is not that this criterion is more easily achieved, merely that it has received more attention from a number of scholars (House, 1976; Lehne, 1978; Strike, 1982, see also Guba and Lincoln, 1985).

Ontological Authentication. If each person's reality is constructed and reconstructed as that person gains experience, interacts with others, and deals with the consequences of various personal actions and beliefs, an appropriate criterion to apply is that of improvement in the individual's (and group's) conscious experiencing of the world. What have sometimes been termed *false consciousness* (a neo-Marxian term) and *divided consciousnes* are part and parcel of this concept. The aim of some forms of disciplined inquiry, including evaluation (Lincoln and Guba, 1985b) ought to be to raise consciousness, or to unite divided consciousness, likely via some dialectical process, so that a person or persons (not to exclude the evaluator) can achieve a more sophisticated and enriched construction. In some instances, this aim will entail the realization (the "making real") of contextual shaping that has had the effect of political, cultural, or social impoverishment; in others, it will simply mean the increased appreciation of some set of complexities previously not appreciated at all, or appreciated only poorly.

Educative Authentication. It is not enough that the actors in some contexts achieve, individually, more sophisticated or mature constructions, or those that are more ontologically authentic. It is also essential that they come to appreciate (apprehend, discern, understand)—not necessarily like or agree with—the constructions that are made by others and to understand how those constructions are rooted in the different value systems of those others. In this process, it is not inconceivable that accommodations, whether political, strategic, value-based, or even just pragmatic, can be forged. But whether or not that happens is not at issue here; what the criterion of educative validity implies is increased understanding of (including possibly a sharing, or sympathy with) the whats and whys of various expressed constructions. Each stakeholder in the situation should have the opportunity to become educated about others of different persuasions (values and constructions), and hence to appreciate how different opinions, judgments, and actions are evoked. And among those stakeholders will be the evaluator, not only in the sense that he or she will emerge with "findings," recommendations, and an agenda for negotiation that are professionally interesting and fair but also that he or she will develop a more sophisticated and complex construction (an emic-etic blending) of both personal and professional (disciplinary-substantive) kinds.

How one knows whether or not educative authenticity has been reached by stakeholders is unclear. Indeed, in large-scale, multisite evaluations, it may not be possible for all—or even for more than a few—stakeholders to achieve more sophisticated constructions. But the techniques for ensuring that stakeholders do so even in small-scale evaluations are as yet undeveloped. At a minimum, however, the evaluator's responsibility ought to extend to ensuring that those persons who have been identified during the course of the evaluation as gatekeepers to various constituencies and stakeholding audiences ought to have the opportunity to be "educated" in the variety of perspectives and value systems that exist in a given context.

By virtue of the gatekeeping roles that they already occupy, gatekeepers have influence and access to members of stakeholding audiences. As such, they can act to increase the sophistication of their respective constituencies. The evaluator ought at least to make certain that those from whom he or she originally sought entrance are offered the chance to enhance their own understandings of the groups they represent. Various avenues for reporting (slide shows, filmstrips, oral narratives, and the like) should be explored for their profitability in increasing the consciousness of stakeholders, but at a minimum the stakeholders' representatives and gatekeepers should be involved in the educative process.

Catalytic Authentication. Reaching new constructions, achieving understandings that are enriching, and achieving fairness are still not enough. Inquiry, and evaluations in particular, must also facilitate and stimulate action. This form of authentication is sometimes known as feedback-action validity. It is a criterion that might be applied to conventional inquiries and evaluations as well; although if it were virtually all positivist social action, inquiries and evaluations would fail on it. The call for getting "theory into action"; the preoccupation in recent decades with "dissemination" at the national level; the creation and maintenance of federal laboratories, centers, and dissemination networks; the non-utilization of evaluations; the notable inaction subsequent to evaluations that is virtually a national scandal—all indicate that catalytic authentication has been singularly lacking. The naturalistic posture that involves all stakeholders from the start, that honors their inputs, that provides them with decision-making power in guiding the evaluation, that attempts to empower the powerless and give voice to the speechless, and that results in a collaborative effort holds more promise for eliminating such hoary distinctions as basic versus applied and theory versus practice.

Tactical Authenticity. Stimulation to action via catalytic authentication is in itself no assurance that the action taken will be effective, that is, will result in a desired change (or any change at all). The evaluation of inquiry requires other attributes to serve this latter goal. Chief among these is the matter of whether the evaluation is empowering or impoverishing, and to whom. The first step toward empowerment is taken by providing all persons at risk or with something at stake in the evaluation with the opportunity to control it as well (to move toward creating collaborative negotiation). It provides practice in the use of that power through the negotiation of construction, which is joint emic-etic elaboration. It goes without saying that if respondents are seen simply as "subjects" who must be "manipulated," channeled through "treatments," or even deceived in the interest of some higher "good" or "objective" truth, an evaluation or inquiry cannot possibly have tactical authenticity. Such a posture could only be justified from the bedrock of a realist ontology and an "objective," value-free epistemology.

Summary

All five of these authenticity criteria clearly require more detailed explication. Strategies or techniques for meeting and ensuring them largely remain to be devised. Nevertheless, they represent an attempt to meet a number of criticisms and problems associated with evaluation in general and naturalistic evaluation in particular. First, they address issues that have pervaded evaluation for two decades. As attempts to meet these enduring problems, they appear to be as useful as anything that has heretofore been suggested (in any formal or public sense).

Second, they are responsive to the demand that naturalistic inquiry or evaluation not rely simply on parallel technical criteria for ensuring reliability. While the set of additional authenticity criteria might not be the complete set, it does represent what might grow from naturalistic inquiry were one to ignore (or pretend not to know about) criteria based on the conventional paradigm. In that sense, authenticity criteria are part of an inductive, grounded, and creative process that springs from immersion with naturalistic ontology, epistemology, and methodology (and the concomitant attempts to put those axioms and procedures into practice).

Third, and finally, the criteria are suggestive of the ways in which new criteria might be developed; that is, they are addressed largely to ethical and ideological problems, problems that increasingly concern those involved in social action and in the schooling process. In that sense, they are confluent with an increasing awareness of the ideology-boundedness of public life and the enculturation processes that serve to empower some social groups and classes and to impoverish others. Thus, while at first appearing to be radical, they are nevertheless becoming mainstream. An invitation to join the fray is most cheerfully extended to all comers.

References

Guba, E. G. "Criteria for Assessing the Trustworthiness of Naturalistic Inquiries." *Educational Communication and Technology Journal*, 1981, *29*, 75–91.
Guba, E. G., and Lincoln, Y. S. "Do Inquiry Paradigms Imply Inquiry Methodologies?" In D. L. Fetterman (Ed.), *The Silent Scientific Revolution*. Beverly Hills, Calif.: Sage, in press.

Guba, E. G., and Lincoln, Y. S. *Effective Evaluation: Improving the Usefulness of Evaluation Results Through Responsive and Naturalistic Approaches.* San Francisco: Jossey-Bass, 1981.

Guba, E. G., and Lincoln, Y. S. "The Countenances of Fourth Generation Evaluation: Description, Judgment, and Negotiation." Paper presented at Evaluation Network annual meeting, Toronto, Canada, 1985.

House, E. R. "Justice in Evaluation." In G. V. Glass (Ed.), *Evaluation Studies Review Annual, no. 1.* Beverly Hills, Calif.: Sage, 1976.

Lehne, R. *The Quest for Justice: The Politics of School Finance Reform.* New York: Longman, 1978.

Lincoln, Y. S., and Guba, E. G. *Naturalistic Inquiry.* Beverly Hills, Calif.: Sage, 1985a.

Lincoln, Y. S., and Guba, E. G. "Ethics and Naturalistic Inquiry." Unpublished manuscript, University of Kansas, 1985b.

Morgan, G. *Beyond Method: Strategies for Social Research.* Beverly Hills, Calif.: Sage, 1983.

Strike, K. *Educational Policy and the Just Society.* Champaign: University of Illinois Press, 1982.

Yvonna S. Lincoln is associate professor of higher education in the Educational Policy and Administration Department, School of Education, the University of Kansas. Egon G. Guba is professor of educational inquiry methodology in the Department of Counseling and Educational Psychology, School of Education, Indiana University. They have jointly authored two books, Effective Evaluation *and* Naturalistic Inquiry, *which sketch the assumptional basis for naturalistic inquiry and its application to the evaluation arena. They have also collaborated with others on a third book,* Organizational Theory and Inquiry, Sage, 1985.

24

Research as Praxis

Patti Lather

The author, who is concerned with the methodological implications of critical theory, explores issues in the developing area of emancipatory research. She defines the concept of "research as praxis," examines it in the context of social science research, and discusses examples of empirical research designed to advance emancipatory knowledge. The primary objective of this essay is to help researchers involve the researched in a democratized process of inquiry characterized by negotiation, reciprocity, empowerment — research as praxis.

> The attempt to produce value-neutral social science is increasingly being abandoned as at best unrealizable, and at worst self-deceptive, and is being replaced by social sciences based on explicit ideologies. (Hesse, 1980, p. 247)

> Since interest-free knowledge is logically impossible, we should feel free to substitute explicit interests for implicit ones. (Reinharz, 1985, p. 17)

> Scientists firmly believe that as long as they are not *conscious* of any bias or political agenda, they are neutral and objective, when in fact they are only unconscious. (Namenwirth, 1986, p. 29)

Fifty years ago the Italian neo-Marxist, Gramsci, urged intellectuals to adhere to a "praxis of the present" by aiding "developing progressive groups" to become increasingly conscious of their own actions and situations in the world (quoted in Salamini, 1981, p. 73). This essay explores what it means to do empirical research in an unjust world. In it I discuss the implications of searching for an emancipatory approach to research in the human sciences.[1] It is written from the perspective of one who believes that, just as there is no neutral education (Freire, 1973), there is no neutral research (Hall, 1975; Reason & Rowan, 1981; Westkott, 1979). Bearing in mind the words of Gramsci, my objective is to delineate the parameters

---

[1] Polkinghorne (1983) traces the history of the term "human science." He argues that "behavioral science" retains the specter of behaviorism and its prohibition against including consciousness as a part of scientific study. "Social science" carries connotations of seeking a knowledge characteristic of the natural sciences in its law-seeking mode of inquiry. "Human science," he argues, is more inclusive, using multiple systems of inquiry, "a science which approaches questions about the human realm with an openness to its special characteristics and a willingness to let the questions inform which methods are appropriate" (Appendix, p. 289).

of a "praxis of the present" within the context of empirical research in the human sciences.[2]

I base my argument for a research approach openly committed to a more just social order on two assumptions. First, we are in a postpositivist period in the human sciences, a period marked by much methodological and epistemological ferment. There has been, however, little exploration of the methodological implications of the search for an emancipatory social science. Such a social science would allow us not only to understand the maldistribution of power and resources underlying our society but also to change that maldistribution to help create a more equal world. Second, research that is explicitly committed to critiquing the status quo and building a more just society — that is, research as praxis[3] — adds an important voice to that ferment.

My exploration of postpositivist, praxis-oriented research draws on three research programs — feminist research,[4] neo-Marxist critical ethnography (Masemann, 1982; Ogbu, 1981), and Freirian "empowering" or participatory research (Hall, 1975, 1981). Each of these research programs opposes prevailing scientific norms as inherently supportive of the status quo; each is premised on a "transformative agenda" with respect to both social structure and methodological norms; each is, in other words, concerned with research as praxis (Rose, 1979, p. 279). All three of these postpositivist research programs are examples of what Hesse (1980), borrowing from Althusser,[5] terms the "epistemological break" of developing a critical social science with an openly emancipatory intent (p. 196). After brief overviews of praxis-oriented, new paradigm research and of recent efforts in radical educational theorizing aimed at creating an empirically informed Marxism, the essay focuses on the development of empowering approaches to generating knowledge.

---

[2] In another article (Lather, 1984), I explore what Gramsci's concept of "developing progressive groups" means in a contemporary context by arguing that women presently constitute a "developing progressive group" ripe with potential for assuming a position at the center of a broad-based struggle for a more equal world.

[3] Morgan (1983) distinguishes between positivist, phenomenological, and critical/praxis-oriented research paradigms. While my earlier work used the term "openly ideological," I find "praxis-oriented" better describes the emergent paradigm I have been tracking over the last few years (Lather, in press). "Openly ideological" invites comparisons with fundamentalist and conservative movements, whereas "praxis-oriented" clarifies the critical and empowering roots of a research paradigm openly committed to critiquing the status quo and building a more just society.

Praxis-oriented means "activities that combat dominance and move toward self-organization and that push toward thoroughgoing change in the practices of . . . the social formation" (Benson, 1983, p. 338). Praxis is, of course, a word with a history. In this essay, I use the term to mean the dialectical tension, the interactive, reciprocal shaping of theory and practice which I see at the center of an emancipatory social science. The essence of my argument, then, is that we who do empirical research in the name of emancipatory politics must discover ways to connect our research methodology to our theoretical concerns and commitments. At its simplest, this is a call for critical inquirers to practice in their empirical endeavors what they preach in their theoretical formulations.

[4] Feminist research is not monolithic: some researchers operate out of a conventional positivist paradigm, others out of an interpretive/phenomenological one, while others still — an increasing number — use a critical, praxis-oriented paradigm concerned both with producing emancipatory knowledge and with empowering the researched. (see Acker, Barry, & Esseveld, 1983; Bowles & Duelli-Klein, 1983; Roberts, 1981; Westkott, 1979).

[5] It was actually French philosopher Bachelard who originated the concept of epistemological break, which Althusser then applied to the work of Marx (see Lecourt, 1975). Epistemological break means a rupture in the established way of conceptualizing an issue, a rupture which essentially *inverts*

The Postpositivist Era

Research paradigms inherently reflect our beliefs about the world we live in and want to live in (Bernstein, 1976; Fay, 1975; Habermas, 1971; Hesse, 1980). Currently we are in a period of dramatic shift in our understanding of scientific inquiry. Lecourt (1975) has termed this present era "the decline of the absolutes" (p. 49; see also Bernstein, 1983; Smith & Heshusius, 1986). No longer does following the correct method guarantee true results, rather, "method does not give truth; it corrects guesses" (Polkinghorne, 1983, p. 249). It is increasingly recognized that the fact/value dichotomy simply drives values underground. Facts are never theory-independent (Hesse, 1980, p. 172); they are as much social constructions as are theories and values. Whereas positivism insists that only one truth exists, Rich (1979) argues: "There is no 'the truth,' [nor] 'a truth'—truth is not one thing, or even a system. It is an increasing complexity" (p. 187). Postpositivism has cleared methodology of prescribed rules and boundaries. The result is a constructive turmoil that allows a search for different possibilities of making sense of human life, for other ways of knowing which do justice to the complexity, tenuity, and indeterminacy of most of human experience (Mishler, 1979).

Broadly speaking, postpositivism is characterized by the methodological and epistemological refutation of positivism (Bernstein, 1976, 1983; Mitroff & Kilmann, 1978); much talk of paradigm shifts (Eisner, 1983; Phillips, 1983; Smith, 1983); and by the increased visibility of research designs that are interactive, contextualized, and humanly compelling because they invite joint participation in the exploration of research issues (Reason & Rowan, 1981; Reinharz, 1979, 1983; Sabia & Wallulis, 1983). Postpositivism is marked by approaches to inquiry which recognize that knowledge is "socially constituted, historically embedded, and valuationally based. Theory serves an agentic function, and research illustrates (vivifies) rather than provides a truth test" (Hendrick, 1983, p. 506). What this means is that "scholarship that makes its biases part of its argument" has arisen as a new contender for legitimacy.[6]

Research programs that disclose their value-base typically have been discounted, however, as overly subjective and, hence, "nonscientific." Such views do not recognize the fact that scientific neutrality is always problematic; they arise from a hyperobjectivity premised on the belief that scientific knowledge is free from social construction (Fox-Keller, 1985; Harding, 1986). Rather than the illusory "value-free" knowledge of the positivists, praxis-oriented inquirers seek emancipatory knowledge. Emancipatory knowledge increases awareness of the contradictions hidden or distorted by everyday understandings, and in doing so it directs attention to the possibilities for social transformation inherent in the present configuration of social processes. Admittedly, this approach faces the danger of a rampant subjectivity where one finds only what one is predisposed to look for, an outcome that parallels the "pointless precision" of hyperobjectivity (Kaplan, 1964). Thus a central task for praxis-oriented researchers becomes the con-

---

meaning. Hesse (1980), for example, uses the term to characterize those who argue not only *against* the possibility of an "objective" social science but *for* the possibilities inherent in an explicitly value-based social science with emancipatory goals.

    [6] Phrase used by Anyon in a session of the annual meeting of the American Educational Research Association, Montreal, April 1984.

frontation of issues of empirical accountability — the need to offer grounds for accepting a researcher's description and analysis — and the search for workable ways of establishing the trustworthiness of data in new paradigm inquiry.

Research as Praxis

The foundation of postpositivism is the cumulative, trenchant, and increasingly definitive critique of the inadequacies of positivist assumptions[7] in light of the complexities of human experience (Bernstein, 1976; Cronbach, 1975; Feinberg, 1983; Giroux, 1981; Guba & Lincoln, 1981; Kaplan, 1964; Mishler, 1979). Postpositivism argues that the present orthodoxy in the human sciences is obsolete and that new visions for generating social knowledge are required (Hesse, 1980; Reason & Rowan, 1981; Rose, 1979; Schwartz & Ogilvy, 1979). Those committed to the development of a change-enhancing, interactive, contextualized approach to knowledge-building have amassed a body of empirical work that is provocative in its implications for both theory and, increasingly, method.

.Several examples of this work are available. Consider Bullough and Gitlin's (1985) case study of one middle school teacher, a study designed to encourage rethinking the meaning of resistance and its place in theories of cultural and economic reproduction within the context of teachers' work lives. Their research design included the teacher's written response to a preliminary interpretation of the data, which is an example of the most common form of an emancipatory approach to research — the submission of a preliminary description of the data to the scrutiny of the researched. In an earlier study, Willis (1977) focused on the school-to-work transition in the lives of twelve working-class British "lads." The most oft-cited example of neo-Marxist critical ethnography, Willis's work both identifies the area of resistance to authority as a corrective to the overly deterministic correspondence theories then popular in neo-Marxist circles (see Apple, 1980–81; Bowles & Gintis, 1976) and builds into his research design an attempt to take the research findings back to the lads for further dialogue. McRobbie (1978) conducted a similar study inquiring into the effects of socialization into femininity on the lives of working-class British females. Finally, a more praxis-oriented example is Mies's (1984) action-research project in Germany, designed to respond to violence against women in the family. A high visibility street action attracted people who were then interviewed regarding their experience with and views on wife-beating. The resulting publicity led to the creation of a Women's House to aid victims of domestic abuse. A desire for transformative action and egalitarian participation guided consciousness-raising in considering the sociological and historical roots of male violence in the home through the development of life histories of the women who had been battered. The purpose was to empower the oppressed to come to understand

---

[7] The basic assumptions of positivism are four: (1) the aims, concepts, and methods of the natural sciences are applicable to the social sciences; (2) the correspondence theory of truth which holds that reality is knowable through correct measurement methods; (3) the goal of social research is to discover universal laws of human behavior which transcend culture and history; and (4) the fact-value dichotomy, the denial of both the theory-laden dimensions of observation and the value-laden dimensions of theory. For an overview and critique of each of the three paradigms, the positivist, the interpretive, and the critical/praxis-oriented, see, respectively, Bredo and Feinberg (1982), Carr and Kemmis (1983), and Bernstein (1976).

and change their own oppressive realities (see also Anyon, 1980, 1981, 1983; Berlak & Berlak, 1981; Everhart, 1983; Hall, 1981; McNeil, 1984; Miller, 1986; Roberts, 1981; Tripp, 1984).

Such examples are part of a rich ferment in contemporary discourse about empirical research in the human sciences, a discourse that spans epistemological, theoretical, and, to a lesser degree, methodological areas. Within radical educational circles, for example, there have been several calls for eliminating the dichotomy between empirical work and the construction of emancipatory theory (Anyon, 1982; Ramsay, 1983; Wexler, 1982). There are, however, few clear strategies for linking critical theory and empirical research.

This failure to probe the methodological implications of critical theory has led to a number of difficulties for praxis-oriented research. The abundance of theoretically guided empirical work affiliated with the "new sociology of education" attests both to the conceptual vitality offered by postpositivist research programs and to the danger of conceptual overdeterminism. This nondialectical use of theory leads to a circle where theory is reinforced by experience conditioned by theory. Marxism's history of sectarianism and "theoretical imperialism" (Thompson, 1978; see also Bottomore, 1978) gives evidence of the need for open, flexible theory-building grounded in a body of empirical work that is ceaselessly confronted with, and respectful of, the experiences of people in their daily lives. Far too often, however, one is left with the impression that neo-Marxist empirical work is conducted to provide empirical specificities for a priori theory (Hargreaves, 1982; Lather, in press). Such work demonstrates the continued relevance of Thompson's (1978, p. 13) assertion that too much of Marxist social theory is an "immaculate conception which requires no gross empirical impregnation"[8] (see also Comstock, 1982, p. 371; Kellner, 1975, p. 149; Krueger, 1981, p. 59; Wright, 1978, p. 10).

Additionally, neo-Marxist empirical studies are too often characterized by an attitude toward the people researched that is captured in the words of one research team: "We would not expect the teachers interviewed to either agree with or necessarily understand the inferences which were made from their responses" (Bullough, Goldstein, & Holt, 1982, p. 133). Given the all-male research team and the largely female teacher subjects, one could make much of the gender politics involved in such a statement. But the issue here is the implications of such a stance for the purposes of emancipatory knowledge-building and the empowerment of the researched. One of the central tasks of my argument is to encourage those of us who do critical inquiry to demonstrate how our attitude differs from what Reinharz (1979) has termed the "rape model of research" (p. 95) so characteristic of mainstream social science: career advancement of researchers built on their use of alienating and exploitative inquiry methods.

The difficulties which continue to characterize critical inquiry raise two central questions about the effort to develop a style of empirical research that advances

---

[8] Two examples of the dangers of conceptual overdeterminism leading to theoretical imposition (the lack of a reciprocal relationship between data and theory) in the new sociology of education are correspondence theory, which posited an overly deterministic mirror-image relationship between schools and the needs of corporate capitalism (Apple, 1979; Bowles & Gintis, 1976), and the wishful thinking which saw resistance in every inattentive student and recalcitrant teacher (for critiques, see Bullough & Gitlin, 1985; Giroux, 1983).

emancipatory knowledge. First, what is the relationship between data and theory in emancipatory research? In grounded theory-building the relationship between data and theory, according to Glasser and Strauss (1967), is that theory follows from data rather than preceding it. Moreover, the result is a minimizing of researcher-imposed definitions of the situation, which is an essential element in generating grounded theory. Given the centrality of a priori theory in praxis-oriented research, it is evident that emancipatory theory-building is different from grounded theory-building. Understanding those differences requires a probing of the tensions involved in the use of a priori theory among researchers who are committed to open-ended, dialectical theory-building that aspires to focus on and resonate with lived experience and, at the same time, are convinced that lived experience in an unequal society too often lacks an awareness of the need to struggle against privilege. Second, growing out of the first question, how does one avoid reducing explanation to the intentions of social actors, by taking into account the deep structures—both psychological and social, conscious and unconscious—that shape human experience and perceptions, without committing the sin of theoretical imposition? This question is tied to both the issue of false consciousness (defined later in this essay) and the crucial role of the researcher vis-à-vis the researched in emancipatory inquiry. An exploration of both of these central questions comprises the remainder of this essay.

For praxis to be possible, not only must theory illuminate the lived experience of progressive social groups; it must also be illuminated by their struggles. Theory adequate to the task of changing the world must be open-ended, nondogmatic, informing, and grounded in the circumstances of everyday life; and, moreover, it must be premised on a deep respect for the intellectual and political capacities of the dispossessed. This position has profound substantive and methodological implications for postpositivist, change-enhancing inquiry in the human sciences.

Empowering Approaches to the Generation of Knowledge

> For persons, as autonomous beings, have a moral right to participate in decisions that claim to generate knowledge about them. Such a right . . . protects them . . . from being managed and manipulated . . . the moral principle of respect for persons is most fully honored when power is shared not only in the application . . . but also in the generation of knowledge . . . doing research on persons involves an important educational commitment: to provide conditions under which subjects can enhance their capacity for self-determination in acquiring knowledge about the human condition. (Heron, 1981, pp. 34–35)

Krueger (1981) notes that "there are hardly any attempts at the development of an alternative methodology in the sense of an 'emancipatory' social research to be explored and tested in substantive studies" (p. 59). Along these lines, Giddens (1979) suggests that the task of a critical social science is to explore the nature of the intersection between choice and constraint and to center on questions of power. Is this not equally true of the research situation itself? Insofar as we have come to see that evolving an empowering pedagogy is an essential step in social transformation, does not the same hold true for our research approaches?

I am arguing for an approach that goes well beyond the action-research concept proposed over thirty years ago by Lewin, which has given rise to "a very active and lively field" in Britain and Australia over the past decade (Tripp, 1984, p. 20). While Tripp (1984) and Grundy (1982) note the existence of some critical and emancipatory teacher-based action research, the vast majority of this work operates from an ahistorical, apolitical value system which lends itself to subversion by those "who are tempted to use merely the technical form as a means of engineering professional teacher development" (Tripp, 1984, p. 20).

An emancipatory social research calls for empowering approaches to research whereby both researcher and researched become, in the words of feminist singer-poet Chris Williamson, "the changer and the changed." For researchers with emancipatory aspirations, doing empirical research offers a powerful opportunity for praxis to the extent that the research process enables people to change by encouraging self-reflection and a deeper understanding of their particular situations. In an attempt to reveal the implications that the quest for empowerment holds for research design, I will focus on three interwoven issues: the need for reciprocity, the stance of dialectical theory-building versus theoretical imposition, and the question of validity in praxis-oriented research.

The Need for Reciprocity

No intimacy without reciprocity. (Oakley, 1981, p. 49)

Reciprocity implies give-and-take, a mutual negotiation of meaning and power. It operates at two primary points in emancipatory empirical research: the junctures between researcher and researched and between data and theory. The latter will be dealt with in the next section of this essay; I here address reciprocity between researcher and researched.

Reciprocity in research design is a matter of both intent and degree. Regarding intent, reciprocity has long been recognized as a valuable condition of research fieldwork, for it has been found to create conditions which generate rich data (Wax, 1952). Everhart (1977), for example, presents reciprocity as "an excellent data gathering technique" (p. 10) because the researcher moves from the status of stranger to friend and thus is able to gather personal knowledge from subjects more easily. He traces his evolution from detachment to involvement in a study of student life in a junior high school where he comes to recognize "the place of reciprocity in productive fieldwork" (p. 8). I argue that we must go beyond the concern for more and better data to a concern for research as praxis. What I suggest is that we consciously use our research to help participants understand and change their situations. I turn now to those who build varying degrees of reciprocity into their research designs for the purpose of empowering the researched.

Laslett and Rapoport (1975), who studied school dropouts in Britain, build a minimal degree of reciprocity into their research designs. They term their approach "collaborative interviewing and interactive research." A central component of their strategy is to repeat interviews at least three times. The repetition is "essential to deal with the feelings roused, often covertly, in order to 'unlock' deeper levels of data content" (p. 973). Furthermore, they urge "giving back" to respondents a picture of how the data are viewed, both to return something to the participants and to check descriptive and interpretive/analytic validity.

A Marxist survey researcher, Carr-Hill (1984), expands the use of reciprocity to identify, through initial interviews, a group of twelve to fifteen people with whom the researcher engaged in a series of open discussions about the mismatch between formal education and the way people live their lives. This resulted in a collectively generated survey given to one hundred people, a survey couched in the language of respondents and "in terms of the social categories through which they perceive the world" (p. 281). Additionally, interested participants attended evaluation seminars where survey results stimulated respondents "to critically analyze their own educational history and its relation to their present life-styles" (p. 281).

A maximal approach to reciprocity in research design can be found in the work of two evaluators involved in a four-year project to assess the curricular reform movements of the 1960s (Kushner & Norris, 1980–81). The goal of their research was to move people from articulating what they know to theorizing about what they know, a process the researchers term "collaborative theorizing" (p. 27). This methodology is characterized by negotiation: negotiation of description, interpretation, and the principles used to organize the first-draft report. While they admit that final drafts are usually the preserve of the researcher, Kushner and Norris suggest that the attractiveness of this approach is that all participants, within time constraints, are allowed a role in negotiation of the final meanings of the research. Such collaboration, they contend, offers "an opportunity to extend the range of theories and meanings . . . to give participants the dignity of contributing to theorizing about their worlds . . . [and] through sharing meaning-production . . . [to] develop significant understandings of schooling and education" (p. 35).

A final example is provided by Tripp (1983). He explores what it means for interviews to be coauthored and negotiated in a conscious effort to democratize the research situation. In his case studies of alienation and the school-to-work transition, Tripp held one-to-one and group discussions "as a means of developing participants' views" (p. 32). The resulting coauthored statements constituted an agreed-upon account of the views of the participants. Tripp cautions, however, that "the negotiation process must be clearly bounded" (p. 38) because participants often wish to "unsay" their words. In Tripp's view, "the right to negotiate [on the part of research participants] was replaced by the right to comment" (p. 39). Researchers are not so much owners of data as they are "majority shareholders" who must justify decisions and give participants a public forum for critique.

Tripp's research design, however, is not fully interactive. Reciprocity in the negotiation of meaning is limited to the early stages of investigation. No attempt is made to involve research participants in either the interpretation of the descriptive data or the construction of empirically grounded theory. The lack of involvement of research participants in these later stages of the research process makes possible a situation where the entire issue of false consciousness is skirted. False consciousness is the denial of how our commonsense ways of looking at the world are permeated with meanings that sustain our disempowerment (Bowers, 1984; Gramsci, 1971; Salamini, 1981); it is a central issue in any maximal approach to reciprocity.

In order to address this issue, Fay (1977) argues that we must develop criteria/ theories to distinguish between people's reasoned rejections of interpretations and theoretical arguments and false consciousness. Fay pinpoints this as a glaring omission, a black hole,[9] if you will, in critical theory: a lack of knowledge about "the conditions that must be met if people are going to be in a position to actually consider it [critical theory] as a possible account of their lives" (p. 218). Fay is pointing out that the creation of emancipatory theory is a dialogic enterprise. Both the substance of emancipatory theory and the process by which that theory comes to "click" with people's sense of the contradictions in their lives are the products of dialectical rather than top-down impositional practices.

Dialectical practices require an interactive approach to research that invites reciprocal reflexivity and critique, both of which guard against the central dangers to praxis-oriented empirical work: imposition and reification on the part of the researcher. As Comstock (1982) argues, "dialogic education is integral to every research program which treats subjects as active agents instead of objectifying them and reifying their social conditions" (p. 386). Yet, notably more often than in either feminist or Freirian praxis-oriented research, the neo-Marxist researcher's self-perceived role is as "interpreter of the world" (Reynolds, 1980–81, p. 87), exposer of false consciousness. This nondialectical, nonreciprocal perception of the role of the researcher confounds neo-Marxist researchers' intent to demystify the world for the dispossessed. Respondents become objects—targets of research— rather than active subjects empowered to understand and change their situations. As a result, neo-Marxist praxis–oriented work too often falls prey to what Fay (1977) notes as the irony of domination and repression inherent in most of our efforts to free one another (p. 209). In the name of emancipation, researchers impose meanings on situations rather than constructing meaning through negotiation with research participants.

There are at present few research designs which encourage negotiation of meaning beyond the descriptive level. The involvement of research participants in data interpretation as well as (to take one further step toward maximal reciprocity) theory-building remains largely an "attractive aspiration" (Kushner & Norris, 1980–81, p. 35). But as Fay notes, feminist consciousness-raising groups provide a model for how to begin to flesh-out the nature of maximal reciprocity: the involvement of research participants in the construction and validation of knowledge.

Throughout the late 1960s and 1970s, thousands of small grassroots groups formed to provide a way for women to exchange thoughts, experiences, and feelings. From this movement emerged the feminist maxim: the personal is political. What were once thought to be individual problems were redefined as social problems that require political solutions. For Fay (1977), the lesson from these groups is that

> coming to a radical new self-conception is hardly ever a process that occurs simply by reading some theoretical work; rather, it requires an environment of trust,

[9] Sears (1983) first used this term in a conference paper.

openness, and support in which one's own perceptions and feelings can be made properly conscious to oneself, in which one can think through one's experiences in terms of a radically new vocabulary which expresses a fundamentally different conceptualization of the world, in which one can see the particular and concrete ways that one unwittingly collaborates in producing one's own misery, and in which one can gain the emotional strength to accept and act on one's new insights.

The experience of the Women's Movement confirms that radical social changes through rational enlightenment require some mechanism for ensuring that those conditions necessary for such enlightenment will be established and maintained. (p. 232)

Following Fay (1977), I propose that the goal of emancipatory research is to encourage self-reflection and deeper understanding on the part of the persons being researched at least as much as it is to generate empirically grounded theoretical knowledge. To do this, research designs must have more than minimal reciprocity. The following is a summary of some of the procedures and theory necessary to attain full reciprocity in research:

— Interviews conducted in an interactive, dialogic manner, that require self-disclosure on the part of the researcher. An example of self-disclosure can be found in Oakley's (1981) research with women and their experience of motherhood. Arguing the need for interactive self-disclosure, Oakley emphasizes a collaborative, dialogic seeking for greater mutual understanding. This is opposed to mainstream interview norms where interview respondent's questions about the interviewer's own life are deflected (see also Acker, Barry, & Esseveld, 1983; Hanmer & Saunders, 1984).

— Sequential interviews of both individuals and small groups to facilitate collaboration and a deeper probing of research issues.

— Negotiation of meaning. At a minimum, this entails recycling description, emerging analysis, and conclusions to at least a subsample of respondents. A more maximal approach to reciprocity would involve research participants in a collaborative effort to build empirically rooted theory.

— Discussions of false consciousness which go beyond simply dismissing resistance to Marxist interpretations as such. We need to discover the necessary conditions that free people to engage in ideology critique, given the psychological hold of illusion — "the things people cling to because they provide direction and meaning in their lives" (Fay, 1977, p. 214). There is a dialectic between people's self-understandings and researcher efforts to create a context which enables a questioning of both taken-for-granted beliefs and the authority that culture has over us (Bowers, 1984). There, in the nexus of that dialectic, lies the opportunity to create reciprocal, dialogic research designs which not only lead to self-reflection but also provide a forum in which to test the usefulness, the resonance of conceptual and theoretical formulations.

Dialectical Theory-Building versus Theoretical Imposition

I do not believe that imposing Marxist rather than bourgeois categories is socialist practice. (Carr-Hill, 1984, p. 290)

The goal of theoretically guided empirical work is to create theory that possesses "evocative power" (Morgan, 1983, p. 298). By resonating with people's lived concerns, fears, and aspirations, emancipatory theory serves an energizing, catalytic role. It does this by increasing specificity at the contextual level in order to see how larger issues are embedded in the particulars of everyday life. The result is that theory becomes an expression and elaboration of politically progressive popular feelings rather than an abstract framework imposed by intellectuals on the complexity of lived experience.

Building empirically grounded theory requires a reciprocal relationship between data and theory. Data must be allowed to generate propositions in a dialectical manner that permits use of a priori theoretical frameworks, but which keeps a particular framework from becoming the container into which the data must be poured. The search is for theory which grows out of context-embedded data, not in a way that automatically rejects a priori theory, but in a way that keeps preconceptions from distorting the logic of evidence. For example, Ramsay (1983) aptly criticizes Anyon's critical ethnographies (which focus on the effects of class and gender on the structure of U.S. public school classrooms) for telling us more about her predispositions than about the phenomena studied. Anyon's (1980, 1981) *certainty* and *clear-cutness* are particularly problematic, for, as Ramsey notes, "while we would agree that there is no such thing as 'value-free' or objective research, we would argue that there is a need to keep as open a frame of reference as is possible to allow the data to generate the propositions" (p. 316).

Theory is too often used to protect us from the awesome complexity of the world. Yet, "the road to complexity" is what we are on in our empirical efforts (Clark, 1985, p. 65). Moving beyond predisposition requires a set of procedures that illuminates the ways that investigators' values enter into research (Bredo & Feinberg, 1982, p. 439; Feinberg, 1983, pp. 159–160). Anchoring theoretical formulations in data requires a critical stance that will reveal the inadequacies of our pet theory and be open to counter-interpretations. Apple (1980–81), in cautioning that conceptual validity precedes empirical accuracy, neglects the largely undialectical role that theory plays in most critical ethnography. Empirical evidence must be viewed as a mediator in a constant mutual interrogation between self and theory. Otherwise, neo-Marxist theory will fail to transcend "the hubris of the social sciences" still present in the two emergent alternatives to positivist orthodoxy— the interpretive and critical paradigms (Moon, 1983, p. 28). As Acker, Barry, and Esseveld (1983) note, "An emancipatory intent is no guarantee of an emancipatory outcome" (p. 431). The struggle, of course, is to develop a "passionate scholarship" (Du Bois, 1983) which can lead us toward a self-reflexive research paradigm that no longer reduces issues of bias to canonized methodology for establishing scientific knowledge (Cronbach, 1980; Godddard, 1973, p. 18).

The search for ways to operationalize reflexivity in critical inquiry is a journey into uncharted territory. Sabia and Wallulis (1983) make clear the danger: too often critical self-awareness comes to mean "a negative attitude towards competing approaches instead of its own self-critical perspective" (p. 26). Guidelines for developing critical self-awareness, hence, are rare. Nevertheless, while the methodological implications of critical theory remain relatively unexplored (Bredo & Feinberg, 1982, p. 281), the need for research approaches which advance a more equal world is receiving some attention (Acker, Barry, & Esseveld, 1983; Apple, 1982; Comstock, 1982; Fay, 1975, 1977). Various suggestions for operationalizing reflexivity in critical inquiry can be drawn from that small body of work.

First, critical inquiry is a response to the experiences, desires, and needs of oppressed people (Fay, 1975). Its initial step is to develop an understanding of the world view of research participants. Central to establishing such understandings is a dialogic research design where respondents are actively involved in the construction and validation of meaning. The purpose of this phase of inquiry is to provide accounts that are a basis for further analysis and "a corrective to the investigator's preconceptions regarding the subjects' life-world and experiences" (Comstock, 1982, p. 381).

Second, critical inquiry inspires and guides the dispossessed in the process of cultural transformation; this is a process Mao characterized as "teach[ing] the masses clearly what we have learned from them confusedly" (quoted in Freire, 1973, p. 82). At the core of the transformation is "a reciprocal relationship in which every teacher is always a student and every pupil a teacher" (Gramsci quoted in Femia, 1975, p. 41). Thus, critical inquiry is a fundamentally dialogic and mutually educative enterprise. The present is cast against a historical backdrop while at the same time the "naturalness" of social arrangements is challenged so that social actors can see both the constraints and the potential for change in their situations.

Third, critical inquiry focuses on fundamental contradictions which help dispossessed people see how poorly their "ideologically frozen understandings" serve their interests (Comstock, 1982, p. 384). This search for contradictions must proceed from progressive elements of participants' current understandings, or what Willis (1977) refers to as "partial penetrations": the ability of people to pierce through cultural contradictions in incomplete ways that, nevertheless, provide entry points for the process of ideology critique.

Fourth, the validity of a critical account can be found, in part, in the participants' responses. Fay (1977) writes: "One test of the truth of critical theory is the considered reaction by those for whom it is supposed to be emancipatory. . . . Not only must a particular theory be offered as the reason why people should change their self-understandings, *but this must be done in an environment in which these people can reject this reason*" (pp. 218–219, italics in original). The point is to provide an environment that invites participants' critical reaction to researcher accounts of their worlds. As such, dialogic research designs allow praxis-oriented inquirers both to begin to grasp the necessary conditions for people to engage in ideology critique and transformative social action, and to distinguish between what Bernstein (1983) calls "enabling" versus "blinding" biases on the part of the researcher (p. 128).

Fifth, critical inquiry stimulates "a self-sustaining process of critical analysis and enlightened action" (Comstock, 1982, p. 387). The researcher joins the participants in a theoretically guided program of action extended over a period of time.

Earlier in this essay, I argued for reciprocity as a means to empower the researched. Here reciprocity is employed to build more useful theory. Research designs can be more or less participatory, but dialogic encounter is required to some extent if we are to invoke the reflexivity needed to protect research from the researcher's own enthusiasms. Debriefing sessions with participants provide an opportunity to look for exceptions to emerging generalizations. Submitting concepts and explanations to the scrutiny of all those involved sets up the possibility of theoretical exchange—the collaborative theorizing at the heart of research which both advances emancipatory theory and empowers the researched.

A strictly interpretive, phenomenological paradigm is inadequate insofar as it is based on an assumption of fully rational action.[10] Sole reliance on the participants' perceptions of their situation is misguided because, as neo-Marxists point out, false consciousness and ideological mystification may be present. A central challenge to the interpretive paradigm is to recognize that reality is more than negotiated accounts—that we are both shaped by and shapers of our world. For those interested in the development of a praxis-oriented research paradigm, a key issue revolves around this central challenge: how to maximize the researcher's mediation between people's self-understandings (in light of the need for ideology critique) and transformative social action *without becoming impositional*.

Comstock (1982) says that the critical researcher's task is to stimulate research participants into "a self-sustaining process of critical analysis and enlightened action" (p. 387). Doing such work in a nonelitist and nonmanipulative manner means that one wants to be not a "one-way propagandist," but rather like the Cobbett written about by Thompson (1963): Cobbett acknowledged "the aid which he is constantly deriving from those new thoughts which his thoughts produce in their minds." Thompson notes: "How moving is this insight into the dialectical nature of the very process by which his own ideas were formed! For Cobbett, thought was not a system but a relationship" (p. 758).

For theory to explain the structural contradictions at the heart of discontent, it must speak to the felt needs of a particular group in ordinary language (Fay, 1975, p. 98). If it is to spur toward action, theory must be grounded in the self-understandings of the dispossessed even as it seeks to enable them to reevaluate themselves and their situations. This is the central paradox of critical theory and provides its greatest challenge. The potential for creating reciprocal, dialogic research designs is rooted in the intersection between people's self-understandings and the researcher's efforts to provide a change-enhancing context. Such designs would both lead to self-reflection and provide the forum called for by Fay (1977) whereby the people for whom the theory is supposed to be emancipatory can participate in its construction and validation.

In sum, the development of emancipatory social theory requires an empirical stance which is open-ended, dialogically reciprocal, grounded in respect for human capacity, and yet profoundly skeptical of appearances and "common sense." Such an empirical stance is, furthermore, rooted in a commitment to the long-term, broad-based ideological struggle to transform structural inequalities.

Issues of Validity

The job of validation is not to support an interpretation, but to find out what might be wrong with it. . . . To call for value-free standards of valid-

---

[10] The inadequacies of an overreliance on rationality in human behavior are eloquently captured in Ascher's letter to de Beauvoir, a letter written to "clear the air" after Ascher had written a biography of de Beauvoir: "I don't think you ever grasped sufficiently the way the unconscious can hold one back from grasping a freedom consciously chosen. Too often I see your sense of freedom being based on

ity is a contradiction in terms, a nostalgic longing for a world that never was. (Cronbach, 1980, pp. 103–105)

What does empirical rigor mean in a postpositivist context?[11] If validity criteria are the products of the paradigms which spawn them (Morgan, 1983), what validity criteria best serve praxis-oriented research programs? The need to systematize as much as possible the ambiguity of our enterprise does not mean that we must deny the essential indeterminacy of human experience — "the crucial disparity between the being of the world and the knowledge we might have of it" (White, 1973, p. 32). My point is, rather, that if illuminating and resonant theory grounded in trustworthy data is desired, we must formulate self–corrective techniques that check the credibility of data and minimize the distorting effect of personal bias upon the logic of evidence (Kamarovsky, 1981).

Currently, paradigmatic uncertainty in the human sciences is leading to the reconceptualization of validity. Past efforts to leave subjective, tacit knowledge out of the "context of verification" are seen by many postpositivists as "naive empiricism." Inquiry is increasingly recognized as a process whereby tacit (subjective) knowledge and propositional (objective) knowledge are interwoven and mutually informing (Heron, 1981, p. 32; Polanyi, 1967). The absence of formulas to guarantee valid social knowledge forces us to "operate simultaneously at epistemological, theoretical and empirical levels with self-awareness" (Sharp & Green, 1975, p. 234). Our best tactic at present is to construct research designs that demand a vigorous self-reflexivity.

For praxis-oriented researchers, going beyond predisposition in our empirical efforts requires new techniques and concepts for obtaining and defining trustworthy data which avoid the pitfalls of orthodox notions of validity. The works of Reason and Rowan (1981) and Guba and Lincoln (1981) offer important suggestions in this regard. Reason and Rowan advise borrowing concepts of validity from traditional research but caution us to revise and expand those concepts in ways appropriate to "an interactive, dialogic logic" (p. 240). Their notion of validity is captured in the phrase "objectively subjective" inquiry (p. xiii). Guba and Lincoln argue for analogues to the major principles of orthodox rigor. They state that in order to fulfill the minimum requirement for assessing validity in new paradigm research the techniques of triangulation, reflexivity, and member checks should be enlisted. Building on these, I offer a reconceptualization of validity appropriate for research that is openly committed to a more just social order.

First, *triangulation* is critical in establishing data-trustworthiness, a triangulation expanded beyond the psychometric definition of multiple measures to include multiple data sources, methods, and theoretical schemes. The researcher must consciously utilize designs that allow counterpatterns as well as convergence if data are to be credible.

---

a rationalism that denies that murky inner world over which we have as little, or much, control as the world outside us. And, in fact, control would be your word, not mine. For I believe we have to love this deep inner self and try to be in harmony with it" (Ascher, De Salvio, & Ruddick, 1984, p. 93; see also Harding, 1982).

[11] Issues of validity in openly ideological research are dealt with much more fully in Lather (in press).

Second, *construct validity* must be dealt with in ways that recognize its roots in theory construction (Cronbach & Meehl, 1955). Our empirical work must operate within a conscious context of theory-building. Where are the weak points of the theoretical tradition we are operating within? Are we extending theory? Revising it? Testing it? Corroborating it? Determining that constructs are actually occurring, rather than they are merely inventions of the researcher's perspective, requires a self-critical attitude toward how one's own preconceptions affect the research. Building emancipatory social theory requires a ceaseless confrontation with and respect for the experiences of people in their daily lives to guard against theoretical imposition. A *systematized reflexivity* which reveals how a priori theory has been changed by the logic of the data becomes essential in establishing construct validity in ways that contribute to the growth of illuminating and change-enhancing social theory.

As an example, Acker, Barry, and Esseveld (1983), in a noteworthy effort to reconstruct "the social relations that produce the research itself" (p. 431), write that "our commitment to bringing our subjects into the research as active participants [has] influenced our rethinking of our original categories . . . " (p. 434). As part of their self-reflexive essay on their research into the relation between changes in the structural situation of women and changes in consciousness, they explore the tension "between letting the data speak for itself and using abstracted categories." They ask, "How do we explain the lives of others without violating their reality?" (p. 429). Contrast this with Willis's (1977) classic ethnography where there is no clear indication how the researcher's perspectives were altered by the logic of the data. Without this account, one is left viewing the role of theory in this research (which is so strongly shaped by a priori conceptions) as being non-dialectical, unidirectional, an imposition that disallows counter-patterns and alternative explanations (see also Lather, in press; Walker, 1985).

Third, *face validity* needs to be reconsidered. Kidder (1982) contends that although it has been treated lightly and dismissed, face validity is relatively complex and inextricably tied to construct validity. "Research with face validity provides a 'click of recognition' and a 'yes, of course' instead of 'yes, but' experience" (p. 56). Face validity is operationalized by recycling description, emerging analysis, and conclusions back through at least a subsample of respondents: "Good research at the nonalienating end of the spectrum . . . goes back to the subjects with the tentative results, and refines them in light of the subjects' reactions" (Reason & Rowan, 1981, p. 248). The possibility of encountering false consciousness, however, creates a limit on the usefulness of "member checks" (Guba & Lincoln, 1981) in establishing the trustworthiness of data. False consciousness, an admittedly problematic phenomenon (Acker, Barry, & Esseveld, 1983), however, does exist. For reasons illuminated by Gramsci's (1971) theories of hegemony, most people to some extent identify with and/or accept ideologies which do not serve their best interests. Thus, an analysis which only takes account of actors' perceptions of their situations could result in research being incorrectly declared invalid. The link between face and construct validity and the possible false consciousness of research participants is an area that very much needs empirical exploration. Perhaps the best that can be suggested at this point is that, just as reliability is necessary but not sufficient to establish validity within positivism, building face validity into new paradigm research should become a necessary but not sufficient approach to establishing data credibility.

Fourth, given the emancipatory intent of praxis-oriented research, I propose the less well-known notion of *catalytic validity* (Brown & Tandom, 1978; Reason & Rowan, 1981, p. 240). Catalytic validity represents the degree to which the research process reorients, focuses, and energizes participants toward knowing reality in order to transform it, a process Freire (1973) terms conscientization. Of the guidelines proposed here, this is by far the most unorthodox; it flies directly in the face of the positivist demand for researcher-neutrality. The argument for catalytic validity is premised not only within a recognition of the reality-altering impact of the research process, but also in the desire to consciously channel this impact so that respondents gain self-understanding and, ultimately, self-determination through research participation.

Efforts to produce social knowledge that will advance the struggle for a more equitable world must pursue rigor as well as relevance. By arguing for a more systematic approach to triangulation and reflexivity, a new emphasis for face validity, and inclusion of catalytic validity, I stand opposed to those who claim that empirical accountability either is impossible to achieve or is able to be side-stepped in praxis-oriented, advocacy research. Lack of concern for data credibility within praxis-oriented research programs will only decrease the legitimacy of the knowledge generated therein. Praxis-oriented research can only benefit from agreed-upon procedures which make empirical decision-making public and hence subject to criticism. Most important, if we do not develop such procedures, our theory-building will suffer from a failure to protect our work from our passions and limitations. I join Lecourt (1975) in his call for an "ardent text" (p. 49) grounded in "the real motion of knowledge" (p. 79) which is as tied to passion as to "objectivity." The tension between advocacy and scholarship, however, can be fruitful only to the extent that it pushes us toward becoming vigorously self-aware in our efforts to develop a praxis-oriented research paradigm.

Summary

This essay has one essential argument: a more collaborative approach to critical inquiry is needed to empower the researched, to build emancipatory theory, and to move toward the establishment of data credibility within praxis-oriented, advocacy research. The present turmoil in the human sciences frees us to construct new designs based on alternative tenets and epistemological commitments. My goal is to move research in many different and, indeed, contradictory directions in the hope that more interesting and useful ways of knowing will emerge. Rather than establishing a new orthodoxy, we need to experiment, document, and share our efforts toward emancipatory research. To quote Polkinghorne (1983): "What is needed most is for practitioners to experiment with the new designs and to submit their attempts and results to examination by other participants in the debate. The new historians of science have made it clear that methodological questions are decided in the practice of research by those committed to developing the best possible answers to their questions, not by armchair philosophers of research" (p. xi). Let us get on with the task.[12]

References

Acker, J., Barry, K., & Esseveld, J. (1983). Objectivity and truth: Problems in doing feminist research. *Women's Studies International Forum, 6*(4), 423-435.

Anyon, J. (1980). Social class and the hidden curriculum of work. *Journal of Education, 62*, 67-92.

Anyon, J. (1981). Social class and school knowledge. *Curriculum Inquiry, 11*, 3-42.

Anyon, J. (1982). Adequate social science, curriculum investigations, and theory. *Theory into Practice, 21*, 34-37.

Anyon, J. (1983). Accommodation, resistance, and female gender. In S. Walker & L. Burton (Eds.), *Gender and education* (pp. 19-38). Sussex, Eng.: Falmer Press.

Apple, M. (1979). Ideology and curriculum. Boston: Routledge & Kegan Paul.

Apple, M. (1980-1981). The other side of the hidden curriculum: Correspondence theories and the labor process. *Interchange, 11*(3), 5-22.

Apple, M. (1982). *Education and power.* Boston: Routledge & Kegan Paul.

Ascher, C., De Salvio, L., & Ruddick, S. (Eds.). (1984). *Between women.* Boston: Beacon Press.

Benson, J. K. (1983). A dialectical method for the study of organizations. In G. Morgan (Ed.), *Beyond method: Strategies for social research* (pp. 331-346). Beverly Hills, CA: Sage.

Berlak, A. (1986). *Teaching for liberation and empowerment in the liberal arts: Toward the development of pedagogy that overcomes resistance.* Unpublished paper.

Berlak, A., & Berlak, H. (1981). *Dilemmas of schooling: Teaching and social change.* New York: Methuen.

Bernstein, R. (1976). *The restructuring of social and political theory.* New York: Harcourt Brace Jovanovich.

Bernstein, R. (1983). *Beyond objectivism and relativism: Science, hermeneutics, and praxis.* Philadelphia: University of Pennsylvania Press.

Bottomore, T. (1978). Marxism and sociology. In T. Bottomore & R. Nisbet (Eds.), *A history of sociological analysis* (pp. 118-148). London: Hunemann.

Bowers, C. A. (1984). *The promise of theory: Education and the politics of cultural change.* New York: Longman.

Bowles, G., & Duelli-Klein, R. (Eds.). (1983). *Theories of women's studies.* Boston: Routledge & Kegan Paul.

Bowles, S., & Gintis, H. (1976). *Schooling in capitalist America: Educational reform and the contradictions of economic life.* New York: Basic Books.

Bredo, E., & Feinberg, W. (Eds.). (1982). *Knowledge and values in social and educational research.* Philadelphia: Temple University Press.

Brown, D., & Tandom, R. (1978). Interviews as catalysts. *Journal of Applied Psychology, 63*, 197-205.

Bullough, R., & Gitlin, A. (1985). Beyond control: Rethinking teacher resistance. *Education and Society, 3*, 65-73.

[12] To avoid becoming "an armchair philosopher of research" myself, I am presently engaged in what I see as a long term effort to explore student resistance to liberatory curriculum in an introductory women's studies course (Lather, 1986). My theoretical concern is with the processes of "ideological consent" (Kellner, 1978, p. 46), especially the enabling conditions which open people up to ideology critique and those which limit these processes (A. Berlak, 1986).

Bullough, R., Goldstein, S., & Holt, L. (1982). Rational curriculum: Teachers and alienation. *Journal of Curriculum Theorizing, 4*, 132–143.

Carr, W., & Kemmis, S. (1983). *Becoming critical: Knowing through action research.* Deakin, Australia: Deakin University Press.

Carr-Hill, R. (1984). Radicalizing survey methodology. *Quality and Quantity, 18*, 275–292.

Clark, D. (1985). Emerging paradigms in organizational theory and research. In Y. Lincoln (Ed.), *Organizational theory and inquiry: The paradigm revolution* (pp. 43–78). Beverly Hills, CA: Sage.

Comstock, D. (1982). A method for critical research. In E. Bredo and W. Feinberg (Eds.), *Knowledge and values in social and educational research* (pp. 370–390). Philadelphia: Temple University Press.

Cronbach, L. (1975). Beyond the two disciplines of scientific psychology. *American Psychologist, 30*, 116–127.

Cronbach, L. (1980). Validity on parole: Can we go straight? *New Directions for Testing and Measurement, 5*, 99–108.

Cronbach, L., & Meehl, P. (1955). Construct validity in psychological tests. *Psychological Bulletin, 52*, 281–302.

Du Bois, B. (1983). Passionate scholarship: Notes on values, knowing and method in feminist social science. In G. Bowles and R. Duelli-Klein (Eds.), *Theories of Women's Studies* (pp. 105–116). Boston: Routledge & Kegan Paul.

Eisner, E. (1983). Anastasia might still be alive, but the monarchy is dead. *Educational Researcher, 12*(5), 13–14, 23–24.

Everhart, R. (1977). Between stranger and friend: Some consequences of "long term" fieldwork in schools. *American Educational Research Journal, 14*, 1–15.

Everhart, R. (1983). *Reading, writing and resistance: Adolescence and labor in a junior high school.* Boston: Routledge & Kegan Paul.

Fay, B. (1975). *Social theory and political practice.* London: Allen & Unwin.

Fay, B. (1977). How people change themselves: The relationship between critical theory and its audience. In T. Ball (Ed.), *Political theory and praxis* (pp. 200–233). Minneapolis: University of Minnesota Press.

Feinberg, W. (1983). *Understanding education: Toward a reconstruction of educational inquiry.* New York: Cambridge University Press.

Femia, J. (1975). Hegemony and consciousness in the thought of Antonio Gramsci. *Political Studies, 23*, 29–48.

Fox-Keller, E. (1985). *Reflections on gender and science.* New Haven, CT: Yale University Press.

Freire, P. (1973). *Pedagogy of the oppressed.* New York: Seabury.

Giddens, A. (1979). *Central problems in social theory.* Berkeley: University of California Press.

Giroux, H. A. (1981). *Ideology, culture, and the process of schooling.* Philadelphia: Temple University Press.

Giroux, H. A. (1983). Theories of reproduction and resistance in the new sociology of education: A critical analysis. *Harvard Educational Review, 53*, 257–293.

Glaser, B., & Strauss, A. (1967). *The discovery of grounded theory: Strategies for qualitative research.* Chicago: Aldine.

Goddard, D. (1973). Max Weber and the objectivity of social science. *History and Theory, 12*, 1–22.

Gramsci, A. (1971). *Selections from the prison notebooks of Antonio Gramsci* [1929–1935] (Q. Hoare & G. Smith, Eds. & Trans.). New York: International Publishers.

Grundy, S. (1982). Three modes of action research. *Curriculum Perspectives, 3*(2), 22–34.

Guba, E., & Lincoln, Y. (1981). *Effective evaluation.* San Francisco: Jossey-Bass.

Habermas, J. (1971). *Theory and practice.* Boston: Beacon Press.

Hall, B. (1975). Participatory research: An approach for change. *Prospects, 8*(2), 24–31.

Hall, B. (1981). The democratization of research in adult and non-formal education. In P. Reason and J. Rowan (Eds.), *Human inquiry* (pp. 447–456). New York: Wiley.

Hanmer, J., & Saunders, S. (1984). *Well-founded fear: A community study of violence to women.* London: Hutchinson.

Harding, S. (1982). Is gender a variable in conceptions of rationality? *Dialectica, 36,* 225–242.

Harding, S. (1986). *The science question in feminism.* Ithaca, NY: Cornell University Press.

Hargreaves, A. (1982). Resistance and relative autonomy theories: Problems of distortion and incoherence in recent Marxist analyses of education. *British Journal of Sociology of Education, 3,* 107–126.

Hendrick, C. (1983). A middle-way metatheory. [Review of *Toward transformation in social knowledge.*] *Contemporary Psychology, 28,* 504–507.

Heron, J. (1981). Experimental research methods. In P. Reason and J. Rowan (Eds.), *Human inquiry* (pp. 153–166). New York: Wiley.

Hesse, M. (1980). *Revolution and reconstruction in the philosophy of science.* Bloomington: Indiana University Press.

Kamarovsky, M. (1981). Women then and now: A journey of detachment and engagement. *Women's Studies Quarterly, 10*(2), 5–9.

Kaplan, A. (1964). *The conduct of inquiry: Methodology for behavioral science.* San Francisco: Chandler.

Kellner, D. (1975). The Frankfurt School revisited. *New German Critique, 4,* 131–152.

Kellner, D. (1978). Ideology, Marxism, and advanced capitalism. *Socialist Review, 42,* 37–65.

Kidder, L. (1982, June). Face validity from multiple perspectives. In D. Brinberg and L. Kidder (Eds.), *New directions for methodology of social and behavioral science: Forms of validity in research* (No. 12, pp. 41–57). San Francisco: Jossey-Bass.

Krueger, M. (1981). In search of the "subjects" in social theory and research. *Psychology and Social Theory, 1*(2), 54–61.

Kushner, S., & Norris, N. (1980–1981). Interpretation, negotiation and validity in naturalistic research. *Interchange, 11*(4), 26–36.

Laslett, B., & Rapoport, R. (1975). Collaborative interviewing and interactive research. *Journal of Marriage and the Family, 37,* 968–977.

Lather, P. (1984). Critical theory, curricular transformation, and feminist mainstreaming. *Journal of Education, 166,* 49–62.

Lather, P. (1986, June). *Empowering research methodologies: Feminist perspectives.* Paper presented at the annual meeting of the National Women's Studies Association, Champaign, IL.

Lather, P. (in press). Issues of validity in openly ideological research: Between a rock and a soft place. *Interchange.*

Lecourt, D. (1975). *Marxism and epistemology.* London: National Labor Board.

Masemann, V. (1982). Critical ethnography in the study of comparative education. *Comparative Education Review, 26,* 1–15.

McNeil, L. (1984, April). *Critical theory and ethnography in curriculum analysis.* Paper presented at annual meeting of American Educational Research Association, New Orleans, LA.

McRobbie, A. (1978). Working class girls and the culture of femininity. In Women's Study Group (Ed.), *Women take issue: Aspects of women's subordination* (pp. 96–108). London: Hutchinson.

Mies, M. (1984). Towards a methodology for feminist research. In E. Altbach, J. Clausen, D. Schultz, & N. Stephan (Eds.), *German feminism: Readings in politics and literature* (pp. 357–366). Albany: State University of New York Press.

Miller, J. (1986). Women as teachers: Enlarging conversations on issues of gender and self-control. *Journal of Curriculum and Supervision, 1*(2), 111–121.

Mishler, E. (1979). Meaning in context: Is there any other kind? *Harvard Educational Review, 49,* 1–19.

Mitroff, I., & Kilmann, R. (1978). *Methodological approaches to social science.* San Francisco: Jossey-Bass.

Moon, J. D. (1983). Political ethics and critical theory. In D. Sabia & J. Wallulis (Eds.), *Changing social science: Critical theory and other critical perspectives* (pp. 171–188). Albany: State University of New York Press.

Morgan, G. (Ed.). (1983). *Beyond method: Strategies for social research*. Beverly Hills, CA: Sage.

Namenwirth, M. (1986). Science through a feminist prism. In R. Bleir (Ed.), *Feminist approaches to science* (pp. 18–41). New York: Pergamon Press.

Oakley, A. (1981). Interviewing women: A contradiction in terms. In H. Roberts (Ed.), *Doing feminist research* (pp. 30–61). Boston: Routledge & Kegan Paul.

Ogbu, J. (1981). School ethnography: A multilevel approach. *Anthropology and Education Quarterly, 12*, 3–29.

Phillips, D. C. (1983). After the wake: Postpositivistic educational thought. *Educational Researcher, 12*(5), 4–12.

Polanyi, M. (1967). *The tacit dimension*. Garden City, NY: Anchor Books, Doubleday.

Polkinghorne, D. (1983). *Methodology for the human sciences: Systems of inquiry*. Albany: State University of New York Press.

Ramsay, P. (1983). A response to Anyon from the Antipodes. *Curriculum Inquiry, 13*, 295–320.

Reason, P., & Rowan, J. (1981). Issues of validity in new paradigm research. In P. Reason & J. Rowan (Eds.), *Human inquiry* (pp. 239–252). New York: Wiley.

Reinharz, S. (1979). *On becoming a social scientist*. San Francisco: Jossey-Bass.

Reinharz, S. (1983). Experiential analysis: A contribution to feminist research. In G. Bowles & R. Duelli-Klein (Eds.), *Theories of women's studies* (pp. 162–191). Boston: Routledge & Kegan Paul.

Reinharz, S. (1985). *Feminist distrust: A response to misogyny and gynopia in sociological work*. Unpublished manuscript. [Expanded version of Reinharz, S. (1985). Feminist distrust: Problems of context and content in sociological work. In D. Berg & K. Smith (Eds.), *Clinical demands of social research* (pp. 153–172). Beverly Hills, CA: Sage.]

Reynolds, D. (1980–1981). The naturalistic method and educational and social research: A Marxist critique. *Interchange, 11*(4), 77–89.

Rich, A. (1979). *On lies, secrets, and silence: Selected prose, 1966–1978*. New York: Norton.

Roberts, H. (1981). *Doing feminist research*. Boston: Routledge & Kegan Paul.

Rose, H. (1979). Hyper-reflexivity: A new danger for the counter-movements. In H. Nowotny & H. Rose (Eds.), *Counter-movements in the sciences: The sociology of the alternatives to big science* (pp. 277–289). Boston: Reidel.

Sabia, D., & Wallulis, J. (Eds.). (1983). *Changing social science: Critical theory and other critical perspectives*. Albany: State University of New York Press.

Salamini, L. (1981). *The sociology of political praxis: An introduction to Gramsci's theory*. Boston: Routledge & Kegan Paul.

Schwartz, P., & Ogilvy, J. (1979, April). *The emergent paradigm: Changing patterns of thought and belief*. (Values and Lifestyles Program Report No. 7). Menlo Park, CA: Stanford Research Institute (S.R.I.) International.

Sears, J. T. (1983, October). Black holes of critical theory: Problems and prospects of ethnographic research. Paper presented at Fifth Annual Curriculum Theorizing Conference, Dayton.

Sharp, R., & Green, A. (1975). *Education and social control: A study in progressive primary education*. Boston: Routledge & Kegan Paul.

Smith, J. K. (1983). Quantitative vs. qualitative research: An attempt to clarify the issue. *Educational Researcher, 12*(3), 6–13.

Smith, J., & Heshusius, L. (1986). Closing down the conversation: The end of the quantitative-qualitative debate among educational inquirers. *Educational Researcher, 15*(1), 4–12.

Thompson, E. P. (1963). *The making of the English working class*. New York: Pantheon Books.

Thompson, E. P. (1978). *The poverty of theory and other essays*. New York: Monthly Review Press.

Tripp, D. H. (1983). Co-authorship and negotiation: The interview as act of creation. *Interchange, 14*(3), 32–45.

Tripp, D. H. (1984, August). *Action research and professional development*. Discussion paper for the Australian College of Education Project, 1984-1985. Murdock, Australia: Murdock University.

Walker, J. C. (1985). Rebels with our applause: A critique of resistance theory in Paul Willis's ethnography of schooling. *Journal of Education, 167*(2), 63-83.

Wax, R. (1952). Reciprocity as a field technique. *Human Organization, 11*, 34-41.

Westkott, M. (1979). Feminist criticism of the social sciences. *Harvard Educational Review, 49*, 422-430.

Wexler, P. (1982). Ideology and education: From critique to class action. *Interchange, 13*(1), 53-78.

White, H. (1973). Foucault decoded: Notes from underground. *History and Theory, 12*, 23-54.

Willis, P. (1977). *Learning to labor: How working class kids get working class jobs*. New York: Columbia University Press.

Wright, E. O. (1978). *Class, crisis and the state*. London: National Labor Board.

This essay is a revision of papers originally presented at the Sixth Annual Curriculum Theorizing Conference, Dayton, October 1984, sponsored by the *Journal of Curriculum Theorizing* and the University of Dayton, and the annual meeting of the American Educational Research Association, Chicago, March 1985.

25

Postpositivist Critical Multiplism

Thomas D. Cook

This chapter is concerned with what I think is the most pressing methodological problem of our day: How can scientific practice be justified in light of the cogent criticisms of its most basic premises by philosophers, historians, and sociologists of science? This difficulty is felt more acutely within the social than the natural sciences, and perhaps most acutely by those who have worked at the interface between social science and social policy. This is because social science theory and method were used in the 1960s and 1970s to help design and evaluate social programs aimed at ameliorating social problems, but the results from these programs were disappointing. Was this because social science is an inappropriate source of input into social policy and cannot produce effective programs or clear-cut evaluations? If so, the reasoning goes, might social policy benefit no more from social *science* knowledge than from other forms of knowledge about society and human nature?

Commentators have responded to the doubts about science in general and about the role of social science in policy analysis by attempting to justify science in what I call a multiplist mode. Among other things, multiplism is associated with the call for (1) *multiple* operationalism (e.g., Webb, Campbell, Schwartz & Sechrest 1966); (2) *multimethod* research (e.g., Campbell & Fiske, 1959); (3) planned research programs based on *multiple* interconnected studies (e.g., Lakatos & Musgrave, 1970); (4) the synthesis of *multiple* studies related to each other in haphazard fashion (e.g., Glass, McGaw, & Smith, 1981); (5) the con-

From Thomas D. Cook, "Postpositivist Critical Multiplism," in R. Lance Shotland and Melvin M. Mark, eds., *Social Science and Social Policy*, pp. 21-62. Copyright © 1985 by Sage Publications, Inc.

struction of complex *multivariate* causal models instead of simple univariate ones (e.g., Simon, 1957; Blalock, 1961); (6) the competitive testing of *multiple* rival hypotheses rather than testing a single hypothesis (e.g., Popper, 1972); (7) the use of *multiple* stakeholders to formulate research questions (e.g., Cronbach et al., 1980); (8) the use of *multiple* theoretical and value frameworks to interpret research questions and findings (e.g., Cronbach, 1982; Dunn, 1982); (9) the advocacy that *multiple* analysts examine important data sets (e.g., Mosteller & Moynihan, 1972); and (10) the desirability of *multitargeted* research that seeks to probe many different types of issue within a single study (e.g., Chen & Rossi, 1980; 1983).

The purpose of this chapter is to examine how well a multiplist approach meets the total set of challenges that come from the philosophy, history, and sociology of science and from experiences using social science during the social reform years of the 1960s and 1970s.

THE ORIGINS OF MULTIPLISM

In a world where one way of conducting research was universally considered to be "correct," scientific practice would be easy. Researchers would simply do what is correct. It is the current absence of total certainty about what constitutes correct practice that leads to the advocacy of multiplism in perspectives and methods. The current uncertainty arises, I think, from two principle sources. The first is the systematic attack on the theory of knowledge that was dominant until 20 years ago in most philosophy of science; the second is the move social scientists made toward causal research in field settings. This meant a move away from the laboratory and the traditions of causal research it represents based on control over stimulus materials and external events, and also a move away from the descriptive theory and cross-sectional research methods then prevalent among sociologists and political scientists. Given these moves, lessons had to be learned from experience about what happens when control is reduced while the ambition to infer is simultaneously increased—the state of affairs during the Great Society years.

A. The Attack on Positivism

An amusing incident took place in 1961 in Tubingen during a special symposium held on epistemological issues in the social sciences. Popper was the first speaker, and Adorno was the second. It was widely expected that Popper would defend epistemological positions believed to be "positivist" and that Adorno would challenge these positions. However, because Popper unequivocably denounced positivism, the anticipated confrontation did not materialize. It was then left to Dahrendorf, the rapporteur, to reveal why. He noted that Popper defined positivism in terms of the "empty bucket" theory of induction. This assumes that some associations repeatedly occur in nature that can be validly observed by senses that bring no prior knowledge to bear, and from these observations general laws can be induced. This conception of positivism is quite different from the more hypothetico-deductive version that Adorno attacked. The latter assumes that totally explicit theories are possible from which hypotheses can be deduced that can subsequently be confronted with empirical data that will confirm or reject the theory from which the hypotheses were derived.

The difficulties Popper and Adorno had in agreeing on a definition of positivism incline me not to offer my own. Because many varieties of positivism can be constructed, I will outline the ontological, epistemological, and methodological assumptions that characterize the scientific beliefs and practices that are today more likely to be labeled "positivist," irrespective of their links to past theories of positivism. I do not want to suggest that any social (or natural) scientist has ever subscribed to all these assumptions, or that they adequately describe scientific practice as it occurs, or that practice has evolved only from positivism or from any other single philosophy of science for that matter. Scientific practice has multiple origins that include the trial-and-error behavior of practitioners, selective adaptations from prior philosophies, and research on research. Nonetheless, the assumptions I call positivist were widely disseminated after 1930 and were used to justify a particular set of scientific practices. These assumptions were partly based on logic and partly on how philosophers thought physicists went about the business of doing research and constructing theories.

1. Ontological assumptions Positivists are realists and assume the existence of the world outside of the mind. They further assume that this world is lawfully ordered and that the major task of science is to describe this order. The order is assumed to be deterministic in its manifestations (rather than probabilistic) so that once the laws of nature are known, perfect prediction will result. Indeed, only when perfect prediction has been achieved do positivists want to speak of having discovered a law. Laws are preferred if they are general and apply to many phenomena, if they are functional in form and specify how observable forces are related to each other, and if they are parsimonious because few forces need to be invoked. Einstein's $e = mc^2$

meets these criteria. It applies to all motion and subsumes all prior theories of motion; it specifies the form of a relationship; and because one parameter is a constant only one other needs to be estimated. Most positivists further assume that the terms in their laws will be ahistorical, based on forces that are permanent fixtures of the external world, and nonmentalistic, devoid of conceptions based on intentions and wishes.

All these ontological assumptions have come under attack. Some are probably false. For instance, to assume determinism flies in the face of discoveries from particle physics and molecular biology suggests that the most basic elements of the universe are related probabilistically. The assumptions have come under attack in the social sciences because of their dubious relevance to human nature, social organization, and the current status of social theory. Practicing social scientists know that perfect prediction (i.e., $R^2 = 1$) is impossible with current theories. They also realize that to increase prediction nearly always entails adding more constructs to a theoretical system. But this jeopardizes parsimony. They also believe that most research areas are circumscribed in coverage (i.e., they apply only to, say, attitude change or intergroup cooperation) and that making them more general would probably lead to highly abstract verbal theories with little predictive power for particular instances. To take perfect prediction as a criterion for inferring laws and generalities seems inordinately unrealistic to many of those who criticize the relevance of physics to the social sciences.

Positivists gravitate to prediction because it depends on observing the correlation between variables; they want to avoid constructs like "causation" that cannot be directly observed. But prediction does not necessarily lead to causal or explanatory knowledge (Bhaskar, 1979; Scriven, 1971) and does not guarantee control over events (Collingwood, 1940). For instance, we can almost perfectly predict the length of any day from the length of prior days and the length of the same day one year ago. But that hardly helps either to explain the length of a day or to modify its length. Because prediction, whether in a deterministic or probabilistic mode, does not necessarily entail explanation or manipulation, some critics of positivism reject it as the sole, or even major, criterion for judging the adequacy of theories. Most want to replace it with causal explanation.

But in the social sciences such explanation is not likely to take the simple form of the laws of physics. Most social phenomena are multiply determined; each unique cause may be related to other causes in complex ways; and each cause may itself be complexly and multiply determined by other forces that are not themselves direct causes of what is being explained. To practicing social scientists, causal explanation is not likely—in the near term, at least—to involve simple relationships that look like parsimonious laws. Instead, multiple causal determinants, multiple causal paths, and multiple causal contingencies have to be assumed, making human nature and social relationships seem more like pretzels than single-headed arrows from A to B or simple functional equations—more like convoluted multivariate statistical interactions than simple main effects (e.g., Cronbach & Snow, 1976; House, 1980; McGuire, 1984).

It is difficult to assume that the circumscribed level of prediction that social scientists now attain will remain stable over settings and times. To exemplify this, replace the analogy of physics with that of macrobiology. Unlike the case with physical objects, animals (including man) seek to control their environments, and the knowledge they achieve is often stored as genetic mutations or as the teachings of priests, grandmothers, law books, and even methodology texts. The past lives on in the behavioral and cognitive present, influencing how we define problems, select possible solutions, and envisage future opportunities. Because it is rare that only one response will be adequate for meeting individual or species' "needs," a macrobiological perspective suggests that the same set of external contingencies can result in a wide variety of apparently adaptive responses, with the form of the response depending on what unfolds from within, what has transpired in the past, and what is available in the present, including chance and present plans for the future. The argument is, then, that laws about human nature and social life cannot be inferred using the physicists' assumptions of ahistoricity and nonmentalism.

The preceding arguments are about how human nature and social relationships are organized in the real world. They are not about whether there is an external world. However, even this fundamental assumption has come under attack from scholars who contend that humans have a compulsion to understand their world, and, in so doing, construct meanings in their minds. Because people respond to such constructions rather than to the external world itself, critics like Habermas (1972) or Harré and Secord (1972) contend that it is mind that determines behavior and not the world outside of the mind, if there is one. Note that this denial of realism is not based on a direct refutation. Rather, it postulates that we do not need to assume an external world if we can never prove that one exists and if we believe that humans react anyway to mental constructions of the world rather than to the world itself.

2. Epistemological assumptions Crucial to positivism is the assumption that "objective" knowledge is possible—that theory-neutral observations can be made that tap directly into nature and are not affected by the wishes, hopes, expectations, category systems, etc. of observers. So pervasive is the role of observation that positivists espouse a definitional operationalism that makes an entity no more or less than its measure. From this belief follows the dictum that "IQ is what IQ tests measure"; IQ is not seen to be a hypothetical entity defining the cognitive skills that are considered most useful for manipulating abstract knowledge.

Attacks on the neutrality or objectivity of observation have come from many quarters, largely on the grounds that science is conducted by people, and people cannot divorce themselves from their prior knowledge and expectations. The subjective components in observation may come from many sources—the social class biases stressed by Marxists, the paradigmatic biases emphasized by Kuhn (1962), or the investigator expectancies stressed by Merton (1957) and Rosenthal (Rosenthal & Jacobson, 1968). To those who crave certain knowledge from the senses no consolation is offered from modern developments in epistemology, metascience, or human perception (Campbell, 1974). And to those who believe that individuals may be biased but multiple observers may not be in the aggregate, it must be pointed out that Kuhn's work (1962) became so salient because his thesis was that *all* the scientists in a particular field at a particular time may share the same set of fallacious and unacknowledged assumptions that enter into all observations of nature.

Critics have also taken issue with according a special status to observables. Science has often progressed because bold thinkers were willing to postulate the unobservable, and, in some cases, were eventually proven correct. We still today cannot see the core of the earth, and yet geologists and mineralogists do research on how it might be composed. Moreover, some theories have only improved explanatory power by invoking constructs that cannot be directly observed, as with recent shifts by behaviorists to incorporate cognitive and affective phenomena (e.g., Bandura, 1977; Bower, 1981). The pragmatic case, then, is that neither prediction or explanation is enhanced by restricting oneself to observables.

The epistemological basis of positivism goes beyond postulating the possibility of observation that is both theory-neutral and comprehensive. Logic is also involved. Inductivist versions of positivism rely on abstracting general statements from observed regularities. To achieve this requires a defensible theory of induction, but none is yet available (Popper, 1959). Although attempts have been made to construct defenses of induction, it is not clear that they can deal with the logical problem inherent in inferring from past regularities that the same regularity will continue into the future. Among social scientists, a hypothetico-deductive version of positivism has had more adherents than a pure inductivist version. Accepting this critique of induction, hypothetico-deductivists recommend that scientists should strive to deduce unique observable hypotheses from a theory and they should then confront these hypotheses with observational data that will definitively confirm or disconfirm the hypotheses and their parent theory.

One of the many assumptions behind the hypothetico-deductive approach is that the theory being scrutinized is totally explicit in the constructs and patterns of relationship it specifies and in the ways it specifies how each construct should be measured. If a theory is not specific on these matters, disconfirming observations can be used, not to reject the theory—as is required in positivism—but rather to add novel theoretical contingencies that encompass the disconfirmations by specifying when a particular relationship should and should not be found or how a construct should and should not be measured. Unfortunately, nearly all of the social science theories of today are so "squishy" or "incommensurable" that little ingenuity is required to accommodate disconfirming results. Moreover, the passion that leads individuals to develop theories may often incline them to reject deviant findings in preference to accepting them as the new "truth." And when many of the major scholars in a field are proponents of a particular theory, disconfirmations will have an even more difficult battle because they then need to prevail against a powerful "invisible college" of scientific opinion-makers.

3. Methodological assumptions The primacy of indentifying functional relationships between observables means that observation and quantitative measurement play large roles in positivism. Without such data one cannot sensitively test the specific equations that predict an outcome. From the importance of quantified observation follow several important methodological consequences. The first is a stress on developing better techniques of measurement, e.g., more powerful telescopes, microscopes, x-rays, attitude scales, physiological measures, etc. The second is a move toward experimentation and laboratory sciences. Measurement is easier when the objects of study do not change in unknown ways, as occurs in much physics in which inert objects are studied and all the external sources of change in these objects have been earlier identified and can either be kept out of the explanatory system by such means as lead-lined walls or can be directly measured in credible ways.

However, the objects of study are not inert in the human sciences. They mature. They react to historical events. Moreover, we do not know all of the factors to which people react, and many of those we do know about are not measurable. From this arises the rationale for laboratory research, with its goal of isolation and control over extraneous variables. However, humans are adaptable and can construct beliefs and behaviors that help them adapt to the unique ecology of the laboratory. For instance, we know that humans often react to the suspicion they are being observed. But sometimes they react negatively, sometimes with resignation, and sometimes even with a misguided sense of helpfulness (Weber & Cook, 1972). Unfortunately, we do not know when they react each way; and even if we did we could not easily quantify how much the knowledge of being observed influenced particular responses. Because these theoretical irrelevancies cannot be totally specified, some scholars believe that it is preferable to prevent them from occurring at all. This means leaving the lab and conducting field research with unobtrusive measurement.

The concern with perfect prediction leads positivists to methods based on analytic reductionism—breaking an observed relationship down into the components that are necessary and sufficient for a relationship to occur. Positivists would not be satisfied with establishing that X is sometimes related to Y. They would like to discover what it is about X that is invariably related to some particular aspect of Y. To do this they decompose X and Y into their constituent elements, each of which will eventually be studied in its own right. But decomposing X into its causally efficacious components (say X') and Y into its causally impacted elements (say Y') may still not be enough. Perfect prediction may further depend on relating X' and Y' to "third variables" that codetermine their relationship, especially the more microscopically specified variables that occur after X' has changed and before Y' has been influenced. The upshot of the urge to improve prediction through decomposition and the discovery of substantively relevant mediating variables is a science that slowly gravitates to a more reductionist level of analysis, relatively closed systems as testing sites (e.g., the laboratory), and a form of research in which the control afforded by experimentation is valued more than the holism faciliated by naturalism.

Positivism is also associated with the belief that a single "crucial experiment" can definitively test a theory (or the difference in viability between one or more theories). Brute empiricism of the kind, "what will happen if I do X?" is not prized; nor is descriptive research that is devoid of hypothesis testing or willful intrusions into nature. The emphasis on the crucial experiment also leaves out of science phenomena that cannot be easily quantified or controlled, thereby running the risk that substantive importance may play less of a role in selecting research topics than the degree to which quanitification, control, prediction, experimentation, and theory testing are possible. We can see in the attack on positivist methods a rejection of the primacy of observation over introspection, quantification over understanding, micro-level over macro-level analysis, control over naturalism, theory testing over discovery, and crucial experiments conducted on select parts of nature over more tentative probing of all of nature.

4. The consequences of such attacks When scientists share a common set of assumptions it is presumably easier to decide how to proceed with the practice of science. One simply selects the kinds of problems and methods commensurate with the guiding assumptions. But when—as today—foundations are under attack, question and method choice become more problematic. It is now not easy to assume one is trying to describe a social world that is lawfully fixed, deterministically ordered, and can be perfectly described with elegant and simple functional relationships; it is not now easy to assume that everything of importance can be measured, that value-free measurement is possible, and that our theories are perfectly specified. It is not now easy to assume that closed-system methods generalize to open-system contexts, that crucial experiments are possible that provide definitive tests of theories, and that little value should be accorded to methods of discovery as opposed to methods of testing. Multiplism arose partly in response to such questioning of old certainties about question and method choice. But that was not its only origin, at least not in policy-related research.

B. Social Reform in the 1960s and 1970s

The Kennedy, Johnson, and Nixon presidencies were associated with social reforms in many sectors of the social welfare system. By and large, these proved to be disappointing in their effects. The major reasons for this were probably (1) inadequacies in the knowledge of society undergirding the design and implementation of social programs; (2) inadequacies of the social science methods used to evaluate these programs; and (3) limitations in the range of values and interests incorporated into both the definition of social problems and the selection of approaches designed to ameliorate these problems. Because these diagnoses overlap with the critique of positivism and disappointment with the gains of the Great Society and its offshoots occurred at about the same time positivism came under attack, it is difficult—if not impossible—to distinguish which parts of the advocacy of multiplism followed from the attack on positivism and which from the intellectual inquests on the Great Society.

We turn now to a discussion of *how* disappointment with social reform attempts influenced practice among social scientists. We argue that uncertainty was created about the degree of authority warranted by substantive social theory, by the research techniques then most widely accepted, and by the use of formal decisionmakers as the sole source for generating policy-relevant research questions.

1. The decrease in authority experienced by substantive theory Every social program is implicitly or explicitly undergirded by theoretical postulates about factors that will ameliorate a social problem, whether it is poor academic achievement, underemployment, or prison recidivism. Not surprisingly, social planners and program developers looked to social scientists for some of the knowledge they needed to design into specific practices that might ameliorate these problems. In retrospect, we can see that such expectations were inappropriate.

One difficulty that quickly became obvious was that most of the hypotheses used were internally inadequate. That is, doubts quickly became clear about the validity of such hypotheses as better food promotes learning in poor children; more police visibility reduces crime; rehabilitation lowers prison recidivism, largely because the relevant theories failed to specify the types of conditions under which a given relationship did and did not hold. The contact hypothesis in race relations is an instructive example in this regard because some contingencies were specified from its earliest days in the 1930s (Allport, 1935), but these were inadequate and new contingencies were added (Amir, 1969). But these, in their turn, did not turn out to be comprehensive enough, and we still cannot structure interracial contact that reliably decreases prejudice except in certain very controlled settings in schools.

A second problem with the substantive theories was that they were not comprehensive enough to use as action blueprints. In order to tell service deliverers about the specific acts they should perform under various sets of circumstances much improvisation had to take place on the part of program developers and local personnel. They were forced to build some forms of knowledge into program design that were not contained in the substantive theories of social scientists. Instead, they came from practitioner knowledge or from trial and error learning.

Finally, a new awareness emerged of how problematic it was to implement well in practice those relatively few activities about which substantive theories were indeed explicit. Pressman and Wildavsky (1979) stressed the implementation problems stemming from chaotic events that occur at the site of service delivery where the activities of multiple actors have to be coordinated; Williams (1980) stressed the problems of communication, commitment, and capacity that occur in trying to implement changes in multilevel organizational hierarchies; Fullan (1982) stressed practitioners' reluctance to accede to changes that were asked of them by superiors or outsiders who did not seem to understand or appreciate the pressures on service deliverers; and, finally, Berman (1980) and Bardach (1977) stressed how much implementation depends on system-level considerations of power, language, and history that bind or separate different groups in organizational contexts.

By the middle of the 1970s the authority of substantive social science theory for girding program design was under heavy attack, and alternatives and supplements were sought. Thus, the decrement in authority attributed to theory was accompanied by a corresponding increase in the authority attributed to other forms of knowledge, particularly practitioner wisdom. The claims on its behalf went beyond stressing how it was needed to fill in the gaps in social science knowlege. Claims were also heard that the practices advocated by social service professionals might be just as legitimate as scientific knowledge. The rationale offered was that in a vast nation like the United States, practice is likely to invent many variants, most of which never enter into the "permanent" stock of professional wisdom because they do not seem to be effective or only seem effective in restricted contexts. This suggests that the practices remaining in the permanent stock should include many that have repeatedly withstood unsystematic tests of their adequacy. The implication is that practice should be treated more like a legitimate, alternative form of relevant knowledge than as an ugly stepsister to science.

During the same period, a new value was accorded to observing closely what goes on in programs as they are first implemented. The expectation was that such observational studies would help improve the internal operations of programs and would also lay down a body of general knowledge from which principles about the design, implementation, and revision of social programs could be induced. Implicit in the advocacy of grounded observation was the critique that substantive social theory is often too abstract, too little tested in multiple action contexts, and too rarely formulated with implementation in mind. Consequently it fails to reflect, or be responsive to, the contextual density in which clients and practitioners actually operate and on which the effectiveness of programs depends. The growing pessimism about substantive theory was leavened, then, by growing optimism about the validity and utility of practitioner wisdom and about the roles that grounded observation can play when it is not guided by preordained theoretical concepts.

2. The decrease in authority experienced by particular social science methods In positivist science decision rules were clear and justified "authoritative" statements about scientific practice. As applied to the social sciences, most of the rules were about which methods to use in pursuing particular types of question; thus, to probe causal questions, randomized experiments were advocated; to probe descriptive questions about populations, sample surveys were proposed; and to probe descriptive issues about system relationships, participant observation was proposed. Rules were further formulated about how to do experiments, surveys, and observational studies and about the types of invalid inference that would result if inappropriate methods were chosen. In the 1950s and 1960s it was not difficult to know what were the proper things to do in the social sciences. But experience in the evaluation of social programs led to a weakening of the old links between research functions and methods. Previously advocated methods came to be seen as less deserving of hegemony for the tasks for which they were originally designed; other methods came to be seen as deserving more merit than had previously been allotted to them.

Perhaps the most famous example of this concerns methods for probing the causal effects of programs. Pessimism arose about the efficacy of randomized experiments for this purpose because so many experiments proved to be difficult to mount or to maintain in the desired form over time, especially because of the frequency of treatment-correlated attrition from the study. Moreover, the findings of most experiments were greeted, not with universal approval, but with cacophonous discord about what had really been discovered (Lindblom & Cohen, 1979). Although some of the criticisms were not relevant to random assignment per se, others were. One criticism stressed how random assignment exacerbated invidious comparisons between groups receiving treatments of different value; another stressed the differential attrition that can arise when treatments differ in desirability; and yet another mentioned how random assignment often led to undesirable restrictions to the external validity of studies. Thus, the crucible of experience forced out many of the problems inherent in conducting randomized experiments in open-system contexts. The same identification of weaknesses through experience happened with other forms of experimentation. The authority of many quasi-experimental designs came to suffer from an enhanced realization of the difficulty of specifying all the relevant ways in which treatment groups were nonequivalent and perfectly measuring all the constructs specified in models of such initial nonequivalence.

As might be expected, the identification of problems with particular methods also led to attempts to improve them. Thus arose the advocacy of randomized experiments in which all irrelevant sources of desirability between treatments were reduced; in which the units receiving one treatment could not communicate with those receiving another; and in which the implementation of the experimental design was monitored so as to detect differential attrition early in order to deal with it before it became too late (Cook and Campbell, 1979). (It was also hoped that such monitoring would improve the chances of detecting side effects and of specifying the different populations and settings in which a treatment might have an impact.) In the quasi-experimental domain, the identification of problems led to more self-consciousness about the need for explicit and defensible selection models and to attempts to circumvent the nonequivalence problem in other ways than through measurement and subsequent statistical manipulation; e.g., by means of dry-run experiments in which pretest measurement occurs on two separate occasions; by means of switching replication experiments in which treatments are eventually given to controls; or by means of nonequivalent dependent variables, only one of which is supposed to be affected by a treatment but each of which should be affected by the most plausible alternative interpretations of a treatment effect (Cook & Campbell, 1979). But although experimental methods were improved because of the knowledge generated from the problems identified during the course of social reform attempts, perfection did not result. Experimental methods were still stigmatized.

Some critics of the experiment argued that it was not enough to "band-aid" marginal improvements onto methods that, in their opinion, were fundamentally flawed. The most radical critics of the experiment wanted to search for truly novel methods of causal inference. In particular, a variety of qualitative alternatives were espoused. They were espoused not only on grounds that they facilitated inferences about simple causal relationships, but it was also stressed that they made it easier to assess the quality of treatment implementation, to detect unanticipated side effects, and to provide contextual understanding

(Patton, 1978). Supporting this advocacy were theories that explicitly set out to create a logical basis for inference based on qualitative data (e.g., Scriven's 1976 *modus operandi* approach and Campbell's apparent renunciation of the monolithic supremacy of experiments in Cook & Reichardt, 1979). With qualitative techniques added to the list of possible causal methods and with doubts being so public about the efficacy of randomized experiments, the authority of experiments shrank and method choice became all the more difficult for those who wanted to answer causal questions.

It would be wrong to believe that a decrement in authority was only experienced with experimental methods. As a means for describing populations, survey research methods have been much advocated and are regularly employed. However, recent critiques have stressed the practical difficulties that sometimes occur when trying to implement them; e.g., when resources permit mounting a demonstration project at only a few sites but generalization to the nation at large is desired (Cook, Leviton, & Shadish, in press). Also, ethical and political pressures demand that social research be increasingly conducted with groups and organizations that are fully informed about the research and can opt not to participate. Volunteer biases arise, and need adding to those associated with telephone ownership, being away from the home by day, etc.

As with experiments, the absolute decrement in authority attributed to survey methods was accompanied by an increase in the authority attributed to alternative means of generalization. Cook and Campbell (1979) proposed basing inferences about generalizability in terms of the degree to which relationships were dependably replicated across purposive but heterogeneous samples of respondents and settings, or on the degree to which the samples studied were impressionistically modal of a desired target population (see also St. Pierre & Cook, in press). The popularity of meta-analysis seems also to have added credibility to the idea that generalized statements are often warranted when findings have been multiply replicated across heterogeneous samples of respondents, settings, and times, none of which were chosen with known probability from a designated population. Although inferences based on continuities across heterogeneous instances do not have the same logical warrant as inferences based on samples in which the probability of selection is known, they are nonetheless not completely without worth. This being so, we can see that the authority of the sample survey was squeezed from two ends: Increased doubts arose about its absolute adequacy, and an enhanced justification was offered for some alternatives that are more easily implemented. This double squeeze is exactly what occurred with experiments.

The experiences gained in designing and evaluating social reforms in the 1960s and 1970s led to another important insight about method choice. Such choice is made all the more difficult, not only because many methods exist for fulfilling any one research function, but also because multiple functions have to be met in most individual research studies. To be more specific, in the 1960s and 1970s applied social scientists with backgrounds in psychology became increasingly aware that experimental design was only a part of research design, and that the latter involved choices about sampling, measurement, data collection, data analysis, and strategies for disseminating results. Correspondingly, researchers with backgrounds in sociology and economics became more aware of causal concerns and experimental design.

More important than the realization of more decision points and more alternatives at each point was the realization that the methods chosen for one research function might constrain the range of methods available for fulfilling another function. Thus, when a particular experimental design was chosen, this constrained sampling options, and vice versa. Likewise, if a particular data collection procedure was chosen, the choice of data analysis was constrained, and vice versa. Research design came to be seen more as the art of reconciling conflicting demands imposed by the constraints that followed once a particular method was chosen for fulfilling a particular research function. Scholars even came to realize that one may sometimes choose a generally inferior method on the dual grounds that it provides valid "enough" results about, say, causal connections *and* also makes it easier to select a different method for fulfilling a different research function; say, generalization. Methods have to be selected not only for their logical adequacy, but also for their fit to the rest of an overall research design and to the priorities built into that design. Because of this realization method choice became even more difficult.

3. The decrease in authority experienced by formal decisionmakers
Most social scientists in the 1960s seem to have been willing to work within a system for defining and solving social problems that was set by formal decisionmakers from the executive and legislative branches of government. Social scientists were widely seen to be the servants of such persons, helping them to plan policy and programs and test how efficacious they were. So long as this source of policy-relevant questions remained unproblematic, it was not especially difficult for researchers interested in social policy to formulate the issues and questions they sought to investigate.

But experience in the 1960s and 1970s made it clear that in the world of social policy it is rare to find clear definitions of problems, potential solutions, and research questions, for a lack of specificity helps create the political consensus required for obtaining agreements about action from a group of heterogeneous and powerful interests. Moreover, decisionmakers do not operate in a void. They are open to multiple sources of influence and to many conflicting values. In deciding what to support, decisionmakers consider many points of view—national ideology, personal preference, political survival, and personal advantage. They also sometimes consider social science evidence. But this is only one of many inputs into decisionmaking and will rarely be of sufficient centrality to determine decisions (Weiss & Weiss, 1981). The political system is a world where many statements are deliberately unclear and do not reflect what is intended, many conflicting forces operate, many different forms of knowledge are respected, and action is multiply determined. But although the political system is open and includes many actors representing many points of view, formal decisionmakers may themselves be relatively homogeneous in some respects. They may be especially inclined, for instance, to blame social groups and individuals in need for their plight, to propose solutions that are marginally ameliorist and not radical, to favor solutions that directly or indirectly favor the interests of business, and to press for actions that promise seemingly dramatic results in a short period. Given the growing evidence about how the political system operates, it is not surprising that a decrement occurred among some social scientists in the authority they were prepared to attribute to formal decisionmakers as the sole, or even the major, source of problem definitions, potential solutions, and information needs.

As with theories and methods, the decline of formal decisionmakers as the major source of priorities and values was associated with the rise of other alternatives. Foremost among these was a pluralist conception based on conducting policy research whose assumptions and questions reflect the values and information needs of multiple stakeholders. Researchers were no longer encouraged to see themselves as servants of powerful, formal decisionmakers. Instead, they were urged to consider and consult with all interested parties. In the health system, this meant not only federal agencies and congressional committees and their staffs, but also hospital administrators and the professional associations representing them; physicians and nurses and the associations representing them; insurance companies; hospital patients; and health policy researchers. These groups have different interests concerning health matters and different information needs about particular health programs. Formal decisionmakers can only imperfectly represent these multiple interests, each of which could probably represent itself much better. Consequently, pluralists emphasize that researchers should avoid building the restricted set of assumptions of the powerful into their research; they want researchers to consult with all the relevant stakeholder groups in the sector under study.

Some theroists advocate pluralism in the formulation of policy questions, not only because this reflects the form of democracy in which they believe, but also because they believe that consulting with multiple stakeholders is more likely to lead to research results being used in policy debates. This is because the results should be relevant to more groups, and more groups should then know of them (Leviton & Hughes, 1981). Other theorists see pluralism as a means of raising the researcher's consciousness about the social values latent in how formal decisionmakers interpret problems and questions. However, stakeholder analysis is not the only means of forcing out hidden assumptions and values. Other means to this end include procedures such as the Science Court and substantive standing committees in the manner of the National Research Council (briefly reviewed in Hennigan, Flay, & Cook, 1980), as well as textual analysis in the manner of hermeneutics and the Delphi technique. However, the major point is not that techniques exist to make assumptions explicit; rather, it is that in the last 20 years a decline in the authority of formal decisionmakers has taken place that required the development or use of such techniques. It is not now easy to see formal decisionmakers as the major, legitimate source of research priorities and of the values built into the design of research or the interpretations of findings. Related to this decline is an increase in the authority of alternative sources of questions and values, particularly pluralist sources or sources based on some form of critical analysis.

4. Declines are not disappearances With theory, methods, and values I have described a decrease in the authority of established choice alternatives and a growth in the authority of other alternatives, some of them previously discredited. It is important in this respect to note that the decreases in authority were not to a level that made the dominant alternatives lose all their authority. Substantive theory is still useful for program design; certain methods are still useful for generating particular forms of knowledge; and formal decisionmakers are still useful for producing research that gets used. Indeed, in all three cases it is probably still possible to argue that, of all the possible alternatives, the old one is the best. In the last 20 years we have witnessed the overthrow of the hegemony previously attributed to particular choices and a consequent increase in the difficulties of choice for practicing social scientists. It is within this context of old certainties unthroned, but not abolished, that the call for multiplism arose.

MULTIPLISM

1. The theory The fundamental postulate of multiplism is that when it is not clear which of several options for question generation or method choice is "correct," all of them should be selected so as to "triangulate" on the most useful or the most likely to be true. If practical constraints prevent the use of multiple alternatives, then at least more than one should be chosen, preferrably as many as span the full range of plausible alternative interpretations of what constitutes a useful question or a true answer. To make this concrete, consider one of the oldest explicit rationales for multiplism—that offered for multiple operationalism (Campbell & Fiske, 1959; Webb, Campbell, Schwartz, & Sechrest, 1966).

Once the notion has been rejected that an entity is equivalent to its measure, four major difficulties arise in deciding how to measure entities or constructs. Deciding on a clear definition is crucial to measurement. Yet in every scholarly field or policy domain there is active disagreement about definitions. Even after one or more conceptual definitions has been selected, each still has to be operationally specified in terms of manipulable or measurable procedures. The second difficulty is that each operational definition will inevitably include components not in the conceptual definition. These components can be of many kinds. One that often occurs is when a measure is made in a particular mode but the mode is not part of the definition; e.g., aggression is measured in a paper-and-pencil mode (Campbell & Fiske, 1959). Another is when a measure is made at one time, but the situational factors that might have influenced responding at that one time are not part of the definition. The third problem is that operational measures will sometimes fail to include necessary components of the conceptual definition; e.g., the "intent to harm" that is crucial in some definitions of aggression. Finally, with multidimensional constructs, the weights implicitly assigned to dimensions in the operational measure may correspond imperfectly to the weights implicit or explicit in conceptual definitions. Thus, a mathematics test might be designed to measure knowledge of algebra, trigonometry, and arithmetic equally, but, in practice, may assign more weight to algebra than the other two components. In this case, all the substantive components are present, but their weights deviate from what has been defined. For these four reasons, a single measure will inevitably be inadequate.

Because it is not clear what a "correct" measure is, it is desirable to measure or manipulate a construct in several ways. From a multiple operationalist perspective, the choice of operations is constrained by several requirements. First, each representation should by itself be a "reasonable" measure of the target construct. Second, the various measures should differ in the dimensions they contain that are irrelevant to the target construct but might influence how it is measured. This implies that across all the instances there should be a "heterogeneity of irrelevancies" so that the same irrelevancies are not present with all the representations of a construct, as would happen if we had several measures of X but all were collected in a face-to-face interview. Third, at least one measure should contain all of the dimensions considered necessary to the target construct so that the full definition of a construct is present in at least one of its representations, even though other irrelevancies are also likely to be present with that representation.

The purpose of multiple operationalism is to examine whether comparable results are obtained with each measure or manipulation. If they are, researchers can conclude that a triangulation of results is achieved across measures that are similar to each other in theoretically relevant sources of shared variance but differ from each other in the theoretically irrelevant sources of variance each contains that might have influenced the relationships obtained with any one of the measures. The multiple measures are meant to converge on a single interpretation by fulfilling two functions: (1) Demonstrating replication; and (2) ruling out all alternative interpretations of the measures because no single alternative is present across all the heterogeneous instances in which a particular construct-defining empirical relationship was obtained.

When the obtained results do not converge across different measures of the same construct, an empirical puzzle results. In synthesizing many causal studies, for example, the implication would be that X and Y are only related under some conditions, and the need arises to specify these conditions. If an irrelevancy in one of the measures were eventually isolated as the crucial causal contingency, one would then specify that X and Y are related, when, say, direct observation occurs but not when paper-and-pencil measures are used. In this particular case, the contingency is of minor theoretical importance. However, other controlling contingencies can be of greater theoretical or practical utility, as when one specifies that a particular substantive component of construct X is crucial for bringing about the observed X-Y relationship.

One can then specify that Y is related to X' but not X'', e.g., mandatory desegregation is related to minority achievement gains but voluntary desegregation is not. Whatever the outcome, multiple operationalism is always useful. Empirical convergences increase confidence about dependability; and failures to converge present empirical puzzles whose solution will often specify the particular operational formulations on which a relationship depends.

2. The forms of multiplism Although I outlined the theory of multiplism as it was developed to circumvent the problems inherent in definitional operationalism, a similar conceptualization based on multiple verification and the falsification of identified alternative interpretations undergirds all forms of multiplism. Because, in my construction, multiplism was a response to the attacks on positivism and to the experiences gained in studying the social reforms of the 1960s and 1970s, we might expect the forms multiplism takes to correspond to the specifics of these attacks and experiences. In general, they do.

One form multiplism takes is in the search to discover systems of causal determination that are more complex than the predictive equations of positivism or the simple bivariate causal connections of most laboratory research. Following leads from population biology, social scientists have increasingly turned to path analysis or structural equation modeling. This technique is based on using theory to identify the hypothesized—and usually multiple—determinants of a particular phenomenon, including the ways in which these determinants are linked to each other and are themselves determined by outside forces. Such causal modeling assumes a social world whose structure is more "multivariate-complex" than the physical world, and the links in this structure are thought to be probabilistic rather than deterministic, for the coefficients that link constructs in path analysis are expressed as probability statements. The world that social scientists seek to describe is also assumed to be influenced by many types of constructs, not just the physical and immediate. Indeed, sociological models of status attainment include historical constructs (e.g., mother's education), motivational constructs (e.g., need for achievement), cognitive constructs (e.g., achievement level), and observable structural constructs (e.g., the number of positions available at each level in an organizational pyramid). Although realist, the operational ontology of most social scientists differs from the positivists' world of parsimonious, deterministic, ahistorical, and nonmentalist observable forces.

Many social scientists now assume a highly contingent world in which few relationships are so dependable that they hold across a wide variety of persons, settings, and times. Statistical main effects will not describe this world as well as higher-order statistical interactions. But to isolate these interactions requires, at a minimum, sampling across multiple groups, settings, and times. This necessarily entails probing how generalizable particular relationships are. Postpositivist social science cares more than its predecessors for heterogeneous sampling and data analyses that examine the degree of dependability achieved across subpopulations.

But because of obvious resource constraints, this preference cannot always be well addressed in the design and analysis of individual studies. This helps explain the higher status recently accorded to literature reviews, for they can be used to probe the degree of dependability achieved across the range of populations, settings, and times sampled in the multiple studies conducted in the past. As a reflection of this renewed interest in reviews, Cronbach (1982) has sought to raise evaluators' awareness of the gains to be made by fitting one's findings into the existing literature without necessarily doing any new data analyses. However, novel methods of quantitative syntheses have recently become available thanks largely to the work of Glass, Rosenthal, and Light, recently summarized by Light and Pillemer (in press). The hope is that through syntheses of multiple studies one will be able to identify relationships of such stability that they hold across a wide range of populations, settings, and times, as well as across a wide range of operational representations and previously unexamined threats to internal validity. The value of single studies is reduced in the postpositivist world, especially the value of studies that claim to be crucial experiments.

It is perhaps in the epistemological domain that multiplism is most obvious in recent practice. I have previously outlined the general move from definitional to multiple operationalism. Within the context of causal modeling, multiple operationalism is best exemplified by maximum likelihood factor analytic models such as LISREL (Joreskog & Sorbum, 1978), which require researchers to make theoretical models as explicit as possible and to specify the nature of the links between theoretical constructs and the multiple imperfect measures that have been made of each construct. This form of causal modeling makes it more difficult than heretofore to squirm away from disconfirming data by arguing that hypothesis tests were inadequate because the substantive theory was poorly specified, the constructs were poorly measured, or the links between measures and latent constructs were not clear. Do not get me wrong. Even with causal modeling done by LISREL, one can still argue that the quality of measurement was too low to provide a convincing test. The present argument is only that sustaining such a case is more difficult when multiple measures have been collected that obviously triangulate on a construct than when a single measure has been used to represent each of the theoretical constructs.

In postpositivist multiplism, researchers do not aspire to the single perfect test that will confirm or falsify a hypothesis. Indeed, they may even reject single tests altogether. Statisticians like Tukey (1977) consider all inferential data analyses as exploratory and they note that inferences are better based on multiple probes of a relationship than single tests. In quasi-experimental research, multiple data analyses will particularly raise the quality of interpretations because many different and plausible models of selection can be invoked to describe pretest group differences. The aspiration is to triangulate on the same inference despite any presumed differences in bias built into the various selection models used as part of a data analysis strategy. With causal explanatory models, the advocacy is to pit multiple models in competition with each other rather than to test the goodness of fit of a single model. The problem with testing a single model is that, even if the obtained data are consistent with the model, they might be even more consistent with other models. When multiple explanatory models are explicitly pitted against each other, the aim is to see which one is superior rather than which one is necessarily "true." Notice at this point the many levels at which multiplism is possible. First, multiple causal models should be placed in competition with each other; second, each of the models should include multiple constructs; third, each construct should be multiply measured; and fourth, the constructs can be of multiple types—mentalist, historical, or whatever. Finally, multiple probes of the relative fit of the models may be needed if ambiguities of interpretation should occur after the first analysis.

In policy research that follows a social science model we have recently witnessed a growing advocacy of studies with a multitask focus (Chen & Rossi, 1980, 1983). The 1960s were dominated by a social experimentation model that explicitly assumed the priority of research tasks designed to probe questions about how program-related variables affected outcomes that seemed to be related to the amelioration of social problems. No one was more associated with this position than Campbell (e.g., 1969). But at the same time in econometrics, and later in both sociology and evaluation, the priority shifted from exploring bivariate causal relations to exploring multivariate explanatory models that specify why something causes something else. This entails investigating within the programmatic black box so as to probe what there is in it that might make a program effective. But because most programs were less effective than hoped, opening up the black box was most important for determining why the effects obtained were so modest in size and range. Of the many reasons for disappointment, one was that program services sometimes failed to reach their target beneficiaries; another was that even when they did, the services were not implemented as often or as well as had been hoped. These hypotheses helped put onto the research agenda the study of how services were targeted and implemented.

Policy studies were thus expected to fulfill multiple descriptive and explanatory tasks simultaneously. At a minimum, they were supposed to provide descriptions of program clients, service implementation, and program effects. It was also expected they would explain why some clients were reached and not others, why some patterns of implementation were obtained and not others, and why some effects came about and not others. As the popularity of hermeneutics increased, policy studies came increasingly under pressure to include analyses of the implicit value assumptions in how a social program was formulated and in how the results might be interpreted. Also, calls were increasingly heard to expand the researcher's role so that he or she was made increasingly responsible, not only for producing relevant and valid results, but also for acting to bring the results to the attention of relevant parties and to help them interpret the results in terms of their interests (Cronbach et al., 1980).

The multiplicity of tasks is inevitably associated with a multiplicity of methods. But multiple methods were not now advocated for making heterogeneous the method variance associated with a single test of a single research question. Now multiple methods were espoused because it seemed more important to answer a wider range of questions than those concerned with describing the causal effects of social programs. The hegemony of causal questions justified the near-exclusive advocacy of experimental methods. But once questions about populations, service delivery, the range of effects, the nature of causal contingency variables, the use of research results, and their value assumptions became more important, so too did issues of sampling, measurement, data collection, data analysis, and textual criticism. The primacy of quantification also seemed less obvious, and qualitative methods came to be more openly espoused and made relevant to more research tasks. Indeed, the rationale for them subtly shifted. No longer were they promoted to describe implementation, to discover unplanned side effects, and to give grounded and firsthand understanding. They also came to be promoted because they can sometimes facilitate inferences about causal relationships and causal explanations. The legitimization of a wider range of tasks in policy research meant not only that multiple questions and issues were raised, but also that multiple methods were increasingly used in individual studies.

The advocacy of qualitative data collection methods goes beyond their flexibility and potential for describing, discovering, explaining, and communicating. Also involved is their potential for prioritizing research issues. If researchers take seriously their own firsthand experiences in the field and those of the managers, service providers, clients, and experts with whom they come into contact, then grounded knowledge may emerge from which it may be possible to infer new research priorities. This suggests a new source of research questions over and above derivations from substantive theory or catering to the presumed information needs of formal policymakers. Indeed, in a democracy with pretensions to pluralism, formal policymakers should probably not be the only group whose information needs, and hence whose political interests, evaluators should meet. Every policy decision has the potential to impact on multiple stakeholder groups, and discussions with these groups often teach us that they want to learn different things. For instance, although formal policymakers in the federal or state capitals might want to know how school desegregation influences white flight, the academic achievement of black children, and classroom discipline, judges and school districts facing desegregation decisions may want to know how different desegregation plans influence public acceptance of desegregation. They want to identify the options they should choose, and the label "desegregation" is far too global to be helpful in their planning. On the other hand, officials in school districts that have already desegregated may want to identify classroom practices that prevent resegregation within classrooms or that enhance cross-race contact; parents in those districts may want to know how desegregation has influenced academic achievement and discipline; local political officials may want to know how desegregation affects taxpayer identification with the school district and approval of the school board; and local business leaders may want to know how desegregation influences property values, sales tax revenues, and the type of families moving into the district. A respect for direct experience and for the experiences and wishes of multiple stakeholders means that multiple sources and types of research questions become legitimate. This, in turn, creates more sources of uncertainty for the social researcher interested in policy. Where should he or she look for guidance about which research issues are worth tackling and about how these issues should be phrased?

Once it was realized that social science is concerned, not with guaranteeing truth or utility, but with offering defensible interpretations of what is in the outside world, the problem arose as to who should offer such interpretations. In a culture that claims to be libertarian and pluralist, it is not surprising that the answer was that multiple interpretations and values should be offered that cover a broad spectrum of individual and group interests. This went beyond the call for multiple stakeholders research; it also included the call for secondary analysis in which multiple researchers have the chance to criticize others' formulations of issues, choice of methods, and interpretations of results. The purposes of multiple competing analyses are to estimate the degree of correspondence between investigators who differ in their value and method preferences and to use any differences in findings to discover the nature of the analysts' implicit assumptions. The important point is that investigators who actively seek to reexamine another's work are likely to be especially motivated to detect errors or limitations in the assumptions made (Cook, 1974). The presumption is that no one is better able to identify factors that restrict interpretations than one's professional "enemies." Without their motivated criticism, plausible alternative interpretations are less likely to be identified and probed, and knowledge claims are all the more likely to turn out to be false in the long run.

The advantages of heterogeneous review were also associated with the call to have policy research be actively monitored by advisory boards composed both of scholars with substantive or methodological expertise and members of heterogeneous interest groups. Also heard were calls to provide funding for multiple, simultaneously conducted studies on the same issue from different value perspectives. To this end, the National Institute of Education recently asked six experts to conduct meta-analyses of the school desegregation literature. Two of the scholars had publicly claimed that desegregation increases the achievement of minority children; two others had claimed that desegregation does not influence achievement; and the other two seemed more value-neutral judging by what they had published on the issue. But perhaps the most salient response to the value-ladenness of science has been the call to use a variety of different iterative techniques to discover all the hidden assumptions in research, whether this be in a science court context, through hermeneutic textual analysis, or through invited debates involving publicly identified proponents of multiple value positions. In all of these suggestions is the assumption that parochial value perspectives can be easily slipped into that run throughout all the research on a topic. By making multiple and heterogeneous the preferences and values of investigators, the aim is to infuse research with multiple value perspectives and to analyze completed research from a variety of different value positions. In all cases, the concern is the same: To identify commonalities of finding and interpretation through processes that vigorously attempt to falsify all the claims made about knowledge and utility.

3. The advantages of multiplism Multiplism is meant to raise consciousness about what should be learned to help increase the likelihood that knowledge claims are true. It aims to do the former by discovering as wide a range of perspectives on utility as is possible, probing for correspondence and differences, and using the differences to analyze why they occur so as to achieve a better understanding of the reasons to prefer some formulations of what is useful over others. Multiplism aims to foster truth by establishing correspondences across many different, but conceptually related, ways of posing a question and by ruling out whether any obtained correspondences are artifacts of any epiphenomena of value, substantive theory, or method choice that have been inadvertently incorporated into individual tests.

Multiplism is attractive inferentially because the greater the heterogeneity of irrelevancies across which a relationship holds, the greater is the likelihood that threats to any kind of validity can be ruled out. Thus, when results are demonstrably stable across populations, settings, and times, external validity is enhanced. When results are stable across many ways of assessing covariation (and not just a single statistical test), statistical conclusion validity is enhanced. When results are stable across multiple potential threats to causal inference, internal validity is enhanced. And when interpretation of the meaning of relationships in theoretical and value terms is common across a wide variety of perspectives, objectivity—defined as intersubjective verifiability—is enhanced. Multiplism does not guarantee that all the threats to each of these kinds of validity are ruled out, but it does increase the likelihood. Moreover, the gain in validity should be associated with a gain in credibility. This may, in turn, increase the likelihood that results based on a multiplist approach will be used as part of the total input into decisions about social action. Multiplism promises payoffs, then, for generalization, theoretical meaning, dependability of associations, the validity of causal knowledge, and the social utility of research knowledge. This is a considerable potential.

But multiplism also promises greater specificity. When data patterns do not converge across multiple measures, methods, populations, settings, times, and the like, the search begins to identify the contingencies controlling the relationship. Being able to specify such contingencies helps avoid misinterpretations about generality. This is especially important if X and Y are related positively under some conditions but negatively or not at all under others, as opposed to the case in which X and Y are related by the same sign but the magnitude of the relationship varies. Being able to specify causal contingencies also helps create a specificity about domains of relevance, as when one learns that *Sesame Street* increases knowledge of the alphabet but not problem solving. Even when resources or ingenuity have not allowed all the relevant theoretical and value interpretations to be directly examined empirically, a multiplist frame of mind is still useful. It identifies more of the still untested assumptions on which provisionally identified knowledge depends, thus creating an environment in which the consumers of research are invited to make up their own minds about the explicitly acknowledged assumptions on which their acceptance of findings should depend.

Multiplism also promises to provide us with more comprehensive pictures of how policies impact on the social world than those to which we are used. It teaches us that question formulation benefits from considering multiple sources, such as competing theoretical models, the information needs of multiple stakeholder groups, and the use of one's own and others' grounded experience to trust novel issues to the fore. If all of these sources are used to identify research issues, the latter will be framed at a higher level of consciousness. Moreover, it is highly likely that they will eventually create a more comprehensive understanding of which policy changes are needed, of what the changes implemented to date have achieved, and of why they have achieved what they have. From a multiplist perspective it would be well-nigh impossible to have learned how school desegregation influences white flight without also having probed how it affects property values, black achievement, school discipline, racial prejudice, or parental cooperation in the PTA; it would be almost impossible to have learned something about such a global and variable entity as school desegregation while remaining ignorant of the effects of various forms it takes, e.g., magnet schools, metropolitan desegregation plans, etc. Multiplism breeds knowledge about a broad universe of effects, a large set of contingency conditions, and differentiated conceptions of the social policy or social program under analysis.

Finally, multiplism promises to make policy research more intellectual, value conscious, and debate-centered. This promise follows from the frank recognition that social science research, although it strives to minimize the intrusion of values or deliberately tries to make them heterogeneous, can never totally rule them out. From this arises the multiplist's impulsion to explicate latent value and interest assumptions. Multiplists hope that primary authors will do this in a self-conscious fashion. But they know that it is best achieved through critical commentary by scholars, practitioners, and other interested parties who hold different values and methodological preferences from those of primary authors. Although some persons may deplore the social and possibly contentious nature of the knowledge so achieved and still aspire to nuggets of truth revealed by some divine methodological hand, these nuggets will not be forthcoming. Multiplism has the potential to breed honesty rather than self-delusion and to force out assumptions for more enlightened public debate. But in such debates it is important to realize that although points of disagreement may generate the most heat, there will often be some points of convergence. These promise to be sources of light and so deserve special scrutiny in case they have attained their special status by withstanding all attempts to refute them, and so reflect more than an underexamined social consensus.

THE LIMITATIONS OF MULTIPLISM

Despite its real and potential advantages, multiplism is no panacea. Among its limitations, I want to discuss two: The problem of constant bias across heterogeneous instances; and the absence of an algorithm for specifying what should be made heterogeneous in a single study granted that for practical reasons not everything that should be made heterogeneous can be. In discussing this last point we shall discuss the danger of falling into a flabby relativism about question and method preferences that makes all sources equally legitimate and equates truth with social consensus.

1. Constant bias: The single source The old story according to which Tycho Brahe and all before him saw the sun move to set behind the stationary earth illustrates that some biases—in this case a perceptual, geocentric one—are so widely shared socially that they cannot be made heterogeneous. No one can conceive of the bias being a bias. Kuhn (1962) has discussed the same issue in more recent times. In the more mundane setting of current survey research we are mindful of the constant biases potentially produced when, despite multiple versions of a question, all the interviewers are middle class and ask questions face-to-face. While question-wording is heterogeneous in this case, the mode of data collection is not. Similarly, if parental reports, peer reports, and playground observation each indicate increased children's aggression, this makes heterogeneous the observer and the mode of data collection. But if for each measure the response categories are limited to verbal aggression, pushing, and shoving many laymen might want to label the tests as measuring boisterousness or incivility rather than aggression, for none of the measures is explicitly based on intending to do harm or on leaving the other person in physical pain. In the previously discussed meta-analyses of school desegregation (National Institute of Education, 1984), the 19 school districts studied were from all parts of the United States, the studies covered a 20-year period, and the desegregation plans varied considerably. But still, the latest study was published in 1971; nearly all the school districts desegregated voluntarily rather than as a result of court mandates; achievement gains were assessed after one or two years of desegregation; and no reasonable estimates could be made of the gains of children who had never attended segregated schools before transferring to desegregated ones. Once again we see that, despite considerable heterogeneity, a number of different biases were constant throughout the studies. As a final example of constant bias consider Director's (1979) research on job training programs. He surveyed many studies that differed in many ways, all of which concluded that the programs in question failed to benefit graduates. However, in all cases, the persons receiving training had poorer employment histories than the control groups, resulting in what Campbell and Boruch (1975) would call a constant underadjustment of the initial differences between people in job programs and their controls. If it occurred, this source of constant bias would underestimate the effects of job training.

When many sources of potential bias have been made heterogeneous in a study or across a set of studies, the danger always is that the obviousness of the heterogeneity so achieved may lull researchers out of a critical frame of mind. They may be less likely to ask whether any other sources of bias-inducing homogeneity might still be operating that produce repeated convergence on the wrong answer! The origins of this danger go beyond the human preference to attribute a law-like status to multiple repeated instances of a relationship (Tversky & Kahnemann, 1977). They also stem from the fact that, *ceteris paribus*, even mindless multiplism entails a wider range of demonstrated convergences and the ruling out of more threats to validity. Thus, a review of job corps studies is likely to include centers with different operating philosophies and different populations of job seekers; the centers are likely to be located in many different parts of the country;

seen as a whole, the evaluations are likely to have many different measures of job preparation, earnings, and job performance; and, finally, some of them are likely to have been set up quasi-experimentally and others (post-Director!) as randomized experiments. In light of such achieved heterogeneity it would indeed be tempting to claim that the obtained results hold for job corps centers in general (and not just for those with particular philsophies), for job seekers of all backgrounds (and not those of a certain ethnic group or education level), for all parts of the country (rather than certain regions), for all measures of earnings (and not just self-reports), and for studies in which the various treatment groups were initially constituted in a similar or dissimilar fashion. However, the relationship between the degree of multiplism and the likelihood of more valid inferences is governed by a *ceteris paribus* clause. What multiplism makes more likely, it does not necessarily guarantee. It does not follow from multiple heterogeneous replication that all sources of constant bias have been identified and ruled out.

2. Constant bias: Multiple sources operating in the same direction It is important to differentiate between a constant source of bias (as illustrated in the examples above) and a constant direction of bias. The two are related; all things being equal, a constant source of bias will result in a constant direction of bias. Note, though, that a constant direction of bias can also result when all the individual sources of identified doubt have been made heterogeneous across all of the tests examined. To exemplify this, consider the literature on the effects of television violence, recently reviewed by Huesmann as part of the NIMH Report on *Television and Behavior* and studied meta-analytically by Hearold (1979). Only a minor part of Huesmann's chapter deals with whether television violence increases aggression; for like most others, he believes that the issue is closed. His belief rests on the consistency of past findings from laboratory and field experiments, cross-sectional surveys, and panel studies. To accept such consistency as a basis for believing that television causes aggression, one must logically accept that the different methods do not share biases operating in the same direction and the past studies using unbiased methods have been accurately reviewed.

It is obvious why laboratory experiments may exaggerate any link between television violence and aggression for normal children in everyday settings. Experiments have to produce aggression to discriminate between the outcomes of different treatments. Yet aggression is a relatively rare event. So, experiments are designed to minimize inhibitions against aggression, to minimize external cues sanctioning aggression, and to maximize the clarity and intensity of short-term experimental treatments that have been deliberately chosen because they are likely to foster aggression. Although appropriate for discriminating between treatments, this strategy is not obviously relevant to drawing conclusions about regular television programming in the home, in which internal cues against aggression may operate more powerfully, situational cues sanction aggression, and television aggressors are punished, usually by characters with prosocial qualities that are themselves presumably worthy of emulation. Also, the violent scenes on television are interspersed with many different types of activity, and viewers are free to watch intermittently or with low levels of involvement.

Positive bias is also likely in cross-sectional surveys in which the amount of exposure to violence is correlated with aggression scores, holding constant background variables that are thought to correlate with viewing and aggression. The adequacy of this approach depends on how completely selection differences between heavier and lighter viewers are modeled and how well the constructs in the model are measured. Usually, the selection models are primitive, involving demographic variables such as age, sex, race, etc. that are presumably proxies for the true (and unknown) psychological and social factors that cause differences in exposure to violence. Campbell and Boruch (1975) have argued that "underadjustment" is likely to occur in this situation so that although some of the true selection differences will be removed; not all of them will. The synchronous correlation between viewing and aggression is positive, although usually small: In the .15 to .25 range. If Campbell and Boruch are correct, some of the background differences between heavier and lighter viewers will not have been removed, and estimates of the relationship between television and aggression will be somewhat inflated. Not everyone agrees with Campbell and Boruch. Cronbach, Rogosa, Floden, & Price (1977) believe that overadjustment can sometimes occur, as can perfect adjustment. However, in the last case we do not yet know when it will be! The point is *not* that underadjustment bias has occurred in all past cross-sectional studies of television and aggression; it is only that a plausible case can be made that the bias might have operated.

Huesmann mentions six reports of field experiments involving random assignment in nonlaboratory settings. Four were said to have yielded evidence of a positive relation between violence viewing and aggression, the exceptions being Feshbach and Singer (1971) and Wells (1973). However, the study of Loye, Gorney, and Steele (1977) is also an exception because the data show that the group assigned to a television diet of high violence was no more likely to commit hurtful behaviors than the controls. Moreover, the experiment of Stein and Friedrich (1972) showed weak effects confined to a subgroup of initially more aggressive children, and, according to Parke, Berkowitz, Legens, West, and Sebastian (1977), this result failed to replicate it (Sawin, 1973). Thus, four of the six studies are problematic. Of the two others, the work of Loye et al. is also included as one of three experiments reported in Parke et al. (1977) that therefore emerges as the crucial report claiming to find effects of television violence. However, these field experiments deal with institutionalized children; regular television viewing was forbidden, possibly creating frustration; and in two studies the boys assigned to view aggressive films were intially more aggressive. In our view, the field experiments on television violence produce little consistent evidence of effects despite claims to the contrary and the instances in which an effect is claimed involve populations that seem to be initially more aggressive.

It is widely agreed that the best method for studying television effects involves longitudinal panel studies. Unfortunately, the state of the analytic art has recently changed. The formerly advocated analysis based on cross-lagged panel correlations is misleading when test-retest correlations differ between variables. Then, the less reliable measure will spuriously appear to be causal (Cook & Campbell, 1979; Rogosa, 1980). Television viewing is nearly always less stable than aggressiveness, as in the study by Lefkowitz, Eron, Walder, and Huesmann (1972) in the Surgeon-General's report and in the original data that Huesmann includes in his chapter in the NIMH report. It may also be the case with Singer and Singer (1980), who used cross-lagged panel analysis. Thus, a bias may also have operated in past panel studies to produce a spurious relationship between television viewing and aggression. Indeed, two recent panel studies that used more appropriate analytic models resulted in one case that concluded that no relationship exists between television violence and aggression (Milavsky, Kessler, Stipp, & Rubens, 1982) and in another case that concluded that at most only a very modest relationship might exist (Huesmann, Lagerspetz, & Eron, 1982).

Like most summaries of television violence and its effects, the NIMH Report is somewhat uncritical in its claim that the question has been answered and in its implication that the effect is widespread. The reliance on evidence from multiple methods is admirable—in the abstract. But the viability of such a strategy depends on the absence of biases operating in the same direction across all of the methods. However, this absence cannot be assumed. Although it is indeed the case that what was problematic with the laboratory experiments was made heterogeneous across the other kinds of research and what was problematic with the surveys was made heterogeneous across some of the other forms of research, there is nonetheless presumptive evidence that in each form of research a unique form of bias operated to overestimate the effects of television. We do not, then, have a constant *source* of bias; but we do have a constant direction of bias despite demonstrated heterogeneity in every currently conceived source of bias.

3. Constant bias: Identifying plausible sources of constant bias The likelihood of avoiding a constant direction of bias depends on identifying all the plausible source of such bias. There are by now enough lists of threats about enough kinds of validity that one would think it unlikely that any sources of bias remain undiscovered. But they may, particularly if some sources are unique to particular topics. Besides, human ingenuity is restricted, and sources of spuriousness that cannot be imagined at this time will seem self-evident to future generations. Hence, even the best means of discovering sources of constant bias are fallible. Nonetheless, they are useful because they at least sensitize us to many viable contending interpretations.

After examining the published list of validity threats, it is desirable to consult with a wide variety of persons with very different methodological and value preferences and to induce them to be as critical as possible in conceptualizing alternative interpretations to those that primary analysts first prefer. This is undoubtedly a social process; and those who labored to produce particular results may not always be too keen to have their work and themselves be critically scrutinized in public. Yet some form of public commentary is probably the best technique available for generating a comprehensive list of plausible alternative interpretations of a piece of research, even research conceived in a multiplist mode. Although such scrutiny is needed at all stages of a research project, it is perhaps most needed when a study is initially planned and when preliminary results have been extracted.

It is one thing to claim that research should be offered for public critical scrutiny, and quite another thing to achieve such a diversity of conflicting and even antagonistic points of view that all the plausible threats to valid interpretation will emerge. It is only because of personal hostilities between scholars, the passions engendered by ideology and personal intellectual commitments, and the ambitions of young scholars and outsiders who want to overthrow the conventional wisdom that science and critical reason can flourish. Without these forces, conventional wisdom will restrict the range of alternative interpretations and "paradigm dominance" is likely to continue. Science belongs in an open society committed to respect for one's intellectual enemies; it requires the passion to pursue one's ideas, the courage to welcome criticism, and the openness to take it very seriously. Although the spirit of dispute does not, and cannot, guarantee that the ineffable truth will emerge, it does increase the likelihood that the knowledge achieved will approximate the truth because all the relevant heterogeneous parties have reflected on the research at a high level of consciousness and have agreed that no alternative interpretation of a particular relationship is plausible right now. This is a consensus; but it is a consensus that no viable alternatives exist to a knowledge claim after a process of open criticism from multiple, conflicting perspectives. Consensus about alternatives to a relationship count more in science than consensus about a relationship. It is this process of encouraging heterogeneity in world views and beliefs about method and of encouraging the critical and even skeptical application of all these sources of heterogeneity to knowledge claims that characterizes science and best discriminates tentative and critically achieved truth from social consensus.

2. The absence of an algorithm for choosing what to make heterogeneous Once sensitivity has been raised to the necessity of avoiding a constant direction of bias, the problem then confronting everyone who designs a single study is in deciding what to make heterogeneous. If a conceptually important factor sometimes remains homogeneous even though scores of studies have been conducted on the topic—as with television violence and its effects on children—how can the individual researcher hope to have the insight and resources to make heterogeneous within a single study all the factors that should be made so? After all, a study that is truly multiplist requires the capacity not only to answer multiple research questions but also to uncover novel questions and issues. It also requires multiple constructs; multiple measures of each construct; and multiple populations of persons, settings, and times. Also needed are multiple mechanisms for triangulating on inferences about cause; multiple data analyses for every important substantive issue; and commentary by many people who have unique values and method preferences that relate to research questions and procedures. Who has the resources to do all these things? And even if one did, might not the logistics of so much probing compromise the quality of the answers provided? Guidelines are needed in any practical theory of multiplism to help individual researchers decide what to make heterogeneous, given that not everything can be.

But specifying in cookbook form the aspects of research that should be made hetereogeneous smacks of rigidly codifying what scientific practice should be. Critics have always held it against positivism that its tenets were so easily codified into slogans for practice (e.g., science requires hypothesis testing; all knowledge depends on observation) or into lists of recommendations (as with the lists of threats to validity of Campbell & Stanley, 1966, and Cook & Campbell, 1979). Nonetheless, because scientists often look to theorists of methods for help in deciding what to do (just as practitioners look to substantive theorists in other fields), so theorists of methodology have some responsibility to enlighten though not to try to force behavior into specific channels. As part of this responsibility it is not difficult to suggest some modest general guidelines to consider in deciding what can and should be made heterogeneous within the resource constraints of a single study.

The decision should depend in part on factors that have been left homogeneous in past studies and that can be easily defended as important. Thus, if school desegregation research were exclusively based on studies of voluntary desegregation, it would be useful to conduct the next study in districts with both voluntary and court-mandated desegregation because most of the districts now desegregating are doing so in response to legal pressure. If only a single district could be studied, this would be a district where the courts have forced desegregation. Although this involves sampling districts homogeneously when seen from the perspective of the single study, it would also entail sampling with some heterogeneity when seen from the perspective of the whole research tradition. The strategy of creating a single case that goes contrary to an undesirable source of past homogeneity is apparent among meta-analysts. In order to examine whether an average effect size is due to a methodological artifact or is restricted in generality, meta-analysts often compute average effect sizes for the majority of studies and contrast them with the effect sizes from the one or two studies in which there has been random assignment (e.g., Zdep, 1967; Crain & Mahard, 1983), from the few studies in which respondents are in placebo control groups as opposed to no-treatment controls (Devine & Cook, 1983), or from the few school districts that desegregated under court mandate (Cook, 1984). In all such cases the comparisions are suspect, not only because of low sample sizes and nonindependent errors when some studies provide more than one effect size estimate, but also because the few studies are inevitably different from the main body of studies in many ways other than the form of the treatment assignment, the nature of the control group, or who authorized school desegregation. Nonetheless, multiplism suggests a new rationale for the single study: To create heterogeneity where formerly homogeneity reigned.

But one has to be careful, for not all sources of homogeneity are equally important in their implications. One has to look for homogeneities discussed by informed commentators from different value perspectives;

further, these informed discussions should lead the researcher to conclude that the homogeneities in question reduce the interpretability or relevance of what is known. For instance, many commentators on school desegregation believe that kindergarten and the first grade are important ages to study. Children who enter desegregated schools at this level have usually not previously experienced segregated schooling and are unlike their older cohorts who moved to desegregated schools from previously segregated ones. If it is seen as particularly crucial to get good estimates from the younger grades, this might lead to a preference for sampling these grades at the cost of gathering little or no information on later grades. But even so, it should not be forgotten that multiple features of the research can be made heterogeneous even when working with a single grade. Because multiplism is a multilevel concept, more outcomes can be measured; particularly important outcomes like academic achievement can be measured with a new set of tests, the tests can be given under different (but still relevant) social conditions, etc. The art is to make heterogeneous on a priority basis while always bearing in mind the difficulties inherent when one person or group decides what these priorities should be.

It should not be forgotten that the costs of multiplism are partly related to what is being made heterogeneous. In general, it costs considerably more to add sites to a single study design than to operationalize constructs in multiple ways. It costs much more to make heterogeneous the times of study and measurement than to add a measure of, say, gender to the measurement plan. It costs more to add face-to-face commentary on a design plan from a wide variety of people with different value and methodology preferences than it does to, say, conduct multiple analyses of the same quasi-experimental data set in order to vary the selection models employed to control for initial group nonequivalence. These cost differentials mean that some forms of multiplism should verge on the routine, especially those relating to more measurement on the same persons. I am not trying to argue that this is universally possible, for obvious limits of time and energy constrain what can be measured and many scholars have a preference to measure more constructs rather than to measure fewer constructs in more ways. Nonetheless, measurement involves one of the least expensive ways of facilitating multiplism. In this context, it should not be forgotten that multiple options exist for answering some questions, and they vary in expense. Using the past literature to provide additional sites is less costly than sampling new sites and collecting data in them, whereas puzzling over one's findings from the personally imagined perspectives of managers, practitioners, and clients, or from libertarian, elitist, pluralist, socialist, and Marxist perspectives, will be less costly than holding a Science Court or doing multi-attribute utility analyses with multiple stakeholder groups. I am not trying to argue that all the alternative techniques produce equally valid findings—only that they are available, each helps, and they vary considerably in the resources they require.

A final point to consider is that multiplism can degenerate into the mindless relativism implicit in assuming that no question is more justified than any other and no method is more justified than any other for a particular purpose. The decreases in authority mentioned earlier for substantive theory, particular methods, and formal decision-makers did not involve either total losses or decreases to a point at which all the available options for question generation and method choice are equally appropriate. Some methods are still superior to others for particular purposes when judged from a variety of logical perspectives; moreover, some types of questions promise better payoffs than others. But because their superiority does not involve hegemony and is not universally acknowledged, it seems to us to be both politic and logically necessary for all social scientists interested in policy to point out and publicly defend their decisions about the features of research they have left homogeneous because they believe that the gains expected from making them heterogeneous would be minimal. Presumably a greater likelihood exists of persuasive rationales for those sources of homogeneity that are deliberately allowed to remain if researchers do not rely exclusively on their own judgment about what is the "best" single version of a question or method, but instead subject their initial beliefs to active scrutiny from multiple perspectives. Thus, even the decision not to act heterogeneously should be based on multiplist principles.

CONCLUSION

In response to attacks on a more positivist conception of science in general and of social science in particular, a new and more tentative approach to knowledge growth has taken place. It stresses multiplism: Approximating the ultimately unknowable truth through the use of processes that critically triangulate from a variety of perspectives on what is worth knowing and what is known. Triangulation requires generating multiple instances of some entity and then testing whether the instances converge on the same theoretical meaning despite the irrelevant sources of uniqueness that any one instance may contain. Such multiplism can be seen in the advocacy of multiple stakeholder research, multiple competing data analyses and interpretations, multiple definitionalism, multimethod research, multitask research, multivariate causal modeling, putting multiple plausible hypotheses into competition with each other, and assessing the generality of relationships across multiple populations, settings, and times.

The problems with a multiplist approach are largely practical. Multiplism calls for judgment based on knowledge of the assumptions behind the choice of particular methods, and knowledge of how to reconcile the various methods that might be used for each of the ends that usually have to be represented within a single study. Although we might like to triangulate on many things and take account of the perspectives of all stakeholder groups, this is manifestly not possible in most single studies. Nor is multiplism invariably desirable, given what is already known about a particular substantive issue or the characteristics of a particular feature of research design. After all, decades of research on research have identified some research procedures that are superior to others, e.g., when survey interviewers and interviewees are of a similar race. But because so much still is unknown, sensitivity to multiplism is a crucial adjunct to research design so as to reduce the chances of parochial question formulation and of generating research findings that are unnecessarily method-specific.

However, multiplism is no panacea, for we can multiply replicate the same mistake or the same parochial set of assumptions. At issue is a critical multiplism that never gives up being self-questioning and never abandons the search to discover hidden sources of inadvertent, constant biases in past work. And to ensure that hidden assumptions are likely to emerge, it is crucial for multiplists to cultivate intellectual and interest "opponents" who hold different value and method preferences and to elicit from them commentary on what has been done and any knowledge claims that have been made. Such criticism is most likely in open societies that thrive on differences, encourage idiosyncracies of perspective, and allow the young and ambitious to challenge the established. From a multiplist point of view, truth is provisionally attained when a powerful consensus of many disparate parties agrees that no alternative interpretations are plausible other than those offered publicly. Such knowledge claims deserve more of a status as facts than do consensual interpretations that have not been critically probed at a high level of consciousness from all the currently identified perspectives of relevance, however "wild" they may seem to be.

Many of the more fervent critics of positivism will reject all the foregoing remarks and will interpret them as an ad hoc attempt to save positivism by improving it at the margin while retaining many of its most fundamental and flawed assumptions. Their criticism may be that we have recreated in this chapter the process whereby substantive theorists add contingencies to their theories to preserve them from disconfirming observations. They would probably acknowledge that we are postpositivist in some of our beliefs, but would refuse to accept two assumptions that buttress multiplism: That there is a real world, and that we can know it to be a useful, but imperfect, degree through observation based on multiplist procedures that have been critically selected after considering multiple perspectives about what the purposes of the research should be, what prior research indicates is known, and what the preferred methods of study might be.

We are happy to retain these assumptions. To reject them would probably mean rejecting nearly all of the achievements of the social sciences to date. Although it is debatable how fundamental or extensive they have been, it is hardly debatable that some progress has been made. Moreover, the current generation of researchers is not likely to reject all they have learned and practiced for which they have also often been rewarded. They will not begin their careers again under a radically different set of assumptions about knowledge and its growth, especially in the absence of well-articulated *practical* alternatives for conducting research. Perhaps they should, but they won't. What multiplism offers is indeed incrementalist, for it builds on past theory and practice in methodology as well as on critiques of these same theories and practices. Multiplism is not as revolutionary as other alternatives to pure positivism. However, this should not blind us to how difficult it is to implement multiplism in research practice and how it subtly undermines the motivation of researchers who hope for more from single studies than multiplism leads us to believe can realistically be achieved. The long-term payoff of multiplism, though, should be more incisive and comprehensive research questions as well as results that are more dependable. These are not trivial expected gains, and will only be hard-won. They will not come easily or quickly, but they will come.

REFERENCES

Allport, G. W. (1935). Attitudes. In C. M. Murchison (Ed.), *Handbook of Social Psychology*. Worcester, MA: Clark University Press.

Amir, Y. (1969). Contact hypothesis in ethnic relations. *Psychological Bulletin, 71,* 319-342.

Bandura, A. (1977). Toward a unifying theory of behavioral change. *Psychological Review, 84,* 191-215.

Bardach, E. (1977). *The implementation game*. Cambridge, MA: MIT Press.

Berman, P. (1980). Thinking about programmed and adaptive implementation: Matching strategies to situations. In H. M. Ingram & D. E. Mann (Eds.), *Why policies succeed or fail.* (pp. 205-227). Beverly Hills, CA: Sage.

Bhaskar, R. (1979). *The possibility of naturalism.* Sussex: Harvester.

Blalock, H. M., Jr. (1961). *Causal inferences in nonexperimental research.* Chapel Hill, NC: University of North Carolina Press.

Bower, G. H. (1981). Emotional mood and memory. *American Psychologist, 36,* 129-148.

Campbell, D. T. (1969). Reforms as experiments. *American Psychologist, 24,* 409-429.

Campbell, D. T. (1974). Evolutionary epistemology. In P. A. Schlipp (Ed.), *The philosophy of Karl Popper. The library of living philosophers.* (Vol. 14, 1). LaSalle, IL: Open Court Publishing.

Campbell, D. T., & Boruch, R. F. (1975). Making the case for randomized assignment to treatments by considering the alternatives: Six ways in which quasi-experimental evaluations tend to underestimate effects. In C. A. Bennett & A. A. Lumsdaine (Ed.), *Evaluation and experience: Some critical issues in assessing social programs.* New York: Academic Press.

Campbell, D. T., & Fiske, D. W. (1959). Convergent and discriminant validation by the multitrait-multimethod matrix. *Psychological Bulletin, 56,* 81-105.

Campbell, D. T., & Stanley, J. C. (1963). Experimental and quasi-experimental designs for research on teaching. In N. L. Gage (Ed.), *Handbook of research on teaching.* Chicago: Rand McNally.

Chen, H. T., & Rossi, P. H. (1980). The multi-goal, theory-driven approach to evaluation: A model linking basic and applied social science. *Social Forces, 59,* 106-122.

Chen, H. T., & Rossi, P. H. (1983). Evaluating with sense: The theory-driven approach. *Evaluation Review, 7,* 283-302.

Collingwood, R. G. (1940). *An essay on metaphysics.* Oxford, England: Clarendon Press.

Cook, T. D. (1974). The potential and limitations of secondary evaluations. In M. W. Apple, M. J. Subkoviak, & H. S. Lufler, Jr. (Eds.), *Educational evaluation: Analysis and responsibity* (pp. 155-235). Berkeley: McCutchan.

Cook, T. D. (1984). What have black children gained academically from school desegregation? A review of the meta-analytic evidence. Special volume to commemorate *Brown v. School of Education.* In *School desegregation.* Washington, DC: National Institute of Education.

Cook, T. D., & Campbell, D. T. (1979). *Quasi-experimentation: Design and analysis issues for social research in field settings.* Boston: Houghton Mifflin.

Cook, T. D., Leviton, L. L., & Shadish, W. (in press). Program evaluation. In G. Lindsey & E. Aronson (Eds.), *Handbook of social psychology,* (3rd ed.). Boston: Addison-Wesley.

Cook, T. D., & Reichardt, C. S. (Eds.). (1979). *Qualitative and quantitative methods in evaluation.* Beverly Hills, CA: Sage.

Crain, R. L., & Mahard, R. E. (1983). Minority achievement: Policy implications of research. In W. D. Hawley (Ed.), *Effective school desegregation: Equity, quality and feasibility.* Beverly Hills, CA: Sage.

Cronbach, L. J. (1982). *Designing evaluations of educational and social programs.* San Francisco: Jossey-Bass.

Cronbach, L. J., Rogosa, D. R., Floden, R. E., & Price, G. G. (1977). *Analysis of covariance in nonrandomized experiments: Parameters affecting bias.* Occasional paper, Stanford University, Stanford Evaluation Consortium.

Cronbach, L. J. et al. (1980). *Toward reform of program evaluation: Aims, methods, and institutional arrangements.* San Francisco: Jossey-Bass.

Cronbach, L. J., & Snow, R. E. (1976). *Aptitudes and instructional methods.* New York: Irvington.

Devine, E. C., & Cook, T. D. (1983). Effects of psyco-educational interventions on length of hospital stay: A meta-analytic review of 34 studies. In R. J. Light (Ed.), *Evaluation studies review annual* (Vol. 8). Beverly Hills, CA: Sage.

Director, S. M. (1979). Underadjustment bias in the evaluation of manpower training. *Evaluation Quarterly, 3,* 190-218.

Dunn, W. (1982). Reforms as arguments. *Knowledge: Creation, Diffusion, Utilization, 3,* 293-326.

Feshbach, S., & Singer, R. D. (1971). *Television and aggression: An experimental field study.* San Francisco: Jossey-Bass.

Fullan, M. (1982). *The meaning of educational change.* New York: Teachers College Press.

Glass, G. V., McGaw, B., & Smith, M. I. (1981). *Meta-analysis in social research.* Beverly Hills, CA: Sage.

Habermas, J. (1972). *Knowledge and human interests.* London: Heinemann.

Harré, R., & Secord, P. (1972). *The explanation of social behaviour.* Oxford: Basil Blackwell.

Hearold, S. L. (1979). *Meta-analysis of the effects of television on social behavior.* Unpublished doctoral dissertation. University of Colorado.

Hennigan, K. M., Flay, B. R., & Cook, T. D. (1980). "Give me the facts!": The use of social science evidence in formulating national policy. In R. F. Kidd & M. J. Saks (Eds.), *Advances in applied social psychology* (Vol. 1) (pp. 113-148). Hillsdale, NJ: Erlbaum.

House, E. R. (1980). *Evaluating with validity.* Beverly Hills, CA: Sage.

Huesmann, L. R., Lagerspetz, K., & Eron, L. D. (1982). *Intervening variables in the television violence-aggression relation: A binational study.* Unpublished manuscript, University of Illinois at Chicago.

Joreskög, K. G., & Sörbom, D. (1978). *LISREL IV, analysis of linear structural equation systems by the method of maximum likelihood: User's guide.* Chicago: International Educational Services.

Kuhn, T. S. (1962). *The structure of scientific revolutions.* Chicago: University of Chicago Press.

Lakatos, I., & Musgrave, A. (Eds.). (1970). *Criticism and the growth of knowledge.* Cambridge, England: Cambridge University Press.

Lefkowitz, M., Eron, L. Walder, L., & Huesmann, L. (1972). Television violence and child aggression: A follow-up study. In *National Institute of Mental Health Television and Social Behavior Reports and Papers,* (Technical report to Surgeon General's Scientific Advisory Committee on Television and Social Behavior, Vol. III). Washington, DC: Government Printing Office.

Leviton, L. C., & Hughes, E. F. (1981). Research in the utilization of evaluations: Review and snytheses. *Evaluation Review, 5,* 525-548.

Light, R. J., & Pillemer, D. B. (1984). Summing up. Research synthesis. Cambridge, MA: Harvard University Press.

Lindblom, C. E., & Cohen, D. K. (1979). *Usable Knowledge.* New Haven, CT: Yale University Press.

Loye, D., Gorney, R., & Steele, G. (1977). Effects of television: An experimental field study. *Journal of Communication, 27,* 206-216.

McGuire, W. J. (1984). Contextualism. In L. Berkowitz (Ed.), *Advances in experimental social psychology.* New York: Academic Press.

Merton, R. K. (1957). Bureaucratic structure and personality. In *Social theory and social structure.* New York: Free Press.

Milavsky, J. R., Kessler, R. C., Stipp, H., & Rubens, W. S. (1982). *Television and aggression: The results of a panel study.* New York: Academic Press.

Mosteller, F., & Moynihan D. P. (1972). *On equality of educational opportunity.* New York: Vintage Books.

National Institute of Education. (1984). *The effects of school desegregation on the achievement of black children.* Washington, D.C.

Parke, R. D., Berkowitz, L., Leyens, J. P. West, S., & Sebastian, R. J. (1977). Some effects of violent and nonviolent movies on the behavior of juvenile delinquents. In L. Berkowitz (Ed.), *Advances in experimental and social psychology* (Vol. 10). New York: Academic Press.

Patton, M. Q. (1978). *Utilization-focused evaluation.* Beverly Hills, CA: Sage.

Popper, K. R. (1959). *The logic of scientific discovery.* New York: Basic Books.

Popper, K. R. (1972). *Objective knowledge: An evolutionary approach.* Oxford, England: Clarendon Press.

Pressman, J., & Wildavsky, A. (1979). *Implementation: How great expectations in Washington are dashed in Oakland* (2nd ed.). Berkeley: University of California Press.

Rogosa, D. (1980). A critique of cross-lagged correlation. *Psychological Bulletin, 88,* 245-258.

Rosenthal, R., & Jacobson, L. (1968). *Pygmalion in the classroom.* New York: Holt, Rinehart and Winston.

Sawn, D. B. (1973). *Aggressive behavior among children in small polygroup settings with violent television.* Unpublished doctoral dissertation, University of Minnesota.

Scriven, M. (1971). The logic of cause. *Theory and Decision, 2,* 3-16.

Scriven, M. (1976). Maximizing the power of causal investigation: The modus operandi method. In G. V. Glass (Ed.), *Evaluation studies review annual* (Vol. 1). Beverly Hills, CA: Sage.

Simon, H. A. (1957). *Models of man.* New York: John Wiley.

St. Pierre, R., & Cook, T. D. (in press). Sampling strategies in program evaluation. In R. Conner (Ed.), *Evaluation studies review annual* (Vol. 9). Beverly Hills, CA: Sage.

Singer, J. L., & Singer, D. G. (1980). *Television, imagination and aggression: A study of preschoolers' play.* Hillsdale, NJ: Erlbaum.

Stein, A. H., & Friedrich, L. K. (1972). Television content and young children's behavior. In J. P. Murray, E. A. Rubenstein, & G. A. Comstock (Eds.), *Television and social behavior* Vol. 2: *Television and social learning,* Washington, DC: Government Printing Office.

Tukey, J. W. (1977). *Exploratory data analysis.* Reading, MA: Addison-Wesley.

Tversky, A., & Kahneman, D. (1977). Judgment under uncertainty: Heuristics and biases. *Science, 185,* 1124-1131.

Webb, E. J., Campbell, D. T., Schwartz, R. D., & Sechrest, L. (1966). *Unobtrusive measures.* Skokie, IL: Rand McNally.

Weber, S. J., & Cook, T. D. (1972). Subject effects in laboratory research: An examination of subject roles, demand characteristics, and valid inferences. *Psychological Bulletin, 77,* 273-295.

Weiss, J. A., & Weiss, C. H. (1981). Social scientists and decision makers look at the usefulness of mental health research. *American Psychologist, 36,* 837-847.

Wells, W. D. (1973). *Television aggression: Replication of an experimental field study.* Unpublished manuscript, University of Chicago.

Williams, W. (1980). *The implementation perspective.* Berkeley: University of California Press.

26

Trends in the Logic of Policy Inquiry

A Comparison of Approaches and a Commentary

Rita Mae Kelly

In the 1980s critiques of the positivist approach to policy analysis have intensified (see, e.g., Campbell, 1984; Deising, 1982; Lincoln & Guba, 1985; Miller, 1984; Paris & Reynolds, 1983; Scriven, 1984); and alternative foundations for the logic of policy inquiry have been presented (Cook, 1985; Fischer, 1980; Lincoln & Guba, 1985; Miller, 1984; Palumbo & Nachmias, 1984; Paris & Reynolds, 1983). These alternatives question the appropriateness and possibility of value-neutral philosophic postures. They also question assumptions about reality, the role of substantive theory in policy inquiry, and the trustworthiness of extant methodologies and measurement tools. Though as of 1986 no single alternative has become dominant, several commonalities among the alternatives exist, indicating more consensus than one might think. These commonalities suggest that a basic shift in the logical foundations undergirding policy inquiry has taken place.

To explicate this position I briefly compare Lasswell's (1951) view of the policy sciences with the applied social science approach as articulated by Coleman (1972) and revised into "multiplism" in 1985 by Cook (1985). I then examine how Miller's (1984) design science, and Lincoln and Guba's (1985) naturalistic inquiry approaches differ from the applied social science approaches. I conclude by identifying the commonalities.

POLICY SCIENCE

The policy sciences are often viewed as applied social sciences, i.e., as forms of social engineering. At its simplest, the applied social science approach has been interpreted to mean that knowledge accumulated in the various disciplines will be used to improve social programs and policies. Researchers will remain within the disciplinary framework to build theory, test hypotheses, and expand explanatory and predictive power. Applied social scientists can cull through the resulting body of knowledge for ideas and theories applicable to real world problems. This understanding of the relationship of social science to policy is obviously restrictive; it makes the policy analyst dependent on the disciplinary researcher. Applying social science knowledge to the world of action is necessarily slow; the concern for "truth" and the advancement of theory overrides the concern for providing a decisionmaker the best information possible at a given point in time.

Harold Lasswell, the founding father of the policy sciences, rejected a narrow, instrumental relationship between the social sciences and policy research (Lasswell, 1951). He defined the policy sciences as "The disciplines concerned with explaining the policy-making and policy-executing

From Rita Mae Kelly, "Trends in the Logic of Policy Inquiry: A Comparison of Approaches and a Commentary," *Policy Studies Review*, Vol. 5, pp. 520-528. Copyright © 1986 by the Policy Studies Organization. Reprinted by permission.

process, and with locating data and providing interpretations which are relevant to the policy problems of a given period" (p. 14). Lasswell (1951) emphasized that pursuing a policy orientation does *not* mean dissipating energy on a variety of topical issues. Rather the policy scientist is to study "fundamental and often neglected problems which arise in the adjustment of man in society" (p. 14), and develop a policy science of democracy. Lasswell argued that having a policy orientation does not mean abandoning objectivity. Nor does it mean reducing an emphasis on theory and model building. According to Lasswell:

> The policy frame of reference makes it necessary to take into account the entire context of significant events (past, present, and prospective) in which the scientist is living. This calls for the use of speculative models of the world revolutionary process of the epoch, and puts the techniques of quantification in a respected though subordinate place. (Lasswell, 1951, pp. 14-15)

APPLIED SOCIAL SCIENCE

While Lasswell (1951) and others (such as Dror, 1984, for example) were advancing a broad view of policy inquiry, others in the positivist, behavioral tradition were articulating a more modest but nonetheless major role for the social sciences. Campbell (1971) and Coleman (1972) were instrumental in linking the social sciences (economics, sociology, psychology, and political science in particular) to the notion of an experimenting society. This society would be scientific not in that it would be based on social science theory, but rather in that it would rely on scientific methods as its evolutionary mechanism. "The relation of the policy sciences to such a society is a relation in which social science theory plays a small and secondary part, but methods of the social sciences play a central part" (Coleman, 1972, p. 2).

According to Coleman, policy researchers live in two worlds: one is their discipline and the other is the world of action. Their job is to act as a translator between the two, realizing that action-oriented research has a different philosophical base than disciplinary research. The major properties distinguishing policy research from disciplinary research are its concern for timeliness, action, and the use of everyday language and concepts, the ever present involvement of special interests, conflict, and struggle over resources, and a need for redundancy rather than an economy of information.

Coleman's (1972) resolution of these differences are all methodologically and procedurally based. In contrast to Lasswell's (1951) call for more speculative models encompassing entire epochs, Coleman (1972) emphasizes statistical models and research design. Moreover, "Models used as the basis for analysis should be relatively simple and robust under conditions of only partially-met assumptions" (p. 5). He also specifies the need to be concerned with policy variables that can be manipulated and to distinguish them from situational variables that may be causally related to outcomes but not manipulable. The general principle being stressed is: "For policy research, the ultimate product is not a 'contribution to existing knowledge' in the literature, but a social policy modified by the research results" (p. 6).

Coleman's emphasis on the scientific method, statistical models and research designs seemed appropriate largely because of the acceptance of

the correspondence theory of truth undergirding positivism and assumptions made about reality within the behavioralist framework. In brief,
these assumptions are that reality is tangible, separate from the observer,
stable over time and space, and fragmentable with the whole being the sum
of its parts. With proper designs, appropriate operational definitions,
measuring instruments, and research techniques reality could be apprehended and linked to extant theories. Reality is viewed as being objective,
discernible to skilled researchers, and capable of being interpreted correctly in sentences exhibiting isomorphism between the empirical world and
theories about the world. Value neutrality could be maintained by the
researcher. The policy researcher envisioned by Coleman in the 1970s was
self-consciously aware of values but did not necessarily analyze or advance
them.

By the 1980s many of the assumptions undergirding Coleman's approach
had been rejected. Cronbach (1982) and Miller (1984), among others,
pointed out that generalizations have not held over time and space; and
that the large-scale, highly funded studies that were supposed to produce
solutions to society's problems by means of large sample sizes, sophisticated methodologies, and the inclusion of large numbers of variables simply
did not do so. Campbell (1984, p. 35, italics in the original), bemoaned
the *"gross overvaluing of, and financial investment in, external validity,*
in the sense of representative samples at the nationwide level" and he
condemned even more strongly definitional operationalism calling it "positivism's worst gift to the social sciences" (Campbell, 1984, p. 27). There
is no longer the same confidence that behavioral methods can ensure
objectivity and enable the observer to assess reality reliably and validly,
thereby making generalization and linkage with theories possible.

Along with the loss of confidence in methods came a recognition that
values are an integral part of policy inquiry. As far as I know, no
defender of the applied social science approach to policy inquiry has ever
argued that values do not influence policy inquiry. The issues, rather,
revolve around the extent and fashion in which policy analysts/researchers
must deal with values. Suggested resolutions of these issues have taken a
variety of forms, two of which I will discuss here. In literature written
by political scientists the most typical resolution appears to be simply to
add evaluative and normative analyses to the applied social science approach. The second resolution, which has become increasingly more
popular in the 1980s, denies the possibility of value neutral, objective
policy inquiry and identifies ways to address problems within given ideological positions.

Dunn (1981), in his widely used textbook *Public Policy Analysis: An
Introduction*, defines policy analysis as "an applied social science discipline
which uses multiple methods of inquiry and argument to produce and
transform policy-relevant information that may be utilized in political
settings to resolve policy problems" (p. 35). Dunn (1981) goes beyond
Coleman (1972) in emphatically asserting that policy studies must include
evaluative and normative analysis as well as empirical analysis. According
to Dunn (1981), the separation of fact and value and the compartmentaliza-
tion of values do not advance either policy analysis or decisionmaking.
Dunn (1981) focuses on the structure of the policy cycle and policy arguments to develop a conceptual framework for policy analysis as an applied
social science discipline. He does not go so far as Lasswell (1951), however, in asserting that a policy science of democracy ought to be the goal
of this discipline. Dunn (1981), like Coleman (1982) and Campbell (1972),
develops a logic of policy inquiry that is geared toward preparing a cadre

of professional experts with sophisticated quantitative, methodological, and analytical skills who can provide the supportive research to political decisionmakers. Dunn (1981) systematizes and codifies a rational, instrumental model of policy studies, tacking on values to his logic of policy inquiry. He does not place values at the core of the enterprise; nor does he demonstrate how different values influence either the method or results of policy inquiry.

The effort to separate and compartmentalize values and the more recent effort to make them the heart of the policy inquiry enterprise has, as Scriven (1984) has noted, promoted a managerial and relativist ideology. These ideologies are most compatible with the value neutrality notions of logical positivism. In evaluations, for example, the goal-achievement evaluation model permits passing value judgments back to program managers and governmental policymakers who in turn can pass responsibility back to legislators. By focusing on the effectiveness of the means to attain ends specified by others, researchers are able to convince themselves that they are maintaining their value neutrality (Scriven, 1984). In the late 1960s and the early 1970s such value neutrality was considered an appropriate professional norm. By the 1980s this positivistic position had come to be roundly condemned by many as not only an unethical abdication of moral responsibility by social scientists, but also as being illogical and philosophically wrong (Scriven, 1984).

In the 1980s the philosophical foundations for determining what is objective reality have become fuzzy. Donald Campbell (1984) describes the current situation as follows:

> This rejection (of logical positivism), in which I have participated, has left our theory of science in disarray. Under some interpretations it has undermined our determination to be scientific and our faith that validity and truth are rational and reasonable goals. (p. 27)

If facts and values cannot be separated and if perceptions of reality cannot be empirically grounded with one perception being found more valid than the others, then are we left with only a random walk through time and space? What has happened to empirical objectivity? To validity?

The responses to this crisis in the applied social science approach to policy inquiry has varied. Some, such as Majchrzak (1984), have tried to retain the essence of the approach by recognizing that policy inquiry is part craftlore and art as well as an applied type of science. According to Majchrzak (1984), policy research is distinctive in that it is multidimensional in focus, uses an empirico-inductive research orientation rather than a hypothesis testing approach, incorporates the future as well as the past, responds to study users, and explicitly incorporates values into the research process. No disciplinary theory or ideology about the relationship of cause and effect guides applied policy research. "Instead, the researcher engages in an iterative process whereby information and model building are constantly interchanged. This type of research approach has been termed by some as the 'grounded theory' approach to research" (Majchrzak, 1984, p. 19). Tangible reality is still accessible to the appropriately trained researcher but value neutrality and the application of time- and context-free generalizations from a body of substantive theory is less frequently and less strongly asserted.

The attack on positivism and the lessons of research conducted on Lyndon Johnson's Great Society programs have led Cook (1985) to articulate the methodological strategy of multiplism to justify and guide the applied social science approach to policy inquiry. "The fundamental postulate of multiplism is that when it is not clear which of several options for question generation or method choice is 'correct', all of them should be selected so as to 'triangulate' on the most useful or the most likely to be true" (Cook, 1985, p. 38). Multiple measures allow examining the comparability of findings from several different measures and modes of measurements (e.g., using pen-and-paper tests, personal interviews or unobtrusive measures). If the multiple measures produce similar results, replication is demonstrated and alternative interpretations can be eliminated. Multiplism rests on the notion that the reality being studied can be perceived in multiple ways. While reality is tangible and observable, what is measured is perceived reality.

According to Cook, multiplism also helps specify causal contingencies, enabling the researcher to identify time and space limitations of relationships. Cook (1985, p. 40) recognizes that "Although realist, the operational ontology of most social scientists differs from the positivists' world of parsimonious, deterministic, ahistorical, and observable nonmentalist forces." He also states that "Statistical main effects will not describe this world as well as higher-orders statistical interactions .... Postpositivist social science cares more than its predecessors for heterogeneous sampling and data analyses that examine the degree of dependability achieved across subpopulations" (p. 41). Because the resources are not always available to do the multiple sampling and analyses required by mutliplism, literature reviews and meta-analyses of several studies are recommended. No one single study, even carefully designed true experiments, can claim to have found truth. Returning to a Lasswellian notion, Cook (1985, p. 44) justifies using qualitative data from multiple stakeholders as a way of advancing a pluralist democracy.

Cook (1985, p. 42) also revises the positivist notion of the purpose of testing causal models. "With causal explanatory models, the advocacy is to pit multiple models in competition with each other rather than to test the goodness of fit of a single model .... When multiple explanatory models are explicitly pitted against each other, the aim is to see which one is superior rather than which one is necessarily 'true'."

Multiplism is clearly an advance over earlier methodology. It places multiple causal models in competition with each other, uses multiple constructs, multiple measures of each construct, multiple types of constructs--mentalist and historical as well as empirical, and examines the fit of the models to the data and interpretations multiple times. In addition, qualitative data are systematically gathered to help set research priorities, describe, discover, explain, and communicate the study's results and to provide the context for interpreting the information, i.e., to ground the knowledge.

Multiplism is postpositivist. It breaks away from the correspondence theory of truth and moves to a consensus theory of truth. Cook (1985, p. 45) readily admits to the change. "... social science is concerned, not with guaranteeing truth or utility, but with offering defensible interpretations of what is in the outside world ...." Given this ambiguity, democracy requires that multiple investigators conduct analyses of the data so that rival plausible interpretations will be disclosed. Research on critical national policy issues requires multiple value perspectives and multiple meta-analyses "to identify commonalities of findings and interpretation through processes that rigorously attempt to falsify all the claims made about knowledge and utility" (Cook, 1985, p. 46).

The movement away from the correspondence theory of truth is linked to changing perceptions of reality. Lasswell's policy science and Coleman's applied science approach to policy inquiry assumed a tangible reality existing separate from humans. Cook's multiplism reflects a sharp drop in confidence in these assumptions, and from other logic of inquiry perspectives even this concern for realism is not meaningful.

Paris and Reynolds (1983) present a more dramatic alternative to the applied social science approach. They would put "rational ideologies" at the heart of policy inquiry. The policy argument, the "reasons for the adoption of a policy" (p. 3), would determine the shape and course of policy inquiry. Analysis from this "rational ideology" perspective does not focus on cause-effect relationships so much as it focuses on exploring the premises of the policy argument.

From the "rational ideology" stance of Paris and Reynolds (1983), the positivist concern for a stable, constant, empirical reality existing external from the observer is of no great significance. A perception of truth as being eternal and objective has little meaning in their logic of policy inquiry. The truth sought within the rational ideological perspective also relies on a consensus theory of truth. To illustrate, with the "rational ideology" approach empirical legitimacy comes from rating alternative policy arguments. Truth resides in the eye of the beholder as much as it resides in the argument or findings themselves. This methodology is also similar in basic ways to philology or hermeneutics in the humanities where scholars persistently explore the meaning of a phrase or text for a particular time period. Consensus on meaning rather than agreement about objective truth is the goal.

Miller's (1984) design science and Lincoln and Guba's (1985) naturalist inquiry approaches reject the postpositivist as well as the positivist assumptions about reality. Both assume reality is created or constructed by humans.

DESIGN SCIENCE

The design science approach has recently been proposed by Miller (1984), but goes back to Simon's (1969) notion that design is a tool not only for acting, but also for understanding. As with Lasswell's (1951) policy science, design science requires the conscious articulation of a desired state or goal. The goal posited by Miller (1984) is improved public sector performance. Miller rejects the positivist notion of value neutrality and the assumptions that there are deterministic laws governing human behavior that are beyond human control, and that "the units of analysis in social systems are highly similar over time and space" (p. 262).

In Miller's (1984) judgment, reality does not fit the assumptions undergirding the applied social science approach. As she sees it, the empirical reality explored by policy inquiry is largely made by humans; it is not "natural" and autonomous as the phenomena studied in the physical sciences tend to be. It is subject to incremental and qualitative change, and is diverse at its core. It is not consistent over time and space. As a consequence, our models and specification of variables are incomplete. Things and people change, with events overtaking our articulation of policy options. Our data are inadequate or inappropriate for the questions raised and problems addressed. Moreover, human beings are not passive but rather impose their own will and meanings on events and problems. Humans and the entities they create, such as cities, institutions, programs, governments, and agencies do not remain static, passive units content to be analyzed by others. They change; their social, economic and political contexts change; and as they do, comparability of our units of analysis disappear (Miller, 1984).

Miller (1984) asserts that, because policy inquiry focuses on performance of humans and the entities they create, measures of central tendency, which undergird most of our statistical models, are inappropriate. To assess performance, to ascertain the patterns and structures most likely to raise performance in the future, she argues that exploration of extreme cases, not the general or average case, is necessary.

Miller (1984) argues that policy inquiry cannot be unobtrusive. By measuring we intrude on reality and, therefore, change it. We cannot separate ourselves from the phenomena being studied (see also, Scriven, 1984). We interact with it, and because humans are involved, reality is willfully reshaped. The resulting variations in our units of analysis make generalizations unreliable and invalid. According to Miller (1984), policy inquiry based on the logic and methods of traditional applied social science of such changeable entities, such moving targets, is not realistic, not empirical, and not useful for improving public sector performance.

Miller's (1984) design science stresses creation over observation. In her judgment, neither physical nor social scientists any longer simply observe and identify patterns of behavior that can be extrapolated to the future. Rather, by their very observations and interventions, scientists increasingly alter basic structures. Since the basic structures (the patterns of relations and relationships) are altered, extrapolations to the future based on extant social science methodology are not possible. It follows that the hypotheses of design science are not generalizations or predictions about current behavior but are assertions that new levels of performance can be attained and diffused under the right conditions.

The purpose of design science is to increase the number of reform options open to decisionmakers, enhancing the probability of attaining prespecified goals. Miller (1984) also believes a design science, based on recent quantitative advances in the hard sciences, will "remove apparent conflicts between getting things done and being scientists" (p. 285). According to Miller (1984), design science is an improvement over traditional political science and applied social science because it will enable the quantification of "diversity as well as central tendency, disequilibrium as well as equilibrium, disorder as well as order, and human laws as well as natural laws" (p. 285).

NATURALISTIC INQUIRY

Lincoln and Guba (1985) present the most radical alternative to the applied science approach. They argue that there is only a constructed reality, a reality that is multiple, holistic, existing essentially in the minds of individuals. Positivism and postpositivism are rejected. Only ideographic statements specifying particular times, particular spaces, and particular contexts are possible. Value neutrality is rejected, as is the notion of causality. "All entities are in a state of multiple simultaneous shaping, so that it is impossible to distinguish causes from effect" (Lincoln & Guba, 1984, p. 37).

Fourteen characteristics of the naturalistic inquiry are posited. These include focusing on research in natural rather than in experimental settings so the holistic reality can be apprehended; using humans rather than survey instruments as the data gathering devices; using intuitive, felt, tacit knowledge to reflect "more fairly and accurately the value patterns of the investigator"; using qualitative rather than quantitative methodologies; using purposive rather than random, representative sampling; conducting inductive rather than deductive data analyses; using grounded rather than a priori substantive theory; using emergent research designs; negotiating analysis outcomes with the subjects so their meanings and constructions of reality will be incorporated in the final report; reporting results in the case study mode rather than in scientific or technical reports; interpreting data ideographically, not nomothetically (i.e., not in lawlike generalizations); applying findings only tentatively, limiting the study, interpretations, and applications to boundaries determined by the particular study's focus; and finally, using new criteria for judging the trustworthiness of the data. These new criteria are credibility, transferability, dependability, and confirmability.

According to Lincoln and Guba (1985, p. 43), internal validity is inappropriate "because it implies an isomorphism between research outcomes and a single, tangible reality on to which inquiry can converge." External validity is rejected because it assumes "absolute stability and replicability," and objectivity is rejected because values are inherent in all inquiry and the observer interacts with the observed. Within the naturalistic inquiry approach truth is established by dialectical discourse when consensus exists among participating parties.

From the naturalistic inquiry perspective research, evaluation, and policy analysis are different forms of inquiry. The phrase "evaluation research" is confusing and illogical, since it brings together apples and oranges. According to Lincoln and Guba, empirical, objective science is impossible.

COMMONALITIES AMONG THE DIFFERENT APPROACHES

Though the new approaches of the 1980s to policy inquiry differ markedly from each other, as already noted, they nonetheless have much in common. Some of the commonalities include the following: (1) Values are seen as being intimately and properly involved in social science research and policy inquiry. (2) Grounded theory rising from the phenomenological tradition is a vital part of policy inquiry. (3) Qualitative analyses are considered essential to establish the context and boundaries of the inquiry. (4) The correspondence theory of truth is rejected by all new approaches described, and a consensus theory of truth is being substituted for it. (5) Among those still concerned about the scientific study of social phenomena, the physics model of science emphasizing prediction and control of the physical world is being replaced with a biological model that stresses contingency and chance. (6) There is more explicit recognition in each of the described approaches of a sense of responsibility for consciously promoting an improved democracy as well as improving a particular program.

In my judgment these commonalities reflect a basic shift from the logic of policy inquiry existing in the early 1970s. The boundaries of discourse have definitely been altered. Much work, however, remains to be done before a fully satisfactory logic of policy inquiry is elaborated. A major problem, for example, exists in the shift to a consensual theory of truth. Intersubjective consensus alone is insufficient for establishing truth. There was a consensus among the Nazis that was not advantageous to the world. Linking the consensus theory to defensible goals established for society, such as developing a policy science of democracy, might help prevent gross, unethical aberrations, but care would need to be taken to ensure that a particular vision or ethic of the good society and best political system does not become the test of truth.

REFERENCES

Campbell, D.T. (1971, September). *Methods for the experimenting society.* Paper presented at the meeting of the American Psychological Association, Washington, DC.

Campbell, D.T. (1984). Can we be scientific in applied social science? In R.F. Conner, D.B. Altman, & C. Jackson (Eds.), *Evaluation studies review annual, 9* (pp. 26-48). Beverly Hills, CA: Sage.

Coleman, J.S. (1972). *Policy research in the social sciences.* Morristown, NJ: General Learning Press.

Cook, T.D. (1985). Post positivist critical multiplism. In R.L. Shotland & M.M. Mark (Eds.), *Social science and social policy* (pp. 21-62). Beverly Hills, CA: Sage.

Cronbach, L.J. (1982). Prudent aspirations for social inquiry. In W. Kruskal (Ed.), *The social sciences: The nature and uses.* Chicago: The University of Chicago Press.

Diesing, P. (1982). *Science and ideology in the policy sciences.* New York: Aldine.

Dror, Y. (1984). On becoming more of a policy scientist. *Policy Studies Review, 4*(1), 13-21.

Dunn, W.N. (1981). *Public policy analysis: An introduction.* Englewood Cliffs, NJ: Prentice-Hall.

Fischer, F. (1980). *Politics, values and public policy.* Boulder, CO: Westview Press.

Lasswell, H.D. (1951). The policy orientation. In D. Lerner & H.D. Lasswell (Eds.), *The policy sciences* (pp. 3-15). Stanford, CA: Stanford University Press.

Lincoln, Y.S., & Guba, E.G. (1985). *Naturalistic inquiry.* Beverly Hills, CA: Sage.

Majchrzak, A. (1984). *Methods for policy research.* Beverly Hills, CA: Sage.

Miller, T.C. (1984). Conclusion: A design science perspective. In T. Miller (Ed.), *Public sector performance* (pp. 261-279). Baltimore, MD: Johns Hopkins University Press.

Palumbo, D.J., & Nachmias, D. (1984). The preconditions for successful evaluation: Is there an ideal paradigm? In R.F. Conner, D.G. Altman, & C. Jackson (Eds.), *Evaluation studies review annual, 9* (pp. 102-114). Beverly Hills, CA: Sage.

Paris, D.C., & Reynolds, J.F. (1983). *The logic of policy inquiry.* New York: Longman.

Scriven, M. (1984). Evaluation ideologies. In R.F. Conner, D.G. Altman, & C. Jackson (Eds.), *Evaluation studies review annual, 9* (pp. 49-80). Beverly Hills, CA: Sage.

Simon, H.A. (1969). *The sciences of the artificial.* Cambridge, MA: MIT Press.

I would like to thank Carol Weiss and Dennis Palumbo for the exchange of ideas that led to this paper. They should, of course, be absolved of any responsibilities for errors in the text.

PART VI

EDITORS' COMMENTS
Evaluation Practice

The first article we reprint on evaluation practice is by Ascher (1986) and provides an overview of the policy sciences. Ascher reminds evaluators that their historical roots were nourished in a broad, multidisciplinary policy studies movement that predates World War II. Bemoaning the tendency for policy sciences to move toward narrow specialization, Ascher shows evaluators how to retain both an interdisciplinary perspective and a focus on broad problems and policy issues.

The next article is by Shadish (1986). He reviews alternative perspectives about the numerous, often underarticulated decisions that lead to an evaluation. Those decisions include whether an evaluation is needed, what purpose the evaluation is to serve, what questions are worth asking, and what technologies are available to answer those questions, given available time and resources. More careful consideration of these decisions will help avoid unnecessary evaluations, useless evaluations, evaluations that ask the wrong questions, and evaluations that use an inferior technology to answer questions.

The next five articles concern the design of evaluations to estimate the effects of treatments. Recognizing that treatments will be most effective and attractive if they are matched carefully to the needs of individual clients, Finney and Moos (1986) describe the fundamental problems of effective matching and explain what is required to solve them. Then, Maxwell, Bashook, and Sandlow (1986) illustrate how they used qualitative observation techniques within the context of a quasi-experiment. These authors suggest that they were able to detect differences that would have been lost if either the qualitative observations or the quasi-experiment had not been used. While circumstances prevented them from implementing their study in the context of a randomized experiment, we see no logical reason why this could not be done with obvious beneficial results.

The next article, by LaLonde (1986), provides an important and original empirical comparison of the results of a randomized experiment with the results of the latest econometric approaches to analyzing data from quasi-experiments. LaLonde finds that, in spite of their mathematical elegance, the econometric approaches tend to contain large and unknown specification biases. The article by Haveman (1986) that follows reviews the recent edited book entitled *Social Experimentation* by Hausman and Wise (1985). Haveman agrees with LaLonde that randomized experiments in principle tend to provide more reliable estimates of effects than econometric analyses of quasi-experiments. But he finds much to criticize about the cost-effectiveness and feasibility of randomized experiments, based on a review of accumulated experience with such experiments in 10 major social programs from 1965 to 1980. In the next article, Glymour and Scheines (1986) describe the development and use of the TETRAD program for discovering plausible alternative causal models. They illustrate the value of their approach by applying it to a model involving multiple indicators of latent constructs. This article is a rare example of how philosophy of science can have an impact on scientific practice.

Two more articles address techniques for reviewing and synthesizing the results of multiple studies. Bangert-Drowns (1986) contrasts five approaches to meta-analysis that have evolved in the research literature. Slavin (1986) then offers "best-evidence synthesis," an alternative intended to combine the best of quantitative synthesis with the best of traditional narrative reviews. The final article is by Kaplan (1986), who reveals how to report evaluations of policy alternatives by creating and telling stories.

REFERENCES

Hausman, J., & Wise, D. (Eds.). (1985). *Social experimentation.* Chicago: University of Chicago Press, for the National Bureau of Economic Research.

27

The Evolution of the Policy Sciences

Understanding the Rise and Avoiding the Fall

William Ascher

The recent growth of public policy programs seems to demonstrate that the science of public policy has found a secure place in academe as an intellectually sound as well as practically relevant profession. However, we should temper our optimism. History shows that there are strong and chronic pressures that push many practitioners away from solid public policy studies, back toward disciplinary specialization and irrelevance.

The best of today's public policy research has distinctive and exciting features that we should fight to maintain. It is problem and solution oriented, simultaneously saying something to the real world while avoiding the sterility of academic parlor games. In focusing on prescription as well as description, it makes clear its commitment to particular values, thus avoiding the "value neutral" stance that social science ought to be totally "objective"—a highly problematic stance, given that the very decision to focus on a particular issue requires a value judgment as to what is important.

The policy sciences' multidisciplinary approach is sensitive to the broad social matrix in which policies are formulated and applied. It thus emphasizes context (many aspects are relevant), and how these many aspects fit together (relevant factors are connected in complex ways that cannot be straightforwardly aggregated via statistical summation). Rather than being static, or regarding decision as a single-moment event, it is sensitive to dynamic processes, including policymaking itself. It has an empirical focus on human behavior, and, rather than regarding this behavior as mechanistically determined, it emphasizes the "intentionalist" principle that individuals' usual efforts to maximize valued outcomes provide the most fundamental basis for understanding their behavior. It is scientific, but in the general sense of pursuing verifiable knowledge rather than in the specific (and terribly limiting) sense of searching for general laws.[1]

From William Ascher, "The Evolution of the Policy Sciences: Understanding the Rise and Avoiding the Fall," *Journal of Policy Analysis and Management*, Vol. 5, pp. 365-383. Copyright © 1986 by John Wiley & Sons, Inc. Reprinted by permission.

The policy sciences movement that was founded and is still symbolized by Harold D. Lasswell, his many collaborators, and their students exemplifies these qualities.[2] But let us not separate ourselves from other people who agree with us on fundamentals but use different labels. We need all the true allies we can get, and the work of many others fits these criteria even if it is not called "policy sciences." I focus here on the evolution of the policy sciences because it is a clearly definable and important intellectual movement, not because it is the only story of development of better approaches to public policy.

Early Behavioralism: The Good Guys
In this century, the earliest precursor to the policy sciences movement was an early but robust form of multidisciplinary behavioralism that arose in reaction against the social sciences and legal studies of the 1920s and 1930s. Previously, the broad departments of social philosophy of the late nineteenth century had given way to the "modern," fragmented departments or schools of political science, sociology, law, psychology, economics, and so on—each jealous of its own boundaries and scornful of interlopers. Relevance and empiricism beyond the armchair variety were rare; the typical "gentleman" academic was as loathe to dirty his hands with practical details or data gathering as the gentleman farmer was to get behind the plow. This reluctance made analysis formalistic, legalistic, and often vapid. Studies put more emphasis on the organization chart than on how individuals and institutions actually operate. Without hard information or real-world relevance, the analysis was bound to be vacuous. To make matters even more parochial, many of the studies of the era were strongly prejudiced against non-American institutions and practices.

The counterreaction was a movement toward multidisciplinary behavioralism. It was "behavioral" in the most basic sense: human behavior—individual action—was its starting point. This focus drove it to cross disciplinary boundaries precisely because it is obvious that human behavior has many interconnected determinants—political, legal, social, economic, and psychological. Having recognized that no one discipline with its specialized methods held the key, these behavioralists became dedicated eclectics in their choice of methods. Any form of verifiable knowledge, whether gathered through psychoanalytic interviews or from counting war casualties, could prove useful.

From an early start at Columbia, behavioralism blossomed at the University of Chicago, and was endorsed by the intellectual mavericks in the bolder universities. These were not people incapable of making it in the mainstream disciplines. Many were, or became, highly respected pioneers and leaders in their fields: Charles E. Merriam and Lasswell in political science, Edward Sapir in linguistics, Robert Park in sociology, George Herbert Mead, Clyde Kluckhohn, and Margaret Mead in anthropology, Myres McDougal in law, Harry Stack Sullivan in psychiatry, and Gilbert White in geography. Without overindulging in intellectual hagiography, one can demonstrate that the early multidisciplinary, reform-minded behavioralism was not a marginal movement (which makes the later near-eclipse of this movement after World War II all the more surprising and troubling).

Another reason for this reintegration of social science was the commitment these behavioralists felt to public affairs. Although this movement articulated no self-conscious focus on policy *per se*, it nonetheless concerned itself with political reform, democracy, education, and social and economic welfare, inspired by John Dewey's pragmatism of integrating philosophy and public affairs. It also seemed obvious that pragmatic work on such worldly issues called for well-rounded analysis. Charles E. Merriam, the chairman of the University of Chicago political science department who stimulated and coordinated much of the interdisciplinary collaboration at his university and founded the Social Science Research Council, was also heavily involved in the reform efforts in Chicago city politics. As a prototype "man of knowledge and man of action," he was the primary symbol of the pragmatic aspect of early behavioralism.[3] Lasswell, however, came to be the intellectual leader of the effort to develop a systematic approach to integrating knowledge and action.

How could these scholars be both activists and scientists? Their answer was to start with normatively important issues selected by clarifying their goals and the goals of the community, making no bones about their commitment to a particular outcome. They would then analyze objectively the preexisting trends, conditions ("how things work"), and likely future developments in order to explore possible alternative actions for achieving those goals. Lasswell explicitly enumerated the five key "intellectual tasks" as the clarification of goals, trends, conditions, projections, and alternatives. The implicit message was that objective analysis can help make value-based choices, yet remain scientific in its separation from "goal clarification" as an intellectual exercise.

How can the analyst or scholar be both an expert and a partisan? Lasswell, for one, reconciled these roles in two ways. He asserted a broadly defined partisanship that everyone ought to share: the commitment to human dignity. This conception accepts that human dignity may legitimately be defined differently by various people in different countries. The analyst should facilitate the achievement of human dignity as it is defined in the given context. However, this does not mean that the analyst from one culture or community must stay close to home or consider every bit of advice as only narrowly applicable. Virtually all societies hold common general notions of human dignity and human rights, even if these norms are frequently violated in practice.

Lasswell also asserted that the analyst–scholar's objectivity can help to clarify which partisan political conflicts are legitimate because they reflect significant differences in interests, and which are destructive to human dignity because people's objectives are distorted from what would truly increase the satisfaction of the winners. But sorting out the real issues from the nonissues should not be narrowly technocratic, nor should it put the analyst in the position of dictator. Instead, the analyst must help the society to reach its own insights, much as psychoanalysts guide their clients to self-understanding.[4]

Marxism and other theories that explained change through macro-level factors (such as the mode of production, the social divisions of society, the level of economic development, and so on) threatened the pragmatists' objectives because these theories implied that significant outcomes are hardly affected by reform and pragmatism. But the early behavioralists had a response to such sociological or economic determinism. They emphasized the processes of political competition and the selection of policies, showing that politics and policy choice did make a difference. Thus, the commitment to activism was reinforced by a framework that mapped out where intervention would be possible.

These pre-World War II developments laid the philosophical and practical groundwork for today's field of public policy. Applications of such thinking in New Deal programs increased confidence that social science could have practical application, and methodological developments in operations research and other fields during World War II showed that approaches that are both rigorously systematic *and* broad-gauged are technically feasible.

Backsliding with Postwar "Neo-Behavioralism" Behavioralism excited many social scientists in many fields. Yet after the second world war, some practitioners distorted early behavioralism, betraying many of the pioneers' principles. The shift began with a seemingly innocuous notion that if the focus were on behavior, then the most scientific approach would be to discover and "prove" behavioral laws. The implications for policy-relevant work were anything but innocuous.

First, "proof" required testing of explicitly formulated general laws. Ultimately, only simple relationships that were applicable to all contexts were deemed worthy of consideration. Whereas the early behavioralism had tried to develop ways to map and explore the context of a specific behavior, the new behavioralism searched for a limited number of variables that would stand in consistent relation with one another.

Second, the search for general laws promoted attempts to establish—usually quantitatively—the relative importance of variables. Even many who gave up on finding general laws came to focus on the question of "Which factor is the most important?" In contrast, the early behavioralists had seen real life as very complex. They had felt that the best question was "How do all the relevant factors hang together?" But the coefficients in regression equations came to be the focal point of later "behavioral research." The numerous studies on whether socioeconomic status was more important than race in explaining political party preferences, or whether integration was more important than school expenditures for educational accomplishment, and so on, were bad enough in their disregard for the importance of putting it all together. But these gave way to even more fragmented efforts to find pairwise correlations between any and all variables, based on the usually false presumption that the correlations themselves were context-free and hence generalizable. The discovery of correlations does not tell us how things work; it does not tell us how policy instruments operate. One could perhaps make a weak argument that discovering which variables correlate with one another (e.g., educational levels correlate with political activism) is a useful first step for orienting further research. But this approach disregards both the importance of context and the relevance of choices made by individual actors. And, as the final product of policy research, this approach is deficient because it offers no useful policy actions that could be implemented to achieve explicitly defined goals.

Third, this neo-behavioralism also reintroduced the disciplinary boundaries that the forerunners had sought to transcend. Under the guise of being more scientific, many neo-behavioralists adopted one procedural idea from systems theory, namely, that analysis can usefully explore each separate subsystem. But they rarely got around to the main point of putting the whole system back together. The neo-behavioralists thus paid lip service to systems theory, while violating its basic spirit by focusing exclusively on economics, politics, demography, or some other fragment of an issue, calling it a "subsystem."

Fourth, the neo-behavioralists' quest to state and prove general laws that hold across all cases required practitioners to find a "lowest common denominator" measure for all the cases to be considered. In contrast, the early behavioralists had measured everything they could get their hands on, recognized that quantification was an aid to objectivity, and put no bounds on the sources and elaborateness of measurement.[5] Quincy Wright of the older generation had filled volumes with an astonishing variety of insightful statistics about war[6]; the neo-behavioralists sought to come up with a few measures of "violence" that would hold equally in France, Nepal, or Togo. Right after World War II, some expected that public opinion research would quickly deliver on its promise to account for political and policy outcomes by objectively measuring attitudes and developing a general theory linking outcomes to mass public attitudes. When this failed,[7] the neo-behavioralists' search for variables measured in common-denominator terms led to a heavy reliance on gross sociological and economic variables (class, region, educational levels, income). These broad factors certainly influence behaviors, but for many neo-behavioralists the ease of gathering "hard" socioeconomic data as opposed to attitudinal and other "soft" data led to skipping the subjective aspects entirely. This neglect led to mechanistic analyses that ignored the importance of motives; events seemed to "happen to" various classes of people. Predicting and explaining change, and, even more importantly, engineering change, was simply beyond the capability of such work.

Finally, the neo-behavioralists enshrined "value-free science." Given a primary objective of theory building and testing, "guarding against value biases" seemed more important than policy relevance. As "scientists" they lacked the motivation and means to clarify goals, or to reconcile the clarification of goals with the analysis of dynamics. They were thus left with trying to eliminate goal clarification entirely, an impossible pursuit since the very selection of "dependent variables" reflects at least a value commitment to the importance of the outcomes represented by those variables.

The Policy Sciences Response

By the early 1950s, Lasswell and his postwar colleagues (Daniel Lerner, Yehezkel Dror, Abraham Kaplan, Myres McDougal, to name a few) responded with a second-generation behavioralism that they called the "policy sciences." They added a greater emphasis on policy issues and on the role of the policy scientist to the theoretical foundations of early behavioralism. The emphasis on policy was meant to guarantee that the focus on problems and the search for solutions would not be lost in "scientific" analysis. To counter the conception that socioeconomic factors make people behave in deterministic ways, the policy sciences also highlighted the role of individuals' intentions and choices by seeing policy outcomes as the result of individuals' efforts to maximize what they value.

The theoretical conception resembled the microeconomic assumption of rationality on the part of individual firms and consumers, but Lasswell's "maximization postulate" went beyond material costs and benefits to include all rewards and punishments that individuals regard as significant. The importance of considering process and how all factors hang together was reemphasized through an elaboration of the decision- or policymaking process. So, in the new ideal, a policy scientist must examine "how well or how poorly the policy process is operating," and be sensitive "to the effective and formal factors responsible for results."[8] To encourage social scientists to desert the sterile role model of the detached observer, policy scientists were exhorted to clarify policy issues and to facilitate constructive resolutions of legitimate differences in interests and objectives, returning to Lasswell's original conception of 1930.[9]

More generally, the policy sciences movement gave greater explicit emphasis to the importance of beginning work by setting out the broad range of potentially relevant factors, and its theoreticians devoted much effort to develop guidelines for accomplishing this initial mapping. The *scientific* objective of analysis is to create a catalog of behavioral dynamics that made no claim to universality, to learn as much as possible about predisposing factors, and to monitor these factors carefully. The possibility of discovering general laws was dismissed on several grounds. Socioeconomic correlations are unstable because the measures are unstable. Apparently similar objective conditions turn out differently because they are subjectively different from one context to another. And small differences in how all relevant factors interrelate often lead to very different outcomes. Efforts to measure subjectivity meaningfully have also led away from simple propositions to more complex and hence richer propositions about attitudes and behavior.[10]

The policy sciences philosophy also rejected the neo-behavioralists' claims to the "scientific" high ground. It asserted that analyzing and prescribing policy is *more* demanding than simply addressing the "big theoretical questions." Adequate performance of the "five intellectual tasks"—clarifying goals, trends, conditions, projections, and alternatives—for a particular policy problem is hardly trivial. Given that all aspects of the social behavior interrelate, one cannot do an adequate job of prescription, even on a relatively narrow issue, without understanding how the whole interconnected system works. In fact, the focus on policy actually increases the likelihood of addressing important intellectual issues by weeding out the questions that are sterile or phony because they are unconnected to real outcomes.

Where Are We Now? Many people would now consider public policy and policy sciences in ascendancy. Public policy training programs, publications, and research organizations have increased in number and visibility, even as many traditional disciplines have faltered. At first glance, the outlook for multidisciplinary public policy would seem to be continued growth and acceptance in academe, government, and business.

The outlook seems less bright, however, in historical perspective. The old conflicts with the narrower single-discipline approaches are chronic, and any victories or losses may prove only temporary turns in a longer-run cycle. The struggle is chronic because some personal temptations and institutional tensions will not go away. For one thing, superspecialization always offers the attraction that it is simply easier for researchers to be narrow than broad, to seek closure rather than to try to expand the scope of what must be examined, to use system-wide variables rather than to integrate micro and macro analyses, to devise "scientific" but crude measures rather than context-specific measures. For those who enjoy theoretical work, it remains more fashionable and rewarding in many disciplines to attack single-faceted intellectual riddles than complex real-world problems. The policy sciences have argued that any decent analysis of such problems must address all meaningful intellectual challenges, and that narrow competence is not competence at all. But they have not carried the day. In general, specialists can *feel* less intellectually precarious than policy scientists who are trying to master the multidisciplinary world of theory and action. For many who enjoy empirical work, theory testing seems to be a solid, scientific endeavor even if no theories really pass the test. Moreover, specialists still have better job security. Because of these attractions it is unreasonable to expect that social scientists will stop trying to mimic the natural sciences.

Within policy analysis itself, there are similar dangers. Creeping technical specialization erodes the original multidisciplinary framework. Some practitioners take the task of policy analysis to be strictly technical, isolated from political and social processes. Overreliance on otherwise useful analytical techniques, such as simulation models, operations research, or cost–benefit analysis, can abstract policy problems from their contexts. Some policy studies overlook the importance of process because they treat the problem and decision as that of the policy analyst alone. Large-scale complex modeling is also abused. Although designed to allow the analyst to express the connections among many factors, its arcane complexity can be used to hide analytical fragmentation and narrowness from the analyst's client.[11] Again, it is simply easier in any given analysis to narrow the context, especially when the results superficially seem to be more solid and technically elegant. It is particularly difficult to maintain our vigilance on these matters when the main-line disciplines seem to accept the principles of the policy sciences through reforms that fasten onto the key labels but remain only superficial.

Finally, it is also troubling that this latest round of apparent victories for the policy sciences has not been marked by more general academic excitement. Although such subjective factors are not readily measured systematically, this author's clear impression is that although there are some enthusiasts in academia, the expansion of public policy programs has been driven by demand (agencies clamoring for more broadly trained recruits and students seeking careers) than sparked by wide enthusiasm on campus. There are a few enthusiasts, to be sure, but nothing like the wave of intellectual excitement that met the unveiling of early behavioralism. Partly, this nonresponse may reflect the control that traditional disciplines still maintain over Ph.D. training and the certification of professional standing, itself evidence that the policy sciences mindset has not penetrated deeply enough. But it may also result from behavioralism's success: the single-discipline competition has adopted many of the same "bells and whistles," such as big models, used by solid policy analysis. The competition has also appropriated many of the symbols. The number of narrow-gauged professional societies giving out Harold D. Lasswell Awards to scholars who have done narrow work has driven some of my policy sciences colleagues to the brink of cynicism. Today, it is simply much more difficult to identify work done in the multi-disciplinary, contextual, eclectic, intentionalist, process-sensitive spirit by examining the obvious methodological and symbolic cues.

Should self-defined policy scientists and like-minded practitioners from other movements and disciplines now feel optimistic or pessimistic? Neither one. We should remain vigilant in defense of hard-won gains. We must continue to work toward creating a new intellectual and practical identity. We should continue to mix scholarship with participation in the real world, without looking askance at real-world participation as less intellectual, nor abandoning the scholarship because it does not pay as well. We should support our publication network that emphasizes this new identity, even if publishing in the main-line disciplinary journals still offers a bit more prestige. We should insulate our students and junior colleagues from attacks by the single-discipline competition, and inoculate them (and ourselves) from backsliding.

WILLIAM ASCHER is professor of public policy studies and political science at the Institute of Policy Sciences and Public Affairs, Duke University.

NOTES   1. See Lasswell, Harold D., *A Pre-View of Policy Sciences* (New York: Elsevier, 1971); Harold D. Lasswell and Daniel Lerner, Eds., *The Policy Sciences: Recent Developments in Scope and Method* (Stanford: Stanford University Press, 1951); Brunner, Ronald D., "Policy Sciences as Science," *Policy Sciences, 15* (1982): 115–135.

2. The framework is most explicitly outlined in Lasswell, Harold D., and Kaplan, Abraham, *Power and Society* (New Haven: Yale University Press, 1950).

3. See Karl, Barry D., *Charles E. Merriam and the Study of Politics* (Chicago: University of Chicago Press, 1974).

4. Lasswell, Harold D., *Psychopathology and Politics* (Chicago: University of Chicago Press, 1930).

5. See Merriam, Charles E., *New Aspects of Politics* (Chicago: University of Chicago Press, 1925), ch. 5. See also Barry Karl's forward to the 1970 edition.

6. Wright, Quincy, *The Study of War* (Chicago: University of Chicago Press, 1942).

7. See Brunner, Ronald D., "An Intentionalist Alternative in Public Opinion Research," *American Journal of Political Science, 21*(3) (August 1977): 435–464.

8. Lasswell, *A Pre-View of Policy Sciences, op. cit.,* p. 76.

9. Lasswell, *Psychopathology and Politics, op. cit.,* ch. 10.

10. See Brown, Steven R., *Political Subjectivity* (New Haven: Yale University Press, 1980).

11. See Brewer, Garry, *Politicians, Bureaucrats, and the Consultant* (New York: Basic Books, 1973), p. 218.

28

Sources of Evaluation Practice

Needs, Purposes, Questions, and Technology

William R. Shadish, Jr.

Many evaluators point to 1965 as the origin of modern social program evaluation, the year Senator Robert Kennedy amended Title I (compensatory education) of the Elementary and Secondary Education Act to require evaluation of the activities funded by that act (House, 1980). If that date is accurate, then the field has reached its 20th birthday. Evaluations of Title I have continued over that time (House, 1980); and evaluations have since proliferated from education into all major fields of social intervention, including health, mental health, criminal justice, housing—and to interventions to help handicapped children and their families, the topic of this book.

A previous version of this chapter was presented at the Conference on Evaluating Early Intervention Programs for Severely Handicapped Children and Their Families, held at Vanderbilt University, March 13–15, 1983. The author acknowledges the helpful comments of Len Bickman, Tom Cook, Nick Smith, and Dave Weatherford on that previous version.

Evaluators continue to profit from this accumulating practical experience concerning when, where, why, and how evaluation should be conducted. One result of this experience is the realization that the event we call an evaluation is the product of a number of complicated decisions that are generally unarticulated and poorly understood by most evaluators themselves. The purpose of this chapter is to more clearly pinpoint some of these decisions so that evaluators can begin to make explicit and rational what is often implicit and irrational in their work.

To introduce these decisions, consider the following analogy: Conducting an evaluation is a lot like buying a used car. Suppose, for the moment, that you wanted to buy a car. How would you decide? One strategy would be to choose on the basis of some simple, relatively invariant rules. For example, "I always buy a Volkswagen because that is what my father bought, and he told me it was a good choice"; or "I've been buying Oldsmobiles for 15 years, and I've always been pleased; I will buy another one in expectation of continuing this pleasure." In fact, some consumers do buy their cars using such rules. Most, however, give somewhat more thought to the matter. They consider whether or not they need and can afford a car at this time, what they intend to do with the car, what characteristics a car should have to fill this purpose, and what kinds of cars are being sold at the moment that are both affordable and possess these characteristics. Through thoughtful examination, consumers hope to avoid wasting money on a car they do not need, cannot use, or that is technically inferior to other models.

Evaluators can learn from this example about the decisions involved in conducting an evaluation. Some evaluators, like some car buyers, rely on simple rules: "My teacher told me that the randomized field experiment was superior to other methods"; or "I have always used the case study method with good results; so I will continue to use it." Other evaluators (perhaps fewer than we care to acknowledge), ask if an evaluation is really needed at this time, what the intent of the evaluation is, what kinds of evaluation could fulfill that intent, and what methods are available to implement such evaluation within the constraints of available resources.

Final evaluations should not be the product of a simple rule, but rather contingent upon a host of other decisions. Four such decisions seem relevant here (Table 1). An evaluation is the product of decisions that (a) the evaluation is needed in the first place, (b) the evaluation will serve a particular purpose, (c) a good evaluative question is being asked, and (d) the method is the best technology for answering that question, given available technology and existing resources and constraints. To the extent that such considerations go unexamined, evaluators risk conducting

TABLE 1

Decisions Involved in an Evaluation

1. Is Evaluation Needed?

2. Evaluation for What Purpose?

3. What Evaluative Question to Ask?

4. What Technologies are Available to Answer Those Questions?

unnecessary evaluations, evaluations that ask the wrong questions, and evaluations that use unnecessarily weak or inappropriate technologies.

The Decision to Evaluate

The decision to purchase an automobile is implicitly a judgment that a benefit will accrue from the purchase, and that such a benefit will outweigh the benefits that would be obtained if the money were invested a different way—for a child's education, in the stock market, or on a vacation, for example. Similarly, the decision to evaluate a particular program ought to hinge on the same factors: expectation of a benefit, and of a better outcome than if the money were spent another way.

What is the benefit of evaluation? How can it be compared to other benefits? Ideally, a set of rules or a well-explicated theory would suggest answers to these questions. Unfortunately, such rules or theories do not exist in any formally developed way. Consequently, most evaluators decide to evaluate for largely atheoretical reasons, and not as the result of serious contemplation of the benefits of evaluation. They evaluate because they are enticed with money to do so, or are mandated by those in authority to evaluate, or they simply enjoy doing evaluation research.

Symbolic of the state of the field in this regard is Standard #5 of the new Standards for Program Evaluation developed by the Evaluation Research Society (Rossi, 1982): ["Agreement should be reached at the outset that the evaluation is likely to produce information of sufficient value, applicability, and potential use to justify its cost"](ERS Standards Committee, 1982, p. 12). But since so many of the central terms in this standard are undefined—value, applicability, use—the standard is effectively reduced to this: Early agreement should be reached that the client

is willing to pay the cost of the evaluator producing the information. T.
is a pragmatic standard—the decision to evaluate is a good one if bo\
parties agree to it. It is, in fact, a criterion that is eminently well-suited
to the marketplace economy in which much of evaluation exists, the principle of supply and demand. As such, it is justified by marketplace
theorists who argue that the most efficient system of producing and
distributing goods and services—including evaluation—is the free
marketplace (Lindblom, 1977).

Different Standards in Different Sectors

From this perspective, it is not surprising that the profession of
evaluation has not developed more explicit prescriptions about when
evaluation is needed. Carter (1982), commenting on how the Standards
might affect private, for-profit evaluation firms, notes that few such firms
would have any incentive to implement Standard #5. After all, such firms
make their money by obtaining evaluation contracts, not by questioning
the need for them. Evaluators have been willing to assume that if their
services are purchased it is because the consumer wants the product and
that consumer wants are an adequate expression of consumer needs. In
the marketplace, these wants shape the services offered by evaluators
(Shadish, 1982).

Still, not all evaluation is produced in response to marketplace contingencies; some evaluation takes place under varying degrees of central
planning by, for example, government personnel, local personnel, or
university faculty. Unlike marketplace evaluation, such evaluations are
more likely to be accompanied by guidelines to indicate when evaluation
is a worthy investment of social resources. But even these guides are still
fairly primitive. Glass and Ellett (1980), for example, note that ''although
evaluation theorists claim that their views will lead to a better society,
nearly all of them fail to advance any conception of what that society is
or what will count as improvement and why'' (p. 225). Glass and Ellett
(1980) suggest that the answer to this question must be in terms of the
utility of evaluation: Is it yielding net benefits; is it doing more good than
harm; by what criteria?

To illustrate Glass and Ellett's point, the decision to evaluate is
sometimes justified with simple claims that society requires knowledge
about the effectiveness of its programs, or that society must have a means
of holding programs accountable. Such statements may be true, but they
are not sufficiently developed to justify the practice of evaluation. For
example, claims about the need to search for effective programs—if these
claims are to be anything more than window dressing—presume some

theory of why and how such information might be useful. Such a theory must discuss why and to whom such information might be of interest, the place of such information in improving the functioning of social policy, and the kinds of information that are most likely to result in such improvements. Such points cannot be taken for granted, and do not have intuitive answers. For example, many stakeholders to a social program have little interest in program effects; rather, they may want information on costs, on who is being served, or on local implementation (e.g., Shadish, Thomas, & Bootzin, 1982). In addition, data about the effectiveness of large social programs have little effect on social policy. Such programs begin for political and economic reasons, and rarely end. Even when they *do* end—as with the program rolled into block grants under the Reagan administration—they do so not on account of evaluative data but for political or ideological reasons (Cook, 1981; Cronbach et al., 1980). Claims that we need evaluation to establish effectiveness amount to rhetoric unless those claims are backed by more detailed theory.

Cost-Free Evaluation

Scriven (1976a) suggests assessing the potential utility of evaluation by his concept of "cost-free evaluation." According to Scriven, in most cases "the crucial and proper justification of evaluation is that it improves the efficiency of yield of programs and projects" (p. 220). Even more stringently, this criterion implies that evaluations "should meet the standard of providing a positive cost-benefit balance" (p. 217) to the purchaser of the evaluation; and if this cannot be demonstrated, the evaluation should not be done. Scriven suggests in his own work that he has been able to demonstrate this kind of profit to his clients; unfortunately, these examples apparently remain unpublished, as do the detailed criteria with which he works. Therefore, like Standard #5, and claims of the need to know program effects, Scriven's criterion is provocative but of little immediate use to the practicing evaluator who needs more specified prescriptions concerning how to proceed.

Evaluability Assessments

Wholey (1983) provides more specific guides. He begins by suggesting that it is only worth evaluating when management is able and willing to make changes in a program on the basis of anticipated evaluation results. The logic behind Wholey's position is that evaluation ought to have the immediate effect of improving social programs; he presumes that working with management is the most likely way to obtain such improvement. He prescribes an evaluability assessment to see if this condition is met. Evaluability assessment is arguably the best developed tool for helping evaluators to decide whether to evaluate. In fact, the Standards for Program Evaluation prescribe an "evaluability assessment" (Wholey, 1979) to help decide when an evaluation is needed (Cronbach, 1982b). Still, not all evaluators will agree with Wholey that it is necessary to work with program management to obtain program improvement. Cronbach (1982a) and Cronbach et al. (1980), for example, might advocate working with service providers. But this difference with Wholey need not vitiate the worth of evaluability assessment. It is likely that evaluability assessment can be adopted to stakeholders other than management, retaining the emphasis on assessing whether or not stakeholders are willing to make changes in the program on the basis of anticipated evaluation results.

A Preliminary Decision Rule

Taking the above modifications of the prescriptions of Scriven and Wholey together, then, suggests the following criterion for deciding to evaluate: Evaluation is beneficial when direct program improvements are likely to be identified that can save more money than the cost of evaluation. Is this a reasonable criterion? Not yet. Both cost-free evaluation and evaluability assessment share a common flaw—neither assesses the benefits of evaluation relative to other uses of the resources. Evaluability assessment, for example, is undertaken in order to clarify whether it is worth conducting an evaluation "given a management decision to allocate resources to program evaluation" (Wholey, 1979, p. 49). How management is to make that decision, and the role evaluators ought to play in that decision, are not discussed. Similarly, an evaluation might be cost-free, but still be a poorer investment than some alternative investment of social funds, or might not be cost-free but still be the best available investment.

Some insight into the relative need for evaluation can be gleaned from a comparison of the benefits of evaluation to the benefits of some salient alternatives (see Table 2, which is illustrative, not exhaustive, of such alternatives). The benefit from evaluation is relatively immediate: empirical information about the worth or merit of an entity (Cook, Leviton, & Shadish, 1985; Scriven, 1980). Therefore, evaluation is deemed beneficial when its results are needed more than benefits provided by alternative allocations of resources.

TABLE 2

Evaluation and Some Alternatives

Activity	Anticipated Benefit
Evaluation	Immediate empirical knowledge of the merit or worth of program activities and objectives
Basic Research	Knowledge that may someday yield payoffs
Program Design	Clarification of program activities and objectives
Organizational Development	Assisting management to find ways to efficiently manage the program
Service Delivery	Immediate aid to needy clients

Alternatives to Evaluation

Some of the alternatives to evaluation retain a focus on program improvement. For instance, when an evaluability assessment suggests it is not worth evaluating a program, Wholey suggests that a reasonable alternative is to "embark on a *program design* effort to define the measurable objectives and explicit, testable assumptions linking expenditures, program activities, intended outcomes, and intended impact on the problem addressed by the program" (Wholey, Nay, Scanlon, & Schmidt, 1975, p. 187). This option may be preferable when the evaluability assessment reveals that the program is too poorly specified to allow clearly formulated variables. If the program is clearly formulated, but no party anticipates using evaluative information to initiate change, the need might be for organizational development and consultation to see if any parties to the program can anticipate using evaluative information under any circumstances to make program improvements.

Problem Solving Alternatives. But these are not really radical alternatives to evaluation, since they aim partly to make evaluation a more likely event. A larger step away from evaluation is to continue an emphasis on research, but to abandon the hope for short-term program improvement that is implicit in evaluation. A number of important critics of the relationship between science and social problem solving might take this position. Lindblom and Cohen (1979), for example, argue that social problem solving ordinarily proceeds without authoritative input from social scientists, through social interactions—endless transactions of an economic, political, and social nature, in a vast and complex social system, under no particular rational control. They argue, in effect, that evaluation will rarely be an improvement over these social interactions, at least in the short term. Similarly, Weiss points out that some social programs are not worth improving because they are so fundamentally flawed that incremental improvements are unlikely to produce important effects on the relevant social problem:

> For the social scientist who wants to contribute to the improvement of social programming, there may be more effective routes at this point than through evaluation research. There may be greater potential in doing research on the processes that give rise to social problems, the institutional structures that contribute to their origin and persistence, the social arrangements that overwhelm efforts to eradicate them, and the points at which they are vulnerable to social intervention. (1973, pp. 44-45)

Common to these authors is the contention that it is overly optimistic to hope for important, short-term, instrumental benefit in program improvement based on the results of research. They believe research to be important, but not for its short-term payoff.

Social Alternatives.   Another alternative is to abandon research altogether, and instead to spend money on service provision. Such a position is rationally justified from many perspectives: for example, if one doubts that social science can in the foreseeable future (or ever) develop sufficiently powerful theories to impact on social problems; or if one believes that correct social theories, such as Marxism, already exist so that further research detracts from their implementation; or if one thinks that the remaining social problems faced by this nation are a function of fundamental flaws in its social system that cannot be remedied by incremental program improvement; or if one simply cannot bring oneself to abandon the short-term good that can be done for needy clients in favor of the nebulous and long-term benefits that might occur through research and development. Rational, informed advocates of each of these positions can be found; evaluators encounter the last rationale, for example, when service providers argue that their own funds ought not to be reduced in order to fund evaluation.

The Libertarian Alternative.   One more alternative is to abandon not only research, but also large scale social interventions entirely, in favor of a libertarian emphasis on allowing individuals to solve their own problems within the limits of their resources, or to rely on the charity of others for solutions. Social scientists would seem unlikely to adopt this latter philosophy, since such scientists tend to "cluster on the left-liberal end of the political spectrum" (Weiss, 1978, p. 25) that tends to favor government intervention in social problems. But such scientists do not make the decisions to allocate social resources to evaluation; clearly, some of those who do make such decisions in the political arena would consider this libertarian option a viable one.

To Evaluate, or Not to Evaluate . . .

So where does all this leave the evaluator who is deciding whether or not to evaluate a particular program now? It leaves that evaluator with a complicated rule of thumb that might read something like this: Evaluate when direct program improvements are likely to be identified, if you believe that improvements in the program might vitally increase its chances to deal with the problem, if you judge that the benefit from the program improvement will exceed the benefit that would occur from spending the money on service provision, and if you believe that society ought to spend money on social interventions to deal with social problems. Is this a satisfactory rule of thumb? Yes, in that it makes conceptual sense and begins to reflect the complexities that exist in the decision to evaluate; but no, because it is still too incompletely specified to tell the evaluator how to make this judgment. In the interests of enhancing the specificity of this rule, three points seem worth pursuing both by evaluation theorists and by individual evaluators trying to decide whether to evaluate a particular program or project.

The first point is that they ought to try to define evaluation explicitly enough to distinguish it from other ways they could expend their resources (Cook et al., 1985; Glass & Ellett, 1980; Scriven, 1980). For starters, they might compare their own points of reference to the standards of the present chapter: that for most important purposes in social policy we really only evaluate when we aim to produce empirical information about the merit of programs, information that is immediately useful in some nontrivial sense. (Few who say they are doing evaluation probably take much of this description seriously.) Rather, work is often labeled as evaluation simply because it is popular to do so, or because it might increase the chances of funding—a trend noted by Wholey who found that agencies self-servingly "expand the definition of activities eligible for funding under the heading 'evaluation' to include efforts that do not actually result in the evaluation of federal programs" (Wholey, Nay, Scanlon, & Schmidt, 1975, p. 90). This trend was also noted by Scriven (1980), who states that if evaluation is the assessment of merit or worth, then a great deal of research would not qualify as evaluation. This first point might be called the "truth in labeling" rule; cogent arguments about the true meaning of evaluation are, of course, welcome.

If this writer's definition of the purpose of evaluation is accepted, a second point to consider is that evaluators and theorists should think about the relationship between evaluation findings and change. If evaluation is to be immediately useful, it must in some sense involve change. Prerequisite to this task are theories of change that delineate the limits of what changes are possible to expect under what circumstances. Examples of this kind of work include Cronbach (1982a) and Cronbach et al. (1980), who tie evaluation design to the process of policymaking; Spencer (1982), who discusses the benefit-cost of social science; and Leviton and Hughes (1981) or Weiss (1977), who discuss factors that bear on the use of evaluation findings in policy. Evaluation provides input into existing change processes; it can be no better than the change processes in which it is embedded. And evaluation for its own sake may not be worthy of the vast amount of social funding it has received to date, particularly compared to the alternatives.

Third, evaluators should ask themselves how they would evaluate their own evaluations—this is partly a validity check to ensure that the first two points were not simply an exercise in good intentions. Evaluators who are interested in this third task can use one of the general analytic frameworks available in the literature (Cook & Gruder, 1978; Cook & Shadish, 1982; Scriven, 1980). Evaluators who become seriously interested in assessing the worth of their work will find a burgeoning literature on the matter. Glass and Ellett (1980), for example, would have evaluations be scientific, ethical, and about values; House (1980) would have them be true, beautiful, and just. Presumably, one's own evaluations ought to possess these qualities in increasing quantity as the evaluator learns more about the craft; presumably, evaluation ought to possess more of these qualities more than the alternatives to evaluation.

When is evaluation needed? Probably not as often as it is done. In a world of unlimited resources, of course, it probably does no harm to conduct an unnecessary evaluation. But limited resources are characteristic of society, so unnecessary evaluations may take resources away from more worthy social endeavors.

The Purposes of Evaluation

To return for a moment to the analogy between buying a car and designing an evaluation, recall that some tasks are performed better by one kind of car than another. Jeeps, for example, are better at traversing rough terrain than are Continentals; pickup trucks are better at hauling wood than are sports cars. Some cars attempt to do many tasks well; some versions of Chevrolet Blazer trucks, for example, have large cargo space, four wheel drives, high clearance, and relatively luxurious interiors. But these all-purpose cars rarely do a particular task as well as a more specialized car does that task—as anyone who has compared the ride of a Blazer to a Continental can attest. Car buyers, therefore, take into account the purposes they want the car to serve when they make their purchase.

Need-Based Theories

Evaluators must take into account the purposes they want the evaluation to serve. Most theorists suggest that the ultimate purpose of evaluation is to help society to solve social problems; at least, language to this effect can be found in their writings (Campbell, 1971; Cook et al., 1985; Cronbach et al., 1980; Guba & Lincoln, 1981; House, 1980; Patton, 1978; Rossi, Freeman, & Wright, 1979). But this ultimate goal leaves considerable room for interpretation about the best intermediate means of getting there.

Some theorists advocate the immediate search for major solutions that will fill social needs, solutions that can then be transmitted to policymakers for their consideration. We might call these *need-based theories of evaluation*. Campbell (1969, 1971), for example, advocated an experimental attitude toward social problem solving, in which the evaluator introduced major variations of potential solutions into society, and then experimentally determined which ones did best at solving problems. The best would be adopted as policy. Similarly, Scriven (1980) wants evaluators to judge programs by how well they meet social needs; anything less than that is a failure to do the job of evaluation. For these theorists, good evaluations identify solutions to social problems.

Use-Based Theories

Other theorists, however, counter that a major justification for evaluation is the production of immediately useful knowledge. We might call these *use-based theories of evaluation*. These theorists argue that a focus on social problem solving can too easily become basic research of no apparent usefulness to the society that is paying for it, and also that evaluation results cannot contribute to solving social problems unless those results are used. For these reasons, they focus on producing information that can and will be used (Guba & Lincoln, 1981; Patton, 1978; Wholey, 1979, 1983). For such theorists, good evaluations produce information that is used by one or more of the stakeholders to a social program.

Both use-based and need-based evaluation theories make sense. Unfortunately, experience suggests that there is often a trade-off between them (Bryk & Raudenbush, 1983; Shadish, 1984; Weiss, 1978). The trade-off has not been particularly well articulated, but reads something like this: Information is more likely to be immediately used to the extent that it does not threaten the status quo. But important social problems such as racism, unemployment, and rising health care costs often involve needs that *are* very threatening to the status quo. Evaluations that address these important issues are more likely to threaten the status quo and are less likely to be used.

This trade-off is more than academic interest, since evaluators will proceed to conceptualize, design and conduct their work differently depending how they stand on the matter. Table 3, for example, presents some of the many differential practices that might emerge from use-based theories compared to need-based theories. The figure is meant to illlustrate potential implications of different treatment of the purposes of evaluation—it does not represent the views of any particular author. The contrast is between two approaches to evaluation that represent polar extremes of conceivable purposes for evaluation. Other conceptions (e.g., Cronbach, 1982a) fall somewhere in between and tend to be subject to the advantages and disadvantages of the extreme to which they are closer.

Information Needs Versus Material Needs

Perhaps the most important difference in the two approaches concerns the need to which the evaluation is presumed to respond— information needs versus material needs. In use-based theories of evaluation, emphasis is on determining what information potential users want. Extensive communication between the evaluator and potential users is advised, so the evaluator can thoroughly understand and respond to their information needs; close communication with users is maintained throughout the evaluation; and a great deal of effort is expended to see that the user of the information is committed to using the evaluation

TABLE 3

Assorted Characteristics of Use-Based Versus
Need-Based Theories of Evaluation

Use-Based Theories Tend to Emphasize:[a]

- Relevance of information to the needs of potential information users
- Extensive communication between potential users and evaluators
- Translation of evaluations into their implications for policy and programs
- Credibility or trust placed in evaluations
- Commitment or advocacy of individual users

Need-Based Theories Tend to Emphasize:[b]

- Relevance to a social problem
- Constructiveness of information in suggesting a solution
- Manipulability of the solution
- Evidence that the solution will be generalizable over settings
- Importance of the information in terms of size of effect, number of people affected, and dollars

---

[a](Leviton & Hughes, 1981)
[b](Cook, Leviton, & Shadish, 1985)

results (Guba & Lincoln, 1981; Wholey, 1979). All this is easier if the evaluator focuses on single information users rather than multiple users.

In needs-based theories, on the other hand, the evaluation intends to produce information relevant to the material needs that program clients experience. The evaluator must understand the material needs giving rise to the problem and suggest solutions to these needs that are manipulable and transferable over settings and that are likely to have an important effect on the problem (Cook et al., 1985; Scriven, 1980). Whether the information is immediately useful is not much of a concern; in fact, some theorists with this bent specifically prohibit evaluators from contacting some of the potential users of the information for fear of being contaminated by their biases (Scriven, 1980).

But emphasizing both concerns in any given evaluation may be difficult at best, because different social groups are likely to have somewhat different needs and are likely to experience those needs in different ways and to different degrees (Shadish et al., 1982) The existence of severely handicapped children, for example, has different implications for different groups—teachers will need educational advice, parents may face financial and familial needs, and legislators may face political problems from families who want more resources. No single information user is likely to have all these different perspectives, nor to want to use information about each of them. An evaluator who focuses on the material needs of handicapped children is likely to produce results that are at best irrelevant to the information needs of many groups. At worst, information that might help some groups could threaten others, who will then fight against its use.

Tradeoffs

However, myopic focus on either use of social problem solving is not a viable solution in the long run. Early evaluation theorists who focused on meeting material needs (Campbell, 1969, 1971) were justifiably criticized for being politically and economically unrealistic (Shaver & Staines, 1971). Evaluators who relied on such theories produced social interventions that solved particular social problems in experimental demonstrations but which often were not greatly used because they were politically or economically incompatible with American society (Fairweather, 1980; Graziano, 1969; Shadish, 1984).

Conversely, some evalutors have focused so much on producing usable information that any significant relevance to important material needs has been sacrificed. An example is the system of Community Mental Health Center (CMHC) evaluation that emerged subsequent to the 1975 CMHC amendments in Congress (Cook & Shadish, 1982). The National Institute of Mental Health (NIMH) encouraged a "local use" system of evaluation that resulted in much information about how many patients were seen, by whom, for how long, and at what cost, which was then used primarily by CMHC managers for accounting, reporting to funding agencies, and public relations (Cook & Shadish, 1982). The information thus generated had little to do with any important mental health needs, although it was used extensively by the most powerful local stakeholder— the CMHC manager. Looking back on this system of evaluation, one influential mental health evaluator concluded: "We frittered away our potential in many, badly flawed, little studies of small problems of local agencies, while these agencies suffer from serious technical and organizational defects" (Windle, 1982, p. 296).

Granted, rationales exist for exclusive focus on information needs versus material needs. For example, a relatively exclusive focus on material needs might be justified if the evaluator believed that existing social programs were so fundamentally flawed that using evaluative information

to improve them was futile; or believed that the real client of an evaluation was "the public good" rather than the organization funding the
evaluation. A focus on information needs might be justified for those
evaluators whose organizational positions force them to respond to informational needs or for those who believe that the client has the right to
demand particular information by virtue of having paid for the evaluation. But when evaluators take these more limited focuses, they need to
be aware of the liabilities they incur and inform the consumer of them.

Finding A Compromise

However, at least some theorists of evaluation have struggled with
how to combine use and social problem solving, despite the apparent
trade-offs betweeen the immediate utility of information and the
magnitude of the social problem to which the program responds. One
characteristic of these theories is that they recognize that it is more
politically and economically realistic to improve existing social programs
than it is to invent major new programs (Cook et al., 1985; Cronbach et
al., 1980). After all, social programs are relatively permanent fixtures in
the policy arena; programs begin for political and economic reasons, and
if programs terminate, it is due to political and economic reasons and not
by virtue of their positive or negative effects. It is unlikely that society
would implement a major innovative social program even if evaluation
were to identify one. Therefore, even if an existing program is fundamentally flawed in some way that prevents it from having a major impact
on the problem, it is still the only realistic means of immediately reaching
large numbers of needy clients.

But the relative permanency of social programs leads such theorists
to avoid evaluating the programs themselves—such programs as a whole
would not be affected by evaluative information. Such theorists think that
the best way to produce evaluative information that will be used to solve
social problems is to focus on critical leverage points in the existing program, rather than on the whole program. For Cronbach et al. (1980):

> Leverage refers to the proability that the information—*if* believed—will change
> the course of events. This means that the information must bear on aspects
> of the program that could be altered. It is much easier to change administrative
> procedures and allocation rules than it is to abandon a program or change
> its basic thrust. Consequently, even Congress finds more use for process infor-
> mation (especially information on who gets what and on costs per person
> served) than for reports on effects of services. (p. 265)

Under his theory, Cronbach tells the evaluator to search for "changes at the margin" (Cronbach et al., 1980, p. 245) of social programs as the leverage point.

Cook et al. (1985) have a similar conception of leverage in evaluation—a focus on those points in existing social programs that could be changed. As a heuristic aid, Cook (1981) distinguishes among program, projects, and elements. Programs are adminstrative umbrellas providing regulatory and fiscal support but not usually direct services; programs are heterogeneous in implementation from local project to project. Projects are local organizations that administer direct services under the auspices of the program. Elements are the presumably efficacious direct service components within projects. Of the three, elements naturally turn over quickest, and programs slowest, with projects falling in between. Elements offer the greatest opportunity for quick changes; but their disadvantage is that they have a smaller potential for impact on clients than do projects or programs that consist of multiple elements and multiple client groups.

Using this terminology, Cook et al. (1985) come to three conclusions about leverage. First, studying the effects of social programs has little leverage, since those programs as a whole are probably not affected by evaluative information. Second, Cook et al. agree with Cronbach that information about the implementation of social programs has leverage for federal and state policymakers and program managers. Those groups can respond to obvious problems in implementation with remedial actions and have often done so (Leviton & Boruch, 1983). Third, Cook et al. add another leverage point—information about robustly effective types of projects and elements that are derived from multiple instances of an intervention. The instances may appear to be only loosely related to each other, but they share the same hypothesized casual mechanism and bring about the same effect even when implemented in different settings. An example in education is Wiley's (1976) "time on task," which can be operationalized in many ways—longer school days, more homework, briefer recesses, and so forth—and which robustly increases student achievement over different settings.

Emergent Elements

By combining information that has leverage in the senses just discussed with an assessment of the important social needs to which the program and its constituent parts respond, both Cronbach et al. (1980)

and Cook et al. (1985) hope to produce useful information that responds to social needs. But the evaluator needs to keep one more issue in mind: Information has leverage only to the extent that is about an intervention that can be implemented (Cronbach et al., 1980; Shadish, 1983; Shadish, 1984). As the preceding paragraphs suggest, such interventions are likely to be small, manipulable, and technical (i.e., discrete activities or elements rather than entire local projects or social programs). But in addition, these elements must be consistent with the value, traditions, and systems in which they must be implemented. They must be emergent, an outgrowth from the system itself, leading the system forward toward solving its needs without attempting the almost impossible task of making it change its values and practices in important ways.

An example of this kind of ''emergent element'' is the phenothiazine medication for the treatment of psychotic disorders. These drugs significantly met many needs in the mental health system while remaining consistent with a health delivery system that values professional care, reduction of deviant behavior, and medical treatments more than social interventions.

Not all elements have this emergent quality. Lichstein (in press), for example, points out that many relaxation strategies—meditation, for example—were introduced thousands of years ago in India as part of a lifestyle that supported their use. But today they are introduced abruptly into an individual's life despite the fact that they may be orthogonal to, or even hostile to, that person's world view. Using progressive muscle relaxation as a treatment for Type A (psychologically coronary prone) personalities, for example, is often intrinsically hostile to that person's way of life. As a result, such relaxation strategies are not used consistently by patients who need them despite their demonstrated efficacy in helping the problem; Americans are prone to prefer a pill to an active behavioral strategy.

Formulating Evaluation Questions

When buying a used car, the consumer could ask a wide array of questions: How powerful is the engine? What does the odometer read? How many passengers does it seat comfortably? What is the cost? What is the gas mileage? How reliable has the car proven in the past? Car buyers are often insufficiently aware of all the questions they could be asking, hence they sometimes fail to ask an important question about the car. It is equally important that the consumer ask questions that are tailored to the purpose the consumer wants the car to serve; buyers who know the purpose they want the car to serve can limit the number of questions they ask and devote the bulk of their resources to getting good answers to those questions. For example, buyers who have good mileage, reliability, and low cost as priorities can explore these questions thoroughly with the dealer, friends, and through such sources as Consumers Union. But buyers who have hauling wood as a priority will ask about cubic feet and tonnage capacities and may be relatively uninterested in gas mileage.

Similarly, evaluators need to be aware of the array of questions they could ask about social programming in order to ensure that important questions are not overlooked. Then, they need to prioritize these questions so that the resulting evaluation will best meet their purposes; and so they know to which questions they need to devote the most resources, and which questions are relatively expendable, if choices among questions must be made. The questions that could be asked about social programs will generally fall into one of six categories (See Table 4):

Questions of Audience

Audience questions concern the number and characteristics of real and potential service recipients. For example, for programs for handicapped children and their families, the evaluator might want to know who is served by particular programs for handicapped children, the potential demand for services, characteristics of handicapped children such as their educational needs, children who receive services from programs for the handicapped but who may not be eligible, or the different groups in society that would be affected by attempts to help such children. This kind of information assists in planning social programs and in ensuring that the intended audience is reached. The Health Care Financing Administration (HCFA), for example, recently postponed indefinitely the implementation of a National Plan for the Chronically Mentally Ill because of a demand for services that was unknown but feared to be high (Shadish & Bootzin, 1981).

Program Implementation

Implementation questions concern the manner in which the program is actually implemented in the field. Here, the evaluator might want to

TABLE 4

Types of Questions

Question Types	Examples
Audience	1. Who is being served by the social program? 2. Who experiences the social problem that gives rise to the program?
Implementation	1. What is the kind and frequency of services provided under the program? 2. Who provides services? 3. Do program activities bear on the social problem that prompted the program?
Effect	1. What effects, intended or not, does the program have on service recipients? 2. Do program effects ameliorate the social problem giving rise to the program?
Impact	1. Who besides service recipients themselves are affected by the program—families, friends? 2. Does this program change the functioning of other social programs that deal with the client?
Cost	1. How much does it cost to provide services to program clients? 2. Is this program cost-beneficial, or cost-effective?
Causal Process	1. Given that the program has identifiable effects and impacts, by what means are these outcomes produced? 2. What social theories account for this particular solution to this particular social problem?

know about the kinds and frequency of services provided to handicapped children and their families, the number of social programs available to provide these services relative to demand, whether these are model (demonstration) projects or conventional care programs, and whether or not intended services are actually occurring. Such questions not only inform the client about what is happening in the program but ensure that intended activities are occurring. Nvasky and Paster (1976), for example, found that few planned activities of the Law Enforcement Assistance Administration (LEAA) were actually implemented. This finding prevented a premature conclusion that the program was ineffective.

Questions of Effect

Effect questions concern the changes in service recipients brought about by programs. If, for example, a program goal is to improve the quality of life for handicapped children, then the question may be whether this goal is obtained. But to the same degree, the evaluator ought to be interested in unintended effects. Provision of financial aid to families of the handicapped may ease their financial plight in coping with the costs of catastrophic illness, but at the same time may make such children more dependent on federal or state sources of support and less likely to seek other forms of help or income. Finally, the evaluator will also want to know about the magnitude of the effect. With some handicapped children, for example, educational advances of any practical significance are difficult or impossible to obtain.

Questions of Impact

Impact questions concern outcomes that are linked to the social program by a longer causal chain than are effects. A program to help the handicapped may also provide jobs in the community to people who equip vans for transporting the handicapped, may force local schools to develop new programs for the handicapped, and may require local welfare agencies to hire new staff to administer the new program.

Program Costs

Cost questions hold a special place in the hearts of program administrators and legislators, and answering such questions requires a somewhat specialized technology (Levin, 1975, 1983). One interest here, for example, might be the amount of money currently being spent on handicapped children and their families. A similar interest concerns the money that could be spent on such children if enough social programs were provided to serve the needs of all such children. After all, given recent experience with the exploding Medicaid budget, legislators are unlikely to mandate new entitlement programs for handicapped children if the demand for such services is potentially large, but unknown. Cost questions also deal with relative cost-benefit of programs for handicapped children. Since society is characterized by scarce resources, giving funds to the handicapped may take funds away from programs ranging from defense to unemployment to cleaning up toxic chemicals. Society wants to know which of these many investments will yield the greatest dividend.

The Causal Process

Finally, causal process questions are concerned with theories and explanations about the variables that mediate the relationship between program implementation and effects. Knowledge of these relationships allows more confident transfer of effective social programs from one site to another and advances social theory about the amelioration of social problems.

Asking All These Questions—Pros and Cons

A comprehensive evaluation of programs to help severely handicapped children and their families might ask all these questions (Rossi et al., 1979). For several reasons, however, asking all these questions in a particular evaluation is not a wise strategy (Cook et al., 1985). For one thing, to the extent that the evaluation is being conducted to fill identified information needs, answers to all these questions are probably not wanted by the information user. If the evaluation is to meet social needs, not all questions will yield answers that could be used as solutions to social problems. If, for example, the evaluation concerns a national social program, information about program effects may not alter policy, since such programs as a whole are largely uninfluenced by data about their effectiveness (Cook, 1981). Evaluation must ask questions about the effectiveness of interventions that are most likely to change (Cronbach et al., 1980)—about projects within programs, or elements within local projects. Questions about interventions that probably cannot be changed are unlikely to produce information that can solve social problems.

Methods for Generating Questions

In most evaluations, a primary source of questions about a social program is likely to be a client—whether that client is a single user of information or all stakeholders with an interest in a social problem. Other sources will include past research, social theory, key informants about the program of interest, and such sources as program goals (Cronbach et al., 1980). In fact, multiple sources ought to be consulted in forming evaluations, in order to avoid unnecessarily parochial or naive questions. Unless the evaluator is a substantive expert in the field of interest, this means contacting someone who is such an expert and including them as much as possible in the question formation process.

Multiple Sources. Why multiple sources? Why not single information users who understand the most important social problem to which a program is relevant, for example? The answer is that one cannot be sanguine about finding such a stakeholder. Single information users are primarily concerned with their own problems, which are at best one small piece of any important social problem. Even experts on the program are unlikely to have a complete, unbiased point of view. Moreover, single information users are unlikely to want to pay for information that does not bear directly on their problems.

One might try to include multiple stakeholders in designing evaluations, with the hope that this mechanism would increase the chances that all aspects of the problem would be identified and that each group would be more likely to use the information because each group had a hand in identifying its own needs. This approach is successful to some degree in that it may inform the evaluator about different aspects of the problem (Bryk & Raudenbush, 1983). But at least some of the evaluators who have tried this approach have concluded that it is exceedingly time-consuming, expensive, and cumbersome, and that it may not have the payoff for use to justify the cost (Bickman & Rog, this volume; Bryk & Raudenbush, 1983; Weiss, 1983). A variant on this approach is proposed by Cohen (1983), who suggests that each stakeholder group have its own evaluator, who would produce the information it wanted to use to solve its problems. Even if this solution were theoretically desirable, limited evaluation resources make it impractical.

Evaluators, therefore, will likely have to strike a compromise between devoting all the resources to one stakeholder versus trying to serve multiple stakeholders. One such compromise is to work primarily with duly elected or appointed representatives of the public—legislators, federal policymakers, and Congressional staffs. Such representatives may have somewhat more power to use information instrumentally; and they may at the same time, by virtue of the pluralistic political forces that impinge on their social position, be forced to represent a pluralistic set of interests that is larger than that of any single group.

In addition, the evaluator should use a broad array of inputs into the formation of evaluation questions—past evaluations, stakeholder interviews, social theory, and pilot studies—and use this information to educate both themselves and the most salient users (usually the group that pays for the evaluation) to ask more informed, less parochial questions (Cronbach, 1982a, 1982b). They might also (a) obtain knowledge about a new area by teaching a course on it, writing a review paper or grant proposal, or taking responsibility for special projects on the topic; (b) actively involve themselves in related experiences such as conferences and conventions, interdisciplinary contact, real world involvement with the topic, or an intensive case study; and (c) engage in such activities as brainstorming, group discussion and consensus techniques such as the Nominal Group Technique, and dialectic thinking about the opposites of the conventional wisdom about a topic (Campbell, Daft, & Hulin, 1982; Cook et al., 1985).

Priorities.   Once a sufficiently exhaustive set of questions has been compiled, the evaluator faces the task of prioritizing those questions, since resources rarely exist to answer all questions well. Questions are prioritized according to their promise for fulfilling the purposes of the evaluation; a needs-based evaluation, for example, might devote more resources to determining if the intervention had effects that met the relevant social needs to some degree (Scriven, 1980). Other questions might be directly or indirectly related to this question as aids in answering it; it may be useful to have at least a brief description of the intervention so as to be able to verify the kind of program it is. A use-based evaluation, on the other hand, might devote more resources to answering a question that was coming up for debate among the users; if Congress is debating aspects of the implementation of a compensatory education program, for example, the evaluator might provide data relevant to this question. Again, other questions may prove useful in an ancillary sense in answering this implementation question, and they would have second priority.

Questions cannot be completely prioritized, however, until the evaluator considers the available methods for answering the questions—the topic of the next section.

Choosing Methods from Available Technology

Evaluators can choose from a huge array of methods for use in answering the high-priority questions (see Table 5). Unfortunately, however, the relationship between the question to be asked and the method to be used is far from perfect. Knowledge of the question does not lead directly to the best method to be used. On the other hand, particular methods usually are not good for answering all kinds of questions; some methods are more

TABLE 5

Question Types and Available Technology

Question Types	Available Technology
Audience	1. Census 2. Sample survey 3. Structured or unstructured interview 4. Onsite observation
Implementation	1. Onsite observation 2. Surveys of clients or service providers 3. Quantitative Time Sampling 4. Management information systems
Effect	1. Experimental and quasi-experimental design 2. Measurement with statistical adjustment 3. Occasionally, case studies 4. Investigative journalism, modus operandi
Impact	1. Time series 2. Archival data 3. Participant observation for discovery 4. Construction of and comparison to standards
Costs	1. Description of costs 2. Cost-benefit 3. Cost-effectiveness
Causal Process	1. Structural modelling for confirmation 2. Participant observation and interviews for discovery 3. The role of theory

or less useful in answering each kind of question. As a start on this task, Table 5 presents a nonexhaustive list of some general classes of methods that might be useful in answering particular kinds of questions (see Morgan, 1983, for a sense of the incompleteness of Table 5).

Bandwidth Versus Fidelity

Several points are worth noting from Table 5. First, some methods, such as surveys, appear frequently across many question types. These methods can provide low to medium quality information about a broad array of questions. Other methods, randomized experiments for example, appear to be rather limited in application. These latter methods provide very high quality answers to a narrow set of questions. The difference between the two kinds of methods is one of bandwidth versus fidelity (Cronbach et al., 1980); the more narrowly targeted the information provided by the method (fidelity), the higher the quality of the answers but the fewer the questions to which it is applicable.

Multidisciplinary Methods

Second, note that the choice of methods is limited by the available technology. A good evaluator must be familiar with the available technology and with the advantages and disadvantages of each method for answering particular questions in particular situations. The knowledge required is multidisciplinary. No single evaluator is likely to have all the methodological skills listed in Table 5. Hence, multidisciplinary cooperation fosters the conduct of good evaluation (Shadish & Cook, 1983).

Sometimes No Method Is Clearly Best

Third, sometimes no available technology is entirely satisfactory for answering particular questions. Take, for example, the question of program effects. Randomized field experiments are desirable methods for this question, but in field settings such experiments almost inevitably suffer from attrition, vitiating much of the unique worth of the experiment (Cronbach, 1982a). Individual quasi-experimental methods, for the most part, suffer from identifiable threats to validity that make none of them ideal by themselves (Cook & Campbell, 1979). Causal modeling approaches are useful; but such approaches fail to rule out significant threats to validity. Even if some threats can be ruled out by recent econometric developments (Heckman, 1980)—which is not yet established (LaLonde, 1984; Murnane, Newstead, & Olsen, 1985)—computer algorithms have not yet been developed to estimate robustly the necessary parameters (Cronbach, 1982a). Case study methods, under some limited circumstances, can yield confident causal inference (Campbell, 1979; Scriven, 1976b). But the conditions under which such confidence obtains nearly never occur in practice in social program evaluation (Cook et al., 1985). The solution, in such cases, is the use of multiple methodologies, each with competing strengths and weaknesses, to increase confidence that the important threats to validity of causal inference have been ruled out (Shadish, 1986; Shadish, Cook, & Houts, in press).

The Reality of Trade-Offs

Finally, note that trade-offs between methods will have to be made in practice, so that any single study will be unlikely to implement methods that can answer all questions well. Some of these trade-offs involve limited resources. If many resources are devoted, for example, to quantitative observation with time sampling in order to assess implementation, relatively few resources may be left for other methods. Yet such time sampling will fail to provide good answers to many other questions. Other trade-offs are logical. Sites that are willing to cooperate in a randomized field experiment are probably not representative of all sites of interest. They may be more cooperative, for example. The converse is true, too, about the random sampling of sites that might facilitate generalizability; many of the sites so sampled will be unwilling to cooperate in a randomized experiment (Cronbach, 1982a).

Clearly, then, the choice of methods in evaluation must take into account available technology, trade-offs between methods that stem from resources or logic, and trade-offs between high quality answers to limited questions versus answers of less quality to a broad array of questions. At this stage, therefore, question and method choices become iteratively interdependent; one explores different ways of fitting different methods and different questions together (Cook et al., 1985), trying to honor both the priorities among the questions of interest and the extant practical constraints.

A Constant Process Throughout Evaluation

At this stage, the evaluator will want to go back to the questions asked earlier in this chapter to see if the answers have changed in view of subsequent developments. For example, the evaluator might want to ask whether or not, in view of the costs or of the feasibility of implementing a particular method to answer the question of interest, is it still worth doing the evaluation? The questions asked in this chapter—about needs, purposes, questions, and technology—are not really sequential, but are iterative. The evaluator asks these questions again and again as the evaluation proceeds, changing past decisions as new learning occurs and as new decisions change the feasibility of implementing old decisions.

Further Discussion of Methods

The preceding discussion of specific methods and method choices is necessarily brief. Its purpose is not to discuss the strengths and weaknesses of particular methods, but rather to characterize the relationship between methods and the decisions that precede methodological choices. Until such issues are more thoroughly elaborated, attempts to prescribe specific methods as most useful or preferable for the evaluation of programs for handicapped children are premature. Such prescriptions depend too heavily on decisions about which questions are most important in these programs; about the kinds of resources available to evaluators of these programs at the local, state, and federal level; about the kinds of changes in programming that these evaluators and their clients expect; and about the justification for any evaluation at all.

This chapter, therefore, is meant to intrigue the reader to learn more about these decisions and the factors that bear on them. For those who are intrigued, more complete discussions are available in many of the references provided in this chapter. For a more complete elaboration of the relative strengths and weaknesses of particular methods in Table 5, and of the trade-offs among them, the reader is referred to Cook et al. (1985), the source from which Table 5 was abstracted; and to Cronbach (1982a), who also discusses the issues in this chapter. More thorough discussions of individual methods include the following:

1. *Case Study and Participant Observation*—Cook and Reichardt (1979); Guba and Lincoln (1981); Patton (1980)

2. *Surveys and Questionnaires*—Babbie (1973); Bradburn, Sudman, and Associates (1980); Nunnally (1978); Thorndike (1971); Warwick and Lininger (1975)

3. *Management Information Systems*—Attkisson, Hargreaves, Horowitz, and Sorenson (1978)

4. *Experimental and Quasi-Experimental Methods*—Cook and Campbell (1979); McCleary and Hay (1980)

5. *Regression, Structural Modeling*—Cohen and Cohen (1975); Huitema (1980); Joreskog and Sorbom (1979); Kenny (1979)

6. *Analysis of Secondary Data Sources*—Boruch, Wortman, and Cordray (1981); Glass, McGaw, and Smith (1981)

7. *Cost*—Levin (1975, 1983); Rothenberg (1975); Thompson (1980)

The Political Economy of Evaluation

This chapter began with an analogy between conducting an evaluation and choosing a used car. The point of the analogy was that the decisions made for both choices are fundamentally similar—asking about needs, purposes, questions, and technology. The astute reader, however, may have noticed a flaw in the analogy: It holds true only if the evaluator shares one critical characteristic with the car buyer, that both act as critical and informed consumers of their respective products. Unfortunately, the evaluator is not often analogous to the car buyer as an informed consumer—in the spirit of the present analogy, the evaluator is more often analogous to the used car salesman. Presumably, both the used car salesman and the evaluator, as sellers of a product, have little intrinsic incentive to help the consumer make an informed choice (Carter, 1982). The result may be that even if the issues outlined in this chapter are clear to evaluators, they may have little reason to follow them. This problem leads one to ask about possible institutional safeguards for good evaluation.

Will Self-Regulation Help?

One might argue that the profession of evaluation is different from that of used car salesmen in that evaluation has promulgated the Standards for Program Evaluation, thereby policing the actions of its members and ensuring that the rights of evaluation consumers are protected (Rossi, 1982). For an array of reasons, however, one cannot be overly confident that such efforts will result in better products to the consumer. For one thing, current evaluation standards are necessarily quite vague (Cronbach, 1982b). They allow virtually any method to be used in virtually any situation, and they proscribe hardly anything at all; Sechrest (1981) refers to them as moral prescriptions. Also, no mechanism exists to enforce the Standards (Carter, 1982), which may be appropriate given their ambiguities, but which further lessens their power to influence evaluator behavior. Finally, some have argued that self-policing among any of the professions—law, medicine, clinical psychology—has never been particularly successful. To judge from complaints by evaluators themselves of unethical practices, evaluation seems to be no exception (Winter, 1982).

Licensure and Accreditation.   Becker and Kirkhart (1981) suggest using such standards as a starting point toward development of licensure and accreditation procedures. Training programs in evaluation could then ensure that their students were appropriately exposed to the issues and trained in methods for their resolution, at least to the extent that technology allows. States could be encouraged to establish licensure laws modeled after such standards, formulating examinations for prospective evaluators to pass and judging their performance against the standards. Professional evaluation organizations could establish procedures for censure or expulsion of errant members. Are these good ideas? Probably so, at least in that they might allow for the expulsion from practice of evaluators who engage in grossly unethical behavior, and in that they might allow evaluators to demonstrate competency at the time of the examination. But such procedures would probably not offer much benefit beyond this. They are limited by the ambiguities of the Standards themselves, so there would be few clear cut criteria of unethical practice. And licensure procedures, despite their avowed purpose to protect the public, are poor predictors of future behavior (Kane, 1982).

Problems of Regulation.   One reason that such difficulties exist in the regulation of practice is relatively intractable—evaluation exists in an American marketplace economy which is in many ways intrinsically hostile to consumer regulation of producer behavior (Lindblom, 1977), and this fact is not likely to change significantly. Whether it be in the provision of medical care, life insurance, automobiles, steel, or cigarettes, the producer has the advantage of a free hand to put a product on the market, and the consumer fights an uphill battle to encroach on this free hand. Informed consumers make better fighters. But it is difficult to hope that consumers of evaluation can be truly informed about important decisions that affect their purchase, given the technical nature of those decisions and the lack of consensus in the field itself about proper answers. Lacking this information, consumers seem unlikely to make an informed choice from among the diverse proposed evaluations the field tries to sell them. The profession of evaluation need only look to the experience of other professions with the regulation of professional practice—law, medicine, clinical psychology—to see some of the limits on how well that approach is likely to succeed.

This is not to suggest that the marketplace has no redeeming merits as a mechanism for weeding out good from bad evaluation. It does help ensure that consumers will be availed of services they want. In this light it is no wonder that Wholey's (1979, 1983) approach to evaluation at the federal level has been so remarkably pervasive; it is not the only approach to evaluation being presented to federal consumers of evaluation, but it may be the one that comes closest to providing them with the kind of evaluation they want, so they purchase it. And consumers sometimes do become informed, and then purchase better products. Wholey, for example, has used evaluability assessment to educate federal policymakers about some of the factors that should bear on their purchase of evaluation; and has convinced them that it is in their interests to organize evaluation so that, for example, program managers should not evaluate their own programs (Wholey et al., 1972).

Evaluation Policy as Social Policy.   But another reason difficulties exist in the regulation of practice is that the profession of evaluation is still young, and it has not yet developed answers to all the questions posed in this chapter. Answers are diverse, often contradictory, hotly debated, widely scattered throughout the literature (Reichardt & Cook, 1979; Wortman, 1983) and only occasionally consolidated into major, comprehensive theories (Shadish, Cook, & Leviton, in preparation). Even where sensible institutional mechanisms for reducing bias have been proposed (Cook & Shadish, 1982; Cordray, 1982; Scriven 1976c), evaluators have devoted insufficient attention to the economic and political realities of implementing those mechanisms in evaluation policy. The existence of such mechanisms is not enough; evaluation policies that are incompatible with the American political-economic system are no more likely to be implemented than social policies with such incompatibilities. The need here is for a new specialty in evaluation—theories of the political economy of evaluation.

Let the Buyer Beware

As in all marketplace economies, however, consumers must learn to protect themselves. They can start by simply remembering that they are consumers, not partners, in the production of good evaluations. They should take the same attitude toward their purchase of evaluation that they take toward the purchase of a car. The information in the present chapter is intended to help them assume a more critical attitude. One more piece of advice should be added: Consumers should remember that the extent to which an evaluator will consider the client's best interests, from the need for evaluation to the final choice of methods, probably depends in no small part on the personal characteristics of the evaluator—integrity, honesty, consideration, knowledge of the field. Indeed, it is just such qualities of character that lead a car buyer to trust and to recommend a particular used car salesman—integrity, honesty, consideration, knowledge. In fact, the personal character of the used car salesman has become a minimum standard by which consumers judge those who sell a product: "Would you buy a used car from this person?" has become a well known question that is asked of all those people whose character, and hence whose product, is suspect. The question concisely conveys consumer concern with purchasing a product that meets their needs. Perhaps consumers of evaluation ought to recall this standard when they are purchasing an evaluation. Perhaps the evaluation client should ask, in essence, "Would I buy a used car from this evaluator?" Evaluators about whom the answer to this question is negative are probably unlikely to provide a good evaluation.

References

Attkisson, C. C., Hargreaves, W. A., Horowitz, M. J., & Sorenson, J. E. (Eds.). (1978). *Evaluation of human services programs.* New York: Academic Press.

Babbie, E. R. (1973) *Survey research methods.* Belmont, CA: Wadsworth Publishing.

Becker, H., & Kirkhart, K. (1981). The Standards: Implications for professional licensure and accreditation. *Evaluation News, 2,* 153–156.

Boruch, R. F., Wortman, P. M., & Cordray, D. S. (Eds.). (1981). *Reanalyzing program evaluations.* San Francisco: Jossey-Bass.

Bradburn, N. M., Sudman, S., & Associates (1980). *Improving interview method and questionnaire design.* San Francisco: Jossey-Bass.

Bryk, A. S., & Raudenbush, S. W. (1983). The potential contribution of program evaluation to social problem solving: A view based on the CIS and Push/ Excel experiences. In A. S. Bryk (Ed.), *Stakeholder-based evaluation* (pp. 97–107). San Francisco: Jossey-Bass.

Campbell, D. T. (1969). Reforms as experiments. *American Psychologist, 24,* 409–429.

Campbell, D. T. (1971, September). *Methods for the experimenting society.* Paper presented to the Annual Meeting of the American Psychological Association, Washington, DC.

Campbell, D. T. (1979). "Degrees of freedom" and the case study. In T. D. Cook & C. S. Reichardt (Eds.), *Qualitative and quantitative methods in evaluation research* (pp. 49–67). Beverly Hills, CA: Sage Publications.

Campbell, J. P., Daft, R. L., & Hulin, C. L. (1982). *What to study: Generating and developing research questions.* Beverly Hills, CA: Sage Publications.

Carter, L. F. (1982). The standards for program evaluation and the large for-profit social science research and evaluation companies. In P. H. Rossi (Ed.), *Standards for evaluation practice* (pp. 37–48). San Francisco: Jossey-Bass.

Cohen, D. K. (1983). Evaluation and reform. In A. S. Bryk (Ed.), *Stakeholder-based evaluation* (pp. 73–82). San Francisco: Jossey-Bass.

Cohen, J., & Cohen, P. (1975). *Applied multiple regression/correlation analysis for the behavioral sciences.* Hillsdale, NJ: Lawrence Erlbaum.

Cook, T. D. (1981). Dilemmas in evaluation of social programs. In M. B. Brewer & B. E. Collins (Eds.), *Scientific inquiry and the social sciences: A volume in honor of Donald T. Campbell* (pp. 257–287). San Francisco: Jossey-Bass.

Cook, T. D., & Buccino, A. (1979). The social scientist as a provider of consulting services to the federal government. In J. Platt & J. Wicks (Eds.), *The psychological consultant* (pp. 103–134). New York: Grune and Stratton.

Cook, T. D., & Campbell, D. T. (1979). *Quasi-experimentation: Design and analysis issues for field settings.* Chicago: Rand-McNally.

Cook, T. D., & Gruder, C. L. (1978). Metaevaluation research. *Evaluation Quarterly*, 2, 5–51.

Cook, T. D., Leviton, L. C., & Shadish, W. R. (1985). Program evaluation. In G. Lindzey & E. Aronson (Eds.), *Handbook of social psychology* (3rd ed.) (pp. 699–777). New York: Random House.

Cook, T. D., & Reichardt, C. S. (Eds.). (1979). *Qualitative and quantitative methods in evaluation research.* Beverly Hills, CA: Sage Publications.

Cook, T. D., & Shadish, W. R. (1982). Metaevaluation: An assessment of the Congressionally mandated evaluation system for community mental health centers. In G. J. Stahler and W. R. Tash (Eds.), *Innovative approaches to mental health evaluation* (pp. 221–253). New York: Academic Press.

Cordray, D. S. (1982). An assessment of the utility of the ERS standards. In P. H. Rossi (Ed.), *Standards for evaluation practice* (pp. 67–82). San Francisco: Jossey-Bass.

Cronbach, L. J., Ambron, S. R., Dornbusch, S. M., Hess, R. D., Hornick, R. C., Phillips, D. C., Walker, D. F., & Weiner, S. S. (1980). *Toward reform of program evaluation.* San Francisco: Jossey-Bass.

Cronbach, L. J. (1982a). *Designing evaluations of educational and social programs.* San Francisco: Jossey-Bass.

Cronbach, L. J., (1982b). In praise of uncertainty. In P. H. Rossi (Ed.), *Standards for evaluation practice* (pp. 49–58). San Francisco: Jossey-Bass.

ERS Standards Committee. (1982). Evaluation research society standards for program evaluation. In P. H. Rossi (Ed.), *Standards for evaluation practice* (pp. 7–20). San Francisco: Jossey-Bass.

Fairweather, G. W. (Ed.). (1980). *The Fairweather Lodge: A twenty-five year retrospective.* San Francisco: Jossey-Bass.

Glass, G. V., & Ellett, F. S. (1980). Evaluation research. In M. R. Rosenzweig and L. W. Porter (Eds.), *Annual review of psychology, Vol. 31* (pp. 211–228). Palo Alto, CA: Annual Reviews.

Glass, G. V., McGaw, B., & Smith, M. L. (1981). *Meta-analysis in social research.* Beverly Hills, CA: Sage Publications.

Graziano, A. M. (1969). Clinical innovation and the mental health power structure: A social case history. *American Psychologist*, 24, 10–18.

Guba, E. G., & Lincoln, Y. S. (1981). *Effective evaluation.* San Francisco: Jossey-Bass.

Heckman, J. J. (1980). Sample selection bias as a specification error. In E. W. Stromsdorfer & G. Farkas (Eds.), *Evaluation Studies Review Annual, Vol. 5* (pp. 60–74). Beverly Hills, CA: Sage Publications.

House, E. R. (1980). *Evaluating with validity*. Beverly Hills, CA: Sage Publications.

Huitema, B. E. (1980). *The analysis of covariance and its alternatives*. New York: Wiley.

Joreskog, K. G., & Sorbom, D. (1979). *Advances in factor analysis and structural equation modelling*. Cambridge, MA: Abt Books.

Kane, M. T. (1982). The validity of licensure examinations. *American Psychologist, 37*, 911–918.

Kenny, D. A. (1979). *Correlation and causality*. New York: Wiley.

LaLonde, R. J. (1984). *Evaluating the econometric evaluations of training programs with experimental data*. (Working Paper No. 183). Princeton University: Industrial Relations Section.

Levin, H. M. (1975). Cost-effectiveness analysis in evaluation research. In E. Struening & M. Guttentag (Eds.), *Handbook of evaluation research, Vol. 2* (pp. 89–122). Beverly Hills, CA: Sage Publications.

Levin, H. M. (1983). *Cost-effectiveness: A primer*. Beverly Hills, CA: Sage Publications.

Leviton, L. C., & Boruch, R. F. (1983). Contributions of evaluation to education programs and policy. *Evaluation Review, 7*, 563–598.

Leviton, L. C., & Hughes, E. F. X. (1981). Research on the utilization of evaluations: A review and synthesis. *Evaluation Review, 5*, 525–548.

Lichstein, K. L. (in press). *Clinical relaxation strategies*. New York: Wiley.

Lindblom, C. E. (1977). *Politics and markets: The world's political-economic systems*. New York: Basic Books.

Lindblom, C. E., & Cohen, D. K. (1979). *Usable knowledge: Social science and social problem solving*. New Haven, CT: Yale University Press.

McCleary, R., & Hay, R. A. (1980). *Applied time series analysis for the social sciences*. Beverly Hills, CA: Sage Publications.

Morgan, G. (Ed.). (1983). *Beyond method: Strategies for social research*. Beverly Hills, CA: Sage Publications.

Murnane, R. J., Newstead, S., & Olsen, R.J. (1985). Comparing public and private schools: The puzzling role of selectivity bias. *Journal of Business and Economic Statistics, 3*, 23–35.

Nunnally, J. C. (1978). *Psychometric theory* (2nd Ed.). New York: McGraw-Hill.

Nvasky, V. S., & Paster, D. (1976). (background paper). In law enforcement: The federal role. *Report of the Twentieth Century Fund Task Force on the Law Enforcement Assistance Administration* (pp. 25–134). New York: McGraw-Hill.

Patton, M. Q. (1978). *Utilization-focused evaluation*. Beverly Hills, CA: Sage Publications.

Patton, M. Q. (1980). *Qualitative evaluation methods*. Beverly Hills, CA: Sage Publications.

Reichardt, C. S., & Cook, T. D. (1979). Beyond qualitative versus quantitative methods. In T. D. Cook & C. S. Reichardt (Eds.), *Qualitative and quantitative methods in evaluation research* (pp. 7–32). Beverly Hills, CA: Sage Publications.

Rossi, P. H. (Ed.). (1982). *Standards for evaluation practice*. San Francisco: Jossey-Bass.

Rossi, P. H., Freeman, H. E., & Wright, S. R. (1979). *Evaluation: A systematic approach.* Beverly Hills, CA: Sage Publications.

Rothenberg, J. (1975). Cost-benefit analysis: A methodological exposition. In E. Struening & M. Guttentag (Eds.), *Handbook of evaluation research, Vol. 2* (pp. 4–88). Beverly Hills, CA: Sage Publications.

Scriven, M. (1976a). Payoffs from evaluation. In C. C. Abt (Ed.), *The evaluation of social programs* (pp. 217–224). Beverly Hills, CA: Sage Publications.

Scriven, M. (1976b). Maximizing the power of causal investigations: The modus operandi method. In G. V. Glass (Ed.), *Evaluation studies review annual (Vol. 1)* (pp. 101–118). Beverly Hills, CA: Sage Publications.

Scriven, M. (1976c). Evaluation bias and its control. In G. V. Glass (Ed.), *Evaluation studies review annual (Vol. 1)* (pp. 119–139). Beverly Hills, CA: Sage Publications.

Scriven, M. (1980). *The logic of evaluation.* Inverness, CA: Edgepress.

Sechrest, L. (1981). The Standards: A general review. *Evaluation News, 2,* 145–147.

Shadish, W. R. (1982). Evaluation during fiscal stringency. *Evaluation News, 3,* 89–91.

Shadish, W. R. (1983, October). *Planning for implementability.* Paper presented at the annual convention of the Evaluation Research Society, Chicago.

Shadish, W. R. (1984). Policy research: Lessons from the implementation of deinstitutionalization. *American Psychology, 39,* 725–738.

Shadish, W. R. (1986). Planned critical multiplism: Some elaborations. *Behavioral Assessment, 8,* 75–103.

Shadish, W. R., & Bootzin, R. R. (1981). Long-term community care: Mental health policy in the face of reality. *Schizophrenic Bulletin, 7,* 580–585.

Shadish, W. R., & Cook, T. D. (1983). Evaluation of social programs. In B. B. Wolman (Ed.), *International encyclopedia of psychiatry, psychology, psychoanalysis, and neurology, first progress volume* (pp. 413–416). New York: Aesculapius Press.

Shadish, W. R., Cook, T. D., & Houts, A. C. (in press). Quasi-experimentation in a critical multiplist mode. In W. M. K. Trochim (Ed.), *Advances in quasi-experimental design and analysis.* San Francisco: Jossey-Bass.

Shadish, W. R., Cook, T. D., & Leviton, L. C. (in preparation). *Evaluating social programs: Theorists and theories.*

Shadish, W. R., Thomas, S., & Bootzin, R. R. (1982). Criteria for success in deinstitutionalization: Perceptions of nursing homes by different interest groups. *American Journal of Community Psychology, 10,* 553–566.

Shaver, P., & Staines, G. (1971). Problems facing Campbell's "Experimenting Society." *Urban Affairs Quarterly, 7,* 173–186.

Spencer, B. D. (1982). Feasibility of benefit-cost analysis of data programs. *Evaluation Review, 6,* 649–672.

Thompson, M. S. (1980). *Benefit-cost analysis for program evaluation.* Beverly Hills, CA: Sage Publications.

Thorndike, R. L. (1971). *Educational measurement* (2nd ed.). American Council on Education, Washington, DC.

Warwick, D. P., & Lininger, C. A. (1975). *The sample survey: Theory and practice.* New York: McGraw-Hill.

Weiss, C. H. (1973). Where politics and evaluation research meet. *Evaluation, 1,* 37–45.

Weiss, C. H. (Ed.). (1977). *Using social research in public policy making.* Lexington, MA: Lexington Books.

Weiss, C. H. (1978). Improving the linkage between social research and public policy. In L. E. Lynn (Ed.), *Knowledge and policy: The uncertain connection* (pp. 23–81). Washington, DC: National Academy of Sciences.

Weiss, C. H. (1983). Toward the future of stakeholder approaches in evaluation. In A. S. Bryk (Ed.), *Stakeholder-based evaluation* (pp. 83–96). San Francisco: Jossey-Bass.

Wholey, J. S. (1979). *Evaluation: Promise and performance.* Washington, DC: The Urban Institute.

Wholey, J. S. (1983). *Evaluation and effective public management.* Boston: Little, Brown.

Wholey, J. S., Duffy, H. G., Fukumoto, J. S., Scanlon, J. W., Berlin, M. A., Copeland, W. C., & Zelinsky, J. G. (1972). Proper organizational relationships. In C. H. Weiss (Ed.), *Evaluating action programs: Readings in social action and education* (pp. 118–122). Boston: Allyn & Bacon.

Wholey, J. S., Nay, J. N., Scanlon, J. W., & Schmidt, R. E. (1975). Evaluation: When is it really needed? *Evaluation, 2,* 89–93.

Wiley, D. E. (1976). Another hour, another day: Quantity of schooling, a potent path for policy. In J. E. Wiley (Ed.), *Schooling and achievement in American society.* New York: Academic Press.

Windle, C. (1982). Limited and limiting perspectives. *Evaluation and Program Planning, 5,* 296–298.

Winter, N. B. (1982). (Letter to the editor). *Evaluation News, 3,* 92–93.

Wortman, P. M. (1983). Evaluation research: A methodological perspective. In M. R. Rosenzweig & L. W. Porter (Eds.), *Annual Review of Psychology, (Vol. 34)* (pp. 223–260). Palo Alto, CA: Annual Reviews.

29

Matching Patients with Treatments

Conceptual and Methodological Issues*

John W. Finney and Rudolf H. Moos

ABSTRACT. The current enthusiasm for matching patients with optimal treatments rests on limited conceptual analyses. In addition, much of the existing research on patient-treatment matching has been based on methodological assumptions that are not commensurate with the complexity of the matching problem. Six key conceptual and methodological issues that underlie attempts to match patients with optimal forms of treatment and to conduct research on patient-treatment matching are outlined. The conceptual issues are: (*1*) selecting effective matching variables, (*2*) specifying the end result that matching is to enhance and (*3*) determining the stage(s) in the treatment process at which matching decisions are to be made. The three methodological issues deal with the type of patient-treatment match or interaction effect and include: (*1*) nonlinear interaction effects, (*2*) higher-order interaction effects and (*3*) multilevel interaction effects. Examples clarifying these issues are drawn from the literature on treating alcohol-dependent persons, but the issues are discussed at a broad level that permits generalization to treatment for many disorders. Implications for research on and the practice of "prescriptive treatment" are considered. (*J. Stud. Alcohol* **47:** 122-134, 1986)

THERE IS widespread support currently for the idea of matching alcohol-misusing or alcohol-dependent persons with optimal treatment approaches: a process sometimes referred to as prescriptive or differential treatment. In many cases, however, the enthusiasm for prescriptive treatment is uncritical, resting on limited conceptual analyses. Moreover, the methodological assumptions that have guided most studies of differential treatment have not adequately reflected the complexity of the phenomenon. This article considers some key conceptual and methodological issues that are raised by efforts to apply prescriptive treatment and by research on such efforts. (The specific focus is on prescriptive treatment for alcohol misusing or alcohol-dependent patients, but the issues raised are relevant to the differential treatment of other psychological and behavioral disorders.) Some implications of the issues for the practice of patient-treatment matching and some promising avenues for research in this area also are discussed.

The global perspective taken and the issues raised

highlight the complexity of the matching problem. Thus they afford one explanation of why powerful differential treatment systems have not yet been developed. By the same token, however, consideration of the complexity of the matching problem can promote realistic expectations that, in turn, should provide a more solid foundation for the sustained efforts that will be needed to produce more effective matching systems.

Enthusiasm for Differential Treatment in the Alcoholism Field

Scientific research on alcoholism treatment spans a period of 40 to 50 years. Although Bowman and Jellinek (1941) called for research on matching patients with optimal forms of treatment more than four decades ago, and although some scattered studies of differential treatment have been conducted during the last 25 years (for a review, see Glaser, 1980), treatment providers and researchers in the alcoholism field currently seem more eager to apply and explore prescriptive treatment principles than ever before. Indeed, many appear to espouse the view Cronbach (1957) set forth in his well-known article, "The Two Disciplines of Scientific Psychology." In that article, Cronbach outlined some of the shortcomings of both the experimental and correlational approaches for searching for "main effects" in psychology and proposed "aptitude-treatment interaction" research as a method of synthesizing and going beyond them.

Received: 3 May 1985.
* This article is based in part on a presentation by the first author at a Conference on Substance Abuse Assessment held at the Menlo Park Division of the Palo Alto Veterans Administration Medical Center, Menlo Park, California, December 1982. Preparation of the article was supported by Veterans Administration Medical and Health Services Research and Development Service research funds and National Institute on Alcohol Abuse and Alcoholism grant AA 02863.

In the field of alcoholism treatment research, the search for main effects via experimental and correlational studies likewise has been disappointing. As portrayed by the hypothetical data in Figure 1A, experimental and quasi-experimental studies of alternative treatment approaches typically have yielded similar modest treatment effects (Emrick, 1975). For example, Kissin et al. (1968) randomly assigned (for the most

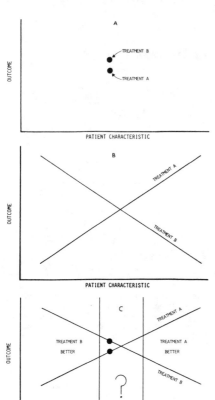

FIGURE 1. Hypothetical data illustrating: A, similar (modest) average outcomes for two treatment modalities; B, inconsistent relationships between a patient pretreatment characteristic and outcome in two treatment modalities; and C, an interaction between a patient pretreatment characteristic and two treatment modalities.

part) men to three treatment conditions: (1) outpatient pharmacologic therapy (a combination of a tranquilizer and an antidepressant), (2) outpatient group psychotherapy and pharmacologic therapy and (3) an inpatient rehabilitation ward. At a follow-up 1 year after treatment entry, the proportion of patients in each treatment group who were rated as "successes" (abstinent or almost so and significant improvement on social and vocational criteria during the 6 months prior to follow-up) varied only slightly and nonsignificantly from 17.4 to 20.0%. No treatment has been demonstrated to be consistently superior for the entire population of alcohol-misusing persons.

With respect to the correlational approach, investigators have sought to identify patient intake characteristics that are consistently associated with outcome within a variety of treatment programs. However, with the possible exception of indicators of "social stability," the search for consistent prognostic indicators has not been fruitful (Emrick and Hansen, 1983; Gibbs and Flanagan, 1977),[1] as illustrated by the hypothetical data in Figure 1B. For instance, Ritson (1968) found that persons with long histories of heavy drinking tended to experience better outcome, whereas Stinson et al. (1979) observed that patients who had fewer years of problem drinking exhibited better posttreatment functioning. In other studies, specific patient characteristics have been unrelated to treatment outcome. Edwards (1966), for example, found no relationship between treatment outcome and age, duration of drinking history or intelligence. Overall, patient pretreatment characteristics have not been good predictors of posttreatment functioning, with such variables typically accounting for 20% or less of the variance in outcome dimensions (Cronkite and Moos, 1978; Luborsky and McLellan, 1978).

Like Cronbach in 1957, many treatment providers and researchers in the alcoholism field today are ready to deemphasize the search for main effects and pursue the multiple, divergent and more promising paths implied by patient–treatment interaction effects. The appeal of patient–treatment interactions stems from the idea that they can "explain" the discouraging results of past main effects studies and hold the promise of producing

---

[1] Certain patient characteristics are more consistently related to treatment outcome variables at the program level. For example, in a meta analysis of treatment outcome studies, Costello (1980) found that programs that treated married and employed individuals tended to have higher success or improvement rates than programs treating clients without these characteristics. As Cronbach et al. (1976) observed, measures at different analysis levels are likely to assess different constructs. The aggregate patient characteristics that Costello linked with program-level outcomes may be indirect indicators of a more positive treatment climate, may reflect the fact that programs treating affluent patients attract more able treatment providers or may be proxies for other treatment program factors.

more powerful and applicable findings. Alternative treatments produce similar (modest) effects, but different groups of patients may be helped by different types of treatment. Although any given patient characteristic is not consistently associated with treatment outcome within a variety of treatment programs, perhaps persons high on that characteristic are helped by one treatment whereas persons low on that variable benefit from another. For "multimodal" or "shotgun" treatment programs in which patients are exposed to a number of different treatment components in the hope that something will "take," a finding of no relationship between a particular patient characteristic and outcome also is consistent with the possibility of an underlying patient–treatment interaction effect. Again, patients high on the variable may be helped by one therapeutic component, whereas those low on that variable may benefit from another. These expectations are diagrammed in Figure 1C. (Note that Figure 1C, illustrating an interaction effect, can be produced by overlaying Figures 1A and 1B.)

Given the enthusiasm among treatment providers and researchers for differential treatment, it is fortunate that this area is not totally uncharted. We can draw on efforts that have been made in the alcoholism field over the last 25 years, starting with the study by Wallerstein et al. (1957), and including the contributions of Glaser (1980) and colleagues (1978), the research of Annis and Chan (1983), Kissin et al. (1970), Lyons et al. (1982) and McLellan et al. (1983) and the essays by Gibbs (1981) and Pattison (1979). In addition, there are relevant conceptual and empirical analyses in the general field of psychotherapy (e.g., Beutler, 1979; Frances et al., 1984). Finally, the work of Cronbach and his colleagues (Cronbach and Snow, 1977; Cronbach and Webb, 1975) can be extrapolated to provide valuable conceptual and methodological insights. Indeed the present article draws heavily on Cronbach's work.

Research in these fields highlights six important conceptual and methodological issues inherent in efforts to match patients and treatments and to carry out research to inform such matching. The issues involve each of the four basic components of the matching hypothesis: patients, treatments, outcomes and the form of the patient–treatment match or interaction effect. The first three issues are more conceptual in nature: (1) selecting effective matching variables from the vast arrays of patient and treatment characteristics; (2) specifying the end result(s) that matching is to enhance; and (3) determining the stage(s) in the treatment process at which matching decisions are to be made. The other three issues are more methodological in nature. Each deals with a different, more complex form of patient–treatment interaction effect than the simple interaction effect that has been assumed among some treatment

providers and in the studies of most researchers. These three issues are: (1) nonlinear interaction effects, (2) higher-order interaction effects and (3) multilevel interaction effects.

Conceptual Issues

Selecting potential matching variables

The first issue is to determine the patient and treatment variables on which to base a differential treatment system. The overwhelming array of potential matching variables can be appreciated more readily by considering two broad categories within both the patient and treatment domains. (We will return to these categories later when considering promising avenues for matching research.)

Patient variables. Persons seeking treatment can be differentiated by any of a large number of variables. Some of these variables can be arrayed along a global dimension of patient deficits–resources. Variables toward the deficit end of this dimension—such as excessive drinking, alcohol dependence symptoms, depressive symptoms and occupational problems—are involved in patients seeking treatment and represent the main foci for the therapeutic efforts of most treatment providers. At the other end of the dimension are patient resources, such as "ego strength." These resource variables represent relatively stable patient factors that, especially if reinforced and augmented during the treatment process, may enable patients to prevent and resist relapse-inducing situations and thus promote recovery.

A second broad category in the patient domain consists of information processing variables—such as cognitive abilities (e.g., abstract reasoning and problem-solving skills) and patient "motivation." Most psychosocial interventions involve cognitively mediated learning processes. Information processing skills affect how and to what extent patients organize and process the information presented to them during the course of treatment, and the degree to which they are able to retain information and apply it in relevant situations following treatment. Thus these characteristics play an important role in determining the level at which a particular therapeutic approach is implemented across individual patients.

Patient variables are usually thought of in terms of personal characteristics. Another subcategory of patient variables that has been largely overlooked in patient–treatment matching consists of aspects of patients' extra treatment environments. Some of these life context factors represent deficits (e.g., chronic life strains), whereas others constitute resources (e.g., social support). Still others are related to information processing, such as a spouse who can clarify and reinforce the treatment approach being employed with his or her alcoholic partner.

Treatment variables. Turning to the treatment domain, one again encounters great diversity. In fact, Glaser (1980) argues that specifying appropriate matching dimensions in the treatment domain may prove more difficult than specifying relevant patient attributes because we are more familiar with and have more concepts and measures to choose from in the patient domain. For the sake of brevity, only two broad classes of treatment variables are outlined here. The first category consists of "therapeutic" components—those aspects of treatment that are aimed at reducing or remedying patient deficits and producing positive posttreatment functioning. These components range from broad treatment modalities (e.g., behavior therapy, Alcoholics Anonymous, therapeutic community approach) to specific acts of therapists during the treatment process (e.g., confrônting denial). Also included here are treatment goal or patient growth-oriented aspects of treatment environments, such as those tapped by the personal problem and practical orientation subscales of the Ward Atmosphere Scale (Moos, 1974).

The second set of treatment variables consists of components of the treatment delivery process. Included here is the manner in which the treatment process is organized and presented to clients, such as its sequencing, repetition and duration. This category also encompasses relevant aspects of the treatment provider such as his or her cognitive style, as well as broad aspects of the "quality" of the treatment setting, such as its clarity and organization (Moos, 1974).

Strategies for selecting relevant matching variables. These categories of patient and treatment variables are neither comprehensive nor mutually exclusive. However, they provide a broad overview of the two domains and highlight the diversity of patient and treatment factors that are potential bases for matching. The first problem encountered by a treatment provider or researcher is how to select variables from the two domains to produce effective matching (or yield significant interaction effects). Any one or more of at least five approaches can be employed: (*1*) reliance on clinical judgment, (*2*) the "cafeteria" approach, (*3*) exploratory data analysis, (*4*) data reduction techniques and (*5*) theoretical analysis. Some of these approaches are more likely to be employed by treatment providers, whereas others are more likely to be selected by researchers.

Treatment providers often rely on their clinical judgment in attempting to "individualize" or match their treatment approaches to different patients. Indeed, this approach accounts for much of the "naturalistic" matching that currently takes place. Although indivi-

dualized treatment undoubtedly represents an improvement over the rigid imposition of a standardized approach, dissatisfaction with treatment effectiveness remains. Part of the problem stems from the inaccuracy of clinical judgment (Meehl, 1954; Wiggins, 1973), so that individualized treatment approaches are unlikely to be reliable or systematic within clinicians over time. Methods can be applied to make clinical judgments more accurate (Fischhoff, 1982). In addition, however, more rigorously derived principles are needed to assist treatment providers as they apply differential treatment.

A second method for effecting a patient-treatment match is to employ the cafeteria approach to treatment allocation-selection (Ewing, 1977; Parker et al., 1979). The idea is that patients are offered a menu of treatment options from which they select the components of their individual treatment regimen, usually with some help from staff. Ewing sees this approach as a short-run alternative until more reliable data are available on which to base differential treatment, whereas Parker et al. appear to view it as more of a long-term solution. Both argue that the cafeteria approach can increase treatment attractiveness and retention. As we indicate later, however, treatment attractiveness and treatment effectiveness are not necessarily related positively and a number of studies (for a review, see Finney et al., 1981) have shown that the relationship between duration of treatment and treatment outcome is not straightforward. Given that patients may select treatment options on the basis of their preferences rather than their needs, the value of the cafeteria approach may lie in the greater sense of control it gives to patients, rather than in the appropriateness of the resulting patient-treatment match.

The next three approaches are more systematic. Two of them (exploratory data analysis and data reduction techniques) are of special appeal to researchers. The exploratory approach consists of obtaining data without specific consideration of matching hypotheses (or using data already gathered for other purposes) and, with the appropriate computer-assisted analysis, determining what patient and treatment variables interact. For example, Smart (1978) employed data on 31 patient variables (e.g., demographic characteristics, drinking variables, physical health, social isolation) and six treatment dimensions (e.g., type of treatment received, profession of the patient's principal therapist) and examined the resulting 186 first-order interactions (i.e., one patient variable in interaction with one treatment variable). However, he found no statistically significant interaction effects in this purely empirical study.

The data reduction procedure occupies the middle ground between exploratory empirical and theoretical analyses. The basic approach is to use factor or variable cluster analysis to reduce an array of variables to a few general dimensions for the patient and treatment domains. The interactions of these general dimensions with respect to outcome criteria then can be explored. To the extent that variable selection is not theoretically driven and an unconstrained analysis is employed, the approach is quite similar to exploratory data analysis, albeit at a higher level of generality or abstraction. On the other hand, confirmatory factor analytic techniques (Joreskog, 1969) can be employed when the selection of variables and their organization is guided by theory. However, no example of the data reduction approach for exploring patient-treatment interaction effects in the alcoholism field was found.

The fifth method, one with appeal to both treatment providers and researchers, is to rely on theory to guide the selection of appropriate patient and treatment variables. Coordinated concepts for patients and treatments—that is, constructs in each domain that have theoretical implications for constructs in the other—can be identified from existing theory or generated in a fresh conceptualization. For example, McLachlan (1974) used conceptual systems theory (Harvey et al., 1961) to formulate a specific patient-treatment matching hypothesis. Patients were assessed in terms of their conceptual level (CL), ranging from stage 1 (poorly socialized, impulsive and cognitively simple) to stage 4 (empathic, interdependent and cognitively complex). Treatment was differentiated in terms of the degree of "structure" provided during inpatient treatment and in aftercare. The matching hypothesis was that low CL patients benefit more from highly structured treatments that compensate for their lack of ability to structure their own experience. On the other hand, high CL patients benefit from a less structured environment that encourages individuals to use their own resources to organize their experiences (an environment that presumably would create confusion in low CL patients). McLachlan (1974) found no main effects for patient CL or treatment structure; however, there was a significant interaction effect. Among patients matched with both inpatient and aftercare services, 77% were rated as "recovered" at a 12- to 16-month follow-up; only 38% of mismatched patients were in the recovered category (for another example, see Spoth, 1983).

With respect to the three systematic approaches, the results of the Smart (1978) and McLachlan (1974) studies, although admittedly extreme, suggest that in any single empirical study a conceptual approach to identifying patient-treatment interaction effects is likely to prove more productive than a purely empirical one. They thus support Lewin's well-known contention that "there is nothing so practical as a good theory" (cited in Wrightsman et al., 1972, *p. 3*). Indeed, the formulation of relevant theories is probably the most pressing current need in the matching field.

Along these lines it is worthwhile to consider an informative paper on patient-treatment matching by Skinner (1981). He outlined several conditions that he felt were necessary for a rigorous test of a matching hypothesis, including the use of distinctive treatments and experimental designs with random assignment of patients to treatment conditions. He arrayed the results of nine tests of matching hypotheses and noted that, with the exception of McLachlan's (1974) study, those yielding statistically significant interaction effects employed experimental designs, whereas nonsignificant results were obtained in nonexperimental studies. Skinner concluded that only true experiments are likely to yield statistically significant results in tests of matching hypotheses, due to their greater power relative to nonexperimental studies.

Although we agree that true experiments are more sensitive, we believe that the "superiority" of the experiments Skinner (1981) reviewed in yielding significant results may be due less to their statistical power and more to the fact that they generally were driven by theories, whereas the nonexperimental studies generally were not. In addition, in that their specifications were guided by theory, the alternative treatment modalities examined in the experiments typically were more distinctive than the treatments in the nonexperimental studies. Again, formulating powerful theories seems more important than methodology as the primary key to developing effective matching schemes.

Exploratory analyses also can play an important role in the search for effective prescriptive treatment approaches. Such analyses—for example, using product-terms in multiple regression analyses (Cohen, 1978; Southwood, 1978)—can compensate for their lack of systematic focus by the ease with which they can be mounted in large numbers. Exploratory analyses can trigger fruitful theoretical insights and yield findings that may be confirmed under more controlled, hypothesis-testing conditions (e.g., McLellan et al., 1983a, 1983b).

The end result matching is to enhance

Typically, the end result that patient-treatment matching is supposed to enhance is presumed to be the effectiveness of treatment—that is, increased positive treatment outcome. In the alcoholism field, abstinence was once the singular outcome toward which treatment was directed. In more recent years, some treatment providers and researchers have come to view a reduction of alcohol consumption to a level of "moderate drinking" as an acceptable outcome of treatment for some patients whose drinking problems are less severe.

In addition to excessive alcohol consumption, many clients at treatment intake exhibit deficits in other life areas. Because treatment providers recognize that such deficits may contribute to relapse into patterns of alcohol misuse, they often are addressed during treatment. Consequently, treatment outcome has come to be viewed in multidimensional terms, and multiple outcome measures usually are reported in evaluations of alcoholism treatment programs. The multivariate nature of treatment outcome, reflecting the "biopsychosocial" perspective on alcohol misuse held by many treatment providers and researchers (Kissin and Hanson, 1982), obviously complicates the decision-making process in differential treatment. One form of patient–treatment matching might enhance a patient's psychological functioning, whereas another might produce better social relationships.

Matching does not have to focus solely on enhancing the effectiveness of treatment, however. For individuals who are not coerced into treatment, it is necessary to consider the attractiveness of particular treatment modalities to different types of potential patients as well as the extent to which such modalities are likely to retain specific types of patients once they enter treatment. Unfortunately, the most effective treatments may not be the most attractive and may not exert the greatest "holding power."

For example, Worden (1980) evaluated a halfway house program for chronic alcoholic men that initially was loosely structured and had no systematic educational or treatment components. Not surprisingly, the program was ineffective. Almost all of the residents were drinking when they left the program (usually after only a 1- or 2-week stay), and many did not have jobs at treatment termination. The program was subsequently restructured into an intensive 30-day regimen including education and therapy groups, individual counseling and scheduled recreational and physical activities, followed by structured reentry into the work force and the community.

Two effects of the new program quickly became apparent: treatment retention increased (men who entered the program stayed longer), but treatment attractiveness declined markedly. Over a 20-month period, occupancy plummeted from almost full capacity under the old program to 13% (only 2 of 15 beds occupied). Agencies were less likely to refer patients to the new program. Some wanted their patients working right away (not waiting 30 days), whereas others provided intensive treatment of their own and saw no need to refer patients to a similar program. In addition, potential patients shied away from the new program, opting for less demanding programs. Worden (1980) wrote: "We found ourselves in the absurd position of having a high-powered program (we thought) without clients" (*p. 158*).

As another example, Sanchez-Craig et al. (1984) randomly assigned early-stage problem drinkers to virtually identical treatment regimens with either abstinence or controlled drinking as the treatment goal. No significant differences were found between the two groups in either treatment attrition or, at a 2-year follow-up, in treatment outcome. However, the controlled drinking goal was more attractive in that fewer persons assigned that goal expressed reservations about it in comparison to those assigned the abstinence goal. The authors conclude that controlled drinking is a more suitable goal for early-stage problem drinkers—a goal that might attract more individuals to treatment at a point when their drinking may be more amenable to change. These two examples suggest that in formulating treatment options for different types of patients, program developers will have to consider treatment attractiveness and retention, as well as treatment effectiveness.

Multistage matching

It is tempting to think of matching as representing a single decision: a patient is assessed at treatment intake and assigned to the specific treatment modality presumed to provide the greatest benefit. In actuality, however, a number of decisions regarding patient–treatment matching may be required during the course of treatment. Some of these decisions will be in response to patient change during the treatment process. In the early stages of treatment, "course adjustments" may have to be directed toward keeping a patient in treatment (forming a treatment alliance), rather than toward enhancing treatment effectiveness. Once a sufficient degree of treatment motivation has been established, the process of behavior change is likely to be the primary treatment focus. After a behavior change has been effected, the treatment focus may shift to maintaining it.

Other patient–treatment matching decisions may arise in regard to the varied aspects of the biopsychosocial disorder of alcohol dependence. Abroms (1981) states that logically, but not always practically, a treatment provider should address biological deficits first, followed by psychological and then social problems. His argument for such treatment "serialism" is based on the assumption that adequate biological functioning (appropriate levels of alertness, cognitive organization, drive strength and affective regulation) is a necessary foundation for effecting change in psychological functioning, and that adequate psychological functioning is a prerequisite for therapy oriented toward achieving a proper balance between social ties and individual freedom. This perspective is consistent with our earlier point concerning an adequate match of treatment delivery and patient information-processing capabilities as necessary for the implementation of therapeutic treatment components.

The idea of multistage matching suggests two basic approaches for exploring patient–treatment interactions (Cronbach and Snow, 1977). First, broad patient variables (such as personality traits) can be explored for their interactions with general treatment modalities. Such macrolevel studies can inform the initial assignment of patients to different types of treatment programs. Second, microprocess studies and observations of treatment providers can be brought to bear on the interactions of more specific and malleable patient characteristics with specific acts of therapists. Such studies should help to clarify the dynamics of adapting treatment to intrapatient change.

Methodological Issues

A number of methodological issues can be raised in connection with research on patient–treatment matching. We focus on three that deal with the form of the patient–treatment interaction effect or the nature of the patient–treatment match. Thus these "methodological" issues have implications for formulating conceptualizations of effective prescriptive treatment systems.

Nonlinear effects

To this point, we have assumed linear relationships between patient variables and outcome within different treatment programs. However, nonlinear relationships undoubtedly are present at times, and can be detected if one looks for them (Abbott, 1984). An extreme case is graphed in Figure 2. As an example, age and treatment goals may interact in a curvilinear fashion. Young (particularly unmarried) persons who are not heavily dependent on alcohol may be more likely to

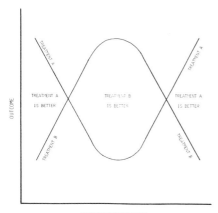

FIGURE 2. Hypothetical data illustrating a curvilinear interaction between a patient pretreatment characteristic and two treatment modalities.

improve following treatment if they adopt a moderate drinking goal (Treatment A in Figure 2). Such a goal may be more consistent with the press toward drinking in the social environments of young persons, and thus may generate fewer stressful situations that could precipitate full-blown relapses (Polich et al., 1981). Likewise, older problem drinkers (persons 60 years and older), especially "late-onset" problem drinkers, may benefit socially and physiologically from the ingestion of small quantities of alcohol. A moderate drinking goal may be appropriate for them. On the other hand, for persons (especially married individuals) in the middle of the adult age range, abstinence may be the more effective treatment goal (Treatment B in Figure 2). Abstinence is more likely to be consistent with the expectations of family members regarding the treatment goal that should be pursued by a person who has a drinking problem (Polich et al., 1981).

The data graphed in Figure 2 also illustrate how nonlinear interactions may cause investigators to obtain seemingly conflicting results when their samples have restricted ranges on a treatment allocation variable. A researcher working with persons on the lower half of the distribution of the allocation variable "X" shown in Figure 2 would conclude that persons "low" on that variable should be assigned to Treatment A, whereas those "high" on X should enter Treatment B. In contrast, an investigator studying persons on the upper half of the distribution would argue that persons low on X should be in Treatment B, and those high on X should be assigned to Treatment A.

Higher-order interaction effects: Entering the "hall of mirrors"

Of course, the task facing practitioners and researchers committed to differential treatment is more difficult than simply choosing one or two critical patient variables (e.g., X_1 and X_2), each of which interacts with a single treatment dimension (e.g., $X_1 \times T_1$ and $X_2 \times T_2$). In his 1957 essay, Cronbach argued that main effects of both treatment and recipient variables are often of limited generalizability due to interaction effects. When he later wrote "Beyond the Two Disciplines of Scientific Psychology," Cronbach (1975) lamented, "I was shortsighted not to apply the same argument to the interaction effects themselves" (p. 119). He pointed out that interaction effects can be moderated by other variables in higher-order interactions (e.g., $X_1 \times X_2 \times T_1$): "Once we attend to interactions, we enter a hall of mirrors that extends to infinity" (p. 119).

Effective patient–treatment matching systems are likely to be more complicated than those modeled by first-order interactions. Even if a first-order matching scheme proved effective in a particular treatment setting, conditions at other sites (or changes over time in the original setting) probably would limit the generalizability or transportability of the original matching system and require a higher-order system. For instance, it might be found in one program that introverted persons respond better to individual psychotherapy, whereas extroverted ones have better outcomes in group therapy. Later, it might be noted in another program that only introverted people of above-average intelligence respond better to individual psychotherapy. An original first-order patient–treatment interaction thus might be further specified in the form of a higher-order interaction from a study having a more diverse patient sample than was available for the original research.

Multilevel effects

Most discussions of prescriptive treatment assume an individual treatment model—that is, a model in which individual patients are exposed and react to treatment independently. In fact, for most alcohol-dependent patients, treatment has a strong social (not just a dyadic) component. Inpatient treatment occurs in a social context. Even with such individualized approaches as aversion conditioning, patients have ample time to interact with each other informally and during on-site group therapy and Alcoholics Anonymous meetings. For outpatients, group therapy is a widely used social treatment approach.

When treatment is a social process, at least three levels of interaction effects may occur (Cronbach and Snow, 1977; Cronbach and Webb, 1975): (*1*) an individual effect as is usually assumed, (*2*) a group effect and (*3*) an individual-within-group or comparative effect. In an individual effect, a patient pretreatment characteristic (X) interacts directly with the treatment variable; the interaction is not affected by the social context (if any) in which the treatment is provided. In a group effect, a group-level variable (such as the mean of group members on an individual difference variable, $\overline{X}$) interacts with the treatment variable. For example, with an especially verbal group (in terms of the average of the group members), a therapist may accomplish more than he or she would with a more reticent group.

Finally, in a comparative or individual-within-group effect, it is a patient's standing on some variable relative to the other persons in the setting (X-$\overline{X}$) that interacts with treatment. For example, a patient with below-average verbal skills may elicit more attention from the leader and consequently experience a better outcome in a group that, on average, was composed of reticent as opposed to gregarious members. Another example of a comparative interaction effect may be reflected in the differential outcome for men and women patients following group and individual therapy. The lesser responsiveness of women to group therapy may be due not to a general aversion to group therapy, but to a reluctance to express their feelings openly in groups that are composed mainly of men (Cronkite and Moos, 1984).

Cronbach and Webb (1975) note that, given the mathematical interdependence of X, $\overline{X}$ and X–$\overline{X}$, the three types of interaction effects just described cannot be completely disentangled. However, one can examine between- and within-group regressions in multilevel analyses (Boyd and Iversen, 1979; Burstein, 1980). Group-level processes affect between-group regressions, whereas comparative or "frogpond" processes (Firebaugh, 1980) influence within-group effects. Individual effects are reflected in both between- and within-group regressions (Cronbach and Snow, 1977).

Figure 3A illustrates a between-group interaction effect involving the average level of a patient allocation variable X and Treatments A and B. However, there is no interaction involving within-group processes since the within-group slopes are constant across groups. Given the considerable within-group variance shown on the patient allocation variable, it is likely that if these data had been analyzed in the usual way—that is, with individuals collapsed across groups within treatment categories—no significant interaction effect would have been found. Clearly, the group-level interaction effect would not have been detected in such an analysis.

In Figure 3B a cross-level interaction effect between within-group X and between-group (average) X is graphed—that is, the within-group slopes vary as a function of group-level or average X. Such effects highlight the possibility that "what's good for the goose" may not be good for the "gaggle" or vice versa. Again, had these data been analyzed after collapsing individuals across groups, it is likely that no significant interaction effect would have emerged. Finally, Figure 3C depicts a cross-level, higher-order interaction among within-group X, between-group (average) X and treatment. The within-group slopes vary as a function of both the treatment modality and the group-level (average) patient characteristic.

These hypothetical, multilevel data illustrate two important points. First, experimental designs in which all eligible patients are randomly assigned to social treatments may not provide a sound basis for generalization to subsequent situations in which patients are assigned to the identified "optimal" treatment program. Researchers typically assume only an individual effect when employing an experimental research design. However, the heterogeneous groups created by random assignment may exert different group level effects and contribute to different comparative effects than would the more homogeneous groups created after the adoption of a matching system.

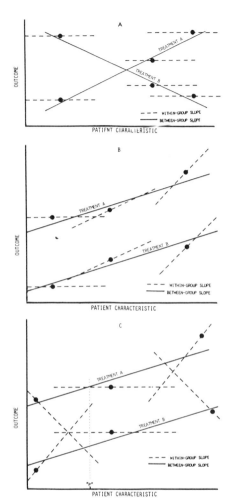

FIGURE 3. Hypothetical data illustrating: A, a group-level interaction between an average patient pretreatment characteristic and two treatment modalities; B, a cross-level interaction between a within-group patient pretreatment characteristic and group-level (average) patient characteristic; and C, a cross-level, higher-order interaction among a within-group patient pretreatment characteristic, between-groups (average) patient characteristic and two treatment modalities.

Second, interaction effects at three levels (or perhaps more when one recognizes multiple subgroups in treatment settings) represent a substantial increment in complexity as compared with an individual model. The hypothetical data in Figure 3C suggest that treatment assignment should take into account treatment modality and both the individual patient's and the treatment group's score on the allocation measure. For example, person P in Figure 3C should be assigned to Treatment A if there were a treatment group available that had a moderate average score on X. If that option were not available (i.e., if the only treatment groups open had low mean scores on X), P would be better off in Treatment B.

It may be tempting to dismiss contextual effects as a trivial concern in regard to treatment effectiveness. However, a recent study of smoking cessation treatment (Etringer et al., 1984) found that experimenter-induced group cohesiveness had a significant, positive impact on short-term outcome across two behavioral treatment modalities. In addition, contextual effects have been found repeatedly in the educational field (e.g., Cronbach and Webb, 1975). Moreover, even in studies of the impact of drugs among rats, "cage" effects have been isolated (Chiapella, 1982). Coupled with the considerable progress that has been made in developing appropriate statistical techniques to probe such effects (Boyd and Iverson, 1979; Tate and Wongbundhit, 1983), these findings suggest that multilevel effects represent an important perspective for future research on the matching problem.

Implications for Efforts to Match Patients and Treatments

Several implications for future efforts to match patients with treatments flow from the issues discussed here.

Incremental progress

One implication of the complexity that pervades differential treatment is that the incremental benefits from matching levels of any one patient variable with different forms of treatment are likely to be small. In short, there are likely to be no dramatic breakthroughs. Even modest increments in treatment success rates (e.g., 5–10%) are meaningful, however, when one considers that each year over one million persons are treated for alcohol misuse in the United States alone (Saxe et al., 1983). Moreover, as knowledge about modestly effective patient–treatment matches accumulates, eventually it should be possible to develop more elaborate approaches (i.e., systems that mirror the complexity of the task) whose effectiveness will be more impressive.

The science and art of differential treatment

A second implication is that effective matching always is likely to be more than a technical exercise in which an initial assessment is followed by consulting a graph (such as the one presented in Figure 1C) to make a single, final decision about treatment assignment (see Cronbach and Snow, 1977). Research can produce more effective principles on which differential treatment can be based with respect to both initial treatment assignment and during-treatment course adjustments. However, there undoubtedly always will be an "intuitive" component in patient-treatment matching. Treatment providers will have to remain responsive to the subtle individual differences among patients at treatment intake and to changes in individual patients during treatment.

Administrative feasibility and cost-effectiveness

Finally, practical issues involved in initiating and administering prescriptive treatment systems should be considered. One administrative issue is the cost-effectiveness of matching patients with treatments. A prescriptive treatment system might be more effective (e.g., 50% of patients showing improvement versus 40% under the old treatment system). However, it also may be less efficient due to the added costs of implementing new assessment procedures, providing alternative forms of treatment and developing and operating a system to allocate clients to different treatments, e.g., a central evaluation unit (for a discussion of cost-benefit analysis as it applies to differential treatment, see Jeffers, 1977). To ensure that the absolute number of patients experiencing improvement increases, additional resources may have to be committed to the treatment system. In short, more effective prescriptive treatments may be more expensive. More generally, the paucity of patient-treatment matching programs to date may be due, in part, to their greater administrative complexity relative to that of simpler allocation systems. Researchers and clinicians will need to develop methods to reduce the administrative burden of matching systems so that they are easier to get off the ground and less susceptible to collapse once they have been implemented.

Promising Avenues for Future Research

As noted earlier, a great deal of "naturalistic" patient-treatment matching already takes place, both between and within treatment programs. At both these levels, the emphasis tends to be on matching patient deficits (in terms of personal characteristics) with specific therapeutic approaches. Matching at the between-program level often results from program administrators' efforts to address the needs of the particular clientele their programs tend to attract (Kern et al., 1978). Within

programs, treatment providers often attempt to individualize the therapy offered to patients with different needs. Patients, at times, also have some latitude in selecting the specific components that will make up their own treatment regimen (although not usually to the extent suggested by the cafeteria approach). With additional research, the effectiveness of matching patients' personal deficits and therapeutic approaches can be increased. In addition, at least two other promising bases for matching patients and treatments are beginning to be explored.

Information processing capabilities and treatment delivery

Goldman (1983) recently observed that "to profit from psychological treatment, an individual must be capable of receiving new information, integrating it with existing informational stores, and then, hopefully, changing some aspect of his or her behavior" (*p. 1045*). Given the growing awareness of the cognitive deficits of alcoholic patients, increasing attention no doubt will be focused on matching patient information processing capabilities with the manner in which treatment is delivered (Guthrie and Elliott, 1980; Wilkinson and Sanchez-Craig, 1981). As noted earlier, a mismatch between patient cognitive capabilities or styles and treatment delivery implies inadequate implementation of whatever therapeutic components are employed. To deliver an effective treatment, a treatment provider may well have to apply sound principles of both therapy and "instructional science."

For example, Sanchez-Craig and Walker (1982) instructed alcoholic halfway house residents in a five-step problem-solving or coping process. During treatment, problem-solving skills were taught to criterion, so there was no variation in treatment implementation across individuals at that point. One month after training, however, only five of the 15 residents (33.3%) were able to repeat at least four of the five steps (only two residents recalled all five steps). Not surprisingly, no differences in outcome were found between the skills-training group and either of two control groups. Sanchez-Craig and Walker concluded that the cognitive deficits experienced by many alcoholics need to be considered in order to implement this conceptually promising treatment approach adequately. Rehabilitation techniques to accelerate cognitive recovery (Hansen, 1980) could be employed in the early stages of the treatment process, and memory aids could be incorporated in teaching problem-solving skills.

Work already is underway to explore the matching of patient information processing capabilities with the manner in which treatment for alcoholism is delivered. O'Leary and Donovan (1979) hypothesized that a longer period of treatment may provide patients who have substantial cognitive impairment with the opportunity for the "overlearning" necessary to compensate for information processing deficits and to "assimilate the benefits of a therapeutic program" (*p. 376*). On the other hand, it was argued that for patients without serious cognitive impairment, a long period of treatment was unnecessary and might even produce deterioration effects. To test this hypothesis, Walker et al. (1983) categorized patients into three levels of neuropsychological functioning and randomly assigned them to a 2-week or a 7-week milieu-oriented inpatient treatment program followed by an aftercare program. Although there was no interaction between neuropsychological functioning and length of stay in a multivariate test across several outcome measures, the authors conclude that the possible interaction between cognitive capabilities and treatment delivery deserves further study. A more differentiated approach to treatment delivery—that is, one that goes beyond a simple difference in treatment duration—might prove more productive.

Matching patients' extra-treatment environments to treatments

One of the current trends in alcoholism treatment is to consider the life contexts in which patients function outside of treatment (Azrin, 1976). As we have pointed out elsewhere (Moos and Finney, 1983; Moos et al., 1980), matching treatment regimens to patients' environmental circumstances as well as their personal characteristics is a potentially fruitful avenue for future research on differential treatment. Along these lines, Longabaugh and Beattie (1985) have outlined a conceptually guided research program to test the effectiveness of matching patients who enjoy social environmental resources with an individually focused treatment program and patients who have social environmental deficits with an environmentally oriented treatment modality. The results of this project should be instructive regarding the utility of the general approach of matching treatments to patients' environmental circumstances. (For a purely empirical exploration of environmental resource × treatment modality interaction effects, see Ward et al., 1982.)

Conclusion

Given the "strength" and "dosage levels" of current treatment modalities, the matching hypothesis seems the best hope for improving treatment services for alcohol-dependent patients, as well as for persons suffering from other types of psychological-behavioral disorders. As we have seen, however, patient–treatment matching may involve multiple patient (personal and environmental) and treatment (therapeutic and delivery) dimensions

interacting in multiple forms or "powers" (linear and nonlinear), in multiple orders, at multiple levels and during multiple stages of the treatment process to influence multiple end results or outcomes. Thus, developing effective differential treatment systems poses a substantial challenge.

There is a danger in pointing out the complexity of any task: that it will immobilize persons who otherwise would undertake it (Weick, 1984). A simplified view of a problem may spur people to action, but such responses tend to be coupled with overly optimistic expectations about their effects. When reality intrudes and those expectations are disconfirmed, efforts are likely to be abandoned. The dilemma may be resolved by trying to achieve a greater understanding of a (complex) phenomenon. Thus, we have considered some of the dimensions or parameters of the matching problem. This perspective has at least two benefits. First, it offers a general framework within which specific foci for individual research projects (e.g., attempting to learn more about the interaction between patient information-processing capabilities and the manner in which treatments are delivered, or exploring multilevel interaction effects) can be located. At the same time, it provides what seem to us to be realistic expectations regarding the likely effectiveness of relatively simple matching schemes. With realistic expectations, one can have a greater appreciation for modest matching effects. These "small wins" (Weick, 1984) are valuable, as noted earlier, because even a small improvement in treatment effectiveness (proportion of patients experiencing improvement) is important when a large patient population is receiving treatment. Realistic expectations also prepare one for the sustained efforts that are needed to achieve more powerful matching systems. As information on the results of simpler matching systems accumulates, it should be possible to develop approaches that systematically consider more of the complexity of the phenomenon and that yield more substantial improvements in patient functioning.

Acknowledgments

Our thanks to Andrew Billings, Charles J. Holahan and Roger Mitchell for their comments on earlier drafts.

References

ABBOTT, M. W. Locus of control and treatment outcome in alcoholics. J. Stud. Alcohol **45:** 46-52, 1984.

ABROMS, G. M. Psychiatric serialism. Compreh. Psychiat. **22:** 372-378, 1981.

ANNIS, H. M. AND CHAN, D. The differential treatment model: Empirical evidence from a personality typology of adult offenders. Crim. Just. & Behav. **10:** 159-173, 1983.

AZRIN, N. H. Improvements in the community-reinforcement approach to alcoholism. Behav. Res. Ther. **14:** 339-348, 1976.

BEUTLER, L. E. Toward specific psychological therapies for specific conditions. J. Cons. Clin. Psychol. **47:** 882-897, 1979.

BOWMAN, K. M. AND JELLINEK, E. M. Alcohol addiction and its treatment. Q. J. Stud. Alcohol **2:** 98-176, 1941.

BOYD, L. H. AND IVERSEN, G. R. Contextual Analysis: Concepts and Statistical Techniques, Belmont, Calif.: Wadsworth Publishing Co., 1979.

BURSTEIN, L. The analysis of multilevel data in educational research and evaluation. In: BERLINER, D. E. (Ed.) Review of Research in Education, Vol. 8, Washington, D.C.: American Educational Research Association, 1980, pp. 158-233.

CHIAPELLA, A. P. Methodology for Studies on Behavior-Related Enzymes: Adrenal Phenylethanolamine N-Methyltransferase as the Model System, Ph.D. dissertation, Stanford University, 1982.

COHEN, J. Partialed products are interactions; partialed powers are curve components. Psychol. Bull. **85:** 858-866, 1978.

COSTELLO, R. M. Alcoholism treatment effectiveness: Slicing the outcome variance pie. In: EDWARDS, G. AND GRANT, M. (Eds.) Alcoholism Treatment in Transition, Baltimore: Univ. Park Press, 1980, pp. 113-127.

CRONBACH, L. J. The two disciplines of scientific psychology. Amer. Psychologist **12:** 671-683, 1957.

CRONBACH, L. J. Beyond the two disciplines of scientific psychology. Amer. Psychologist **30:** 116-127, 1975.

CRONBACH, L. J., DEKEN, J. E. AND WEBB, N. Research on Classrooms and Schools: Formulation of Questions, Design and Analysis, Stanford, Calif.: Stanford University, School of Education, Stanford Evaluation Consortium, 1976.

CRONBACH, L. J. AND SNOW, R. E. Aptitudes and Instructional Methods: A Handbook for Research on Interactions, New York: Irvington Pubs., 1977.

CRONBACH, L. J. AND WEBB, N. Between-class and within-class effects in a reported aptitude × treatment interaction: Reanalysis of a study by G. L. Andersen. J. Educ. Psychol. **67:** 712-724, 1975.

CRONKITE, R. C. AND MOOS, R. H. Evaluating alcoholism treatment programs: An integrated approach. J. Cons. Clin. Psychol. **46:** 1105-1119, 1978.

CRONKITE, R. C. AND MOOS, R. H. Sex and marital status in relation to the treatment and outcome of alcoholic patients. Sex Roles: J. Res. **11:** 93-112, 1984.

EDWARDS, G. Hypnosis in treatment of alcohol addiction: Controlled trial, with analysis of factors affecting outcome. Q. J. Stud. Alcohol **27:** 221-241, 1966.

EMRICK, C. D. A review of psychologically oriented treatment of alcoholism. II. The relative effectiveness of different treatment approaches and the effectiveness of treatment versus no treatment. J. Stud. Alcohol **36:** 88-108, 1975.

EMRICK, C. D. AND HANSEN, J. Assertions regarding effectiveness of treatment for alcoholism: Fact or fantasy? Amer. Psychologist **38:** 1078-1088, 1983.

ETRINGER, B. D., GREGORY, V. R. AND LANDO, H. A. Influence of group cohesion on the behavioral treatment of smoking. J. Cons. Clin. Psychol. **52:** 1080-1086, 1984.

EWING, J. A. Matching therapy and patients: The cafeteria plan. Brit. J. Addict. **72:** 13-18, 1977.

FINNEY, J. W., MOOS, R. H. AND CHAN, D. A. Length of stay and program component effects in the treatment of alcoholism: A comparison of two techniques for process analyses. J. Cons. Clin. Psychol. **49:** 120-131, 1981.

FIREBAUGH, G. Groups as contexts and frog ponds. In: ROBERTS, K. H. AND BURSTEIN, L. (Eds.) Issues in Aggregation: New Directions for Methodology of Social and Behavioral Science, Vol. 6, San Francisco: Jossey-Bass, Inc., Pubs., 1980, pp. 43-52.

FISCHHOFF, B. Debiasing. In: KAHNEMAN, D., SLOVIC, P. AND TVERSKY, A. (Eds.) Judgment under Uncertainty: Heuristics and Biases, Cambridge, England: Cambridge Univ. Press, 1982, pp. 422-444.

FRANCES, A., CLARKIN, J. AND PERRY, S. Differential Therapeutics in Psychiatry: The Art and Science of Treatment Selection, New York: Brunner-Mazel, Inc., 1984.

GIBBS, L. E. The need for a new design for evaluating alcoholism treatment programs. Drug Alcohol Depend. **8:** 287-299, 1981.

GIBBS, L. AND FLANAGAN, J. Prognostic indicators of alcoholism treatment outcome. Int. J. Addict. **12:** 1097-1141, 1977.

GLASER, F. B. Anybody got a match? Treatment research and the matching hypothesis. In: EDWARDS, G. AND GRANT, M. (Eds.) Alcoholism Treatment in Transition, Baltimore: Univ. Park Press, 1980, pp. 178-196.

GLASER, F. B., GREENBERG, S. W. AND BARRETT, M. A Systems Approach to Alcohol Treatment, Toronto: Addiction Research Foundation, 1978.

GOLDMAN, M. S. Cognitive impairment in chronic alcoholics. Amer. Psychologist **38:** 1045-1054, 1983.

GUTHRIE, A. AND ELLIOTT, W. A. The nature and reversibility of cerebral impairment in alcoholism: Treatment implications. J. Stud. Alcohol **41:** 147-155, 1980.

HANSEN, L. Treatment of reduced intellectual functioning in alcoholics. J. Stud. Alcohol **41:** 156-158, 1980.

HARVEY, O. J., HUNT, D. E. AND SCHRODER, H. M. Conceptual Systems and Personality Organization, New York: John Wiley & Sons, Inc., 1961.

JEFFERS, J. R. Cost-benefit analysis as applied to differential treatment models. In: DAVIS, C. S. AND SCHMIDT, M. R. (Eds.) Differential Treatment of Drug and Alcohol Abusers, Palm Springs, Calif.: ETC Publications, 1977, pp. 88-106.

JORESKOG, K. G. A general approach to confirmatory maximum likelihood factor analysis. Psychometrika **34:** 183-202, 1969.

KERN, J. C., SCHMELTER, W. AND FANELLI, M. A comparison of three alcoholism treatment populations: Implications for treatment. J. Stud. Alcohol **39:** 785-792, 1978.

KISSIN, B. AND HANSON, M. The bio-psycho-social perspective in alcoholism. In: SOLOMON, J. (Ed.) Alcoholism and Clinical Psychiatry, New York: Plenum Press, 1982, pp. 1-19.

KISSIN, B., PLATZ, A. AND SU, W. H. Social and psychological factors in the treatment of chronic alcoholism. J. Psychiat. Res. **8:** 13-27, 1970.

KISSIN, B., ROSENBLATT, S. M. AND MACHOVER, S. Prognostic factors in alcoholism. Psychiat. Res. Rep. **24:** 22-43, 1968.

LONGABAUGH, R. AND BEATTIE, M. Optimizing the cost effectiveness of treatment for alcohol abusers. In: MCCRADY, B., NOEL, N. E. AND NIRENBERG, T. D. (Eds.) Future Directions in Alcohol Abuse Treatment Research. NIAAA Research Monograph No. 15, DHHS Publication No. (ADM) 85-1322, Washington: Government Printing Office, 1985, pp. 104-136.

LUBORSKY, L. AND MCLELLAN, A. T. Our surprising inability to predict the outcomes of psychological treatments—with special reference to treatments for drug abuse. Amer. J. Drug Alcohol Abuse **5:** 387-398, 1978.

LYONS, J. P., WELTE, J. W., BROWN, J., SOKOLOW, L. AND HYNES, G. Variation in alcoholism treatment orientation: Differential impact upon specific populations. Alcsm. Clin. Exp. Res. **6:** 333-343, 1982.

MCLACHLAN, J. F. C. Therapy strategies, personality orientation and recovery from alcoholism. Canad. Psychiatry Assoc. J. **19:** 25-30, 1974.

MCLELLAN, A. T., LUBORSKY, L., WOODY, G. E., O'BRIEN, C. P. AND DRULEY, K. A. Predicting response to alcohol and drug abuse treatments. Arch. Gen. Psychiat. **40:** 620-625, 1983a.

MCLELLAN, A. T., WOODY, G. E., LUBORSKY, L., O'BRIEN, C. P. AND DRULEY, K. A. Increased effectiveness of substance abuse treatment: A prospective study of patient-treatment "matching." J. Nerv. Ment. Dis. **171:** 597-605, 1983b.

MEEHL, P. E. Clinical Versus Statistical Prediction, Minneapolis:

Univ. of Minnesota Press, 1954.

Moos, R. H. Evaluating Treatment Environments: A Social Ecological Approach, New York: John Wiley & Sons, Inc., 1974.

Moos, R. H. and Finney, J. W. The expanding scope of alcoholism treatment evaluation. Amer. Psychologist 38: 1036-1044, 1983.

Moos, R. H., Finney, J. W. and Cronkite, R. C. The need for a paradigm shift in evaluations of treatment outcome: Extrapolations from the Rand research. Brit. J. Addict. 75: 347-350, 1980.

O'Leary, M. R. and Donovan, D. M. Male alcoholics: Treatment outcome as a function of length of treatment and level of current adaptive abilities. Eval. Hlth Prof. 2: 373-384, 1979.

Parker, M. W., Winstead, D. K. and Willi, F. J. P. Patient autonomy in alcohol rehabilitation. I. Literature review. Int. J. Addict. 14: 1015-1022, 1979.

Pattison, E. M. The selection of treatment modalities for the alcoholic patient. In: Mendelson, J. H. and Mello, N. K. (Eds.) The Diagnosis and Treatment of Alcoholism, New York: McGraw-Hill Book Co., 1979, pp. 125-227.

Polich, J. M., Armor, D. J. and Braiker, H. B. The Course of Alcoholism: Four Years After Treatment, New York: John Wiley & Sons, Inc., 1981.

Ritson, B. The prognosis of alcohol addicts treated by a specialized unit. Brit. J. Psychiat. 114: 1019-1029, 1968.

Sanchez-Craig, M., Annis, H. M., Bornet, A. R. and MacDonald, K. R. Random assignment to abstinence and controlled drinking: Evaluation of a cognitive-behaviorial program for problem drinkers. J. Cons. Clin. Psychol. 52: 390-403, 1984.

Sanchez-Craig, M and Walker, K. Teaching coping skills to chronic alcoholics in a coeducational halfway house. I. Assessment of programme effects. Brit. J. Addict. 77: 35-50, 1982.

Saxe, L., Dougherty, D., Esty, K. and Fine, M. The Effectiveness and Costs of Alcoholism Treatment. Health Technology Case Study 22, prepared for U.S. Congress Office of Technology Assessment, Washington: Government Printing Office, 1983.

Skinner, H. A. Different strokes for different folks: Differential treatment for alcohol abuse. In: Meyer, R. F., Babor, T. F., Glueck, B. C., Jaffe, J. H., O'Brien, J. E. and Stabenau, J. R. (Eds.) Evaluation of the Alcoholic: Implications for Research, Theory, and Treatment. NIAAA Research Monograph No. 5, DHHS Publication No. (ADM) 81-1033, Washington: Government Printing Office, 1981, pp. 349-367.

Smart, R. G. Do some alcoholics do better in some types of treatment than others? Drug Alcohol Depend. 3: 65-75, 1978.

Southwood, K. E. Substantive theory and statistical interaction: Five models. Amer. J. Sociol. 83: 1154-1203, 1978.

Spoth, R. Differential stress reduction: Preliminary application to an alcohol-abusing population. Int. J. Addict. 18: 835-849, 1983.

Stinson, D. J., Smith, W. G., Amidjaya, I. and Kaplan, J. M. Systems of care and treatment outcomes for alcoholic patients. Arch. Gen. Psychiat. 36: 535-539, 1979.

Tate, R. L. and Wongbundhit, Y. Random versus nonrandom coefficient models for multilevel analysis. J. Educ. Stat. 8: 103-120, 1983.

Walker, R. D., Donovan, D. M., Kivlahan, D. R. and O'Leary, M. R. Length of stay, neuropsychological performance, and aftercare: Influences on alcohol treatment outcome. J. Cons. Clin. Psychol. 51: 900-911, 1983.

Wallerstein, R. S., Chotlos, J. W., Friend, M. B., Hammersley, D. W., Perlswig, E. A. and Winship, G. M. Hospital Treatment of Alcoholism: A Comparative, Experimental Study. Menninger Clinic Monograph Series No. 11, New York: Basic Books, Inc., 1957.

Ward, D. A., Bendel, R. B. and Lange, D. A reconsideration of environmental resources and the posttreatment functioning of alcoholic patients. J. Hlth Social Behav. 23: 310-317, 1982.

Weick, K. E. Small wins: Redefining the scale of social problems. Amer. Psychologist 39: 40-49, 1984.

Wiggins, J. C. Personality and Prediction: Principles of Personality Assessment, Reading, Mass.: Addison-Wesley Publishing Co., Inc., 1973.

Wilkinson, D. A. and Sanchez-Craig, M. Relevance of brain dysfunction to treatment objectives: Should alcohol-related cognitive deficits influence the way we think about treatment? Addict. Behav. 6: 253-260, 1981.

Worden, M. The vagaries of program evaluation: A case study. J. Psychedelic Drugs 12: 157-164, 1980.

Wrightsman, L. S., Oskamp, S., Davis, K. E., Baker, N. J., Smead, A., O'Connor, J., Sigelman, C. K., Young, C. E. and Kaats, G. R. Social Psychology in the Seventies, Monterey, Calif.: Brooks/Cole Publishing Co., 1972.

30

Combining Ethnographic and Experimental Methods in Educational Evaluation

A Case Study

Joseph A. Maxwell, Philip G. Bashook, and Leslie J. Sandlow

T here has been a long-standing disagreement over the relative superiority of "quantitative" and "qualitative" research methods for the study of social phenomena; Pelto and Pelto (1978:ix) refer to this as "the central methodological debate of the 1970s." To a large extent this debate has been a confrontation between two schools of social research, each with its own paradigm for the conduct of valid inquiry. On one side are the "hard science" advocates of precisely defined variables, objective methods of data collection, and statistical analysis of results, with the controlled experiment as the ideal of rigorous research design. On the other are the proponents of "naturalistic," "humanistic," or "holistic" investigations, who emphasize inductive and phenomenological approaches and present ethnographic field investigation as a model for research. Each school has tended to portray its own paradigm as an integrated package, forcing a choice between two alternative and incompatible ways of conducting research (Reichardt and Cook 1979:9).

More recently, however, there has been a reaction against this polarization of the issue. Not only have proponents of one paradigm been more willing to recognize the merits of the other, but there have been numerous suggestions for combining the two approaches (e.g., Pelto and Pelto 1978; Campbell 1978; Reichardt and Cook 1979;

AUTHORS' NOTE: This project was supported by the National Fund for Medical Education and the Schering-Plough Foundation (Project SP/H-77).

From Joseph A. Maxwell, Philip G. Bashook, and Leslie J. Sandlow, "Combining Ethnographic and Experimental Methods in Educational Evaluation: A Case Study," in David M. Fetterman and Mary Anne Pitman, eds., *Educational Evaluation: Ethnography in Theory, Practice, and Politics*, pp. 121-143. Copyright © 1986 by Sage Publications, Inc.

Meyers 1981). Reichardt and Cook (1979:8) claim that seeing the problem as a choice between conflicting paradigms has obscured the real issues in the debate and created unnecessary schisms. They argue that methods are *not* necessarily linked to paradigms, and that nothing prevents the researcher from "mixing and matching" techniques to achieve the combination most appropriate to a particular research problem and setting. Meyers (1981:152-154, 170) repudiates both the conventional distinctions between qualitative and quantitative methods, and the use of the term "paradigm" to refer to these. He proposes that we speak of qualitative and quantitative *data*, instead of methods, and argues that both can easily be used in the same study.

This deemphasis of the connection between methods and paradigms has been attacked in turn by some proponents of qualitative methods. Ianni and Orr (1979), Rist (1980), and Fetterman (1982) charge that the growing interest in qualitative and ethnographic techniques by researchers who lack sufficient grounding in the conceptual framework and training underlying these techniques, has led to shallow, poorly conducted research that fails to utilize the real strengths of qualitative methods. Britan (1978) and Guba and Lincoln (1981) claim that the presuppositions of qualitative and quantitative methods make them appropriate for different goals and situations, while Smith (1983) sees the two approaches as epistemologically incompatible given our present knowledge.

We take a middle position on this debate, combining arguments from both of these perspectives. We agree with Britan and Fetterman that research methods cannot be used productively without taking account of their theoretical and methodological presuppositions, and that these presuppositions impose certain constraints on the overall research design and the combined use of different methods. However, we disagree with the claim that the presuppositions of all "quantitative" and "qualitative" methods are *necessarily* in conflict. Specifically, we argue that the two methods often considered the most "extreme" examples of quantitative and qualitative research, experimental design and ethnographic investigation, can be productively combined within a single research framework.

We are not referring simply to the parallel or sequential use of quantitative and qualitative investigations of a single social setting or program (e.g., Trend 1979; Ianni and Orr 1979; Green and Wallat 1981; Rodin, Rowitz, and Rydman 1983; Patel and Cranton 1983). Such use has gained widespread acceptance (Conner, Altman, and Jackson 1984; Whyte 1984:129-151), and can be seen as one form of "triangulation" (Webb et al. 1966; Denzin 1978; Jick 1983), in which the results of several different lines of investigation are used to mutually support one another. What we are proposing, in contrast, is an integral joining of two methods, ethnography and experimental design, that have usually been seen as polar opposites.

A similar argument for the compatibility of quantitative and qualitative approaches has been presented by Jacob (1982), whose research involved the ethnographic study of Puerto Rican children's development within the basic framework of a quantitative model. Our approach differs from Jacob's in employing an explicitly experimental design, rather than simply a quantitative one, thus combining ethnographic investigation with experimental controls. (Fetterman [in press] also describes a study combining experimental design with ethnographic investigation, but focuses on the use of ethnography to evaluate the experimental findings and the use of experimental findings to provide insights in ethnography, rather than the use of experimental controls *in* ethnography.)

This joining of the two methods can be conceptualized from the point of view of either the experimentalist or the ethnographer. From the experimentalist's perspective, our proposal resembles a standard experimental design, with an intervention, pre- and postintervention collection of data, and a variety of control conditions. However, the data are collected not by the standard quantitative techniques, but through ethnographic investigation. From the ethnographer's point of view, the design is essentially ethnographic but involves the comparison of the ethnographic results, both over time and between different groups, to assess the impact of a particular intervention.

We demonstrate this proposal with a study of the educational value of physicians' participation in what are called medical care evaluation (MCE) committees. These committees, also known as medical audit or peer review committees, are found in most hospitals; they review patient records against explicit criteria for the treatment of particular disorders in order to identify patterns or instances of inappropriate care and make recommendations for dealing with these problems.

We began our study by conducting an ethnographic investigation of existing MCE committees and systematically comparing the descriptions of these committees to identify the factors that contributed to their educational value. We then designed and implemented an experimental program intended to increase this educational value and continued the ethnographic investigation in order to assess the program's impact on the committees' functioning and on the learning that took place in committee meetings. In addition, we used a number of quantitative techniques to measure the committees' educational value and the effect of the experimental program on the participating physicians. Before presenting this example, however, we will examine the presuppositions of ethnography and experimental design in order to demonstrate that they are not inherently incompatible.

THE PRESUPPOSITIONS OF ETHNOGRAPHIC AND EXPERIMENTAL RESEARCH

The basic presuppositions of ethnographic investigation can be summarized as follows (compare Knapp 1979; Wilson 1977; Smith 1982):

(1) It is based on the relatively intensive and long-term involvement of the investigator in the setting being studied.
(2) It requires a holistic, contextual approach to the setting and to the problems chosen for investigation rather than analytically separating out some aspect of the setting for study without considering its connection to the rest of the sociocultural context.
(3) It describes and analyzes the setting from the participants' point of view rather than from that of an outside observer. It therefore requires an initially exploratory and open-ended approach. Ethnography can go beyond the participants' perspective, but it must begin with and be grounded in this perspective.

This view of ethnography does not prohibit its use for causal explanation. Some practitioners of qualitative research (e.g., Lofland 1971; Geertz 1973) deliberately reject the search for causes, arguing that this is inappropriate for qualitative or ethnographic methods. Instead, they see their goal as the description or interpretation of social phenomena. However, Cook and Campbell (1979:93-94) claim that

careful linguistic analysis of their reports shows that they are rarely successful. Their understandings, insights, meanings, analysis of intentions and the like are strongly colored by causal conclusions even when the terms "effects," "gains," "benefits" and "results" are carefully avoided.

Kidder (1981) likewise states that causal assertions are often incorporated in the conclusions of qualitative studies. She suggests that many qualitative researchers are reluctant to say "this caused that" because their work does not satisfy the assumptions of statistical hypothesis testing in quantitative research, and that they therefore retreat to the "safe" position of claiming that their work is only descriptive. She argues, however, that careful qualitative research contains implicit checks on threats to causal validity and thus allows the researcher legitimately to draw causal conclusions.

This is a position that has recently received considerable support (Light and Pillemer 1982; Runciman 1983; Goetz and LeCompte 1984:220-228; Huberman and Miles 1985). In our opinion, the rejection of causation is neither necessary nor desirable; ethnographic investigation *can* be used to understand causal relationships (Maxwell 1984). In fact, one of the strengths of qualitative methods is that they can directly investigate causal processes that are unavailable to correlational studies or to "black box" experimental designs (Bennis 1968; Britan 1979; Fetterman 1982).

The presuppositions of the experimental method are less easy to define. Both Kaplan (1964:144-170) and Cook and Campbell (1979:2-8) focus on the concept of *control* as the crucial feature of the experiment. Cook and Campbell (1979:7-8) define several different senses of "control," and state that "whatever its manifestation, the major function of control is the same: to rule out threats to valid inference" (1979:8).

In nineteenth-century physical science this was accomplished by actual physical shielding and control of conditions, allowing the manipulation of a single variable and observation of its effects. Subsequently, educational and biological researchers developed methods for the systematic assignment of subjects to treatments and the explicit comparison of these groups of subjects in order to determine the effect of different treatments; this is the origin of the "control group" design (Boring 1954; Campbell 1984). According to Cook and Campbell, "All experiments involve at least a treatment, an outcome measure, units of assignment, and some comparison from which change can be inferred and hopefully attributed to the treatment" (1979:5).

Some writers restrict the term "experiment" to a research design in which units are randomly assigned to "treatment" or "control" groups, and the influences on the groups are identical except for the presence or absence of the "treatment." Others, such as Cook and Campbell (1979:5-6), use the term "experiment" more broadly to refer to a variety of designs that involve the systematic comparison of particular groups or settings with others that are similar in important respects, or with the same group or setting at different times, in order to determine the effect or influence of some event or intervention. Cook and Campbell distinguish several types of experiments, including randomized experiments and a variety of quasi-experiments such as nonequivalent group designs and interrupted time-series designs. We therefore take the basic presupposition of experimental research to be the use of controlled comparison to decide between alternative causal interpretations, rather than the use of randomized assignment.

However, our purpose in this chapter is not to defend a particular definition of the term "experiment." Instead, it is to demonstrate that particular types of controlled comparisons can be combined with ethnographic methods to provide a greater understanding of program settings and processes. We do not see our use of such controls as a radical departure from traditional anthropological methods. The concept of "controlled comparison" has a long and respected history in anthropology (Eggan 1954), and our use of specific comparisons incorporated in the research design is a logical extension of Eggan's use of historical and geographic controls in comparing societies.

We therefore see no inherent incompatibility in the presuppositions of experimental and ethnographic research methods. Ethnographic investigation, employing inductive, holistic and emic categories of analysis, can be conducted within a research framework that involves the systematic comparison of different groups in order to determine the effect of some intervention.

COMBINING EXPERIMENTAL CONTROLS AND ETHNOGRAPHY

The theoretical possibility of combining ethnographic investigation with experimental controls has been suggested by Reichardt and Cook, who propose "using randomized experiments with participant observers as the measuring instruments" (1979:22). Similarly, Campbell (1978:199) has argued that anthropologists studying an experimental program in a school system would be better able to draw causal conclusions if they spent half their time studying another school system without the program or studying the school system prior to the program implementation, adding that "this has apparently not been considered."

More recently, Firestone and Herriot (1984) and Miles and Huberman (1984) have provided extensive discussions of multisite qualitative research, but are concerned almost entirely with using this approach to achieve greater generalizability of results, rather than to increase internal causal validity. On the other hand, Kidder (1981) has claimed that qualitative researchers often *do* utilize quasi-experimental controls to increase internal validity, but do so implicitly, without employing the language of experimentation.

We are aware of only one other study that explicitly used ethnographic methods in combination with experimental controls. This was an evaluation of a computerized medical information system in a hospital ward (Lundsgaarde, Fischer, and Steele 1981). The evaluation employed two comparable medical wards, which were initially studied while both were using a manual medical record system; one of the wards then converted to a computerized record system, while the "control" ward retained the manual system. The researchers employed both ethnographic and quantitative methods to determine what effect the computerized system had on the clinical activities of the ward.

The ethnographic component of the evaluation involved participant observation and informal interviewing, behavioral observations, structured interviews and a questionnaire, and document analysis. Fieldwork was conducted on both wards for eight months. The overall goals of the ethnographic research were to describe the local context within which the computerized system was implemented, to provide a more meaningful interpretation of the quantitative outcome measures, and to document the events surrounding the implementation of the computerized system and the experiences of the health care providers using the system (Lundsgaarde, Fischer, and Steele 1981:1-16).

A CASE STUDY: MEDICAL CARE EVALUATION

Our study likewise involved the use of ethnographic methods within an overall experimental design. The study was concerned with the educational effect on physicians of participation in the MCE committees at Michael Reese Hospital and Medical Center in Chicago. There have been numerous anecdotal accounts of the educational value of serving on MCE committees. However, when we began our investigation, no one had attempted systematically to identify or document this educational effect or to influence the operation of the committees so as to make them more educational. Through a two-year study of these committees at Michael Reese Hospital (Sandlow et al. 1981; Bashook et al. 1982; Maxwell et al. 1984), we sought to determine the committees' influence on physicians' knowledge and performance, to identify the committee characteristics that contributed to this influence, and to design and evaluate a program for improving the educational value of the committees.

The MCE committees at Michael Reese were of two types: (1) criteria development committees, which formulated criteria for the diagnosis and treatment of particular disorders, and (2) audit committees, which reviewed the hospital's overall performance against these criteria, examined individual patient records, and made recommendations for improving the quality of care. Both types of committees were composed mainly of physicians from a single clinical department and were chaired by a physician member. (At the time of the study, a small number of the committees involved physicians from several departments, working on a topic of joint relevance; a few committees also included nurses or other health professionals.) Membership of the committees that we studied ranged from four to eight physicians, with the exception of two committees that had fewer physician members and a majority of nurses.

During the period of the study (1978 to 1980), the committee meetings also involved two members of the hospital MCE staff: a facilitator, usually a physician, who led the meetings and provided information on the MCE procedures, and a program coordinator, who prepared summaries of each meeting, wrote the instructions for the personnel who abstracted the medical records for comparison with the criteria, and handled the administrative tasks of the committee. The committees met either biweekly or monthly; meetings generally lasted for one hour.

The criteria development committees that we studied usually began by developing a list of possible topics for further study. These topics were usually specific diagnoses, but were sometimes particular medical or surgical procedures. The selection of topics was based on the morbidity and mortality associated with the diagnosis or procedure, the possibility for reducing these, and the overall impact on the health care system at Michael Reese Hospital. The topics were then ranked according to their potential for improvement in patient care practices.

Having selected a topic, the committee developed a set of criteria for the care of patients with that diagnosis or undergoing that procedure. These criteria addressed both the processes and outcomes of care. The criteria were defined in explicit terms to allow a non-physician abstractor to determine from the patient's record whether each criterion had been met or not. Once developed, the criteria were tested by means of a trial audit of 25 patient records and revised if necessary.

When the criteria had received final approval, a full audit of patient records was performed (usually the 100 most-recent cases with that diagnosis or procedure), and the results presented to the audit committee. The data were summarized in a tabular form that allowed the committee both to review overall compliance with each criterion and to select particular problematic cases for in-depth review. The latter cases were reviewed by individual physicians, and a summary of each case was normally presented to the whole committee. The committee then discussed the management of the case and decided whether any action was warranted. It also made recommendations for the overall improvement of care, and, if necessary, for changes in the criteria.

The study involved three researchers: an anthropologist (Maxwell); an educator who had been involved in establishing the MCE program at Michael Reese (Bashook); and a physician who had developed the program, was currently responsible for its operation, and chaired one of the committees (Sandlow). The fact that two of the researchers were insiders, known to many of the committee members, greatly facilitated the study. The original research design was developed by two of the investigators (Bashook and Sandlow) with backgrounds in biology and education, and psychology and medicine, respectively, and was explicitly intended as an experiment—or, to use Cook and Campbell's term, a quasi-experiment. It was only with the involvement of the third investigator that ethnographic methods were incorporated into the research design.

The initial stage of the research was primarily ethnographic. One of the authors (Maxwell) acted as a participant observer in 13 committees over a seven-month period; although his role was largely passive, he assisted the MCE staff with some tasks during the meetings. He also audiotaped the meetings, and took written notes on what occurred. The observer was treated for the most part simply as a member of the MCE staff by the committee members. A total of 52 committee meetings were observed during this stage of the research. The goal of this stage was to identify the naturally occurring learning that took place in committee meetings and to determine the factors affecting this learning.

Following each meeting, the audiotape was reviewed by the observer, and an edited transcript prepared, based on the tape and the observation notes. This transcript was indexed for information pertaining to the leader's style and goals, the character of committee interaction, and evidence of learning. A coding system was then developed to identify and categorize "learning opportunities" occurring during committee meetings. These learning opportunities were occasions on which information was presented, or discussion took place, that appeared to be of potentially educational value to participants. The initial categories for coding learning opportunities were primarily "etic" in nature; they distinguished learning opportunities by who initiated them, how this occurred, the type of content presented, their duration, and whether they consisted of a presentation by one person or a discussion.

However, the categories were grounded in the extensive experience of two of the researchers with the MCE committees at Michael Reese and in the interviews with physician committee members described below. In addition, the identification of the learning opportunities was largely based on the observed reactions of the committee members. In many instances, physicians would comment, "This was a very interesting case," or "I don't understand why this was done," or indicate their interest by paying close attention; for other cases, they would comment, "There's nothing to learn from this one," or engage in side conversations during a presentation. The identification of learning opportunities was also validated by having all three investigators listen to selected tapes and independently identify learning opportunities. All of the coding of learning opportunities was done by the observer.

The observer interviewed eight physician members of the committees. These interviews were open-ended, exploring the educational value of MCE committees, their structure and operation, and the physician's attitudes toward MCE. The interviews averaged 30 minutes in length and were audiotaped, transcribed, and analyzed. In addition, information on committee operation and the educational value of the committees was obtained informally from committee members and from the MCE staff, providing a better understanding of the data obtained from observation and interviews.

All but one of the 13 committees could be unambiguously classified as having high or low educational value based on the number and significance of the learning opportunities. Five committees (three criteria development and two audit) were of high educational value, while seven (three criteria development and four audit) were of low educational value. (The thirteenth committee was intermediate in educational value and was not observed often enough to permit a definite classification.) These two groups of committees could be most clearly defined on the basis of two characteristics: the number of potentially educational *discussions* per meeting that focused on the medical problem under consideration and its appropriate management and the total amount of time per meeting spent in learning opportunities related to this problem (Table 6.1). In addition, qualitative differences in the educational value of the two groups of committees were substantial.

The observations, interviews, and data from the MCE staff were then used to develop an ethnographic description, or portrayal, of each committee. These portrayals were analyzed and compared to discover the differences between the committees with high and low educational value, and to determine how these differences affected the educational value of the committees. We found the following contrasts:

(1) Criteria development committees with high educational value dealt primarily with the optimal (rather than the minimally acceptable) management of the medical problem under consideration. This led to an exploration of alternative approaches to the problem and the presentation and justification of committee members' views on these. In contrast, criteria development committees with low educational value tended to focus on the minimal, generally held standards of acceptable care; as a result, most points raised in meetings were ones on which the members already agreed.

(2) In audit committees with high educational value, members reviewed records prior to the meeting and presented them at the meeting as case problems which were then discussed by the committee. In audit committees with low educational value, on the other hand, records were reviewed (often at the meeting itself) primarily to determine whether the criteria were met or not. Cases were rarely discussed by the committee unless there was a question as to whether the patient's treatment was justified.

(3) The attitude and goals of the committee chairperson had an important influence on the educational value of committee meetings. A majority of the committees with high educational value were led by physicians who saw the committees as having an important educational function, as evidenced by their statements and actions. In contrast, none of the leaders of committees with low educational value felt that education was an important function of the committees.

(4) There appeared to be a "critical mass" of physicians required to regularly sustain an educationally valuable interaction. Committee meetings with fewer than four physicians present had significantly ($p < .01$) fewer learning opportunities than those with four or more

TABLE 6.1

Comparison of Medical Care Evaluation Committees Having
High and Low Educational Value, Michael Reese Hospital

Committees	Number of Committees	Number of Discussions of Problems per Meeting		Minutes Spent in Learning Opportunities per Meeting	
		Mean	Range of Committee Means	Mean	Range of Committee Means
High value	5	3.2	2.0 to 5.0	10.1	4.3 to 18.2
Low value	7	0.3	0.0 to 0.7	0.9	0.0 to 1.8

SOURCE: Sandlow et al. (1981).

physicians. However, high attendance was not in itself sufficient to generate educational interaction.

The identification of these four characteristics as important influences on the educational potential of the committees was not based simply on their correlation with the frequency and significance of learning opportunities. Using the participant-observational data, we were able to demonstrate *how* each characteristic acted to increase this educational potential. This illustrates the point made earlier: that qualitative data can provide direct evidence regarding causal processes that is not available to traditional experimental or correlational designs.

Our original plan for improving the educational value of the committees had been to develop a formal educational structure, with predefined learning objectives and distinct educational activities. However, the ethnographic research revealed two important points about the committees. First, it became clear that the educational strength of the committees lay primarily in the informal, unplanned interaction that occurred during meetings. The most informative exchanges that occurred during committee meetings were often peripheral to the stated topic and would have been largely unpredictable to someone attempting to design the committee's educational "curriculum." It also became clear that most physicians considered the educational value of the committees to be secondary to their functions of criteria development and record review, and would resent any substantial interference with the latter tasks.

We therefore designed a model MCE program that was intended to increase the *informal* discussion among physicians that occurred as part of the criteria development and audit process. This model program has been described in detail elsewhere (Bashook et al. 1982); it was structured to ensure that committee discussion considered the optimal management of particular disorders or the optimal care of individual patients, that committee members prepared draft criteria or reviewed records prior to the meeting, that the committee leaders emphasized educational aspects of the committee's activities, and that a sufficient number of physicians was present to generate an educationally optimal amount of discussion. At the same time, the model program was designed to meet the hospital's needs for effective record review.

We gained permission from three clinical departments in the hospital to institute this program in their MCE committees. Five committees in these departments were already in operation; we established a sixth committee, so that each department had one criteria development and one audit committee. Members of existing committees were reoriented to the model program, and new members were selected by the department head. One of the investigators served as MCE facilitator for each of the committees.

The model program was studied in each of these six committees for a period of 12 to 15 months. We continued the participant observation methods of the previous phase of the research, with one of the investigators attending and audiotaping meetings, preparing an edited transcript, and indexing the transcript for learning opportunities and committee operation. These transcripts were circulated and discussed by all three investigators.

In addition, we attempted to measure the committees' effect on participants' knowledge and performance. To do this, we used multiple-choice knowledge tests and a review of the records of patients treated by physicians participating in the study. We also developed a form of stimulated-recall interview, which we call the "clinical case recall interview," to investigate how physicians participating on the committees changed their management of a particular disorder following committee discussion of the disorder. This involved questioning a physician in detail about how specific patients with particular diagnoses were managed following the committee's discussion of these diagnoses, and whether committee participation had resulted in any changes in the physician's management strategy. Twelve physicians were interviewed in this manner. Finally, we sent questionnaires dealing with their perception of and attitudes toward the committees to all of the participating physicians, and conducted follow-up interviews with a sample of these physicians.

We used several types of quasi-experimental controls in this phase of research. First, we compared the same committees before and after the model program was introduced. Second, we established control groups of physicians who did not serve on the committees, but who participated in the knowledge testing and record review. The members of the control group in each department were approximately equivalent to the experimental subjects in subspecialty training and in type and length of practice. Third, for the knowledge tests and record review, we utilized several "control" topics that were not discussed by the committees, in addition to the topics that the committees dealt with. Fourth, we found that the model program was successfully established in only three of the six committees, as determined by adherence to the four characteristics stated above. This allowed us to compare the "successful" and "unsuccessful" committees and thus to separate the effects of the model program (which was fully realized in only three committees) from the influence of the investigative methods (which were employed in all six committees). The categorization of the committees as "successful" or "unsuccessful" was made before the results of the knowledge tests and performance audit were obtained.

The six experimental committees had a relatively high number of learning opportunities in comparison with the preintervention committees, and there was a statistically significant increase in the number of learning opportunities in three of the four committees for which pre-intervention data exist (Table 6.2). Far more significant than these quantitative differences between committees, however, was the qualitative difference in the educational interchange. In the three "successful" committees (Criteria Development committees A and B and Audit Committee A), there was often a high-level discussion of the issues surrounding a problem or patient. These learning opportunities often were extended discussions, with citation of literature. In Audit Committee B and Criteria Development Committee C, on the other hand, learning opportunities tended to be shorter and lower-level, and in the Audit Committee C they were normally quite brief and of minimal educational significance. The questionnaire showed that all but one member of the "successful" committees saw their participation as "very" or "moderately" educational, while less than half of the members of the "unsuccessful" committees considered their participation to be "very" or "moderately" educational.

TABLE 6.2

Learning Opportunities Occurring During Committee Meetings

	Preintervention		Postintervention		
	Committees with High Educational Value	Committees with Low Educational Value	Dept A***	Dept B***	Dept C
Criteria Development Committees					
Learning opportunities per meeting	5.9	2.2	11.3**	5.8	3.6**
Standard deviation	3.0	2.5	6.4	5.1	2.6
Number of meetings	13	12	9	17	9
Audit Committees					
Learning opportunities per meeting	5.1	1.2	6.9*	5.9*	3.6*
Standard deviation	2.0	1.2	2.1	3.4	2.4
Number of meetings	14	10	15	7	9

SOURCE: Bashook et al. (1982).
*Difference from preintervention value is statistically significant at p < .05.
**No preintervention data.
***"Successful" committees.

The physicians we interviewed were divided on what they saw as the major educational impact of the committees. Some members felt that these committees were useful mainly for review and updating. These members tended to emphasize the value of presentations by experts. Other members cited the value of committee meetings in forcing them to reexamine basic definitions and management principles. These physicians usually felt that the most educational aspect of the meetings was the discussion among members; many of them mentioned the importance of learning how others do things, and of being exposed to different points of view. On the whole, the second group of physicians had a higher opinion of the committees' educational value than the first group; they also tended to be older, and were somewhat more likely to be in private practice.

There was a striking difference between physicians in Departments A and B in terms of what they saw as the main educational impact of the committees. Members of the committees in Department A emphasized the educational value of the committee meetings themselves, while members of the committees in Department B tended to see the major influence as being the development and distribution of criteria sets and audit reports, and the sanctions against physicians whose practice did not meet departmental standards. Members of the committees in Department C were intermediate between Departments A and B in this respect.

The results of the quantitative measures of the impact of committee participation (the knowledge tests and the medical record review) were positive but inconclusive. The committees showed an overall gain in knowledge test scores on the experimental topics. For the committees in Department A, which conformed most closely to the model program, this gain was statistically significant (p < .05); for the committees in departments B and C, the gain was not statistically significant. The gains by members of the three successful committees were statistically significant by comparison with the gains of their matched controls on the experimental topics, and by comparison with the members' gain on the control topics (p < .01). However, the magnitude of the gains was small.

The medical record audit did not reveal any statistically significant changes in the physicians' performance, due primarily to two problems that were not foreseen when the audit was planned. First, following the committee's discussion of the experimental topics, there were usually too few records for each physician to allow meaningful statistical comparison. Second, the audit procedures turned out to be insensitive to the actual changes in performance that occurred, as these changes were revealed by the clinical case recall interviews.

Despite the failure of the record audit to demonstrate changes in behavior, the clinical case recall interviews identified four instances (all from committees in Department A) in which members had made substantial changes in the way they treated patients with particular disorders, and which they unequivocally attributed to the committees' discussion of these disorders. The committees' role in these changes was verified by comparing the physicians' accounts with the meeting transcripts, to confirm that the meetings were a plausible impetus for the reported changes.

These changes were not incremental improvements in performance, the type of change that the medical record review was designed to detect, but were instead shifts in overall management strategy for these disorders. One gastroenterologist said that he had been made more aware of the fact that there's no single recipe for treating patients with gastrointestinal bleeding. Prior to the Criteria Development Committee's discussion of this topic, he had tended to use endoscopy as a routine initial procedure. Now he tends to individualize his management; he described a middle-aged male patient with gastrointestinal bleeding whom he had put at bedrest for several days and then began plans for workup. Previously, he would have used immediate endoscopy without considering the particular factors indicating a different approach for this patient.

Another member of the Criteria Development Committee, a general internist, also changed his management of patients with gastrointestinal bleeding. Prior to the committee's discussion of this topic, he had employed X-rays as his main diagnostic procedure. He now uses endoscopy as his procedure of choice, and when there is no immediate danger, waits 24 to 36 hours after the acute episode before having a gastroenterologist see the patient. Formerly, he would have admitted the patient immediately and sent them for X-rays the next morning; most of the time he would not have used endoscopy even if the source of bleeding was not located. There was no question in his mind that his method of management had changed as a result of his participation in the committee's discussion of the topic.

Two members of the Audit Committee in Department A cited significant changes in their management of diabetics as a result of the committee's discussion of this topic. One, an older physician who maintains a part-time practice, now places much more emphasis on outpatient management of patients with elevated blood sugar; he recently had a patient with a blood sugar of 550 mg/dl whom he successfully treated as an outpatient. He had tended to use outpatient management for less extreme cases before the committee's audit of this topic, but said that he would never have had the nerve to attempt it in this case, or even been sure it was the best approach, without the influence of the committee discussion. He was quite enthusiastic about the success of this approach, and was positive that participation on the committee had provided the impetus for him to change his practice.

Another Audit Committee member, a general internist who had completed his residency a few years earlier, reported a similar shift in his approach to the management of diabetics. He gave as an example an older woman, a newly diagnosed diabetic, whom he had managed as an outpatient despite pressure from her children to have her admitted to the hospital. The management was quite successful; the patient was asymptomatic the whole time and was "thrilled" that she did not have to leave work and go to the hospital. He had no doubt that before the committee's discussion of diabetes, he would have admitted the patient, because he would have lacked the confidence to stand up to the pressure. Now, he feels he has completely changed his practice in this area.

The interviews also showed that the changes were not the result of a simple "updating" of knowledge, as much continuing medical education has assumed, but resulted from a major rethinking of the physician's previous practice. In fact, two physicians emphasized that the committee discussions had *not* provided new medical knowledge but instead had given them the confidence to *apply* knowledge that they already had. This aspect of the committees' educational value was confirmed by the follow-up interviews with other physicians and was an outcome of committee participation that had not been anticipated in designing the quantitative measures of knowledge and performance change.

IMPLICATIONS FOR ETHNOGRAPHIC EVALUATION

The ethnographic component of the study thus turned out to be more productive than the quantitative procedures in terms of understanding the educational processes that occur in MCE committees. There were two main advantages to the ethnographic approach: It allowed us to discover aspects of the committees' educational functioning that we had not anticipated and would have missed had we relied entirely on quantitative methods, and it provided insight into the processes by which the committees influenced physicians' knowledge and performance.

However, the value of the ethnographic research was substantially increased by the experimental controls incorporated in the research design. For the ethnographic portion of the research, these controls were the comparison of the high-value and low-value committees, the comparison of the same committees before and after the model program was introduced, and the comparison of the "successful" and "unsuccessful" committees.

The experimental controls, in combination with the quantitative results, helped us to rule out certain alternative explanations for the results we obtained; these alternative explanations included the possibility that the changes that took place for members of the "successful" committees were due to learning from sources other than committee meetings, or to a "Hawthorne effect" of the research on the committees. The fact that the knowledge gains did not occur in the matched control groups, or for the control topics included in the knowledge tests, and that the major changes took place in the "successful" committees, strengthened our conclusion that the features of the model MCE program had a causal role in the changes in knowledge and performance that we identified.

Our joint use of ethnographic, quantitative, and experimental methods differs from most reported combinations of quantitative/experimental and qualitative/ethnographic methods in which the two types of investigation are conducted separately and their *results* are combined. What we have done is to use ethnographic methods *within* an experimental framework incorporating particular types of controls. These controls were employed with both the quantitative and ethnographic methods, allowing us to address certain validity threats that would have been much more serious in the absence of these controls.

The importance of controls against bias in qualitative research has recently been emphasized by Huberman and Miles (1985), who argue that "clinical judgments ... are consistently less accurate than statistical/actuarial ones," and that "any 'clinical' researcher operating in a natural setting had best be well-armed with the safeguards against bias described in the social judgment literature." We believe that the sorts of experimental controls that we describe can reduce these biases without sacrificing the richness of data and access to participants' meanings provided by ethnographic methods. Experimental controls can also permit the researchers to evaluate competing explanations that may all have some plausibility on ethnographic grounds.

On the other hand, exclusively experimental designs usually treat the setting being studied as a "black box," providing no information about the actual causal processes operating in the setting. Ethnographic investigation can identify these causal processes, increasing the interpretability of experimental outcomes and contributing to the development of a causal model.

Our advocacy of the use of ethnographic investigation in conjunction with an experimental framework is grounded in the concept of causal validity, which is in turn based on the examination of plausible alternative causes ("validity threats") that must be ruled out in order to validate the proposed causal relationship (Cook and Campbell 1979:38; Kidder 1981). This procedure has been labeled "strong inference'' by Platt (1964), and has been further elaborated by Scriven (1976) in what he refers to as the "modus operandi" method. In our view, it is this critical examination of alternative hypotheses, and not the use of specific research techniques, that is the essence of scientific research and evaluation.

We have tried to demonstrate, through a description of our study of the educational value of a model medical care evaluation program, that it is both possible and productive to combine ethnographic methods with experimental controls in evaluation research. We have also analyzed the presuppositions of the two approaches, attempting to show that they are not methodologically or philosophically incompatible. If our example and arguments are valid, the joint use of these two methods should produce research and evaluations that have significantly greater validity than those employing either method alone.

REFERENCES CITED

Bashook, P. G., L. J. Sandlow, and J. A. Maxwell
    1982 Increasing the Educational Value of Medical Care Evaluation: A Model Program. Journal of Medical Education 57:701-707.
Bennis, W. G.
    1968 The Case Study. Journal of Applied Behavioral Science 4:227-231.
Boring, E. G.
    1954 The Nature and History of Experimental Control. American Journal of Psychology 57:701-707.
Britan, G. M.
    1978 Experimental and Contextual Models of Program Evaluation. Evaluation and Program Planning 1:229-234.
Campbell, D. T.
    1978 Qualitative Knowing in Action Research. In The Social Contexts of Method. M. Brenner, P. Marsh, and M. Brenner, eds. New York: St. Martin's.
    1979 Degrees of Freedom and the Case Study. In Qualitative and Quantitative Methods in Evaluation. T. D. Cook and C. S. Reichardt, eds. pp. 49-67. Beverly Hills, CA: Sage.
    1984 Can We Be Scientific in Applied Social Science? In Evaluation Studies Review Annual, Vol. 9. R. F. Connor, D. G. Altman, and C. Jackson, eds. pp. 26-48. Beverly Hills, CA: Sage.
Connor, R. F., D. G. Altman, and C. Jackson
    1984 1984: A Brave New World for Evaluation? In Evaluation Studies Review Annual, Vol. 9. R. F. Connor, D. G. Altman, and C. Jackson, eds. Beverly Hills, CA: Sage.
Cook, T. D., and D. T. Campbell
    1979 Quasi-Experimentation: Design and Analysis Issues for Field Settings. Boston: Houghton Mifflin.

Cook, T. D., and C. S. Reichardt, eds.
1979 Qualitative and Quantitative Methods in Evaluation Research. Beverly Hills, CA: Sage.

Denzin, N. K.
1978 The Research Act. 2nd ed. Chicago: Aldine.

Eggan, F.
1954 Social Anthropology and the Method of Controlled Comparison. American Anthropologist 56:743-763.

Fetterman, D. M.
1982 Ethnography in Educational Research: The Dynamics of Diffusion. Educational Researcher (March): 17-29. Reprinted in Ethnography in Educational Evaluation. D. Fetterman, ed. Beverly Hills, CA: Sage.
in press Ethnographic Educational Evaluation. *In* Toward an Interpretive Ethnography of Education at Home and Abroad, G. D. Spundler, ed. Beverly Hills, CA: ·Sage.

Firestone, W. A., and R. E. Herriott
1984 Multisite Qualitative Policy Research: Some Design and Implementation Issues. *In* Ethnography in Educational Evaluation. D. M. Fetterman, ed. Beverly Hills, CA: Sage.

Geertz, C.
1973 The Interpretation of Cultures. New York: Basic Books.

Goetz, J. P. and M. D. Le Compte
1984 Ethnography and Qualitative Design in Educational Research. New York: Academic Press.

Green, J. L., and C. Wallat
1981 Ethnography and Language in Educational Settings. Norwood, NJ: Ablex.

Guba, E. G., and Y. S. Lincoln
1981 Effective Evaluation. San Francisco: Jossey-Bass.

Huberman, A. M., and M. B. Miles
1985 Assessing Local Causality in Qualitative Research. *In* Exploring Clinical Methods for Social Research. D. N. Berg and K. K. Smith, eds. Beverly Hills, CA: Sage.

Ianni, F.A.J., and M. T. Orr
1979 Toward a Rapprochement of Quantitative and Qualitative Methodologies. *In* Qualitative and Quantitative Methods in Evaluation. T. D. Cook and C. S. Reichardt, eds. pp. 87-98. Beverly Hills, CA: Sage.

Jacob, E.
1982 Combining Ethnographic and Quantitative Approaches: Suggestions and Examples From a Study on Puerto Rico. *In* Children In and Out of School: Ethnography and Education. P. Gilmore and A. A. Glatthorn, eds. Washington, DC: Center for Applied Linguistics.

Jick, T. D.
1983 Mixing Qualitative and Quantitative Methods: Triangulation in Action. *In* Qualitative Methodology. J. Van Maanen, ed. Beverly Hills, CA: Sage.

Kaplan, A.
1964 The Conduct of Inquiry: Methodology for Behavioral Science. San Francisco: Chandler.

Kidder, L. H.
1981 Qualitative Research and Quasi-Experimental Frameworks. *In* Scientific

Inquiry and the Social Sciences: M. B. Brewer and B. E. Collins, eds. San Francisco: Jossey-Bass.

Knapp, M. S.
1979 Ethnographic Contributions to Evaluation Research: The Experimental Schools Program Evaluation and Some Alternatives. *In* Qualitative and Quantitative Methods in Evaluation. T. D. Cook and C. S. Reichardt, eds. pp. 118-139. Beverly Hills, CA: Sage.

Light, R. J., and D. B. Pillemer
1982 Numbers and Narrative: Combining Their Strengths in Research Reviews. Harvard Educational Review 52:1-26.

Lofland, J.
1971 Analyzing Social Settings: A Guide to Qualitative Observation and Analysis. Belmont, CA: Wadsworth.

Lundsgaarde, H. P., P. J. Fischer, and D. J. Steele
1981 Human Problems in Computerized Medicine. Publications in Anthropology 13. Lawrence: University of Kansas, Department of Anthropology.

Maxwell, J. A.
1984 Using Ethnography to Identify Causes. Paper presented at the Annual Meeting of the American Anthropological Association, Denver.

Maxwell, J. A., L. J. Sandlow, and P. G. Bashook
1984 The Effect of a Model Medical Care Evaluation Program on Physician Knowledge and Performance. Journal of Medical Education 59: 33-38.

Meyers, W. R.
1981 The Evaluation Enterprise. San Francisco: Jossey-Bass.

Miles, M. B., and A. M. Huberman
1984 Qualitative Data Analysis: A Sourcebook of New Methods. Beverly Hills, CA: Sage.

Patel, V. L., and P. A. Cranton
1983 Transfer of Student Learning in Medical Education. Journal of Medical Education 58:126-135.

Pelto, P. J., and G. Pelto
1978 Anthropological Research: The Structure of Inquiry. Cambridge: Cambridge University Press.

Platt, J. R.
1964 Strong Inference. Science 146:347-353.

Reichardt, C. S., and T. D. Cook
1979 Beyond Qualitative Versus Quantitative Methods. *In* Qualitative and Quantitative Methods in Evaluation. T. D. Cook and C. S. Reichardt, eds. pp. 7-32. Beverly Hills, CA: Sage.

Rist, R. C.
1980 Blitzkrieg Ethnography: On the Transformation of a Method into a Movement. Educational Researcher (February):8-10.

Rodin, M. B., L. Rowitz, and R. Rydman
1983 Levels of Analysis and Levels of Need: Cultural Factors and the Assessment of Need for Alcoholism Treatment Services in an Urban Community. Human Organization 41:299-306.

Runciman, W. G.
1983 A Treatise on Social Theory. Vol. 1: The Methodology of Social Theory. Cambridge: Cambridge University Press.

Sandlow, L. J., P. G. Bashook, and J. A. Maxwell
   1981 Medical Care Evaluation: An Experience in Continuing Medical Education. Journal of Medical Education 56:581-586.
Scriven, M.
   1976 Maximizing the Power of Causal Investigations: The Modus Operandi Method. *In* Evaluation Studies Review Annual, Vol. 1. G. V. Glass, ed. pp. 101-118. Beverly Hills, CA: Sage.
Smith, J. K.
   1983 Quantitative Versus Qualitative Research: An Attempt to Clarify the Issue. Educational Researcher (March):6-13.
Smith, L. M.
   1982 Ethnography. *In* Encyclopedia of Educational Research. 5th ed. H. Mitzel, ed. pp. 587-592. New York: Macmillan.
Trend, M. G.
   1979 On the Reconciliation of Qualitative and Quantitative Analyses: A Case Study. *In* Qualitative and Quantitative Methods in Evaluation. T. D. Cook and C. S. Reichardt, eds. pp. 68-86. Beverly Hills, CA: Sage.
Webb, E. J. et al.
   1966 Unobtrusive Measures: Nonreactive Research in the Social Sciences. Chicago: Rand McNally.
Whyte, W. F.
   1984 Learning from the Field: A Guide from Experience. Beverly Hills, CA: Sage.
Wilson, W.
   1977 The Use of Ethnographic Techniques in Educational Research. Review of Educational Research 47:245-265.

31

Evaluating the Econometric Evaluations of Training Programs with Experimental Data

Robert J. LaLonde*

This paper compares the effect on trainee earnings of an employment program that was run as a field experiment where participants were randomly assigned to treatment and control groups with the estimates that would have been produced by an econometrician. This comparison shows that many of the econometric procedures do not replicate the experimentally determined results, and it suggests that researchers should be aware of the potential for specification errors in other nonexperimental evaluations.

Econometricians intend their empirical studies to reproduce the results of experiments that use random assignment without incurring their costs. One way, then, to evaluate econometric methods is to compare them against experimentally determined results.

This paper undertakes such a comparison and suggests the means by which econometric analyses of employment and training programs may be evaluated. The paper compares the results from a field experiment, where individuals were randomly assigned to participate in a training program, against the array of estimates that an econometrician without experimental data might have produced. It examines the results likely to be reported by an econometrician using nonexperimental data and the most modern techniques, and following the recent prescriptions of Edward Leamer (1983) and David Hendry (1980), tests the extent to which the results are sensitive to alternative economet-

ric specifications.[1] The goal is to appraise the likely ability of several econometric methods to accurately assess the economic benefits of employment and training programs.[2]

Section I describes the field experiment and presents simple estimates of the program effect using the experimental data. Sections II and III describe how econometricians evaluate employment and training programs, and compares the nonexperimental estimates using these methods to the experimental results presented in Section I. Section II presents one-step econometric estimates of the program's impact, while more complex two-step econometric estimates are presented in Section III. The re-

*Graduate School of Business, University of Chicago, 1101 East 58th Street, Chicago, IL 60637. This paper uses public data files from the National Supported Work Demonstration. These data were provided by the Inter-University Consortium for Political and Social Research. I have benefited from discussions with Mariam Akin, Orley Ashenfelter, James Brown, David Card, Judith Gueron, John Papandreou, Robert Willig, and the participants of workshops at the universities of Chicago, Cornell, Iowa, Princeton, and MIT.

[1] These papers depict a more general crisis of confidence in empirical research. Leamer (1983) argues that any solution to this crisis must divert applied econometricians from "the traditional task of identifying unique inferences implied by a specific model to the task of determining the range of inferences generated by a range of models." Other examples of this literature are Leamer (1985), Leamer and Herman Leonard (1983), and Michael McAleer, Adrian Pagan, and Paul Volker (1985).

[2] Examples of nonexperimental program evaluations are Orley Ashenfelter (1978), Ashenfelter and David Card (1985), Laurie Bassi (1983a,b; 1984), Thomas Cooley, Thomas McGuire, and Edward Prescott (1979), Katherine Dickinson, Terry Johnson, and Richard West (1984), Nicholas Kiefer (1979a,b), and Charles Mallar (1978).

From Robert J. LaLonde, "Evaluating the Econometric Evaluations of Training Programs with Experimental Data," *American Economic Review,* Vol. 76, pp. 604-620. Copyright © 1986 by the American Economic Association. Reprinted by permission.

sults of this study are summarized in the final section.

I. The Experimental Estimates

The National Supported Work Demonstration (NSW) was a temporary employment program designed to help disadvantaged workers lacking basic job skills move into the labor market by giving them work experience and counseling in a sheltered environment. Unlike other federally sponsored employment and training programs, the NSW program assigned qualified applicants to training positions randomly. Those assigned to the treatment group received all the benefits of the NSW program, while those assigned to the control group were left to fend for themselves.[3]

During the mid-1970s, the Manpower Demonstration Research Corporation (MDRC) operated the NSW program in ten sites across the United States. The MDRC admitted into the program AFDC women, ex-drug addicts, ex-criminal offenders, and high school dropouts of both sexes.[4] For those assigned to the treatment group, the program guaranteed a job for 9 to 18 months, depending on the target group and site. The treatment group was divided into crews of three to five participants who worked to-gether and met frequently with an NSW counselor to discuss grievances and performance. The NSW program paid the treatment group members for their work. The wage schedule offered the trainees lower wage rates than they would have received on a regular job, but allowed their earnings to increase for satisfactory performance and attendance. The trainees could stay on their supported work jobs until their terms in the program expired and they were forced to find regular employment.

Although these general guidelines were followed at each site, the agencies that operated the experiment at the local level provided the treatment group members with different work experiences. The type of work even varied within sites. For example, some of the trainees in Hartford worked at a gas station, while others worked at a printing shop.[5] In particular, male and female participants frequently performed different sorts of work. The female participants usually worked in service occupations, whereas the male participants tended to work in construction occupations. Consequently, the program costs varied across the sites and target groups. The program cost $9,100 per AFDC participant and approximately $6,800 for the other target groups' trainees.[6]

The MDRC collected earnings and demographic data from both the treatment and the control group members at the baseline (when MDRC randomly assigned the participants) and every nine months thereafter, conducting up to four post-baseline inter-

---

[3] Findings from the NSW are summarized in several reports and publications. For a quick summary of the program design and results, see Manpower Demonstration Research Corporation (1983). For more detailed discussions see Dickinson and Rebecca Maynard (1981); Peter Kemper, David Long, and Craig Thornton (1981); Stanley Masters and Maynard (1981); Maynard (1980); and Irving Piliavin and Rosemary Gartner (1981).

[4] The experimental sample included 6,616 treatment and control group members from Atlanta, Chicago, Hartford, Jersey City, Newark, New York, Oakland, Philadelphia, San Francisco, and Wisconsin. Qualified AFDC applicants were women who (i) had to be currently unemployed, (ii) had spent no more than 3 months in a job in the previous 6 months, (iii) had no children less than six years old, and (iv) had received AFDC payments for 30 of the previous 36 months. The admission requirements for the other participants differed slightly from those of the AFDC applicants. For a more detailed discussion of these prerequisities, see MDRC.

[5] Kemper and Long present a list of NSW projects and customers (1981, Table IV.4, pp. 65–66). The trainees produced goods and services for organizations in the public (42 percent of program hours), nonprofit (29 percent of program hours), and private sectors.

[6] The cost per training participant is the sum of program input costs, site overhead costs, central administrative costs, and child care costs minus the value of the program's output. These costs are in 1982 dollars. If the trainees' subsidized wages and fringe benefits are viewed as a transfer instead of a cost, the program costs per participant are $3,100 for the AFDC trainees and $2,700 for the other trainees. For a more detailed discussion of program costs and benefits, see Kemper, Long, and Thornton.

TABLE 1—THE SAMPLE MEANS AND STANDARD DEVIATIONS OF
PRE-TRAINING EARNINGS AND OTHER CHARACTERISTICS FOR
THE NSW AFDC AND MALE PARTICIPANTS

| | Full National Supported Work Sample | | | |
| | AFDC Participants | | Male Participants | |
Variable	Treatments	Controls	Treatments	Controls
Age	33.37	33.63	24.49	23.99
	(7.43)	(7.18)	(6.58)	(6.54)
Years of School	10.30	10.27	10.17	10.17
	(1.92)	(2.00)	(1.75)	(1.76)
Proportion	.70	.69	.79	.80
High School Dropouts	(.46)	(.46)	(.41)	(.40)
Proportion Married	.02	.04	.14	.13
	(.15)	(.20)	(.35)	(.35)
Proportion Black	.84	.82	.76	.75
	(.37)	(.39)	(.43)	(.43)
Proportion Hispanic	.12	.13	.12	.14
	(.32)	(.33)	(.33)	(.35)
Real Earnings	$393	$395	1472	1558
1 year Before	(1,203)	(1,149)	(2656)	(2961)
Training	[43]	[41]	[58]	[63]
Real Earnings	$854	$894	2860	3030
2 years Before	(2,087)	(2,240)	(4729)	(5293)
Training	[74]	[79]	[104]	[113]
Hours Worked	90	92	278	274
1 year Before	(251)	(253)	(466)	(458)
Training	[9]	[9]	[10]	[10]
Hours Worked	186	188	458	469
2 years Before	(434)	(450)	(654)	(689)
Training	[15]	[16]	[14]	[15]
Month of Assignment	−12.26	−12.30	−16.08	−15.91
(Jan. 78 = 0)	(4.30)	(4.23)	(5.97)	(5.89)
Number of				
Observations	800	802	2083	2193

Note: The numbers shown in parentheses are the standard deviations and those in the
square brackets are the standard errors.

views. Many participants failed to complete these interviews, and this sample attrition potentially biases the experimental results. Fortunately the largest source of attrition does not affect the integrity of the experimental design. Largely due to limited resources, the NSW administrators scheduled a 27th-month interview for only 65 percent of the participants and a 36th-month interview for only 24 percent of the non-AFDC participants. None of the AFDC participants were scheduled for a 36th-month interview, but the AFDC resurvey during the fall of 1979 interviewed 75 percent of these women anywhere from 27 to 44 months after the baseline. Since the trainee and control group members were randomly scheduled

for all of these interviews, this source of attrition did not bias the experimental evaluation of the NSW program.

Naturally, the program administrators did not locate all of the participants scheduled for these interviews. The proportion of participants who failed to complete scheduled interviews varied across experimental group, time, and target group. While the response rates were statistically significantly higher for the treatment as opposed to the control group members, the differences in response rates were usually only a few percentage points. For the 27th-month interview, 72 percent of the treatments and 68 percent of the control group members completed interviews. The differences in response rates were

TABLE 2—ANNUAL EARNINGS OF NSW TREATMENTS, CONTROLS, AND
EIGHT CANDIDATE COMPARISON GROUPS FROM THE *PSID* AND THE *CPS-SSA*

Year	Treatments	Controls	PSID-1	PSID-2	PSID-3	PSID-4	CPS-SSA-1	CPS-SSA-2	CPS-SSA-3	CPS-SSA-4
							Comparison Group[a,b]			
1975	$895	$877	7,303	2,327	937	6,654	7,788	3,748	4,575	2,049
	(81)	(90)	(317)	(286)	(189)	(428)	(63)	(250)	(135)	(333)
1976	$1,794	$646	7,442	2,697	665	6,770	8,547	4,774	3,800	2,036
	(99)	(63)	(327)	(317)	(157)	(463)	(65)	(302)	(128)	(337)
1977	$6,143	$1,518	7,983	3,219	891	7,213	8,562	4,851	5,277	2,844
	(140)	(112)	(335)	(376)	(229)	(484)	(68)	(317)	(153)	(450)
1978	$4,526	$2,885	8,146	3,636	1,631	7,564	8,518	5,343	5,665	3,700
	(270)	(244)	(339)	(421)	(381)	(480)	(72)	(365)	(166)	(593)
1979	$4,670	$3,819	8,016	3,569	1,602	7,482	8,023	5,343	5,782	3,733
	(226)	(208)	(334)	(381)	(334)	(462)	(73)	(371)	(170)	(543)
Number of Observations	600	585	595	173	118	255	11,132	241	1,594	87

[a] The Comparison Groups are defined as follows: *PSID*-1: All female household heads continuously from 1975 through 1979, who were between 20 and 55-years-old and did not classify themselves as retired in 1975; *PSID*-2: Selects from the *PSID*-1 group all women who received AFDC in 1975; *PSID*-3: Selects from the *PSID*-2 all women who were not working when surveyed in 1976; *PSID*-4: Selects from the *PSID*-1 group all women with children, none of whom are less than 5-years-old; *CPS-SSA* − 1: All females from Westat *CPS-SSA* sample; *CPS-SSA*-2: Selects from *CPS-SSA*-1 all females who received AFDC in 1975; *CPS-SSA*-3: Selects from *CPS-SSA*-1 all females who were not working in the spring of 1976; *CPS-SSA*-4: Selects from *CPS-SSA*-2 all females who were not working in the spring of 1976.
[b] All earnings are expressed in 1982 dollars. The numbers in parentheses are the standard errors. For the NSW treatments and controls, the number of observations refer only to 1975 and 1979. In the other years there are fewer observations, especially in 1978. At the time of the resurvey in 1979, treatments had been out of Supported Work for an average of 20 months.

larger across time and target group. For example, 79 percent of the scheduled participants completed the 9th-month interview, while 70 percent completed the 27th-month interview. The AFDC participants responded at consistently higher rates than the other target groups; 89 percent of the AFDC participants completed the 9th-month interview as opposed to 76 percent of the other participants. While these response rates indicate that the experimental results may be biased, especially for the non-AFDC participants, comparisons between the baseline characteristics of participants who did and did not complete a 27th-month interview suggest that whatever bias exists may be small.[7]

[7] This study evaluates the AFDC females separately from the non-AFDC males. This distinction is common in the literature, but it is also motivated by the differences between the response rates for the two groups.

Table 1 presents some sample statistics describing the baseline characteristics of the AFDC treatment and control groups as well as those of the male NSW participants in the other three target groups.[8] As would be expected from random assignment, the

The Supported Work Evaluation Study (*Public Use Files User's Guide*, Documentation Series No. 1, pp. 18–27) presents a more detailed discussion of sample attrition. My working paper (1984, tables 1.1 and 2.3), compares the characteristics and employment history of the full NSW sample to the sample with pre- and postprogram earnings data. Randall Brown (1979) reports that there is no evidence that the response rates affect the experimental estimates for the AFDC women or ex-addicts, while the evidence for the ex-offenders and high school dropouts is less conclusive.

[8] The female participants from the non-AFDC target groups were not surveyed during the AFDC resurvey in the fall of 1979 and consequently do not report 1979 earnings and are not included with the AFDC sample. Excluding these women from the analysis does not affect the integrity of the experimental design.

TABLE 3—ANNUAL EARNINGS OF NSW MALE TREATMENTS, CONTROLS, AND
SIX CANDIDATE COMPARISON GROUPS FROM THE *PSID* AND *CPS-SSA*

Year	Treatments	Controls	Comparison Group[a,b]					
			PSID-1	*PSID*-2	*PSID*-3	*CPS-SSA*-1	*CPS-SSA*-2	*CPS-SSA*-3
1975	$3,066	$3,027	19,056[a]	7,569	2,611	13,650	7,387	2,729
	(283)	(252)	(272)	(568)	(492)	(73)	(206)	(197)
1976	$4,035	$2,121	20,267	6,152	3,191	14,579	6,390	3,863
	(215)	(163)	(296)	(601)	(609)	(75)	(187)	(267)
1977	$6,335	$3,403	20,898	7,985	3,981	15,046	9,305	6,399
	(376)	(228)	(296)	(621)	(594)	(76)	(225)	(398)
1978	$5,976	$5,090	21,542	9,996	5,279	14,846	10,071	7,277
	(402)	(227)	(311)	(703)	(686)	(76)	(241)	(431)
Number of Observations	297	425	2,493	253	128	15,992	1,283	305

[a] The Comparison Groups are defined as follows: *PSID*-1: All male household heads continuously from 1975 through 1978, who were less than 55-years-old and did not classify themselves as retired in 1975; *PSID*-2: Selects from the *PSID*-1 group all men who were not working when surveyed in the spring of 1976; *PSID*-3: Selects from the *PSID*-1 group all men who were not working when surveyed in either spring of 1975 or 1976; *CPS-SSA*-1: All males based on Westat's criteria, except those over 55-years-old; *CPS-SSA*-2: Selects from *CPS-SSA*-1 all males who were not working when surveyed in March 1976; *CPS-SSA*-3: Selects from the *CPS-SSA*-1 unemployed males in 1976 whose income in 1975 was below the poverty level.

[b] All earnings are expressed in 1982 dollars. The numbers in parentheses are the standard errors. The number of observations refer only to 1975 and 1978. In the other years there are fewer observations. The sample of treatments is smaller than the sample of controls because treatments still in Supported Work as of January 1978 are excluded from the sample, and in the young high school target group there were by design more controls than treatments.

means of the characteristics and pretraining hours and earnings of the experimental groups are nearly the same. For example, the mean earnings of the AFDC treatments and the AFDC controls in the year before training differ by $2, the mean age of the two groups differ by 3 months, and the mean years of schooling are identical. None of the differences between the treatment's and control's characteristics, hours, and earnings are statistically significant.

The first two columns of Tables 2 and 3 present the annual earnings of the treatment and control group members.[9] The earnings of the experimental groups were the same in the pre-training year 1975, diverged during the employment program, and converged to some extent after the program ended. The

post-training year was 1979 for the AFDC females and 1978 for the males.[10]

Columns 2 and 3 in the first row of Tables 4 and 5 show that both the unadjusted and regression-adjusted pre-training earnings of the two sets of treatment and control group members are essentially identical. Therefore, because of the NSW program's experimental design, the difference between the post-training earnings of the experimental groups is an unbiased estimator of the training effect, and the other estimators described in columns 5–10(11) are unbiased estimators as well. The estimates in column 4 indicate that the

[9] All earnings presented in this paper are in 1982 dollars. The NSW Public Use Files report earnings in experimental time, months from the baseline, and not calendar time. However, my working paper describes how to convert the experimental earnings data to the annual data reported in Tables 2 and 3.

[10] The number of NSW male treatment group members with complete pre- and postprogram earnings is much smaller than the full sample of treatments or the partial sample of control group members. This difference is largely explained by the two forms of sample attrition discussed earlier. In addition, however, (i) this paper excludes all males who were in Supported Work in January 1978, or entered the program before January 1976; (ii) in one of the sites, the administrators randomly assigned .4 instead of one-half of the qualified high school dropouts into the treatment group.

TABLE 4—EARNINGS COMPARISONS AND ESTIMATED TRAINING EFFECTS FOR THE NSW
AFDC PARTICIPANTS USING COMPARISON GROUPS FROM THE *PSID* AND THE *CPS-SSA*[a,b]

| Name of Comparison Group[d] | Comparison Group Earnings Growth 1975-79 (1) | NSW Treatment Earnings Less Comparison Group Earnings | | | | Difference in Differences: Difference in Earnings Growth 1975-79 Treatments Less Comparisons | | Unrestricted Difference in Differences: Quasi Difference in Earnings Growth 1975-79 | | Controlling for All Observed Variables and Pre-Training Earnings | |
| | | Pre-Training Year, 1975 | | Post-Training Year, 1979 | | | | | | | |
		Unadjusted (2)	Adjusted[c] (3)	Unadjusted (4)	Adjusted[c] (5)	Without Age (6)	With Age (7)	Unadjusted (8)	Adjusted[c] (9)	Without AFDC (10)	With AFDC (11)
Controls	2,942 (220)	−17 (122)	−22 (122)	851 (307)	861 (306)	833 (323)	883 (323)	843 (308)	864 (306)	854 (312)	–
PSID-1	713 (210)	−6,443 (326)	−4,882 (336)	−3,357 (403)	−2,143 (425)	3,097 (317)	2,657 (333)	1746 (357)	1,354 (380)	1664 (409)	2,097 (491)
PSID-2	1,242 (314)	−1,467 (216)	−1,515 (224)	1,090 (468)	870 (484)	2,568 (473)	2,392 (481)	1,764 (472)	1,535 (487)	1,826 (537)	–
PSID-3	665 (351)	−77 (202)	−100 (208)	3,057 (532)	2,915 (543)	3,145 (557)	3,020 (563)	3,070 (531)	2,930 (543)	2,919 (592)	–
PSID-4	928 (311)	−5,694 (306)	−4,976 (323)	−2,822 (460)	−2,268 (491)	2,883 (417)	2,655 (434)	1,184 (483)	950 (503)	1,406 (542)	2,146 (652)
CPS-SSA-1	233 (64)	−6,928 (272)	−5,813 (309)	−3,363 (320)	−2,650 (365)	3,578 (280)	3,501 (282)	1,214 (272)	1,127 (309)	536 (349)	1,041 (503)
CPS-SSA-2	1,595 (360)	−2,888 (204)	−2,332 (256)	−683 (428)	−240 (536)	2,215 (438)	2,068 (446)	447 (468)	620 (554)	665 (651)	–
CPS-SSA-3	1,207 (166)	−3,715 (226)	−3,150 (325)	−1,122 (311)	−812 (452)	2,603 (307)	2,615 (328)	814 (305)	784 (429)	−99 (481)	1,246 (720)
CPS-SSA-4	1,684 (524)	−1,189 (249)	−780 (283)	926 (630)	756 (716)	2,126 (654)	1,833 (663)	1,222 (637)	952 (717)	827 (814)	–

[a] The columns above present the estimated training effect for each econometric model and comparison group. The dependent variable is earnings in 1979. Based on the experimental data, an unbiased estimate of the impact of training presented in col. 4 is $851. The first three columns present the difference between each comparison group's 1975 and 1979 earnings and the difference between the pre-training earnings of each comparison group and the NSW treatments.
[b] Estimates are in 1982 dollars. The numbers in parentheses are the standard errors.
[c] The exogenous variables used in the regression adjusted equations are age, age squared, years of schooling, high school dropout status, and race.
[d] See Table 2 for definitions of the comparison groups.

earnings of the AFDC females were $851 higher than they would have been without the NSW program, while the earnings of the male participants were $886 higher.[11] Moreover, the other columns show that the econometric procedure does not affect these estimates.

[11] It is commonly believed that the NSW program had little impact on the earnings of the male participants (see MDRC; A. P. Bernstein et al., 1985). My working paper discusses why this estimated impact differs from the results discussed elsewhere. The 1978 earnings data were largely collected during the 36th-month interview, where the difference between the male treatment and control group members' earnings averaged $175 per quarter.

II. Nonexperimental Estimates

In addition to providing researchers with a simple estimate of the impact of an employment program, MDRC's experimental data can also be used to evaluate several nonexperimental methods of program evaluation. This section puts aside the NSW control group and evaluates the NSW program using some of the econometric procedures found in studies of the employment and training programs administered under the MDTA, CETA, and JTPA.[12]

[12] These acronyms refer to the Manpower Development and Training Act-1962, the Comprehensive Em-

TABLE 5—EARNINGS COMPARISONS AND ESTIMATED TRAINING EFFECTS FOR THE NSW MALE PARTICIPANTS USING COMPARISON GROUPS FROM THE *PSID* AND THE *CPS-SSA*[a,b]

Name of Comparison Group[d]	Comparison Group Earnings Growth 1975–78 (1)	NSW Treatment Earnings Less Comparison Group Earnings				Difference in Differences: Difference in Earnings Growth 1975–78 Treatments Less Comparisons		Unrestricted Difference in Differences: Quasi Difference in Earnings Growth 1975–78		Controlling for All Observed Variables and Pre-Training Earnings (10)
		Pre-Training Year, 1975		Post-Training Year, 1978		Without Age (6)	With Age (7)	Unadjusted (8)	Adjusted[c] (9)	
		Unadjusted (2)	Adjusted[c] (3)	Unadjusted (4)	Adjusted[c] (5)					
Controls	$2,063	$39	$–21	$886	$798	$847	$856	$897	$802	$662
	(325)	(383)	(378)	(476)	(472)	(560)	(558)	(467)	(467)	(506)
PSID-1	$2,043	–$15,997	–$7,624	–$15,578	–$8,067	$425	–$749	–$2,380	–$2,119	–$1,228
	(237)	(795)	(851)	(913)	(990)	(650)	(692)	(680)	(746)	(896)
PSID-2	$6,071	–$4,503	–$3,669	–$4,020	–$3,482	$484	–$650	–$1,364	–$1,694	–$792
	(637)	(608)	(757)	(781)	(935)	(738)	(850)	(729)	(878)	(1024)
PSID-3	($3,322	($455	$455	$697	–$509	$242	–$1,325	$629	–$552	$397
	(780)	(539)	(704)	(760)	(967)	(884)	(1078)	(757)	(967)	(1103)
CPS-SSA-1	$1,196	–$10,585	–$4,654	–$8,870	–$4,416	$1,714	$195	–$1,543	–$1,102	–$805
	(61)	(539)	(509)	(562)	(557)	(452)	(441)	(426)	(450)	(484)
CPS-SSA-2	$2,684	–$4,321	–$1,824	–$4,095	–$1,675	$226	–$488	–$1,850	–$782	–$319
	(229)	(450)	(535)	(537)	(672)	(539)	(530)	(497)	(621)	(761)
CPS-SSA-3	$4,548	$337	$878	–$1,300	$224	–$1,637	–$1,388	–$1,396	$17	$1,466
	(409)	(343)	(447)	(590)	(766)	(631)	(655)	(582)	(761)	(984)

[a] The columns above present the estimated training effect for each econometric model and comparison group. The dependent variable is earnings in 1978. Based on the experimental data an unbiased estimate of the impact of training presented in col. 4 is $886. The first three columns present the difference between each comparison group's 1975 and 1978 earnings and the difference between the pre-training earnings of each comparison group and the NSW treatments.
[b] Estimates are in 1982 dollars. The numbers in parentheses are the standard errors.
[c] The exogenous variables used in the regression adjusted equations are age, age squared, years of schooling, high school dropout status, and race.
[d] See Table 3 for definitions of the comparison groups.

The researchers who evaluated these federally sponsored programs devised both experimental and nonexperimental procedures to estimate the training effect, because they recognized that the difference between the trainees' pre- and post-training earnings was a poor estimate of the training effect. In a dynamic economy, the trainees' earnings may grow even without an effective program. The goal of these program evaluations is to estimate the earnings of the trainees had they not participated in the program. Researchers using experimental data take the earnings of the control group members to be an estimate of the trainees' earnings without the program. Without experimental data, researchers estimate the earnings of the trainees by using the regression-adjusted earnings of

ployment and Training Act–1973, and the Job Training Partnership Act–1982.

a comparison group drawn from the population. This adjustment takes into account that the observable characteristics of the trainees and the comparison group members differ, and their unobservable characteristics may differ as well.

Any nonexperimental evaluation of a training program must explicitly account for these differences in a model describing the observable determinants of earnings and the process by which the trainees are selected into the program. However, unlike in an experimental evaluation, the nonexperimental estimates of the training effect depend crucially on the way that the earnings and participation equations are specified. If the econometric model is specified correctly, the nonexperimental estimates should be the same (within sampling error) as the training effect generated from the experimental data, but if there is a significant difference between the nonexperimental and the experimental estimates, the econometric model is misspecified.[13]

The first step in a nonexperimental evaluation is to select a comparison group whose earnings can be compared to the earnings of the trainees. Tables 2 and 3 present the mean annual earnings of female and male comparison groups drawn from the *Panel Study of Income Dynamics* (*PSID*) and Westat's Matched *Current Population Survey – Social Security Administration File* (*CPS-SSA*). These groups are characteristic of two types of comparison groups frequently used in the program evaluation literature. The *PSID*-1 and the *CPS-SSA*-1 groups are large, stratified random samples from populations of household heads and households, respectively.[14] The other, smaller, comparison groups are composed of individuals whose characteristics are consistent with some of the eligibility criteria used to admit applicants into the NSW program. For example, the *PSID*-3 and *CPS-SSA*-4 comparison groups in Table 2 include females from the *PSID* and the *CPS-SSA* who received AFDC payments in 1975, and were not employed in the spring of 1976. Tables 2 and 3 show that the NSW trainees and controls have earnings histories that are more similar to those of the smaller comparison groups, whose characteristics are similar to theirs, than those of the larger comparison groups.[15]

The second step in a nonexperimental evaluation is to specify a model of earnings and program participation to adjust for differences between the trainees and comparison group members. Equations (1) through (4) describe a conventional model of earnings and program participation that is typical of the kind econometric researchers use for this problem:

$$(1) \quad y_{it} = \delta D_i + \beta X_{it} + b_i + n_t + \varepsilon_{it}$$

$$(2) \quad \varepsilon_{it} - \rho \varepsilon_{it-1} = \nu_{it}$$

$$(3) \quad d_{is} = y_{is} + \gamma Z_{is} + \eta_{is}$$

$$(4) \quad D_i = 1 \quad \text{if } d_{is} > 0; \quad D_i = 0 \quad \text{if } d_{is} < 0.$$

In equation (1), earnings in each period are a function of a vector of individual characteristics, X_{it}, such as age, schooling, and race for individual i in time t; a dummy variable indicating whether the individual participated in training in period $s + 1$, D_i; and an error with individual- and time-specific components and a serially correlated transitory disturbance. The transitory disturbance follows the first-order serial corre-

---

[13] Thomas Fraker, Maynard, and Lyle Nelson (1984) describe a similar study using the NSW AFDC and Young High School Dropouts. Instead of focusing the study on models of earnings and program participation, their study evaluates several strategies for choosing matched comparison groups. They use grouped Social Security earnings data when comparing the annual earnings of the NSW treatments to the earnings of each of the comparison groups.

[14] The *PSID* file including the poverty subsample selects only women and men who were household heads continuously from 1975 to 1979, and 1978, respectively. The *CPS-SSA* file matches the March 1976 *Current Population Survey* with Social Security earnings. Only individuals in the labor force in March 1976 with nominal income less than $20,000 and household income less than $30,000 are in this sample. In 1976, 2 percent of the females and 21 percent of the males had earnings at the Social Security maximum. In this paper, females younger than 20 or older than 55 and males older than 55 are excluded from the comparison groups.

[15] Not only are the pre-training earnings of the *PSID*-3 comparison group in Table 2 similar to the earnings of the NSW experimental groups, but the characteristics of these groups are similar as well. The mean age for the *PSID*-3 women is 40.95; the mean years of schooling is 10.31; the proportion of high school dropouts is 0.63; the proportion married is 0.01; the proportion black is 0.85; and the proportion Hispanic is 0.03. I experimented with matching the comparison groups even more closely to the pre-training characteristics of the experimental sample. However, these closely matched comparison groups are extremely small. For example there were 57 women from the *PSID* who received welfare payments in 1975, were not employed at the time of the survey in 1976, resided in a metropolitan area, and had only school-age children. The mean earnings of this group were $1,137 in 1975; $673 in 1976; $743 in 1977; $1,222 in 1978; and $1,697 in 1979.

lation process described in equation (2). Equations (3) and (4) specify the participation decision: an individual participates in training and is admitted into the program in period $s + 1$ if the latent variable d_{is} rises above zero. The participation equation is typically rationalized by the notion that the supply of individuals who decide to participate in training depends on the net benefit they expect to receive from participation and on the demand of the program administrators for training participants. The participation latent variable is typically a function of a vector of characteristics Z_{is}, current earnings y_{is}, and an error.

The estimators described in the column headings in Tables 4 and 5 (as well as many others in the literature) are based on econometric specifications that place different restrictions on the training model represented by equations (1)–(4) (although one common restriction assumes that the unobservables in the earnings and participation equations are uncorrelated). These estimates are consistent only insofar as their restrictions are consistent with the data. The restrictions can be tested provided the nonexperimental data base has sufficient information on the pre-training earnings and demographic characteristics of the trainees and comparison group members. An econometrician is unlikely to take seriously an estimate based on a model that failed one of these specification tests. Therefore, the results of such tests can often aid the researcher in choosing among alternative estimates. It follows, then, that simply checking whether the nonexperimental estimates replicate the experimental results and whether these estimates vary across different econometric procedures is not the only motivation for comparing experimental to nonexperimental methods. By making this comparison, we can also discover whether the nonexperimental data alone reliably indicate when an econometric model is misspecified and whether specification tests, which are supposed to ensure that the econometric model is consistent with the data, lead researchers to choose the "right" estimator.

In practice, the available data affect the composition of the comparison groups and the flexibility of the econometric specifica-

tions. For example, since there is only one year of pre-training earnings data, we cannot evaluate all of the econometric procedures that have been used in the literature, nor can we test all of the econometric specifications analyzed in this paper with the nonexperimental data alone.[16]

Nevertheless, several one-step estimators are evaluated in Tables 4 and 5, starting with the simple difference between the treatment and comparison group members' post-training earnings in column 4. Column 5 presents this earnings difference controlling for age, schooling, and race. This cross-sectional estimator is based on a model where these demographic variables are assumed to adequately control for differences between the earnings of the trainees and comparison group members. Column 6 presents the difference between the two nonexperimental groups' pre- and post-training earnings growth. This estimator allows for an unobserved individual fixed effect in the earnings equation and for the possibility that individuals with low values of this unobservable are more likely to participate in training. The cross-sectional estimator described in column 5 is now biased since the training dummy variable is correlated with the error in the earnings equation. Differencing the earnings equation removes the fixed effect, leaving[17]

$$(5) \quad y_{it} - y_{is} = \delta D_i + \beta \cdot AGE_i + (\eta_t - \eta_s) + \varepsilon_{it} - \varepsilon_{is}.$$

---

[16] One limitation of the NSW Public Use File is that there is only one year of pre-experimental data available in calendar time as opposed to experimental time. Consequently, there are several nonexperimental procedures which require more than a year of pre-training earnings data that are not evaluated in this paper. If additional data were available, it is possible that these procedures would adequately control for differences between the NSW treatments and comparison group members and that the results of the specification tests would correctly guide an econometrician away from some of the estimates presented in this paper to the estimates based on these other procedures. See John Abowd (1983), Ashenfelter, Ashenfelter and Card, Bassi (1983b, 1984), and James Heckman and Richard Robb (1985).

[17] The other demographic variables, schooling and race, are constant over time.

The comparison group's earnings growth represents the earnings growth that the trainees would have experienced without the program. However, since the trainees may experience larger earnings growth than the comparison group members simply because they are usually younger, column 7 presents the difference between the earnings growth of the two groups controlling for age.

Column 8 presents the difference between the post-training earnings of the treatment and comparison group members, holding constant the level of pre-training earnings, while the estimator in column 9 controls both for pre-training earnings and the demographic variables. These estimators are consistent when the model of program participation stipulates that the trainees' pre-program earnings fell (see Table 1) because some of the training participants experienced some bad luck in the years prior to training. In this case, we would expect the trainees' earnings to grow even without the program.[18] The difference in differences estimator in columns 6 and 7 is now biased, since the training dummy variable is correlated with the transitory component of pre-training earnings in equation (5).[19] Finally, columns 10 and 11 report the estimates of the training effects controlling for all observed variables. Besides the variables described earlier, the additional regressors are employment status in 1976, AFDC status in 1975, marital status, residency in a metropolitan area with more than 100,000 persons, and number of children.

Unlike the experimental estimates, the nonexperimental estimates are sensitive both to the composition of the comparison group and to the econometric procedure. For example, many of the estimates in column 9 of Table 4 replicate the experimental results, while other estimates are more than $1,000 larger than the experimental results. More specifically, the results for the female participants (Table 4) tend to be positive and larger than the experimental estimate, while for the male participants (Table 5), the estimates tend to be negative and smaller than the experimental impact.[20] Additionally, the nonexperimental procedures replicate the experimental results more closely when the nonexperimental data include pre-training earnings rather than cross-sectional data alone or when evaluating female rather than male participants.

The sensitivity of the nonexperimental estimates to different specifications of the econometric model is not in itself a cause for alarm. After all, few econometricians expect estimators based on misspecified models to replicate the results of experiments. Hence the considerable range of estimates is understandable given that inconsistent estimators are likely to yield inaccurate estimates. Before taking some of these estimates too seriously, many econometricians at a minimum would require that their estimators be based on econometric models that are consistent with the pre-training earnings data. Thus, if the regression-adjusted difference between the post-training earnings of the two groups is going to be a consistent estimator of the training effect, the regression-adjusted pre-training earnings of the two groups should be the same.

Based on this specification test, econometricians might reject the nonexperimental estimates in columns 4–7 of Table 4 in favor of the ones in columns 8–11. Few econometricians would report the training effect of $870 in column 5, even though this estimate differs from the experimental result

---

[18] Researchers have observed this dip in pre-training earnings for successive MDTA and CETA cohorts since 1964. See Ashenfelter (Table 1); Ashenfelter and Card (Table 1); Bassi (1983a, Table 4.1); and Kiefer (1979a, Table 4-1).

[19] This estimator is similar to one devised by Arthur Goldberger (1972) (or see G. S. Maddala, 1983) to evaluate the Head Start Program where participation in the program depended on a child's test score plus a random error. Similarly, participation in a training program can be thought of as a function of pre-training earnings and a random error. My working paper shows that this estimator is consistent as long as the unobservables in the earnings and participation equations are uncorrelated, and all of the observable variables in the model are used as regressors in the earnings equation.

[20] The magnitude of these training effects is similar to the estimates reported in studies of the 1964 MDTA cohort, the 1969–70 MDTA cohort, and the 1976–77 CETA cohort. (See my working paper, Table I.1.)

by only $19. If the cross-sectional estimator properly controlled for differences between the trainees and comparison group members, we would not expect the difference between the regression adjusted pre-training earnings of the two groups to be $1,550, as reported in column 3. Likewise, econometricians might refrain from reporting the difference in differences estimates in columns 6 and 7, even though all these estimates are within two standard errors of $3,000. As noted earlier, this estimator is not consistent with the decline in the trainees' pre-training earnings.

This point can also be made with the estimates for the NSW male participants (Table 5). For example, all but one of the difference in differences estimates in column 6 are within one standard error of the experimental estimate. Yet for two reasons it is unlikely econometricians would report these estimates. First, as the results in column 7 suggest, since the trainees are younger their earnings might be expected to grow faster than the earnings of the comparison group members even without training. Second, as shown in Table 1, the pre-training earnings of the male participants fell in the period before training, suggesting that the trainees' earnings will grow even if the program is ineffective. Here again, econometricians might turn to the considerable range of estimates in columns 8–10.

The results of these specification tests suggest that an econometrician might report one of the estimates in columns 8–11. However, even without the experimental data, a researcher would find that the estimated training effect is still sensitive to the set of variables included in the earnings equation and to the composition of the comparison group. In Table 4, the estimates using the female household heads with school-age children (PSID-4) as a comparison group differ by more than $1,000. The largest estimate overstates the experimental result by $1,300, while the smallest estimate is within $100 of the experimental estimate. Likewise in column 11, we find that the same estimator with different comparison groups yields a set of estimates that vary by more than $1,000. The estimates for the male participants ex-

hibit the same sensitivity to the choice of a comparison group and to the set of variables used as regressors in the earnings equation. However, the estimated standard errors associated with these training effects are larger than for the female estimates, making it more difficult to draw many conclusions from these results.

Without additional data it is difficult to see how a researcher would choose a training effect from among estimates. Moreover, the nonexperimental data base alone does not allow the econometrician to test whether these estimates are based on econometric models that adequately control for differences between the earnings of the trainees and comparison group members. In this case, comparisons between the experimental and nonexperimental estimates is the best specification test available.[21]

Specification tests that use pre-training earnings data are an appealing means to choose between alternative estimates, but these tests are not themselves always sufficient to identify unreliable estimators. This point becomes clear when we compare the estimates using the PSID-3 comparison group (as defined in Table 2) and those using the NSW control group. The characteristics of these two groups are nearly the same, as are their unadjusted and adjusted pre-training earnings. In each case the cross-sectional estimator in column 5 appears to be an unbiased estimate of the training effect. Moreover, both sets of estimates are unaffected by alternative econometric procedures. Thus both the experimental and nonexperimental estimates pass the same specification tests; nevertheless the nonexperimental estimate is approximately $2,100 larger than the experimental result. If a researcher did not know that one set of estimates was based on an experimental data set, it is hard to see how she or he would

[21]Ashenfelter, Ashenfelter and Card, and Bassi (1984) have noted in their studies using nonexperimental data that their results are sensitive to alternative econometric specifications and that there is evidence for male training participants that the econometric models are misspecified.

choose between two estimates where one training effect is roughly 3.5 times larger than the other.

III. Two-Step Estimates

The unobservables in the earnings equation were uncorrelated with those in the participation equation in all of the econometric models analyzed in the previous section. If, instead, the unobservables are correlated, none of the one-step least squares procedures are consistent estimators of the training effect. Individuals with high unobservables in their participation equation are more likely to participate in training. Yet if the unobservables in the earnings and participation equations are negatively correlated, these individuals are likely to have relatively low earnings, even after controlling for the observable variables in the model. Consequently, least squares underestimates the impact of training.

James Heckman (1978) proposes a two-step estimator that controls for the correlation between the unobservables by using the estimated conditional expectation of the earnings error as a regressor in the earnings equation. If the errors in the earnings and participation equations are jointly normally distributed, this conditional expectation is proportional to the conditional expectation of the error in the participation equation. Using the notation introduced in the last section, this relationship is expressed formally as

$$(6) \quad E(b_i + \varepsilon_{it} | Z_i, D_i) = \rho \sigma_\varepsilon \left[D_i \frac{\phi(\gamma Z_i)}{1 - \Phi(\gamma Z_i)} \right.$$

$$\left. - (1 - D_i) \frac{\phi(\gamma Z_i)}{\Phi(\gamma Z_i)} \right] = rH_i,$$

where Z_i is a vector of observed variables, ρ is the correlation between the unobservables in the model, σ_ε^2 is the variance of the unobservables in the earnings equation, and $\phi(\cdot)$ and $\Phi(\cdot)$ are the normal density and distribution functions. Therefore the earn-

ings equation can be rewritten as

$$(7) \quad Y_{it} = \delta D_i + \beta X_{it} + rH_i + v_i^*,$$

where v_i^* is an orthogonal error by construction. To estimate the training effect, δ, the researcher first uses the coefficients from a probit estimate of the reduced-form participation equation to calculate the conditional expectation, H_i, for both the trainees and comparison group members,[22] and, second, uses this estimate, $\hat{H}_i$, as a regressor in the earnings equation. The training effect is then estimated by least squares.[23]

Table 6 presents estimates for the female and male training participants using the NSW controls, the PSID-1 and CPS-SSA-1 as comparison groups.[24] Unless some variables are excluded from the earnings equation, the training effect in this procedure is identified by the nonlinearity of the probit function. Hence, the rows of Table 6 allow us to evaluate the sensitivity of these estimates to different exclusion restrictions. The second column associated with each set of training effects presents the estimated participation coefficient. If the unobservables are uncorrelated, this estimate should not be significantly different from zero. Therefore, these estimates allow us to test whether this restriction on the correlation between the unobservables is consistent with the nonex-

---

[22] This is a choice-based sampling problem, since the probability of being in the nonexperimental data set is high for the NSW treatment group members and low for the comparison group members. The estimated probability of participation depends not only on the observed variables but on the numbers of trainees and comparison group members. Heckman and Richard Robb (1985) show that this procedure is robust to choice-based sampling. For an example of an application of this estimator in the evaluation literature, see Mallar.

[23] Since the estimated value of this conditional expectation is used as a regressor instead of the true value, the estimated standard errors associated with the least squares estimates are inconsistent and must be corrected. See Heckman (1978,: 1979); William Greene (1981); John Ham (1982); and Ham and Cheng Hsiao (1984).

[24] The two-step estimates using the smaller comparison groups were associated with large estimated standard errors.

TABLE 6—ESTIMATED TRAINING EFFECTS USING TWO-STAGE ESTIMATOR

Variables Excluded from the Earnings Equation, but Included in the Participation Equation	Comparison Group	NSW AFDC Females		NSW Males	
		Heckman Correction for Program Participation Bias, Using Estimate of Conditional Expectation of Earnings Error as Regressor in Earnings Equation			
		Estimate of Coefficient for			
		Training Dummy	Estimate of Expectation	Training Dummy	Estimate of Expectation
Marital Status, Residency in an SMSA,	PSID-1	1,129	−894	−1,333	−2,357
Employment Status in 1976,		(385)	(396)	(820)	(781)
AFDC Status in 1975,	CPS-SSA-1	1,102	−606	−22	−1,437
Number of Children		(323)	(480)	(584)	(449)
	NSW Controls	837	−18	899	−835
		(317)	(2376)	(840)	(2601)
Employment Status in 1976, AFDC Status	PSID-1	1,256	−823	−	−
in 1975, Number of Children		(405)	(410)		
	CPS-SSA-1	439	−979	−	−
		(333)	(481)		
	NSW Controls	−	−	−	−
Employment Status in 1976,	PSID-1	1,564	−552	−1,161	−2,655
Number of Children		(604)	(569)	(864)	(799)
	CPS-SSA-1	552	−902	13	−1,484
		(514)	(551)	(584)	(450)
	NSW Controls	851	147	889	−808
		(318)	(2385)	(841)	(2603)
No Exclusion Restrictions	PSID-1	1,747	−526	−667	−2,446
		(620)	(568)	(905)	(806)
	CPS-SSA-1	805	−908	213	−1,364
		(523)	(548)	(588)	(452)
	NSW Controls	861	284	889	−876
		(318)	(2385)	(840)	(2601)

Notes: The estimated training effects are in 1982 dollars. For the females, the experimental estimate of impact of the supported work program was $851 with a standard error of $317. The one-step estimates from col. 11 of Table 4 were $2,097 with a standard error of $491 using the PSID-1 as a comparison group, $1,041 with a standard error of $503 using the CPS-SSA-1 as a comparison group, and $854 with a standard error of $312 using the NSW controls as a comparison group. Estimates are missing for the case of three exclusions using the NSW controls since AFDC status in 1975 cannot be used as an instrument for the NSW females. For the males, the experimental estimate of impact of the supported work program was $886 with a standard error of $476. The one-step estimates from col. 10 of Table 5 were $ −1,228 with a standard error of $896 using the PSID-1 as a comparison group, $ −805 with a standard error of $484 using the CPS-SSA-1 as a comparison group, and $662 with a standard error of $506 using the NSW controls as a comparison group. Estimates are missing for the case of three exclusions for the NSW males as AFDC status is not used as an instrument in the analysis of the male trainees.

perimental data, and to examine whether this specification test leads econometricians to choose the "right" estimator.

The experimental estimates in Table 6 are consistent with MDRC's experimental design. All of these estimates are nearly identical to the experimental results presented in Tables 4 and 5. And furthermore, since the unobservables are uncorrelated by design, the estimated participation coefficients are never significantly different from zero.

Turning to the nonexperimental estimates we find that although the instruments used to identify the earnings equation have some effect on the results, generally these estimates are closer to the experimental estimates than are the one-step estimates (in column 11 of Tables 4 and 5). For the females, the difference between the two-step and one-step estimates are small relative to the estimated standard errors, and the estimates of the participation coefficient are only marginally significantly different from zero. Interestingly, in one case when the $PSID$-1 sample is used as a comparison group, the estimated participation coefficient is significant (the t-statistic is 2.25) and the training effect of $1,129 is $968 closer to the experimental result than the one-step estimate. Additionally, this estimate is identical to the estimate using the CPS-SSA-1 comparison group, whereas the one-step estimates differed by $1,056. However, if an econometrician reported this training effect, she or he would have to argue that variables such as place of residence and prior AFDC status do not belong in the earnings equation. Otherwise, the econometrician is left to choose between a set of estimates that vary by as much as $1,308.

The two-step estimates are usually closer than the one-step estimates to the experimental results for the male trainees as well. One estimate, which used the CPS-SSA-1 sample as a comparison group, is within $600 of the experimental result, while the one-step estimate falls short by $1,695. The estimates of the participation coefficients are negative, although unlike these estimates for the females, they are always significantly different from zero. This finding is consistent with the example cited earlier in which individuals with high participation unobservables and low earnings unobservables were more likely to be in training. As predicted, the unrestricted estimates are larger than the one-step estimates. However, as with the results for the females, this procedure may leave econometricians with a considerable range ($1,546) of imprecise estimates; although, like the results for the females, there is no evidence that the results of the specification tests would lead econometricians to choose the "wrong" estimator.

IV. Conclusion

This study shows that many of the econometric procedures and comparison groups used to evaluate employment and training programs would not have yielded accurate or precise estimates of the impact of the National Supported Work Program. The econometric estimates often differ significantly

from the experimental results. Moreover, even when the econometric estimates pass conventional specification tests, they still fail to replicate the experimentally determined results. Even though I was unable to evaluate all nonexperimental methods, this evidence suggests that policymakers should be aware that the available nonexperimental evaluations of employment and training programs may contain large and unknown biases resulting from specification errors.[25]

This study also yields several other findings that may help researchers evaluate other employment and training programs. First, the nonexperimental procedures produce estimates that are usually positive and larger than the experimental results for the female participants, and are negative and smaller than the experimental estimates for the male participants. Second, these econometric procedures are more likely to replicate the experimental results in the case of female rather than male participants. Third, longitudinal data reduces the potential for specification errors relative to the cross-sectional data. Finally, the two-step procedure certainly does no worse than, and may reduce the potential for specification errors relative to, the one-step procedures discussed in Section II.

More generally, this paper presents an alternative approach to the sensitivity analyses proposed by Leamer (1983, 1985) and others for bounding the specification errors associated with the evaluation of economic hypotheses. This objective is accomplished by comparing econometric estimates with experimentally determined results. The data from an experiment yield simple estimates of the impact of economic treatments that are independent of any model specification. Successful econometric methods are intended to

[25] There is some evidence that this message has been passed on to the appropriate policymakers. See Recommendations of the Job Training Longitudinal Survey Research Advisory Panel to Office of Strategic Planning and Policy Development, U.S. Department of Labor, November 1985. This has led to at least a tentative decision to operate some part of the Job Training Partnership Act program sites using random assignment. (See Ernst Stromsdorfer et al., 1985.)

reproduce these estimates. The only way we will know whether these econometric methods are successful is by making the comparison. This paper takes the first step along this path, but there are other experimental data bases available to econometricians and much work remains to be done. For example, there have been several other employment and training experiments testing the effect of training on earnings, four Negative Income Tax Experiments testing hypotheses about labor supply, a medical insurance experiment testing hypotheses about insurance and medical demand, a housing experiment testing hypotheses about housing demand and supply, and a time-of-day electricity pricing experiment testing hypotheses about electricity demand.[26] There clearly remain many opportunities to use the experimental method to assess the potential for specification bias in the evaluation of social programs, and in other areas of econometric research as well.

[26]See Linda Aiken and Barbara Kehrer (1985), Abt Associates (1984), Gary Burtless (1985), Barbara Goldman (1981), Goldman et al. (1985), Jerry Hausman and David Wise (1985), J. Ohls and G. Carcagno (1978), and SRI International (1983).

REFERENCES

Abowd, John, "Program Evaluation," Working Paper, University of Chicago, 1983.

Aiken, Linda and Kehrer, Barbara, *Evaluation Studies Review Annual,* Vol. 10, Beverly Hills: Sage Publications, 1985.

Ashenfelter, Orley, "Estimating the Effect of Training Programs on Earnings," *Review of Economics and Statistics,* February 1978, *60,* 47–57.

_____ **and Card, David,** "Using the Longitudinal Structure of Earnings to Estimate the Effect of Training Programs," *Review of Economics and Statistics,* November 1985, *67,* 648–60.

Bernstein, A. P. et al., "The Forgotten Americans," *Business Week,* September 2, 1985, 50–55.

Bassi, Laurie, (1983a) "Estimating the Effect of Training Programs With Non-Random Selection," Princeton University, 1983.

_____ , (1983b) "The Effect of CETA on the Post-Program Earnings of Participants," *Journal of Human Resources,* Fall 1983, *18,* 539–556.

_____ , "Estimating the Effects of Training Programs with Nonrandom Selection," *Review of Economics and Statistics,* February 1984 *66,* 36–43.

Brown, Randall, "Assessing the Effects of Interview Nonresponse on Estimates of the Impact of Supported Work," Mathematica Policy Research Inc., Princeton, 1979.

Burtless, Gary, "Are Targeted Wage Subsidies Harmful? Evidence from a Wage Voucher Experiment," *Industrial and Labor Relations Review,* October 1985, *39,* 105–114.

Cooley, Thomas, McGuire, Thomas and Prescott, Edward, "Earnings and Employment Dynamics of Manpower Trainees: An Exploratory Econometric Analysis," in Ronald Ehrenberg, ed., *Research in Labor Economics,* Vol. 4, Suppl. 2, 1979, 119–47.

Dickinson, Katherine and Maynard, Rebecca, *The Impact of Supported Work on Ex-Addicts,* New York: Manpower Demonstration Research Corporation, 1981.

_____ , **Johnson, Terry and West, Richard,** *An Analysis of the Impact of CETA Programs on Participants' Earnings,* Washington: Department of Labor, Employment and Training Administration, 1984.

Fraker, Thomas, Maynard, Rebecca and Nelson, Lyle, *An Assessment of Alternative Comparison Group Methodologies for Evaluating Employment and Training Programs,* Princeton: Mathematica Policy Research Inc., 1984.

Goldberger, Arthur, "Selection Bias in Evaluating Treatment Effects," Discussion Paper No. 123–72, Institute for Research on Poverty, University of Wisconsin, 1972.

Goldman, Barbara, "The Impacts of the Immediate Job Search Assistance Experiment," Manpower Demonstration Research Corporation, New York, 1981.

_____ **et al.,** "Findings From the San Diego Job Search and Work Experience Demonstration," New York: Manpower Demonstration Research Corporation, 1985.

Greene, William, "Sample Selection Bias as a Specification Error: Comment," *Econometrica*, May 1981, *49*, 795–98.

Ham, John, "Estimation of a Labor Supply Model with Censoring Due to Unemployment and Underemployment," *Review of Economic Studies*, July 1982, *49*, 335–54.

_____ and Hsiao, Cheng, "Two-Stage Estimation of Structural Labor Supply Parameters Using Interval Data From the 1971 Canadian Census," *Journal of Econometrics*, January/February 1984, *24*, 133–58.

Hausman, Jerry A. and Wise, David A., *Social Experimentation*, NBER, Chicago: University of Chicago Press, 1985.

Heckman, James, "Dummy Endogenous Variables in a Simultaneous Equations System," *Econometrica*, July 1978, *46*, 931–59.

_____, "Sample Selection Bias as a Specification Error," *Econometrica*, January 1979, *47*, 153–61.

_____ and Robb, Richard, "Alternative Methods for Evaluating the Impact of Interventions: An Overview," Working Paper, University of Chicago, 1985.

Hendry, David, "Econometrices: Alchemy or Science?" *Economica*, November 1980, *47*, 387–406.

Kemper, Peter and Long, David, "The Supported Work Evaluation: Technical Report on the Value of In-Program Output Costs," Manpower Demonstration Research Corporation, New York, 1981.

_____, _____, and Thornton, Craig, "The Supported Work Evaluation: Final Benefit-Cost Analysis," Manpower Demonstration Research Corporation, New York, 1981.

Kiefer, Nicholas, (1979a) *The Economic Benefits of Four Employment and Training Programs*, New York: Garland Publishing, 1979.

_____, (1979b) "Population Heterogeneity and Inference from Panel Data on the Effects of Vocational Training," *Journal of Political Economy* October 1979, *87*, S213–26.

LaLonde, Robert, "Evaluating the Econometric Evaluations of Training Programs With Experimental Data," Industrial Relations Section, Working Paper No. 183, Princeton University, 1984.

Leamer, Edward, "Let's Take the Con Out of Econometrics," *American Economic Review*, March 1983, *73*, 31–43.

_____, "Sensitivity Analysis Would Help," *American Economic Review*, June 1985, *75*, 308–13.

_____ and Leonard, Herman, "Reporting the Fragility of Regression Estimates," *Review of Economics and Statistics*, May 1983, *65*, 306–12.

McAleer, Michael, Pagan, Adrian and Volker, Paul, "What Will Take the Con Out of Econometrics?," *American Economic Review*, June 1985, *75*, 293–306.

Maddala, G. S., *Limited Dependent and Qualitative Variables in Econometrics*, Cambridge: Cambridge University Press, 1983.

Mallar, Charles, "Alternative Econometric Procedures for Program Evaluations: Illustrations From an Evaluation of Job Corps Book," *Proceedings of the American Statistical Association*, 1978, 317–21.

_____, Kerachsky, Stuart and Thornton, Craig, *The Short-Term Economic Impact of the Jobs-Corps Program*, Princeton: Mathematica Policy Research Inc., 1978.

Masters, Stanley and Maynard, Rebecca, "The Impact of Supported Work on Long-Term Recipients of AFDC Benefits," Manpower Demonstration Research Corporation, New York 1981.

Maynard, Rebecca, "The Impact of Supported Work on Young School Dropouts," Manpower Demonstration Research Corporation, New York, 1980.

Ohls, J. and Carcagno, G., *Second Evaluation of the Private Employment Agency Job Counsellor Project*, Princeton: Mathematica Policy Research Inc., 1978.

Piliavin, Irving and Gartner, Rosemary, "The Impact of Supported Work on Ex-Offenders," Manpower Demonstration Research Corporation, New York, 1981.

Stromsdorfer, Ernst et al., "Recommendations of the Job Training Longitudinal Survey Research Advisory Panel to the Office of Strategic Planning and Policy Development, U.S. Department of Labor," unpublished report, Washington, November 1985.

Abt Associates, "AFDC Homemaker-Home

Health Aid Demonstration Evaluation," 2nd Annual Report, Washington, 1984.

Manpower Demonstration Research Corporation, *Summary and Findings of the National Supported Work Demonstration*, Cambridge: Ballinger, 1983.

SRI International, *Final Report of the Seattle-Denver Income Maintenance Experiment: Design and Results*, Washington: Department of Health and Human Services, 1983.

32

Social Experimentation *and*
Social Experimentation

Robert H. Haveman

Social experimentation was a major social research innovation, introduced with the War on Poverty and pursued vigorously from 1965
through 1980; *Social Experimentation* is a review and evaluation of that
research development. In this essay, I will discuss each of these enterprises,
both of which have serious shortcomings.

I. Social Experimentation

The War on Poverty and Great Society initiative of the mid-
1960s was a major break with previous policymaking. A wide variety of
policy interventions into social affairs were undertaken to change social
positions, the nature of social interactions, and the behavior and performance of low-income people. Because U.S. policymakers had little experience in such matters and substantial uncertainty about how to proceed,
many of the interventions were called "demonstration projects." Unlike
earlier social policy efforts, they represented a major, nonmarginal, activist
attempt to alter individual behavior and economic status.

Into this environment social experimentation was born. While the U.S.
Office of Economic Opportunity (OEO) was initiating numerous demonstration projects through its Community Action Program, it was also considering a major income support proposal—a negative income tax (NIT) to
replace much of the nation's welfare system with a uniform, family-size-
conditioned income guarantee that would gradually diminish as earnings
rose above zero. The NIT would provide income support to families headed
by men as well as women, reduce large differences among the states in
benefit levels, and minimize work disincentives because dollars earned
would not result in equivalent benefits lost. Relative to the existing income
support system, the NIT was also a major break with past policy; its
adoption would have been better characterized as an "overhaul" than a
reform.

In discussions of the NIT within OEO, the work-incentive issue was
considered crucial in determining its political feasibility (Lampman 1976).
Many saw the notion of a guaranteed income as inviting large reductions in

From Robert H. Haveman, "*Social Experimentation* and Social Experimentation," *Journal of
Human Resources*, Vol. 21, pp. 586-605. Copyright © 1986 by the Board of Regents of the University
of Wisconsin System. reprinted by permission. Editor's Note: The following is a book review of a
volume by Hausman and Wise (1985) entitled *Social Experimentation*.

work effort, primarily by male adults who were the heads of families. To those involved in the debates, it was clear that the labor-supply effects of an NIT could not be adequately evaluated from existing studies based on available cross-sectional data, or from a "field test." It required an evaluation of the work-effort behavior of those covered by an NIT relative to those who were not covered; in short, a controlled experiment.

While such experiments had long been practiced in the biological sciences and psychology, for a variety of reasons—ethics, cost, complexity—this research technique had been little used by economists and other social scientists to evaluate policy interventions. Yet it had been discussed at length by some economists (Orcutt and Orcutt 1968, Rivlin 1971), and it appeared ideally suited for reliably estimating the labor-supply effects of an NIT. Relative to past social science research and research techniques, a social experiment was also a major break from past approaches to gaining policy relevant knowledge.

The idea behind a social experiment as applied to an NIT was simple: design a basic NIT and establish a set of benefit-reduction rates and income guarantees that are judged to be in the relevant range; choose a sample of households for whom a negative income tax is a viable policy option; randomly assign these households to an NIT group (the experimental group), the remainder being a control group; administer the NIT plan to households in the experimental group for some period of time; measure the work-effort patterns of those in the experimental group relative to the patterns of those in the control group; adjust for any other factors not taken into account in the experimental design; and attribute the remaining difference in labor supply to the NIT.

Lurking behind this simple idea are a wide variety of technical, empirical, and implementation issues, of which the following are the most important:

- What variables should be emphasized in the experimental design? How many combinations of income guarantees and tax rates should be tested?

- What experimental units should be included? Individuals? Couples? Intact families? Single-parent families? In what environment should the experiment be placed in order to secure the desired level of relevance and generality of results? Urban or rural areas? Large towns or small? Suburbs or inner cities?

- How large a sample is required in order to achieve acceptable levels of statistical reliability for each plan tested? How should those in the experimental group be allocated across the plans tested so as to maximize the statistically reliable information obtained, given the cost?

- What behavioral variables should be measured for units in both the experimental and control groups? Should only labor-supply responses (hours worked, weeks worked, earnings) be measured, or should a variety of other variables of interest (e.g., consumption patterns, family structure) also be measured?

• For how long should the experimental treatment be administered in order to secure a reliable measure of long-run response? One year? Three? Five?

• How is the experiment to be "fielded"—how are observation units to be chosen, enrolled, and how is the treatment to be administered? How can its administration be structured so as to minimize Hawthorne effects (positive effects resulting not from the treatment but just from the stimulation of participating in the experiment)?

• What statistical techniques are to be employed in analyzing the results of the experiment? Simple control-experimental comparisons? Complex models to reflect design characteristics of the experiment or to adjust for the self-selection of units of observation into the experiment or their attrition over the course of the experiment?

• To what extent can the observed responses of a sample of randomly selected and isolated individuals be taken as evidence of the impact of a national program?

Although the difficulties of these issues were, at some level, recognized by the economists and other social scientists who became involved in the OEO-sponsored NIT experiments of the late 1960s, the pressures of the moment propelled an experiment into the field before many of them could be adequately thought through and resolved. In 1968, the three-year New Jersey Income Maintenance Experiment enrolled 1,375 intact poor and near-poor families, each headed by a man of working age, 725 of which were randomly assigned to one of eight negative income tax plans.

The results of the experiment indicated that the response of the husbands of the families was small and not statistically significant. Wives, however, showed statistically significant and relatively large reductions in labor supply due to the experiment. Family labor supply reductions fell into the 5 to 10 percent range. In contrast with the other groups, blacks showed very little response to the NIT incentives.[1]

As the first controlled social experiment, the New Jersey project was subjected to detailed scrutiny from the research community. Within six months of the presentation of the final report on the experiment, the Brookings Institution sponsored a conference of nearly 50 social scientists and policy analysts to review the results of the experiment (Pechman and

---

1. The most comprehensive description of the experiment and evaluation of its labor supply results is Watts and Rees (1977).

Timpane 1975). Five papers were commissioned from researchers not associated with the experiment to review and evaluate the design, the analyses of
effects, and the policy implications of the experiment. In addition, an
in-depth review of the history and conduct of the experiment and an evaluation of its results was sponsored by the Russell Sage Foundation (Rossi and
Lyall 1976).

These reviews produced a wide-ranging critique, and documented concerns with a number of aspects of the experiment and its design which had
been voiced since the inception of the experiment by a variety of observers.
To some, the focus of the experiment on the labor-supply issue was too
restrictive, making the project an empirical test of micro-economic theory,
rather than an effort designed to yield policy-relevant information. The
choice of the experimental units was criticized as being too restrictive; e.g.,
little could be said about the work response of female family heads to an NIT
or to the national costs of such a program. Further, the treatments chosen
were sufficiently similar as to preclude evaluation of the relative effects of
tax rates and guarantees, and the choice of sites so restrictive as to eliminate
the possibility of generalizing the results to larger population groups. The
basic analytical criticisms were the following:

1. Limiting the eligible population in the experiment to families with
   incomes under 150 percent of the poverty line resulted in a trun-
   cated sample with important implications for achieving unbiased
   estimates of response.

2. The experiment was plagued with problems of attrition, in part
   caused by a decision by the state of New Jersey to institute a welfare
   plan for male-headed families after the start of the experiment.
   This also created substantial difficulty in achieving unbiased estimates of response.

3. The pre-experimental values of important variables related to labor
   supply (e.g., wage rates, hours worked, and earnings of all household members) were measured in less than perfect fashion in the
   survey instruments.

4. The duration of the experiment, three years, may be too short to
   enable reliable estimates of the effects of a permanent program.

The New Jersey project represented the general acceptance of large-scale
social experimentation as a valid research tool for estimating important
behavioral responses to proposed policy interventions. The fact that it was
successfully designed and fielded, and that it yielded estimated responses
that passed the scrutiny of the research community, led to a wide variety of
additional publicly funded social experiments.

Table 1 provides a listing of the most significant of these experiments, and some basic facts regarding each. The table proceeds chronologically through each category: income maintenance (1–4), labor market (8–9), and electricity pricing (10) experiments.[2]

Two developments in the evolution of the experiments described in the table are noteworthy. First, the early experiments were primarily in the income maintenance or welfare area. They were followed by experiments designed to test major alterations in the provision of education, health, and housing subsidies to low-income families. The latest experiments, beginning in the mid-1970s, emphasized the work effort and productivity effects of public employment and training interventions or the extent of electricity usage response under various utility pricing arrangements. The second development concerns the complexity of the experiments through time. While the early ones involved relatively simple treatments with relatively straightforward hypotheses to be tested, the later labor market experiments involved more complex treatments, often with several interventions designed to be mutually supporting (e.g., income support plus counseling plus training). Because these treatments were not independently assigned, the findings of these more complex experiments are difficult to interpret.

Stated in constant (1983) dollars, the ten social experiments listed in the table involved a total cost of about $1.1 billion, of which about $450 million was allocable to research and administrative costs. Relative to the total volume of annual poverty research and poverty-related research expenditures—which were in 1980 (current dollars) about $75 million and $300 million, respectively (Haveman 1986),[3] this support for social experimentation research is large indeed. A brief examination of the most significant of these projects is in order.

The Seattle-Denver income maintenance experiment was the largest and most comprehensive of the NIT experiments. Approximately 4,800 families were enrolled, and the families assigned to experimental NIT plans were potentially eligible for payments for a period of three, five, or, for a few families, 20 years. The experiment had two main goals, reflected in its rather elaborate design. The first was to determine the effect of alternative NIT plans on work effort, the same objective as that of the New Jersey experiment. The work-effort findings from the experiment (OISP 1983, Robins and West 1983) showed that the tested NIT plans caused substantially larger reductions in labor-market activity than those estimated in the New Jersey

2. Greenberg and Robins (1985), the main source for Table 1, identify, in addition to those indicated in the table, 29 social experiments in the post-1965 period with total costs of about $150 million.
3. The $75 million and $300 million estimates exclude expenditures on social experimentation. These are classified as demonstrations.

experiment, particularly for persons enrolled in longer duration (5-year) plans. Prime-aged men reduced their annual hours of work by 9 or 10 percent in response to the tested plans; their spouses reduced annual hours by 17 to 20 percent; and women heading single-parent families reduced annual hours by more than 20 percent—and perhaps by as much as 30 percent. According to simulations based on these results, replacing current cash welfare and food stamp programs with an NIT with a guarantee of three-fourths of the poverty line and a 50 percent tax rate would cost the government $1.79 in transfer outlays to raise the net income of poor two-parent families by $1.00. In other words, 44 percent of the net program costs of the NIT would be "consumed" by breadwinners in the form of leisure (Aaron and Todd 1979).[4]

The second objective of the experiment was to test the effectiveness of issuing education and training vouchers to low-income breadwinners. It found that they used much of the subsidy to pay for schooling they would have obtained in the absence of the program; moreover, there was little payoff to the incremental investment.

The National Supported Work Demonstration and the Employment Opportunity Pilot Project (EOPP) were both designed to test alternative interventions assisting hard-to-employ workers in finding jobs. The Supported Work experiment (MDRC 1980; Hollister, Kemper, and Maynard 1984) provided jobs for individuals with severe employment problems (four groups: long-term AFDC recipients, recently released convicts, former addicts, and school dropouts with delinquency records). It gave them one year of work experience under conditions of gradually increasing demands, close supervision, and in association with a crew of peers. EOPP's purpose was to estimate the employment effects of a guaranteed jobs program similar to that proposed by President Carter, as well as new approaches to job finding among the hard-core unemployed (Mathematica Policy Research 1984). It was terminated prior to its original design, and no benefit-cost appraisal was made. Neither experiment was able to claim substantial success in generating long-duration increases in employment or earnings; both were most successful with a group with high welfare incidence—single women with no recent work experience.

In terms of size and cost, the Housing Allowance Demand (Friedman and Weinberg 1982, Bradbury and Downs 1981) and Health Insurance (Newhouse et al. 1982) experiments were among the largest. Both examined families' responses to differentially subsidized prices for rental housing and health care services. They tested the efficiency of improving the economic status of low-income families through permitting them to choose between

---

4. The net program cost of the NIT is the amount by which NIT transfers exceed those now paid under the cash welfare and food stamp programs.

Table 1
The Major Social Experiments

Experiment	Date of Field Work	Final Report Date	Nature of Treatment	Response Measured	Number of Participants	Research and Administrative Costs (1983 dollars)	Total Costs (1983 dollars)
1. New Jersey Income Maintenance Experiment	1968–72	1974	NIT	Head-spouse-family labor supply	1,216 families	$15.4 million	$22.2 million
2. Rural Negative Income Tax Experiment	1970–72	1976	NIT	Head-spouse-family labor supply	809 families	$9.5 million	$15.6 million
3. Gary Income Maintenance Experiment	1971–74	—	NIT plus day care	Head-spouse-family labor supply, use of day care	1,780 families	$33.0 million	$45.2 million
4. Seattle-Denver Income Maintenance	1971–78	1983	NIT plus employment counseling and educational vouchers	Head-spouse-family labor supply, marital stability, earnings capacity	4,784 families	$97.8 million	$132.7 million
5. Education Performance Contracting	1970–71	1972	Cash payment as incentive for academic performance	Educational improvement of junior high students	19,399 students[1]	n.a.	$14.3 million
6. National Health Insurance	1974–81	n.a.	Different fee for service health insurance plans with alternative coinsurance rates and deductibles plus a prepaid group health insurance plan	Demand for health care and change in health status	2,823 families	$94.4 million	$115.0 million

7. Housing Allowances[2]	1973–77	1980	Cash housing allowance	Use of allowance; effect on quality, supply, and costs of housing; administrative feasibility	—[3]	$160.4 million	$352.2 million
8. National Supported Work Project	1975–79	1980	Temporary Public Services Employment (PSE), work discipline, and group support	Administrative costs, effects on antisocial behavior and earnings	6,606 individuals	$16.9 million[4]	$126.8 million
9. Employment Opportunity Pilot Project (EOPP)[5]	1979–81	1982	PSE preceded by required job search and training (if necessary)	Effect on welfare caseload, private sector labor market, use of program, administrative costs, and feasibility	Open to all heads of households on public assistance	n.a.	$246.0 million
10. Electricity Time-of-Use Pricing (15 Experiments)	1975–	1979–	Time-of-use electricity price schedules	Alterations in electricity use levels and patterns of residential consumers	n.a.	n.a.	≈50.0 million

Source: Greenberg and Robins (1985); author's data.

1. The number of students remaining in the program the entire school year. The initial sample comprised 24,000 students split evenly between control and experimental groups.
2. There were three different housing allowance experiments during the 1970s. They have been grouped together here for brevity.
3. One of the housing allowance experiments was open enrollment while the other two involved random selection.
4. Research only.
5. The EOPP was ended long before completion.

services provided at subsidized prices and outright public provision of the same services. The instrument was rent subsidization in the housing case, and coinsurance in the health insurance experiment. Both experiments were complex in their design, and attended mainly to the nature of demand-side responses to alternative subsidization arrangements. The housing allowance experiment had difficulties in obtaining reliable responses because only a small number of eligible households accepted the subsidies. While the health experiment also experienced design problems, it did reveal that families economize on their demand for health services when confronted with the need to pay for some fraction of the cost of the services provided.

Finally, there are the 15 time-of-use residential electricity pricing experiments which have been completed or are ongoing (Aigner 1985). The purpose of these experiments is to test the elasticity of demand of residential electricity users to price variation by time of day or season. These experiments established that usage at peak periods is responsive to prices, and that usage reductions at the peak are not fully offset by increases in off-peak usage. They support the conclusion that total electricity usage and capacity requirements can be reduced by time-specific pricing arrangements.

II. *Social Experimentation*

It was to assess this body of experimental research and evaluation that the National Bureau of Economic Research convened a conference, "Social Experimentation" in 1981. Numerous questions were addressed by the conference, and by the 1985 conference volume, edited by Jerry Hausman and David Wise. The primary ones are:

1. For the income maintenance, housing, health, and electricity pricing experiments, what are the primary objectives, design characteristics, estimation methods, and findings? What are the central weaknesses of the designs, and the potential biases affecting the estimates?

2. What is the value of the findings of the experiments in comparison to what could have been learned from existing data, and relative to the cost? What is the social willingness-to-pay for improved elasticity estimates of particular economic relationships?

3. Is there agreement among analysts regarding the optimal design of experiments, the circumstances under which they are the desired evaluation strategy, and the statistical procedures appropriate for accounting for the special issues to which social experiments give rise (sample selection, treatment assignment, and attrition)?

4. Are there net benefits attributable to the experiments, over and above their contributions to knowledge regarding behavioral responses to policy interventions?

5. Have the findings from the experiments had an influence on public policy decisions? Should policymakers be influenced by their findings?

Question 1 is the concern of the first four chapters of the volume: electricity pricing, Dennis Aigner; housing, Harvey Rosen; income maintenance, Frank Stafford; health, Jeffrey Harris. Each chapter has two discussants. In these three presentations on each experiment, questions 2 and 3 are also addressed, although often not explicitly.

Question 4 is the subject of the chapter by Hausman and Wise, the most analytical chapter in the volume. Their position is that experimental designs should be as simple as possible, testing a single behavioral response, with a large random sample of the population randomly assigned to treatment and control groups. Discussants John Conlisk and Daniel McFadden agreed with the objective of this strategy—avoidance of the difficult explanation problems posed by the endogenous stratification present in most of the past experiments—but they questioned its desirability and feasibility in real-world, budget constrained circumstances.

Question 5 is the subject of papers by Ernst Stromsdorfer and David Mundel, and each of these papers also has two discussants. An additional paper, by Frederick Mosteller and Milton Weinstein, draws from experience with medical experimentation to flesh out a framework for determining when experimentation is the optimal research strategy, and raises the important question of when and under what circumstances experimental findings are likely to influence policy choices.

Overall, the conference participants' answers to these questions make for discouraging reading. At the risk of oversimplifying, I will characterize the primary answers to the five questions in the following paragraphs.

Answering the first question requires a wealth of factual information and interpretive comment. The four experiment-specific papers provide a solid source of such material for each of the experiments discussed. Aigner's paper on the electricity pricing experiments emphasizes the differential welfare effect of time-of-use pricing on various population subgroups, and the implications of these differences on participation in a time-of-use pricing program. It is the only paper in the volume that discusses this important welfare economics and program implementation point. The Rosen paper on housing experimentation and the paper's discussants emphasize the critical problem of a short-duration experiment for analyzing the consumption of the services of a durable commodity such as housing, noting the important implications of the assumption that consumers are observed to be in equilib-

rium positions both prior to and after the experimental treatment is administered. The duration problem may well explain why the estimated income
elasticity from the experiment is at the very low end of the range of elasticities estimated from prior studies. Stafford, in dealing with the income-
maintenance experiments, makes a special contribution in emphasizing that
standard theory based on continuous supplies and linear budget constraints
may misguide the designers of experimental studies when actual work
behavior is intermittent and responds to nonconvex budgets. The Harris
paper on the health experiment seems more intent on suggesting an alternative research strategy—macro-experimentation (more on this later)—than
on describing and appraising what was actually done. While the other
experiment-specific studies compared the experimental findings to existing
estimates, the counterfactual for Harris' appraisal is some ideal, but not-yet-
observed, experiment.

It is with respect to the evaluation of the design and findings of these
experiments that one struggles against a sense of déjà vu. The book's litany
of problems and their impacts on the reliability of the empirical findings
reads like a recital of the analytical criticisms of the New Jersey experiment
that has existed informally since the inception of that experiment in 1968,
and that were documented in the formal critiques of its design and findings.
This litany includes:

1. Insufficient sample sizes, insufficient variation in the treatment
   variables, and inadequate definition of the treatment variables
   (Aigner, p. 11; Rosen, pp. 60 ff., p. 69; Stafford, pp. 102 ff.; Harris,
   p. 150).

2. Selectivity problems involving restrictions imposed on the participating population, or self-selection possibilities for participation (Aigner, p. 19; Rosen, p. 65; Stafford, pp. 97 ff.; Harris, pp.
   148 ff.).

3. Sensitivity of results to the specification of the estimating model,
   with no basis for testing the accuracy of the assumed statistical
   properties (Aigner, p. 33; Rosen, pp. 59 ff., p. 63, p. 68; Stafford,
   pp. 98 ff.; Harris, p. 152).

4. Short duration of the experiments, precluding the estimation of
   long-run impacts (Aigner, pp. 18 ff.; Rosen, pp. 64 ff.; Stafford,
   pp. 101 ff.).

5. Self-selected attrition of participants from the experiment (Aigner,
   pp. 12 ff.; Rosen, p. 65; Stafford, pp. 97 ff.; Harris, pp. 150 ff.).

6. Estimation of behavior which responds to nonconvex budget constraints and which is intermittent with simple linear constraint

models assuming continuous demands or supplies (Aigner, p. 19; Rosen, p. 63; Stafford, pp. 98 ff.; Harris, pp. 153 ff.).

7. The difficulty of estimating market effects from the individual response estimates available from micro-experiments (Aigner, p. 31; Rosen, pp. 71 ff.; Stafford, p. 103; Harris, pp. 153 ff.).

8. The presence of Hawthorne-type effects (Rosen, p. 66; Harris, pp. 151 ff.).

9. Inadequate data on both important "shift" variables and pre-experimental data on the primary response variables (Rosen, p. 66; Harris, pp. 151 ff.).

There are several explanations for this persistent catalog of problems with social experimentation, none of which are particularly encouraging. For some of these problems, the theoretical and empirical requirements for avoiding them lay beyond the financial and intellectual resources available to those who designed and fielded the experiments. These problems include nonrandom attrition from or selection into the sample, estimation of behavior given complex and ultimately unknown budget constraints, and inadequate data on the backgrounds of respondents or their previous behavior. Most of these problems, it should be noted, affect both social experimental research and standard micro-data analysis, and are typically more serious in the latter than in the former. While modeling and data collection advances have been made with respect to all of these, financial resources are scarce and the pool of technical expertise on these issues is spread thin. Progress has been painfully slow.

A second explanation is that avoiding the problems or reducing them to more tolerable levels is very costly; budget constraints imposed on each experiment resulted in the occurrence of the same set of problems, but of various intensities. The problems in this category concern deviations from the pure random assignment experimental model, and include the restrictions imposed on participating populations, inadequate sample sizes, insufficient variation in treatment variables, ad hoc specification of response models, and the short-run nature of the experiments. Presumably, these problems will exist at some level so long as constraints on social experimental research budgets exist.[5]

5. This is not to suggest that all of these problems have plagued each of the experiments with equal intensities, or that experiments with less constrained budgets were not able to reduce the problems confronted by earlier projects, or those with more binding budget constraints. Robert Moffitt has emphasized, for example, that the SIME-DIME experiment did have a much larger sample size than the New Jersey experiment, as well as cells with multiple durations, higher income truncation points, a more diverse population, and a wider range of program parameters.

Finally, the problems may have persisted because the later designers of experiments learned little from the experience of the earlier experimenters.[6] This explanation appears to have some basis, especially across the substantive areas over which experimentation was done. For example, in his discussion of the reasons for the poor designs of the electricity pricing experiments, the first of which started in 1975, Paul Joskow states:

> When the earliest experiments were structured, those involved had simply not thought very deeply about what the data generated might be used for. [They] were motivated more by narrow adversarial and litigation concerns than by an interest in sound economic analysis. . . . There was no *inherent* reason for these early experiments to have been so poorly designed (pp. 43–44).

While all of these problems cited by the authors have, to some extent, detracted from the reliability of the experimental findings, they vary widely in both their seriousness and in the extent to which they can be avoided. While some of them can be minimized by larger experimental budgets or more technical expertise (e.g., sample sizes, estimates of responses to complex budget constraints), others are not easily correctable (e.g., problems of attrition from or self-selection into the experiment).

The second question has to do with the value of the findings of the experiments relative to existing estimates, and to the costs of obtaining them. By and large, the authors of the four experiment-specific papers and their discussants did not find the experimental results to be notably more reliable than existing estimates based on cross-sectional data. For example, in assessing the findings of the housing allowance experiments, Rosen concludes that "if the goal was to obtain new and improved estimates of the behavioral responses to housing allowances, . . . the money would have been better spent on augmenting conventional data sources" (p. 72). In discussing the findings of the health insurance experiment, Harris concludes that "economists and other social scientists have spent disproportionately too much effort on the design and interpretation of microexperiments" (p. 145). And, in the case of the electricity pricing experiments, Aigner concludes that "It is difficult to summarize the empirical results . . . since the elasticity

---

6. To some extent, of course, this was unavoidable. Some of the earlier experiments—for example, SIME-DIME, housing allowances, and health insurance—were being designed prior to the formal evaluations of the design and findings of the New Jersey project. However, the basic concerns with the design of the New Jersey project were clearly debated and discussed well before the final report was published. While this timing point is surely relevant, I cannot agree with those who argue that, in fact, there has been only one phase of experimentation and that the proper question is: Given what we have learned from this first phase, would the benefits outweigh the costs of a new experiment that we would design today? I am indebted to Robert Moffitt for raising this point.

estimates frequently conflict with each other . . . no consistent overall pattern emerges" (p. 20). His discussants state this conclusion even more strongly. Finally, for the income maintenance experiments, Stafford is the most optimistic, concluding that "at a minimum, the experiments have reduced the variance of labor supply parameters, even if they have not shifted the means very much" (p. 121). Such a claim, it should be noted, is not great praise when the ten conventional male labor-supply analyses reviewed by Stafford have a range of uncompensated wage elasticities of $+.11$ to $-.55$, a range of compensated wage elasticities of $+.86$ to $-.04$, and a range of income elasticities of $-.06$ to $-.51$. It would be surprising if estimates from any new study added to this set failed to reduce the variance.[7]

These generally pessimistic conclusions, it should be noted, rest largely upon the numerous design and analysis weaknesses noted above, rather than on any comprehensive comparison of the magnitudes, the strengths, and the weaknesses of both experimental and nonexperimental estimates. When the experimental findings are set against potential estimates from some ideally designed and unflawed experiment, such an assessment is probably appropriate. However, when set against the reliability of existing estimates from nonexperimental research, this conclusion seems exaggerated. Most of the same problems affecting the experiments also plague nonexperimental empirical studies on behavioral responses, and appear in even more virulent form in such research. Moreover, nonexperimental analyses are burdened by additional problems that are at least partially avoided by the experiments. The absence of pre-observation measures of the variables of interest and the weakness of the variables available for control come immediately to mind. My own judgment is that the parameter estimates from the social experiments are, in general, more reliable than those available from nonexperimental studies. They set the standard in the labor supply, housing demand, medical demand, and electricity demand areas; they are the best game in town. Any new estimates are—and should be—judged by comparison to them. This assessment, of course, does not say that the contribution to knowledge provided by the experiments is worth the cost.

The third question concerns the lessons from the experiments for the design of future research on behavioral responses to policy incentives. In the face of the serious reservations of the conference participants regarding the findings of the experiments, it would be reassuring if there were agreement on the characteristics of the optimal research design for response estima-

---

7. Indeed, Stafford's conclusion regarding the "rather clear consensus" on labor supply parameters seems overdrawn, as has been discussed in detail by Killingsworth (1983), and noted by Sherwin Rosen in his discussion comments.

tion. With such agreement, one could anticipate that a second generation of experiments would yield more reliable results.

Jerry Hausman and David Wise present the most concrete case for an experimental research design that would minimize many of the problems that have plagued past experiments. They advocate a simple micro-experiment with few treatments, large sample sizes, and full randomization so as to avoid the need for complicated structural models based on strong and nontestable specification assumptions. While agreeing with the objective of avoiding endogenous stratification, John Conlisk finds their advice "incomplete," and "sees no reason to suppose that a good design will be the sort of simple design Hausman and Wise have in mind. Nor [does he] see a useful way to substitute simple rules of thumb . . . for a full-blown, optimal design analysis specific to the context at hand" (p. 212). While Conlisk's criticism is telling, neither he nor the authors discuss the substantial additional research costs that the proposal implies, and the trade-off between the benefits attributable to these costs and the value of other expenditures on knowledge acquisition. Given the enormous costs of the experiments, together with the design compromises which budget constraints have imposed on them, the failure to address this issue explicitly is unfortunate. Moreover, even in the pure experimental model proposed by Hausman and Wise, *unavoidable* problems of selection into and attrition from the experiment will exist. And, while they advocate a variety of sophisticated statistical techniques to correct for these problems, there is little assurance that estimates derived from them will be similar, and if not, which model is to be preferred.

Harris finds the shortfalls in the health insurance experiment to be overwhelming and offers a second design proposal: the substitution of macro-experimentation—the assignment of treatments to randomly selected groups, communities, or markets, with others, also randomly selected, serving as controls—for micro-experimentation. Larry Orr, his discussant, finds this enthusiasm for macro-experiments to be "seriously overdrawn," and cites a variety of difficulties with such an approach—cost, political feasibility (and, hence, self-selection), control and administration, and the lack of a true control group—to be sorely and unrealistically understated. One senses from reading the volume that most conference participants agreed with this critique.

The fourth question concerns the possibility of other benefits from social experimentation, given the disappointing conclusion that the response estimates—their primary purpose, output, and benefit—are not markedly more reliable than those from other studies. Indeed, conference participants attribute a variety of other "benefits" to social experimentation. Virtually all of these are side (or secondary) effects—often, unanticipated—from experimentation, and include:

1. The initiation and fostering of more thoughtful and comprehensive discussions of the policy measures under consideration (p. 48);

2. the development of economic concepts and statistical techniques which will be useful in subsequent scientific work (pp. 98 ff., 121 ff., 136);

3. increased knowledge regarding the efficient administration and monitoring of programs (pp. 56, 78);[8]

4. estimates of (or at least insights into) take-up rates to new or altered policies and hence, improved cost estimates (pp. 87, 92);

5. generation of valuable longitudinal micro-data sets enabling subsequent analyses of economic behavior (pp. 72, 78, 90, 121);

6. use of the experimentation mantle to present results regarding economic behavior that are also available from other studies in a more persuasive, convincing way (pp. 93, 251 ff.); and

7. contributions to scientific progress by pointing up behaviors inconsistent with standard theory, hence stimulating the development of new or extended theories (pp. 121 ff., 136, 138).

While many of these benefits may have accrued from the experiments, in this volume anecdotal evidence serves as the primary basis for assessing their value. Discussion of them consists of little more than a set of catalog entries. The analogy to the claims of advocates of increased space and military research is obvious, and the volume does nothing to document the gains claimed.

Moreover, while such side benefits of social experimentation can be noted, the associated costs of experimentation must also be weighed. While one is left with the impression that these secondary effects net out to be positive, that conclusion is not obvious. The substantial research resources and brainpower devoted to experimentation would have been employed in some other enterprise in the absence of this heady new social research endeavor. The secondary or side-effect benefits that would have accrued from these activities would likely have been as significant as those attributed to the experiments. These forgone side benefits are secondary costs allocable to experimentation; they fit into many of the same categories as the side benefits credited to experimentation and are equally as unmeasured and unseen. The lesson from the early benefit-cost literature could be

---

8. The monthly reporting procedure now incorporated into welfare administration legislation came directly from experience in the Rural Negative Income Tax Experiment, and has demonstrated efficiency gains in program administration and financial control.

profitably applied in this case as well: unless there are overriding considerations of asymmetric information, deviations from full employment, or other identifiable market failures, assume that the secondary benefits and costs from a public investment—anticipated or imagined—are a wash!

The final question concerns the impact of the experiments on public policy decisions. In the volume, this impact is regarded as a mixed bag. And, as with the discussion of the secondary benefits of social experimentation, the evaluation provided is anecdotal, impressionistic, and contradictory. Ernst Stromsdorfer points to both the positive effects of the income maintenance experiments on welfare policy and to noneffects elsewhere; Henry Aaron emphasizes (twice) that the "serendipitous findings of the income-maintenance and housing-allowance experiments will more than repay the U.S. Treasury the cost of the experiments in short order" (p. 276), and notes that "social experiments . . . have been a force for slowing the adoption of new policies"[9] (p. 276); Joskow points out that policymakers "do not understand what deadweight losses are, would not care much about them if they did, and, as a result, more rarified calculations are unlikely to have any policy impacts" (p. 45).

Laurence Lynn reacted strongly to this discussion of the policy impacts of experimentation: "I find this subject . . . boring. . . . [T]he number of interesting things one can say is limited. . . . [T]he interesting things have already been said quite well by others. . . . The authors reach opposite conclusions . . ." (pp. 277–78). As with the previous point, the discussion in this area seems to ignore the need for a comprehensive framework in which all effects are considered. No meaningful conclusion is possible by tracing the policy impacts of a single activity (e.g., social experimentation) in the absence of a similar tracing of the policy impacts of the forgone activities—both research and nonresearch—which would have occurred but never did. In the absence of any evidence about these offsetting effects, I find no reason to consider them anything but equal to and opposite in sign from those anecdotal impacts mentioned—in sum, again a wash. One could have expected more from this National Bureau volume.

In summary, the volume's primary value lies in the unified collection of a set of assessments of a wide range of social experiments by a well-known and highly competent group of economists and analysts. While these assessments raise few issues that have not already been exposed in more in-depth reviews (see, for example, the Brookings Institution conference volumes on social experimentation), the perspectives brought by new critics are both stimulating and provocative. The overall impression—that if the resources used for the experiments could have been reallocated among alternative

---

9. This same point has also been emphasized in Burtless and Haveman (1985) and Greenberg and Robins (1985).

social research and data collection efforts, the social payoff would likely be greater—is not a particularly satisfying one, however. A second contribution of the volume lies in the prescriptions for experimental designs which can avoid or at least mitigate some of the weaknesses of past experiments and other research on behavioral responses. While provocative, these prescriptions are also contentious.

A message which the volume conveys with persistence, if not with clarity, is that if we were seriously contemplating a new round of social experimental research today, we would do things differently and probably better than we did them before. We would be more discerning regarding the particular issues on which social experimentation would be justified, more sensitive to the interaction between the nature and design of the experiment (e.g., micro- versus macro-experimentation) and the policy question of interest, more careful in designing the experiment to avoid problems of selectivity and attrition bias and inadequate specification of treatments and response, and more thorough in administering and monitoring the implementation of the experiment. In terms of the design of micro-experiments, we would opt for simpler, less complicated treatments, and invest more in collecting pre-experimental data on the relevant aspects of behavior. While being aware of the consequences of truncating the population eligible for participation, we would not necessarily proceed to full randomization in sample selection and treatment assignment as proposed by Hausman and Wise.

The book is seriously uneven, however. For my tastes, the unsubstantiated "schmoosing" about the unintended benefits of experimentation and their impacts on policymakers which is scattered throughout the volume detracts from the substantive analyses in the book. The same holds for the 20-page discussion of essentially extraneous issues (viz., statistical decision theory, nonstandard time diary studies, and his own agenda for future labor economics research) tagged on to the end of the Stafford paper, the (in essence) reprinting of the Stromsdorfer paper on the impact of social research on policy from a 1979 volume, and inclusion of the Mosteller-Weinstein paper on evaluating how, when, where, and why to perform health care—as opposed to social—experiments. Interestingly, several of the more interesting and insightful passages in the volume are found in the discussants' comments, especially those of Joskow, John Quigley, Gregory Ingram, Orr, Aaron, and Conlisk. Finally, one might wonder why the proceedings of a 1981 conference on this important issue were not available to a general audience until 1985.

References

Aaron, H., and J. Todd. 1979. "The Use of Income Maintenance Experiment Findings in Public Policy, 1977–78." In *Industrial Relations Research Association Proceedings*, 46–56.

Aigner, D. 1985. "The Residential Electricity Time-of-Use Pricing Experiments: What Have We Learned?" In *Social Experimentation*, ed. Hausman and Wise. Chicago: University of Chicago Press, for the National Bureau of Economic Research.

Bradbury, K. A., and A. Downs, eds. 1981. *Do Housing Allowances Work?* Washington, D.C.: The Brookings Institution.

Burtless, G., and R. Haveman. 1985. "Policy Lessons from Three Labor Market Experiments." In *Employment and Training R&D: Lessons Learned and Future Directions*, ed. R. T. Robins. Kalamazoo: The Upjohn Institute.

Friedman, J., and D. Weinberg. 1982. *The Economics of Housing Vouchers*. New York: Academic Press.

Greenberg, D., and P. Robins. 1985. "The Changing Role of Social Experiments in Policy Analysis." In *Evaluation Studies Review Annual*, vol. 10, ed. L. Aiken and B. Kehrer. Beverly Hills: Sage.

Hausman, J., and D. Wise, eds. 1985. *Social Experimentation*. Chicago: University of Chicago Press, for the National Bureau of Economic Research.

Haveman, R. 1986. "The War on Poverty and Social Science Research, 1965–1980." *Research Policy* (forthcoming).

Hollister, R. G., Jr., P. Kemper, and R. A. Maynard. 1984. *The National Supported Work Demonstration*. Madison, Wis.: University of Wisconsin Press.

Lampman, R. 1976. "The Decision to Undertake the New Jersey Experiment." In *The New Jersey Income Maintenance Experiment*, D. Kershaw and J. Fair, vol. 1, *Operations, Surveys, and Administration*. New York: Academic Press.

Killingsworth, M. 1983. *Labor Supply*. Cambridge: Cambridge University Press.

[MDRC] Manpower Demonstration Research Corporation. 1980. *Summary and Findings of the National Supported Work Demonstration*. Cambridge, Mass.: Ballinger.

Mathematica Policy Research. 1984. *Final Report: Employment Opportunity Pilot Project: Analysis of Program Impacts*. Princeton, N.J.: MPR.

Newhouse, J., W. Manning, C. Morris, et al. 1982. *Some Interim Results from a Controlled Trial of Cost Sharing in Health Insurance*. Rand Report R-2847-HHS. Santa Monica, Calif.: Rand Corporation.

[OISP] Office of Income Security Policy, U.S. Department of Health and Human Services. 1983. *Overview of the Seattle-Denver Income Maintenance Experiment Final Report*. Washington, D.C.: GPO.

Orcutt, G., and A. Orcutt. 1968. "Incentive and Disincentive Experimentation for Income Maintenance Policy Purposes." *American Economic Review* 58:754–72.

Pechman, J., and M. Timpane. 1975. *Work Incentives and Income Guarantees: The New Jersey Negative Income Tax Experiment*. Washington, D.C.: The Brookings Institution.

Rivlin, A. 1971. *Systematic Thinking for Social Action*. Washington, D.C.: The Brookings Institution.

Robins, P. K., and R. W. West. 1983. "Labor Supply Response." In *Final Report of the Seattle-Denver Income Maintenance Experiment*, vol. 1, *Design and Results*. Stanford, Calif.: SRI International.

Rossi, P. H., and K. C. Lyall. 1976. *Reforming Public Welfare: A Critique of the Negative Income Tax Experiment*. New York: Russell Sage Foundation.

Watts, H., and A. Rees, eds. 1977. *The New Jersey Income-Maintenance Experiment*, vol. 2, *Labor Supply Responses*. New York: Academic Press.

33

Causal Modeling with the TETRAD Program

Clark Glymour and Richard Scheines

ABSTRACT. Drawing substantive conclusions from linear causal models that perform acceptably on statistical tests is unreasonable if it is not known how alternatives fare on these same tests. We describe a computer program, TETRAD, that helps to search rapidly for plausible alternatives to a given causal structure. The program is based on principles from statistics, graph theory, philosophy of science, and artificial intelligence. We describe these principles, discuss how TETRAD employs them, and argue that these principles make TETRAD an effective tool. Finally, we illustrate TETRAD's effectiveness by applying it to a multiple indicator model of Political and Industrial development. A pilot version of the TETRAD program is described in this paper. The current version is described in our forthcoming *Discovering Causal Structure: Artificial Intelligence for Statistical Modeling*.

1. INTRODUCTION

Linear causal models are used throughout the social sciences, in social psychology and psychometrics, in educational research, market research, epidemiology and areas of biology. One of the most challenging tasks facing researchers who use such models or theories to account for their data is to search for plausible alternatives. No conclusions can reasonably be drawn until some such search has been made, even when the researcher has in hand a theory that explains the data and fares acceptably by statistical tests. Alternative theories which do as well or better by statistical criteria might produce significantly different parameter estimates, or might exhibit different causal relations. The number of alternative models – even linear models – that might account for any body of data is typically astronomical. The problem is to devise a method which will generate most or all of the best alternatives to a given linear causal model. The practical problem is to find a procedure for locating the best alternatives which is quick, convenient, and relatively reliable. By using ideas from the philosophy of science, statistics, graph theory, and some programming approaches typical of artificial intelligence work, we think we have taken a step toward solving this problem.

This paper describes a computer program, TETRAD, that we have developed in collaboration with K. Kelly and P. Spirtes. TETRAD

From Clark Glymour and Richard Scheines, "Causal Modeling with the TETRAD Program," *Synthesis*, Vol. 68, pp. 37-63. Copyright © 1986 by D. Reidel Publishing Company. Reprinted by permission.

helps the user to find plausible alternatives to an initial linear causal model. The results obtained with the program have been impressive and surprising. The program depends essentially on three ideas. They are:

(1)   Linear causal models, or structural equation models, can be represented by directed graphs.

(2)   There is a natural correspondence between graph-theoretic properties of causal models and a principle of explanatory virtue taken from Charles Spearman and from contemporary philosophy of science.

(3)   Employing these graph-theoretic properties with principles from artificial intelligence leads to an efficient, program-mable search strategy which generates a set of alternative models which typically do well, in relation to an initial model's performance, on standard statistical tests.

2. LINEAR CAUSAL MODELS AND DIRECTED GRAPHS

Linear causal models are typically represented as systems of linear functional equations of interval scaled variables, together with statistical constraints on the joint distribution of the variables. The statistical constraints typically assume something about the form of the joint distribution (that it is multinormal, for example) and impose restrictions on means, variances or covariances. Distributional assumptions, other than the existence of second moments, do not matter to the TETRAD program. The program may be used with theories that do not assume a multinormal distribution.

Linear models are usually meant to have a causal interpretation of some kind. Causal relations are often indicated in the psychological literature by calling some variables "dependent" and others "in-dependent", and in econometrics by calling some variables "exo-genous" and others "endogenous". Many linear models are accom-panied by a directed graph which gives the causal relations explicitly. Vertices of the directed graph represent variables and a directed edge goes from vertex v to vertex u ($v \rightarrow u$) if v is claimed to have a direct effect on u. "Structural coefficients", which may be either particular numbers or algebraic labels for unknown numbers, are attached to each directed edge and are identical to the linear coefficient in the cor-responding functional equation. We call variables which are unmeasured "latent variables" or "error variables", and those which are measured we call "measured variables".

Two examples of linear causal models, including both graphs and equations, are given below. Structurally, they are typical of many measurement models in sociology, psychometrics and social psychology. Initially it may not be obvious how it is that the equations are determined from the graph, but rules which determine the connection between the graph and its associated equations are given shortly.

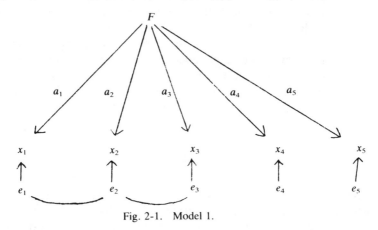

Fig. 2-1.   Model 1.

The equations for Model 1 are:

$$x_1 = a_1 F + e_1$$
$$x_2 = a_2 F + e_2$$
$$x_3 = a_3 F + e_3$$
$$x_4 = a_4 F + e_4$$
$$x_5 = a_5 F + e_5$$

or in matrix form

$$\mathbf{X} = \mathbf{A}(\mathbf{F}) + \mathbf{E}$$

Here $\mathbf{X}$ is the column vector of the x_i, $\mathbf{A}$ is the column vector of the a_i, $(\mathbf{F})$ is the matrix whose one element is F, and $\mathbf{E}$ is the column vector of e_i. To get the covariance matrix for this model we multiply each side of the matrix equation by its transpose and take the expectation value of both sides of the resulting matrix equation. (We assume that the means of all variables are zero and that F has unit variance).

The result is

$$\Sigma = \text{Exp}(\mathbf{X}\mathbf{X}^t) = \mathbf{A}\mathbf{\Pi}\mathbf{A}^t + \mathbf{T} + \text{Exp}(\mathbf{A}(\mathbf{F})\mathbf{E}^t) + \text{Exp}(\mathbf{E}(\mathbf{F})\mathbf{A}^t)$$

The graph implies (by rules we will describe shortly) that the last two terms on the right-hand side are zero. Intuitively this is because the model implies that the error terms are independent of the latent factor F. Here $\mathbf{\Pi}$ is just the one element matrix consisting of the variance of F. $\mathbf{T}$ is a symmetric matrix with nonzero diagonal and with its $(1, 2)$, $(2, 1)$, $(2, 3)$ and $(3, 2)$ members also nonzero. The independent parameters of the model consist of the five members of $\mathbf{A}$ (the a_i), the variance of F, the five diagonal members of $\mathbf{T}$ and any two independent nondiagonal nonzero members of $\mathbf{T}$. A statistical model is not yet fully determined until one specifies what family of probability distributions the parameters parametrize. If, as is commonly assumed, the distribution is multinormal, then Σ parametrizes the distributions since the means are all assumed to be zero.

To explain how it is that the graph for this model determines that these are the appropriate equations, we need two simple definitions:

Define a **PATH** from vertex u to vertex v in a directed graph to be a sequence of directed edges $u \rightarrow u_2 \rightarrow \cdots \rightarrow v$, with all arrows running in the same direction.

Define a **TREK** between u and v to be either a path from v to u, or a path from u to v, or a pair of paths from some vertex w to u and to v such that no more than one vertex occurs in both paths, or an undirected or bidirected arrow connecting u and v.

For example, in Graph 1, which we show in Figure 2-2, there are three treks between variables 2 and 3. The first is a direct edge from 3 to 2, with label y. The second is a common cause from latent variable F, with labels b and c. The third is a common cause from F through variable 1, with labels a and x on the path from F through 1 to 2, and label c on the path to 3 directly from F.

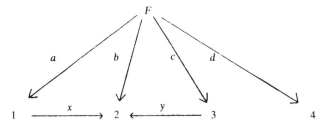

Fig. 2-2.   Graph 1.

Say that vertex *u* is *into* vertex *w* in a directed graph if and only if there is a directed edge (a single headed arrow) from *u* to *w*. The rules for determining the structural equations and statistical constraints from the graph are as follows:

(1)   Each variable *v* in the graph is a linear functional of all of the variables that are into *v*.

(2)   If there is no trek between variables *u* and *v*, then *u* and *v* are statistically independent.

(3)   Variables connected by an undirected or double headed arrow are *not* assumed to be statistically independent.

In effect, a double headed or undirected arrow signifies a covariance that receives no causal explanation in the model. These rules are illustrated in a second model, shown in Figure 2-3. The equations for

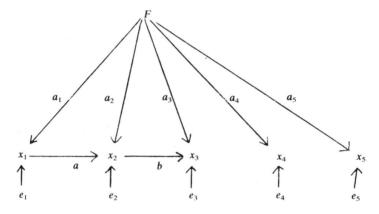

Fig. 2-3.   Model 2.

this model are:

$$x_1 = a_1 F + e_1$$
$$x_2 - ax_1 = a_2 F + e_2$$
$$x_3 - bx_2 = a_3 F + e_3$$
$$x_4 = a_4 F + e_4$$
$$x_5 = a_5 F + e_5$$

In matrix form these equations are

$$\mathbf{BX} = \mathbf{A(F)} + \mathbf{E}$$

or equivalently,

$$X = B^{-1}A(F) + B^{-1}E$$

where X is a column vector of the x_i variables, A is the column matrix of the a_i, E is the column vector of the variables e_i, and

$$B = \begin{vmatrix} 1 & 0 & 0 & 0 & 0 \\ -a & 1 & 0 & 0 & 0 \\ 0 & -b & 1 & 0 & 0 \\ 0 & 0 & 0 & 1 & 0 \\ 0 & 0 & 0 & 0 & 1 \end{vmatrix}$$

The matrix B^{-1} looks like B except that $-a$ is replaced by a and $-b$ is replaced by b and the (3, 1) element is not zero but ab. The reader can easily check that these equations are those obtained by the first of the preceding rules for reading equations from a graph. The covariance matrix is again obtained by multiplying both sides of the matrix equation by their respective transposes, and taking expectation values. This gives:

$$\Sigma = \text{Exp}(XX^t) = B^{-1}A\Pi A'B^{-1t} + B^{-1}TB^{-1t} \\ + \text{Exp}(B^{-1}E(F)A'B^{-1t}) + \text{Exp}(B^{-1}A(F)E'B^{-1t})$$

where Π is the variance matrix of F, and T is the covariance matrix of the e_i variables. The last two terms on the right vanish. That is because of rule 2 for reading equations from graphs: There is no trek between any e_i variable and F. Therefore by rule 2 F and each e_i must be statistically independent, which implies, since all variables have zero means, that the expected value of Fe_i is zero for all i. For the same reason the expected value of the product of any two distinct e_i variables is zero. All of the off-diagonal elements of T are therefore zero.

3. SEARCHING FOR ALTERNATIVE MODELS

There are many circumstances in which a theorist may have a linear causal model in mind, but should want to search for alternatives. Perhaps most commonly, a theorist has a model that fails some statistical test and wants to find a modification that will meet 0.05 muster. But even when a linear causal model passes a statistical test, good science requires a search for alternatives.[1] Otherwise, one can have little or no confidence that there are not theories which are much better than the one proposed, and which, if they had been presented, would deserve as much or more credence. A common situation of this kind concerns the determination of particular causal effects – for example, the effect of summer Head Start participation on test scores. Making a case for (or against) such an effect has too often rested on estimating a parameter representing the effect within some one linear causal model. But to be confident that there is an effect, or that there is not, one would want to know the estimates of the parameters representing the effect in each theoretically and statistically plausible model of the Head Start data, or at least in as many such models as possible. To obtain the estimates one must first locate the models.

Several procedures have been proposed for searching for alternative linear causal models, given an initial model. They include the following:

(1)   Examination of residuals. One strategy is to locate the correlation with the largest residual, and to free a structural parameter associated with the correlation of error terms for the measured variables involved in the correlation. Costner and Schoenberg [5] have shown that the strategy is, as one might expect, often misleading. A closely related strategy examines normed residuals, in which the residuals are assumed to be normally distributed and are represented in units of the variance of the distribution.

(2)   Partial derivatives of a fitting statistic. Byron [3] and in a modified form Sorbom [18], have proposed a strategy that is now embodied in the LISREL programs. The strategy is to treat a statistic as a function, for given sample S, of the fixed parameters of the model, and to consider the partial derivatives of the function with respect to each parameter. The parameter with the largest squared partial derivative (and appropriate second derivative) is freed. The strategy is embodied in LISREL V in the form of "modification indices". Sorbom noted that the strategy may be misleading because it is applied sequentially, one parameter at a time, and also because a large change in a parameter with a small partial derivative may produce better fit than a small change in a parameter with a larger partial derivative. Costner and Herting [13] have explored the limitations of this strategy,

and suggested that it is not reliable for detecting connections between indicators of a common latent variable. They also point out that it may lead to errors if it is *not* applied one parameter at a time.

(3)   Testing sub-models. For multiple indicator models, Costner and Schoenberg described a mixed strategy for specifying revisions. Part of the strategy amounted to examining two factor submodels, each with two indicators (as in Figure 4-1) and freeing the appropriate parameter in such sub-models when they fail chi square tests. Costner and Schoenberg did not propose carrying out an analogous procedure, however, for other kinds of submodels.

Any strategy for finding good alternatives to an initial model is bound to be heuristic, and that means that it is bound to fail in some circumstances. There are nonetheless some clearly desirable features we should like to have in a procedure that searches for alternatives.

(1)   The procedure should be fast enough. A researcher may be willing to spend a day or a weekend in the search for good alternative models, but not a lifetime.

(2)   The procedure should be robust. When it leads to good alternative models (including in simulated data sets, the true one) it should do so even when normality assumptions are violated.

(3)   The procedure should not be confined to the addition of one or two edges to an initial model. It should also be able to consider models that differ from an initial model by deleting directed edges or correlations or by having a quite different theoretical structure.

(4)   The procedure should in cases of difficult real data, help us to produce models that perform much better statistically than the models we propose without the help of the procedure. For difficult real data it should generate models that make correct nonstatistical predictions where those are appropriate.

(5)   The procedure should not necessarily give us a unique alternative theory when several alternatives are plausible.

(6)   The procedure should permit the user to employ his or her

knowledge of the domain to guide the search for alternative models.

(7)   By performing statistical tests on one or two appropriate models for a data set, the procedure should be calibrated so that the user has a reasonable indication of the statistical performance over suggested alternatives prior to actually estimating and testing the models.

An ideal procedure might permit us to start with an initial model, M, form a much more restricted model, M_0, and search the "space" of all models that can be obtained by freeing some of the parameters of M_0 for alternatives to M. The TETRAD program does exactly that. The program has all of the desiderata just enumerated. It can be viewed as a systematic extension of the submodel strategy suggested by Costner and Schoenberg which employs Spearman's principle as a heuristic guide.

4. CONSTRAINTS ON THE COVARIANCE MATRIX

Suppose σ_{ij} is the (i, j) element of the matrix Σ for Model 1. Recalling that F has unit variance, it is easy to verify that

$$\sigma_{ij} = a_i a_j$$

for any distinct i and j equal to 1, 3, 4 or 5 (because for these values of i, j the (i, j) elements of T are zero). It follows that this model implies that

$$\sigma_{13}\sigma_{45} = \sigma_{14}\sigma_{35} = \sigma_{15}\sigma_{34}.$$

These three equations (only two of which are independent) represent constraints on the covariance matrix. The constraints are determined by the particular model. Thus Model 2 does *not* imply that the first term in the triple of equalities above is equal to the other two. The models are not equivalent. Constraints of this form were called **tetrad equations**[2] by Charles Spearman [19], for an obvious reason, and we will retain his terminology.

Constraints on the covariance matrix represent claims that a model or theory makes about the domain to which it is applied. Nothing guarantees us a priori that the covariance values we find upon measuring the variables will be in agreement with these constraints. If, however, the model is literally true, then the population covariances must satisfy the constraints the model implies. Such constraints are routinely called "overidentifying constraints" in the social science literature, because they usually indicate that the model implies that there is more than one way to estimate or identify structural parameters in the model [6, 8]. For testing a model and for comparing the adequacy of alternative models, however, the important thing is that *these implications of a model establish constraints on measurable features of the population.* For structural equation models of the kind treated by TETRAD, these are restrictions on covariances.

Constraints on covariances may take several forms, including:

(1)   That certain covariances vanish.
(2)   That certain covariances are equal to one another.
(3)   That certain partial correlations vanish.
(4)   That certain partial correlations are equal to one another.
(5)   Tetrad equations, i.e., equations of the form $\rho_{12}\rho_{34} - \rho_{13}\rho_{24} = 0$.
(6)   Higher order equations, e.g., sextet equations.

For multiple indicator models, tetrad equations are the most commonly occurring, and therefore the most important, kind of constraint. For models in which few or no measured variables depend on latent variables, however, vanishing partial correlations are usually more frequent [2], although such models can also imply tetrad constraints. Higher order constraints certainly can arise in multiple indicator models, but they are not so numerous as tetrad constraints.

4.1. *The Directed Graph Representation*

Representing causal models as directed graphs allows us to easily compute which tetrad equations a model implies. The rules for calculating the correlations and thus the tetrad equations implied by a graph are given by Heise [12]. Any trek between two measured variables contributes to the correlation between them. The exact contribution from any trek is the product of the edge labels, or linear coefficients, along that trek. The correlation between any two measured variables is just the sum of the contributions from each distinct trek. Consider a simple model, Graph 2, represented as a direct graph in Figure 4-1.

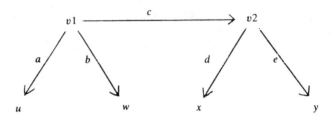

Fig. 4-1.   Graph 2.

If all variables are standardized, then

$$\rho_{uw} = ab \qquad \rho_{xy} = de$$
$$\rho_{ux} = acd \qquad \rho_{wy} = bce$$
$$\rho_{uy} = ace \qquad \rho_{wx} = bcd$$

Thus

$$\rho_{ux}\rho_{wy} = \rho_{uy}\rho_{wx}$$

reduces to

$$(acd)(bce) = (ace)(bcd)$$

an algebraic identity that must hold no matter what the values of a, b, c, d, and e may be.

In contrast, the equation

$$\rho_{uw}\rho_{xy} = \rho_{ux}\rho_{wy}$$

reduces to

$$(ab)(de) = (acd)(bce)$$

which will only hold if either one of a, b, d, e is 0, or if $c = 1$. We say that the graph **implies** the equation

$$\rho_{ux}\rho_{wy} = \rho_{uy}\rho_{wx}$$

but does **not imply** the equation

$$\rho_{uw}\rho_{xy} = \rho_{ux}\rho_{wy}$$

or the equation

$$\rho_{uw}\rho_{xy} = \rho_{uy}\rho_{wx}$$

Suppose, however, that we add an edge to Graph 2 in Figure 4-1 and thus had Graph 3 which we picture in Figure 4-2.

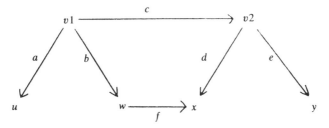

Fig. 4-2.   Graph 3.

In this case,

$$\rho_{uw} = ab \qquad\qquad \rho_{xy} = de + ecbf$$
$$\rho_{ux} = acd + abf \qquad \rho_{wy} = bce$$
$$\rho_{uy} = ace \qquad\qquad \rho_{wx} = bcd + f$$

Thus

$$\rho_{ux}\rho_{wy} = \rho_{uy}\rho_{wx}$$

reduces to

$$(acd + abf)(bce) = (ace)(bcd + f)$$

which is only an identity for particular values of a, b, c, d, e, and f. Thus by adding the edge from w to x we have defeated the implication of the tetrad equation implied by the same graph without that edge. It can be shown[3] that the standardization assumption is unnecessary.

The tetrad equations implied by a model are determined solely by the directed graph.

4.2. *Tetrad Residuals*

Given a linear causal model M and an empirical covariance matrix, S, determined from a sample, we can ask how close S comes to satisfying the constraints that M implies on the covariances. For example, if the constraints are of tetrad form, and σ_{ij} are the members of S and

$$\rho_{ij}\rho_{kl} = \rho_{ik}\rho_{jl}$$

is a constraint implied by the model, we can measure how closely S satisfies the constraint by the *squared tetrad residual*

$$T^2(ijkl, ikjl) = (\sigma_{ij}\sigma_{kl} - \sigma_{ik}\sigma_{jl})^2.$$

We refer to the positive square root of the squared tetrad residual simply as the **tetrad residual**. The sum of all tetrad residuals, **TTR** (total tetrad residual), over all constraints implied by the model M is one measure of how poorly the model fits the data.

We can also use the tetrad residual to determine if there are any equations that "hold" in the data, even though they are not implied by the current model. If the tetrad residual for any equation is small enough, it is natural to suppose that the tetrad equation is approximately true in the population. In the version of the TETRAD program we describe in this paper, this inference is not statistical. (For a description of the current version of the program, see our *Discovering Causal Structure: Artificial Intelligence for Statistical Modeling*). For computational efficiency and greater flexibility we use a purely heuristic criteria. We allow the user to specify a parameter, **delta**, between 0 and 1, which TETRAD uses to decide if an equation "holds" in the data.

TETRAD computes all of the tetrad equations implied by a linear causal model, the tetrad residual of each such equation, all of the tetrad equations that hold to within (a function of) delta, and the sum (TTR) of the tetrad residuals of all of the equations implied by the model. All of this information is available to the user. It then uses this information to search for revisions of the model it was given.

5. SCIENTIFIC EXPLANATION AND SPEARMAN'S PRINCIPLE

The most abstract principles of scientific explanation should apply in common to the social and to the natural sciences. What differs is the mathematical setting and the substance, not the form of a good explanation. Philosophers of science have repeatedly pointed out that scientific explanation addresses both particular facts and regularities or patterns in the data. Thus Newtonian gravitational theory explained those regularities of planetary motion that we call Kepler's laws, and Dalton's atomic theory explained regularities such as the law of definite proportions. Philosophers and historians of science have also suggested various forms for the explanation of regularities or patterns in the data, forms that are supposed to be characteristic of good scientific explanations [4, 7, 16, 17]. The details of philosophical explication are not pertinent here, but one version of an explanatory principle could be crudely described as follows:

Other things being equal, if one theory implies a pattern in the data for all values of its free parameters, and another theory implies that pattern only for specific values of its free parameters, the first theory provides a better explanation of the pattern than does the second theory.

Refinements of this explanatory principle have been used to explicate the superior explanations of planetary regularities provided by Copernican astronomy as against Ptolemaic astronomy in the 16th and 17th centuries, the explanatory superiority of atomic chemistry in the 19th century, and the superior explanation of anomalies of planetary motion given by general relativity early in this century.

The same principle applies to linear causal models. Consider Models 1 and 2 again.[4] Suppose that in the sample from a population to which the theories are applied one finds that

$$\sigma_{13}\sigma_{45} = \sigma_{14}\sigma_{35}.$$

Both Model 1 and Model 2 are consistent with this constraint, but only Model 1 implies the constraint no matter what the values of its free parameters may be. Model 1 provides a better explanation of the constraint than does Model 2. In general:

Other things being equal, a linear causal model that implies a tetrad equation for all values of its free parameters provides a better explanation of that tetrad equation than does a model that implies the equation only for particular values of its free parameters.

We call this preference "Spearman's Principle" since it was the basis for Spearman's "tetrad method" which was influential in psychometrics prior to the development of factor analysis [20]. Spearman's method and his principle ceased to have an explicit influence on causal modeling largely because of computational difficulties [11], which the digital computer has since removed.

Assuming Spearman's principle, if a model is to be revised to prevent the implication of tetrad equations that *do not* hold in the data, then one must prefer those revisions that do not prevent the implication of tetrad equations that *do* hold in the data. Since however, tetrad equations or other constraints rarely hold exactly in any sample data (or in a population, for that matter) the principle can only be used effectively if some approximation criterion is employed to separate tetrad equations that are to be counted as holding (because they hold closely enough) from tetrad equations that are not counted as holding. So understood, Spearman's principle represents a powerful heuristic principle in the search for good linear causal models. TETRAD makes full use of the principle.

6. TETRAD'S SEARCH STRATEGY

At present, TETRAD only considers revisions of an initial model which add edges to the graph, or in the statistical representation, revisions which free structural parameters originally fixed at 0. In practice this is a minor limitation. One can always start with a graph which has a small number of edges and work towards models with more elaborate causal structure. The search problem is then roughly as follows: Which sets of edges, when added to the initial model, will produce the most plausible elaborations. Any attempt to survey the possibilities by hand is clearly hopeless.

TETRAD uses Spearman's principle to search for elaborations of an initial model. The program considers additions to the graph which will defeat the implication of false equations while not defeating the implication of true ones. It does this by first identifying the edges which will defeat the implication of any tetrad equations that hold in the data to within the user specified parameter, delta. We call the set of such edges *DP* (dontpick). If delta is set tolerantly, so a relatively large number of tetrad equations are counted as "holding" in the data, this set of edges will be large. It then eliminates any edge in *DP* from further consideration, thus narrowing the search space.

The number of edges remaining as candidates for addition might still be large. A search through different subsets of these edges for the most plausible elaborations of the initial model might still be prohibitive. TETRAD's search strategy is essentially to solve a big problem by splitting it into many small ones. TETRAD looks at sub-models of the original graph which have precisely four measured variables. TETRAD considers all distinct subgraphs which contain only four measured variables and their adjacent latent variables as vertices, and all the causal connections found among these vertices in the original graph. For a graph with 7 measured variables there are only 35 such subgraphs. Within each subgraph, there are only a few candidates TETRAD need choose between. This is easily done by classifying the subgraph according to a pattern matching algorithm and then going to a lookup table to find which edges will defeat the appropriate equations. All that remains is to combine the information TETRAD has gathered for the local subgraphs into global information about the whole graph.

7. TETRAD'S OUTPUT

To use TETRAD the program must be supplied with the directed graph of a linear causal model, covariance or correlation data for variables with approximately zero means, and a value between 0 and 1 for the approximation parameter, delta. The space of alternative models through which the program searches is bounded by the model that is given to the program: it searches only for alternatives that result from adding edges to the initial model. Thus if one has a model such as Model 1 above and one wants to find alternatives to it, one doesn't just give Model 1 to TETRAD. Instead one gives TETRAD a model that has more parameters fixed at 0 than does Model 1. That means a model whose graph has fewer directed and undirected edges. We recommend giving TETRAD initial models in which every measured variable depends on one and only one latent variable, and in which there is no directed edge or correlation between two measured variables. We call such graphs *skeletal*.

TETRAD calculates

(1)   All of the tetrad equations implied by the initial model.
(2)   All of the tetrad equations that hold in the data to within (a function of) delta.

(3)   The tetrad residual for each tetrad equation implied by the initial model.

(4)   The sum of the tetrad residuals, or *TTR*, for the entire model.

(5)   For each pair of measured variables, how much the sum of tetrad residuals for the entire model will be reduced if the model is modified by the addition of a trek between those measured variables, as well as how much two other indicators of a model's performance, $D+$ and $D-$, will change.

(6)   Sets of suggested additions to the model.

7.1. *Sets of Suggested Additions*

All of the information except for the suggested additions to the model may be obtained for the directed graph of any recursive linear causal model with standardized variables, or for any multiple indicator model with standardized latent variables and with measured variables having zero means. The set of suggested additions is appropriate only for multiple indicator models, and for a few other cases.

The suggested additions may be either connections between measured variables or connections between latent and measured variables. At present TETRAD only considers connections between latent and measured variables to be *from* the latent variable to the measured variable. We denote this kind of suggestion with a "→" in TETRAD's output. Suggested connections between measured variables are ambiguous as to causal direction, so we denote them with a "−". (See section 9.) The additions are found using Spearman's principle. Call a tetrad equation "false" if it does not hold in the data to within (a function of) delta, and "true" otherwise. Each set of suggested additions has the following property:

If the initial model is altered so that a trek is added connecting any pair of variables occurring in a set of suggested additions, and the alterations do not produce a trek connecting any other pair of measured variables, then the modified model will entail all of the true tetrad equations that the initial model does and the modified model will not entail some of the false tetrad equations implied by the initial model.

Each set of suggested edges is as large as it can be for this property. The simultaneous addition of any further treks will not prevent the entailment of any further false tetrad equations unless it also prevents the entailment of true tetrad equations. TETRAD can give the user several alternative sets of suggested additions. Within any set, not all of the suggestions are equally important, but the user can gain an indication of the importance of particular suggestions by looking at the table which shows how much the tetrad residuals will be decreased by particular additions. There is no obligation that the user consider all of the suggestions in any particular set.

How good an alternative model turns out to be depends not only on what pairs of variables are connected by new treks, but also on how the treks work together. If the initial model is the skeleton of Model 1 then both Model 1 and Model 2 are ways of establishing extra treks (hence extra contributions to covariance) between variables 1 and 2 and variables 2 and 3. But Model 2 differs from Model 1 in also establishing a trek between variable 1 and variable 3. Users can easily compare how well alternative ways of introducing treks will perform by running TETRAD on the alternatives and looking at the TETRAD residuals.

Exactly as with indices of fit [1, 14], the TETRAD residuals are not in the usual sense a statistic. They are not sensitive, for example, to sample size. Thus there is no way to tell, a priori, what a unit change in the tetrad residual means in terms of a change in the probability of the chi square statistic. By using TETRAD together with an estimation and testing package such as LISREL, however, it is straightforward to get a useful approximate calibration of the tetrad residuals. Suppose one has a model M with a chi square probability greater than zero. Running TETRAD on M, one gets its tetrad residuals. One can be pretty confident that any model with the same or fewer free parameters and a smaller sum of tetrad residuals will have a chi square statistic with a higher probability. If one has two nested models differing by a single parameter, one can run LISREL and TETRAD on both of them to estimate how much the addition of a parameter must reduce the sum of tetrad residuals in order to preserve or improve the probability of the chi square statistic.

Once one has a feel for the connection between tetrad residuals, the number of free parameters, and the chi square probability for a particular data set, it is easy to use TETRAD to explore for alternative models that have different theoretical causal assumptions (and thus a different causal skeleton and different choice of M_0) from the model with which the theorist began.

7.2. *Other Information*

The output of which equations are implied and held is straightforward. TETRAD forms a separate row for each foursome and enters the appropriate equations under columns labeled "Implied" and "Held". If an equation appears in one side of a row and not in another, then there is a discrepancy between the model's implications and what TETRAD considers as holding in the data. The output of the tetrad residual is equally straightforward. TETRAD lists each equation implied by the model and its residual on a single horizontal row, making the information easy to recover and use.

TETRAD records the **number** of equations which show a discrepancy between what the model implies and what holds in the data. We call the number of equations that a model implies which are not considered to hold in the data **D+**, and the number of equations which do hold in the data but are not implied by the model **D−**.

TETRAD also provides the user with a chart for comparing the relative worth of single trek additions. This chart supplies three pieces of information. First, it tells the user how much TTR will be reduced by adding a single trek to the graph between two variables, called the $Rttr$ value. Second, it tells the user how much $D+$ will be reduced by adding a single trek to the graph between two variables, called the $RD+$ value. Third, it indicates how much $D−$ will be augmented by the same addition, called the $RD−$ value.

We give illustrations of TETRAD's output for $D+$, $D−$, TTR, and sets of suggested additions in the case analysis that follows the next section.

8. HEURISTICS

At present, TETRAD is far from automatic. The user must employ considerable judgment in the course of an analysis. We use the program in conjunction with the following heuristics:

(1)   Eliminate all of the variables that are irrelevant to TETRAD. (These include all variables that have zero indegree and unit outdegree, typically error variables.)

(2)   Proceed in a tree-like search for single edges, depth first. That is, find what is the "best" single edge to add among a

set of candidates. Add it, and find what is the "best" addition to the already revised model, etc.

(3)   Begin with a small (e.g., 0.05) value of delta and increase it until the sets of suggested treks each contain no more than a few treks, even as few as one or two.

(4)   Consider suggested edges from latent variables to measured variables before considering suggested edges from measured variables to measured variables. If the skeleton contains two or more latent variables and no treks from latent to measured variables are suggested, lower delta slightly and see if such treks occur among the recommendations. If so first add the latent to measured edges that are most commonly suggested and most robustly suggested.

(5)   For treks between pairs of measured variables, prefer those treks that have the smallest value of $RD-$ and the largest values of $Rttr$ and $RD+$. Prefer those treks that occur most frequently among the sets of suggested treks at low values of delta.

(6)   If you are considering adding two treks which share a vertex, e.g., 2-3 and 3-4, find out whether or not the trek linking the two unshared vertices, e.g., 2-4, is also desirable to add. If so, add two treks between 2-3 and 3-4 which also produce a trek between 2-4 (e.g., $2 \rightarrow 3$ $3 \rightarrow 4$). If not, add two treks between 2-3 and 3-4 which do not produce a trek between 2-4 (e.g., $2 \rightarrow 3$ $3 \leftarrow 4$).

(7)   Examine the TTR values of the different combinations of ways of adding suggested treks. Prefer those combinations with the lowest TTR values.

9. TETRAD IN SOCIOLOGY: COSTNER AND SCHOENBERG'S MODEL

In 1973, H. Costner and R. Schoenberg proposed a method for identifying multiple indicator misspecifications that is at its core similar to the one TETRAD embodies. They illustrated their technique with a model of Industrial and Political Development.

Costner and Schoenberg consider the model in Figure 9-1. In this model, GNP is gross national product, Energy is the logarithm of total energy consumption in megawatt hours per capita, Labor is a labor force diversification index, Exec is an index of executive functioning, Party is an index of political party organization, Power is an index of power diversification, and CI is the Cutright Index of political representation.

Using their revision procedure, Costner and Schoenberg arrive at the

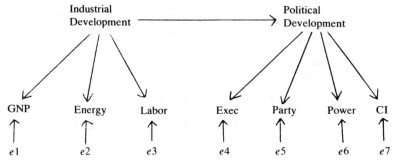

Fig. 9-1. Costner and Schoenberg's initial model.

following modified model in Figure 9-2. The revised model has a chi square of 19.5 with 10 degrees of freedom. The probability of the statistic on the model is 0.034. (Costner and Schoenberg give the model 11 degrees of freedom and $p = 0.053$, presumably because they fix the coefficient of one indicator of political development at unity.) The fit is marginal. One might want to know if there are good alternatives to this model or if its fit can be improved by adding further connections. To answer these questions we begin with Costner and Schoenberg's initial model, which is already skeletal.

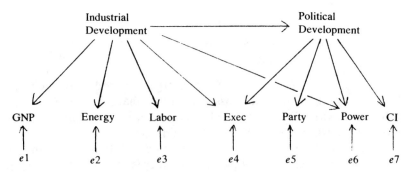

Fig. 9-2. Costner and Schoenberg's revised model.

We first get rid of all of the variables that are irrelevant to TETRAD. In this case that includes all of the error variables and the exogenous source of variance in Political Development. This leaves us with a theoretically plausible skeleton, numbered as in Figure 9-3.

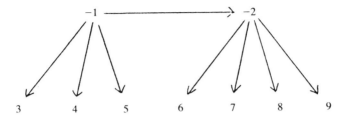

Fig. 9-3.   Costner and Schoenberg numbered skeleton.

The correlations given to the TETRAD program are in Figure 9-4. We begin our search for elaborations of the skeleton by starting with a small (e.g., 0.05) value of delta, and increasing it until each set of suggested treks contains only a few treks.

Generally, if one starts with small values of delta, the size of the suggested sets will decrease as delta increases. The edges that continue to be suggested as delta increases are the most robust. That is, they prevent the implication of the most wildly false tetrad equations implied by the skeleton, but do not prevent the implication of any tetrad equations implied by the skeleton that hold even to a weak approximation.

	4	5	6	7	8	9
3	0.95	0.83	0.66	0.56	0.45	0.67
4		0.83	0.70	0.54	0.38	0.66
5			0.62	0.54	0.38	0.61
6				0.47	0.45	0.60
7					0.64	0.64
8						0.67

Fig. 9-4.   Costner and Schoenberg correlations.

For this case, the relevant part of TETRAD's output is as in Figure 9-5. $D+$ for this model is quite poor at 52, but $D-$ is quite good at only

1. We have a *TTR* value for the skeleton (M_0) of 5.3. The skeleton gives a chi square value with essentially zero probability.

The suggested sets don't contain more than four treks each, but delta is still quite low and we might well reduce the sets to just a few treks if we run TETRAD at higher values of delta. It turns out that the sets

The graph analyzed in this example was:

$1 \rightarrow 2$ $1 \rightarrow 3$ $1 \rightarrow 4$ $1 \rightarrow 5$ $2 \rightarrow 6$ $2 \rightarrow 7$ $2 \rightarrow 8$ $2 \rightarrow 9$

elta was: $5.0E - 02$

Sets of suggested treks

{6-8	7-8	7-9	8-9}
{1→8	7-8	7-9	8-9}
{1→6	6-8	7-8	7-9}
{1→6	6-8	7-8	8-9}
{1→6	6-8	7-9	8-9}
{1→8	6-8	7-8	7-9}
{1→8	6-8	7-9	8-9}
{1→6	1→8	6-8	7-8}
{1→6	1→8	7-8	7-9}
{1→6	1→8	7-8	8-9}
{1→6	1→8	6-8	8-9}
{1→6	1→8	7-9	8-9}

The Total Tetrad Residual, or *TTR*, is: $5.3E + 00$.

The total number of equations implied by the model which do not hold in the data, or $D+$, is: 52.

The total number of equations which hold in the data but which are not implied by the model, or $D-$, is: 1.

The number of equations which hold in the data is 18.

The number of equations explained by this model is 17.

Fig. 9-5.   Costner and Schoenberg output at 0.05.

remain the same until delta is at 0.071, in which case TETRAD gives the set of suggested treks shown in Fig. 9-6. (The values of the Tetrad Residuals are of course unaffected by the choice of delta.)

If we increase delta to 0.072 one further equation holds in the data and the set of suggested treks becomes:

{7-8}

For higher values of delta the sets vanish because it is impossible to defeat the implication of any false equations without defeating true ones. As it stands so far the edge $1 \to 8$ and the trek between 7-8 are our best candidates for addition.

In accordance with our heuristics, we consider suggested edges from

Sets of suggested treks
_____

$\{1 \to 8 \quad 7\text{-}8\}$

The total number of equations implied by the model which do not hold in the data, or $D+(T)$, is: 45.

The total number of equations which hold in the data but are not implied by the graph, or $D-(T)$, is: 1.

The number of equations which hold in the data is 25.

The number of equations explained by this model is 24.

Fig. 9-6.   TETRAD's output for Costner and Schoenberg at 0.071.

latent variables to measured variables before considering suggested treks from measured variables to measured variables.

The reason for this recommendation is that an edge from a latent variable to a measured variable will typically do more good than an edge from a measured variable to a measured variable, especially when the additions are made to a skeleton. For example, the edge from Industrial Development to Power $(1 \to 8)$ creates an extra trek from all three of the indicators of Industrial Development (3, 4, 5) to Power (8). This one additional edge therefore prevents the implication of several tetrad equations that are implied by the skeleton and are false, but it does not prevent the implication of any tetrad equations that are true (otherwise TETRAD would not have suggested it). Adding a latent to measured edge will typically do more to reduce the TTR value than will the addition of any single directed edge between measured variables.

The edge $1 \to 6$ occurs frequently in the sets of suggested treks at lower (0.05) values of delta, as does $1 \to 8$. Adding both $1 \to 6$ and $1 \to 8$ gives the best performance of any model which adds two deges to the skeleton; it reduces the TTR from 5.3 to 1.1, and $D+$ from 52 to 20 while leaving $D-$ at 1. Translating, we see that edges $1 \to 6$ and $1 \to 8$ are the same edges that Costner and Schoenberg include in their model shown in Figure 9-2.

TABLE 9-1.

Edge addition				TTR	$D+$	$D-$	Δ	Π	$p(X^2)$
None (skeleton)				5.30	51	1	0.00	0.00	0.000
$1\to8$				2.90	34	1	0.45	0.40	
$7\to8$				3.30	38	1	0.37	0.33	
$8\to7$				3.30	38	1	0.37	0.33	
$1\to8$	$7\to8$			2.10	26	1	0.60	0.48	
$1\to8$	$8\to7$			1.70	22	3	0.67	0.54	
$1\to8$	$1\to6$			1.10	20	1	0.79	0.60	0.034
$1\to8$	$1\to6$	$8\to7$		0.68	15	3	0.87	0.61	
$1\to8$	$1\to6$	$2\to3$		0.60	10	9	0.886	0.620	0.118
$1\to8$	$1\to6$	$2\to4$		0.56	10	9	0.890	0.623	0.220
$1\to8$	$1\to6$	$2\to5$		0.66	12	11	0.875	0.612	0.029
$1\to8$	$1\to6$	$2\to4$	$8\to7$	0.25	4	12	0.95	0.57	

But we can do better with TETRAD's help. Lowering delta still further, to 0.03, we find that TETRAD's sets of suggestions include edges from Political Development (2) to each of the indicators of Industrial Development (1). The effect on the values of TTR, $D+$, $D-$ of various ways of realizing these suggestions is charted in Table 9-1.

TETRAD's portion of this table took us less than 20 minutes to compute. Δ is Bentler and Bonett's "Normed Index of Fit", using Tetrad Residuals. Π is the "parsiomony index" of James, et al., where the degrees of freedom of the skeleton have been set equal to 10. The X^2 values were calculated by using LISREL IV [15]. We note that the value of Π is a good indicator of goodness of fit, when combined with the TTR, $D+$ and $D-$ values. More simply, when models have the same number of degrees of freedom, the probability of the X^2 increases in every case as TTR decreases.

In this case, one of TETRAD's suggestions agrees with that of LISREL IV: the latter program recommends freeing the parameter in Costner and Schoenberg's model which corresponds to the numbered edge $2\to4$. What TETRAD gives us is not only Costner and Schoenberg's revised model but a much fuller sense of the explanatory possibilities based on the initial skeleton.

This is only one example, and an easy one at that. TETRAD has enabled us to find improved models for a number of other data sets, including data from the Head Start program [9] and data from social psychology [10]. One moral of the program is that science with artificial intelligence assistance can sometimes be better than science without it. Another moral, we hope, is that philosophy of science can have a benign influence not just on scientific rhetoric, but also on scientific practice.

NOTES

[1] Linear theories almost always fail statistical tests of high power against all alternatives.
[2] Tetrad equations involve products of correlations among a set of four variables. There are three possible products of correlations which involve all and only those four variables. For example, if the four variables are w, x, y, and z, then the three possible correlation products are

$$\rho_{wx}\rho_{yz}$$
$$\rho_{wy}\rho_{xz}$$
$$\rho_{wz}\rho_{xy}$$

There are three possible tetrad equations in a set of four variables, two of which are independent. They are

$$\rho_{wx}\rho_{yz} = \rho_{wy}\rho_{xz}$$
$$\rho_{wy}\rho_{xz} = \rho_{wz}\rho_{xy}$$
$$\rho_{wz}\rho_{yz} = \rho_{wz}\rho_{xy}$$

[3] See our *Discovering Causal Structure*, Academic Press, forthcoming.
[4] See section 2.

REFERENCES

[1] Bentler, P.: 1980, 'Multivariate Analysis with Latent Variables: Causal Modeling,' *Annual Review of Psychology* **31**, 419–56.
[2] Blalock, Hubert M.: 1961, *Causal Inferences in Nonexperimental Research*, The University of North Carolina Press, Chapel Hill.
[3] Byron, R.: 1972, 'Testing for Misspecification in Econometric Systems Using Full Information', *International Economic Review* **28**, 138–151.
[4] Causey, Robert L.: 1977, *Unity of Science*, D. Reidel Publishing Company.
[5] Costner, H. and Schoenberg, R.: 1973, 'Diagnosing Indicator Ills in Multiple Indicator Models', in Goldberger, A. and Duncan, O. (eds.), *Structural Equation Models in the Social Sciences*, Seminar Press, New York.
[6] Fisher, F.: 1966, *The Identification Problem in Economics*, McGraw-Hill, New York.
[7] Glymour, C.: 1979, 'Explanations, Tests, Unity, and Necessity', *Nous* **14**, 31–50.
[8] Glymour, C.: 1980, 'The Good Theories Do', in *Construct Validity in Psychological Measurement*, U.S. Office of Personnel Management and Educational Testing Service.
[9] Glymour, C., Scheines, R., Kelly, K., and Spirtes, P.: 1984, 'Computer Aided Theory Specification and the Evaluation of Head Start', Submitted to *Educational Evaluation and Policy Analysis*.

[10] Glymour, C. and Scheines, R.: *Discovering Causal Structure: Artificial Intelligence for Statistical Modeling*. Forthcoming, Academic Press.

[11] Guilford, J.: 1936, *Psychometric Methods*, McGraw-Hill, New York.

[12] Heise, D.: 1975, *Causal Analysis*, John Wiley & Sons, New York.

[13] Herting, J. and Costner, J.: 1985, *Respecification in Multiple Indicator Models*, Forthcoming.

[14] James, L. et al.: 1982, *Causal Analysis: Assumptions, Models and Data*, Sage Publications, Beverley Hills.

[15] Joreskog, K. and Sorbom, D.: 1978, *LISREL IV – User's Guide*, International Educational Services, Chicago.

[16] Riddell, R. C.: 1980, 'Parameter Disposition in Pre-Newtonian Planetary Theories', *Archive for History of Exact Sciences* **23**, 87–157.

[17] Rosenkrantz, R.: 1977, *Inference, Method and Decision*, D. Reidel, Dordrecht, Holland.

[18] Sorbom, D.: 1975, 'Detection of Correlated Error in Longitudinal Data', *British Journal of Mathematical and Statistical Psychology* **28**, 138–151.

[19] Spearman, Charles: 1904, 'General Intelligence Objectively Determined and Measured', *American Journal of Psychology* **15**, 201–293.

[20] Spearman, C.: 1914, 'The Theory of Two Factors', *Psychological Review* **21**, 101–111.

Department of Philosophy
Carnegie-Mellon University
Pittsburgh, PA 15213
U.S.A.

and

Department of History and Philosophy of Science
University of Pittsburgh
Pittsburgh, PA 15260
U.S.A.

34

Review of Developments in Meta-Analytic Method

Robert L. Bangert-Drowns

It is easy to observe that meta-analysis is quickly establishing itself as a useful tool for the social sciences. Perusal of representative journals confirms that meta-analysis has been applied in various ways to diverse literatures. It is imperative, therefore, that reviewers, publishers, consumers, and critics of these reviews be best informed about the method. It is especially important to clarify exactly what the term "meta-analysis" describes. In this article I propose a clarification in two ways. First, a brief history of meta-analysis is given. Second, five different approaches to meta-analytic method are distinguished and suggestions for their use are offered.

When Glass (1976) first coined the term *meta-analysis*, he meant it to refer to no new or specific technique. Instead, Glass advocated the application of familiar experimental methodologies to summarize research findings in the social sciences. As he put it later, " 'Meta-analysis' is nothing more than the attitude of data analysis applied to quantitative summaries of individual experiments . . . it is not a technique; rather it is a perspective that uses many techniques of measurement and statistical analysis" (Glass, McGaw, & Smith, 1981, p. 21).

Recently, there has been disagreement over what exactly constitutes meta-analysis. For example, Hunter, Schmidt, and Jackson (1983) have referred to their meta-analytic work as "state-of-the-art meta-analysis . . . the most complete meta-analysis procedure now known" (p. 140). Hedges and Olkin (1982) regard Glass's original formulation as outdated and present what they believe to be a more technically adequate form. Glass has recently restated his confidence in his original formulation of meta-analysis and called for greater specificity in the use of the term (Glass & Kleigl, 1983).

These disagreements only further obscure what was ironically intended to be a tool of clarification. Readers, researchers, editors, and research reviewers need to be better informed if they are to be intelligent consumers and critics of meta-analytic reviews. Meta-analysis is becoming an increasingly commonplace tool of social science. J. A. Kulik (1984) estimates that about 300 meta-analyses have already been conducted. Despite the increase in meta-analytic literature, S. E. Jackson (1984) found that only 33% of a sample of *Psychological Bulletin* authors described themselves as fairly familiar or very familiar with this type of review. The need for more information about this method is, therefore, also growing.

This article provides some of the needed information. A brief history of the development of meta-analysis is given, and then

five alternative approaches to meta-analysis are distinguished and suggestions for their use made.

Brief History of Meta-Analysis

Research reviews can be arranged into four classes (Cooper, 1982; G. B. Jackson, 1980). The first type of review identifies and discusses new developments in a field. The second uses empirical evidence to highlight, illustrate, or assess a particular theory or to tentatively propose new theoretical frameworks. Third, a reviewer can organize knowledge from divergent lines of research.

Meta-analysis belongs to the fourth class of review, the integrative review. The integrative review is "primarily interested in inferring generalizations about substantive issues from a set of studies directly bearing on those issues." (G. B. Jackson, 1980, p. 438). The meta-analytic reviewer will typically collect a group of studies that investigate the same question through roughly similar procedures. Of course there would be little need for review if this convergence of hypothesis and research design produced identical results in all the studies. On the contrary, the social sciences are replete with research, especially applied research, that has attempted to verify or extend previous research in an unsystematic way (e.g., Shaver & Norton, 1980). Diversity in study outcomes may therefore be due to subtle differences in setting, subjects, and researcher. This is precisely what meta-analysis hopes to answer: Are some regular patterns discernable in a body of studies on a given topic that show divergent outcomes?

Meta-analysis applies statistics to the treatment of quantitative representations of study outcomes. This distinguishes meta-analysis from more informal narrative forms of review. Perhaps the most statistically sensitive type of narrative review is the "vote-counting" or "box-score" review (Light & Smith, 1971).

In a box-score review, the studies are grouped into three sets: those significantly favoring the control group, those significantly favoring the experimental group, and those with nonsignificant outcomes. The modal category is taken as the best representation of the outcomes of this research area. Outcomes of lesser fre-

Correspondence concerning this article should be addressed to Robert L. Bangert-Drowns, Center for Research on Learning and Teaching, 109 East Madison Street, Ann Arbor, Michigan 48109.

From Robert L. Bangert-Drowns, "Review of Developments in Meta-Analytic Method," *Psychological Bulletin*, Vol. 99, pp. 388-399. Copyright © 1986 by the American Psychological Association. Reprinted by permission of the publisher and author.

quency are attributed to chance or undetected experimental error. Counting statistically significant findings gives a crude idea of how large and consistent a particular finding is in a body of research.

Vote counting, however, will only reliably represent the size of a treatment's effect if the collected studies have the same sample sizes and a unimodal distribution reflecting one population. There are two reasons for this. First, statistical significance is a product of both the treatment's effect and the sample size. If the sample sizes of the studies differ, conclusions from studies with larger samples are more likely to be significant even when the underlying treatment effect is small or the same as in the other studies. Secondly, a multimodal distribution could suggest that factors other than the treatment alone are mediating study outcomes. Meta-analysis is not hampered by these problems. It does not rely on frequency counts or statistical significance within studies. Instead it applies statistics to numerical representations of the studies' dependent measures. Further, it typically investigates the influence of mediating factors on the independent variable.

Early Meta-Analytic Studies

Glass cites two reviews that exemplify earlier applications of meta-analytic ingenuity (Glass et al., 1981, p. 24). Underwood (1957) graphed the apparently divergent outcomes of 16 studies on recall interference. He discovered a significant relation between the number of prior lists learned and recall ability. This relation was not detected in any individual study. Sudman and Bradburn (1974) gathered hundreds of studies investigating response effects in survey research. These reviewers applied statistical methods to assess the influence of survey design and use on survey results.

Other well-known examples are not hard to find. Ghiselli (1949, 1955, 1973) averaged correlation coefficients from numerous studies to estimate the validity of different tests in predicting proficiency in different occupations. Bloom (1964) aggregated correlation coefficients to summarize evidence of stability and change in behavior. Cartwright (1971) quantified and cumulated study outcomes to show that group influence is trivial in risky shift research. Erlenmeyer-Kimling and Jarvik (1963) aggregated more than 30,000 correlation pairings from 52 studies to discover orderly relations between intelligence and genetic history.

One can trace meta-analysis to earlier roots (Hedges & Olkin, 1982). In the first third of this century, agricultural experimenters assembled a large body of studies bearing on identical questions. Interpretation of these study findings was hampered as interpretation in the social sciences is today. As Yates and Cochran (1938) observed, "differences in soil, agronomic practices, climatic conditions and other variations in environment" (p. 556) introduced uncontrolled factors into experiments. Secondly, the amount of land needed for an adequate experiment was often not available at a single site. "The agricultural experimenter is thus frequently confronted with the results of a set of experiments on the same problem" (Yates & Cochran, 1938, p. 556).

Tippitt (1931) answered the difficulty by supplying methods to test the statistical significance of results combined from separate experiments. Other researchers, such as Fisher (1932), K.

Pearson (1933), and E. S. Pearson (1938), followed in this tradition. They sought ways to combine probability values from tests of significance.

Cochran (1937) and Yates and Cochran (1938) set out to answer the difficulty in a different way. They developed methods to estimate the mean effect and variability of a particular treatment examined at different agricultural centers. Furthermore, Cochran (1943) discussed the importance of comparing different dependent measure criteria for compatibility and relative accuracy before combining study findings.

Wilkinson (1951) proposed a method to interpret multiple outcomes from single studies in the social sciences. He observed that, because study results are either significant or nonsignificant, the binomial distribution could be used to determine the expected number of significant results given a true null hypothesis. This estimate of expected studies could be tested against the actual number of significant findings as a check on the assumption about the null hypothesis.

Jones and Fiske (1953) went further to import the meta-analytic attitude of agricultural research to the social sciences. They extended Wilkinson's proposition and argued that Fisher's (1932) and K. and E. S. Pearson's methods of combining probabilities could be used to combine findings in education and psychology. Mosteller and Bush (1954) also established combined probabilities as a useful tool in social science integration.

As early as the 1950s, therefore, combining probabilities was advocated as a reasonable way of statistically integrating social science research. However, no integrative technique similar to Cochran's was formally developed for the social sciences. That is, no one advocated a coherent method to estimate the mean and variation of a social or psychological treatment. Two remaining methodological problems blocked this development.

Two Obstacles to Meta-Analysis

Dissimilar dependent measures and variations in study features presented difficult obstacles to the translation of the meta-analytic attitude into a coherent meta-analytic method. Though a group of studies might investigate the same question with similar methods, the reviewer could not be sure to what degree the combined results were distorted due to differences in the criterion scale used and differences in study features. Three important articles offered solutions to these problems and in many ways anticipated what would become modern meta-analytic method.

In his well-known article "The statistical power of abnormal-social psychological research," Cohen (1962) indirectly spoke to some of the gaps in meta-analytic method. He set out to review the power of all the studies appearing in Volume 61 of the *Journal of Abnormal and Social Psychology*. He made three calculations of statistical power for each article, each calculation corresponding to hypothetical population effects of different degrees: low, medium, or large. Given such calculations, Cohen showed that the 78 articles were poorly designed to detect false null hypotheses when effect sizes were medium or low.

To the historian of research integration, Cohen's review contributed to meta-analytic theory in three important ways. First, he showed a way of statistically summarizing a diverse literature without taking recourse to counting or combining significance levels. Each study was represented in the review by three power estimates. These estimates were summarized in terms of central tendency (mean and median) and variation.

Secondly, because effect size is a factor in determining a study's power, any call to power analysis must also be an encouragement for an analysis of effect size. Cohen did not calculate the effect size for each study, a procedure that is common in modern meta-analysis. He did, however, underscore the convenience of the use of effect size in statistical research integration. Faced with "diverse content areas, utilizing a large variety of dependent variables and many different types of statistical tests . . . size of effect was expressed quantitatively in terms not dependent on the specific metric of the variable(s) involved" (1962, p. 446).

Third, Cohen suggested a rudimentary form by which the relations between study features and study findings could be examined. He realized that the power of major statistical tests, tests on the central hypotheses of the article, may be greater than the power of more peripheral statistical tests. He classified these separately, performing his analysis on the major tests, then analyzing the power of the peripheral tests to see if there were differences between the classes. In this way, the influence of a study feature on findings was empirically assessed.

In their article "The teaching–learning paradox: A comparative analysis of college teaching methods." Dubin and Taveggia (1968) attempted an ambitious statistical integration of findings from 74 studies comparing forms of college teaching. Like many reviewers before them, they categorized findings into three groups (favored treatment A, favored treatment B, and no difference) and performed simple sign tests on the frequency distributions.

However, these researchers complained that "the sign test does not give us any indication of the magnitude or distribution of differences between any two methods of teaching" (Dubin & Taveggia, 1968, p. 59). Fifty-six of the 74 studies reported group means, standard deviations, and sample sizes. They calculated t values for the findings of these studies as a measure of the magnitude of the difference between means. These t values were averaged and the average was tested to see if it differed significantly from zero. They concluded that the various college teaching methods did not differ significantly.

From a meta-analytic perspective, this review suffered from at least two faults. (a) The t value is inferior to Cohen's effect size as a measure of treatment magnitude because it is dependent on sample size. Two applications of a treatment may produce effects of identical magnitude, yet if one application involved a larger sample, its corresponding t value would also be larger. (b) In addition, the authors did not attempt to examine any relations between treatment effects and features of the studies.

However, Dubin and Taveggia (1968) did anticipate meta-analysis in several ways. First, they recognized the value of using a standardized measure of magnitude that can be compared across studies and across criterion scales. Second, they insisted on the review of research from a probabilistic standpoint. As Taveggia (1974) later put it, "Research results are *probabilistic. . . .* In and of themselves, the findings of any single research is meaningless—they may have occurred simply by chance" (p. 398). Third, the authors believed that measures of treatment effect representing each study could be treated as data points and summarized and tested statistically.

A third article speaks to the development of meta-analytic method. In "Accumulating evidence: Procedures for resolving contradictions among research studies," Light and Smith (1971) proposed an alternative to narrative methods of research integration. Their alternative, called "cluster analysis," involves five steps.

First, only studies that are methodological replications are admitted to cluster analysis. Second, the reviewer must gather the original data reflected in the studies' findings. Third, the reviewer must determine natural aggregations or clusters into which the data can be regrouped. Fourth, the reviewer must investigate differences among the clusters, comparing means, variances, relations between independent and dependent variables, subject/treatment interactions, and subject/cluster interactions, to see if differences among clusters explain study outcome variation.

Finally, in those cases in which no differences are found, clusters can be combined to increase sample sizes. At the end of a cluster analysis, a reviewer should be able to draw conclusions from larger samples or attribute differences in study findings to identifiable differences among the clusters. Of course, such an analysis may also fail and the variation in the original studies be found to be unexplainable.

In many ways, cluster analysis is distinguishable from the meta-analytic tradition. Cohen (1962) and Dubin and Taveggia (1968) were willing to quantitatively represent each study in their reviews and perform analyses on these statistical representations. This resembles modern meta-analytic procedure. Light and Smith, on the other hand, relied on original data. In this way, cluster analysis is more a form of secondary analysis, the reanalysis of original data, than a form of meta-analysis and is impossible to do in the numerous cases in which original data is unavailable (Cordray & Orwin, 1983; Glass, 1976).

Yet Light and Smith (1971) made an important theoretical contribution to the maturation of meta-analysis. Their interest was, after all, in the synthesis of diverse study outcomes. They reaffirmed the importance of finding a statistically sensible way to resolve apparent contradictions in research findings. More importantly, their work underscores the necessity of the search for subject/setting interactions as an essential focus of any research integration and an essential means for explaining variation in study findings.

Five Forms of Meta-Analytic Method

In 1976, the same year that Glass first coined the term "meta-analysis," Rosenthal published his book *Experimenter effects in behavioral research* and Schmidt and Hunter were working on a validity generalization technique. These three concurrent efforts established three distinguishable meta-analytic approaches. Since the late 1970s, two other coherent methods have been formulated as elaborations of Glass's approach (Hedges, 1982a; Mansfield & Busse, 1977).

It would be incorrect to think that these five approaches are the last word in meta-analysis. They only indicate the present moment in the continuing evolution of review methodology. Users may in fact select and apply elements of these five without committing themselves to all the features of any one approach. I present these approaches as five separate and coherent methods

Table 1
Five Methods of Meta-Analysis

Descriptive label	Purpose	Unit of analysis	Treatment of study variation	Outcomes of analysis
Glassian meta-analysis	To review what a literature says about the scientific process in a given area	Study finding	Examine relations between effect sizes and preestablished categories	Average effect size; comparisons of effect sizes in preestablished categories; regression models
Study effect meta-analysis	To review what a literature says about a treatment's effectiveness	Study	Examine relations between effect sizes and preestablished categories; apply strict study inclusion criteria	Average effect size; comparisons of effect sizes in preestablished categories; regression models
Combined probability method	To estimate a treatment effect and the reliability of this finding	Study, for effect size; subject, for combined probability	Crude division of studies into groups analyzed separately	Average effect size; combined probability; fail-safe N
Approximate data pooling with tests of homogeneity	To estimate population treatment effects	Subject	Apply tests of homogeneity	Average effect sizes for homogeneous groups
Approximate data pooling with sampling error correction	To estimate population treatment effects	Subject	Compare variation among studies to variation attributable to sampling error; test for moderating variables	Average effect size; study variation; variation attributable to sampling error; list of moderators accounting for remaining variation; regression models

because they have been most frequently used this way and because no one has yet documented the differences among all five methods. They are distinguishable on four factors: purpose, unit of analysis, treatment of study variation, and products of the meta-analysis (Table 1).

Glassian Meta-Analysis

Scientific literature does not just record the measured effects of controlled treatments. It is also an enduring record of the way scholars think about their field, the way they conduct research, the way they organize their data, and the assumptions implicit in their taxonomies and interpretations. An ambitious integrative project would evaluate such features of research as well as summarize study outcomes to assess the scientific enterprise in a given area.

Glass has endeavored to apply meta-analysis in this way. The meta-analyses of psychotherapy effectiveness and class size influence are classics of research integration (Glass, Cahen, Smith, & Filby, 1982; Smith, Glass, & Miller, 1980). Other reviewers have followed his lead (e.g., Hansford & Hattie, 1982; Hartley, 1978; Walberg & Haertel, 1980, pp. 103–133; White, 1982).

Glassian meta-analysis proceeds through three steps. First, all studies relevant to a defined question are collected. Glass uses liberal criteria for inclusion, accepting studies of widely varying methodological quality to his synthesis. Second, the outcomes of each study are transformed to a common metric to allow comparisons across the different scales of different dependent measures. Glass's effect size (*ES*), a modified form of Cohen's

d, divides the difference between experimental and control means by the control group's standard deviation.

The study finding is the unit of analysis in Glass's method. That is, one study may produce several findings from several dependent measures. Each finding is transformed into a separate effect size. The more dependent measures a study has, the more frequently it is represented in the overall meta-analysis.

After the first two steps, a Glassian meta-analyst can describe an average outcome of a group of studies and the variance of those outcomes. Glass wants to additionally search for significant relations between independent variables and dependent measures. Every study is coded on a number of quantitative dimensions (e.g., number of sessions of psychotherapy) and categorical variables (e.g., random assignment of subjects vs. nonrandom assignment). For example, Smith and Glass (1977) coded at least 16 independent variables for each study. Variables are preselected by the reviewer as potential determinants of variability in study findings. They represent differences in treatment application, methodological differences and controls for validity, differences in publication history, and differences in experimental setting. Parametric tests are applied to identify relations between study outcomes and the coded study features.

Critics of Glassian meta-analysis have found fault with four features that are peculiar to this approach. These features are the inclusion of methodologically poor studies in the review (the "garbage in–garbage out" complaint), the use of overly broad categories in averaging effects across independent and dependent variables (the "apples-and-oranges" problem), and the representation of individual studies by multiple effect sizes, resulting in nonindependent data points (the nonindependence problem) and misleadingly large samples (the problem of "inflated Ns"). These complaints can be recast in terms of threats to internal, construct, statistical conclusion, and external validities (Cook & Campbell, 1979; Wortman, 1983).

Glass's liberal inclusion of studies regardless of methodological quality flies in the face of integrative tradition. The traditional reviewer gives greater weight to findings of greater internal validity. Mansfield and Busse (1977) argued for the elimination of methodologically inferior studies from meta-analysis. Eysenck (1978) more disparagingly referred to meta-analysis as "mega-silliness" and complained that the inclusion of methodologically inadequate research only demonstrates the axiom "garbage in-garbage out."

Replying to this criticism, Glass takes an empirical stand (e.g., Glass et al., 1981, pp. 220–226). He agrees that internal validity can effect the outcome of research, but he argues that this is an empirical question, one that meta-analysis is equipped to handle. By coding studies for various threats to internal validity, relations between effect sizes and these threats can be determined, if they exist.

Some authors have found fault with this reply (Bryant & Wortman, 1984; Cook & Leviton, 1980). It makes sense to look for relations between effect size and methodological flaws only if the available research provides a wide range of experimental rigor. If studies with numerous threats to validity predominate a review's sample, there may not be a sufficient number of well-controlled studies to provide a comparison. "When all studies share a common bias, this all-inclusive approach can be misleading. . . . Without well-designed studies that can be used as a baseline for comparison, it is impossible to determine how methodological quality affects results" (Bryant & Wortman, 1984, p. 12).

Critics also complain about the apples-and-oranges problem. At the level of the independent variable, Glass's form of meta-analysis can obscure critical differences among subgroups of studies. For example, Glass's investigation of psychotherapy effectiveness included psychodynamic, Adlerian, eclectic, transactional analysis, rational-emotive, Gestalt, client-centered, systematic desensitization, implosion, and behavior modification therapies (Smith & Glass, 1977). These were collapsed into two "superclasses," behavioral and nonbehavioral, and even averaged across all groups for a total "psychotherapy effect" measure. Presby (1978) complained that important differences "are cancelled in the very use of broad categories, which leads to the erroneous conclusion that research results indicate negligible differences among outcomes of different therapies" (p. 514).

In question then is the construct validity of Glassian meta-analyses. Do the categories established by the Glassian meta-analyst accurately reflect relevant underlying constructs? Glass has said that the construct validity can only be assessed against the purposes of the reviewer. Whether the reviewer has a specific hypothesis in mind or is simply trying to summarize a literature in broad strokes will determine to a great degree the validity of the categories used (Glass et al., 1981). Cooper (1982) has defined "integrative review" by the fact that it can encompass more operational definitions than primary research. As Wortman (1983) put it, "If a policy decision to reimburse clinical psychologists

for psychotherapy is being considered, then a general question concerning the effectiveness of all therapies seems appropriate" (p. 240). Besides, an overall effect size can later be broken into effects related to specific treatments.

An apples-and-oranges treatment of dependent measures, however, seems less defensible (J. A. Kulik, 1984; Landman & Dawes, 1982). Glassian meta-analysis records and uses an effect size from every finding, even if a study produces more than one finding. In studies of computer-based instruction, for example, achievement test scores, ratings of attitudes toward computers, and ratings of attitudes toward course content can all be said to measure the same construct. How would one interpret their combination? "Computer-based instruction produces increases of 0.30 standard deviations in . . ." what? Meta-analysis may quantify a combined effect, but readers of reviews are generally not interested in such abstractions; effects of a treatment, however defined, must be effects on something specific.

Another difficulty arising from the calculation of effect sizes for every dependent measure is the nonindependence of the resulting data points. Even Glass et al. (1981) recognized this as a cogent criticism. Landman and Dawes (1982), in their reanalysis of a sample of Glass's psychotherapy data, found five different types of violation of the assumption of independence. Inferential statistics are less reliable when applied to such data and this poses a significant threat to the statistical conclusion validity of the review.

A fourth criticism results from the calculation of effect sizes for every dependent measure. That is, studies are represented in the meta-analysis by the number of findings they report. Thus, any report, even if it is atypical or of marginal quality, can have greater influence on meta-analytic findings if it uses many dependent measures. The ratio of study findings to studies can be extreme at times. Burns (1981), for example, gathered 413 effect sizes from 33 reports. Some studies contributed as many as 120 effect sizes, others as few as 1.

"Inflated Ns" threaten the generalizability or external validity of meta-analyses. Because individual studies can be arbitrarily overrepresented in a review, the definitions of the sample and target population become unclear. The problem is compounded when effect sizes are divided into study feature categories. Categories that only represent data from one or two studies do not offer generalizable information, even if they have a large number of effect sizes.

An example of the potential confusion is offered by the Educational Research Service's (1980) critique of Glass's class size meta-analysis. Fourteen of the 76 studies were considered well-controlled. These 14 well-controlled studies produced 110 comparisons, but 73% of the 110 came from 4 of the 14 studies. Glassian meta-analysts must use some procedure to protect against biases that may result when a small group of studies contributes too much data.

Glass has been disappointed by the dearth of variables found to significantly explain diversity in study findings (Glass, 1979). However, Glass recently restated his confidence in the general robustness and usefulness of his method (Glass & Kleigl, 1983). He also made his view of the purposes of meta-analysis explicit. The goal of meta-analysis is larger than simply summarizing the outcomes of a sample of research, according to Glass. It endeavors "to determine how and in what ways the judgments, decisions, and inclinations of persons (scholars, citizens, officials, administrators, policy makers) ought to be influenced by the literature of empirical research" regarding a defined enterprise (Glass & Kleigl, 1983, p. 35). To accomplish this, the meta-analyst evaluates not only a treatment and its effect but the method of research and the taxonomical structure used by researchers in a field.

Study Effect Meta-Analysis

Mansfield and Busse (1977) were early critics of Glass's meta-analytic approach. They outlined an alternative specifically designed to summarize study findings on the effect of a particular treatment and to avoid the problems of study inclusion and apples-and-oranges combinations. Since 1979, J. A. Kulik and his colleagues have produced about 15 meta-analyses that are consistent with the suggestions of Mansfield and Busse (e.g., Bangert-Drowns, Kulik, & Kulik, 1983; J. A. Kulik & Bangert-Drowns, 1983/1984; J. A. Kulik, C.-L. C. Kulik, & Cohen, 1979). Other examples of this type of meta-analysis are offered by Landman and Dawes (1982) and Wortman and Bryant (1985).

Perhaps the most significant feature of this form of meta-analysis is that it differs from Glassian meta-analysis regarding the appropriate unit of analysis. For Glass, the unit of analysis is the study finding; an effect size is calculated for every study outcome. In the alternative form of meta-analysis, the study itself is the unit of analysis. If a study uses more than one dependent measure, the corresponding effect sizes are either combined if they represent the same construct (e.g., academic achievement) or they are sent to separate analyses if they represent different constructs (e.g., one analysis for academic achievement data, another for attitude toward school data).

By using the study as the unit of analysis, this meta-analytic type avoids several pitfalls of Glass's approach, such as nonindependence of effect sizes, inflated *N*s, and the apples-and-oranges problem. Dependent measures are analyzed separately if they are assumed to gauge different constructs, protecting construct validity. The number of studies reviewed is equal to the number of effect sizes, protecting the overall results from being biased by a small number of studies that may produce many outcomes. The independence of the effect sizes allows the reviewer to use statistics with more confidence.

Because using the study as the unit of analysis is a central feature of this approach, I refer to it as *study effect meta-analysis* (SEM) to distinguish it from Glassian meta-analysis. Study effect meta-analysis and Glassian meta-analysis are similar in some ways. Both use quantitative and categorical variables to code study features as independent variables. Glass's *ES* is used as an outcome measure and parametric statistical tests are used to identify relations between study features and study outcomes. Study effect meta-analysis is usually more exclusive than the Glassian form in selecting studies for review. In Kulik's research, for example, if any study suffers from flaws that may obscure treatment effects or if the study's method deviates too greatly from standard experimental practice, the study is rejected. All studies must possess experimental and control groups. If subjects are not randomly assigned to these groups, there must at least be evidence that the two groups show pretreatment equivalence. Any study whose treatment specifically trains the experimental group on the dependent measure is excluded. The experimental treatment in each accepted study must roughly fit criteria established by experts in the area under review. Control groups must undergo treatment that is roughly equivalent across studies.

In addition to Kulik, other meta-analysts have applied the study effect approach. Wortman and Bryant (1985), for example, developed 33 criteria for study exclusion in their meta-analysis of desegregation research. Threats to construct and external validity were used to determine a study's relevance for the review. Threats to internal and statistical conclusion validity were used to decide whether a relevant study was of acceptable quality (Bryant & Wortman, 1984).

In addition, the dependent measures that were examined by Wortman and Bryant (1985) were fairly homogeneous; that is, mathematics and reading achievement test performances were used to calculate effect sizes. In some ways, their treatment of effect sizes resembled the Glassian approach. Effect sizes were calculated for grade level and for reading and mathematics achievement, resulting in 106 effect sizes for 31 studies. "The overall analyses, however, used the study as the unit of analysis by averaging the results within each study and combining these average effect sizes" (Wortman & Bryant, 1985, p. 302).

Landman and Dawes (1982) used SEM to reanalyze a sample of studies randomly selected from Smith and Glass's (1977) psychotherapy review. Their results suggest that the inclusion of methodologically poorer studies and the calculation of more than one effect size for each study may have served to lower the average effect sizes Smith and Glass computed. Landman and Dawes found that the apples-and-oranges problem at both the independent and the dependent variable level may have more seriously obscured some potentially important relations.

The differences between the study effect method and Glass's method are few, but they betray the different purposes in these meta-analytic approaches. Glass, with his liberal standards of inclusion and empirical attitude toward methodological flaws and differences in dependent criteria, seeks to use quantitative means to assess a scholarly subculture, to examine modes of inquiry and construct definition as well as to estimate treatment effects. Study effect meta-analysis, on the other hand, seeks to represent what the available research says about a treatment's effectiveness. In doing so, SEM seems especially sensitive to the limits that the quality, quantity, and historical context of published research impose on integrative interpretations.

This approach is not without its shortcomings. With stricter inclusion standards and only one effect size from each study, one should expect a smaller sample size than with Glass's approach. If less than 10 studies pass the screening stage, such small samples would be prohibitive. Study exclusion may also provide an undesirable opportunity for a reviewer's biases to creep into the review, and it deprives a meta-analyst of the chance to determine whether and how some methodological shortcomings affect study outcomes. However, if a reviewer has a group of 20 or more studies, if it is likely that differential representation of studies will effect the meta-analytic findings, if the reviewer has a focused concern in mind and is not as interested in a general evaluation of a scientific field, and if the reviewer is willing to explicitly define and adhere to standards for inclusion, SEM is an attractive alternative to Glass's approach.

Combined Probability Method

Since 1976, Rosenthal and his colleagues (Cooper, 1979; Rosenthal, 1976, 1978, 1983; Rosenthal & Rubin, 1982a, 1982b) have developed two distinguishable meta-analytic methods; the more recent form is discussed later in this article. The combined probability method, discussed here, has been used to survey a number of areas (e.g., Arkin, Cooper, & Kolditz, 1980; Cooper, 1979; Dusek & Joseph, 1983; Rosenthal, 1976; Rosenthal & Rubin, 1978; Wolf, Savickas, Saltzman, & Walker, 1983).

Meta-analyses based on these techniques have a typical format (e.g., Cooper, 1979). The reviewer specifies an area of interest and all relevant studies are collected. For each study, exact one-tailed p values are calculated and their corresponding standard normal deviate (Z) listed. Additionally, Cohen's d is calculated for each study as a measure of effect that is more independent of sample size than is a p value. (Cohen's d is sometimes also represented as Cohen's U_3, the percentage of control group subjects with dependent measures less than the mean of the experimental group.)

Finally, the average effect size and a combined probability measure are calculated. The ds (and U_3s) are averaged to provide an overall effect size measure. Stouffer's method (Rosenthal, 1978) is used to combine the Zs corresponding to each study. The resulting Stouffer's Z defines the probability that the pooled subjects would be distributed among treatments as they are in the collected studies. The "fail-safe N" is calculated using an extension of the Stouffer method and is a more intuitively understandable form of the combined Z. The fail-safe N indicates the number of additional studies of no effect needed to reduce a significant combined probability to nonsignificance. (Note that the fail-safe N represents the number of unlocated studies of *zero effect*. There may in fact be a smaller number of *negative* studies, studies favoring the control group, that would reduce the meta-analytic outcome to nonsignificance [Cooper, 1979; Rosenthal, 1979].)

The unit of analysis in the calculation of the average d is clearly the study. Each study contributes one effect size and these are simply averaged across studies. Stouffer's Z, however, is not a simple average across studies, but a Z score of a cumulation of Z scores. Because the probabilities corresponding to each Z are already sensitive to sample size, the unit of analysis in determining overall probability is the subject.

This meta-analytic approach is not as comprehensive as the others. What is most conspicuously absent from this form of meta-analysis is rigorous attention to differences in study features. This method is not as attentive to outcome variation as it is to the degree of outcome convergence. Decisions regarding the inclusion or exclusion of methodologically inferior studies are left to the reviewer's discretion. Only very few or very basic differentiations are made in a literature, for example, the differentiation between studies examining race and studies examining sex as bases of teacher expectation (Dusek & Joseph, 1983). A reviewer might use this approach to gain a rough impression of a group

of studies but must borrow from other approaches for more subtle analysis.

Unlike Glassian and study effect meta-analysis, the implicit purpose of the combined probability approach is not to review a literature but to estimate a treatment effect and provide some measure of the estimate's reliability. These measures are intended to be broadly generalizable. Cooper (1979), for example, went so far as to use his meta-analytic findings to predict the results of future research. In keeping with this goal of deriving generalizable conclusions, Rosenthal's method has begun to focus on the subject as the unit of analysis, an effort to draw conclusions from large samples of subjects. Rosenthal's combined probability method can be seen as a transitional form of meta-analysis between, on the one hand, meta-analyses whose conclusions are interpreted as specific to the studies reviewed and, on the other hand, meta-analyses that attempt to determine population parameters and "true" treatment effects.

Approximate Data Pooling With Tests of Homogeneity

Rosenthal's combined probability method hints at an alternative use of meta-analysis. Instead of critically reviewing a body of studies, perhaps studies' summary statistics could be used to approximate the pooling of all the subjects from all the studies into one large comparison. That is, perhaps meta-analysis could be used to approximate data pooling.

Two methodological modifications are immediately implied. If we are concerned with pooling data across studies, we must attend not only to variability among studies as Glass prescribes, but also to the variance associated with each effect size as a summary statistic. Second, Glassian meta-analysis is meant to test differences between a priori categories. An alternative is to provide some overall test to determine whether such categorical tests are necessary at all. If a group of effect sizes is found to be homogeneous, the effect sizes can be averaged without further fuss. The crucial question is whether the variation among effect sizes is due to real mediators or simply to sampling error.

Hedges (1982a) and Rosenthal and Rubin (1982a) have devised tests for the homogeneity of effect sizes. Variability among study outcomes is represented as the sum of squared differences between each effect size and the weighted average effect size. The ratio of this sum of squared differences to the sum of sampling variances in all the effect sizes is distributed as a chi-square. If this ratio, designated H, is approximately 1, variation among studies is approximately the same as sampling error of the studies. If H is large or statistically significant, the variation among studies cannot be attributed to sampling error only.

Hedges (1982b) extends the use of this test of homogeneity. If the overall H is large, the effect sizes can be broken into smaller categories that may differ in average effect size. If H within a category is small, the effect sizes within the category are assumed to be homogeneous and to represent a single population treatment effect. A variant of the H statistic, H_B, describes the degree to which the categories vary among each other. As with the partitions of variation in an analysis of variance, the overall H is equal to the sum of the within-category H and between-categories H_B. By sensitizing regression to the sampling error of the effect sizes, the H statistic can be applied to continuous data as well (Hedges, 1982c).

Rosenthal and Rubin (1982a, 1982b) suggest a simple formula to test for significant differences among effect sizes in a heterogeneous group. The concept is analogous to contrasts in analysis of variance. The sum of appropriately weighted effect sizes is distributed as a standard normal deviate. This Z can be easily tested for statistical significance.

Hedges (1981) proposed several adjustments to increase the accuracy of the effect size as an estimator. Some of these are not practically important. For example, using Hedge's correction for estimator bias, Bangert-Drowns et al. (1983) found a correlation of .999 between corrected and uncorrected effect sizes in a meta-analysis of 27 studies. Corrected and uncorrected estimators are virtually equivalent for greater than 10 df (Hedges, 1982a, p. 492; Rosenthal & Rubin, 1982a, p. 504). Similarly Hedge's corrections for unreliability and invalidity of dependent measures are generally impractical because they require information that is rarely available, such as the reliabilities of the dependent measure and of a valid response measure, and the correlation between the two measures.

However, Rosenthal and Rubin (1982a) and Hedges (1981) also sought a weighting procedure that would minimize the variance of the cumulated effect size. The frequency-weighted effect size, that is, the effect size multiplied by the ratio of its sample size to the sum of all sample sizes, appears to adequately approximate the optimally weighted effect size (Hunter et al., 1983).

The use of the test of homogeneity bears some resemblance to Light and Smith's (1971) cluster analysis. Cluster analysis attempted to group original data into natural clusters of homogeneity. Hedges and Rosenthal have weighted effect sizes to reflect differences in sample size and sampling error. These subject-sensitive statistics are clustered and reclustered as they form natural aggregations of greater homogeneity, tested by subject-sensitive significance criteria. The subject is the unit of analysis even though this unit is mediated by the summary statistic, effect size.

Hedges appears to be as willing as Glass to include studies of diverse quality and treatment features. The tests of homogeneity can be used to empirically determine whether this diversity produces heterogeneous outcomes (Hedges & Olkin, 1982). However, Hedges will not allow the averaging of effects from dependent measures representing different constructs. To estimate single population effects, effect size estimates must come from dependent measures that can be assumed to be linearly equatable.

The practical usefulness of tests of homogeneity is unclear. Rosenthal and Rubin (1982a) warn that the behavior of statistics used in this meta-analytic type is not fully understood for small or nonnormal samples. Hedges and Stock (1983) reexamined the continuous model offered by Glass relating class size to student achievement. Their conclusions largely duplicated Glass's findings.

In addition, some authors have spoken against the use of tests of homogeneity. Hunter et al. (1983), for example, developed a test of homogeneity for use with the correlation coefficient. This test is identical to Hedges's and Rosenthal and Rubin's. However, Hunter et al. (1983) "do not endorse this significance test because it asks the wrong question. Significant variation may be trivial

in magnitude, and even nontrivial variation may still be due to research artifacts" (p. 46). Hedges (1982a) warns, "When the sample sizes [within studies] are *very* large, it is probably worthwhile to consider the actual variation in [the effect sizes] because rather small differences may lead to large values of the test statistic" (p. 493).

Approximate Data Pooling With Sampling Error Correction

Hunter and Schmidt became interested in quantitative research synthesis as a tool to investigate the differential validity of employment tests for blacks and whites (Hunter & Schmidt, 1978; Hunter, Schmidt, & Hunter, 1979; Schmidt, Berner, & Hunter, 1973). They found in summarizing test validity research that "72% of the variation across studies is accounted for by four artifacts: sampling error, variation in criterion reliability, variation in test reliability, and variation in range restriction" (Hunter & Schmidt, 1981, p. 7). Their meta-analytic technique, therefore, is designed to check for such artifactual mediators.

In many ways this fifth and final form of meta-analysis is a variation of that advocated by Hedges and by Rosenthal and Rubin. The two methods agree in basic purpose and analytic strategy. Their greatest difference is that Hunter and Schmidt will not use tests of homogeneity.

Studies are collected; each study is represented in the analysis by one effect size. All studies that bear on the question of interest are included regardless of methodological adequacy. Effect sizes for each study are individually corrected for unreliability or other statistical artifacts when appropriate information is given. If such information is sporadically given, say in only 20 of 50 collected studies, Hunter and Schmidt recommend using the average of the measures found in the 20 studies to correct all the effect sizes.

To measure the overall variability of the effect sizes, the sum of squared differences between each effect size and the estimated population effect is calculated and weighted by proportional sample sizes. The amount of variation attributable to sampling error is calculated next. This calculation is identical to the sampling error approximations used by Hedges and by Rosenthal and Rubin. However, Hunter and Schmidt do not test for homogeneity. Instead, they subtract the variation due to sampling error from the total variation. If sampling error removes approximately 75% of the overall variation, the effect sizes are assumed to estimate one parameter (i.e., they are homogeneous), and the frequency-weighted effect is the best estimate of the parameter.

If the variation is still large after correcting for sampling error, the meta-analyst should investigate the influence of moderator variables. The meta-analyst develops and codes a set of independent variables representing study and treatment features suspected of producing outcome variation. Effect sizes can be divided into groups according to these categories. If a variable really acts as a moderator, the means of the categories should be different, and their variation should be less than variation for the mixed group. Alternatively, correlations can be taken between effect sizes and study features (and these correlations can be corrected for sampling error in the effect sizes) to assess the influence of moderators.

This type of meta-analysis has a number of products. There is an overall mean and standard deviation corrected for statistical artifacts. Once moderating variables have been identified, Hunter and Schmidt recommend the use of regression on the effect sizes as individual data points in much the way Glass recommends. Such a procedure allows the meta-analyst to estimate the distribution of the treatment effects when study characteristics are at their means and when they are varied.

The Hunter-Schmidt procedure is consistent with the goals of meta-analysis described by Hedges and by Rosenthal and Rubin. These researchers wish to base causal conclusions on larger groups of subjects. When primary data is not available, meta-analysis can approximate cluster analysis by grouping effect sizes into natural aggregations. However, instead of testing for statistical significance, Hunter and Schmidt resort to real measures of variance and approximate sampling error. Using these, the meta-analyst is more aware of the real magnitude of variation being examined, not just its statistical significance.

Use of the real measures allows for more creative manipulations of data variation. DerSimonian and Laird (1983), for example, used a meta-analytic procedure that approximates data pooling without recourse to homogeneity tests. They showed that in studies of Scholastic Aptitude Test coaching, sampling error could be estimated more exactly than the estimation routinely used in the test of homogeneity.

When tests of homogeneity calculate sampling error for a group of studies, they assume that each study is a "posttest only" design (C.-L. C. Kulik & J. A. Kulik, 1985). Sampling error estimates are not adjusted when additional information is available from pretests or covariates. DerSimonian and Laird estimated sampling error from gain scores, that is, with variation reduced by information about subjects' pretreatment aptitude. Thus, by *not* applying statistical tests, these reviewers more flexibly and accurately examined the magnitude of variation produced by different categories of effect sizes.

Discussion

Research outcomes vary in ways that make generalizable interpretations difficult. Such variation comes from a number of sources. It may reflect real population variation, the effects of different treatment features or study settings, sampling error, selection biases of the reviewer, publication biases, the effects of erroneous or insufficient reporting (unreported spurious influences, computational errors, typographical errors), differing degrees of validity and reliability in the outcome measures, and differences in the range or intensity of the independent variable. The task is enormous, but the power of social scientific inquiry would greatly increase if patterns could be found amid this outcome variation.

A number of processes have been used to attempt this task. These processes can be arranged on a continuum according to the degree of quantification. At one extreme, there is the informal narrative review that, at its simplest, lists the outcomes of some sample of studies and presents the reviewer's reasoned speculations regarding their interpretation. At the other extreme, there are the forms of secondary analysis, such as cluster analysis (Light & Smith, 1971). Cluster analysis groups original data from varied research sources into smaller, natural aggregations. Where no differences are found among aggregations, original data is pooled into samples of larger sizes.

Meta-analysis lies between these two extremes. Its procedures are more approximate than those of cluster analysis. Yet meta-analysis is more statistically rigorous than is the typical narrative review. It attempts to identify some central tendency in the outcomes of a group of studies and additionally to analyze their variation without resorting to original data.

Because meta-analysis is not a single method, the user must make a number of decisions in conducting such a review. This article does not advocate any particular approach as entirely superior to the others. Instead, general guidelines and cautions are offered regarding the applications of elements of these approaches.

Purpose

The meta-analytic reviewer must first decide the intention of the review. Two alternatives are possible. A reviewer may primarily want to describe a body of literature. Such analyses seek to answer questions of the form "What does available research say about treatment X's effects?" (Glass et al., 1981; J. A. Kulik, C.-L.C. Kulik, & Cohen, 1979). On the other hand, some meta-analyses attempt to approximate an increased sample size in order to test a specific hypothesis and to determine a generalizable estimate of a treatment effect. In intent, these reviews are similar to cluster analyses or data pooling and seek to answer questions of the form "What is the real effect of treatment X?" (Hedges, 1980; Hunter et al., 1983; Rosenthal & Rubin, 1982a).

The difference between these alternatives is not a trivial one. A meta-analyst's choice will determine how outcome variation is treated and how the findings are interpreted and generalized. Indeed, it will determine how the meta-analyst conceives of the whole meta-analytic enterprise.

Meta-analysts who stand closer to the cluster analysis/data pooling/secondary analysis traditions identify their work with the work of primary researchers. They attempt to answer the same questions as primary researchers, only these meta-analysts hope to use larger samples. "In meta-analysis, the parameter of interest is the population standardized mean difference" (Hedges, 1980, p. 25); "Only cumulation of results across studies can generate [adequate] sample sizes in most areas of contemporary research" (Hunter & Schmidt, 1981, p. 6); and, "We are able to extend traditional limits of meta-analysis to obtain results previously available only when the original data were analyzed" (DerSimonian & Laird, 1983, p. 6).

Other meta-analysts, whose concerns are more in the tradition of "literature review," have pointedly distinguished their work from the work of primary researchers. As Glass put it, "The literature on psychotherapy outcomes is distinct from psychotherapy outcomes themselves by a sequence of translations too obvious to enumerate" (Glass & Kleigl, 1983, p. 35). For Glass, the work of the primary researcher is to construct and test theory; for the meta-analyst, it is to accurately summarize research as it is reported.

Glass's comment is sobering. It reminds us that publicly available reports may not be simple indicants of all the research being done nor of the real effects of a specific treatment. It has been repeatedly observed, for example, that effect sizes taken from published articles are consistently higher than those found in dissertations (Bangert-Drowns, Kulik, & Kulik, 1984; Smith, 1980). There is the forbidding possibility that a meta-analyst's findings may say more about editorial preference, the politics of research finance, or the differential capabilities and biases of professionals and graduate students than about real treatment effects. This dilemma is more serious for meta-analyses that propose to estimate treatment parameters. Those reviews that more modestly claim to only characterize the available findings can fulfill their purposes whether or not publication histories differentiate those findings.

Treatment of Study Variation

Once a purpose is clarified, the meta-analyst must decide how variations among studies will be handled. The meta-analyst must consider three kinds of variation. First, differences in research quality must be considered. Most meta-analysts are fairly liberal in their inclusion of studies of differing quality. However, some (e.g., J. A. Kulik, C.-L.C. Kulik, & Cohen, 1979; Wortman & Bryant, 1985) may eliminate many studies on the grounds of methodological inferiority.

Glass has criticized the use of inclusion standards. Disregarding studies a priori from review because their quality introduces the reviewer's biases and removes a large sample of findings that may in fact differ little from more controlled research. It militates against the possibility of discovering some potentially important relations between methodological variety and outcome variance.

Even the most liberal reviewers will exclude some studies, such as those with insufficient or obviously incorrect reports. Because all meta-analysts deal with inclusion decisions to some degree, two rules should apply. First, criteria for inclusion must be so explicitly stated that others may replicate the results or evaluate the limitations of the review. Second, the meta-analyst must test to determine whether differences in quality are related to differences in outcome. The reviewer can then decide whether research features are confounding treatment effects.

The second issue regarding study variation is the apples-and-oranges problem. A reviewer's interest may be broader than the primary researcher's, for example, an interest in psychotherapy rather than just behavior modification (Cooper, 1982; Wortman, 1983). A reviewer may therefore mix independent variables that primary researchers had tested separately. Such "mixed" independent variables can at times be somewhat artificial or remote from real applications. However, reviewers should define a research area according to their purposes, remembering that a broadly defined independent variable can later be split into smaller components.

Mixing dependent measures that examine different constructs is less justifiable, however. Treatments may influence many phenomena but averaging measures of all these phenomena only confuses our picture of the treatment. A drug may cure cancer but make colds worse. Averaging these effects would obscure important information about the drug and produce a single effect size that is difficult to interpret. It seems better to let every averaged effect size represent one type of dependent measure.

The third issue regarding study variation is the management of outcome variance. Two approaches are available. The first is to treat each study or study finding as a single data point. Traditional statistical tests are applied to relate these collected data points to features of the studies from which they came. This approach is consistent with the use of meta-analysis for literature review (Glassian and study effect meta-analysis).

The alternative is to recognize that each effect size is a summary statistic describing the varied performance of a group of subjects. Each effect size, therefore, has its own sampling error. By accounting for this sampling error, perhaps more accurate estimates can be made of the treatment effects. This is consistent with the use of meta-analysis to approximate data pooling either with or without tests of homogeneity.

Users should note some final cautions regarding the homogeneity tests. Rosenthal and Rubin (1982a) warn that the accuracy of the homogeneity tests for small or nonnormal samples is not certain. Studies that have compared the homogeneity procedures with Glass's have largely replicated Glass's findings. In addition, Hunter and Schmidt offer an alternative, a method that allows the reviewer to approximate data pooling without resorting to homogeneity tests. Their procedure attends to the real magnitude of variation instead of significance tests and thereby encourages more flexible treatment of sampling error, as in DerSimonian and Laird (1983).

Unit of Analysis

Meta-analysts must also decide which will be the review's unit of analysis, the study itself or the study finding. For cases in which a meta-analyst is approximately data pooling, procedures applied to effect sizes are subject-sensitive and the subject may be regarded as the unit of analysis. Even in these cases, however, one must still decide which will be the basis of the effect sizes, the study or the finding.

There are too many difficulties associated with the study finding as unit of analysis to warrant its continued use. Multiple effect sizes from any one study cannot be regarded as independent and should not be used with statistical tests that assume their independence. Differential contributions of effect sizes from the studies means that some studies will have greater influence on overall findings than others. If effect sizes are divided into smaller categories, whole categories can be dominated by one or two studies and therefore not provide reliably generalizable information. As a rule, each study should be represented only once to an analysis.

Outcomes of Analysis

Of course the outcomes of the analysis are highly dependent on the methods used. Of the five described here, Rosenthal's combined probability method is perhaps the most unique. Its products are an average effect size, a measure of the combined probability of the study outcomes, and the fail-safe N. Even more notable, however, is what is lacking. This approach to meta-analysis makes little or no attempt to examine the relation between study features and study outcomes.

Meta-analysis at its present level of development should be

expected to provide more than just measures of central tendency. It should also systematically attempt to relate study features or treatment characteristics to the study outcomes. The combined probability method therefore must be used only in conjunction with elements of other approaches that will better address study outcome variation.

Conclusion

The systematic differences in meta-analysis have been largely overlooked. It is time they are clarified so the limitations of this approach to research integration can be more realistically assessed. These differences should not be taken as evidence of some inherent weakness of meta-analysis. It is merely a reflection of the natural evolution of a new social scientific tool. Perhaps meta-analytic methods appropriate to different purposes and different research areas will ultimately be distinguished.

Meta-analysis is not a fad. It is rooted in the fundamental values of the scientific enterprise: replicability, quantification, causal and correlational analysis. Valuable information is needlessly scattered in individual studies. The ability of social scientists to deliver generalizable answers to basic questions of policy is too serious a concern to allow us to treat research integration lightly. The potential benefits of meta-analysis method seem enormous.

References

Arkin, R., Cooper, H., & Kolditz, T. (1980). A statistical review of the literature concerning the self-serving bias in interpersonal influence situations. *Journal of Personality, 48,* 435–448.

Bangert-Drowns, R. L., Kulik, J. A., & Kulik, C.-L. C. (1983). Effects of coaching programs on achievement test performance. *Review of Educational Research, 53,* 571–585.

Bangert-Drowns, R. L., Kulik, J. A., & Kulik, C.-L. C. (1984, August). *The influence of study features on outcomes of educational research.* Paper presented at the 92nd annual meeting of the American Psychological Association, Toronto.

Bloom, B. S. (1964). *Stability and change in human characteristics.* New York: Wiley.

Bryant, F. B., & Wortman, P. M. (1984). Methodological issues in the meta-analysis of quasi-experiments. In W. H. Yeaton & P. M. Wortman (Eds.), *Issues in data synthesis* (pp. 5–24). San Francisco: Jossey-Bass.

Burns, P. K. (1981). A quantitative synthesis of research findings relative to the pedagogical effectiveness of computer-assisted mathematics instruction in elementary and secondary schools. *Dissertation Abstracts International, 42,* 2946A. (University Microfilms No. 81-28, 378)

Cartwright, D. (1971). Risk taking by individuals and groups: An assessment of research employing choice dilemmas. *Journal of Personality and Social Psychology, 20,* 361–378.

Cochran, W. G. (1937). Problems arising in the analysis of a series of similar experiments. *Journal of the Royal Statistical Society, 4* (Suppl.), 102–118.

Cochran, W. G. (1943). The comparison of different scales of measurement for experimental results. *Annals of Mathematical Statistics, 14,* 205–216.

Cohen, J. (1962). The statistical power of abnormal–social psychological research: A review. *Journal of Abnormal and Social Psychology, 65,* 145–153.

Cook, T. D., & Campbell, D. T. (1979). *Quasi-experimentation: Design and analysis issues for field settings.* Boston, MA: Houghton Mifflin.

Cook, T. D., & Leviton, L. C. (1980). Reviewing the literature: A comparison of traditional methods with meta-analysis. *Journal of Personality, 48,* 449–472.

Cooper, H. M. (1979). Statistically combining independent studies: A meta-analysis of sex differences in conformity research. *Journal of Personality and Social Psychology, 37,* 131–146.

Cooper, H. M. (1982). Scientific guidelines for conducting integrative reviews. *Review of Educational Research, 52,* 291–302.

Cordray, D. S., & Orwin, R. C. (1983). Improving the quality of evidence: Interconnections among primary evaluation, secondary analysis, and quantitative synthesis. In R. J. Light (Ed.), *Evaluation Studies Review Annual: Vol. 8* (pp. 91–119). Beverly Hills, CA: Sage.

DerSimonian, R., & Laird, N. M. (1983). Evaluating the effect of coaching on SAT scores: A meta-analysis. *Harvard Educational Review, 53,* 1–15.

Dubin, R., & Taveggia, T. C. (1968). *The teaching–learning paradox: A comparative analysis of college teaching methods.* Eugene: University of Oregon Press.

Dusek, J. B., & Joseph, G. (1983). The bases of teacher expectancies: A meta-analysis. *Journal of Educational Psychology, 75,* 327–346.

Educational Research Service (1980). Class size research: A critique of recent meta-analyses. *Phi Delta Kappan, 62,* 239–241.

Erlenmeyer-Kimling, L., & Jarvik, L. F. (1963). Genetics and intelligence: A review. *Science, 142,* 1477–1479.

Eysenck, H. J. (1978). An exercise in mega-silliness. *American Psychologist, 33,* 517.

Fisher, R. A. (1932). *Statistical methods for research workers* (4th ed.). London: Oliver & Boyd.

Ghiselli, E. E. (1949). The validity of commonly employed occupational tests. *University of California Publications in Psychology, 5,* 253–288.

Ghiselli, E. E. (1955). The measurement of occupational aptitude. *University of California Publications in Psychology, 8,* 101–216.

Ghiselli, E. E. (1973). The validity of aptitude tests in personnel selection. *Personnel Psychology, 26,* 461–477.

Glass, G. V. (1976). Primary, secondary, and meta-analysis research. *Educational Researcher, 5,* 3–8.

Glass, G. V. (1979). Policy for the unpredictable. *Educational Researcher, 8,* 12–14.

Glass, G. V., Cahen, L. S., Smith, M. L., & Filby, N. N. (1982). *School class size: Research and policy.* Beverly Hills, CA: Sage.

Glass, G. V., & Kliegl, R. M. (1983). An apology for research integration in the study of psychotherapy. *Journal of Consulting and Clinical Psychology, 51,* 28–41.

Glass, G. V., McGaw, B., & Smith, M. L. (1981). *Meta-analysis in social research.* Beverly Hills, CA: Sage.

Hansford, B. C., & Hattie, J. A. (1982). The relationship between self and achievement/performance measures. *Review of Educational Research, 52,* 123–142.

Hartley, S. S. (1978). Meta-analysis of the effects of individually paced instruction in mathematics. *Dissertation Abstracts International, 38,* 4003A. (University Microfilms NO. 77–29, 926)

Hedges, L. V. (1980). Unbiased estimation of effect size. *Evaluation in Education: An International Review Series, 4,* 25–27.

Hedges, L. V. (1981). Distribution theory for Glass's estimator of effect size and related estimators. *Journal of Educational Statistics, 6,* 107–128.

Hedges, L. V. (1982a). Estimation of effect size from a series of independent experiments. *Psychological Bulletin, 92,* 490–499.

Hedges, L. V. (1982b). Fitting categorical models to effect sizes from a series of experiments. *Journal of Educational Statistics, 7,* 119–137.

Hedges, L. V. (1982c). Fitting continuous models to effect size data. *Journal of Educational Statistics, 7,* 245–270.

Hedges, L. V., & Olkin, I. (1982). Analyses, reanalyses, and meta-analysis. *Contemporary Education Review, 1,* 157–165.

Hedges, L. V., & Stock, W. (1983). The effects of class size: An examination of rival hypotheses. *American Educational Research Journal, 20,* 63–85.

Hunter, J. E., & Schmidt, F. L. (1978). Differential and single-group validity of employment tests by race: A critical analysis of three recent studies. *Journal of Applied Psychology, 63,* 1–11.

Hunter, J. E., & Schmidt, F. L. (1981). *Cumulating results across studies: Correction for sampling error. A proposed moratorium on the significance test and a critique of current multivariate reporting practices.* Unpublished manuscript, Michigan State University, East Lansing.

Hunter, J. E., Schmidt, F. L., & Hunter, R. (1979). Differential validity of employment tests by race: A comprehensive review and analysis. *Psychological Bulletin, 86,* 721–735.

Hunter, J. E., Schmidt, F. L., & Jackson, G. B. (1983). *Meta-analysis: Cumulating research findings across studies.* Beverly Hills, CA: Sage.

Jackson, G. B. (1980). Methods for integrative reviews. *Review of Educational Research, 50,* 438–460.

Jackson, S. E. (1984, August). *Can meta-analysis be used for theory development in organizational psychology?* Paper presented at the 92nd annual meeting of the American Psychological Association, Toronto.

Jones, L. V., & Fiske, D. W. (1953). Models for testing the significance of combined results. *Psychological Bulletin, 50,* 375–382.

Kulik, C.-L. C., & Kulik, J. A. (1986). *Estimating effect sizes in quantitative research integration.* Manuscript submitted for publication.

Kulik, J. A. (1984, April). *The uses and misuses of meta-analysis.* Paper presented at the meeting of the American Educational Research Association, New Orleans.

Kulik, J. A., & Bangert-Drowns, R. L. (1983/1984). Effectiveness of technology in precollege mathematics and science teaching. *Journal of Educational Technology Systems, 12,* 137–158.

Kulik, J. A., Kulik, C.-L. C., & Cohen, P. A. (1979). A meta-analysis of outcome studies of Keller's personalized system of instruction. *American Psychologist, 34,* 307–318.

Landman, J., & Dawes, R. M. (1982). Psychotherapy outcome. *American Psychologist, 37,* 504–516.

Light, R. J., & Smith, P. V. (1971). Accumulating evidence: Procedure for resolving contradictions among different research studies. *Harvard Educational Review, 41,* 429–471.

Mansfield, R. S., & Busse, T. V. (1977). Meta-analysis of research: A rejoinder to Glass. *Educational Researcher, 6,* 3.

Mosteller, F. M., & Bush, R. R. (1954). Selected quantitative techniques. In G. Lindzey (Ed.), *Handbook of social psychology: Vol. 1. Theory and method.* Cambridge, MA: Addison-Wesley.

Pearson, E. S. (1938). The probability integral transformation for testing goodness of fit and combining tests of significance. *Biometrika, 30,* 134–148.

Pearson, K. (1933). On a method of determining whether a sample size n supposed to have been drawn from a parent population having a known probability integral has probably been drawn at random. *Biometrika, 25,* 379–410.

Presby, S. (1978). Overly broad categories obscure important differences between therapies. *American Psychologist, 33,* 514–515.

Rosenthal, R. (1976). Interpersonal expectancy effects; A follow-up. In R. Rosenthal, *Experimental effects in behavioral research* (pp. 440–471). New York: Irvington.

Rosenthal, R. (1978). Combining results of independent studies. *Psychological Bulletin, 85,* 185–193.

Rosenthal, R. (1979). The "file drawer problem" and tolerance for null results. *Psychological Bulletin, 86,* 638–641.

Rosenthal, R. (1983). Assessing the statistical and social importance of the effects of psychotherapy. *Journal of Consulting and Clinical Psychology, 51,* 4–13.

Rosenthal, R., & Rubin, D. B. (1978). Interpersonal expectancy effects; The first 345 studies. *Behavioral and Brain Sciences, 1,* 377–386.

Rosenthal, R., & Rubin, D. B. (1982a). Comparing effect sizes of independent studies. *Psychological Bulletin, 92,* 500–504.

Rosenthal, R., & Rubin, D. B. (1982b). Further meta-analytic procedures for assessing cognitive gender differences. *Journal of Educational Psychology, 74,* 708–712.

Schmidt, F. L., Berner, J. G., & Hunter, J. E. (1973). Racial differences in validity of employment tests: Reality or illusion? *Journal of Applied Psychology, 58,* 5–9.

Shaver, J. P., & Norton, R. S. (1980). Randomness and replication in ten years of the *American Educational Research Journal. Educational Researcher, 9,* 9–16.

Smith, M. L. (1980). Publication bias and meta-analysis. *Evaluation in Education, 4,* 22–24.

Smith, M. L., & Glass, G. V. (1977). Meta-analysis of psychotherapy outcome studies. *American Psychologist, 32,* 752–760.

Smith, M. L., Glass, G. V., & Miller, T. I. (1980). *The benefits of psychotherapy.* Baltimore, MD: Johns Hopkins University Press.

Sudman, S., & Bradburn, N. M. (1974). *Response effects in surveys: A review and synthesis.* Chicago: Aldine.

Taveggia, T. (1974). Resolving research controversy through empirical cumulation. *Sociological Methods and Research, 2,* 395–407.

Tippett, L. H. C. (1931). *The methods of statistics.* London: Williams & Norgate.

Underwood, B. J. (1957). Interference and forgetting. *Psychological Review, 64,* 49–60.

Walberg, H. J., & Haertel, E. H. (Eds.). (1980). *Evaluation in education: An international review series (Vol. 4).* Oxford, England: Pergamon Press.

White, K. R. (1982). The relation between socioeconomic status and academic achievement. *Psychological Bulletin, 91,* 461–481.

Wilkinson, B. (1951). A statistical consideration in psychological research. *Psychological Bulletin, 48,* 156–158.

Wolf, F. M., Savickas, M. L., Saltzman, G. A., & Walker, M. L. (1983). *A meta-analytic evaluation of an interpersonal skills curriculum for medical students: Synthesizing evidence over successive occasions.* Unpublished manuscript, University of Michigan, Ann Arbor. (Preliminary version presented at the meeting of the American Educational Research Association, Montreal, April 1983)

Wortman, P. M. (1983). Evaluation research: A methodological perspective. *Annotated Review of Psychology, 34,* 223–260.

Wortman, P. M., & Bryant, F. B. (1985). School desegregation and black achievement: An integrative review. *Sociological Methods and Research, 13,* 289–324.

Yates, F., & Cochran, W. G. (1938). The analysis of groups of experiments. *Journal of Agricultural Science, 28,* 556–580.

35

Best-Evidence Synthesis: An Alternative to Meta-Analytic and Traditional Reviews

Robert E. Slavin

ABSTRACT: This paper proposes an alternative to both meta-analytic and traditional reviews. The method, "best-evidence synthesis," combines the quantification of effect sizes and systematic study selection procedures of quantitative syntheses with the attention to individual studies and methodological and substantive issues typical of the best narrative reviews. Best-evidence syntheses focus on the "best evidence" in a field, the studies highest in internal and external validity, using well-specified and defended a priori inclusion criteria, and use effect size data as an adjunct to a full discussion of the literature being reviewed.

In the decade since Glass (1976) introduced the concept of meta-analysis as a means of combining results of different investigations on a related topic, the practice and theory of literature synthesis has been dramatically transformed. Scores of meta-analyses relating to educa-

Robert E. Slavin is Director, Elementary School Program, Center for Research on Elementary and Middle Schools, Johns Hopkins University, Baltimore, MD 21218. His specializations are cooperative learning, school and classroom organization, field research methods, and research review.

An earlier version of this paper was presented at the 1985 annual meeting of the American Educational Research Association, Chicago. This paper was written under grants from the National Institute of Education (No. NIE-G-83- 0002) and the Office of Educational Research and Improvement (No. OERI-G-86-0006). However, the opinions expressed do not necessarily represent Department of Education policy. I would like to thank Harris Cooper, Gary Gottfredson, Nancy Madden, Robert Stevens, and Noreen Webb for their helpful comments on earlier drafts of this paper.

tional practice and policy have appeared, and the number of articles using or discussing meta-analysis in education has approximately doubled each year from 1979 to 1983 (S. Jackson, 1984). Several thoughtful guides to the proper conduct of meta-analyses have been recently published (see, e.g., Cooper, 1984; Glass, McGaw, & Smith, 1981; Hunter, Schmidt, & Jackson, 1982; Light & Pillemer, 1984; Rosenthal, 1984).

Ever since it was introduced, meta-analysis has been vigorously criticized, and equally vigorously defended. In considering arguments for and against this procedure in the abstract, there is much validity to both sides. Proponents of quantitative synthesis (e.g., Cooper, 1984; Glass et al., 1981; G. Jackson, 1980; Light & Pillemer, 1984) are certainly correct to criticize traditional reviews for using unsystematic and poorly specified criteria for including studies and for using statistical significance as the only criterion of treatment effects. Critics of these procedures (e.g., Cook & Leviton, 1980; Eysenck, 1978; Slavin, 1984; Wilson & Rachman, 1983) are equal-

ly justified in objecting to a mechanistic approach to literature synthesis that sacrifices most of the information contributed in the original studies and includes studies of questionable methodological quality and questionable relevance to the issue at hand.

In an earlier article (Slavin, 1984), I evaluated the actual practice of meta-analysis in education by examining eight meta-analyses conducted by six independent sets of investigators, comparing their procedures and conclusions against the studies they included. I found that all of these meta-analyses had made errors serious enough to invalidate or call into question one or more major conclusions. In reviewing several meta-analyses published after my article went to press, I have seen misapplications of the procedure that are at least as serious (Slavin, 1985). Yet the misuses of meta-analysis in education do not in themselves justify a return to traditional review procedures.

In this paper, I propose an alternative to both meta-analytic and traditional reviews that is designed to draw on the strengths of each approach and to avoid the pitfalls characteristic of each. The main idea behind this procedure, which I call "best-evidence synthesis," is to add to the traditional scholarly literature review application of rational, systematic methods of selecting studies to be included and use of effect size (rather than statistical significance alone) as a common metric for treatment effects.

The Principle of Best Evidence

In law, there is a principle that the same evidence that would be essential in one case might be disregarded in another because in the second case there is better evidence available. For example, in a case of disputed authorship, a typed manuscript might be critical evidence if no handwritten copy is available, but if a handwritten copy exists, the typed copy would be inadmissible because it is no longer the best evidence (since the handwritten copy would be conclusive evidence of authorship).

I would propose extending the principle of best evidence to the practice of research review. For example, if a literature contains several studies high in internal and external validity, then lower quality studies might be largely excluded from the review. Let's say we have a literature with 10 randomized studies of several months' duration evaluating Treatment X. In this case, results of correlational studies, small-sample studies, and/or brief experiments might be excluded, or at most briefly mentioned. For example, Ottenbacher and Cooper (1983) located 61 randomized, double-blind studies of effects of medication on hyperactivity, and therefore decided not to include studies of lower methodological rigor. However, if a set of studies high in internal and external validity does not exist, we might cautiously examine the less well designed studies to see if there is adequate unbiased information to come to any conclusion.

The principle of best evidence works in law because there are a priori criteria for adequacy of evidence in certain types of cases. Comparable criteria could not be prescribed for all of educational research, but could be proposed for

each subfield as it is reviewed. These criteria might be derived from a reading of previous narrative and meta-analytic reviews and a preliminary search of the literature.

Justification for the "Best Evidence" Principle

The recommendation that reviewers apply consistent, well justified, and clearly stated a priori inclusion criteria is at the heart of the best-evidence synthesis, and differs from the exhaustive inclusion principle suggested by Glass et al. (1981) and others, who recommend including all studies that meet broad standards in terms of independent and dependent variables, avoiding any judgments of study quality. Proponents of meta-analysis suggest that statistical tests be used to empirically test for any effects of design features on study outcomes. The rationale given for including all studies regardless of quality rather than identifying the methodologically adequate ones is primarily that the reviewer's own biases may enter into decisions about which studies are "good" and which are "bad" methodologically. Certainly, studies of interjudge consistency in evaluations of journal articles (e.g., Gottfredson, 1978; Marsh & Ball, 1981; Peters & Ceci, 1982; Scarr & Weber, 1978) show considerable variation from reviewer to reviewer, so global decisions about methodological quality are inappropriate as a priori criteria for inclusion of studies in a research synthesis. It is important to recall that much of the impetus for the development of meta-analysis came from a frequent observation that traditional narrative reviews were unsystematic in their selection of studies, and did a poor job (or no job at all) of justifying their selection of studies, arguably the most important step in the review process (see Cooper, 1984; G. Jackson, 1980; Waxman & Walberg, 1982).

However, while it is difficult to justify a return to haphazard study selection procedures characteristic of many narrative reviews, it is also difficult to accept the meta-analysts' exhaustive inclusion strategy. The rationale for exhaustive inclusion depends entirely on the proposition that specific methodological features of studies can be statistically compared in terms of their effects on effect size. Cooper (1984) puts the issue this way:

> If it is empirically demonstrated that studies using "good" methods produce results different from "bad" studies, the results of the good studies can be believed. When no difference is found it is sensible to retain the "bad" studies because they contain other variations in methods (like different samples and locations) that, by their inclusion, will help solve many other questions surrounding the problem area. (pp. 65–66)

In practice, meta-analyses almost always test several methodological and substantive characteristics of studies for correlations with effect size, using a criterion for rejecting the null hypothesis of no differences of .05. However, in order to justify pooling across categories of studies, the meta-analyst must prove the null hypothesis that the categories do not differ. This is logically impossible, and in situations in which the numbers of studies are small and the numbers of categories are large, finding true differences between categories of studies to be statistically significant is unlikely.

One example of this is a recent meta-analysis on adaptive education by Waxman, Wang, Anderson, and Walberg (1985), which coded the critical methodological factor "control method" into eight categories: unspecified, stratification, partial correlation, beta weights in regression, raw or metric weights in regression, factorial analysis of variance, analysis of covariance, or none. In a meta-analysis of only 38 studies, the 8×1 ANOVA apparently used to evaluate effects of methodological quality on study outcome had highly unequal and small cell sizes and an extremely high probability of failing to detect any true differences.

The problem of the reviewer's bias entering into inclusion decisions is hardly solved by exhaustive inclusion followed by statistical tests. The reviewer's bias may just as well enter into the coding of studies for statistical analysis (Mintz, 1983; Wilson & Rachman, 1983). Worse, the reader has no easy way to find out how studies were coded. For example, most of the studies coded as "randomly assigned" in a meta-analysis on mainstreaming by Carlberg and Kavale (1980) were in fact randomly selected from nonrandomly assigned groups. To discover this, it was necessary to obtain every article cited and laboriously recode them (Slavin, 1984).

Reviews of social science literature will inevitably involve judgment. No set of procedural or statistical canons can make the review process immune to the reviewer's biases. What we can do, however, is to require that reviewers make their procedures explicit and open, and we can ask that reviewers say enough about the studies they review to give readers a clear idea of what the original evidence is. The greatest problem with exhaustive inclusion is that it often produces such a long list of studies that the reviewer cannot possibly describe each one. I would argue that all other things being equal, far more information is extracted from a large literature by clearly describing the best evidence on a topic than by using limited journal space to describe statistical analyses of the entire methodologically and substantively diverse literature.

Criteria for Including Studies

Obviously, if a priori criteria are to be used to select studies, these criteria must be well thought out and well justified. It is not possible to specify in advance what criteria should be used, as this must depend on the purposes for which the review is intended (see Light & Pillemer, 1984, for more on this point). However, there are a few principles that probably apply generally.

First, the most important principle of inclusion must be germaneness to the issue at hand. For example, a meta-analysis focusing on school achievement as a dependent measure must explicitly describe what is meant by school achievement and must only include studies that measured what is commonly understood as school achievement on individual assessments, not swimming, tennis, block stacking, time-on-task, task completion rate, group productivity, attitudes, or other measures perhaps related to but not identical with student academic achievement (see Slavin, 1984).

...far more information is extracted from a large literature by clearly describing the best evidence on a topic than by using limited journal space to describe statistical analyses of the entire methodologically and substantively diverse literature.

Second, methodological adequacy of studies must be evaluated primarily on the basis of the extent to which the study design minimized bias. For example, it would probably be inappropriate to exclude studies because they failed to document the reliability of their measures, as unreliability of measures is unlikely in itself to bias a study's results in favor of the experimental or control group. On the other hand, great caution must be exercised in areas of research in which less-than-ideal research designs tend to produce systematic bias. For example, matched or correlational studies of such issues as special education, non-promotion, and gifted programs are likely to be systematically biased in favor of the students placed in regular classes, promoted, or placed in gifted classes, respectively (Madden & Slavin, 1983). In these areas of research, the independent variable is strongly correlated with academic ability, motivation, and many other factors that go into a decision to, for example, promote or retain a student.

Controlling for all these factors is virtually impossible in a correlational study. In research literatures of this kind, random assignment to experimental or control groups is essential. However, in other areas of research, the independent variable is less highly correlated with academic ability or other biasing factors. For example, schools that use tracking may not be systematically different from those that do not. If this is the case, then random assignment, though still desirable, may be less essential; carefully matched or statistically controlled studies may be interpretable.

Third, it is important to note that external validity should be valued at least as highly as internal validity in selecting studies for a best-evidence synthesis. For example, reviews of classroom practices should not generally include extremely brief laboratory studies or other highly artificial experiments. Often, a search for randomized studies turns up such artificial experiments. This was the case with the Glass, Cohen, Smith, and Filby (1982) class size meta-analysis, which found more positive effects of class size in "well controlled" studies than in "less well controlled" studies. Well controlled meant studies using random assignment, but this requirement caused the well controlled study category to include a number of extremely brief artificial experiments, such as a 30-minute study of class size by Moody, Bausell, and Jenkins (1973), as well as a study of effects of class size on tennis "achievement" (Verducci, 1969). Because class size is not strongly correlated with academic ability (see Coleman et al., 1966), this is actually a case in which well designed correlational studies, because of their greater external validity, might be preferred to many of the randomized experimental studies.

One category of studies that may be excluded in some literatures is studies with very small sample sizes. Small samples are generally susceptible to unstable effects. In education, experiments involving small numbers of classes are particularly susceptible to teacher and class effects (see Glass & Stanley, 1970; Page, 1975). For example, if Mr. Jones teaches Class A using Method X and Ms. Smith teaches Class B using Method Y, there is no way to rule out the possibility that any differences between the classes are due to differences in teaching style or ability between Mr. Jones and Ms. Smith (teacher effects) or to effects of students in the different classes on one another (class effects) rather than to any differences between Methods X and Y. To minimize these possibilities, a criterion of a certain number of teachers, classes, and/or students in each treatment group might be established.

In some literatures lacking a body of studies high in internal and external validity, it may be necessary to include (but not pool) germane studies using several methods, each of which has countervailing flaws. For example, if a literature on a particular topic consists largely of randomized experiments low in external validity and correlational studies high in external validity but susceptible to bias, the two types of research might be separately reviewed. If the two groups of studies yield the same result, each buttresses the other. If they yield different results, the reviewer should explain the discrepancy.

Finally, it may be important in some literatures to mention the best designed studies excluded from the review (that is, those that "just missed") to give the reader a more concrete idea of why a study was excluded and what the consequences of that exclusion are. For example, one recent meta-analysis of studies of bilingual education by Willig (1985) devoted considerable attention to describing studies excluded from the review, making the criteria for inclusion clear.

Some arbitrary limitations often placed on inclusion of studies in traditional reviews make little sense, and should be abandoned. Perhaps most common is the elimination of dissertations and unpublished reports (such as government reports or university technical reports). Often, these unpublished reports are better designed than published ones; for example, it may sometimes be easier to get a poorly designed study into a low quality journal than to get it past a dissertation committee. The most important randomized study of special educa-

tion versus mainstream placement (Goldstein, Moss, & Jordan, 1966) and the Coleman Report (Coleman et al., 1966) are two examples of unpublished government reports essential to their respective literatures.

On the other hand, meta-analyses also exclude one type of study that should not be excluded: studies in which effect sizes cannot be computed. It often happens that studies fail to report standard deviations or other information sufficient to enable computation of effect sizes. While effect sizes can be computed directly from t-scores, F's, or p values for two-group comparisons if N's are known (see Glass et al., 1981), there are cases in which important, well designed studies present only p values or F's for complex designs, ANCOVAs, or multiple regression analyses with too little information to allow for computation of effect sizes. Yet there is no good reason to exclude these studies from consideration solely on this basis.

Exhaustive Literature Search

Once criteria for inclusion of studies in a best-evidence synthesis have been established, it is incumbent upon the reviewer to locate every study ever conducted that meets these criteria. Books on meta-analysis (e.g., Cooper, 1984; Light & Pillemer, 1984) give useful suggestions for conducting literature searches using ERIC, Psychological Abstracts, Social Science Citation Index, and bibliographies of other reviews or meta-analyses, among other sources. In some cases, it is necessary to write to authors to request means and standard deviations or other information necessary to understand some aspect of a study. It is particularly important to locate all studies cited by previous reviewers to assure the reader that any differences in conclusions between reviewers are not simply due to differences in the pool of studies located.

Computation of Effect Sizes

In general, effect sizes should be computed as suggested by Glass et al. (1981), with a correction for sam-

ple size devised by Hedges (1981; Hedges & Olkin, 1985). The Hedges procedure produces an unbiased estimate of effect size, reducing estimates from studies with total N's (experimental plus control) less than 50.

There are many statistical issues that are important in computing and understanding effect sizes, and many of these have important substantive implications. For example, there are questions of how to interpret gain scores or posttests adjusted for covariates, how to deal with unequal pretest scores in experimental and control groups, and how to deal with aggregated data (e.g., class or school means). Readers interested in statistical issues should refer to the excellent books on the conduct of quantitative syntheses (e.g., Cooper, 1984; Glass et al., 1981; Hedges & Olkin, 1985; Hunter et al., 1982; Rosenthal, 1984).

Averaging effect sizes within studies. Since many studies report a large number of effects, it may be important to compute averages of some effect sizes across particular subsets of comparisons. The amount of averaging to be done depends on the purpose and focus of the best-evidence synthesis. For example, in a general review of the effects of ability grouping on achievement, different measures of reading and language arts may be averaged. However, in a best-evidence synthesis of research on specific reading strategies, we would want to preserve information separately for reading comprehension, reading vocabulary, oral reading, language mechanics, and so on.

Similarly, in a review of effects of computer-assisted instruction we might average effects for students of different ethnicities, but in a review of compensatory education, separate effects for different ethnic groups might be preserved. However, when pooling effect sizes across studies, each study (or each experimental-control comparison) must count as one observation with effect sizes from similar measures averaged as appropriate. To count each dependent measure as a separate effect size for pooling purposes, as recommended by Glass et al. (1981), creates serious problems as it gives too much weight to studies with large numbers of measures and comparisons and violates assumptions of independence of data points in any statistical analyses (see Bangert-Drowns, 1986).

Table of Study Characteristics and Effect Sizes

No matter how extensive the literature reviewed, all studies should be listed in a table specifying major design and setting variables and effect sizes for principal studies. This table should include the names of the studies, sample size, duration, research design, subject matter, grade levels, treatments compared, and effect size(s). Other information important in a particular area of research might also be included. For example, the table might indicate which effects were statistically significant in the original research. This table is essential not only in summarizing all pertinent information, but also in making it easier to check the review's procedures and conclusions against the original research on which it was based.

In the table of study characteristics and effects sizes, results from studies for which effect sizes could not be computed may be represented as " + " (statistically significant-positive), "0" (no significant differences), or " – " (statistically significant-negative).

For examples of tables of study characteristics and effect sizes, see Willig (1985), Schlaefli, Rest and Thoma (1985), Kulik and Kulik (1984), and Slavin (1986).

Pooling of Effect Sizes

When there are many studies high in internal and external validity on a well defined topic, pooling (averaging) effect sizes across the various studies may be done. For example, let's say we located a dozen studies of Treatment X in which experimental and control students (or classes) were randomly assigned to treatment groups, the treatment was applied for at least 3 weeks, and fair achievement tests equally responsive to the curriculum taught in the experimental and control groups were used. In this case, we might pool the effect sizes by computing a median across the 12 studies. Medians are preferable to

means because they are minimally influenced by anomalous outliers frequently seen in meta-analyses.

In pooling effect sizes, the reviewer must be careful "not to quantitatively combine studies at a broader conceptual level than the readers would find useful" (Cooper, 1984, p. 82). For example, in a quantitative synthesis by Lysakowski and Walberg (1982), it was not useful to pool across studies of cues, participation, and corrective feedback, as these topics together do not form a single well-defined category (see Slavin, 1984).

Pooled effect sizes should be reported as adjuncts to the literature review, not its primary outcome. Pooling and statistical comparisons must be guided by substantive, methodological, and theoretical considerations, not conducted wholesale and interpreted according to statistical criteria alone. For example, many meta-analyses routinely test for differences among effect sizes according to year of publication, a criterion that may be important in some literatures but is meaningless in others, while ignoring more theoretically or methodologically important comparisons (such as plausible interactions among study features).

Pooled effect sizes should never be treated as the final word on a subject. If pooled effects are markedly different from those of two or three especially well designed studies, this discrepancy should be explained. Pooling has value simply in describing the central tendency of several effects that clearly tend in the same direction. When effects are diverse, or the number of methodologically adequate, germane articles is small, pooling should not be done. Hedges and Olkin (1985) have described statistical procedures for testing sets of effect sizes for homogeneity, and these may be useful in determining whether or not pooling is indicated. However, decisions about which studies to include in a particular category should be based primarily on substantive, not statistical criteria.

Literature Review

The selection of studies, computation of effect sizes, and pooling de-

scribed above are only a preliminary to the main task of a best-evidence synthesis: the literature review itself. It is in the literature review section that best-evidence synthesis least resembles meta-analysis. For example, some quantitative syntheses do use a priori selection, do present tables of study characteristics and effect sizes, and do follow other procedures recommended for best-evidence synthesis, but it is very unusual for a quantitative synthesis to discuss more than two or three individual studies or to examine a literature with the care typical of the best narrative reviews.

There are no formal guidelines or mechanistic procedures for conducting a literature review in a best-evidence synthesis; it is up to the reviewer to make sense out of the best available evidence.

Formats for Best-Evidence Syntheses

No rigid formula for presenting best-evidence syntheses can be prescribed, as formats must be adapted to the literature being reviewed. However, one suggestion for a general format is presented below. Also, see Slavin (1986) for an example of a best-evidence synthesis.

Introduction. The introduction to a best-evidence synthesis will closely resemble introductions to traditional narrative reviews. The area being studied is introduced, key terms and concepts are defined, and the previous literature, particularly earlier reviews and meta-analyses, is discussed.

Methods. In a best-evidence synthesis, the methods section serves primarily to describe how studies were selected for inclusion in the review. The methods section might consist of the following three subsections.

Best-Evidence Criteria describes and justifies the study selection criteria employed. Clear, quantifiable criteria must be specified, not global ratings of methodological adequacy. Stringent criteria for germaneness should be applied (e.g., studies of individualized instruction in mathematics that took place over periods of at least 8 weeks in elementary schools, using mathematics achievement measures not specifically keyed to the material being studied in the experimental classes). Among germane studies, criteria for methodological adequacy are established, focusing on avoidance of systematic bias (e.g., use of random assignment or matching with evidence of initial equality), sample size (e.g., at least four classes in experimental and control groups), and external validity (e.g., treatment duration of at least eight weeks). The literature search procedure should be described in enough detail that the reader could theoretically regenerate an identical set of articles. A section titled *Studies Selected* might describe the set of studies that will constitute the synthesis, while a section on *Studies Not Selected* characterizes studies not included in the synthesis, in particular describing excluded studies that were included in others' reviews and studies that "just missed" being included.

Literature Synthesis. The real meat of the best-evidence synthesis is in the *Literature Synthesis* section. This is where the research evidence is actually reviewed. This section would first present and discuss the table of study characteristics and effect sizes and discuss any issues related to the table and its contents. If pooling is seen as appropriate, the results of the pooling are described; otherwise, the rationale for not pooling is presented.

In a meta-analysis, the presentation of the "results" is essentially the end point of the review. In a best-evidence synthesis, the table of study characteristics and effect sizes and the results of any pooling are simply a point of departure for an intelligent, critical examination of the literature (see Light & Pillemer, 1984). In the Literature Synthesis section, critical studies should be described and important conceptual and methodological issues should be explored. A best-evidence synthesis should not read like an annotated bibliography, but should use the evidence at hand to answer important questions about effects of various treatments, possible conditioning or mediating variables, and so on. When conclusions are suggested, they must be justified in light of the available evidence, but also the *contrary* evidence should be

discussed. Effect size information may be incorporated in the Literature Synthesis, as in the following example:

"Katz and Jammer (19XX) found significantly higher achievement in project classes than in control classes on mathematics computations (ES = .45) and concepts (ES = .31), but not on applications (ES = .02)."

In general, the "best-evidence" studies should be described with particular attention to studies with outstanding features, unusually high or low effect sizes, or important additional data. Studies that meet standards of germaneness and methodological adequacy but do not yield effect size data should be discussed on the same basis as those that do yield effect size data. Studies excluded from the main synthesis may be brought in to illustrate particular points or to provide additional evidence on a secondary issue. Except for the references to effect sizes, the bulk of the Literature Synthesis should look much like the main body of any narrative literature review.

One useful activity in many best-evidence syntheses is to compare review-generated and study-generated evidence (see Cooper, 1984). Review-generated evidence results from comparisons of outcomes in studies falling into different categories, while study-generated evidence relates to comparisons made within the same studies. For example, a reviewer might find an average effect size of 1.0 in methodologically adequate studies of Treatment X, and 0.5 in similar studies of Treatment Y and conclude that Treatment X is more effective than Treatment Y. However, this is not necessarily so, as other factors that are systematically different in studies of the two treatments could account for the apparent difference. This issue could be substantially informed by examination of studies that specifically compared treatments X and Y. If such studies exist and are of good quality, they would constitute the best evidence for the comparison of the treatments. Review-generated evidence can be useful in *suggesting* comparisons to be sought within studies, and may

often be the only available evidence on a topic, but is rarely conclusive in itself.

Conclusions. One purpose of any literature review is to summarize the findings from large literatures to give readers some indication of where the weight of the evidence lies. A best-evidence synthesis should produce and defend conclusions based on the best available evidence, or in some cases may conclude that the evidence currently available does not allow for any conclusions.

Summary

The advent of meta-analysis has had an important positive impact on research synthesis in reopening the question of how best to summarize the results of large literatures and providing statistical procedures for computation of effect size, a common metric of treatment effects. It is difficult to justify a return to reviews with arbitrary study selection procedures and reliance on statistical significance as the only criterion for treatment effects. Yet in actual practice (at least in education), meta-analysis has produced serious errors (see Slavin, 1984).

This paper proposes one means, best-evidence synthesis, of combining the strengths of meta-analytic and traditional reviews. Best-evidence synthesis incorporates the quantification and systematic literature search methods of meta-analysis with the detailed analysis of critical issues and study characteristics of the best traditional reviews in an attempt to provide a thorough and unbiased means of synthesizing research and providing clear and useful conclusions. No review procedure can make errors impossible or eliminate any chance that reviewers' biases will affect the conclusions drawn. It may be that applications of the procedures proposed in this paper will still lead to errors as serious as those often found in meta-analytic and traditional reviews. However, applications of best-evidence synthesis should at least make review procedures clear to the reader and should provide the reader with enough information about the primary research on which the review is based to reach independent conclusions.

References

Bangert-Drowns, R.L. (1986). Review of developments in meta-analytic method. *Psychological Bulletin, 99,* 388–399.

Carlberg, C. , & Kavale, K. (1980). The efficacy of special versus regular class placement for exceptional children: A meta-analysis. *Journal of Special Education, 14,* 295–309.

Coleman, J. S., Campbell, E., Hobson, C., McPartland, J., Mood, A., Weinfeld, F., & York, R. (1966). *Equality of educational opportunity.* Washington, DC: U.S. Department of Health, Education, and Welfare.

Cook, T., & Leviton, L. (1980). Reviewing the literature: A comparison of traditional methods with meta-analysis. *Journal of Personality, 48,* 449–472.

Cooper, H.M. (1984). *The integrative research review: A systematic approach.* Beverly Hills, CA: Sage.

Eysenck, H. J. (1978). An exercise in mega-silliness. *American Psychologist, 33,* 517.

Glass, G.V. (1976). Primary, secondary, and meta-analysis of research. *Educational Research, 5,* 3–8.

Glass, G., McGaw, B., & Smith, M. L. (1981). *Meta-analysis in social research.* Beverly Hills, CA: Sage.

Glass, G., Cohen, L., Smith, M. L. & Filby, N. (1982). *School class size.* Beverly Hills, CA: Sage.

Glass, G. & Stanley, J.C. (1970). *Statistical methods in education and psychology.* Englewood Cliffs, NJ: Prentice-Hall.

Goldstein, H., Moss, J., & Jordan, J. (1966). *The efficacy of special class training on the development of mentally retarded children* (Cooperative Research Project no. 619). Washington, DC: U.S. Office of Education.

Gottfredson, S. (1978). Evaluating psychological research reports. *American Psychologist, 33,* 920–934.

Hedges, L.V. (1981). Distribution theory for Glass's estimator of effect size and related estimators. *Journal of Educational Statistics, 6,* 107–128.

Hedges, L., & Olkin, I. (1985). *Statistical methods for meta-analysis.* New York: Academic Press.

Hunter, J. E., Schmidt, F. L., & Jackson, G. B. (1982). *Meta-analysis: Cumulating research findings across studies.* Beverly Hills, CA: Sage.

Jackson, G. B. (1980). Methods for integrative reviews. *Review of Educational Research, 50,* 438–460.

Jackson, S.E. (1984, August). *Can meta-analysis be used for theory development in organizational psychology?* Paper presented at the annual convention of the American Psychological Association, Toronto.

Kulik, J. A., & Kulik, C. L. (1984). Effects of accelerated instruction on students. *Review of Educational Research, 54,* 409–425.

Light, R. J., & Pillemer, D. B. (1984). *Summing up: The science of reviewing research.* Cambridge, MA: Harvard University Press.

Lysakowski, R., & Walberg, H. (1982). Instructional effects of cues, participation, and corrective feedback: A quantitative synthesis. *American Educational Research Journal, 19,* 559–578.

Madden, N. A., & Slavin, R. E. (1983). Mainstreaming students with mild academic handicaps: Academic and social outcomes. *Review of Educational Research, 53,* 519–569.

Marsh, H., & Ball, S. (1981). Interjudgmental reliability of reviews for the *Journal of Educational Psychology. Journal of Educational Psychology, 73,* 872–880.

Mintz, J. (1983). Integrating research evidence: A commentary on meta-analysis. *Journal of Consulting and Clinical Psychology, 51,* 71–75.

Moody, W. B., Bausell, R. B., & Jenkins, J. R. (1973). The effect of class size on the learning of mathematics: A parametric study with fourth grade students. *Journal for Research in Mathematics Education, 4,* 170–176.

Ottenbacher, R.J., & Cooper, H.M. (1983). Drug treatment of hyperactivity in children. *Developmental Medicine and Child Neurology, 25,* 358–366.

Page, E. (1975). Statistically recapturing the richness within the classroom. *Psychology in the Schools, 12,* 339–344.

Peters, D., & Ceci, S. (1982). Peer-review practices of psychological journals: The fate of published articles, submitted again. *The Behavioral and Brain Sciences, 5,* 187–255.

Rosenthal, R. (1984). *Meta-analytic procedures for social research.* Beverly Hills, CA: Sage.

Scarr, S., & Weber, B. (1978). The reliability of reviews for the *American Psychologist. American Psychologist, 33,* 935.

Schlaefli, A., Rest, J. R., & Thoma, S. J. (1985). Does moral education improve moral judgment? A meta-analysis of intervention studies using the defining issues test. *Review of Educational Research, 55,* 319–352.

Slavin, R. E. (1984). Meta-analysis in education: How has it been used? *Educational Researcher, 13* (8), 6–15, 24–27.

Slavin R. E. (1985, March). *Quantitative review.* Paper presented at the annual meeting of the American Educational Research Association, Chicago.

Slavin, R. E. (1986). *Ability grouping and student achievement in elementary schools: A best-evidence synthesis* (Tech. Rep. No. 1). Baltimore, MD: Center for Research on Elementary and Middle Schools, Johns Hopkins University.

Verducci, F. (1969). Effects of class size on the learning of a motor skill. *Research Quarterly, 40,* 391–395.

Waxman, H., & Walberg, H. (1982). The relation of teaching and learning: A review of reviews of process-product research. *Contemporary Education Review, 1,* 103–120.

Waxman, H.C., Wang, M. C., Anderson, K. A., & Walberg, H.J. (1985). Adaptive education and student outcomes: A quantitative synthesis. *Journal of Educational Research, 78,* 228–236.

Willig, A.C. (1985). A meta-analysis of selected studies on the effectiveness of bilingual education. *Review of Educational Research, 55,* 269–317.

Wilson, G.T., & Rachman, S.J. (1983). Meta-analysis and the evaluation of psychotherapy outcome: Limitations and liabilities. *Journal of Consulting and Clinical Psychology, 51,* 54–64.

36

The Narrative Structure of Policy Analysis

Thomas J. Kaplan

Abstract

This paper holds that the prior development of clear external criteria or principles is not always a useful avenue to the resolution of policy dilemmas, and that external criteria are sometimes as likely to emerge from proposed resolutions to policy issues as they are to govern those resolutions. In the absence of external criteria, stories meeting certain characteristics (truth, richness, consistency, congruency, and unity) can integrate necessary considerations, explain the development of current dilemmas, and point the way to resolutions. Not all policy analyses need to be in the narrative form—some analyses appropriately make tenseless arguments for particular principles. However, these principles invariably allow for many possible actions, and only a narrative can explain which particular course of action is desirable and why.

INTRODUCTION Good policy analysis is a demanding task. In recognition of that fact, a body of literature describing for students and practitioners what policy analysis is and how to do it has developed. This paper focuses on one essential step in many descriptions of policy analysis—the establishment of criteria for judging alternative courses of action. The paper argues that, while the establishment of criteria is a perfectly valid and useful step in many problems of policy analysis, it is neither possible nor necessary in every case. The paper further argues that, in cases where no clear criteria are apparent, an informal narrative meeting certain specified tests offers a vehicle for good policy analysis.

The sense that policy problems should be addressed on the basis of broad criteria that, once determined, serve as a guide to appropriate action is widespread. Duncan MacRae thus defines policy analysis as "the choice of the best policy among a set of alternatives with the aid of reason and evidence," and then describes the process of making that choice as a series of discrete tasks: defining

From Thomas J. Kaplan, "The Narrative Structure of Policy Analysis," *Journal of Policy Analysis and Management*, Vol. 5, pp. 761-778. Copyright © 1986 by the Association for Public Policy and Management. Reprinted by permission of John Wiley & Sons, Inc.

the problem, establishing "criteria for choice," and then choosing among alternatives based on the previously established criteria.[1] Nothing is wrong with such a typology of policy analysis. It is desirable, as Theodore Poister argues in a commonly used public administration text, to "make the criteria and standards explicit—clearly identified in all reports—and then to measure performance against these criteria and standards based on empirical evidence."[2] It is also true that the best examples of operations and systems analysis proceed through steps which Oleg Larichev idenified in an article on the subject, with one step being a definition of "the choice criteria to be used in identifying the preferential alternatives."[3]

These writers are surely correct that the establishment of *a priori* criteria can be important to policy analysis. Where a clear and broadly shared social goal exists, policy analysts would be foolish not to judge alternative proposals on the basis of how well they are likely to achieve that goal. Even when no widely shared social commitment exists, but a government agency has a clear and defensible set of its own goals or objectives, policy analysts working for the agency can use those goals or objectives as criteria in judging various proposals. For example, a city planning agency could, in the face of considerable controversy, identify itself as having a primary commitment to downtown economic development, and planners working for the agency could judge a variety of development proposals against that criterion.

Yet it is not always so easy to know what criteria to apply. This is sometimes the case for high-level elected officials, who may face a variety of conflicting pressures, and also happens within executive agencies on particularly complex and troublesome questions. The following true story about a state government agency illustrates both this point and several others I hope to make later in the paper.

A STORY: THE CENTERS FOR THE DEVELOPMENTALLY DISABLED The story concerns a state government human services agency which has for the last seventy years operated institutions for mentally retarded and other developmentally disabled children and adults. Now called Centers for the Developmentally Disabled, the three current institutions have served a variety of missions. At the time of this writing, they are state-operated nursing homes caring for a total of some 2,000 residents, less than half of whom are ambulatory and 80 percent of whom need bathing, feeding, dressing, or toileting care. As is largely true of other nursing homes in the state, a combination of state and federal Medicaid funds supports the three Centers for the Developmentally Disabled.

Episodes of controversy have surrounded the institutions for many years. A state governor in the mid-1960's toured the facilities during his administration and was appalled by what he saw: overcrowded, sterile rooms with no curtains or homelike amenities; residents sitting in corridors on hard benches with nothing to do; no treatment plans for most residents; staff members overwhelmed by the number of residents; and facilities that were uninviting and in poor repair. With the passage of the federal Medicaid program in 1965 and the subsequent development of federal regulations and reimbursement procedures for Intermediate Care Facilities for the Mentally Retarded, it became possible to improve the three institutions with the help of federal financial resources. By the early 1970's, the state had begun an aggressive policy of moving clients from the three institutions into community group homes and nursing homes and, more recently, into independent but supervised placements. The combined population of the three institutions dropped from 3,872 in 1970 to 2,142 in 1980 and to about 2,000 today. Despite the 45-percent population reduction in the 1970's, staffing levels remained almost identical. This was the result of a conscious choice—made easier by the infusion of federal Medicaid funds but a choice which the state might have made anyway—to improve quality of care at the facilities.

The state supported these decisions through a variety of budgetary stratagems. In the first phases of the improvement program, the state budgeted the full costs of the Centers out of general tax funds and then reimbursed the State Treasury with whatever federal Medicaid funds could be claimed. The claiming of federal funds was not difficult in the early 1970's, when the Medicaid program reimbursed all medically related costs, but became harder after the 1976 implementation of a statewide nursing home reimbursement formula that considered factors in addition to cost. To continue the Center improvement program at that point, the state developed a Nursing Home Appeals Board with special funds to supplement nursing homes demonstrating unusual problems. The effect was to allow full funding for the Centers without promoting equivalent increases for other nursing homes.

By the early 1980's, a variety of pressures had combined to weaken the general support for funneling more money to the Centers for the Developmentally Disabled. With increasing attention on Medicaid budget growth, and with the three Centers accounting for nearly 10 percent of all Medicaid expenditures in the state, it became harder to justify the repeated success of the Centers in obtaining full reimbursement from the Appeals Board. This was especially so because other nursing homes making appeals did not enjoy the same success.

A series of 1982 changes in federal Medicaid reimbursement requirements permitted states to tighten their nursing home reimbursement policies. This state took advantage of the opportunity, allowing reimbursement increases averaging only 3 percent annually. To make these rates more acceptable to private and county homes, the state decided to eliminate the Appeals Board and require the three state Centers for the Developmentally Disabled to operate under the same formula governing all other nursing homes.

While the state promulgated no formal announcements in the early 1970's saying that the three facilities would receive preferential Medicaid treatment, or ten years later that the Centers would have to stand on their own as regular nursing homes, these decisions were still reasonably clear and well understood by most interested parties at the times they were made. However, by 1984, just a few years after a concrete decision to make the Centers stand independently as regular nursing homes, the state found itself in the midst of another assessment of the situation. Though the state had imposed major staff and other cost reductions on the Centers, the institutions were not close to being able to meet their current costs under the general nursing home reimbursement formula.

As state government policy analysts and policymakers struggled again with the question of how to handle the Centers, it was tempting to argue that the first issue needing resolution was to define, once and for all, the mission of the institutions. Were they supposed to be just like privately operated nursing homes as the state decided for a brief time in the early 1980's; were they supposed to provide an especially warm, humane, and protective environment for the most disabled as the state decided for a brief time in the 1970's; or were they supposed to concentrate on teaching basic life skills to short-term clients who would soon move to a community placement? Until policymakers had reasonably permanent answers to these kinds of questions, state analysts were tempted to assert, an appropriate policy response to the current problems would not be forthcoming.

LIMITATIONS ON THE USE OF EXTERNAL CRITERIA Despite the wishes of state analysts and policymakers, no clearly agreed upon criteria emerged for judging this issue of how to treat the Centers for the Developmentally Disabled. As is sometimes the case in public policy analysis, a clear understanding of criteria alone would have solved a large share of the problem under analysis, and coming to that understanding was itself a difficult analytic problem, not a mere step in the solution to another problem. Different actors both within and outside the human services agency had different objectives with respect to the Centers for the Developmentally Disabled, and some individuals had multiple and conflicting objectives. Some agency employees wanted most to avoid dividing the agency more than it already was between institutional and community care interests; some emphasized avoiding as much embarrassment as possible over a failure to see earlier how much the Centers were in deficit; some focused on creating the best possible lives for residents remaining in the Centers; some emphasized removing Center residents so as to create the least restrictive environment possible; some concentrated on avoiding past rancorous and unproductive political battles over closing a state institution; and some focused on spending as little as possible to address the problem.

It was impossible to maximize all these objectives simultaneously. The agency could not, for example, avoid embittering its institutional management side and at the same time promote the least-restrictive environment possible for Center residents. Still, agreement on criteria proved impossible to achieve within the executive agency. Despite that lack of agreement, as I will discuss later, the agency was able to develop policy proposals that addressed the Center deficit issue and that were politically and intellectually defensible.

The argument that good policy analysis requires something not achieved in the Centers for the Developmentally Disabled case—clear and generally agreed upon criteria existing separately from the problem under analysis—is by no means trivial. At least since Henry Kissinger's 1962 book on *The Necessity for Choice*, a whole body of efforts to analyze U.S. foreign and military policy has been critical of the United States for having no clear criteria for making strategic choices. Does the United States want to maintain the capacity to intervene militarily anywhere in the world? Should American forces be dedicated primarily to operations in Europe? How much should United States planning depend on the cooperation of European and other allies? To what extent should the United States gear itself for short but intensive conflicts in the Third World? Without knowing in advance the answers to these kinds of questions, some commentators have argued, we have no rational basis for force planning, and we are at a severe disadvantage when an emergency arises.[4]

There doubtless have been world powers—England in the nineteenth and early twentieth centuries, for one—that had a clearer *a priori* conception of their role in the world than the United States now does, and that then applied that conception to a variety of practical foreign policy problems. Few would contest the desirability of generating such criteria whenever possible. But in some cases, the criteria will not be so clear, and we should not expect clarity, yet adequate policy analysis can be performed and should be expected.

THE RECIPROCAL NATURE OF SOLUTIONS AND CRITERIA

While they may not have been right on all questions of epistemology and methodology, the American pragmatists of the early twentieth century are a useful source of insight into the nature of policy analysis. John Dewey's 1910 book on *How We Think* expressed a systematic typology of the thought process that has not yet been much improved. Dewey divided the process into five steps: recognition of a problem or "felt difficulty," identification of the problem's "location and definition" (what we sometimes call data gathering), suggestions of possible solutions (hypotheses), development of the implications of each hypothesis, and testing to see whether the implications of each hypothesis correspond to the problem's "location and definition."[5] Nowhere in the process did Dewey identify a step of comparing proposed solutions to separate, preexisting criteria, and yet it seems perfectly clear that someone following Dewey's process could satisfactorily solve problems. Suppose a man, Dewey writes, returns home to an empty house and sees that his silver is missing. Possible hypotheses immediately leap to his mind. Did burglars steal the silver, did he misplace it, or did his children take it to play house? If he misplaced it, he would likely have put it in the kitchen, but it is not there. If his children took it, the silver would probably be in their rooms. He checks, and it is not there. If burglars took it, the windows must be tampered with. He checks, and they are. Thus, the "moving back and forth between the observed facts and the conditioned idea is kept up till a coherent experience of an object is substituted for the experience of conflicting details—or else the whole matter is given up as a bad job."[6]

Dewey's example of missing silver may, of course, serve as a poor model of policy analysis—one can surely imagine problems that better typify the most common activities of policy analysts. If Dewey had been writing about policy analysis, he might have framed problems like: how should we keep our existing silver stock secure; should we try to accumulate silver or other forms of wealth; or should we sell our existing silver and convert it to other assets? Yet in almost all of these cases, our thought process could function similarly to the thought process described in Dewey's missing silver example; it could be iterative and move back and forth between facts and a "conditioned idea." If we think, for example, about the wisdom of converting our silver to another asset, we might first compare the desirability of silver to the desirability of cash, then compare the desirability of silver to municipal bonds, then to corporate bonds, then to land, etc., until we hit upon something that seems clearly desirable. When we think this way, our decisions on specific comparisons would influence our general principles as much as the principles would influence our specific decisions.

We could, of course, shorten and neaten our thought process by having criteria clearly in mind before we start. We might specify at the outset that we want complete liquidity in our wealth, in which case conversion to cash is the answer and we have no more problem to solve, or that we want the maximum pre-tax return on our investment, in which case we consult our broker and do other forms of research. But when we use criteria like this in our thinking, we have somehow solved the earlier problem of what we want our wealth to do for us—either be maximally available for future decisions or achieve the highest possible current rate of return. We may simply have "known" without much thought what criteria we wanted to apply, or we may have formed the criteria in a messier, more iterative way.

In emphasizing iterative loops between hypotheses and observed facts, rather than comparisons of proposed solutions to external and preexisting criteria, Dewey was following the lead of the American logician Charles S. Peirce. In a 1903 lecture series at Harvard University, Peirce argued that the human mind characteristically moves with lightning speed from the specific to the general and back again, then on to the formation of another general hypothesis which is again tested against specific findings, then on to another hypothesis, etc., until a coherent solution is found. Peirce called this process "abduction," a combination of induction and deduction which remained, according to Peirce, a separate logical process.[7] Dewey's typology of thought argued the same case. "There is a double movement in all reflection," Dewey wrote, "a movement from the given partial and confused data to a suggested comprehensive (or inclusive) entire situation; and back from the suggested whole . . . to the particular facts. . . . Roughly, the first of these movements is inductive; the second deductive. A complete set of thought involves both."[8]

Some of the best of the modern studies of policy analysis have observed this interaction of criteria and solutions in policy analysis. E. S. Quade argues that "although there is widespread belief that goals should and can be set independently of the plans to attain them, there is overwhelming evidence that the more immediate objectives are—possibly more often than not—the result of opportunities that newly discovered or perceived alternatives offer rather than a source of such alternatives. For instance, the objective of landing a man on the moon did not arise until technology made it a feasible attainment."[9] Aaron Wildavsky has similarly argued the need to think interactively about solutions and criteria. Good policy analysis, he has written, "always considers resources and objectives, means and ends together, never separately."[10] Finally, Yehezkial Dror notes that "the interaction between means and ends is most important. Often ends, both operational and general values (though perhaps not final values), change because of innovations in means."[11]

Application of these concepts to such subjects as U.S. military planning results in less surprise at the difficulty of establishing *a priori* criteria. If we could ever irrevocably decide (or at least irrevocably decide for the several year period desirable for weapons procurement) that the defense of Europe and the Western Hemisphere were the primary objective of U.S. military forces, that general principle would help determine the need for, say, new aircraft carriers. In actual fact, however, decisions on whether to build a carrier may be based on a variety of considerations—such as cost, the age and readiness of the current carrier force, the deployment and function of the current carrier force, and the vulnerability of current carriers and any new carriers to enemy attack—in addition to where we want to project our power. All these factors might be integrated, and our decision about whether we want to build a carrier could tell us as much about where we want to project our power as our principle about where we want to project our power would tell us about whether we should procure a carrier.

The present interest in public sector strategic planning, as opposed to "classical" or "rational" planning, partly reflects this understanding of where objectives and criteria fit in the policy analysis process. The establishment of goals and objectives, which in rational planning are the basis for policy and program development, are not even mentioned in many descriptions of strategic planning. The focus is instead on the development of "strategic issues," which arise as much or more from the values of external "stakeholders," perceived opportunities and threats in the external environment, and perceived internal strengths and weaknesses as from a sense of the agency's mission.[12]

Strategic planning provides a useful device for establishing order in policy analysis problems that do not yield easily to *a priori* formulations of objectives and criteria. When there are a wide variety of factors to consider and integrate into a cohesive whole, strategic planning techniques can provide useful assistance. A government agency following these techniques can carefully identify all its stakeholders and assess what they think about the agency, describe briefly all the external political, economic, social, and technological forces that may affect the agency, create a range of scenarios indicating the possible effect of these forces, identify the agency's internal information sources, strengths, and weaknesses, etc. The process can involve numerous nominal group and brainstorming sessions and can go on at great length, all in an effort to impose order on a complex world and ensure the formal consideration of many relevant factors.

THE EXPLANATORY POWER OF STORIES Yet there is another way of imposing order on complexity, considering relevant factors, and making policy recommendations: the narrative structure, or stories, can do all of that, and where no broadly agreed upon criteria exist, do so as validly as other forms of policy analysis. Before I try to demonstrate this contention, two working definitions—one of policy analysis and one of stories—are in order.

By policy analysis, I mean, following Robert D. Behn, the act of helping clients develop a response to public dilemmas.[13] This definition distinguishes policy analysis from much academic social science, in which there is often no direct client. The policy analyst views himself or herself as working for or speaking to a particular decisionmaker or group of decisionmakers and asks this central question: "What should X (or a group of X's) do about Y?"

By stories, I simply mean narratives that describe change over time. Stories are thus not the same as vignettes or case studies about something at a particular point in time. Stories must contain a time element; they describe events. I use the words "story" and "narrative" interchangeably in this paper, even though literary theorists sometimes distinguish the two by defining stories as a special kind of narrative with qualities that encourage the projection of human values upon the material.

The distinction between narratives (or stories) and other forms of discourse is sometimes imprecise, yet a distinction still exists. The same material presented in one way can be a narrative, yet presented another way can be a "description" or a "study" or an "elegy" or something else. The philosopher Nelson Goodman has used the following example: consider "a psychologist's report that recounts a patient's behavior chronologically. It is a story, a history. But rearranged to group the incidents according to their significance as symptoms—of, say, first suicidal tendencies, then claustrophobia, then psychopathic disregard of consequences—it is no longer a story but an analysis, or case study."[14] The distinguishing feature of stories is that they describe events, either events which have already occurred, or (as in a novel) are described as having occurred, or that we predict will occur in the future, or that we want to occur in the future.

Stories are a more pervasive factor in our daily lives than we sometimes realize, and we use them frequently to explain even complex happenings. As an indication of the explanatory powers of stories, consider the following example. Let us say I have a traffic accident and a policeman asks me to account for it. Being a law-abiding citizen, I would normally respond by telling what I believe to be a true story. I might say that I was driving along an arterial, that a car on a cross street failed to stop for a stop sign, that I tried to swerve away but could not, and that the other car then hit mine. If witnesses agree, and if the skid marks and car dents comport with the account, the police officer would no doubt accept my story as a proper explanation of why the event occurred.[15]

Besides using stories in everyday life to explain why events happened, we also frequently use them—and here we move closer to policy analysis—to give complex advice about the future. For example, if someone asks my advice on which presidential candidate to vote for, I might normally respond, if I am willing to give advice at all, by telling a story, perhaps describing how Candidate X voted in the U.S. Senate, what his position papers have said, and what he said in the last televised debate. I could also, of course, give advice by referring to a preexisting principle, such as that one should vote for X because he is a member of a particular political party and one should always support that party, but that would be of little use if I know my questioner is unimpressed with party labels.

Note that it is unnecessary in either of these examples to explain proposals or events—why one should vote for candidate X, or why I had my traffic accident—by explicit reference to some outside, preexisting criteria. The explanations could all be fashioned from within the narrative itself. This is not to say that explanatory narratives never use broad principles which exist outside the narrative. The traffic accident example implicitly rests upon the general proposition that two objects simultaneously approaching the same point will collide unless one of the objects stops or slows down, and the candidate example depends on my judgment that some of candidate X's votes in the Senate were, according to principles which I generally hold, the right votes. I may generally believe in strong environmental protection laws, or I may believe in placing the need for business expansion before the need for environmental protection. In either case, my story about the virtues of X's senatorial voting record is likely to rest implicitly on one of those principles. Yet making implicit use within a story of external criteria is different from, and sometimes more achievable than, going through a formal process of first defining some external criteria and then developing an explanation or proposal that matches those criteria.

Philosophers of science have frequently noted the unique ability of narratives to explain events without explicit reference to external principles, laws, or criteria. Other forms of discourse require, for purposes of formal logic, a "law-like" explanation, as in "This water is steaming because water under a particular pressure boils when it reaches 100° C, and steaming is one property of boiling," or as in "We need to tell the truth in this situation because honesty is always the best policy." Narrative, or "genetic," explanations do not depend for their explanatory power on these explicit outside references.[16] While narrative explanations are traditionally used most frequently in the fields of biology, geology, and history, they could also be useful in policy analysis when criteria-based (or, in more formal terms, law-like) explanations are unavailable.

STORIES IN POLICY ANALYSIS One important virtue of stories in policy analysis is that they provide another way—without having to agree on explicit criteria—to explain how we arrived at a current dilemma, what we should do to address the dilemma, and why a particular proposal about what to do is a good one. When there are no clearly accepted external criteria, policy analysts can think in a narrative form about who should do what, and how, when, and why they should do it in order to address policy dilemmas. The analyst can then write down his or her thoughts in the form of a story and judge the story using criteria I will describe later in this paper. If the story is unsatisfactory, the analyst can rewrite it until it more closely matches the criteria. Policymakers and other analysts can later judge the story using the same criteria, rather than having to apply judgment based on sometimes endless arguments over *a priori* criteria applied to the particular issue at hand. Policy decisions based on these kinds of assessments of total stories may be no better than decisions based on issue criteria, but when gaining agreement on issue criteria is unachievable, narrative-based decisions can provide a useful substitute.

To illustrate this, let us return to the story of the Centers for the Developmentally Disabled. This was a case in which multiple criteria existed, ranging from reducing discord within the agency operating the Centers, to avoiding the expenditure of staff time and energy on achieving unlikely institutional closings, to creating the least-restrictive environment possible for Center residents. High-level agency managers disagreed about which criteria to apply and gave the agency director conflicting advice. As long as policy development remained at this level, a specific set of policy recommendations proved unachievable. Understandably reluctant to seem not to care (or not to care very much) about agency morale, or to seem not to care very much about achieving the least possible restrictive setting for the disabled, the agency director listened to repeated arguments over what criteria to apply by managers developing increasingly hardened positions. Policy analysts deemed to be impartial on these matters because of their distance from either institutional or community program responsibilities were similarly stymied. As soon as they selected one criterion or another as the basis for their analysis, they became identified as just another partisan in this or that camp.

A policy breakthrough came only from the writing of an overall story which avoided explicit selection of *a priori* criteria, and instead simply explained past uses of the Centers, the current dilemmas and how they developed, and a set of proposals designed to address the dilemmas. The end point of the story was a series of requests to move up to 245 Center residents into community settings and meet their costs with Medicaid community waiver money; relocate residents only with the consent of a parent or guardian and the county of residence and only after establishment of a joint state–county services plan; create a special category for the Centers in the state nursing home formula and bill Medicaid for their full costs; and reimburse the Centers for ninety days of "bed hold" after a bed becomes vacant due to a community placement. When confronted with a total story of this nature, agency managers could generally agree that it met their standards. The proposal was advanced to the state Legislature, and after much debate, the Legislature granted most of the request.

The request was not perfectly constructed, and it has failed to work in practice entirely as proposed. For example, it is now clear that fewer than 245 residents will be removed from the Centers as a result of the plan. However, the proposals at least solved the problem of the deficit, and they were superior to the repeated disagreements that resulted from a continued focus on criteria. In this particular case, it is hard to discover from the story that was finally developed the implicit criteria the agency accepted. Sometimes, however, it is possible to ascertain implicit criteria after the fact from a story, and analysts can then apply those criteria more formally to subsequent issues.

Besides offering another way to explain existing dilemmas and the merits of a proposed change, narratives are important to policy analysts for other reasons. Many policymakers, and especially political policymakers, seem to think in terms of stories. If they could, they would observe every program their agency or governmental entity operates or funds. Because they cannot do that, they want to hear stories from people they trust about how the programs operate. At their best, these stories are full of richness and truth, conveying the feel and texture of the programs. Policymakers sometimes want to be able to imagine themselves as employees or service recipients in the program and have a sense of the quality of such an experience, and analysts who can convey these images through rich and accurate stories are often highly valued. This interest in vivid description applies to program changes being proposed for the future as well as to descriptions of existing programs. The narrative form, better than any other, can depict in specific terms how a proposed program will operate and the changes it is intended to accomplish, information that policymakers often like to have before making resource allocation decisions.

Another important use of stories is that they can form the currency of the policymaker's communication on a particular issue to the wider public. "A political leader," Martin Krieger has written, "creates a story that helps persons structure their experience. He draws from their stories to make his more perfect, more encompassing, more capable of attracting a wider following and gaining greater allegiance . . . The archetypes and experiences the leader emphasizes in his story must be sufficiently rich so that others can see themselves in the story, yet at the same time the story will transform how others see themselves."[17] Policy analysts who can help supply these kinds of stories to policymakers perform a useful service.

THE CHARACTERISTICS OF GOOD POLICY ANALYSIS STORIES

Of course, not just any story by a policy analyst will do. If I am to claim that stories describing a policy proposal can be judged in their entirety without reference to explicit policy criteria that exist outside the story, there must at least be criteria that can be applied to policy analysis stories as a genre. This section of the paper discusses the properties of good stories. Readers should note that these properties do not allow for automatic application, and that there may well be disagreement over whether any particular story meets the tests I set out.

The first criterion of good stories is that they must be true, a criterion which is not always easy to satisfy. While most of us recognize statements about "welfare mothers driving around in Cadillacs" as, at best, incomplete anecdotes, untrue stories are often more difficult to recognize and guard against. In part, this is because factual knowledge around many policy issues is often scarce and because, despite rigorous safeguards, we can seldom be sure of the exact consequences of policy change. In addition, untrue stories can be hard to recognize because many true, but still conflicting, stories can often be told about the same event. Examples of this abound. Some influential people in my state believe that state government should purchase prepaid, capitated health insurance for all those not presently insured, charging a substantial fee to those who can afford it and offering the program free to those deemed too poor to pay. To make their case, proponents of the idea tell true stories of problems that have befallen some people who lack insurance and of the increasing difficulty medical providers have in shifting unreimbursed expenses for this population to third-party insurers. Opponents of the proposal tell different, but equally true, stories of the alternative uses to which the funds needed for this program could be applied, the likely administrative complexities of the program, and the already relatively positive health status of our state's citizens even in the absence of such a program.

To take another example of true but conflicting stories, consider the farm crisis of the mid-1980's. On one side of the issue, it is possible to tell a true story of the Soviet grain embargo, sharply rising interest rates, and sharply rising dollar values—all a result of government actions beyond farmers' control—as the factors which suddenly made farming unprofitable and precipitated, through no fault of farmers, an economic crisis on farms. Yet it is just as possible to tell a true story of how some farmers sacrificed the long-term productivity of their land with repeated cultivations of profitable but soil-depleting crops and of how some U.S. farm products cannot compete on the world market even discounting the value of the dollar.

It is thus not enough for policy analysis stories to be true; they must also be rich, which is to say in part that they should encompass all the realistically possible true stories. Good analyses must pick one story or set of stories as the most applicable and show why other stories are either false or inapplicable. This is by no means easy to do and requires careful attention. In judging which of many possible stories to apply, a good analyst may use sophisticated quantitative or other techniques that seem distinctly unstorylike. For example, an analyst evaluating various stories about the farm crisis may develop a complex econometric study to determine how competitive a range of American farm products would be if the dollar value on the international market had held constant. The study might be published as an independent journal article, but its real use for policy analysis purposes would be as a way of filling a gap in a story about government farm policy and allowing other analysts (or the same analyst at a different time) to tell truer and more applicable stories.

Good analytic stories should thus be rich in the sense of conveying a feel for many possible true stories on a subject and performing the difficult task of selecting the most appropriate one. They should be rich in other ways as well. Like any good stories, as Martin Krieger has written, the stories that planners and policy analysts tell should have "actors and settings, and I mean to keep in mind the dramatic and literary associations."[18] The stories should be "commodious and comfortable enough for persons to fit into . . . We want a rich, generous and open, yet specific story that we would understand."[19] Analyses that fail to be rich in this sense are stilted and artificial, sometimes taking the form of a mere outline. They offer no prospect of insight for the reader and often reflect a lack of insight in the writer. Rich analyses are both meaningful and gripping to their audience, allowing readers to put themselves inside the stories while at the same time transforming how readers view the situation.

Good analytic stories are also rich in the sense that they integrate all factors needing consideration. The best stories, indeed, can perform that integrating function as well as any other mechanism, imposing a kind of natural order on a complex world. To return to the Centers for the Developmentally Disabled, a good story on the subject would integrate a complex array of factors, and do so in a way that captures the interest of policymakers. Such an analysis would weave changes over time in the state and federal Medicaid program, the state's nursing home reimbursement formula, the clients served by the Centers, community alternatives to the Centers, the reaction of public employee unions, the reaction of

area legislators, quality control possibilities in community placements, etc., into a story that both richly describes how we arrived
at our current situation and proposes alternative visions of future
development.

Finally, good policy analysis performs this integrating function
in a way that meets the same consistency, congruency, and unity
tests that literacy theorists have applied to fictional narratives.
Under these tests, a story that demonstrates consistency is written
in such a way that any nonnarrative assertion in a narrative is
presupposed by the narrative surroundings. To use an example
developed by the literacy theorist L. B. Cebik, consider the following fictional statement: the prince "mounted his steed with a flourish he had come to learn the crowd expected. Princes are not permitted to grow tired."[20] The first sentence is narrative because it
describes a change—the prince was on the ground at Time A and
on the horse at Time B. While the second sentence is tenseless and
nonnarrative, the juxtaposition of the narrative and nonnarrative
does not jolt the reader in this instance. There would have been a
jolt if the story instead stated, without additional explanation,
that the prince "mounted his steed with a flourish he had come to
learn the crowd expected. Princes must be humble." A similar jolt
would occur if a narrative analysis of a state's Centers for the
Developmentally Disabled read: "Starting at the beginning of the
next fiscal year, we should use Medicaid funds both to assess Center residents and to place at least 40 residents out of the Centers
and into community settings each year. Under federal law, Medicaid funds may be used only for institutional care." The general
statement about Medicaid restrictions does not comport with the
narrative surroundings and would need, at the least, some amplifi-
cation to meet the test of consistency.

Good stories should also demonstrate congruency. The quality of
congruency, in Cebik's formulation, expresses the relationship between narrative statements in a story. Incongruencies exist "whenever the facts or structures in or presupposed by successive narrative sentences conflict without appropriate explanation."[21] If a
story has someone holding aloft some papers which he had formerly thrown in a fire, and if there is no intermediate description
of how the papers got out of the fire, we would flinch. We would
experience a similar jolt if a policy analyst wrote that, "Between
1985 and 1990, we should try to place 1,200 of the current 2,000
Center residents in community settings. By 1990, if our efforts
work as planned, only 1,600 people would remain in the Centers."
These two sentences are not necessarily incompatible; it is possible to imagine a scenario in which 1,200 current Center residents
are transferred out and replaced with 800 new residents during a
five-year period, leaving a total of 1,600 residents. Yet without
some explanation, the juxtaposition is jarring.

Finally, good narratives demonstrate unity, which simply means
that the various sections in a story exhibit some relationship. We
can read and follow loose narratives (for example, a world history
textbook), but we need to have some sense of the overlap or "con-

ceptual relationship" between the sections.[22] A section on how a state provides community support programs for the mentally ill may be appropriate within a narrative on its Centers for the Developmentally Disabled, but the writer of the narrative ought not take for granted that the reader understands the relationship.

These qualities of good analytic narratives—truth, richness, consistency, congruency, and unity—are not surprising, yet they are very hard to write. Stories of this sort provide no forum for unsubstantiated anecdotes or careless thought. Only very skilled analysts are capable of rich, congruent, consistent narratives that describe all relevant true stories, that allow readers to see themselves in stories yet also transform how readers see the stories, and that integrate the many factors needing consideration. The transformational quality is especially hard to achieve. Much skill is required to tell a true story about past events or a rich story of hoped-for future events in a way that, simply through restrained descriptive power, has the ability to change the reader's mind. It is impossible to describe precisely how to go about writing such stories, but it is important to have a sense of what they look like. If one knows one wishes to write a story with particular qualities, one can at least begin by writing a story that meets some of those qualities and then fill in gaps, rewrite the story, fill in more gaps, etc., until one approximates the ideal.

STORIES, SCENARIOS, AND VISIONS

I have so far shown, if my arguments hold, that clear external criteria are not always available as a basis for judging different approaches to policy dilemmas, and that in the absence of external criteria, stories meeting certain characteristics can integrate necessary factors, explain the development of current dilemmas, and point the way to resolutions. I have also tried to describe the characteristics of good stories so that analysts and their critics can judge the worth of various policy narratives. If a story fails to meet those characteristics, the analyst or some other worker in the field can try again to write a better narrative. Note that I have not limited the power of stories to the communication of policy proposals to outside, nontechnical readers who are not expected to be able to follow more technical arguments. Stories can be a useful vehicle for describing the results of careful thought, but they can also serve as a mechanism for developing that thought.

Stories as I have used the term bear a close relationship to what policy analysts sometimes call "scenarios." As Eugene Bardach has described the process, writing scenarios involves "an imaginative construction of future sequences of actions → consequent conditions → actions → consequent conditions. It is inventing a plausible *story* about 'what will happen if . . .' or, more precisely inventing several such *stories*."[23] (My emphasis.) Bardach views scenarios as helping "to illuminate some of the implementation paths that the designer [of a government program] does not want taken. He or she is then in a position to redesign some features of the system . . ." so that the designer or a colleague can "tell stories with happier endings. Trial and error through successive iteration produce better and better endings."[24]

While scenarios of how a program might operate in the future surely do alert designers to potential implementation problems, that is not their only utility. Another use of story-like scenarios is to describe a vision of a future program in a way that lets others judge whether that vision is one which they share. If a story of, for example, how a Health Maintenance Organization might work for Medicaid clients points out possible implementation problems, that is important. But if the story also gives enough of a sense of how such a system might compare to fee-for-service medicine and suggests an alternative vision, then at least policymakers and administrators have an opportunity to judge whether they want to try to manage the implementation problems.

Scenarios conceived as ways of describing a hoped-for vision would be developed in the same way as the implementation scenarios Bardach describes. Scenario writing is, as Bardach notes, "an art. It requires imagination and intuition. One suspects that there is not much that can be formalized or codified about how to do it well."[25] Scenario writing is an unavoidably messy problem. An analyst strives to write something whose general qualities are known, but the analyst only knows if he or she has done so after writing something down, applying the tests I have suggested in this paper, and if necessary (as it usually is) trying again.

CONCLUSION: HOW NECESSARY ARE STORIES TO POLICY ANALYSIS?

Narrative writing is, of course, not the only desirable form of policy analysis. Some arguments flow naturally from widely agreed upon criteria. Other arguments, particularly those which seek to justify the primacy of certain criteria, are tenseless, applying now, in the past, and in the future, and a narrative rendition of such arguments would be awkward. A policy analyst could thus write a treatise, describing no change over time, on why the deinstitutionalization of the mentally ill and the developmentally disabled is a desirable goal. But many policy problems do not benefit from these kinds of tenseless analyses. The principles and generalizations that such analyses generate are often no more useful in explaining a particular future course of action than they are in explaining past events. If, for example, a historian writes the sentence "Extensive reading of British antiauthoritarian, radical political pamphlets helped move Tom Paine to revolutionary action," that narrative explanation of Paine's participation in the American revolution depends on the generalization that human beings can and sometimes do act on what they read. Yet this or any similar generalization allows for many possible actions; Paine could have acted to form a debating society, or to propose a ban on these scurrilous writings, or to lead a revolution. As the philosopher Arthur Danto has made clear, the general principles we may employ (usually implicitly) as explanatory links between past events do not really explain why something occurred. Only the events themselves and the narratives that link them do that. This is because generalizations about human behavior invariably allow for a number of events, not just the one that occurred.[26]

Generalizations and principles are sometimes equally inapplicable to explanations of why future policy changes are desirable. I do not mean that analysts should never write tenseless arguments for or against deinstitutionalization, but policy analysts should not confuse doing that with writing an analysis of the current situation and future course of action for a state's Centers for the Developmentally Disabled. Even if an analyst believed and could persuade all relevant policymakers that "deinstitutionalization" and "normalization" of the disabled are desirable, those general principles would allow for many possible future courses of action regarding the Centers for the Developmentally Disabled. A state could start a pilot community program for 20 Center residents or shut down the Centers completely; a state could force parents of minors in the Centers to take the children home or develop a strictly voluntary program; a state could put an average of $1,000 or $4,000 per month behind each community setting, etc. Only a true, rich, consistent, congruent, and unified narrative can explain which particular course of action is desirable and why.

NOTES

1. Duncan MacRae, Jr., "Concepts and Methods of Policy Analysis," in Bertram H. Raven, ed., *Policy Studies Annual Review*, Vol. 4 (1980), p. 74.

2. Theodore H. Poister, *Public Program Analysis: Applied Research Methods* (Baltimore: University Park Press, 1978), p. 27.

3. Oleg I. Larichev, "Systems Analysis and Decision Making," in P. Humphreys, O. Svenson, and A. Vari, eds., *Analysing and Aiding Decision Processes* (Amsterdam: North-Holland Publishing Company, 1983), p. 127.

4. Henry Kissinger, *The Necessity for Choice: Prospects of American Foreign Policy* (Garden City, N.Y.: Doubleday, 1962); see also Eliot A. Cohen, "When Policy Outstrips Power—American Strategy and Statecraft," *The Public Interest*, Number 75 (Spring, 1984), pp. 3–19.

5. John Dewey, *How We Think* (Boston: D. C. Heath & Co., 1910), p. 72.

6. *Ibid.*, pp. 82–83.

7. Charles S. Peirce, *Lectures on Pragmatism*, in *Collected Papers*, Vol. 5 (Cambridge, Mass.: Harvard University Press, 1965), pp. 106, 113.

8. Dewey, *How We Think*, pp. 79–80.

9. E. S. Quade, *Analysis for Public Decisions* (New York: Elsevier Scientific Publishing Company, 1975), p. 87.

10. Aaron Wildavsky, *Speaking Truth to Power: The Art and Craft of Policy Analysis* (Boston: Little, Brown and Company, 1979), p. 10.

11. Yehezkial Dror, *Public Policy-making Reexamined* (Bedfordshire, England: Leonard Hill Books, 1973), p. 16. See also the discussion of "wicked problems" in Horst W. J. Rittel and Melvin M. Webber, "Dilemmas in a General Theory of Planning," *Policy Sciences*, Vol. 4 (June, 1973), pp. 155–169. David Dery, *Problem Definition in Policy Analysis* (Lawrence, Kansas: The University of Kansas Press, 1984) and Aidan Vining, "The Process of Meta-Strategy Analysis," unpublished manuscript, 1985, also provides useful discussions of the inter-

action between ends and means. While written from the perspective of business rather than public administration, Vining provides an especially strong argument that "in many situations it is futile for the analyst to initially search for organizational goals, objectives or criteria. They will be the outcome of analysis rather than the input to analysis" (p. 10).

12. John Bryson, unpublished materials for a course on "Strategic Management in Public Agencies," Feb. 28–March 1, 1985, Department of Conferences, University of Minnesota—Twin Cities.

13. Robert D. Behn, "Policy Analysts, Clients, and Social Scientists," *Journal of Policy Analysis and Management*, Vol. 4, No. 3 (Spring, 1985), pp. 428-432.

14. Nelson Goodman, "Twisted Tales; or Story, Study, and Symphony," in W. J. T. Mitchell, ed., *On Narrative* (Chicago: The University of Chicago Press, 1981, p. 111); see also Robert Scholes, "Language, Narrative, and Anti-Narrative," in *On Narrative*, pp. 205–206, and Barbara Herrnstein Smith, "Narrative Versions, Narrative Theories," in *On Narrative*, p. 228.

15. This paragraph has been adapted from an earlier article; see Thomas J. Kaplan, "History and the Secondary School Curriculum," *Educational Theory*, Vol. 27, No. 2 (Spring, 1977), p. 122. See also Arthur C. Danto, *Analytical Philosophy of History* (Cambridge: The University Press, 1968).

16. For a summary of genetic explanation, see Ernest Nagel, *The Structure of Science: Problems in the Logic of Scientific Explanation* (London: Routledge and Kegan Paul, Ltd., 1961), pp. 25–26, 564–568; see also Carl G. Hempel, *Aspects of Scientific Explanations and Other Essays in the Philosophy of Science* (New York: The Free Press, 1965), pp. 447–453.

17. Martin H. Krieger, *Advice and Planning* (Philadelphia: Temple University Press, 1981), p. 75.

18. *Ibid.*, p. 51.

19. *Ibid.*, p. 64

20. L. B. Cebik, *Fictional Narrative and Truth* (Lanlow, Md.: University Press of America, 1984), p. 158

21. *Ibid.*, p. 159.

22. *Ibid.*

23. Eugene Bardach, *The Implementation Game* (Cambridge: The Massachusetts Institute of Technology Press, 1977), p. 254.

24. *Ibid.*

25. *Ibid.*

26. Danto, *Analytical Philosophy of History*, pp. 220–232.